Active Citizenship and Disability

IMPLEMENTING THE PERSONALISATION OF SUPPORT

ANDREW POWER

University of Southampton

JANET E. LORD

BlueLaw International LLP

ALLISON S. DEFRANCO

BlueLaw International LLP

CAMBRIDGE
UNIVERSITY PRESS

CAMBRIDGE
UNIVERSITY PRESS

32 Avenue of the Americas, New York NY 10013-2473, USA

Cambridge University Press is part of the University of Cambridge.

It furthers the University's mission by disseminating knowledge in the pursuit of education, learning and research at the highest international levels of excellence.

www.cambridge.org
Information on this title: www.cambridge.org/9781107438682

First published 2013
First paperback edition 2014

A catalogue record for this publication is available from the British Library

Library of Congress Cataloguing in Publication data

Power, Andrew, 1979–
Active citizenship and disability : implementing the personalisation of support / Andrew Power, Janet Lord, Allison DeFranco.
    p.   cm. (Cambridge disability law and policy series)
Includes bibliographical references and index.
ISBN 978-1-107-02991-0 (hardback)
1. People with disabilities – Legal status, laws, etc.   2. Convention on the Rights of Persons with Disabilities and Optional Protocol (2007)   I. Lord, Janet E., 1966–
II. DeFranco, Allison S., 1983–   III. Title.
K637.P69   2012
362.4'04561–dc23   2012033417

ISBN 978-1-107-02991-0 Hardback
ISBN 978-1-107-43868-2 Paperback

ACTIVE CITIZENSHIP AND DISABILITY

This book provides an international comparative study of the implementation of disability rights law and policy focussed on the emerging principles of self-determination and personalisation. It explores how these principles have been enshrined in the United Nations Convention on the Rights of Persons with Disabilities and how different jurisdictions have implemented them to enable meaningful engagement and participation by persons with disabilities in society. The philosophy of 'active citizenship' underpinning the Convention – that all citizens should (be able to) actively participate in the community – provides the core focal point of this book, which grounds its analysis in exploring how this goal has been imagined and implemented across a range of countries. The case studies examine how different jurisdictions have reformed disability law and policy and reconfigured how support is administered and funded to ensure maximum choice and independence are accorded to people with disabilities.

Andrew Power is a Lecturer in Geography and Environment at the University of Southampton in the United Kingdom. He previously worked as a Researcher at the Centre for Disability Law & Policy, National University of Ireland, Galway, where he undertook the fieldwork for this study. His research interests in the field of disability law include independent living, supported decision making and family caregiver policy. Previous research work has included an ESRC postdoctoral fellowship at the Faculty of Health and Medicine (then the Institute for Health Research) at the University of Lancaster. At Southampton, he currently researches and teaches across a range of areas, including social justice, welfare and rights.

Janet E. Lord is a Senior Partner and Director of Human Rights and Inclusive Development at BlueLaw International LLP, a veteran-owned international law and development firm. An expert in human rights treaty negotiations, she participated in all of the negotiations for the UN Convention on the Rights of Persons with Disabilities, serving as legal advisor to several lead governments, expert to the UN and legal advocacy advisor to Disabled Peoples International. She is also Senior Research Associate at the Harvard Law School Project on Disability and Adjunct Professor of Law at the University of Maryland Francis King Carey School of Law.

Allison S. deFranco is a Director of Human Rights and Inclusive Development at BlueLaw International LLP, a veteran-owned international law and development firm. She brings expertise in international education law and policy, disability law and policy and disability-inclusive development programming. DeFranco has worked with major donors and implementing organisations such as the National Council on Disability, Disability Rights International, Disabled Peoples' International and the Harvard Law School Project on Disability to design and implement disability-inclusive democracy and governance, public health and education programmes throughout the world.

Cambridge Disability Law and Policy Series

The Cambridge Disability Law and Policy series examines these topics in interdisciplinary and comparative terms. The books in the series reflect the diversity of definitions, causes and consequences of discrimination against persons with disabilities while illuminating fundamental themes that unite countries in their pursuit of human rights laws and policies to improve the social and economic status of persons with disabilities. The series contains historical, contemporary and comparative scholarship crucial to identifying individual, organizational, cultural, attitudinal and legal themes necessary for the advancement of disability law and policy.

The book topics covered in the series also are reflective of the new moral and political commitment by countries throughout the world towards equal opportunity for persons with disabilities in such areas as employment, housing, transportation, rehabilitation and individual human rights. The series will thus play a significant role in informing policy makers, researchers and citizens of issues central to disability rights and disability antidiscrimination policies. The series grounds the future of disability law and policy as a vehicle for ensuring that those living with disabilities participate as equal citizens of the world.

Books in the Series

Ruth Colker, *When Is Separate Unequal? A Disability Perspective*, 2009

Larry M. Logue and Peter Blanck, *Race, Ethnicity, and Disability: Veterans and Benefits in Post–Civil War America*, 2010

Lisa Vanhala, *Making Rights a Reality? Disability Rights Activists and Legal Mobilization*, 2010

Alicia Ouellette, *Bioethics and Disability: Toward a Disability-Conscious Bioethics*, 2011

Eilionoir Flynn, *From Rhetoric to Action: Implementing the UN Convention on the Rights of Persons with Disabilities*, 2011

Isabel Karpin and Kristin Savell, *Perfecting Pregnancy: Law, Disability, and the Future of Reproduction*, 2012

Arie Rimmerman, *Social Inclusion of People with Disabilities: National and International Perspectives*, 2012

Andrew Power, Janet E. Lord, and Allison S. deFranco, *Active Citizenship and Disability: Implementing the Personalisation of Support*, 2013

Contents

Acknowledgements

In the course of preparation of this book, there were many individuals who kindly provided assistance, insight and encouragement which we would like to acknowledge. We are grateful to all whose names appear here for generously sharing their perspectives, insights and expertise.

Firstly, we offer special thanks to Professor Gerard Quinn, Director of the Centre for Disability Law and Policy at the National University of Ireland, Galway, for his continued support through this project.

We also especially thank the European Network for Independent Living for their extensive support as contributors to the international case studies, including Jamie Bolling, Co–Executive Director, as well as Caroline Lund, Sahand Aleboyeh and Ellen Clifford, all of whom contributed enormously to this work.

Allison S. deFranco and Janet E. Lord also acknowledge the research assistance of Kelly Bunch, Esq., and Katy Carroll in the preparation of their draft work. In addition, we are deeply appreciative of the library facilities of the National Disability Authority.

Andrew Power gives personal thanks to Jenny Rush for supporting him throughout the entire process.

In alphabetical order, those who participated in this research at various stages and merit individual recognition include:

Dr Michael Bach, Executive Vice-President, Canadian Association for Community Living

Professor Jerome Bickenbach, Head of Disability Policy Unit, Swiss Paraplegic Research

Mark Blake-Knox, Chief Executive Officer, Cheshire Ireland

Brendan Broderick, Chief Executive Officer, Muiriosa Foundation

Michael Browne, PhD candidate, Child & Family Research Centre, National University of Ireland, Galway

Dr Deirdre Carroll, former Chief Executive Officer, Inclusion Ireland

Rachel Cassen, Advocacy Co-ordinator, Irish Autism Action

Madeleine Clarke, Founding Director, Genio

Fiona Coffey, Head of Training, Development and Evaluation, Brothers of Charity Galway

Pierrol-Olivier Comin, Employment Support Worker, Association Nationale de Gestion du Fonds pour l'Insertion Professionnelle des Personnes Handicapées

Francis Conaty, Lecturer in Accountancy and Finance, National University of Ireland, Galway

Evelyn Conroy, Co-founder, Irish Centre for Sign-Language Studies

Dr James Cunningham, Director, Centre of Innovation and Structural Change, National University of Ireland, Galway

Aisling de Paor, PhD candidate, Centre for Disability Law and Policy, National University of Ireland, Galway

John Dolan, Chief Executive Officer, Disability Federation of Ireland

Dr Eilionoir Flynn, Senior Research Fellow, Centre for Disability Law and Policy, National University of Ireland, Galway

Focus group participants, Centre for Disability Law and Policy, Local Consultation Group, Ireland

Noelin Fox, PhD candidate, Centre for Disability Law and Policy, National University of Ireland, Galway

Eileen Glynn, Research Assistant, Centre for Disability Law and Policy, National University of Ireland, Galway

Dr Suzanne Guerin, Lecturer, School of Psychology, University College Dublin

Dr Colin Harper, Manager, Disability Action, Northern Ireland

Molly Harrington, ADM, Policy and Research Division, Ministry of Housing and Social Development, British Columbia, Canada

Mary Kealy, Chief Executive Officer, Brothers of Charity Clare

Marion Keigher, former Chief Executive Officer, Brothers of Charity Roscommon

Mary Keogh, PhD candidate, Centre for Disability Law and Policy, National University of Ireland, Galway

Dr Mary Keys, Senior Lecturer, School of Law, National University of Ireland, Galway

John Leinster, Head of Social Work, Brothers of Charity Galway

Mary McQuinn, Administrator, Centre for Disability Law and Policy, National University of Ireland, Galway

Robert E. Myers III, Senior Research Associate, Burton Blatt Institute

Martin Naughton, Co–Executive Director, European Network for Independent Living

Bairbre NicAonghusa, Director, Office for Disability and Mental Health, Department of Health and Children, Ireland

Brian O'Donnell, Chief Executive Officer, National Federation of Voluntary
Bodies, Ireland

James O'Grady, Policy Advisor, Department of Health and Children, Ireland

Charles O'Mahony, PhD candidate, Centre for Disability Law and Policy,
National University of Ireland, Galway

Bernard O'Regan, Chief Executive Officer, Western Care

Jenn Robertson, Law student, Northeastern University, intern at Centre for Disability Law and Policy, National University of Ireland, Galway, Spring 2010

Martin Routledge, Director of Operations, In Control

Rachel Stevens, founding Director, Empower All (former Disability Research
Project Manager and Business Manager, Centre for Disability Law and Policy,
National University of Ireland, Galway)

Katherine Talalas, Law student, William and Mary University, intern at Centre
for Disability Law and Policy, Summer 2009

Edel Tierney, Director of Research and Policy Development, National Federation
of Voluntary Bodies

Maria Walls, Director of Research and Policy Development, Federation of Voluntary Bodies, and PhD candidate, Centre for Disability Law and Policy, National
University of Ireland, Galway

Cormac Walsh, Volunteer, Centre for Disability Law and Policy, National University of Ireland, Galway

Kieran Walsh, Researcher, Irish Centre for Social Gerontology, National University of Ireland, Galway

Dr Sara Woodin, Research Fellow, Sociology and Social Policy, University of
Leeds

There were also many people interviewed and consulted during the fieldwork,
whom we cannot mention individually, but whose helpfulness never went unno-
ticed, and our gratitude is extended to all.

Abbreviations

AAH	Allocation aux Adultes Handicapés (Disabled Adult Allowance) (France)
ACCD	American Coalition of Citizens with Disabilities
ACTP	L'allocation Compensatrice de Tierce Personne (Carer's Compensation Allowance) (France)
AEEH	Allocation d'Education Enfant Handicapé (Education Allowance for Disabled Children) (France)
AES	Allocation d'Education Spéciale (Special Education Allowance) (France)
AFM	Association Française contre les Myopathies (French Muscular Dystrophy Association) (France)
AGEFIPH	L'Association de gestion du fonds pour l'insertion des personnes handicapées (Association for Managing Resources for the Inclusion of Persons with Disabilities) (France)
ANPE	Agence Nationale Pour l'Emploi (National Agency for Employment) (France)
ANPIHM	Association Nationale pour l'Intégration des Handicapés Moteurs (National Association for the Integration of People with Mobility Impairment) (France)
ANSEM	Agence National de l'évaluation et de la Qualité des Etablissements Et Services Sociaux Et Medico-Socio (National Agency for Quality Assessment of Social and Healthcare Services) (France)
AoA	Administration on Aging (United States)
APA	Allocation Personnalisée d'Autonomie (Personal Independence Allowance) (France)
APAJH	L'association pour Adultes et Jeunes Handicapés (Association for Disabled Adults and Young People) (France)

APF	Association des Paralysés de France (French Association for Paralyzed People) (France)
APL	Aide Personnalisée au Logement (Personal Rent Subsidy) (France)
ASPE	Assistant Secretary for Planning and Evaluation (United States)
BACI	Burnaby Association for Community Inclusion (Canada)
BC	British Columbia
BCOD	Base Mensuelle de calcul des Allocations Familiales (Basic Monthly Payment for the Calculation of Family Allowance) (France)
BCOPD	British Council of Organisations of Disabled People
CA	Carer's Allowance (Ireland)
CAF	Caisse d'Allocation Familliale (Family Allowance Fund) (France)
CAMPS	Centre d'Action Médico-Sociale Précoce (Early Years Health and Social Care Centre) (France)
C&AG	Comptroller and Auditor General (Ireland)
C&C	Cash & Counseling (United States)
CCDE	Cash & Counseling Demonstration and Evaluation (United States)
CCDSA	Commission Consultative Départementale de Sécurité et d'Accessibilité (Local Advisory Commission for Civil Protection, Safety and Accessibility) (France)
CDAPH	Commission des Droits et de l'Autonomie des Personnes Handicapées (Commission for the Independence and Rights of Persons with Disabilities) (France)
CDC	Consumer Directed Care (United States)
CDES	Commission Départementale d'Éducation Spéciale (Local Commission for Special Education) (France)
CES	Community Employment Scheme (Ireland)
CFC	Community First Choice (United States)
CHST	Canada Health and Social Transfer
CIB	Citizens Information Board (Ireland)
CIC	Citizen Information Centres (Ireland)
CID	Roman Catholic Institution for the Deaf and Dumb (renamed Catholic Institute for Deaf People in 2007)
CIL	Centre for Independent Living
CLN	Community Living Network
CLS	Community Living Services (United States)
CMP	Centre Medico Psycologique (Healthcare and Psychotherapy Centre) (France)
CMPP	Centre Medico-Pscychopédagogique (Pychotherapeutic Education Centre) (France)
CMS	Centers for Medicare and Medicaid (United States)
CMU	Couverture Maladie Universelle (Universal Health Care Coverage) (France)

CNAM	Commission Nationale d'Assurance-Maladie (National Commission of Health Insurance) (France)
CNAVTS	Caisse Nationale d'Assurance Vieillesse des Travailleurs Salariés (National Old-Age Pension Fund for Employees) (France)
CNCPH	Le Conseil National Consultatif des Personnes Handicapées (National Consultative Council for Persons with Disabilities) (France)
CNSA	Caisse National de Solidarité et d'Autonomie (National Fund for Solidarity and Independence) (France)
COTOREP	Commission Technique d'Orientation et de Reclassement Professionnel (Professional Commission for Occupational Enablement and Rehabilitation) (France)
CRC	Central Remedial Clinic (Ireland)
CRPD	The United Nations Convention on the Rights of Persons with Disabilities
CSCI	Commission for Social Care Inspection (United Kingdom)
CSG	Contribution Sociale Généralisée (The General Social Contribution) (France)
CSIL	Choices in Supports for Independent Living (Canada)
CST	Canadian Social Transfer
CTF	Child Trust Fund (United Kingdom)
CWO	Community Welfare Officer (Ireland)
DDASS	Direction Départementale des Affaires Sanitaires et Sociales (Local Directorate for Health and Social Affairs) (France)
DDTEFP	Direction Departemental du Travail Et de la Formation Professionnelle (Local Directorate for Employment and Professional Development) (France)
DFI	Disability Federation of Ireland
DHHS	Department of Health and Human Services (United States)
DLA	Disability Living Allowance (United Kingdom)
DLCG	Disability Legislation Consultation Group (Ireland)
DO	Discrimination Ombudsman (Sweden)
DPOs	Disabled Persons Organisations
DRA	Deficit Reduction Act 2005 (United States)
DWP	Department of Work and Pensions (United Kingdom)
EC	European Commission
EPSEN	Education for Persons with Special Educational Needs (Ireland)
ERHA	Eastern Regional Health Authority (Ireland)
ESA	Employment and Support Allowance (United Kingdom)
ESAT	Etablissement et Service d'Aide par le Travail (France)
ESF	European Social Fund
EU	European Union

FAM	Foyers d'Accueil Médicalisés (Residential Medical Unit) (France)
FÁS	Foras Aiseanna Saothair (Training and Employment Authority) (Ireland)
FDC	Fond Départementeaux de Compensation (Local Compensation Fund) (France)
FEDESAP	Federation National des Services à la Personne et de Proximité (National Federation of Local Individualized Services) (France)
FI	Fiscal Intermediary
FIPHFP	Fonds pour l'Insertion des Personnes Handicapées dans la Fonction Publique (Fund to Support Persons with Disabilities into Public Roles) (France)
FMAD	Fonds de Modernisation de l'Aide à Domicile (Fund for the Modernisation of Homecare Services) (France)
FMR	Fair Market Rent
FNATH	Fédération Nationale des Accidentés du Travail et des Handicapés (National Federation of Injured and Disabled Workers) (France)
GDP	Gross Domestic Product
GEM	Groupe d'Entraide Mutuelle (Peer Support Group) (France)
GIP	Groupement d'Intérêt Public (Public Interest Group) (France)
GNP	Gross National Income (expressed in purchasing power parity)
GPEC	Gestion Prévisionnelle des Emplois et des Compétences (Forward Management for Workforce and Skills) (France)
HALDE	Haute autorité de lutte contre les discriminations et pour l'égalité (High Authority Against Discrimination and in Favour of Equality) (France)
HCA	Homes and Communities Agency (United Kingdom)
HCBS	Home- and Community-Based Care
HeBE	Health Board Executive (Ireland)
HO	Disability Ombudsman (Sweden)
HSE	Health Service Executive (Ireland)
HUD	Department of Housing and Urban Development (United States)
IAN	Irish Advocacy Network (Ireland)
IASE	Irish Association of Supported Employment (Ireland)
IBA	Individual Budget Allocation
IBSEN	Individual Budgets Evaluation Network
IC	Independent Consultant
ICA	Irish Countrywomen's Association (Ireland)
ICF	International Classification of Functioning, Disability and Health
ICFs/MR	Intermediate Care Facilities for Persons with Mental Retardation
ICTU	Irish Congress of Trade Unions (Ireland)
IDS	Irish Deaf Society (Ireland)

IEM	Institut d'Education Motrice (Mobility Rehabilitation Service) (France)
IES	Institut d'Education Sensorielle (Sensory Rehabilitation Service) (France)
IHSS	In-Home Supportive Services (California)
IME	Institut Médico-Educatif (Health and Education Service) (France)
IMPRO	Institut Medico-Professionnel (Health and Vocational Service) (France)
INMO	Irish Nurses and Midwives Organisation
INO	Irish Nurses Organisation
INSEE	Institut National de la Statistique et des Études Économiques (French National Institute for Statistics and Economic Studies) (France)
IRIS	Include, Respect, I Self-Direct (United States)
ISL	Irish Sign Language (Ireland)
IWA	Irish Wheelchair Association (Ireland)
LOV	Choice Act (Sweden)
LPPR	Liste des Produits et Prestations Remboursables (List of Refundable Products and Services) (France)
MAJ	Meusure d'Accompagnement Judiciaire (Judicial Assistance Measure) (France)
MAPA	Maison d'Acceuil pour Personne Agées (Residential Unit for Older People) (France)
MARPA	Maison d'Acceuil Rurale pour Personne Agées (Rural Residential Unit for Older People) (France)
MAS	Maison d'Acceuil Specialisée (Specialist Residential Unit) (France)
MCCI	Modelling Community Change and Innovation (Canada)
MCFD	Minister of Child and Family Development (Canada)
MCO	Managed Care Organization (United States)
MDPH	Maison Départementale des Personnes Handicapée (Local Agency for Persons with Disabilities) (France)
MFP	Money Follows the Person Grant (United States)
MHC	Mental Health Commission (Ireland)
MSRB	Medico Social Research Board (Ireland)
MSWFP	Making Services Work for People (Canada)
MTP	Majoration pour Tierce Personne (Carer's Allowance) (France)
MVPA	Majoration Pour la Vie Autonome (Additional Allowance for an Independent Life) (France)
NAD	National Association for the Deaf (renamed DeafHear) (Ireland)
NAMHI	National Association for the Mentally Handicapped of Ireland (renamed Inclusion Ireland in 2007)
NCI	National Core Indicators (United States)

NCSE	National Council for Special Education (Ireland)
NDA	National Disability Authority (Ireland)
NDP	National Development Plan (Ireland)
NESC	National Economic and Social Council (Ireland)
NESF	National Economic and Social Forum (Ireland)
NGO	Non-governmental organisation
NHIS	National Health Insurance Society (Ireland)
NHS	National Health Service (United Kingdom)
NI	Northern Ireland
NPIRS	National Psychiatric In-Patient Reporting System (Ireland)
NPM	New Public Management
NRB	National Rehabilitation Board (Ireland)
ODI	Office for Disability Issues (United Kingdom)
ODSP	Ontario Disability Support Program (Canada)
OECD	Organisation for Economic Co-operation and Development (Ireland)
OHM	Office for Health Management (Ireland)
OIC	Order-In-Council
OIG	Office of Inspector General (United States)
PA	Personal Assistant (Ireland)
PAA	Projet d'Accueil et d'Accompagnement (Care and Support Project) (France)
PAS	Personal Advocacy Service (Ireland)
PCH	Prestation de Compensation du Handicap (Disability Compensation Allowance) (France)
PDs	Progressive Democrats (Ireland)
PNA	Psychiatric Nurses Association (Ireland)
POA	Power of Attorney
PPC	Plan Personalisé de Compensation (Personal Compensation Plan) (France)
PPS	Plan Personalisé de Scolarisation (Personal Education Plan) (France)
PRSI	Pay-Related Social Insurance (Ireland)
PTC	Provincial/Territorial Council (Canada)
PwDI	People with Disabilities Ireland
RA	Representation Agreement (Canada)
RAF	Royal Air Force (United Kingdom)
RFP	Request for Proposals
RNID	Royal National Institute for Deaf People (United Kingdom)
RQIA	Regulation and Quality Improvement Authority (United Kingdom)
RRF	Retirement Research Foundation (United States)
RSMH	Swedish National Association for Social and Mental Health

RWJF	Robert Wood Johnson Foundation (United States)
SAAD	Service D'aide et d'Accompagnement a Domicile (Home Assistance and Support Service) (France)
SALAR	Swedish Association of Local Authorities and Regions
SAMSAH	Service d'Accompagnement Medico-Social pour Adulte Handicapé (Health and Social Care Support Service for Disabled Adults) (France)
SAVS	Service d'Accompagnement à la Vie Sociale (Social Life Support Service) (France)
SESSAD	Service d'Éducation Spéciale et de Soins A Domicile (Education and Health Care Services at Home) (France)
SGA	Substantial Gainful Activity (United States)
SMA	State Medicaid Agency (United States)
SPASAD	Service Polyvalant d'Aide et de Soins à Domicile (Multipurpose Assistance and Care Home Service) (France)
SSA	Social Security Administration (United States)
SSAH	Special Services at Home (Canada)
SSDI	Social Security Disability Insurance (United States)
SSI	Supplemental Security Income (United States)
SSIAD	Services de Soins Infirmier a Domicile (Home Nursing Care Service) (France)
SSLU	Support Service Living Unit (Canada)
TB	Tuberculosis
TD	Teachta Daila (member of Dail Eireann, the lower house of the Oireachtas (Irish Parliament)
UCD	University College Dublin (Ireland)
UEROS	d'Evaluation de Réentrainement et d'Orientation Sociale et Professionnelle (Unit for Assessment and Social and Professional Rehabilitation) (France)
UK	United Kingdom
UN	United Nations
UNA	Union Nationale de l'Aide, des soins et des services aux domiciles (National Union of Assistance, Nursing Care and Homecare Services) (France)
UNAPEI	Union nationale des associations de parents, de personnes handicapées mentales et de leurs amis (National Union of Parents, People with Learning Disabilities and Their Friends) (France)
UPIAS	Union of the Physically Impaired Against Segregation (United Kingdom)
US	United States (of America)
VA	Department of Veterans Affairs (United States)
VAT	Value Added Tax

VFM	Value for Money Review (Ireland)
VMRG	Value for Money Review Group
VPN	Valuing People Now
VR	Vocational Rehabilitation
VTS	Visiting Teacher Service
WHO	World Health Organisation
WPG	Woodlands Parents Group (Canada)

PART I

Towards Active Citizenship for Persons with Disabilities

1

Introduction

Since the origins of welfare, there has been a continual debate over the way in which it has developed, with views of how it ought to be organised and what role, if any, the state should play in its provision. Within this debate there has been a more specific question over the role and actions of the state in relation to the lives of persons with disabilities, particularly given the long and close involvement by the state in their 'care'. This involvement has been subject to much attention in recent times over how best people with disabilities are supported to ensure they remain active in society. Welfare and services have been criticised for being paternalistic and no longer encouraging 'independence, social integration and participation in the life of the community'.[1] Accordingly, the general principles of welfare have been called into question by policy makers and disabled people alike regarding how much it promotes and facilitates individual self-determination and participation in society. In considering this agenda, it is important to ask whether or not persons with disabilities should be treated any different from other groups who have traditionally been 'cared for' by the state in the past. These central questions guide the core focus of this book – in particular to re-examine the way in which persons with disabilities have been supported by the state at the domestic level, and how this support has been reconfigured and reframed in accordance with a new generation of values and obligations centred on human dignity and independent living.

These guiding questions are ever more relevant today, given the significant economic downturn affecting many countries around the world. At the same time, the values and expectations that people hold are also changing. Many individuals with support needs are now better educated and no longer want a life of passive and enduring dependency. There is a stronger appreciation of the individual and of

---

[1] As articulated by Article 15 European Social Charter, Council of Europe, 1961.

one's right to shape one's own life. There is also a growing unease at the extent of social disparities, which is compounded by an increased exposure to other countries' standards and practices and greater access to information.[2]

With regard to whether the state has a role in welfare, it is important to revisit the original goals of the concept and purpose of the social institutions of the state. Prior to the beginning of the twentieth century, the overriding philosophy was that economic growth could solve most problems. However, with mass unemployment, gross inequality and widespread deprivation affecting many countries in the Western world, it became clear that growth could also produce costs.[3] Affluence and economic change, it was found, also produced 'diswelfares' and deprivation as well as wealth. For example, higher rates of economic growth often resulted in increased inequality, depending on things such as tax rates and the nature of economic growth.[4] If a society leaves 'the costs where they lie', according to Miller (1987), the least well off often bear the burden for the beneficiaries of growth.[5] When this is left unchecked, as had previously been the case, there are often further associated problems such as a breakdown in social cohesion, emigration and more widespread poor health. The potential alienation caused can also contribute to a loss of political support amongst those who are affected.[6] The wellsprings of the concept of welfare originated as a response to these costs. The goal of social institutions was to help achieve full employment, a share in growing prosperity and the satisfaction of certain basic needs to live and participate in society.

As originally conceived, welfare aimed to give people the opportunity to be active citizens – not to enforce dependency. This was the pivot of Beveridge's social welfare programme, as envisaged in his 1942 and 1944 reports.[7] The welfare institutions he proposed were aimed at increasing the competitiveness of British industry in the post-war period, not only by shifting labour costs like health care and pensions out of corporate ledgers and onto the public account, but also by producing healthier, wealthier and more motivated and productive workers who would also serve as a market themselves for British goods.

Similarly, in Canada, the Canada Assistance Plan in 1966 had two primary objectives according to the 1968 Annual Report of the CAP.[8] These were to 'support the

[2] National Economic and Social Council (2005) *Developmental Welfare State*. NESC, Dublin.
[3] Mishan, E. J. (1993) *The Costs of Economic Growth*. 2nd Edition. Oxford University Press, Oxford.
[4] *Ibid.*
[5] Miller, S. M. (1987) 'Introduction', in Abel-Smith, B. and Titmuss, K. (eds.) *The Philosophy of Welfare: Selected Writings of Richard M. Titmuss*. Allen & Unwin, London. pp. 1–18.
[6] Clarke, J., Cochrane, A. and Smart, C. (1987) *Ideologies of Welfare: From Dreams to Disillusion*. Hutchinson, London.
[7] Beveridge, W. (1942) *Social Insurance and Allied Services* (the Beveridge Report); Beveridge, W. (1944) *Full Employment in a Free Society*.
[8] Canada Assistance Plan Division in the Welfare Assistance and Services Branch (1968) *Annual Report of the Canada Assistance Plan*, Year Ended 31 March.

provision of adequate assistance to persons in need and to encourage the development and extension of welfare services designed to help prevent and remove the causes of poverty and dependence on public assistance'. One of the key factors that supported the development of more effective assistance and welfare service programmes was the growing concern that was being expressed about problems of poverty. It was increasingly recognised that the talents of many Canadians were being wasted because of poverty, illness, inadequate education and training and inequality in opportunities for work.

Meanwhile, in the United States, the 'Great Society' social reforms of the 1960s introduced for the first time general welfare payments, health care through Medicaid, food stamps, special payments for pregnant women and young mothers and federal and state housing benefits. This sought to limit what were seen as dangers in modern American life, including poverty, unemployment and the burdens of widows and fatherless children. With the Welfare Reform Act of 1996, the original emphasis of welfare was revisited and refashioned as 'a finite program built to provide short-term cash assistance and steer people quickly into jobs'.[9]

As originally conceived, there were two interlinked pillars of welfare: *state entitlements* and *social services*. While various mechanisms of state entitlement exist – such as a universal benefit, a means-tested benefit or a tax credit – they are based on a very similar principle that sees welfare as an important agent guaranteeing a minimal level of well-being and social support in order to build a floor under people, on which they can build by their own efforts. Over time, state entitlement increasingly has been given on the basis of contract: that people have to make contributions, that there would be known benefits, that welfare would be much more transparent, and that the cost would be much more clearly designated. The purpose of a non-contributory safety net is to help those who, at various stages in their life, for one reason or another, cannot participate in the contributory mechanisms available.

Alongside this, social services have played an integral part in enabling people to live healthily and to continue to engage in and contribute to society. 'Services' are taken to mean the constellation of actors and organisations necessarily and currently involved in providing supports that are key to social protection, from salaried public employees, to not-for-profit organisations, through to self-employed family doctors.[10] In other words, they offer people the support to move away from a sole reliance on welfare entitlement. In addition to state entitlements, then, access to services – in health, housing, employment, social inclusion and other areas – is also integral to enjoying social protection and becoming active citizens.

9 Goldstein, A. (2008) 'Welfare Rolls See First Climb in Years', *The Washington Post*, 17 December, www.washingtonpost.com/wp-dyn/content/article/2008/12/16/AR2008121602978.html (accessed 4 September 2011).

10 National Economic and Social Council (2005) *Developmental Welfare State*. NESC, Dublin.

Formerly, advances in social protection were largely thought of as a societal dividend which democratic political processes extracted *after* the event from successful economic performance.[11] However, when working together, state entitlements and social services can help to minimise effects of turbulent economic times and to ensure that social disadvantage does not become lasting social exclusion. These joint social institutions can help people adapt to pervasive changes and barriers to societal cohesion over time.

This original purpose of welfare and services arguably got lost in the intervening decades – particularly for people with disabilities, whose non-contribution was assumed in the first place, and services continued to seek to remove them from society. This historic peculiarity was later reflective of the broader 'welfare crisis' in the 1970s in the United Kingdom and in the 1980s in the United States, which sought a reappraisal of the Fabian vision of welfare – particularly its statist, paternalistic form of intervention. It was found that the way in which welfare had developed tended to encourage and enforce dependency rather than promote social and economic re-engagement in society. In particular, welfare became tainted with earlier institutional forms of care which had evolved since the earlier century. People with disabilities were simply being institutionalised and not given the tools or support to help them engage in employment or exercise their freedom. The systems which had been set up to support them in the end had not helped them to be active citizens, nor supported the development of stronger communities. As a result of this legacy, many services today have become standardised, inflexible and unaccountable to those they serve. Too many people are locked into poverty, dependency, social isolation or destructive patterns of behaviour to which the system seems unable to respond.[12] Indeed, many existing services were created to 'look after the helpless' and never sought to promote independence.[13] The legacies of institutionalisation have meant that many services no longer serve the public interest or the interest of people with disabilities. In the past, the 'public interest' served by state funding of such services either was left unsaid or it was simply assumed that passive maintenance was sufficient. Consequently, today, significant erosion has taken place in the legitimacy of traditional sources of such support.

Looking back, one of the key reasons the original welfare effort failed, particularly for people with disabilities, was the uncoupling of state entitlements from social services, which were themselves not supportive of active citizenship. In other words, state entitlements and social services no longer worked in tandem to assist people to become more engaged in society; they had become solely focussed on forcing

---

[11] *Ibid.*

[12] See Duffy, S. (2003) *Keys to Citizenship: A Guide to Getting Good Support for People with Learning Disabilities.* Paradigm, Birkenshead.

[13] McConkey, R. (2004) 'The Staffing of Services for People with Intellectual Disabilities', in Walsh, P. N. and Gash, H. (eds.) *Lives and Times: Practice, Policy and People with Disabilities.* Rathdown Press, Bray. pp. 30–43.

people into separate and non-active lives. For persons with disabilities, this meant that services which were set up to assist them became in themselves barriers to participation. According to the National Economic and Social Council (2005),

> If the social policies adopted are not supportive of continued economic strength, the eventual result will be a return to poor social protection. Part of the challenge to social policy, therefore, is that it facilitate as many people as possible playing a role in the economy and that it provide tangible results – in the form of parallel improvements in the quality of life for everyone – that good economic performance is leveraging the creation of a more just and attractive society.[14]

Rather than meaningful participation being narrowly conceived as solely engaging in open competitive employment however, the active citizenship concept refers to a broader engagement in a range of valued forms of participation, either through supported employment, volunteering, peer support and mentoring, undergoing training, partaking in local activities in the community – or indeed the securing of open competitive employment.[15] In response to this challenge, the wellsprings of reform have come from the recognition that the way in which 'welfare' and social support developed had ignored the original foundations of welfare; it had failed to give people the opportunity to decide the supports they need to meaningfully engage in society. Instead, the ways in which social structures had been established had caused further dislocation.

Given that people with disabilities form a core part of society which to varying extents may require supports to enable freedom, the question needs to be asked: Should persons with disabilities be treated any different from other people? While the debate over new forms of supporting people has relevance for all, the treatment of people with disabilities has its own peculiarities, as touched on earlier. Consistently, throughout the history of welfare, people with disabilities were not given an opportunity to engage or participate in society – and were generally met with pity or revulsion.[16] As a result, people's 'impairments' were medicalised, and the state felt that people with disabilities were best institutionalised, thereby removing any potential for them to socially or economically participate in society.

The advent of community care in the 1970s and 1980s envisaged a new era of participation and inclusion in the community. Significant amounts of money were given to social services to operate community residential centres. However, the

---

14 National Economic and Social Council (2005) *Developmental Welfare State.* NESC, Dublin. p. 1. Please also see pp. xii and 7–11 for a more critical interrogation of how economic and social developments are neither intrinsically opposed nor compelled to occur together in some automatic way. Rather, they *can be made to support each other.*

15 Gilbert, T., Cochrane, A., and Greenwell, S. (2005) Citizenship: locating people with learning disabilities *Int J Soc Welfare,* 14: 287–296.

16 Schweik, S. (2009) *The Ugly Laws: Disability in Public (The History of Disability),* New York University Press, New York.

original proponents of community care quickly saw that the same institutional practices, such as depersonalisation, rigidity of routine, block treatment, social distance
and paternalism, continued to live on in the new community settings which were
built.[17] As a result, there continued to be little chance to guarantee individualised
needs-tailored supports and participation and inclusion in the community. Current
worldwide trends favour a personalisation of supports to meet real as opposed to
assumed need, opening up choice in personal living arrangements and redesigning
supports to enable an active life in the community.[18]

This change in the philosophy of 'support' in the disability field has more recently
been recognised by international human rights instruments, such as the recent UN
Convention on the Rights of Persons with Disabilities (CRPD),[19] which is calling
for a new age of supporting people with disabilities as a core human rights concern.
Importantly, Article 19 of the convention deals with the right to 'independent living
and *being included in the community*.' Among other things it asks States Parties
to guarantee the right to 'have access to a range of in-home, residential and other
community supports services, including personal assistance to support living and
inclusion in the community'.[20] This marks a shift from the earlier philosophy of
rights, which previously had focussed on securing rights to services per se, without
the principles of participation, inclusion and accessibility, as examined in the next
chapter.

The inspiration for reform – that of social and economic re-engagement rather
than continuing social protection in itself – should thus be the same for those with
a disability as for all people. Therefore, while this book is focussed on social support
for persons with disabilities, it nonetheless should have a broader relevance to all
persons, in terms of its focus on the reconfiguration of the very idea of welfare for
all.[21] Here, the emphasis is on the idea of 'active citizenship,' centred on promoting a
life in the community and challenging the socially constructed barriers, behaviours
and attitudes which continue to deny full citizenship, and providing the supports
needed to enable people to realise their citizenship. Significantly, this change means
that people are able to live their own lives as they wish, confident that supports are
of high quality, and have choice and control over the shape of that support.

Underpinning this reform agenda is the idea of a 'developmental welfare state',[22]
meaning a shift from a dependency-creating welfare model towards an enabling

---

[17] European Commission Ad Hoc Expert Group (2009) *Report of the Ad Hoc Expert Group on the Transition from Institutional to Community-Based Care*. European Commission, Brussels.

[18] O'Brien, P. and Sullivan, M. (Eds.) (2005) *Allies in Emancipation: Shifting from Providing Service to Being of Support*. Thomson Dunmore Press, South Melbourne Victoria. pp. 3–19.

[19] United Nations (2006) Convention on the Rights of Persons with Disabilities. Hereafter, CRPD.

[20] Article 19, CRPD (emphasis added).

[21] In Scotland, for example, the *Community Care and Health (Scotland) Act* (2002) stipulated that all persons assessed as having 'community care needs' would be eligible for a direct payment. This covered persons who are frail, receiving rehabilitation after an accident or operation, are fleeing domestic violence, are a refugee, are homeless or are recovering from drug or alcohol dependency.

[22] See National Economic and Social Council (2005) *Developmental Welfare State*. NESC, Dublin.

welfare state. This change in thinking has culminated in many jurisdictions under-going reform processes designed to support people to be active citizens, and to develop stronger communities of support. This has focussed on a more person-alised, *person-driven* approach to meeting needs, providing greater *choice in living arrangements* and a wider range of supports and opportunities that enable people with disabilities to *live and participate in the community*. Personalisation has come to represent this approach focussed on developing a more individualised way to support delivery and the promotion of choice and control in one's own support. Its fundamental principles are contrary to the traditional service-centred response, where the service provider generally decides on a menu of options provided to groups of people with disabilities in segregated settings, with little or no room for choice or personal autonomy.[23] These core guiding principles form the centrepiece (Article 3) of the recent CRPD, which outlines that States Parties must respect a person's inherent dignity, individual autonomy and independence, including the freedom to make his/her own choices, and full and effective participation and inclusion in society.[24] These inform the normative framework of this book.

FOCUS AND SCOPE OF THE BOOK

While the concept of welfare therefore is at a crossroads, the next important question is *how* a state might sculpt such reform, in light of these historical differences in the way people with disabilities have been treated. Achieving such a change suggests the need for reconfiguring traditional welfare structures in such a way as to remove barriers to participation. Examining how different countries have grappled with this reform agenda is the core focus of this book. The central aim is to understand the way in which states have implemented international disability law and policy and reconfigured their systems of welfare and social services in order to facilitate the development of good integrated models of support. To achieve this, the main objectives of the study are to examine:

- the contemporary international and regional (European) disability legal and policy climate, which sets out the moral compass and guiding principles for states to follow;
- the main demand-side and supply-side aspects of reform within the support delivery systems across a comparative sample of jurisdictions including the United States (a selection of states including Wisconsin and Michigan), Canada (British Columbia and Ontario), the United Kingdom (England and Northern Ireland), Sweden and France;

---

[23] Genio (2009) *Disability and Mental Health in Ireland: Searching Out Good Practice*, Genio, http://www.genio.ie/files/publications/Genio_Report_2009_Disability_and_Mental_Health_in _Ireland.pdf (accessed 23 November 2010).
[24] CRPD.

- the context of service delivery within Ireland, a jurisdiction at the cusp of reform, identifying how it has begun to reform its system of support delivery, and the challenges it faces.

In order to inform change at the domestic level, this book is particularly concerned with *how* policy is delivered and implemented. The first consideration in answering this question is how social support is administered by the state. Does the state provide support directly or does it work through intermediaries? Is it operated through a state's health care system or local authority structure? If delivered through intermediaries within the 'independent sector' (non-profit and private agencies), how is the serving of the public interest ensured? More specifically, how do we ensure that the social institutions involved do not fall back into practices which continue to enforce dependency?

In most cases, states have operated a blend of directly provided benefits and services, as well as working through a complex array of intermediaries within the independent sector. To achieve reform throughout this diverse sector, states have had to reconstruct both the demand side of support, by trying to restore power to the consumer, and the supply side of support, by attempting to make the social support market more responsive.

The demand side of reform is seen as pivotal to counteract the effects of people with disabilities being historically devalued and disenfranchised. Without building capacity amongst persons with disabilities, professionals and service managers will continue to reshape their services in ways they see fit, without people themselves being able to insist on the supports they need to guide their own lives. Here, advocacy, independent planning and facilitation in managing one's own support are important mechanisms which can be used, and they are examined in this book. Also, recent welfare policy which has started to gain ground internationally (in the United States, the United Kingdom and Canada), known as 'asset-based welfare policy', where the government fosters saving and asset building, is examined. These policy mechanisms are designed to restore balance to individuals who have previously been left disempowered and solely reliant on the discretion of support providers.

Reforming the supply side is also seen as important in order to carve out new roles for support providers and to inject market forces into service arrangements. This includes an insistence on some form of competitive tendering within the service sector and an enforcement of standards by which they operate. This approach has sought to replace old systems of allocating resources to organisations, which had historically given them unchecked freedom to direct services as they wished. Traditionally, block grants were used to administer funding to the independent sector. These were lump-sum grants of money given to intermediaries to provide loosely defined services to a group of people, without close inspection or state involvement. They therefore did not allow individualised targeting of resources, and as a consequence, individuals were grouped together in depersonalised inflexible service arrangements which were unable to adequately respond to people's wishes to participate more widely in society. In response, states have sought new funding mechanisms, individually earmarked and ring-fenced, to enable people with disabilities to choose the supports which best reflect their needs and wishes. New structures of managing accountability for public money have also been used.

While these mechanisms have been advanced in different ways in each jurisdiction examined in this book, the overall thrust of reform has been centred on a reconfiguration of welfare and social services to empower the person to become actively engaged in choosing the support he or she requires. Some jurisdictions have been involved in this process for some time. The replacement of large residential institutions by a network of community-based person-driven supports is well under way in Canada, the United Kingdom, Sweden and the United States. In addition, France has implemented a system-wide legislative reform to enable people to have more control over the supports they need to live their own lives.

Other countries, such as Ireland, have only begun to transform their disability support systems, and are on the cusp of the reform agenda. By looking at Ireland in international comparison, it is possible to identify how Ireland has responded to the growing international focus on how support systems are helping people to re-engage in society. In effect, Ireland is a test case for transferring a lot of learning from international sources and seeing how it works. There are valuable lessons from other jurisdictions which Ireland can learn from – and perhaps it can avoid the mistakes made by others, such as creating new mini-institutions. It is also a very topical case study at present, as the government has just published a report on the deinstitutionalisation of people with disabilities[25] and is on the cusp of reforming how disability services are managed and funded. Indeed, the Irish case study is an example of a site which is reimagining the role of the welfare state, which should resonate with all other jurisdictions facing challenges to their social care systems. Ireland is therefore at a crossroads in terms of its transformation of congregated services towards the individualisation of support.

This book builds on recent international legal instruments and policy documents which will be outlined in the next chapter. Drawing on the core themes being prioritised within the international and regional (European) legal and policy environment – in particular, the CRPD – the study concentrates on three core focus areas: (1) personalisation; (2) choice in living arrangements; and (3) a life in the community. Each of these fundamental building blocks is being advocated by national jurisdictions committed to personalised forms of support.

At its core, *personalisation* means a more individual approach to the design and delivery of supports which give people more choice over how they best meet their needs. To meet this end, the study focusses on how different governments and providers have grappled with embedding person-driven supports in order to be responsive to their needs and preferences.

---

[25] Health Service Executive (2011) *Time to Move on from Congregated Settings: A Strategy for Community Inclusion*, June 2011.

Meanwhile, in terms of *choice in living arrangements*, as expressed in the CRPD, all people with disabilities should have the opportunity to have more choice and control over their place of residence and where and with whom they live.[26] Inherent in this is an understanding that people with disabilities should have access to the personal assistance necessary to support living and inclusion in the community and to prevent isolation or segregation from the community.[27] The study is therefore concerned with examining steps to ensure this happens, including: general and disability-specific government housing policy; the shaping of the residential support environment (including the extent of independent living arrangements, assured tenancies, etc.); government commitments to deinstitutionalise people from residential centres; and other new housing initiatives.

Finally, a *life in the community* (for all people) involves a shift away from 'providing a service', which has ultimately tied people into segregated services, to 'being of support' in order to improve a person's life chances and ability to achieve dignity and equality in society. According to the Ministry of Community and Social Services in Ontario, 'it's one thing to live in a community, but it's another thing to be *a part of it*'.[28] This goal requires a commitment from government and support providers to promoting community connection (e.g. through the use of Personal Assistants[29]) and fostering the development of social and economic participation (e.g. supported employment[30]) in an effort to help people to get better lives.

To meet this end, the comparative chapters identify challenges countries have faced in the dismantling of conventional block service models in an effort to address these focus areas. It identifies ways in which they have delivered more responsive support, from the demand and supply sides. It is hoped that the successes and challenges of implementation identified in this book will help to inform the development of a clear, targeted and practical map for reform, and to enable rational policy debates to take place.

[26] UN CRPD, Art 19.

[27] Personal Assistance (PA) is a fundamental service provided to people with disabilities ensuring that they can fully participate in society. The tasks of a PA are tailored to the individual needs of the service user (called a 'Leader' within the Centres for Independent Living) and may include personal care, household help, assistance in college or at the workplace, driving, interpretation and so forth. The major difference between a PA and a carer is that in case of personal assistance, the service is designed and managed by people with disabilities directly.

[28] Ontario Ministry of Community and Social Services (2007) *Spotlight on Transformation*, Issue 13 (emphasis added).

[29] Personal Assistants are persons employed to support persons with support needs in their activities of daily living such as: cooking and cleaning; help with personal care like washing and using the toilet; driving or help with getting around; medical tasks like giving injections or changing a catheter; and shopping, banking and paying bills. The aim is to give people the right help at the right time to enable them to have much more choice and control over their lives. Generally, people can choose to get a personal assistant through a home support agency, or employ someone directly.

[30] Supported employment involves the use of support strategies to enable individuals to find jobs that suit their aspirations and abilities, successfully learn the skills and routines of the jobs they obtain and develop career paths in line with personal aspirations and abilities.

METHODS OF STUDY

To meet the requirements of the study, as set out earlier, the research was conducted over a period of two and a half years (late 2008–early 2011). In each jurisdiction, the study adopted a multi-method comparative approach, exploring the central questions identified at the beginning of the chapter across each of the international comparisons. Each comparative study was comprised mainly of a detailed desk-based study. This was supplemented by fieldwork as well as follow up interviews over the phone and by email with service providers and advocacy bodies in each jurisdiction. The desk-based study encompassed an in-depth examination of all available literature, including the texts of national disability law and policy, government reports and reviews, media reporting, shadow reports published by disabled persons organisations, policy submissions and evaluative social policy research from academic sources.

The comparative study fieldwork comprised periods of two-to-four week stays in each of the case-study countries (between May and August 2009), during which time interviews were carried out with the following key stakeholders:

- government officials in relevant departments;
- national and local representative advocacy bodies;
- disabled persons organisations;
- service providers;
- policy researchers.

The interviews were semi-structured and adapted to suit each type of stakeholder with four broad focus areas of questioning: (1) What has been the main focus of reform? (2) What were the main wellsprings and drivers of this reform? (3) How was reform implemented? (4) What challenges or issues have arisen and how have these been dealt with? A more detailed list of comparative questions is provided in the Appendix. Following these periods of fieldwork, supplementary consultative meetings with additional respondents were held over the telephone. The interviews served to cross-check what was emerging from the desk-based study. In addition, the *European Network of Independent Living* also contributed significantly in terms of offering their expertise to the comparative fieldwork and analysis, particularly with the French and Swedish case studies. This multi-targeted approach allowed for a thorough examination of the policy climate in each jurisdiction.[31]

Given the third aim – to examine the context of service delivery within Ireland – the project's main focus at the Irish national scale was to capture a bird's-eye view of the overall infrastructure of disability social support, in which individual service providers have to work. It therefore comprised a multi-method approach including

[31] Ritchie, J. and Lewis, J. (2003) *Qualitative Research Practice: A Guide for Social Science Students and Researchers*. Sage, London.

a detailed historical analysis of the main choke points in Ireland's current disability landscape of support, followed by focus groups and interviews with key stakeholders. This fieldwork took place between September 2009 and April 2010. A wide range of documentation was examined, similar to the other comparative jurisdictions including legislation, planning and policy documents and a variety of other relevant literature. Interviews with key individuals from statutory agencies, service delivery organisations and relevant civil society groups, state/monitoring bodies and disability researchers were carried out to ensure that the research was well grounded.

In addition, day visits were also carried out at eight service provider organisations (five intellectual disability and three physical disability services). Each day visit included interviews with staff and meetings with individuals being supported by the service. Participant observation was also undertaken with an alliance of service providers committed to individualised services. The alliance was used by providers to troubleshoot issues, talk about successful methods and outcomes and identify new ways of tackling organisational barriers. It proved helpful to listen to discussions between service managers over the 'unbundling' of group homes, the individualisation of support plans and the management of more person-driven support arrangements.

Finally, three consultative focus groups were carried out within a local consultation group, established by the Centre for Disability Law and Policy at the National University of Ireland, Galway. The first focus group consisted of individuals with physical and intellectual and developmental disabilities. The second focus group included representatives from the deaf community. Last but not least, a focus group was undertaken with a number of service providers.

A rigorous ethical framework was used throughout the duration of this study. Participants in the focus groups and interviews were given information prior to and subsequent to each meeting to ensure that they understood the nature of the project and the terms to which they were consenting. It was agreed that particular views would not be attributed to individuals. In addition, each individual was given the opportunity to withdraw from the process at any time.

The methodology was mindful that some of the case studies included non-federal polities, like France and Ireland, and others included federal polities, like the United States and Canada. The analysis therefore tried to highlight certain states and provinces in the United States and Canada and devolved territories in the United Kingdom to enable more easily comparable scales. Nonetheless, it is acknowledged that different countries operate in their own specific contexts, and we would not advocate an unproblematic 'transposition' of any one model onto other jurisdictions. Any structural ingredients recommended must always be carefully adapted to suit.

OUTLINE OF THE STUDY

The book is structured in four main parts. Part I consists of three chapters, including the present chapter, which introduces the core conceptual framework which guides the study and sets out the outline of the rest of the study. Chapter 2 begins by examining the international and regional (European) obligations which guide current thinking in the support of persons with disabilities. In particular, it will analyse the background to current international and regional (European) disability law, including hard and soft law and policy instruments, culminating with the UN CPRD. Ultimately, these set the standards by which all stakeholders involved in the lives of persons with disabilities will be judged.

To meet these standards and to overcome dependency-creating welfare structures, as stated, each jurisdiction is having to re-engineer its welfare states and landscapes of support delivery. Chapter 3 thus examines best practice from the international comparative welfare and governance and change management literature to begin to explore ways in which reform *can* be achieved. It will identify the concept of 'smart welfare', which is a governance approach typified by the idea of a 'developmental' or 'enabling' welfare state,[32] and is based on strategic commissioning, developmental funding and the principle of progressive realisation, as articulated by the International Covenant on Economic, Social and Cultural Rights.[33]

Part II of the book draws on the earlier chapters by identifying the implications of the international legal and policy environments, as well as what learning can be applied from best-practice management in support policy. It explores how different comparative jurisdictions – the United States, Canada, the United Kingdom, Sweden and France – have grappled with the reform of their disability landscape of support. Within this part of the book, there are five chapters, each detailing one of the comparative jurisdictions.

Chapter 4 examines the US case in detail. It outlines the governance of disability policy, the law and the policy, funding and delivery of disability support. Drawing from this policy climate, the chapter then identifies the wellsprings of reform and explicates what mechanisms have been used to promote personalisation, choice in living arrangements and a life in the community. Illustrating best-practice examples across the United States, it draws from a range of different states. Finally, the chapter identifies how the United States has grappled with the challenges inherent in its transformation efforts. Chapter 5 follows the same layout as the previous chapter and details how Canada has reformed its support delivery. Given its provincial governance, it examines British Columbia and Ontario in more detail. Chapter 6 explores the reform of support delivery in the United Kingdom. Again, given its devolved governance, the chapter will examine the particular cases within England and Northern Ireland. Chapter 7 examines the emergence of the particular welfare model in Sweden and how it has evolved to ensure people with disabilities can have maximum independence in their lives. Chapter 8 looks at the recent system-wide

---

[32] National Economic and Social Council (2005) *Developmental Welfare State*. NESC, Dublin.

[33] Article 2 of the International Covenant on Economic, Social and Cultural Rights imposes a duty on all parties to: *take steps . . . to the maximum of its available resources, with a view to achieving progressively the full realization of the rights recognized in the present Covenant by all appropriate means, including particularly the adoption of legislative measures.*

reform of law and policy in France and considers how it has changed the way in which people with disabilities are supported.

Part III of the book consists of a detailed case study of Ireland, which is a jurisdiction at the edge of transformation. Two chapters are included in this part of the book. Chapter 9 provides a background history to Ireland's disability support model in order to identify the peculiar blend of service arrangements which emerged. Chapter 10 examines the extent of reconfiguration of this support delivery framework in today's context in Ireland.

Finally, Part IV of the book combines the lessons learned from the earlier review of management literature and each case study chapter and explores options for a new model of disability support consistent with the goals of the UN CRPD. Chapter 11 draws on the findings from the comparative and Irish chapters and sets out the key success factors applicable to all jurisdictions, and specifically to Ireland. The Conclusion at the end of the book aims to serve as the starting point for future dialogue and discussion on the importance of reform and of breaking down barriers to participation faced by people with disabilities in the relevant jurisdictions.

CONCLUSION – TOWARDS REFRAMING 'DISABILITY'

This is a timely opportunity to examine this evolving area, as more and more countries, such as Ireland, transition from traditional service regimes to personalised support systems. With the current economic context in which national policy is framed, as well as the demographic pressures from an ageing population, the need for real and sustainable alternatives is beyond doubt. Moreover, disability is something that cuts through all of society and impacts a wide cross-section of individuals and families. Indeed, the combined number of men, women and children who are born with or can acquire a disability over their life course is estimated to be between 10 per cent and 20 per cent of the global population.[34,35] Additionally, the effects of disability reach spouses, offspring, extended family members and multitudes of people within the community. Disability therefore does not identify a 'minority group'. It affects men and women alike, across different socio-economic, ethnic and age groups and sexual orientations. Alongside these figures, the growing age profile in many Western countries means that levels of acquired cognitive and physical disability amongst the 'general' population (i.e. previously non-disabled) are also increasing.

Cumulatively, the significant rates of people living with disabilities put the notion of 'disability' in a new light. Indeed, the International Classification of Functioning,

---

[34] Priestley, M. (2003) *Disability: A Life Course Approach*. Polity Press, London.

[35] Rates of disability can vary depending on many factors including the age profile of a country, its level of wealth, whether it engages in conflict, the definition used by censuses and so on. It is understood that different definitions of disability are used by different countries' censuses, which can affect the total figures, which in turn makes direct comparison less applicable.

Disability and Health, known more commonly as the ICF,[36] acknowledges that every human being can experience a decrement in health and thereby experience some degree of disability. Disability is not something that only happens to a minority of humanity. The ICF thus 'mainstreams' the experience of disability and recognises it as a universal human experience. Therefore the reforming of disability support is concerned with reaching out to mainstream society for emancipatory understandings of disability. It is understood that the community as a whole is impoverished by the exclusion of individuals who do not altogether conform to the culturally valued images of normality – able in mind and body and occupying customary and socially valued roles.[37]

While the prevalence of people living with disabilities is significant, it is frankly acknowledged in this book that many individuals, particularly within the deaf community and indeed many elderly people, do not consider themselves as having a 'disability'. The main focus of this book is not so much on who is to be labelled 'disabled'. Our starting point is that disability is a 'social construct' – in other words, society's understanding of disability has been socially created through human interpretation, belief and opinion.[38] It thus takes a social model of disability approach, which identifies systemic barriers, negative attitudes and exclusion by society (purposely or inadvertently) as the main contributory factors in disabling people. This book uses some particularised terminology of disability exclusively as an expository device.[39]

Ultimately then, the focal point of this study is to identify the core elements of a framework which promote individually focussed, cost-effective models of support that have applicability in each country. It is hoped that by identifying the adequacy, shortcomings, cost-effectiveness and personal outcomes of this reform in each country, the options and alternatives outlined in Chapter 11 will promote the development of an appropriate framework that has applicability in each jurisdiction.

---

[36] The ICF is a classification of health and health-related domains. These domains are classified from body, individual and societal perspectives by means of two lists: a list of body functions and structure, and a list of domains of activity and participation. Given that an individual's functioning and disability occur in a context, the ICF also includes a list of environmental factors. See http://www.who.int/classifications/icf/en/.

[37] Clark, C. (2001) 'The Transformation of Day Care', in Clark, C. (ed.) *Adult Day Services and Social Inclusion: Better Days*. Jessica Kingsley Publishers Ltd., London. p. 15.

[38] Social Constructivism is a social theory which argues that the meanings we use to understand our world develop in social contexts – through interactions with others – rather than being fixed or 'given' by nature. For more information, please refer to Burr, V. (1995) *An Introduction to Social Constructionism*. Routledge, London.

[39] Throughout the book, it is acknowledged that various different terminologies are used by different jurisdictions to classify people with disabilities. While some localised terminology is used throughout the book (e.g. disabled people in the United Kingdom), generally 'persons/people with disabilities' is used, given its preferred usage in the UN Convention on the Rights of Persons with Disabilities.

2

Supports to Persons with Disabilities in the Context of International and Regional Disability Law and Policy

INTRODUCTION

This chapter considers international as well as regional (European) law and policy frameworks that have particular application to the rights-based provision of disability supports at the domestic level. The chapter begins with an overview of international and regional disability law and policy which are most relevant for the consideration of disability supports. The second part of the chapter examines developments in law and policy with particular reference to the focus areas of the project, namely personalisation, choice in living arrangements and life in the community. The third part provides an analysis of law, policy and process relating to the actual provision of supports to persons with disabilities, including public-sector procurement and competition and consumer complaints mechanisms. The chapter concludes by drawing out the implications of international and regional disability law and policy for ensuring that disability supports are implemented consistent with human rights principles and directed towards fostering full citizenship for persons with disabilities.

The adoption of the Convention on the Rights of Persons with Disabilities (CRPD or Convention)[1] by the UN General Assembly in 2006 marks the culmination of many years of work within the UN system to place disability rights on the international agenda and to fully integrate disability issues into the broader human rights and international development frameworks. At the same time, the adoption of the

---

[1] UN Convention on the Rights of Persons with Disabilities, G.A. Res. 61/106, U.N. Doc. A/61/611 (13 December 2006), *opened for signature* 30 March 2007, 46 I.L.M. 433 [hereinafter Convention or CRPD]. An Optional Protocol providing for additional monitoring mechanisms was adopted at the same time. Optional Protocol to the Convention on the Rights of Persons with Disabilities, *opened for signature* 30 March 2007, 46 I.L.M. 433 [hereinafter Optional Protocol]. The CRPD text, along with its drafting history, resolutions and updated list of signatories and States Parties, is posted on the United Nations Enable Web site at http://www.un.org/esa/socdev/enable/rights/convtexte.htm (accessed 12 March 2012).

CRPD is serving as an impetus for disability law and policy reform at both domestic and regional levels.[2] The CRPD, as the first international human rights convention ever adopted by a regional integration organisation – the European Community – is invigorating disability rights across the Member States of the European Union (EU) and within the institutions of the EU. A EU Disability Strategy 2010–2020[3] was adopted in 2010 and is directed at empowering persons with disabilities to fully realise their human rights and supporting effective implementation of the CRPD consistently across the EU. These developments are further reinforced by the work of the Council of Europe where the CRPD is already serving to guide the interpretation of the human rights instruments adopted within the Council of Europe's regional human rights system.[4] The adoption by the Council of Europe of a Disability Action Plan for the period 2006–2015 also signals its efforts to include disability rights as a core part of the human rights agenda.[5]

Emergence of International Standards on Disability

The starting point for any consideration of international disability rights is the emergence of modern international human rights in the early post–World War Two period, beginning with generalised human rights protections, as opposed to theme-specific or population-focused human rights. At the same time, disability law and policy emerged, but were developed and framed narrowly, and focussed on the rehabilitation of persons wounded during World War II.

Beginning with general human rights provisions in the UN Charter,[6] a framework emerged for the protection of human rights through international treaties to be implemented at the domestic level. The human rights principles and obligations set forth in the International Bill of Rights, comprising the Universal Declaration

---

[2] See generally Lord, J. E. and Stein, M. A. (2008) 'The Domestic Incorporation of Human Rights Law and the United Nations Convention on the Rights of Persons with Disabilities', *U. Wash. L. Rev.* 83: 449.

[3] European Union (2010) *European Disability Strategy 2010–2020: A Renewed Commitment to a Barrier-Free Europe*, available at: http://eur-lex.europa.eu/LexUriServ/LexUriServ.do?uri=COM:2010:0636: FIN:EN:PDF (accessed 12 March 2012).

[4] For more on the CRPD from a European perspective, see generally Arnardóttir, O. and Quinn, G. (eds.), (2009) *Future Prospects for the United Nations Convention on the Rights of Persons with Disabilities*, in The UN Convention on the Rights of Person with Disabilities: European and Scandinavian Perspectives. See also Lawson, A. (2009) 'The UN Convention on the Rights of Persons with Disabilities and European Disability Law: A Catalyst for Cohesion?' in Arnardóttir, O. and Quinn, G. *Ibid.* p. 103. For a helpful international and comparative law perspective written prior to the adoption of the CRPD, see Degener, T. and Quinn, G. (2002) 'A Survey of International, Comparative and Regional Disability Law Reform', in Breslin, M.L. & Yee, S. (eds.), *Disability Rights Law and Policy: International and National Perspectives*, 3–129.

[5] Council of Europe (2006) *Council of Europe Disability Action Plan 2006–2015*, available at: http://www.coe.int/t/e/social_cohesion/soc%2Dsp/Rec_2006_5%20Disability%20Action%20Plan.pdf (accessed 12 March 2012).

[6] UN CHARTER, 26 June 1945, 59 Stat. 1031, T.S. 993, 3 Bevans 1153, *entered into force* 24 October 1945.

of Human Rights,[7] the International Covenant on Civil and Political Rights[8] and the International Covenant on Economic, Social and Cultural Rights,[9] apply to all human beings. In time, specialised treaties pertaining to specific populations or issues were developed, such as the Convention on the Elimination of All Forms of Racial Discrimination[10] and the Convention against Torture,[11] amongst others. While all of these treaties are applicable to persons with disabilities as human beings, they do not explicitly set forth rights for persons with disabilities. They nonetheless form the foundation for international disability law and policy. While disability was largely invisible in these early human rights documents, where referenced, the clear thrust was not equal enjoyment of human rights or social integration and participation, but, more narrowly, on rehabilitation, vocational training and social assistance.[12] As Professor Theresia Degener has emphasised, where disability is addressed in the human rights law, 'it is only in connection with social security and preventive health policy,'[13] and not as a comprehensive human rights issue.

Beginning in the 1970s, the UN turned its attention to the drafting of non-binding standards specifically pertaining to disability. These early efforts included the adoption of the Declaration on the Rights of Mentally Retarded Persons[14] followed by the Declaration on the Rights of Disabled Persons,[15] the first international instruments specifically addressing persons with disabilities. While the adoption of these instruments certainly reflected an important development in terms of placing disability on the international agenda, these were non-binding, did little to shape national law and policy and had no monitoring and implementation measures to facilitate national action. Moreover, they did not fully reflect – and in some cases diverged from –

---

7 Universal Declaration of Human Rights, G.A. res. 217A (III), U.N. Doc A/810 at 71 (1948) [hereinafter UDHR].
8 International Covenant on Civil and Political Rights, G.A. res. 2200A (XXI), 21 U.N. GAOR Supp. (No. 16) at 52, U.N. Doc. A/6316 (1966), 999 U.N.T.S. 171, *entered into force* 23 March 1976 [hereinafter ICCPR].
9 International Covenant on Economic, Social and Cultural Rights, G.A. res. 2200A (XXI), 21 U.N. GAOR Supp. (No. 16) at 49, U.N. Doc. A/6316 (1966), 993 U.N.T.S. 3, *entered into force* 3 January 1976 [hereinafter ICESCR].
10 International Convention on the Elimination of All Forms of Racial Discrimination, G.A. Res. 2106 (XX), U.N. GAOR, Supp. No. 14, at 47, U.N. Doc. A/6014 (1966).
11 Convention against Torture and Other Cruel, Inhuman or Degrading Treatment or Punishment, G.A. Res. 39/46, U.N. GAOR, 39th Sess., Annex, Supp. No. 51 at 197, U.N. Doc. A/39/51 (1984).
12 The UDHR makes only one reference to disability. Article 25 provides that: '[E]veryone has the right to a standard of living adequate for the health and well-being of himself and his family . . . and the right to security in the event of unemployment, sickness, disability, widowhood, old age or other lack of livelihood in circumstances beyond his control'. *See* UDHR, *supra*, n. 7.
13 Degener, T. (1995) 'Disabled Persons and Human Rights: The Legal Framework', in Degener, T. and Koster-Dreese, Y. (eds.), *Human Rights and Disabled Persons: Essays and Relevant Human Rights Instruments*, 9–39. Martinus Nijhoff Publishers, Dordrecht.
14 Declaration on the Rights of Mentally Retarded Persons, G.A. res. 2856 (XXVI), 26 U.N. GAOR Supp. (No. 29) at 93, U.N. Doc. A/8429 (1971). [hereinafter 1971 Declaration], art. 1, Preamble 5.
15 Declaration on the Rights of Disabled Persons, G.A. res. 3447 (XXX), 30 U.N. GAOR Supp. (No. 34) at 88, U.N. Doc. A/10034 (1975).

existing human rights principles, as indicated in the sections that follow.[16] Such early policy responses tended to underscore passivity and dependence which, as the previous chapter discussed, underscored the ethos of welfare policy at the time. However unwittingly, they contributed to separation and segregation, whether in education, employment or other realms, serving to reinforce the isolation of persons with disabilities. They were clearly not directed towards the provision of supports to enable persons with disabilities to live their lives as equal and active citizens.[17]

The designation of the International Year of Disabled Persons in 1981[18] and the adoption of the non-binding World Programme of Action in 1982[19] by the General Assembly as a means of encouraging national-level programmes to achieve equality for persons with disabilities[20] provided a strong impetus for progress on disability rights.

The Decade of Disabled Persons (1983–1992)[21] culminated in the adoption of the Standard Rules on the Equalization of Opportunities for Persons with Disabilities by the General Assembly on 4 March 1994.[22] The Standard Rules are non-binding and consist of twenty-two rules which aim to elaborate the message of the World Programme of Action, providing a basis for technical and economic cooperation amongst States, the UN and other international organisations. The Standard Rules identify as their purpose 'to ensure that girls, boys, women and men with

[16] See generally National Council on Disability, *Understanding the Role of an International Convention on the Human Rights of People with Disabilities* (Principal Author, Lord, J. E. Washington, DC, 2002) [hereinafter NCD Report].

[17] See Quinn, G. (2005) 'The European Social Charter and EU Anti-Discrimination Law in the Field of Disability: Two Gravitational Fields with One Common Purpose', in de Bruca, G. and de Witte, B. (eds.) *Social Rights in Europe*, 279.

[18] International Year of Disabled Persons, G.A. Res. 36/77, at 176, U.N. GAOR, 36th Sess., Supp. No. 77, U.N. Doc. A/RES/36/77 (1981).

[19] The World Programme is a global strategy to enhance disability prevention, rehabilitation and equalization of opportunities. Its three chapters provide an analysis of principles, concepts and definitions relating to disabilities; an overview of the world situation regarding persons with disabilities; and recommendations for action at the national, regional and international levels. Its purpose is to promote effective measures for prevention of disability, rehabilitation and the realisation of the goals of 'full participation' of persons with disabilities in social life and development, and of 'equality.' The World Programme, understood through the lens offered by the CRPD and its general principles and stated purpose, is a hybrid instrument, combining prevention and rehabilitation with more rights-oriented, albeit incomplete, objectives. *See* Implementation of the World Programme of Action Concerning Disabled Persons, G.A. Res. 37/53, at 186–87, para. 11, U.N. GAOR, 37th Sess., Supp. No. 53, U.N. Doc. A/RES/37/53 (Dec. 3, 1982) (hereinafter World Programme of Action 1982).

[20] See World Programme of Action 1982, at paras. 87–90 (providing, inter alia, that 'Member States should urgently initiate national long-term programmes to achieve the objectives of the World Programme of Action; such programmes should be an integral component of the nation's general policy for socio-economic development').

[21] See Decade of Disabled Persons, GA Res. 48/96, U.N. Doc. A/RES/48/96 (4 March 1993), which annexed thereto (resolution 48/96 annex, 20 December 1993), available at http://www1.umn.edu/humanrts/instree/disabilitystandards.html (accessed 12 March 2012).

[22] See Standard Rules on the Equalization of Opportunities for Persons with Disabilities, A/RES/48/96, 85th Plenary Meeting 20 December 1993 (hereinafter, Standard Rules).

disabilities, as members of their societies, may exercise the same rights and obligations as others'.[23] The Rules note the existence of 'obstacles preventing persons with disabilities from exercising their rights and freedoms and making it difficult for them to participate fully in the activities of their societies,' the 'responsibility of States to take appropriate action to remove such obstacles' and the role of persons with disabilities and their organisations in the removal of barriers.[24] The core concept referenced within the section outlining the purpose and objectives of the Standard Rules is the 'equalization of opportunities for persons with disabilities' which is identified as 'an essential contribution in the general and worldwide effort to mobilize human resources'.[25]

Both the World Programme of Action and the Standard Rules emphasise the right of persons with disabilities to the same opportunities as other citizens and to an equal share in the improvements in living conditions resulting from economic and social development. They do not, however, embrace a consistent and coherent human rights approach to disability anchored in core human rights principles of, inter alia, non-discrimination, participation, inclusion and autonomy.

Consensus started to emerge at the close of the last century amongst those working in the fields of disability and international human rights law that the international human rights framework was, in the context of disability, lacking in several fundamental respects.[26] There was no instrument that comprehensively and with specificity focussed on the barriers that persons with disabilities experienced in accessing their human rights, and many governments remained unaware of their legal obligations.[27] Notably, the Office of the High Commissioner for Human Rights issued a pivotal study authored by Professors Gerard Quinn and Theresia Degener demonstrating that the existing UN human rights treaty-monitoring bodies only marginally, if at all, addressed the routine human rights violations to which persons with disabilities were subjected.[28]

Development of a Disability-Specific Human Rights Treaty

In 2001, an initiative to develop a legally binding treaty on the human rights of persons with disabilities was launched by Mexico, following the UN's effort to

---

[23] *Ibid.* at 15.

[24] *Ibid.*

[25] *Ibid.*

[26] See especially Quinn, G. & Degener, T. (2002) *Human Rights and Disability: The Current Use and Future Potential of United Nations Human Rights Instruments in the Context of Disability* 1, available at: www.ohchr.org/Documents/Publications/HRDisabilityen.pdf (accessed 12 March 2012). Two expert seminars on international norms and standards on disability were held in 1998 and 1999 in Berkeley and Hong Kong, respectively, and gave serious consideration to the need for a legally binding convention on the rights of persons with disabilities. *Ibid.*

[27] See generally NCD Report, *supra*, n. 16.

[28] See generally Quinn and Degener, *supra*, n. 26.

include disability as part of the Platform of Action adopted at the World Conference against Racism in Durban, South Africa. In the General Assembly that year, Mexico proposed a resolution calling for the establishment of an Ad Hoc Committee mandated with elaborating 'a comprehensive and integral international convention to promote and protect the rights and dignity of persons with disabilities, based on the holistic approach of the work done in the field of social development, human rights and non-discrimination'.[29] The resolution was adopted and launched the establishment of the Ad Hoc Committee which met for the first time in 2002. The Committee met for a total of eight sessions at UN headquarters in New York and adopted a final text in August 2006.[30] Thereafter, the text was submitted for adoption by the whole General Assembly which occurred on 13 December 2006.

The text of the CRPD is comprised of twenty-five preambular paragraphs and fifty Articles.[31] The aim of the drafters was not to create 'new' rights; rather, the goal was to specify human rights as they apply specifically to persons with disabilities. In other words, the CRPD takes existing human rights obligations and makes clear their relationship to the lives of persons with disabilities. Structurally, the CRPD includes an introductory set of provisions that outline its purpose (Article 1) and key definitions (Article 2), along with articles of general (cross-cutting) application, to be applied across the treaty text (Articles 3 to 9).

The general obligations of States Parties are specified in Article 4 of the Convention which requires that States Parties undertake measures to ensure and promote the full realisation of all human rights and fundamental freedoms for all persons with disabilities without discrimination of any kind on the basis of disability. In

---

[29] See Comprehensive and Integral International Convention to Promote and Protect the Rights and Dignity of Persons with Disabilities, G.A. Res. 56/168, U.N GAOR, 56th Sess., Supp. No. 168, U.N. Doc. A/RES/56/168 (Dec. 19, 2001). A detailed description of the political process behind the United Nations decision to go forward with a disability human rights convention is set forth in the National Council on Disability, Newsroom, *UN Disability Convention–Topics at a Glance: History of the Process*, available at: http://www.ncd.gov/newsroom/publications/2003/history_process.htm (accessed 12 March 2012). Following the adoption of a General Assembly resolution calling for the establishment of a committee to consider proposals for the elaboration of a human rights treaty on the rights of persons with disabilities, an 'ad hoc' committee was established and met for the first time in July 2002. 'Ad hoc' simply connotes a body established for a particular purpose for a time-bound period, as opposed to bodies that operate under the General Assembly for an indefinite period of time.

[30] For more on the CRPD negotiation process, see Kayess, R. & French, P. (2008) 'Out of Darkness into Light? Introducing the Convention on the Rights of Persons with Disabilities', *Hum. Rts. L. Rev.* 8(1): 15; Lord, J. E. (2004) 'Mirror, Mirror on the Wall: Voice Accountability and NGOs in Human Rights Standard Setting', *Seton Hall J. Dipl. & Int'l Rel.* 5: 93.

[31] For comprehensive overviews of the CRPD, see generally Stein, M. A. & Lord, J. E. (2008) 'Future Prospects for the United Nations Convention on the Rights of Persons with Disabilities', in Arnardóttir, O. M. and Quinn, G. (eds.) *The UN Convention on the Rights of Person with Disabilities: European and Scandinavian Perspectives*; Stein, M. A. & Lord, J. E. (2008) 'The United Nations Convention on the Rights of Persons with Disabilities: Process, Substance, and Prospects', in Isa, F. G. and de Feyter, K. (eds.) *International Human Rights Law in a Global Context*, 495.

relation to economic, social and cultural rights, States Parties are obliged to take measures to realise these rights progressively to the maximum extent of available resources. Article 4 obliges States Parties to (1) adopt legislative, administrative and other measures to implement Convention rights; (2) abolish or amend existing laws, regulations, customs and practices that discriminate against persons with disabilities; and (3) adopt an inclusive approach to protect and promote the rights of persons with disabilities in all policies and programmes. Crucially for the provision of disability supports, Article 4 requires States Parties to refrain from conduct that violates CRPD obligations and ensure that the public sector respects the rights of persons with disabilities. Moreover, States Parties must take measures to abolish disability discrimination *by persons, organisations or private enterprises.* In addition, States must undertake research and development of accessible goods, services and technology for persons with disabilities and to promote others to undertake such research; provide accessible information about assistive technology to persons with disabilities; promote professional and staff training on Convention rights for those working with persons with disabilities on the Convention; and consult with and involve persons with disabilities in developing and implementing legislation and policies and in decision-making processes concerning persons with disabilities. This last provision lies at the heart of the CRPD's mandate that implementation requires the full participation by persons with disabilities and their representative organisations.

Following the articles that apply transversally, or across the treaty, the CRPD sets forth specific substantive rights covering civil, political, economic, social and cultural rights (Articles 10 to 30). Finally, it establishes a system of monitoring and implementation (Articles 31 to 40) and includes final provisions that govern the operation of the CRPD (Articles 41 to 50). Significantly for fostering disability rights advocacy, several provisions require active consultations with stakeholders and apply the participation norm to all aspects of implementation, including the requirement that participation be effectuated in all law, policy and programming decisions (Article 4(3) CRPD). A Committee on the Rights of Persons with Disabilities – the CRPD's treaty-monitoring body – is tasked with monitoring implementation in States Parties through its oversight of the mandatory reporting requirement and through the issuance of recommendations. An Optional Protocol[32] to the CRPD, comprised of eighteen Articles, gives the Committee competence to examine individual complaints with regard to alleged violations of the Convention by States Parties to the Protocol. Its purpose is to allow States Parties to opt into participation in individual and group communications procedures, as well as an enquiry procedure, all of which are overseen by the Committee.

---

[32] Optional Protocol, *supra*, n. 1.

International and Domestic Legal Status of CRPD

At the time of this writing, 123 States have ratified the CRPD[33] and 73 have ratified the Optional Protocol.[34] Sixteen States within the EU have ratified the CRPD and twenty-three States did so within the Council of Europe.[35] The CRPD has been signed and the decision taken to conclude it by the European Community (EC) under the EC Treaty. The CRPD requires the regional integration organisations to declare their competence in the areas covered by the Convention and, accordingly, Council Decision 2010/48/EC on the conclusion of the CRPD sets out specific EC instruments that demonstrate the Community's relevant fields of activity.[36]

International human rights standards are designed to be implemented at the domestic level.[37] As a general matter, ratifying States (as well as regional integration organisations such as the EU) are expected to give legal effect to assumed treaty obligations, and the CRPD sets forth general parameters for implementation at the domestic level.[38] The process by which they become part of the domestic law framework varies from country to country.[39] In some States – including, for example, Croatia, Hungary, Slovenia and Spain – the provisions of a human rights convention, including the CRPD, have direct legal effect on the national legal framework and are thus in theory directly applicable, including in courts of law.[40] By contrast, in other States, including the United Kingdom, Australia and Belgium, the international and

---

[33] UNenable, Convention and Optional Protocol Signatures, Countries and Regional Integration Organizations, available at http://www.un.org/disabilities/countries.asp?navid=12&pid=166 (accessed 17 September 2012).

[34] *Ibid.*

[35] *Ibid.*

[36] Areas of competence identified in the Decision include non-discrimination, employment, accessibility, international cooperation, statistics and data collection and monitoring. The competence of the EC is evolving and thus additional areas of competence may indeed emerge over time. Council Decision 2010/48/EC.

[37] Buergenthal, T. Shelton, D. and David Stewart, D. (2002), *International Human Rights*, 347 (2nd ed.).

[38] In order for a treaty to have domestic legal effect, an act of government is frequently required whereby the treaty norm is incorporated into its domestic law. Such legal systems are considered 'dualist' in nature, in contrast with monist systems where the State's legal system is considered to include international treaties without the need for separate, domestic-level action.

[39] There is an extensive literature on the domestic incorporation of human rights standards and the processes by which this occurs. See, e.g., Cassesse, A. (1985) 'Modern Constitutions and International Law', *Hague Recueil Des Cours*, 192: 331; Jacobs, F. G. and Roberts, S. (eds.) (1987) *The Effects of Treaties in Domestic Law*; Seidl-Hohenveldern, I. (1963) 'Transformation or Adoption of International Law Into Municipal Law', *Int'l & Comp. L.Q.* 12: 88; Wildhaber, L. & Breitenmoser, S. (1988) 'The Relationship between Customary International Law and Municipal Law in Western European Countries', *Z.A.O.R.V.* 48: 163 (1988); Higgins, R. (1987) 'United Kingdom', in Jacobs, F. G. & Roberts, S. (eds.) *The Effects of Treaties in Domestic Law* 123, 124–25.

[40] For a detailed analysis, see Anthony Aust, A. (2006) *Modern Treaty Law and Practice*, Cambridge University Press, pp. 146 and 150. For a discussion that relates specifically to the incorporation of the CRPD into domestic law, see *Office of the High Commissioner for Human Rights, Thematic Study by the Office of the United Nations High Commissioner for Human Rights on enhancing awareness and*

national legal systems are regarded as separate and distinct legal spheres. In these countries, international human rights treaties to which the State is a party have no automatic legal force as a matter of domestic law; rather, domestic legislation must be adopted to incorporate the treaty into the domestic legal order.

In terms of the CRPD becoming part of the domestic law framework, Ireland presents an interesting example to review as it signed the CRPD on 30 March 2007,[41] but has not ratified it because of concerns about compliance at the domestic level.[42] Ireland's ratification efforts are coupled with moves to reform domestic disability laws so that Ireland is in full compliance with the CRPD prior to ratification.[43] Similarly, the United States applies an exceedingly strict threshold for ratification, with the State Department undergoing a long and intensive cross-agency review process to assess compliance before the president submits the treaty to the US Senate for its advice and consent which are contingent on ratification. As a result, and partly because of American parochialism when it comes to international treaties in general, the United States has the poorest ratification record of all industrialised states.[44]

The section that follows concentrates on the guiding principles emerging from international and European disability rights law, which have particular relevance to the three focus areas of this study.

GUIDING PRINCIPLES IN INTERNATIONAL AND REGIONAL DISABILITY LAW AND POLICY

General principles which animate and inform international and regional disability law and policy frameworks are important tools in shaping the progressive

---

understanding of the Convention on the Rights of Persons with Disabilities, UN Doc. A/HRC/10/48, 26 January 2009.

[41] An updated list of signatories and States Parties to the CRPD is posted on the United Nations Enable Web site, *supra*, n. 1.

[42] Flynn, E. (2009) 'Ireland's Compliance with the Convention on the Rights of Persons with Disabilities: Towards a Rights-Based Approach for Legal Reform?', *Dublin U. L. J.* 31: 357 (2009); Quinn, G. (2008) Centre for Disability Law and Policy at the NUI Galway School of Law, The United Nations Convention on the Rights of Persons with Disabilities as an Engine of Domestic Law Reform, Presentation given to Conference of States Parties to the Convention on the Rights of Persons with Disabilities (31 October), available at: http://www.un.org/disabilities/images/Message%20G%20 20Quinn%20COP.doc (accessed 12 March 2012).

[43] 'The enactment of the Mental Capacity Bill has already been recognised as a reform which is necessary to facilitate Ireland's ratification of the Convention'; Flynn, E., *supra*, n. 42, p. 357.

[44] The United States has ratified only three of twenty-six international human rights treaties. For more on the US policy of ratification of human rights treaties and the CRPD in particular, see Lord, J. E. & Stein, M. A. (2009) 'Ratify the UN Disability Treaty', *Foreign Policy in Focus* (9 July), available at: http://www.fpif.org/fpiftxt/6247 (accessed 12 March 2012). See also Lord, J. E. & Stein, M. A. (2011), 'The Law and Politics of US Participation in the UN Convention on the Rights of Persons with Disabilities', in Hertel, S. and Libal, K. (eds.) *Explaining the Silence: Human Rights in the United States*.

development of disability supports in advancing disability-inclusive citizenship. The starting point for considering general principles in international disability law is the CRPD, and particularly the provision in Article 3 (General principles). European regional instruments likewise inform the design and provision of disability supports and express principles that should be reflected in domestic disability law and policy. Three core focus areas forming the centrepiece of the present study – personalisation, choice in living arrangements and life in the community – are strongly affirmed in the CRPD. These three areas together define a new paradigm in disability policy in which citizens with disabilities live independently with choice and control over their supports to achieve full social and economic participation. The section which follows provides an overview of these principles and how they apply to personalisation, choice in living arrangements and life in the community. It also considers the application of these principles to the process of support provisions for persons with disabilities.

General principles have an important role in international treaties generally, and in the CRPD in particular. Article 3 identifies the Convention's general principles which include respect for individual dignity, autonomy and independence, respect for difference and acceptance of disability as human diversity, non-discrimination, equal opportunity, complete and meaningful participation, accessibility, sexual equality, respect for children's rights and support of their evolving capabilities.[45] These general principles are to be applied in the drafting of national disability laws and in the formulation of national-level disability policies and should also inform programming and the process of decision making, monitoring and implementation. The inclusion of a general principles article is an innovation which serves to guide the interpretation of the entire text of the treaty.[46]

The general principles set forth in Article 3 firmly anchor the CRPD text in human rights, an important distinction which differentiates the CRPD from all other disability-specific instruments but also, notably, places the CRPD alone amongst all other core human rights conventions which do not specifically articulate general principles.[47] Through its placement in the articles of general and cross-cutting

---

[45] See CRPD, *supra*, n. 1, at art. 3 (a), (b), (c), (d), (e), (f), (g), (h).

[46] The CRPD is the first international human rights convention to include a provision outlining general principles. For more on the important role of general principles in human rights treaties, see Lord and Stein, *supra*, n. 2, at 449.

[47] It should be noted that the treaty committees have elicited general principles to guide the interpretation of human rights treaties, even though they do not have specific provisions outlining general principles. For example the Committee on the Rights of the Child has identified four main principles to guide its interpretation of the CRC. These include: Article 2 (non-discrimination); Article 3(1) (best interests of the child); Article 6 (right to life and maximum possible survival and development); and Article 12 (respect for the views of the child and participation). Convention on the Rights of the Child, G.A. Res. 44/25, Annex, 44 U.N. GAOR Supp. (No. 49) at 167, U.N. Doc. A/44/49 (1989), *entered into force* 2 September 1990.

application, the drafters defined the fundamental principles which must guide the interpretation and application of all of the provisions in the CRPD. Notably, for the purposes of this study, the CRPD outlines a framework which requires disability supports to be specifically targeted to reflect and advance the core principles of autonomy, inclusion and participation and to achieve the objectives of securing human independence and full citizenship.

Principles set forth in European instruments on disability correspond in large part to those reflected in the CRPD. The European Commission first gave expression to the principles contained in the UN Standard Rules in its Green Paper of 1993 concerning social policy where it emphasised that '[s]ocial segregation, even with adequate income maintenance and special provision, is contrary to human dignity and corrosive of social solidarity and community morale'.[48] Gerard Quinn has emphasised the significance of this shift in recognising that 'money alone is not a sufficient answer unless linked to a rights-based reform agenda', and that even expansive funding, if pursued without rights-based principles of participation, inclusion and accessibility, is not an acceptable approach.[49] In 1996, the European Commission set out a clear vision of equal opportunities for persons with disabilities in *Equality of Opportunities for People with Disabilities – A New Community Disability Strategy*.[50] The European Disability Strategy, adopted in 2010, provides further impetus for realising the rights of persons with disabilities and recognises that:

> There are still many obstacles preventing people with disabilities from fully exercising their fundamental rights – including their Union citizenship rights – and limiting their participation in society on an equal basis with others. Those rights include the right to free movement, to choose where and how to live, and to have full access to cultural, recreational, and sports activities.[51]

The Council of Europe has likewise been involved in disability issues, influenced early on by the large population of persons who acquired a disability during World War II. Early activities focussed on rehabilitation, similar to narrowly focussed domestic disability frameworks in both Europe and North America. The first coherent statement of the Council's disability policy was Recommendation R (92), adopted in 1992, following a Ministerial Conference in Paris.[52] A second Council of Europe Ministerial Conference was held in Malaga in 2003 and resulted in the Malaga Political Declaration which identifies as a main aim 'to improve the quality of life

---

[48] *Green Paper on European Social Policy – Options for the Union*, Brussels, COM (93), November 1993, 551 p. 48.

[49] Quinn, G. (2004) *EU Network of Independent Experts on Disability Discrimination.*

[50] *Communication of the Commission on Equality of Opportunity for People with Disabilities – A New European Community Disability Strategy*, Brussels, COM (96) 406, final, 30.07.1996.

[51] European Disability Strategy, *supra*, n. 3 at p. 5, section 2.1.2.

[52] Council of Europe, Recommendation R (1992), *A Coherent Policy for the Rehabilitation of People with Disabilities, available at* http://www.handicapincifre.it/allegati/RECOMMENDATION_R% 2892%296.htm

of people with disabilities and their families, putting emphasis on their integration and full participation in society, since a participative and accessible society is of benefit to the whole population'.[53] Significantly, the Malaga Declaration embraced an approach directed at working 'within anti-discriminatory and human rights frameworks towards mainstreaming quality of opportunity for people with disabilities throughout all policy areas'.[54]

Of particular relevance for ensuring that disability supports are implemented in keeping with human rights in Europe is the Council of Europe's work in the area of social rights. The original European Social Charter of 1961[55] was very much a product of its time and reflected the prevailing rehabilitation model of disability:[56]

Article 15 – The right of physically or mentally disabled persons to vocational training, rehabilitation and social resettlement.

With a view to ensuring the effective exercise of the right of the physically or mentally disabled to vocational training, rehabilitation and resettlement, the Contracting Parties undertake:

1. To take adequate measures for the provision of training facilities, including, where necessary, specialised institutions, public or private;

2. To take adequate measures for the placing of disabled person in employment, such as specialised placing services, facilities for sheltered employment and measures to encourage employers to employment.

The recently Revised European Social Charter[57] (Article 15) takes a decidedly different turn, reflecting as it does the social model of disability and a rights-oriented approach which seeks to ensure the right of persons with disabilities to 'independence, social integration and participation in the life of the community'.[58] Article 15 is tellingly renamed 'the right of persons with disabilities to independence,

---

[53] Political Declaration of the Second Ministerial Conference of Ministers Responsible for Integration Policies for People with Disabilities, 7–8 May 2004, Malaga, Spain, available at http://www.coe.int/T/ E/Social_Cohesion/soc-sp/Integration/ (accessed 12 March 2012).

[54] *Ibid.* at para. 17.

[55] European Social Charter, Turin, 18.X.1961. European Treaty Series (ETS), No. 35.

[56] *See* Quinn, *supra*, n. 17 at 279.

[57] *European Social Charter (Revised)*, 3 May 1996, CETS 163 (hereinafter, European Social Charter), available at: http://www.unhcr.org/refworld/docid/3ae6b3678.html. For an important overview of the European disability rights framework, see Council of Europe, Commissioner for Human Rights, (2008) *Human Rights and Disability: Equal Rights for All*, available at: https://wcd.coe.int/ ViewDoc.jsp?id=1355349&Site=CommDH&BackColorInternet=FEC65B&BackColorIntranet= FEC65B&BackColorLogged=FFC679 (accessed 12 March 2012).

[58] European Social Charter, *supra*, n. 57, at art. 15. There are a number of Council of Europe publications in the field of disability. See, e.g., Council of Europe (2002) *Rehabilitation and Integration of People with Disabilities*; (2003) *Assessing Disability in Europe – Similarities and Differences*; (2003) *Access to Social Rights for People with Disabilities in Europe*; (2003) *Legislation to Counter Discrimination against Persons with Disabilities*; (2003) *Discrimination against Women with Disabilities*; (2003) *Safeguarding Adults and Children with Disabilities against Abuse*.

social integration and participation in the life of the community' and its provisions are more comprehensive and rights-based than the previous articulation of 1961.

While the European Convention for the Protection of Human Rights and Fundamental Freedoms[59] does not explicitly identify disability as a prohibited ground of discrimination, the jurisprudence of the European Court nonetheless applies non-discrimination to persons with disabilities in a succession of cases and, more recently, embraces principles of the CRPD as part of its interpretive lens.[60] European instruments likewise advance non-discrimination as an overarching principle as reflected in the Charter of Fundamental Rights of the European Union[61] (Article 21) and the Treaty of Amsterdam (Article 13).[62]

PERSONALISATION

The CRPD defines, both through its general principles and specific substantive obligations, a framework within which to understand the concept of personalisation and operationalises it in both law and policy. At its core, the concept of personalisation reflects a move away from passive, paternalistic provision of services *for* persons with disabilities and an embrace of individual decision making and autonomy driven by active participation and recognition of legal capacity, together with the provision of supports to promote and facilitate agency and informed decision making and individualised self-determination. Accordingly, under the human rights model reflected in the CRPD, the focus is on basic concepts of justice and human dignity whereby persons with disabilities are empowered to realise their basic needs as a matter of claimed rights rather than as received charity.[63]

---

[59] European Convention for the Protection of Human Rights and Fundamental Freedoms, Nov. 4, 1950, 213 U.N.T.S. 222 (hereinafter ECHR).

[60] See, e.g., *Alajos Kiss v. Hungary*, Eur. Ct. H.R. Application No. 38832/06, 20 May 2010 (holding that the automatic disenfranchisement of a person under guardianship from exercising his or her right to vote was a violation of the European Convention and that the State had to provide weighty reasons when applying a restriction on fundamental rights to a particularly vulnerable group, such as persons with mental disabilities and citing the relevance of the CRPD).

[61] Charter of Fundamental Rights of the European Union, 2000 O.J. (C 364) 1 (hereinafter EU Charter), available at: http://www.unhcr.org/refworld/docid/3ae6b3b70.html (accessed 12 March 2012).

[62] Treaty of Amsterdam, 2 October 2, 1997, 1997 O.J (C 340)1 (hereinafter Treaty of Amsterdam).

[63] The UN High Commissioner for Human Rights emphasised this shift to a rights-oriented perspective on the adoption of the CRPD in December 2006. See UN High Commissioner for Human Rights, Statement by UN High Commissioner for Human Rights on Convention on Rights of Persons with Disabilities, delivered at the adoption of the convention in December 2006 (6 December 2006), available at: http://www.ohchr.org/English/issues/disability/docs/statementhcdeco6.doc (noting that the CRPD dismisses the understanding of persons with disabilities as 'objects of charity, medical treatment and social protection' and instead reaffirms that persons with disabilities are 'subjects of rights, able to claim those rights as active members of society').

Respect for Inherent Dignity, Individual Autonomy and Independence of Persons

Article 3 of the CRPD includes as the first enumerated general principle 'respect for inherent dignity, individual autonomy including the freedom to make one's own choices, and independence of persons'.[64] While the terms 'respect for inherent dignity', 'individual autonomy' and 'independence of persons' are not specifically defined in the CRPD, together they encompass the overall thrust of the CRPD, namely that persons with disabilities, as human beings, have the right to all fundamental human rights and freedoms which protect human dignity and autonomy. In that sense, therefore, they express the concept of personalisation.

The reference to 'respect for inherent dignity' in the CRPD echoes the preamble to the Universal Declaration of Human Rights which emphasises that 'recognition of the inherent dignity and of the equal and inalienable rights of all members of the human family is the foundation of freedom, justice, and peace in the world'.[65] The European Court of Human Rights has recognised human dignity and human freedom as 'the very essence of the Convention'.[66] The Court has also stated that the Convention 'must be understood and interpreted as a whole [and that it forms] an integrated system for the protection of human dignity'.[67] Similarly the EU Charter of Fundamental Rights recognises that the Union is founded on the 'universal values of human dignity, freedom, equality and solidarity'.[68]

The notion of individual autonomy, including the freedom to make one's own choices, is closely aligned with the concept of individual self-determination, a term used frequently within the context of the CRPD negotiations.[69] Even though human rights treaties do not utilise the term 'individual self-determination' or autonomy, there is nonetheless recognition of the term in human rights practice, including in the jurisprudence of the European Court of Human Rights.[70] In addition, in

[64] CRPD, *supra*, n. 1, at art. 3(a).

[65] UDHR, *supra*, n. 7 at prmbl.

[66] See, e.g., *Pretty v United Kingdom* App. No. 2346/02, 29 April 2002, para. 65.

[67] See *Refah Partisi and others v. Turkey* of 31 July 2001, Application no. 41340/98, para.43.

[68] See EU Charter of Fundamental Rights of 2000. It should also be noted that the EU Charter of Fundamental Rights is divided into six chapters on material rights. Chapter One on Human Dignity covers the rights to dignity, life, integrity and the prohibitions against torture and forced labour.

[69] The term 'individual autonomy' was preferred, apparently because the concept of self-determination under international law carries with it a particular meaning – the idea of group self-determination. The literature on the self-determination of peoples springs principally from Article 1 of both Covenants which provide that 'all peoples have the right to self-determination'. See ICCPR & ICESCR, *supra*, n. 8 & 9 at art. 1. See generally Cassese, A. (1995) *Self-Determination of Peoples*; Crawford, J. (ed.) (1988) *The Rights of People*; Thornberry, P. (1989) 'Self-Determination, Minorities, Human Rights: A Review of International Instruments', *INTL & COMP. L. Q.* 38: 867.

[70] See, e.g., *Pretty v. United Kingdom*, para. 61. ('[T]hough no case has established as such any *right to self-determination* as being contained in Article 8 of the Convention, the Court considers that the notion of *personal autonomy* is an important *principle* underlying the interpretation of the Convention'.) *Ibid*.

its General Comment on Persons with Disabilities, the Committee on Economic, Social and Cultural Rights – the body which monitors the International Covenant on Economic, Social and Cultural Rights – recommends the enactment and implementation of antidiscrimination legislation and social-policy programmes, which enable persons with disabilities 'to live an integrated, self-determined and independent life'.[71] The (Revised) European Social Charter and the Charter of Fundamental Rights of the European Union recognise a right to measures designed to ensure 'independence, social (and occupational) integration and participation in the life of the community'.[72] The (Revised) European Social Charter[73] provides important guidance on personalisation in the context of disability support provisions.[74] As noted earlier, Article 15 calls for States 'to take the necessary measures to provide persons with disabilities with guidance, education and vocational training in the framework of general schemes wherever possible' and, in relation to the provision of support services, they are to be directed towards the promotion of 'social integration and participation in the life of the community'.[75]

Human rights jurisprudence reflected in international as well as regional human rights courts and tribunals accepts the principle of autonomy as a founding principle of human rights. Although the European Court of Human Rights has not explicitly found a right to personal autonomy or self-determination in the Convention, it has on numerous occasions stated that it considers the notion of personal autonomy to be an important principle underlying the interpretation of the guarantees contained in the European Convention of Human Rights.[76] The concept of personal autonomy has been taken to embrace broad protections, including the right to establish details of one's identity as a human being, the right to make choices over her/his own body, the right to privacy and the freedoms of thought, conscience and religion.[77]

[71] General Comment No. 5, Persons with disabilities (Eleventh session, 1994), U.N. Doc E/1995/22 at 19 (1995), reprinted in Compilation of General Comments and General Recommendations Adopted by Human Rights Treaty Bodies, U.N. Doc. HRI/GEN/1/Rev.6 at 24 (2003), available at: http://www1 .umn.edu/humanrts/gencomm/epcomm5e.htm (accessed 12 March 2012).

[72] European Social Charter, *supra*, note 57, art. 15; EU Charter, art. 26. The EU Charter includes 'occupational integration'.

[73] European Social Charter, *supra*, n. 57; For an important overview of the European disability rights framework, see Commissioner for Human Rights (2008) *Human Rights and Disability: Equal Rights for All* Council of Europe, Issue Paper, Oct., available at: https://wcd.coe.int/ViewDoc.jsp?id= 1355349&Site=CommDH&BackColorInternet=FEC65B&BackColorIntranet= FEC65B&BackColorLogged=FFC679 (accessed 12 March 2012).

[74] European Social Charter, *supra*, n. 57, at art. 15; See also Maudient, M. (2003) *Access to Social Rights for People with Disabilities*; Council of Europe (2007) *Social security as a human right – The protection afforded by the European Convention on Human Rights* (Human Rights Files No. 23).

[75] European Social Charter, *supra*, n. 57, art. 15.

[76] See Marshall, J. (2010) 'Personal Freedom through Human Rights Law? Autonomy, Identity and Integrity under the European Convention on Human Rights', *Human Rights Law Review* 10: 391–394.

[77] See, e.g., *H.F. v. Slovakia*, ECHR, App. No. 54797/00, judgment 8 November 2005 (Domestic court deprived Applicant of her legal capacity on the basis that she had chronic paranoid schizophrenia and was incapable of entering into legal transactions or managing her affairs. The court had not heard

Participation and Inclusion

The CRPD recognises participation and inclusion as a general principle, which is in keeping with the general trend of international treaty bodies to underscore that the right to participate in decision making is to be understood in broad terms.[78] The CRPD elaborates on the right of persons with disabilities to participate in the political life of their societies and provides specific guidance to States on implementing this right. Participation in the context of the CRPD extends beyond voting – although this aspect is expressed in Article 29 of the CRPD – and encompasses the right of persons with disabilities to participate in decision-making processes where their interests are affected, on an equal basis with others. Thus, the significance of the principle of participation in Article 3 and as applied and in some instances specifically expressed throughout the CRPD is not only that persons with disabilities should be accorded the right to express their views freely, but also that they have the right to be heard and that their views should be accorded due weight.[79] This is central to the

---

evidence from Applicant but relied in its decision on an old psychiatric report and on statements by her ex-husband and his witnesses. Applicant appealed, and without hearing evidence from her or ordering further psychiatric reports, the domestic court rejected her appeal. The ECHR found in favour of the applicant.)

[78] The right to participate in political processes is a well-established principle of human rights law and is expressed in Article 21 of the UDHR.

(1) Everyone has the right to take part in the government of his country, directly or through freely chosen representatives.
(2) Everyone has the right of equal access to public service in his country.
(3) The will of the people shall be the basis of the authority of government; this will shall be expressed in periodic and genuine elections which shall be by universal and equal suffrage and shall be held by secret vote or by equivalent free voting procedures.

UDHR, *supra*, note 7, at art 21.
In addition, Article 25 of the International Covenant on Civil and Political Rights (ICCPR) provides that

[E]very citizen shall have the right and the opportunity . . . without reasonable restrictions . . . to vote and to be elected at genuine periodic elections which shall be universal and equal suffrage and shall be held by secret ballot, guaranteeing the free expression of the will of the electors.

ICCPR, *supra*, note 8, at art. 25, available at: http://www.unhchr.ch/html/menu3/b/a_ccpr.htm

[79] This is in keeping with the development of the concept of participation generally in human rights law and likewise with regard to its specific application in the Convention on the Rights of the Child. See, for example, the statement in the Manual on Human Rights Reporting which comments on Article 12 of the CRC:

This article sets one of the fundamental values of the Convention and probably one of its basic challenges. In essence it affirms that the child is a fully-fledged person having the right to express views in all matters affecting him or her, and having those views heard and given due weight. Thus the child has the right to participate in the decision making process affecting his or her life, as well as to influence decision taken in his or her regard . . . At first sight it might be considered that Article 12 is basically addressing the same reality as Article 13 on freedom of expression and information. It is true that they are closely connected. But the fact they were both incorporated in the Convention and coexist in an autonomous manner, has to be interpreted as to mean that, while article 13 recognizes in a general way freedom of expression, article 12 should prevail in all those cases where the matters

concept of personalisation and has important implications for the terms upon which providers offer their support. Consultation with persons with disabilities and their representative organisations is critical in the design, implementation, monitoring and evaluation of disability support service provision.

Respect for Difference and Acceptance of Disability as Human Diversity

The principle of 'respect for difference and acceptance of persons with disabilities as part of human diversity and humanity' in Article 3 is not defined in the CRPD, nor does it attach to existing human rights convention terminology, and yet it clearly expresses the values that underpin the CRPD and human rights law more generally.[80] It seems to acknowledge, for example, a basic idea of human rights law that individuals with disabilities are active subjects of human rights, as opposed to objects to be acted upon. Moreover, in recognising disability as a natural part of human diversity and in underscoring respect and indeed acceptance – as opposed to the lower threshold of tolerance – of difference, the provision seems an affront to conceptualisations of disability conveying paternalism, pity, charity and the like.

Respect for the Evolving Capacities of Children with Disabilities

Article 3 of the CRPD recognises as a general principle 'respect for the evolving capacities of children with disabilities' and thus requires that the human rights and fundamental freedoms set out in the Convention must be interpreted and applied in a manner that recognises and accommodates the development of children with disabilities towards adulthood and independence. The concept of 'evolving capacities of children with disabilities' is thus directed towards facilitating the exercise of personal autonomy in decision making. The second aspect of Article 3(h) references 'respect for the right of children with disabilities to preserve their identities' and is directed towards ensuring that children with disabilities are legally recognised as persons and that their identity is preserved. The concept was drawn from the Convention on the Rights of the Child (CRC) and reflects 'an acknowledgement that children's development towards independent adulthood must be respected and promoted throughout childhood'.[81] Moreover, the idea is closely linked to the principle of participation, especially Article 12 of the CRC which requires that the views of children shall be given 'due weight in accordance with the age and maturity of the child'.[82] In this regard it links to the recognition accorded in the CRPD of

---

at stake affect the child, while stressing the right of the child to be heard and for the child's views to be taken into account. – United Nations, *Manual on Human Rights Reporting* at 426.

[80] CRPD, *supra*, n. 1, at art. 3.

[81] *Ibid.*

[82] Convention on the Rights of the Child, *G.A. res. 44/25, annex, 44 U.N. GAOR Supp. (No. 49) at 167, U.N. Doc. A/44/49 (1989),* entered into force 2 September 1990, art. 12.

legal capacity, together with the requirement that appropriate supports be provided to facilitate decision making. As applied to disability supports, it requires not only support in keeping with the best interests of the child, but meaningful participation and consultation.

Equality and Non-Discrimination and the Duty to Accommodate

Equality and non-discrimination are core principles of disability rights law, both at the international as well as national levels. The adoption of the CRPD brings into the modern human rights law framework a robust disability discrimination and equality dimension which was implicitly and perhaps incompletely captured in earlier adopted human rights conventions. Moreover, the CRPD is serving to advance the development and reform of disability discrimination law domestically around the world.[83]

Article 5(1) of the CRPD affirms that 'all persons are equal before and under the law and are entitled without any discrimination to the equal protection and equal benefit of the law'.[84] Article 5(2) obliges States Parties to 'prohibit all discrimination on the basis of disability'.[85] Disability discrimination is defined in Article 2 to mean

> any distinction, exclusion or restriction on the basis of disability which has the purpose or effect of impairing or nullifying the recognition, enjoyment or exercise, on an equal basis with others, of all human rights and fundamental freedoms in the political, economic, social, cultural, civil or any other field. It includes all forms of discrimination, including denial of reasonable accommodation.[86]

In addition, Article 5(3) requires that States Parties take steps to ensure that reasonable accommodations are provided.[87] The concept of reasonable accommodation, which was initially expressed in the domestic disability law of the United States,[88] is defined in the CRPD in Article 2 as 'necessary and appropriate modification and adjustments not imposing a disproportionate or undue burden, where needed in a particular case, to ensure to persons with disabilities the enjoyment or exercise on an equal basis with others of all human rights and fundamental freedoms'.[89]

The integration of reasonable accommodation into the formal definition of disability discrimination in Article 2 of the CRPD is important. It establishes that

---

[83] Law reform is currently underway in, for example, Mexico, Vietnam, Zambia, and Jordan, to name a few.

[84] CRPD, *supra*, n. 1, at art 5. Note that the preambular paragraphs of the CRPD reference equality and non-discrimination and Article 1 declares the purpose of the CRPD, and Article 3 articulates non-discrimination as a general principle.

[85] *Ibid.* at art. 5(2).

[86] *Ibid.* at art. 2.

[87] *Ibid.* at art. 5(3).

[88] Rehabilitation Act 1973 § 29 USC § 701 (year); 28 CFR § 41; 29 CFR § 32; 45 CFR § 84.

[89] CRPD, *supra*, note 1, at art. 2.

human rights must be implemented through positive measures in order to address ongoing systemic discrimination against persons with disabilities. Importantly, the failure to provide or denial of reasonable accommodation is thus a separate and distinct basis upon which to found a claim for disability discrimination under the CRPD.

The duty to provide reasonable accommodation in the CRPD extends to a broad array of social actors and thus has substantial relevance for the rights-based appli-cation of disability supports. The State, employers, education providers, health care providers, testing and qualification bodies, providers of goods and services and pri-vate clubs, amongst others, are required to reasonably modify policies, practices and premises that impede the inclusion and participation of persons with disabilities. The provision of reasonable accommodation requires an individual analysis of the appro-priate accommodations for persons with disabilities in various settings, and therefore appropriate accommodations must be tailored to the individual.[90] The individual analysis is important as persons with the same disability are often assumed to need the same reasonable accommodation, but in many instances that is not the case, and it is essential that appropriate accommodations and supports must be determined for the specific person and not by their disability. As it is not possible to foresee all reasonable accommodation interventions that may be required, it is important for domestic legislation to incorporate reasonable accommodation provisions in a flexible, open-ended format in disability support provision.

Legal Capacity and Enabling Personalised Decision Making

Advancing principles of dignity, autonomy and independence, Article 12 of the CRPD recognises that persons with disabilities must be equal before the law. Article 12 confirms that persons with disabilities 'enjoy legal capacity on an equal basis with others in all aspects of life'.[91] This fundamentally important provision reflects and responds to the reality that persons with disabilities have all too often been subjected to laws and practices that deprived them of their legal capacity.[92] As such, their autonomy and freedom to choose how and where to live their lives are effectively removed in such circumstances. This clearly extends to the provision of disability supports.

Article 12(1) reaffirms that all persons, including all persons with disabilities, have the right to recognition before the law, and thus should be recognised as rights holders (as opposed to objects to be acted upon).[93] The right to equal recognition

[90] See Waddington, L. (2008) 'When It Is Reasonable for Europeans to Be Confused: Understanding When a Disability Accommodation Is "Reasonable" from a Comparative Perspective', *Comparative Labor Law & Policy Journal* 29 (3): 101–124.

[91] CRPD, *supra*, note 1, at art. 12.

[92] See, e.g., Mental Disability Advocacy Centre (2007) *Guardianship and Human Rights in Bulgaria: Analysis, Policy and Practice*, 19–20.

[93] CRPD, *supra*, n. 1, at art. 12(1).

before the law encompasses two important elements: (1) recognition of legal personality, in the sense that rights and duties may be imposed; and (2) recognition of the capacity to act, in the sense that one can actually exercise legal rights and duties under the law. Article 12(2) recognises the right to the equal enjoyment of legal capacity.[94] Article 12(3) requires the adoption of supported decision-making mechanisms (assisting the person to make a decision personally), as opposed to substituted decision making (someone else making a decision for the person).[95]

Supported decision-making models must allow and facilitate a person to exercise legal capacity independently in a manner that preserves agency.[96] Such models may not shift decisional power onto a third party (i.e. mentor, guardian, curator). Supported decision-making models will undoubtedly require legal reform at the domestic level, for example the amendment or repeal of guardianship or curatorship regimes and the introduction of an appropriate supported decision-making mechanism which is adequately resourced, individualised and properly implemented. Moreover, supported decision making must meet the diverse needs of persons with disabilities across the wide array of legal transactions and social activities persons encounter. Support provision in this context can take various forms depending on the need in question, for example by means of a personal assistant, peer support, ombudsman or public defendant or, in certain situations, through the use of informal networks.

Minimum safeguards against abuse are required in any supported decision framework used to implement Article 12 of the CRPD. As provided in Article 12(4), these safeguards should include the requirement that the support provider is to assist the person with a disability in making decisions, and not substitute its own will and preferences.[97] Support providers must therefore respect the rights, will and preferences of the person being supported. The type of support to be provided should be proportionate to the person's needs, individualised and free from conflict of interest and undue influence. Further, support arrangements should also be subject to regular review by an independent and impartial authority.

---

94 *Ibid.* at art. 12(2); According to the Office of the High Commissioner for Human Rights, the two terms 'recognition as a person before the law' and 'legal capacity' are distinct. The concept of *legal personality* (derived from art 12(1) CRPD) recognises the individual as a person before the law and is therefore a prerequisite for the enjoyment of any other right, while *legal capacity* is a broader term that includes the capacity of the individual to be subject of rights and obligations as well as the capacity to act. The *capacity to act* is intended as the capacity and power to engage in a particular undertaking or transaction, to maintain a particular status or relationship with another individual, and more in general to create, modify or extinguish legal relationships. Office of the United Nations High Commissioner for Human Rights (2009), *Human Rights Council discussed the human rights of persons with disabilities on 6 March* 2009, available at: http://www.ohchr.org/EN/Issues/Disability/Pages/FirstDebate.aspx (accessed 12 March 2012).

95 CRPD, *supra*, n. 1, at art. 12 (3).

96 This cornerstone idea is also linked to the necessary safeguards set forth in paragraph 4 of art 12, which 'shall ensure that measures relating to the exercise of legal capacity respect the rights, will and preferences of the person'.

97 CRPD, *supra*, note 1, at art. 12 (4).

Finally, Article 12(5) addresses the specific issue of the right of persons with disabilities to own and inherit property and control their own financial affairs. The provision makes clear that persons with disabilities cannot be deprived of their property absent lawful reason. It is thus incumbent upon States Parties to provide the support needed to enable persons with disabilities to manage their financial affairs. Article 12(5) further guards against arbitrary deprivations of property.[98]

In sum, Article 12 explicitly recognises the legal capacity of persons with disabilities and provides measures to support their right to exercise their legal capacity. It essentially requires a continuum of support, thereby acknowledging that some persons with disabilities require no support in making decisions, whereas others may need intensive support. Article 12 thus affirms the position that, irrespective of the level of support needed, States Parties should ensure that this support is not abusive and does not infringe upon the human rights of the support recipient.

CHOICE IN LIVING ARRANGEMENTS

Article 19 of the CRPD, on living independently and in the community, reflects an extension of the right to liberty, namely the freedom to choose one's own living arrangements.[99] As some scholars have emphasised, the CRPD embraces, and articulates for the first time in an international human rights treaty, the right to community integration.[100] Article 19 is thus specifically directed at the elimination of segregated, congregate and socially isolated environments in which persons with disabilities have historically been forced, or obliged, to live.[101] Of particular concern to the CRPD drafters during treaty negotiation was the elimination of living arrangements that segregated and isolated persons with disabilities (e.g. institutions, social care homes, group homes, orphanages), and that all too often represented the choices of others. Trenchantly, Article 19 requires States Parties to ensure that persons with disabilities are able to live *in the community* with living arrangements equal to others, and that these options support the inclusion and participation of persons with disability in community life.[102] It requires that services for disabled people should 'support living and inclusion in the community' and aim to 'prevent isolation or segregation from the community'.[103]

---

[98] *Ibid.*, at art. 12 (5).

[99] *Ibid.*, at art. 19.

[100] *Ibid.*; Rosenthal, E. and Kanter, A. (2002) 'The Right to Community Integration for People with Disabilities under United States and International Law', in Yee, S. & Breslin, M. (eds.) *Disability Rights Law and Policy: International and National Perspectives*, 309–368.

[101] Stein, M. and Quinn, G. (2009) 'Challenges in Realising the Right to Live in the Community', in European Coalition for Community Living, *Focus on Article 19 of The UN Convention On The Rights Of Persons With Disabilities*, 37.

[102] CRPD, *supra*, n. 1, at art. 19.

[103] *Ibid.*

The provision also provides that persons with disabilities must be able to choose with whom they live on an equal basis with others. To this end, States Parties are obliged to ensure that persons with disabilities have access to the support services they require in order to live freely in the community. These support services include in-home support, residential and community support services and personal care. Article 19 also seeks to ensure that mainstream community services and facilities are available and responsive to the needs of persons with disability so as to facilitate their freedom to live in and be a part of the community.

It is still the case that national policies are oriented towards improving – and thus reinforcing – institutional care as opposed to promoting community-based living.[104] Disability Rights International highlights the problem in regard to children in institutions and reports 'governments and international donors spend millions worldwide building and rebuilding these torture chambers for children with disabilities instead of supporting families, substitute families when necessary and community services and education'.[105] These policies are premised on paternalistic assumptions that do not reflect principles of participation, inclusion and other disability rights concepts. As the European Coalition for Community Living has emphasised: 'People with disabilities are able to live in their local communities as equal citizens, with the support that they need to participate in every-day life. This includes living in their own homes or with their families, going to work, going to school and taking part in community activities'.[106]

The implications of the CRPD are quite clear: instead of allocating resources towards rebuilding segregated institutions, such resources should be used to provide proper support for persons with disabilities to live in the community. Further, in cases where national policies promote community-based and independent living, the failure of states to provide direct payments[107] or individualised funding schemes to persons with disabilities stands as a major barrier to managing one's own affairs.

---

[104] This is the case for Bulgaria, for example, where, as ANED comments, national debate is focused on improving the quality of institutional care rather than creating conditions for children and adults to live in their own communities. It should be noted, however, that some small steps towards independent living are currently being taken. See Panayotova, K. (2009) Academic Network of European Disability experts (ANED), *ANED country report on the implementation of policies supporting independent living for disabled people: Bulgaria*, available at: http://www.disability-europe.net/content/pdf/BG-6-Request-07%20ANED_2009_Task_5_template_Bulgaria_to%20publish_to%20EC.pdf (accessed 12 March 2012).

[105] Disability Rights International, *The Worldwide Campaign to End the Institutionalization of Children*, available at: http://www.disabilityrightsintl.org/learn-about-the-worldwide-campaign-to-end-the-institutionalization-of-children/ (accessed 12 March 2012). 'One of the main drivers of institutionalization – particularly in developing countries – is the use of misdirected foreign assistance funding to build new institutions or rebuild old crumbling facilities, instead of providing assistance and access to services for families who want to keep their children at home'. *Ibid.*

[106] European Coalition for Community Living (2008) *Creating Successful Campaigns for Community Living, An advocacy manual for disability organisations and service providers*, November, 71.

[107] A particular method of individual funding where a person receives support funding directly and purchases services or personal assistance.

Clearly, providing a mechanism for direct payments helps to facilitate independent and autonomous decision making. Very often where direct payment options are provided by the State, persons with physical disabilities are more likely to benefit than persons with mental disabilities because of the stigma of certain disabilities, as well as the failure to foster supported decision making. The lack of community-based services, attributable to insufficient funding, is yet another issue. The inadequate allocation of resources for the provision of required hours of personal assistance to support living and inclusion in the community, as envisaged by Article 19, is a common problem.

Review of European Policy on Choice in Living Arrangements

The EU and many Member States have ratified the CRPD, while other European countries have signed it, thus affirming their commitment to uphold the rights of persons with disabilities. The European Commission's office for Employment, Social Affairs and Equal Opportunities published a report that reviewed existing European policy and made recommendations to the EC on how best to transition from institutionalised care to community-based living arrangements in line with the CRPD.[108] The report identified four major problems with institutionalisation: (1) depersonalised treatments and interactions, including the removal of personal possessions – important symbols of one's individuality; (2) rigidity of routine, such as fixed schedules for eating, activities and sleeping, without flexibility for personal preference; (3) block treatment, characterised by 'processing' people in groups without privacy; and (4) social distance and exclusion.[109]

Indeed, in many EU countries, institutional care still accounts for more than one-half of public care expenditures.[110] According to the report, rigid legislative and administrative rules in some EU countries make it difficult to provide services to persons with disabilities outside of large institutions,[111] and therefore persons with disabilities still do not have a choice in their living arrangements and are forced to live in institutional settings for their entire lives. A recent European Coalition for Community Living report on Slovenia provides further evidence of how funding is being channeled to institutions in a way that does not allow for any choice in living arrangements, as the report indicates:

> If a disabled person lives in a long stay residential institution, living expenses are covered by the State, with funds given directly to the institution. Disabled people who choose to live alone or by themselves lose this financial support. This means

[108] European Commission, Employment, Social Affairs, and Equal Opportunities, Ad Hoc Expert Group on the Transition from Institutional to Community-based Care (2009), available at: http://ec.europa.eu/social/BlobServlet?docId=4017&langId=en (accessed 12 March 2012) (hereinafter EC Ad Hoc Expert Group Transition From Institutional to Community Based Care).

[109] *Ibid.*, at 7.

[110] *Ibid.*, at 9.

[111] *Ibid.*

that disabled people who want to live independently need to have a source of income, or be financially supported by their families.[112]

The current disability supports in Slovenia are for persons with disabilities to live in institutions, but do not provide options for persons with disabilities to make their own living arrangements in the community with proper supports. Other EU countries have similar policies; for instance, in Ireland there are seventy-two institutions for persons with disabilities that cost the state €500 million per year to operate.[113] At present, 4,000 persons with disabilities live in institutions that are predominantly operated by voluntary organisations or religious groups.

A recent study carried out in EU Member States and Turkey, *De-institutionalisation and Community Living: Outcomes and Costs* (DECLOC), found that nearly 1.2 million children and adults with disabilities live in long-stay residential institutions.[114] DECLOC reported that in 16 out of 25 countries for which information was available, state funds (local or regional) are used at least in part to support institutions with 100 or more places for persons with disabilities.[115] Further, the report noted that in twenty-one of the countries surveyed state funds are used to support institutions with more than thirty places.[116] The report stressed the importance of transitioning from institutionalised care to community-based supports in line with existing relevant international human rights standards.[117] It also emphasised the importance of Member States to: involve family members and children in decision-making processes, use structural funds for the transition from institutional to community-based care, establish proper monitoring systems to ensure quality of life, create support systems and proper working conditions for professional and informal support providers, and increase coordination between government departments and agencies involved in the transition process.[118] The issue of state funding for institutional care and lack of efficient individualised funding schemes discourage independent living and social inclusion for persons with disabilities.

The Council of Europe Committee of Ministers' *Recommendation on Deinstitutionalization and Community Living of Children with Disabilities* reflects the strong move in favour of community-based living arrangements within a framework

---

[112] European Coalition for Community Living (ECCL) (n.d.) *Focus on Article 19 of the UN Convention on the Rights of Persons with Disabilities, 'We Want Equal, Not Special Treatment!'*, at 34, available at: http://www.community-living.info/index.php?page=308&news=423 (accessed 24 August 2010).

[113] Health Service Executive (2011) *A Time to Move on from Congregated Settings: A Strategy for Community Inclusion*, Report of the Working Group on Congregated Settings, June, Health Service Executive.

[114] Mansell J., Knapp M., Beadle-Brown J., and Beecham J. (2007) *Deinstitutionalisation and community living – outcomes and costs: Report of a European Study*. Volume 2: Main Report. Canterbury: Tizard Centre, University of Kent.

[115] *Ibid.*

[116] *Ibid.*

[117] EC Ad Hoc Expert Group on the Transition from Institutional to Community Based Care, *supra*, n. 108, at 20.

[118] *Ibid.*, at 20–21.

of responsible transition away from institutionalisation.[119] The Recommendation stresses 'the fact that placing children in institutionalized forms of care raises serious concerns as to its compatibility with the exercise of children's rights'[120] and recommends that governments take measures 'in order to replace institutional provision with community-based services within a reasonable timeframe and through a comprehensive approach'.[121] The Recommendation further sets forth principles and actions to be undertaken in order to facilitate the transition from institutionalisation to community-based services with supports. This is keeping with Mansell's work on the issue, which emphasises that it is important for alternatives to institutionalisation to be sensitive to the need to shift from institutional culture so that service provision in the community is directed towards full participation in society.'[122] This approach acknowledges that substituting the same institutional culture in service provision at the community level is unacceptable.

LIFE IN THE COMMUNITY

The foregoing sections have outlined the general principles that amplify current approaches to facilitating full inclusion and participation of persons with disabilities in society, drawn from the international as well as regional disability rights standards, and the concept of personalisation which emphasises independence and respect for individual decision making. The overall thrust of these concepts is to promote full inclusion in a meaningful way and to advance reforms in support systems in a manner that fosters and reinforces participation in the community. The section that follows identifies some of the specific substantive rights, under international law and reflected in European law and policy. In combination, these rights and supporting principles can help to foster engagement in community and tackle exclusionary barriers and isolation for persons with disabilities.

Fostering Accessibility

The CRPD's preamble reminds us that the treaty was motivated in large measure by the continuing exclusion of persons with disabilities[123] and recognition of the many

---

[119] Recommendation CM/Rec (2010)2 of the Committee of Ministers to Member States on Deinstitutionalization and Community Living of Children with Disabilities, 3 February 2010, reprinted in *European Yearbook of Disability Law*, vol. 2 (Lisa Waddgington and Gerard Quinn, eds., 2010), at 385–394.

[120] *Ibid.* at para. 14.

[121] *Ibid.* at para. 17.

[122] Mansell, J. and Beadle-Brown, B. (2010) 'Deinstitutionalisation and Community Living: Position Statement of the Comparative Policy and Practice Special Interest Research Group of International Association for the Scientific Study of Intellectual Disabilities', *Journal of Intellectual Disability Research*, 54: 104–112; 105.

[123] See CRPD, at preamble (k) (expressing concern that in spite of soft laws 'persons with disabilities continue to face barriers in their participation as equal members of society').

benefits that participation in community contributes to society and personhood.[124] Article 9 (Accessibility) aims to dismantle barriers established on the basis of discriminatory attitudes by promoting different forms of accessibility in the public and private spheres, including physical, technological, economic and social accessibility, as well as information and communication accessibility. It imposes a general obligation on States Parties to enable persons with disabilities to live independently and participate fully in all aspects of life by ensuring equal access to the environment. Requiring States Parties to identify and eliminate obstacles and barriers to accessibility and specifically highlighting access to public and domestic buildings, transport and transport infrastructure, information and communication technologies and systems and public services and facilities, the CRPD provides a broad framework within which to achieve accessibility and in respect of different aspects of inclusion.

In addition, Article 9 requires that medical facilities, electronic services and emergency services be accessible to persons with disabilities, that measures such as signage in public buildings should be made available in Braille and in easy-to-read formats and that live assistance and intermediaries should be available, where required, to facilitate access by persons with disabilities to buildings and other facilities open to the public.[125] Article 9, in underscoring the need for States Parties to promote access for persons with disabilities to new information as well as communications technologies and systems, including the Internet, requires States Parties to promote the incorporation of accessibility measures into the design, development, production and distribution of accessible information and communication technologies and systems.[126] Article 9 also requires equivalent levels of accessibility to be available in both urban and rural areas. Crucially, the obligations imposed apply to public services and facilities provided by government and the private sector.[127] Article 9 clarifies that accessibility is to be achieved through a variety of implementation measures, including the development and monitoring of minimum standards and guidelines for accessibility[128] and the provision of training for stakeholders in accessibility issues.[129]

The European Community in Council Decision 2010/48/EC[130] on the CRPD declared its competence to address accessibility in the fields of goods, services, personal mobility (e.g. transport) and information and communication technologies.

---

[124] See *ibid.* at preamble (m) (acknowledging that 'full participation by persons with disabilities will result in their enhanced sense of belonging and in significant advances in the human, social and economic development of society and the eradication of poverty').

[125] See CRPD, *supra*, n. 1, at art. 9.

[126] *Ibid.*

[127] *Ibid. at* art. 9(2)(b).

[128] *Ibid.* at art. 9(2)(a).

[129] *Ibid.* at art. 9(2)(c).

[130] Council Directive (EC) 2010/48.

In the area of goods and services, Council Directive 2001/85/EC[131] aims to guarantee the safety of passengers, and has established special provisions for vehicles used for the carriage of passengers comprising more than eight seats. The Directive also addresses the needs of persons with reduced mobility,[132] through the provision of technical prescriptions to foster accessibility in accordance with EC transport and social policies.

The CRPD supports accessibility in other ways, for example through Article 20 (Personal mobility) requiring States Parties to take effective measures to ensure personal mobility with the greatest possible independence for persons with disabilities.[133] An illustrative but non-exhaustive list provides an indication of the type of measures to be taken, including:

- Facilitating the personal mobility of persons with disabilities in the manner and at the time of their choice, and at affordable cost;
- Facilitating access by persons with disabilities to quality mobility aids, devices, assistive technologies and forms of live assistance and intermediaries, including by making them available at affordable cost;
- Providing training in mobility skills to persons with disabilities and to specialist staff; and
- Encouraging entities that produce mobility aids, devices and assistive technologies to take into account all aspects of mobility for persons with disabilities.[134]

European policy is trending in the direction of facilitating personal mobility. For example, in the context of transport, Regulation 1107/2006[135] is a disability-specific Community measure designed to protect the rights of disabled persons and persons with reduced mobility when travelling by air. Specifically, the basic principles of the Regulation track closely with the requirements of Article 9 – for example, the standard that persons with disabilities may not be denied boarding or booking and that staff dealing directly with the travelling public should receive disability-awareness and disability rights training. While this book does not examine each nation's specific accessibility law and policy, it nonetheless recognises that full

---

[131] Council Directive (EC) 2001/85 relating to special provisions for vehicles used for the carriage of passengers comprising more than eight seats in addition to the driver's seat, and amending Directives 1970/156/EEC and 1997/27/EC [2002] OJ L43/1.

[132] It should be noted that the definition of *persons with reduced mobility*, included in the Directive 2001/85/EC, is broad and includes all people who have difficulty when using public transport, such as disabled people (including people with sensory and intellectual impairments, and wheelchair users); people with limb impairments; people of small stature; people with heavy luggage; elderly people; pregnant women; people with shopping trolleys; and people with children (including children seated in pushchairs).

[133] See CRPD, *supra*, n. 1, at art. 20.

[134] *Ibid.*

[135] Regulation (EC) No 1107/2006 of the Parliament and of the Council of 5 July 2006 concerning the rights of disabled persons and persons with reduced mobility when travelling by air, O.J. L 204 of 26.7.2006.

accessibility for people with disabilities plays an important role in advancing active citizenship.

Giving Full Effect to Social Rights

As noted previously, participation as a value and general principle is firmly embedded in the CRPD text and gives rise to more particular applications across the full range of civil, political, economic, social and cultural realms.[136] The CRPD recognises a number of specific measures designed to enhance participation in various realms of social as well as cultural life. The socialising effects of community inclusion are reinforced through the specification of social rights in the CRPD. Thus, the CRPD signifies a major break from perspectives that saw social programmes as a way of managing or merely maintaining persons with disabilities. Economic, social and cultural rights in the CRPD and now in European disability policy are a means of enhancing freedom and enabling persons with disabilities to attain independence and manage their own lives.

For example, Article 30 of the CPRD on participation in cultural life, recreation, leisure and sport recognises the power of participation as a vehicle for inclusion and as social change conveyor.[137] The recognised right in the CRPD of persons with disabilities to participate in a wide array of cultural, recreational, sporting and leisure activities as central to their full social inclusion is the most detailed expression of this general right in international human rights law generally, and points to its importance for persons with disabilities in particular.[138] Article 30 includes the duty of States to take measures to support access to places where cultural performances or services are held, such as theatres, museums, cinemas, libraries and tourism services.[139] It also includes, as far as possible, access to monuments and sites of national cultural importance.[140] Significantly, the CRPD also affirms the right of people with disabilities to develop their creative, artistic and intellectual potential for both individual and societal benefit.[141]

Other CRPD provisions similarly emphasise social rights as a vehicle for community participation and the advancement of full citizenship. Thus, Article 19 of the CRPD, in addition to creating a right of choice in living arrangements for persons

---

[136] See CRPD, *supra*, n. 1, at art. 3 (c).

[137] For more on Article 30, see generally Stein, M. A. and Lord, J. E., *Jacobus tenBroek: Participatory Justice, and the UN Convention on the Rights of Persons with Disabilities*, 13 *Tex. J. C.L. & C.R.* 167 (2008); Lord, J. E. and Stein, M. A. (2009) 'Social Rights and The Relational Value of the Rights to Participate in Sport, Recreation and Play', BU INTL L J. 27: 249. See also Wolff, E. et al. (eds.) (2007) *Sport in the United Nations Convention on the Rights of Persons with Disabilities* (hereinafter UN Sport), available at: http://www.sportanddev.org/en/learnmore/?uNewsID=42 (accessed 12 March 2012).

[138] See generally UN Sport, *supra*, note 139.

[139] CRPD, *supra*, n. 1, at art. 30(1)(c).

[140] See *ibid*.

[141] See *ibid*. at art. 30(2).

with disabilities, articulates the right to community inclusion and participation for persons with disabilities.[142] In order for persons with disabilities to be included in their community, it is essential to ensure that adequate supports are provided in various community settings. Thus, to realise rights of citizenship and thereby achieve the goal of community inclusion and participation, Article 19 must be read alongside other general provisions of the CRPD dealing with employment,[143] accessibility,[144] education,[145] cultural and recreational activities,[146] decision-making processes[147] and elections,[148] among others, to ensure persons with disabilities are integrated members in their community.

The European Committee on Social Rights has recognised the strong link between social rights and citizenship. In an education complaint, for instance, the applicant, Autism Europe, asserted that France was failing to meet its obligation under, inter alia, Article 15(1) of the revised European Social Charter. The *Autism Europe v. France*[149] claim essentially alleged that children and adults with autism were not able to exercise the effective enjoyment of the right to education in mainstream school settings or in specialised educational institutions because of inadequate support. In other words, the school system was failing to accommodate their individual needs. The Committee found that France had failed to meet its obligations under the Charter insofar as it had failed to demonstrate that it was taking reasonable steps towards the fulfillment of Article 15 and other associated rights, including Article 17 (the right of children to social support) and Article E (equality). Crucially, the Committee stated: 'The underlying vision of Article 15 is one of equal citizenship for persons with disabilities and, fittingly, the primary rights are those of independence, social integration and participation in the life of the community'.[150] The Committee acknowledged that education plays an important role in advancing citizenship rights.[151]

Fostering Community Participation through Meaningful Employment

Article 27 of the CRPD confirms the right of persons with disabilities to employment on an equal basis with others and requires States Parties to recognise the equal right of persons with disabilities to freely chosen or accepted work in an open and inclusive

---

[142] *Ibid.*, at art. 19.
[143] *Ibid.* at art. 27.
[144] *Ibid.* at art. 9.
[145] *Ibid.* at art. 24.
[146] *Ibid.*, at art. 30.
[147] *Ibid.* at art. 4(3).
[148] *Ibid.* at art. 29.
[149] *Autism Europe v. France*, Complaint No. 13/2002, decision on the merits of 4 November 2003.
[150] *Ibid.* at para. 48.
[151] For another decision of the European Social Committee underscoring the importance of quality education for children with disabilities as a means of harnessing social rights and full participation, see *MDAC v Bulgaria*, Complaint No. 41/2007, European Committee of Social Rights, Decision of 3 June 2008.

labour market under just and fair conditions.[152] It enumerates a range of measures to be taken by States Parties in order to give effect to the right to work, including the general prohibition of discrimination on the ground of disability in all forms, sectors and levels of employment which covers, inter alia, conditions of recruitment, hiring, continuity of employment, career advancement and occupational health and safety. Article 27 mandates that States Parties establish, by means of legislation, the duty to provide reasonable accommodation in the workplace for persons with disabilities.[153] States Parties are also required to ensure that persons with disabilities are protected from harassment in the workplace and have effective avenues for the redress of work-related grievances.[154] It reaffirms the right of persons with disabilities to exercise their labour and trade union rights on an equal basis with others, for example by ensuring that labour and trade unions, or associations, are accessible to, and inclusive of, employees with disabilities. Moreover, States Parties should ensure that persons with disabilities have access to comprehensive employment-related support services (e.g. jobseeker and placement services, placement support and job retention services, professional rehabilitation and others), education and training (e.g. technical or vocational training, vocational guidance programmes and others).[155] Other measures set forth in Article 27 relate to the promotion of self-employment, entrepreneurship, and personal business opportunities for persons with disabilities, and affirmative action programmes, or incentives that will encourage the employment of persons with disabilities in the private sector.[156] Such affirmative measures may include, inter alia, tax reliefs, provision of financial subsidies to employers or the determination of employment quotas in the recruitment of persons with disabilities, or others. Finally, Article 27(2) UN CRPD requires States Parties to ensure that persons with disabilities are effectively protected from slavery, servitude and forced and compulsory labour.[157]

Developments in Europe serve to reinforce the concept of full inclusion through employment for persons with disabilities. Notably, the 1997 Amsterdam Treaty[158] accorded to the European Community the authority to combat discrimination on the ground of disability (amongst other grounds). This development provided the point of departure for developing a Directive in 2002 on discrimination, namely the Employment Equality Directive of 2000.[159] Its aim is to prohibit and

---

[152] *Ibid.* at art. 27.
[153] See UN Doc A/HRC/10/48, 17–18.
[154] See CRPD, *supra*, n. 1, at art. 27(1)(b).
[155] *Ibid.* at art 27.
[156] *Ibid.*
[157] *Ibid.* at art. 27(2).
[158] Treaty of Amsterdam amending the Treaty on European Union, the treaties establishing the European Communities and certain related acts, as signed in Nice on 26 February 2001 and published in the Official Journal of the European Communities No. C 80 of 10 March 2001, at art. 5.
[159] Council Directive (EC) 2000/78, establishing a general framework for Equal Treatment in Employment and Occupation [2000] O.J. L303/16, available at: http://eur-lex.europa.eu/LexUriServ/LexUriServ.do?uri=OJ:L:2000:303:0016:0022:EN:PDF (accessed 12 March 2012).

combat discrimination on the grounds of disability as well as religion or belief, age or sexual orientation as regards employment, occupation and vocational training. Article 2 of the Directive defines discrimination, as any 'less favourable' treatment of a person arising from, inter alia, his/her disability and includes both direct and indirect discrimination and harassment; however, it should be noted that it does not provide a clear definition of disability.[160] The Directive does require employers to provide reasonable accommodations for persons with disabilities in Article 5 and requires Member States to ensure that employers take appropriate measures to enable persons with disabilities to have access to, participate in, or advance in employment, thereby promoting qualified candidates with a disability to access the labour market.[161] Unfortunately, and inconsistent with the CRPD, the Directive does not clearly establish that the failure to provide reasonable accommodation constitutes discrimination. It is hoped that future developments will remedy this deficiency.

Innovative Resource Mechanisms

Resource mechanisms will undoubtedly play an essential role in helping to fulfill the far-reaching aims of the CRPD and in advancing full participation in the life of the community for persons with disabilities. Even though the global recession has put tremendous pressure on social funds throughout the world, there are, nonetheless, some innovative funding mechanisms in place that can serve to advance community participation for persons with disabilities. Each of these, where relevant, is discussed at the domestic level in the case-study chapters. It should be mentioned, however, that the drafters of the CRPD did not opt for inclusion of any of the resource mechanisms supported by developing countries, nor did they support those frequently included in other types of international treaties, such as environmental agreements. Some developments in the European context, however, are worth citing.

Structural funds were established to promote implementation of the EU's strategy to reduce disparities between the regions of Europe, otherwise known as the Cohesion policy. Council Regulation (EC) No 1083/2006[162] sets forth general provisions for three such funds: European Regional Development Fund (ERDF), the European Social Fund (ESF) and the Cohesion Fund. The two funding mechanisms of greatest relevance to the development of community-based services for persons with disabilities are the ESF and the ERDF.

The ESF was established to reduce differences in prosperity and living standards across the EU in order to advance economic well-being and aims to support projects directed at promoting employment and to help citizens to advance their education

---

[160] *Ibid.*
[161] *Ibid.* at art. 5.
[162] Council Regulation (EC) No 1083/2006.

and skills to improve their job prospects.[163] It also assists EU Member States to achieve goals established in the European employment strategy and disability action plan and can thus be accessed to fund training for staff working with people with disabilities. The ERDF is directed at financing 'productive investment leading to the creation or maintenance of jobs, infrastructure and local development initiatives and the business activities of small and medium sized businesses'.[164] These investments may include 'investments in health and social infrastructure which contribute to regional and local development and increasing the quality of life'.[165] As the *Ad Hoc Expert Group on the Transition from Institutional to Community based Care* indicated, in some countries it has been applied to finance the construction of new residential institutions or renovate existing residential institutions.[166] That report recommends that guidelines should be developed on the use of funds and that such guidelines should be directed at ensuring that 'projects which aim to build, enlarge or perpetrate institutions are not in line with the Convention on the Rights of Persons with Disabilities and EU's own policies on equal opportunities, social inclusion and discrimination, and are therefore not eligible for funding'.[167] As a Report of the Council of Europe Parliamentary Assembly emphasises:

> In order to enable active participation of persons with disabilities in society, it is necessary that they are given the opportunity to interact with the community. The practice of placing children and adults with disabilities into institutions undermines their inclusion as they are kept segregated from the rest of society and suffer serious damage to their healthy development and obstruction of the exercise of other rights. Deinstitutionalisation is a prerequisite to enabling people with disabilities to become as independent as possible and take their place as full citizens with the opportunity to access education and employment, and a whole range of other services.[168]

Clearly, Structural Funds should not be used to perpetuate and reinforce systems of institutional care. Rather, they should be used to raise awareness about the right

---

[163] Ad Hoc Expert Group on the Transition from Institutional to Community-based Care, *supra*, n. 108 at p. 22. See also European Coalition on Community Living (2010) *Wasted Time, Wasted Money, Wasted Lives… A Wasted Opportunity? A Focus Report on how the current use of Structural Funds perpetuates the social exclusion of disabled people in Central and Eastern Europe by failing to support the transition from institutional care.*

[164] See European Communities (2009) *Ensuring accessibility and non-discrimination of people with disabilities: Toolkit for using Structural and Cohesion Funds*, European Commission, Directorate-General for Employment, Social Affairs and Equal Opportunities, Unit G.3, at 13.

[165] *Ibid.*

[166] Ad Hoc Expert Group on the Transition from Institutional to Community-based Care, *supra*, n. 108, at p. 22.

[167] *Ibid.*

[168] Parliamentary Assembly of the Council of Europe 1 Council of Europe, Parliamentary Assembly (2008) *Access to rights for people with disabilities and their full and active participation in society*, *Report*, Social, Health and Family Affairs Committee, Doc. 11649, 8 August, para. 44.

of persons with disabilities to live in the community, with choices equal to others. Engaging persons with disabilities and their representative organisations in the planning and delivery of such training is essential.

Of particular relevance for disability rights and facilitating the implementation of the CRPD is the requirement laid out in Regulation 1083/2006 that both the Member States and the Commission should take all appropriate measures to prevent any discrimination on the basis of, inter alia, disability, during all phases of implementation of the Funds.[169] Article 16 of the Regulation provides that accessibility for persons with disabilities should be 'one of the criteria to be observed in defining operations co-financed by the Funds and to be taken into account during the various stages of implementation'.[170] The Regulation has relevance for all fields covered by the CRPD, and co-funding awarded by the Funds should respect and promote the CRPD's general principles. Finally, co-funding of national projects of programmes by the Funds should be contingent on inclusion of, and accessibility to, persons with disabilities. In this regard, it can play a key role in the effective implementation of the CRPD.

PROVISION OF PUBLIC SUPPORTS AND SERVICES

In an effort to inform the progressive, rights-based reform of disability supports throughout Europe, international and regional standards that guide government contracting and the issuance of public procurements assume special significance. Government contracting has long been used to provide disability supports throughout the world, but in many European countries and some North American states and provinces, governments provide public funding to organisations and institutions that do not promote the human rights of persons with disabilities. Supports must be provided within a framework directed towards full participation, inclusion and autonomy, as opposed to dependence, segregation and paternalism. In other words, community-based supports should foster the full and active citizenship of persons with disabilities, facilitating inclusion in all aspects of community life. Thus, Ireland has primarily funded church-based organisations that provide 'services' for persons with disabilities, often in institutional settings, as opposed to promoting proper 'supports' to persons with disabilities to live independently as members of their community.[171] Such an approach is not in keeping with a rights-oriented perspective that sees the utilisation of social and economic supports as a way to 'underpin social inclusion and provide the material means by which individuals can make and effectuate their own life'.[172]

---

[169] *Ibid.*
[170] *Ibid.*
[171] Ad Hoc Expert Group on the Transition from Institutional to Community-based Care, *supra*, n. 108.
[172] Quinn, G. and Courtis, C. (2009) 'Poverty, Invisibility and Disability', in Van Bueren, G. (ed.) *Freedom from Poverty as a Human Right*, UNESCO, Paris, 203–206.

The role of public procurement processes in promoting – or unfortunately in many instances restraining – citizenship for persons with disabilities is essential. Government contracting is an important vehicle for the promotion of environmental and corporate social responsibility, with public procurements making up 15–20 per cent of the Gross Domestic Product (GDP) in most EU Member States.[173] As EU Members continue to rely more heavily on government contracts generally, it is essential to consider how Member States ensure public contracts are properly addressing disability supports. The EU's recent ratification of the CRPD marks an important starting point for reviewing the issuance of public procurements and the resulting contracts.

Article 32 of the CRPD addresses the role that international cooperation and disability-inclusive development can play in support of national CRPD implementation efforts.[174] The provision is relevant to the provision of disability supports and services insofar as it obligates States Parties to cooperate internationally through partnerships with other States, with relevant international and regional organisations and civil society in support of national measures to give effect to the CRPD. Importantly, Article 32 of the CRPD requires that all international cooperation efforts, including international development programmes, should be fully accessible to, and inclusive of, persons with disabilities, with obvious implications for the provision of disability supports and services not only across the EC but also between Member States and international development partners.[175]

Specifically, all States Parties are required to make every aspect of their aid programmes, from design to implementation and evaluation, including procurement processes, completely accessible for persons with disabilities.[176] This obligation can be satisfied through legislation, through specific policy pronouncements, or both. Article 32 should be read through the lens of Article 3 (General principles), and thus in implementing the obligation to make development programmes inclusive of persons with disabilities, States Parties must ensure that laws and policies applied to implement Article 32 are consistent with the principles of non-discrimination, participation and accessibility, amongst others.

Further, Article 32 lays out the standard for States Parties to follow in regard to ensuring public procurements are accessible to persons with disabilities and non-discriminatory. To this end, States Parties must ensure that all public procurements meet the obligations laid out in the CRPD, including public procurements for work within the State itself, and not just procurement mechanisms intended for international cooperation efforts. This is particularly relevant in regard to disability

[173] McCrudden, C. (2009) Buying Equality Draft Chapter, available at: http://www.michiganlaw-review.org/articles/mccrudden-buying-social-justice-equality-government-procurement-and-legal-change (accessed 12 March 2012).

[174] See CRPD, *supra*, note 1, at art. 32.

[175] *Ibid.*

[176] *Ibid.*

supports, as many States do not ensure their procurement system is in line with the CRPD's paradigm shift to the social model of disability. These States often award public funding for disability supports to charity or medical groups, rather than award funding to groups which work to provide adequate supports for the individual needs of persons with disabilities. As European countries work to advance the rights set forth in the CRPD, governments must develop models of good practice in their use of public procurements. There is tremendous value behind governments setting best-practice models for private industry and others to follow. Recent EU directives on public procurements were created to ensure 'a European area for public procurement in the context of the internal market. It is based on the fundamental principles enshrined in the Treaty establishing the European Community: equal treatment, a transparent and non-discriminatory call for competition, mutual recognition, the fight against fraud and corruption'.[177] Additionally, the new directives require public procurements to be accessible to persons with disabilities.[178] Clearly the EU is establishing directives for Member States to follow in issuing public procurements which promote equality and non-discrimination. As EU Member States issue public procurements, they should ensure those are accessible and inclusive of persons with disabilities and advance appropriate disability supports for full inclusion in society.

European governments should clearly champion the rights-based implementation of disability supports through issuing public procurements which are accessible to organisations of persons with disabilities and support providers who implement appropriate supports for persons with disabilities to live independently in the community. National-level policies concerning the institutionalisation of persons with disabilities (discussed earlier in the chapter) point to the need for important reforms to disability support systems. As discussed, Ireland spends €500 million per year to institutionalise 4,000 persons with disabilities.[179] In accordance with international and regional human rights standards, the Irish government should reform their public procurement system to reallocate the €500 million to organisations which provide disability supports to the 4,000 persons with disabilities, as well as other persons with disabilities in Ireland, to live in the community. Similarly, other governments which are actively funding institutional living arrangements should, in keeping with the Recommendation of the Committee of Ministers, work to transition to community living with appropriate supports, with benchmarks. Moreover, the development policies of bilateral donors should adhere to the Recommendation

---

[177] EUROPA (2004) *Summaries of EU Legislation, Public procurement in the water, energy, transport and postal services sectors*, available at: http://europa.eu/legislation_summaries/energy/internal_energy_market/l22010_en.htm#key (accessed 25 August 2010); Council Directive 2004/17, 2004 OJ (L134)1,14 (EC) (hereinafter Council Directive 2004/17).

[178] Council Directive 2004/17, *supra*, n. 179.

[179] See O'Brien, C. (2010) 'Institutions for disabled should be closed down, says report', *The Irish Times*, 07 July.

and track expenditures to ensure they are directed towards community living arrangements as opposed to reinforcing segregated institutional living.

CONCLUSION – OPPORTUNITIES AND NEW DIRECTIONS IN ENABLING ACTIVE CITIZENSHIP AND INDEPENDENCE

The twenty-first century has ushered in the disability rights project, both internationally, regionally within Europe and domestically. The CRPD reflects a sharp turn away from charity-driven, passive approaches to disability supports and a clear embrace of disability equality, informed by personalisation, choice in living arrangements and life in the community. The CRPD, along with law and policy in Europe, evokes an appreciation that social programmes aimed at management and maintenance of persons with disabilities, as opposed to full participation, autonomy and inclusion, are no longer an acceptable framework. The challenge, then, is to continue the project of reconfiguring disability supports towards the realisation of disability equality and human rights for all persons with disabilities. This effort requires substantive and processual change, for clearly the realisation of disability equality cannot happen absent the full participation of persons with disabilities themselves and their representative organisations.

These developments in disability law and policy at the international and European level do not exist in a vacuum. They are part of a broader human rights evolution that seeks to apply human rights principles to all persons, in particular groups with a long history of social and economic exclusion. In this sense, disability law informs and is informed by empowerment models in relation to other socially excluded groups, including racial and ethnic minorities, women, children and persons living in poverty. The equality and non-discrimination framework laid out in the CRPD and reflected in European law and policy focusses on individual needs in the manner required by persons with disabilities; States as well as human rights advocates may thus apply this model and the principles it expresses to develop the individual talents of other excluded groups such as those with mental health issues.

In providing specific coverage of a full range of civil, political, economic, social and cultural rights, the CRPD is directed towards enabling independence and full participation within the community for persons with disabilities. In this regard it signals a decisive break from historical practices and indeed many earlier international documents on disability. The thrust turns away from passive, paternalistic approaches which tended to privilege medical care and rehabilitation and embraces fully the rights-oriented provision of essential supports crucial in promoting full citizenship, autonomy and living a full life with dignity. The principles and standards reflected in the CRPD, which relate to the focus of this project, namely personalisation, choice in living arrangements and life in the community, are also emerging as regional, as well as national, standards in Europe. The ratification of the CRPD by many

States in Europe as well as by the European Union will provide further impetus for change, prompting greater alignment with the CRPD in the reform of disability supports. Law and policy reform in this context should be further invigorated by the robust monitoring of compliance with the CRPD not only through the CRPD Committee, but likewise through national human rights institutions, the EU in its areas of CRPD comptence and the Council of Europe. Effective monitoring hinges on the acknowledgement that social rights and supports are *in the service of* personalisation, choice in living arrangements and life in the community, along with the animating principles of dignity, autonomy, non-discrimination and participation.

3

Revitalising Disability Support at the Domestic Level

INTRODUCTION

Given the policy guidance and obligations from international law and policy identified in the previous chapter, in particular the CRPD,[1] there is a significant new emphasis on independent living and encouraging choice and participation. While enabling *choice* is becoming the new paradigm in international, regional and national law and policy, at the heart of the challenge in implementing this is the repositioning of *control* of resources and governance at the domestic level. Therefore, to initiate and sustain this change, countries must readjust their welfare states and community care and social support policy to be more individually led by and responsive to persons with disabilities. This fundamental shift is characterised in many Western jurisdictions by the concepts of 'self-determination', 'personalisation', or the 'choice' agenda. These concepts mean giving people more choice in their own living arrangements, to move beyond what *service* they want, towards what kind of *life* they want.

Similarly, support organisations must try to transform their organisational behaviour and models of support to accommodate individuals in achieving more autonomy in the way they achieve social and economic participation in society. In the United States, for example, these principles are being applied effectively to even those with significant disabilities who are also homeless and who have been otherwise resistant to engaging in treatment and housing services, for instance through the 'Housing First' model.[2]

Before exploring these initiatives and the values underpinning them in more detail in the comparative chapters, this chapter recognises that a vast infrastructure of services already exists which is firmly entrenched in block treatment, institutionalisation

---

[1] CRPD, Article 19.
[2] See Tsemberis, S. (n.d.) *Pathways to Housing*, available at: http://www.pathwaystohousing.org/content/our_model (accessed 25 July 2010).

and group care, which governments and providers must grapple with transforming. Therefore, a significant transition is required which involves moving from traditional funding, management and staffing arrangements in service delivery towards a model which is underpinned by the rights expressed in the last chapter. This chapter attempts to build on the earlier chapter – which sets out what *ought* to be done – to begin to explore what *can* be done. It derives its analysis of best practice from the international comparative welfare and governance literature and change management literature. It focuses on two levels: (1) the system-wide mechanisms used by governments, regulators and commissioners of support providers in promoting and managing change; and (2) the different models of funding, management and evaluation which have been used to leverage cultural and organisational change within public, private and non-profit sector services.

RESHAPING WELFARE: DEVELOPMENTAL FUNDING AND MANAGEMENT

Community support for people with disabilities in most jurisdictions (both developed and developing) is largely delivered through a blend of supports from state and the 'independent sector' made up of non-profit and private sector providers. Given the increasing role of this sector in the disability support field, there is a significant body of international comparative welfare literature, which has examined debates over best practice in state and non-profit relations, particularly regarding commissioning and procurement. Achieving the extension of choice and control as outlined earlier requires changes in the contracting practice of the relevant local governing authority. This section examines the different jurisdictional attempts to develop more personalised funding mechanisms, using strategic commissioning and management, to animate best practice and innovation in the sector.

There are a number of different methods of public administration used by governments in contracting and procurement, such as the length of time of contract, specificity of detail and choice of outcomes. Each of these can have very different outcomes in how the support organisations operate and the types and size of organisations which flourish. Generally, two broad typologies of contracting and procurement exist: those of centralised government approaches and decentralised government approaches. In addition to these typologies, more recent approaches to contracting are emerging over the last few years to support the move to personalisation, such as the use of flexible 'developmental' funding and citizens' commissioning, which are defining a new era of contracting and procurement. Each of these is examined in the following sections.

Centralised Government Approaches

Generally, centralised 'welfare states' fund services such as health care and social support through a national statutory agency. The planning and control of public expenditure are generally administered by the Treasury, which has oversight of economic planning. The Treasury allocates resources to departments, and departments to services. Making block contracts to a national health care provider has been the dominant method of funding used by governments of centralised welfare states. Local authorities have a role in community care; however, they must operate under centralised legal restraints and central government guidance, inspections and audits and financial controls.

Grant-in-aid funding is also generally offered to charitable organisations, which is often used to fill the gaps in statutory provision. This type of funding generally does not tightly prescribe the volume and type of service provided. Unlike contractual grants which are appropriate where government wishes to maintain detailed control over expenditure, grant-in-aid is used where the government has decided that the recipient body should operate relatively independently.[3] Charity bodies are thus often expected to carry out additional fundraising to cover all their costs.

The archetypal centralised government approach has been the UK welfare state as set out by the Beveridge report in the United Kingdom. As noted in the first chapter, Beveridge was the architect of the collectivist welfare approach and proposed comprehensive health and rehabilitation services, unemployment assistance (albeit limited to encourage a return to work) and children's allowance, as well as a commitment to full employment. This approach also signalled an important political shift emphasising the welfare state's importance as a major pillar of support for capitalism rather than a symbol of creeping socialism.[4] Beveridge envisaged a post-war society in which the state could actually strengthen the market economy.

These collectivist solutions were based on Keynesian economics, which advocates for the public sector to step in to intervene and assist the economy generally, and to ensure adequate employment.[5] Intervention would come in the form of government spending and tax breaks during recessionary times in order to stimulate the economy and government spending cuts and tax increases in good times, in order to curb inflation.

The core idea behind centralised welfare approaches is that access to services is theoretically more equitable.[6] Similarly, with regard to the information available to users at the local level, it is often useful to have a centralised point of access.[7] A degree of centralisation also appears to be needed to drive strategic vision and deliver a comprehensive coverage of support.[8] Notwithstanding the later criticisms of hierarchical structures and centralised welfare provision (identified below), without some level of standardisation of information, eligibility and service options, portability also

---

3   See Scottish Public Finance Manual, available at: http://www.scotland.gov.uk/Topics/Government/ Finance/spfm/grants (accessed 7 December 2010).
4   Clarke, J., Cochrane, A. and Smart, C. (1987) *Ideologies of Welfare: From Dreams to Disillusion*. Hutchinson Education, London.
5   Keynes, M. (1936) *General Theory of Employment, Interest and Money*. Palgrave Macmillan, London.
6   De Vries, M. (2007) 'The Rise and Fall of Decentralization: A Comparative Analysis of Arguments and Practices in European Countries', *European Journal of Political Research* 38: 193–224.
7   Hood, C. (1991) 'A Public Management for All Seasons?' *Public Administration* 69: 3–19, 8.
8   Bogdanor, V. (1999) *Devolution in the United Kingdom*. Oxford University Press, Oxford.

becomes a crucial issue, as people end up being blocked from moving from one area to another.

On the other hand, centralised provision of state services has attracted much criticism. One critique from Hood involves an inherent 'claim to universality' which persists in centralised welfare provision.[9] In other words, the idea that one size fits all, or that one form of governance will suit the myriad different types of health provision, is seen to be problematic. Critics argue that remote decision makers have little understanding of what is happening at the local context, and that this is reflected in poor decisions and inappropriate choices for service users.[10] Critics of centralisation such as Osborne and De Vries argue that a heavily centralised system prevents local practitioners from responding quickly and adequately to needs of users.[11] In the United Kingdom, for example, many Primary Care Trusts have expressed disappointment in their inability to pursue locally defined agendas.[12] Additionally, it is argued that, with tighter centralised controls, provider organisations risk losing flexibility, innovation and dynamism.[13]

Decentralised Government Approaches

In response to the criticisms of centralised welfare-type models of managing services and commissioning, public administration entered a new age in the 1980s and 1990s, as 'less' government became the prevailing idea. The core focus became centred on opening up market opportunities for independent providers (private and non-profit) and a reduction in direct state provision. The aim of public administrative decentralisation is to redistribute authority, responsibility and financial resources for providing 'public' services among different levels of governance including local governments, semi-autonomous intermediaries or corporations or area-wide, regional or functional authorities.[14] In the 1990s, central control was gradually loosened, as local providers within the independent sector were commissioned by public health services and local authorities to undertake services.

9 Hood, *supra*, n. 7.
10 Ackroyd, S. (1995) 'From Public Administration to Public Sector Management: A Consideration of Public Policy in the United Kingdom', *International Journal of Public Sector Management* 8 (2): 4–24.
11 See Osbourne, S. (1998) *Voluntary Organisations and Innovation in Public Services*. Routledge, London; De Vries, *supra*, n. 6.
12 Wilkin, D., Coleman, A., Dowling, B. and Smith, K. (2002) *National Tracker Survey of Primary Care Groups and Trusts 2001/2002, Taking Responsibility?* Kings Fund, London.
13 See, for example, Salamon, L., Sokolowski, S. W. and List, R. (2003) *Global Civil Society: An Overview*. Centre for Civil Society Studies, The Johns Hopkins Institute for Policy Studies, Baltimore.
14 For a more extensive discussion of government decentralisation, see Hossain, A. (n.d.) *Administrative Decentralization: A Framework for Discussion and Its Practices in Bangladesh*, available at: http://citeseerx.ist.psu.edu/viewdoc/download?doi=10.1.1.128.6007&rep=rep1&type=pdf (accessed 7 March 2011).

One aspect of this trend has been the emergence of New Public Management (NPM) in highly liberalised countries to manage the increasing numbers of agencies in administering and delivering public services. At the most basic level this concept promotes the use of private-sector management techniques in the administration of public welfare.[15] Under recent NPM initiatives, contract-style outsourcing has begun using quantitative, calculable metrics of 'impact' requiring tight specification of what is to be carried out, and the expected results of the work, by the provider. Increasingly, tightly proscribed contracts have been used to measure progress and impact and to ensure that targets are met by providers.

These contracts are normally for a period of a few years (generally two-to-five years) and specify in advance the volume of service users and type of service offered. Given the length of time involved in tendering, and the acquired rights expectations on providers (taking on other providers' employees), multi-annual funding is preferred to help 'bed in' providers and facilitate a better continuum of support for individuals. This approach was seen as important in reducing the level of direct centralised welfare provision – and the opening up of market forces amongst providers within an 'independent sector'. Countries introducing tighter monitoring models under NPM initiatives have seen increased financial accountability in areas of procurement, for example.[16]

However, despite these ascribed benefits, critics argue that NPM types of performance measurements are inappropriate for health and social care.[17] It has been found that the more competitive architecture often fails to ameliorate problems associated with achieving improvement – competition may drive efficiency but it is not sufficient to drive continuous improvement.[18] A further issue is that the process of negotiating contracts and adhering to monitoring procedures often works in favour of larger over smaller (and often more flexible) organisations.[19]

On the other hand, comparative welfare experts tend to agree that some form of monitoring is vital in order for states to gain a good service from the organisations to which they are entrusting their service provision.[20] In addition, the problem with

---

[15] For a detailed discussion of NPM, see McLaughlin, K., Osborne, S. P. and Ferlie, E. (2002) *New Public Management: Current Trends and Future Prospects*. Routledge, London.

[16] Hood, *supra*, n. 7.

[17] Thomas, R. and Davies, A. (2005) 'Theorizing the Micro-politics of Resistance: New Public Management and Managerial Identities in the UK Public Services', *Organisation Studies* 26 (5): 683–706.

[18] Marsh, I. and Spies-Butcher, B. (2007) *Program design for continuous improvement in human services: a case study of Australia's disability employment sector*, http://www.workplace.gov.au/NR/rdonlyres/AB3C66B1-30E8-424D-A372-75DE41A4FC96/0/182UniversityofSydney.pdf (accessed 20 February 2012).

[19] Barnett, P. and Barnett, J. R. (2006) 'New Times, New Relationships: Mental Health, Primary Care and Public Health in New Zealand', in Milligan, C. and Conradson, D. (eds.) *Landscapes of Voluntarism: New Spaces of Health, Welfare and Governance*. Policy Press, Bristol. pp. 73–90.

[20] Arnold, T. (2007) 'Emerging Questions and Future Directions', in Donnelly-Cox, G. and Breathnach, C. (eds.) *Differing Images: The Irish Nonprofit Sector and Comparative Perspectives*. The Liffey Press, Dublin. pp. 75–81.

autonomous, independent organisations providing disability services without any monitoring is that these organisations can become the sole guarantors of access. Power and Kenny found that in the local governance of the Irish non-profit disability sector, for example, where loosely managed contracting has been a feature, the autonomy of agencies has not necessarily brought about better representation for diverse groups.[21] In fact, one of the core problems in the Irish context has been the discretionary nature of funding, which has given rise to considerable differences between health care authorities in the interpretation of the grant regulations.[22] Despite the rhetoric around local organisational autonomy, it appears that the reality can fall short.

New Directions

It appears that there are a number of positives and negatives with centralised and decentralised forms of public administration discussed earlier. Regardless of whether systems are centralised or not, however, people with disabilities are often required to negotiate a complicated web of fragmented services with little choice over the types of support they require. Moreover, competition as a sole focus of reform often does not drive innovation in commissioned services or the meeting of rights obligations. In response to the issues inherent in both approaches, the following are a number of more recent mechanisms used in order to animate self-determination and ensure cost-effective resource allocation. A summary is provided at the end.

1. Citizens' Commissioning

Newer forms of contracting and managing social support structures have been introduced by governments in the mid- to late 1990s based on the concept of 'citizens commissioning', otherwise known as individual funding.[23] This has involved allowing individuals to receive public funds directly to buy their own supports, thus shaping the market by their choices. This shifts the contracting relationship from the traditional local authority-provider roles to between the person and the provider directly.

In response to this shift in commissioning power, local authorities in the United Kingdom, for example, are beginning to explore new methods of procurement, such as outcomes-focused Framework Agreements, in order to assure quality and

21 Power, A. and Kenny, K. (2011) 'When Care Is Left to Roam: Carers' experiences of grassroots nonprofit services in Ireland', *Health & Place* 17 (2): 422–429.

22 See Donoghue, F. (1998) 'Defining the Nonprofit Sector: Ireland', in Salamon, L. M. and Anheier, H. K. (eds.) *Working Papers of the John Hopkins Comparative Nonprofit Sector Project*, no. 28. The Johns Hopkins Institute for Policy Studies, Baltimore.

23 Social Care Institute for Excellence (2010) *Personalisation: A Rough Guide*, available at: http://www.scie.org.uk/publications/reports/report20.pdf (accessed 23 January 2012).

supply through validation of preferred providers.[24] These agreements are made with high-quality providers as a way of predefining a list of 'preferred providers' which individuals can choose to use in their local area. They are regarded as zero-level contracts, which means that the council does not pay the provider directly; rather, the provider receives its funding through persons themselves with their own individual funding. Whilst the contracts do not guarantee demand, being one of a limited number of preferred providers for a particular area is perceived to reduce the risk to anticipated volume.

The UK Department of Health's *Putting People First* Delivery Programme worked with the Office for Public Management (OPM) and six councils to develop a better understanding of emerging practice in procurement and map the progress being made towards flexible contracting for personalised outcomes. According to their study,[25] the case study councils had begun to use framework agreements with providers. The agreement requires any provider to offer services in more flexible and personalised ways regardless of whether their 'service users' are self- or state-funded. The framework agreement approach also incorporates other means of quality assurance. For example, in Manchester and Wigan, respectively, they have required providers to have attained compliance with the Care Quality Commission standards for inclusion in the framework contract. Other councils have operated a 'supermarket approach' which enables customers to register their views on quality through their purchasing patterns and vendor reviews. Additionally, the 'select list' approach provides a smaller choice of providers pre-approved by the council. All the new contracts are intended to assure that the choice of services available is of a sufficiently high quality.

2. Citizen Involvement and Partnership

In addition to the kinds of previously mentioned commissioning mechanisms, a form of governing that encourages the input of *users of the service themselves*, in the form of 'citizen involvement', is found to be essential.[26] According to a study by the UK Department of Health, *involving people* was a strong factor in shaping the local landscape of support delivery.[27] Most of the case study sites in this study

---

[24] The UK Department of Health is advocating the establishment and use of Framework Agreements as the key contractual vehicle for Local Authorities to work with the provider market under the 'Transforming Social Care' agenda as presented to Cabinet, 'Transforming Social Care', Sue Redmond (22 April 2008) and 'Putting People First', Department of Health (2007). These are discussed in more detail in Chapter 7.

[25] Department of Health (2009) *Contracting for Personalised Outcomes: What We're Learning from Emerging Practice*, DH/Putting People First Programme.

[26] Gardner, J., Carran, D. T. and Nudler, S. (2001) 'Measuring Quality of Life and Quality of Services Through Personal Outcome Measures: Implications for Public Policy', *International Review of Research in Mental Retardation* 24: 75–100.

[27] Department of Health, *supra*, n. 25.

directly engage people with disabilities in various ways in the development of the new framework contracts and service specifications.[28] The Department of Health also has published a guide, called *Working Together for Change*, which describes an approach to user involvement tested with four councils that uses person-centred information from people's support plans and reviews to inform commissioning and strategic planning.[29]

Examples of models which include people with disabilities in high levels of decision-making authority are also evident in the United States. These include the creation of the Director of Recipient Affairs cabinet positions in many State Offices or Departments of Mental Health[30] and the inclusion of people with mental health issues as members of local Community Health Boards with decision-making authority for locally provided mental health services.

In addition to stakeholder involvement, *better partnerships* between commissioners and support providers represent another factor in successfully developing personalisation. The same Department of Health report cited earlier[31] found that, consistent with NPM ideology, a collaborative approach was key to the reform of high-quality support delivery. It reported that a shift from previously adversarial relationships to collaborative practices and partnerships with providers had been essential to their success. This is an important finding – that while competition is needed to foster choice and a more responsive service system, collaboration is key to making it work better.

An important caveat is that the local commissioning authority needs to be given the sufficient resources to adequately develop a marketplace. Experience from some states in the United States has seen a hollowing out of local government, which has meant that they are not capable of managing the social care market. In one U.S. study, three-quarters of county managers felt constrained in their ability to develop competition and provide clients with alternatives because of their own capacity limitations and the political disincentives associated with adding staff or encroaching on private markets.[32] In other words, privatisation does not necessarily lead to a better marketplace. Public managers have said that contract-management

[28] People using services were also involved in provider selection in some council areas, such as Bath and NE Somerset and in Lancashire.

[29] See Department of Health (2009) *Working Together for Change: Using Person-Centred Information for Commissioning*. HMSO, London.

[30] For example, the New York Office for Mental Health Bureau of Recipient Affairs now includes fourteen people in six locations around the state, working to ensure meaningful consumer/survivor participation at all levels of the mental health system, to change policies and practices that interfere with growth and recovery, and to promote and support peer-run alternatives. See http://www.nycvoices.org/article_98.php (accessed 2 August 2011).

[31] Department of Health, *supra*, n. 25.

[32] Van Slyke, D. M. (2003) 'The Mythology of Privatization in Contracting for Social Services', *Public Administration Review* 63 (3): 296–315.

expertise and capacity are needed to develop detailed requests for proposals, solicit bids, evaluate bids, award contracts and provide technical assistance to contractors. Reducing local government resources can limit their ability to monitor and enforce good practice and accountability.

In addition to better partnerships between commissioners and providers, *provider-provider collaboration* is also important. Many of the sites have actively encouraged subcontracting and provider-to-provider collaboration because they consider it unlikely that any one provider would be able to meet the service requirements of all budget holders. In particular, in rural areas, where there might be a small number of providers, more choice is enabled by the encouragement of subcontracting. Ensuring that people have a wide choice of supports does not necessarily equate to having a large number of contracted providers – rather, opportunities for buying other goods and services (such as technology or access to local facilities) which enable independence should be allowed within the community. A Demos report recommends that care should be taken that shaping the local market does not mean inadvertently restricting choice and impeding innovation. To aid this process, rather than large block-contracts, some councils have developed a system of 'mini-tenders' to obtain services to fit an individual's support plan.[33] These are designed to enable collaboration between the providers on an approved list (with framework agreements) for a given locality. Providers are also collaborating to find their own solutions to commonly shared issues such as staff recruitment and rostering.

3. A Learning-by-Doing Approach

In addition to the increased and wider use of citizens' commissioning, citizen engagement and partnership, the change agenda in the delivery of disability supports indicates the need for a system based on an integrated learning process which enables effective ongoing policy development and collaboration. Reflecting these goals, an alternative framework for commissioner-provider relationships in human services has been championed by Charles Sabel.[34] This has been coined the pragmatist or experimentalist approach and transfers the emphasis in exchanges between state and provider from a primarily punitive command-and-control approach to a primarily learning basis.

This broad approach has been widely tested in a variety of human services and other public policy settings in the United States, including child welfare social

---

[33] Bartlett, J. (2009) *At Your Service: Navigating the Future Market in Health and Social Care*. Demos, London. For examples, see Bath and NE Somerset, discussed in Department of Health, *supra*, n. 25.

[34] See Sabel, C. (2006) 'Beyond Principal-Agent Governance: Experimentalist Organisation, Learning and Accountability', in Engelen, E. and Sie Dhian Ho, M. (eds.) *De Staat van de Democratie. Democratie voorbij de Staat*. WRR Verkenning 3: Amsterdam University Press, Amsterdam. pp. 173–195.

work practice in Utah and Alabama[35] and in New Jersey.[36] Experimental principles define an approach to the management of purchaser-provider relations designed to enhance interagency collaboration which is wholly different from the structure which now governs many neo-liberal welfare states.

Under Sabel's schema, a number of decrees exist which guide the experimentalist model. First, basic norms and guidelines must be both learned and elaborated in the course of practice. Reconfigured training of staff, including the introduction of mentoring partnerships with other agencies, is helpful in this regard. Second, a new conception of the relation between central administration (government or relevant department) and the front line (staff dealing with the clients) emerges. The centre articulates general goals, provides support for the front line and monitors its success in vindicating the principles. Third, change should be incremental, to enable the process of learning.[37]

In terms of the tools used to determine best practice and monitor relationships, Sabel's approach proposes to reverse the direction and substance of the exchange between purchasers and providers and to move away from fixed rules and a command-and-control approach towards enabling the continuous evaluation of possible changes in the rules: 'Accountability thus requires not comparison of performance to a goal or rule, but *reason giving*'.[38] In this model, evaluation of a service provider is carried out with the input of other agencies in a process of ongoing mutual appraisal. Here, it is important to emphasise that monitoring must incorporate a user focus, with voices of persons with disabilities themselves being heard.[39] For Sabel, then, monitoring is formative and continuous, or nearly so, rather than occasional or episodic, and is more interested in diagnostic information – information that can redirect the method of provision.[40]

Related to the aforementioned factor is the *degree of flexibility* accorded to providers in order to achieve best practice. The lack of flexibility is often criticised in the independent sector by organisations which feel that they are not accorded enough freedom to innovate their services. Often when service providers fail to follow the rules in command-and-control systems, they stand to be immediately penalised. In pragmatist systems, an inability or unwillingness to improve or respond to change at an acceptable rate triggers initially increased capacity-enhancing assistance from

---

35 Noonan, K. G., Sabel, C. and Simon, W. H. (2008) 'The Rule of Law in the Experimentalist Welfare State: Lessons from Child Welfare Reform', *Columbia Public Law Research Paper*, 08–16.

36 *Ibid.*; Liebman, J. and Sabel, C. (2003) 'A Public Laboratory Dewey Barely Imagined: The Emerging Model of School Governance and Legal Reform', *New York University Review of Law and Social Change*, 184–300.

37 Noonan et al., *supra*, n. 35.

38 Sabel, *supra*, n. 34, at 184 (emphasis added).

39 See Power and Kenny, *supra*, n. 21.

40 Marsh and Spies-Butcher, *supra*, n. 18.

the relevant commissioning authority and an agreed plan to remedy the failure to comply. Repeated failure to respond, even with assistance, is, however, likely to bring about penalties for the offending service.[41] In this system, the autonomy of decentralised, independent service providers must be facilitated by appropriate structures. For example, while local organisations can potentially bring benefits such as a more rapid response to disabled persons' needs, this must be supported by the wider system.

This system-wide support relates to another key factor in developing a smart welfare model, namely *provider development*. This was found by the English Department of Health to be one of the key successful factors in developing more personalised support delivery.[42] This includes continuing training and development opportunities around such topics as: how to work with the self-directed support process; meeting the budget management and accounting requirements of personal budgets; and developing different models of service provision to meet the requirements of personalisation. These workshops have not been dictatorial, but have enabled the exchange of knowledge and experience and mutual problem solving between councils and providers striving to meet the challenge together.

4. Outcome Monitoring

In addition to the developmental approach to making support providers more responsive and restoring power to the consumer, support provision systems are increasingly developing mechanisms for monitoring the personal outcomes for persons with disabilities who use supports in their lives. This can inform policy makers about the outputs for investment, as well as identify the lasting impact of reforming disability support provision. This is an area that has received much attention in disability policy development, as noted in a report by Mansell for the European Union (2007), *Deinstitutionalisation and Community Living – Outcomes and Costs*, which places a strong emphasis on the need for more and better data including data on outcomes in relation to the shift from institutions to the community across Europe.[43]

In reality, outcome measurement – and its link with procurement of best practice – is an area which remains largely underdeveloped in most jurisdictions. The UK Department of Health argues that, while the development of outcome measures is the ultimate goal, as they reflect improvements in health and well-being as well as the experience of services, it can take longer to demonstrate changes in outcome as a

---

[41] Sabel, *supra*, n. 34.
[42] Department of Health, *supra*, n. 25.
[43] Mansell, J., Knapp, M., Beadle-Brown, J. and Beecham, J. (2007) *Deinstitutionalisation and Community Living – Outcomes and Costs: Report of a European Study*. Volume 3: Country Reports. Tizard Centre, University of Kent, Canterbury.

result of service improvement.[44] For this reason, it is likely that statutory agencies will continue to use other forms of indicators alongside outcomes, including input indicators (such as staffing and investment) and process indicators (such as the establishment of new services or better ways of working), to assess early local progress. These are seen as still being relevant as long as changes in these inputs and processes are understood from the research literature to lead to improvements in health and well-being and/or the experience of support.

Despite there being challenges in implementing a robust system of outcome measurement, each of the jurisdictions have begun to develop mechanisms to incorporate outcome performance indicators in assessing quality at both the regional system-wide level and the local support provision level.

For strategic commissioning at the regional level, there is greater scope for measuring system-level performance and including outcome indicators to inform planning across a broad range of areas. In England, for example, local authorities are being inspected and evaluated by the Care Quality Commission (CQC). Each local authority is now required to report annually on social care performance against sixteen essential standards (which include both subjective and objective measures) including increased choice and control, improved quality of life, and freedom from discrimination and harassment.[45] There are also two additional 'domains' in which local authorities must report: leadership and commissioning and use of resources. The Self-Assessment uses an outcomes framework, based on the Department of Health white paper, *Our Health, Our Care, Our Say*, with the two additional domains. It marks a continued move towards a less prescriptive, more localised approach to the performance assessment of adult social care. More details on this process are provided in the UK chapter (Chapter 6) of this book.

In the United States, there is a performance measurement and evaluation system used in the intellectual disability field, called the National Core Indicators (NCI). It uses service-level data and research across an agreed set of outcome indicators. For this purpose, it is useful to compare results across states and inform future planning. However, participation in NCI is voluntary and is not linked with the procurement mechanisms of the state.

Assessment is also carried out at the local level. Performance of individual care providers registered by local authorities are also being inspected and reported by the CQC. From 1 October 2010, the inspection process measures five agreed indicators: Involvement and Information; Personalised Care, Treatment and Support; Safeguarding and Safety; Suitability of Staffing; and Quality and

---

44 Department of Health (2007) *Performance Indicators, NSF Diabetes*, available at: http://www.dh .gov.uk/en/Publicationsandstatistics/Publications/PublicationsPolicyAndGuidance/Browsable/DH_ 4917354 (accessed 18 December 2010).

45 Please refer to: http://www.cqc.org.uk/_db/_documents/CAG_Annex_3.3_SA_guidance_word_ version_19.pdf (accessed 20 December 2010).

Management.[46] Following a key inspection of a service, the CQC publishes a rating that describes the quality of care provided. If the provider is not able to declare that it meets any one or more of the CQC standards, it must state specifically why it does not in each case, and offer an action plan specifying the SMART principles (a plan should be Specific, Measurable, Achievable, Relevant, and Time bound) to remedy the non-compliance.

These examples illustrate the range of mechanisms being developed in the reconfiguration of personal social support systems. It is clear that there is a strong emphasis being placed on continuous monitoring, evaluation and data collection across different jurisdictions. However, this is an area which is still developing and remains constrained by the limitations in the different international, national and local knowledge bases.

Summary

It appears that a model incorporating different forms of monitoring, where organisations are subject to some forms of centralised planning, competitive contracting and strategic commissioning, appears most appropriate. The change agenda in the delivery of disability support indicates the need for a system based on an integrated learning process that enables effective ongoing policy development, collaboration, resourcing, capacity development and implementation of monitoring and evaluation. These changes need to be part of a broader transition within the welfare infrastructure to an enabling 'smart welfare' approach, as set out in Table 3.1.[47]

To meet the aim of this broad transition, there is a need for a tiered approach to different levels of commissioning and managing support delivery. According to the UK Department of Health, their *Commissioning Toolkit*[48] proposes that to implement a new system of self-directed support, there is a need to adopt three levels of commissioning, as follows:

Strategic commissioning is at the local authority or regional level. It often operates across administrative boundaries such as health care, social care and housing. It helps to set the broad conditions so that self-directed support can become established by trying to ensure that all agencies work together towards a common agenda, that the third-sector and user-led organisations are funded and that information and advice services are available on the ground.

One example of this type of commissioning is the large-scale, multi-year competitive grants in the United States administered by the federal Center for Medicare and

---

[46] Each of these indicators has a number of essential outcomes, as listed here: http://www.care-plan-management-system.co.uk/cqc-registration/ (accessed 20 December 2010).

[47] National Economic and Social Council (2005) *The Developmental Welfare State*. NESC, Dublin.

[48] In Control (2010) *Phase 3 Report*. See p. 59.

TABLE 3.1. *Overview of the shift in paradigm of governing public services delivery*

Former welfare state	Developmental welfare state
Crisis-oriented	Seeks balance between prevention and intervention
Centre* sets detailed directives	Centre sets strategic directives
Service deliverer accountable for inputs and compliance	Service deliverer accountable for outputs and quality
Compliance with rules	Attainment of standards
Annual budget	Multi-annual budgeting
Funds isolated projects	Leverages local innovations into improvements in mainstream services
Public bodies with customer service ethos	Autonomous bodies with public service ethos
One size fits all	Assumption of need for diversity

* Centre = state or relevant commissioning authority
Source: NESC (2005) The Developmental Welfare State, NESC, Dublin.

Medicaid Services (CMS) to states to improve employment outcomes for people with disabilities.[49] Although states have implemented different approaches, most states use the funding to address benefits planning and work incentives to reduce the fear of loss of benefits when people with disabilities return to work, create partnerships to increase inter-agency coordination for job creation and model evidence-based and promising employment practices.

Operational commissioning usually covers part of a city, town or larger rural area where population is more thinly spread. It works to get universal services like schools, colleges, health centres, libraries and commercial outlets to deal with people in a more personalised way. It also helps to coordinate these services so that they join up when people use their budgets to buy them.

Citizens' commissioning is the level at which citizens direct their own support using individual funding or their own funds, as discussed earlier.

Of course, in shifting towards an experimentalist architecture, much remains to be done to work out particular details in relation both to the specification of outcomes and the design of an appropriate governance structure. As this section has shown, different countries operate in their own specific contexts, and this book would not advocate an unproblematic 'transposition' of one model onto any national context. For example, disability commissioning in Ireland is still under the remit of the

---

[49] Section 203 of the Ticket to Work/Work Incentives Act of 1999 provides grants to states to develop state infrastructures to support working individuals with disabilities. For eligibility under this grant programme, a state must offer personal assistance services statewide within and outside the home to the extent necessary to enable an individual to be engaged in full-time competitive employment.

Health Service Executive, and is thus not strategically well placed for enabling broader operational commissioning of mainstream (non-health related) services. As Arnold notes, there is huge diversity across countries with regard to welfare provision.[50] In considering these options, it is important to remember that no country is in a position to completely reinvent its welfare provision model, should it so choose. Legacies of previous patterns and systems of service provision persist, for example, the UK's history is one that ranged from an older command-and-control model of state welfare provision to a market-driven, liberal model of contracting between state and service provider.[51] Nonetheless, the main tenets of these new approaches provide a road map of options and alternatives for the management of support structures, which can be carefully adapted to suit.

REVITALISING A DISABILITY SUPPORT ORGANISATION: DEVELOPMENT AND INNOVATION

While the previously mentioned system-wide architectural mechanisms can help to animate change within the independent sector, ultimately organisations themselves must also become more responsive and flexible in working with individuals. This section examines the factors associated with development and innovation within organisational environments, including internal working cultures. At the outset, this book recognises and promotes the expansion of user-led, self-help groups and organisations controlled by people with disabilities. Instead of care and dependency, people with disabilities should ultimately claim independence and control over their services and their everyday life. User-led organisations have been shown to be far more responsive to their service users' needs, both in terms of what is on offer and how it is offered.[52] Centres for Independent Living (CILs) have provided an important dual role in this regard, as both service providers and political advocates for the rights of people with disabilities. Their model advocates that persons with disabilities become 'leaders', which is the term to describe persons with a disability who manage their own personal assistant service on a daily basis. They recruit and retain their own personal assistants and direct the service appropriate for their needs. A leader is in charge and takes full responsibility for the instructions given to the personal assistant, for the actions and consequences that follow from these and for training and day-to-day management of the service.

[50] Arnold, *supra*, n. 20.
[51] Salamon, L., Wojciech, S. and Anheier, H. (2000) 'Social Origins of Civil Society: An Overview', *Working Papers of the John Hopkins Comparative Nonprofit Sector Project*, No. 38. The John Hopkins Center for Civil Society Studies, Baltimore.
[52] Barnes, C. and Mercer, G. (2006) 'Independent Futures. Creating User-led Disability Services in a Disabling Society', *Scandinavian Journal of Disability Research* 8 (4): 317–320.

However, it is acknowledged, particularly in learning disability support services, that there is also a vast infrastructure of residential and day services which are grappling with becoming more individually responsive to persons deemed to have complex or profound impairments or persons who have become institutionalised as a result of earlier, outmoded service regimes. In many cases, people with such support needs are still seen as passive consumers, and there is little consideration of their abilities and resources. Within these support environments, there are significant leadership challenges in changing organisational culture, embedding rights as core values and retraining staff. Moreover, there is a lot of 'people work' needed to empower and support people with disabilities who are unable to become full leaders as envisaged earlier, to become more involved in self-directing their own support arrangements.

The following section draws on the management literature on supporting innovation, particularly the work by Osbourne on innovation in voluntary organisations involved in public service.[53] The innovative capacity of providers, particularly the non-profit sector, like many of their other ascribed characteristics, such as flexibility and a non-bureaucratic structure, has become widely assumed. The basis of this, according to Osbourne,[54] in Britain at least, is certainly within historical fact, for grassroots non-profit providers were the pioneers of many social services.

However, within the management literature, there is much debate over whether there is evidence to support this claim. Moreover, in the disability literature, it is acknowledged that the provider sector in many cases has become resistant to reform.[55] Many writers argue that one cannot justify a blanket claim of an innovative capacity for the voluntary sector in the personal social services, particularly as one considers the size, shape and complexity of the non-profit sector – a sector consisting of many diverse organisations, ranging from the multitude of unregistered and unincorporated associations through to national and international service providers and multimillion-pound organisations.[56]

Given the diversity of the sector, it is thus useful to consider non-profit organisations as existing along a spectrum of development, from 'grassroots' to 'stagnation', as illustrated by the 'non-profit organisational lifecycle'. This posits that non-profit agencies move from a series of stages in their operation as follows:

- *Grassroots – Innovation*: Volunteer driven; perceived need for a programme or service; entrepreneurial and visionary leader.

53 Osbourne, *supra*, n. 11.
54 *Ibid.*
55 There are many examples of disability support workers resisting personalisation. See Think Local, Act Personal (2011) *Shaping the Market for Personalisation: Diagnostic and Action Planning Tool.* Developed by Sam Bennett, Personalisation Advisor to Think Local, Act Personal Partnership.
56 Kendall, J. and Knapp, M. (1995) 'A Loose and Baggy Monster: Boundaries, Definitions and Typologies', in Smith, J. D., Rochester, C. and Hedley, R. (eds.) *An Introduction to the Voluntary Sector.* Routledge, London. pp. 66–95.

- *Start-up – Incubation*: Simple programmes are initiated, often led by single-minded founder(s); mostly led by volunteers.
- *Adolescent – Growing*: Programmes begin to establish themselves in the market; often demand is larger than capacity; staff size increases – still join primarily for mission.
- *Mature – Sustainability*: Core programmes are established and recognized in the community; even larger and more diverse and specialized staff; professional managers are hired.
- *Stagnation and Renewal*: Organisation loses sight of market; programmes developed primarily to attract funding; difficulty in delivering services and reaching goals; low staff morale and high staff turnover; bogged down in structure that may be outdated.
- *Decline and Shutdown*: No longer meeting market needs; loss of credibility with funders and clients; high conflict among staff.[57]

To avoid the last stages of this life cycle, organisations often must make a commitment to readdress their core values and operation or else face the prospect of losing contracts and ultimately shutting down.

Given the degree of professionalisation within the larger non-profit organisations, a more measured evaluation of the extent of innovation comes from Kramer, who argues that although the voluntary sector may indeed develop new services or programmes, they are invariably only minor modifications of existing services, rather than genuine innovations.[58] In the context of disability organisations, it is assumed that innovation involves being *person-driven*, individually responsive and flexible and focused on supporting the inclusion and participation of persons with disability in community life.[59] While innovation is generally thought of as an outcome of an organisation, innovation is better understood as *a process* rather than an outcome. It must involve change, both in terms of the transformation of its idea of how to support people with disabilities into actual reality and of its impact on its host organisation.[60]

In terms of the organisational characteristics which support such an innovation, the management literature suggests that different organisational characteristics are appropriate to different stages of the innovation process. Whereas an open decentralised organisation is regarded as effective for the generation of ideas, a hierarchical and centralised one is thought to be more effective for their implementation.[61]

[57] See Speakman Consulting (n.d.) *Nonprofit Organizational Life Cycle*, available at: http://www.speakmanconsulting.com/pdf_files/NonProfitLifeCyclesMatrix.pdf (accessed 12 February 2012).
[58] Kramer, R. M. (1981) *Voluntary Agencies in the Welfare State*. University of California Press, Berkeley.
[59] *supra*, n. 1.
[60] Robert, M. and Weiss, A. (1988) *The Innovation Formula*. Ballinger, Cambridge, MA.
[61] Tidd, J. (1995) 'Development of Novel Products through Intraorganizational and Interorganizational Networks: The Case of Home Automation', *Journal of Product Innovation Management* 12(4): 307–322.

The extent to which an organisation encourages innovation therefore can depend on the degree to which it is possible to achieve both these organisational states simultaneously.[62] Achieving this in turn can depend on whether the organisational environment is committed to innovative change. The key factor here is the development of organisational values and an organisational environment which encourages and stimulates the type of innovation expressed earlier. In reality, the extent of such innovation is dependent on the staff adhering to the innovative value system, which in many cases does not occur. In terms of the attributes of organisations which are continually committed to innovation, according to Osbourne, distinct foci can be drawn out in terms of (1) their internal organisational culture and (2) their external environment and their relationship to this, to explain their innovative capacity.[63]

1. Internal Organisational Culture

In terms of the internal organisational culture, the two main issues that emerge from the management literature are the nature of organisational leadership and the nature of organisational life. While the size of an organisation obviously is a factor in determining the organisational culture, it is regarded as a weak indicator of innovation alone.[64]

Having good organisational leadership is regarded by Kendrick and Sullivan as essential in achieving social inclusion for persons with disabilities, in particular for organisations which have been traditionally provider-led.[65] There is clear consensus that senior management's commitment to innovation and reform is a key factor in achieving change. To support this commitment, there are three distinct leadership roles which drive successful innovative outcomes within an organisation:

1) the direction of the organisation;
2) the creation and management of an organisational culture;
3) the product champion or hero/innovator.

---

[62] Heap, J. (1989) *The Management of Innovation and Design*, Cassell, London.

[63] Osbourne, *supra*, n. 11.

[64] In terms of size, the debates continue over whether larger organisations are better for innovation than smaller ones. Proponents of size as a predictor, however, often use this as a proxy for resource availability (in terms of capital, personnel and expertise), whereas those supporting smallness are similarly using it as a proxy for a less bureaucratic organisational structure and for greater freedom for individual action. For further discussion, see Herbig, P. (1991) 'A Cusp Catastrophe Model of the Adoption of an Industrial Innovation', *Journal of Product Innovation Management* 8(2): 127–137; Da Rocha et al. (1990) 'Characteristics of Innovative Firms in the Brazilian Computer Industry', *Journal of Product Innovation Management* 7(2): 123–134.

[65] Kendrick, M. J. and Sullivan, L. (2009) 'Appraising the leadership challenges of social inclusion', *The International Journal of Leadership in Public Services*, 5 supplement: 67–75.

The three positions mutually enforce the organisations' commitment towards change and ameliorate the different challenges which arise throughout the implementation stage of introducing new working practices associated with personalisation, resulting from reorganisation fatigue and resistance from workers to change.

Setting the 'direction of the organisation' is usually the role of the senior manager, who must drive the organisational change required to see the innovation through. The research demonstrates that a hands-on, directive managerial approach at the senior level works best to provide leadership and embed innovative values within the organisation. Senior management must be behind the process to enable verification and challenge any resistance to new working practices. There needs to be a good communication channel to facilitate reporting up and down throughout the organisation. Experience shows that the approach needed to sustain change is characterised as a long march – consisting of discretionary and ongoing efforts throughout the organisation.[66]

Secondly, the creation and management of an organisational culture form another key role that leaders must try to propagate. This is about creating a climate conducive to organisational change. This includes generating a specific collection of values and norms shared by people and groups in an organisation and that control the way they interact with each other and with stakeholders outside the organisation.[67] This in turn can stimulate positive psychology, attitudes and experiences amongst staff, thus setting persistent behaviours and working practices based on a set of values. Again, this is a key role for senior managers.

The final role is the 'product champion' or 'hero/innovator'. The role of people with disabilities and individuals who ascribe to the values enshrined in rights is crucial in this process of implementation. This is often a 'lead worker' involved in managing a team of employees to drive the personalisation project.

This last role is particularly important for larger disability provider organisations, which often must operate in bureaucratic environments with tightly proscribed performance measurement systems. In these cases, freeing up talented staff to lead new projects is often essential to develop better personalised outcomes.

The second factor in shaping the internal organisational culture is the nature of organisational life. This can comprise many aspects including the type and quality of communication channels and processes within an organisation and the complexity of organisational tasks.

Albrecht and Hall maintain that internal communication is *the* key factor in organisational capacity to innovate.[68] This is a crucial leadership challenge: to foster good quality and strategic use of communication between the different departments

---

[66] Kanter, R.M. (2000) 'Leaders with passion, Conviction and Confidence can use several techniques to take charge of change rather than react to it'. *Ivey Business Journal*, May/June: 32–36.

[67] Hill, C. and Jones, G. R. (2001) *Strategic Management*. Houghton, Mifflin.

[68] Albrecht, T. and Hall, B. (1991) 'Facilitating talk about new ideas: the role of personal relationships in organisational innovation,' *Communication Monographs*, 58: 273–287.

and key individuals within an organisation. This is examined in more detail in the following section.

The nature of the staff group is also crucial, particularly for disability support organisations in terms of the level of professionalisation of direct support workers. In the talent management literature, it is found that a strategic and systematic approach to finding and sustaining the right staff can have significant positive effects on the organisation.[69] Organisations are also spending a long time teasing out the contractual arrangements which have to be in place for more flexible personalised support arrangements to work. As part of this process, they have to consider all of the revenue implications both for the individuals concerned and for themselves as an organisation.[70]

Many organisations which are beginning a transformation towards more individualised working practices are hiring key workers to fill dedicated roles to kick-start new personalised support plans. Increasingly, disability organisations are reporting that they have begun implementing more person-led approaches to finding the right staff match for individuals, such as self-recruiting as well as psychometric testing to measure a support worker's abilities, attitudes and personality traits conducive to developing high-quality relationships.[71] Significantly, the ability to be comfortable with risk taking was also highlighted as important.[72] This related to the complexity of the tasks they would have to undertake in an individualised support arrangement.

In addition to sourcing talent externally, the cultivation of talent within the organisation's boundaries is also emphasised. For many disability organisations there may be constraints on hiring and firing support workers. In these cases, there are many methods used in reinvigorating staff, such as sending staff on work placements to other organisations, hosting training workshops and going through training modules such as, amongst others, rights, leadership, person-centred approaches, values, ethical issues, 'Right Relationship', advocacy, and consumer and family empowerment.[73]

2. The Organisation's External Environment and Its Relationship to It

Generally, within the management literature, organisational networks are now an essential component of innovation, where expertise and knowledge are so widely dispersed that collaboration with other organisations in their market sector is essential. Although much of this literature focuses on for-profit organisations within a

---

[69] Collings, D. G. and Mellahi, K. (2009) 'Strategic Talent Management: A Review and Research Agenda', *Human Resource Management Review* 19(4): 304–313.

[70] Derived from consultative meetings with disability organisations in 2009–2010.

[71] *Ibid.*

[72] Personal Communication, service manager, July 2010, Ireland.

[73] Examples from Michael Kendrick's *Training on Leadership in the Field of Disability*, available at: http://www.kendrickconsulting.org/default.asp?ppid=&ctid=14&cid=0&tr=SITEMENU (accessed 21 March 2012).

competitive environment, there is much evidence to support the idea that collaboration between agencies within the disability support sector leads to more successful personalised working ways, such as, for example, New Options Alliance in Ireland and Altrum[74] in the United Kingdom.

According to West, there are some essential components of improving an organisation's external environment and its relationship to this.[75] He identifies four features, each of which appears to relate to enabling factors in innovation.

Innovating organisations are collaborators. According to West, knowledge creation takes place through interaction with other organisations and public research institutions. Indeed, empirical research has shown that innovating organisations are almost invariably collaborative, and that collaboration persists over sustained periods.[76] The active role and collaboration of 'end-users' in shaping the innovative capacity of organisation have also been a consistent theme in much of the organisation studies literature. Similarly, as discussed earlier, in the disability service provider sector, meaningful collaboration with persons with disabilities can generate more successful personalised outcomes, as these networks are essential to assure continued independent living arrangements in the community. In this sense, collaborating involves working closely with persons with disabilities in defining ways to meet the vision and values enshrined in the UN CRPD.

Innovating organisations accumulate capability over time. West has also found that past developments tend to be utilised to determine future pathways of innovation. This relates to the earlier discussion of the importance of fostering a learning-by-doing approach, whereby having the right organisational climate can help the progressive achievement of goals. This often involves drawing lines in the sand at various points of reform in order to rule out returning to previous outmoded practices.

Innovating organisations tend to cluster. Multiple studies have suggested that successful organisations gather together geographically, either 'horizontally' – groups of similar disability organisations – or 'vertically' – organisations connected with 'mainstream' local services. Organisations within such clusters tend to be more successful than those standing alone, perhaps because they tap into knowledge bases and related expertise that would not exist separated from the cluster.

Innovating organisations in all sectors employ knowledge not developed internally. Finally, many new processes draw upon knowledge not possessed by organisations. Rather, West argues, cooperation and collaboration amongst other innovating firms, end-users, consultants, universities or research institutes are frequent characteristics

---

74 See Altrum Web site: http://www.altrum.org.uk (accessed 2 December 2010).

75 West, J. (2006) *A Strategy to Accelerate Innovation in NSW Outline for Policy Development. Technical Report.* NSW Department of State and Regional Development (DSRD), New South Wales, Australia.

76 See Basri, E. (2001) 'Inter-Firm Technological Collaboration in Australia: Implications for Innovation and Public Policy', in *OECD Innovation Networks: Co-operation in National Innovation Systems.* OECD, Paris, pp. 143–168.

of modern innovation processes. Disability organisations interviewed in Ireland, for example, often cited getting in external expertise, such as other managers who have transformed their organisations, as well as normalisation and social role valorisation theorists and international consultants such as Michael Kendrick[77] or David Pitonyak, for example.[78] These were useful exercises in kick-starting organisational transformation. In this context, the role of universities, research institutes and private consultants is that of important collaboration partners.

Diffusion and Percolation of Innovation

In terms of scaling up innovation across a sector, the final stage of the innovation process is diffusion. While we often think of innovations as distinct, easily identifiable entities, a closer inspection of studies throughout this last section has revealed that they are anything but: communication channels and social networks play a central role in the widespread adoption of innovations. Furthermore, they can be resolved into smaller sub-steps, making the definition somewhat arbitrary.[79]

Traditionally, it was argued that the pattern of diffusion of an innovation would follow a normal curve, moving from the 'innovators' through to the 'laggards'.[80] However, this idea has been criticised for not incorporating other factors in the process, for example the importance of evaluation in the process, which makes diffusion a cyclical process rather than a linear one.[81] This is particularly important in the disability sector, where properly administered outcome measurement can feed back into further development on an ongoing cyclical basis.

Secondly, the idea of *percolation* has been argued to be preferential to diffusion (or at least a *percolation model* of diffusion), as the notion of percolation concentrates on the environment in which innovation takes place, rather than seeing it as a self-contained or linear process.[82] Here, the spread of certain information and communication-based innovations is responsive to the interaction between the network effect and the heterogeneity of organisations.[83] The network effect can be enriched by introducing policy actions, such as the ones discussed earlier in the chapter, intended to trigger widespread adoption of a new way of working

---

[77] Please refer to: http://www.kendrickconsulting.org (accessed 15 June 2011).

[78] Please refer to: http://www.dimagine.com/index.html (accessed 15 June 2011).

[79] Silverberg, G. and Verspagen, B. (2005) 'A Percolation Model of Innovation in Complex Technology Spaces', *Journal of Economic Dynamics & Control* 29: 225–244. In this article, the authors refer to 'agents' as being heterogeneous rather than solely organisations.

[80] Rogers, E. and Shoemaker, F. (1971) *Communication of Innovation.* Free Press, New York.

[81] See Mohr, L. (1987) 'Innovation Theory: An Assessment from the Vantage Point of New Electronic Technology in Organisations', in Pennings, J. and Buitendan, A. (eds.) *New Technology as Organizational Innovation*, Ballinger, Cambridge, MA, pp. 13–31.

[82] Mort, J. (1991) 'Perspective: The Applicability of Percolation Theory to Innovation', *Journal of Product Innovation Management* 8 (1): 32–38.

[83] Cantonoa, S. and Silverberg, G. (2009) 'A Percolation Model of Eco-Innovation Diffusion: The Relationship between Diffusion, Learning Economies and Subsidies', *Technological Forecasting and Social Change* 76 (4): 487–496.

(e.g. commissioning policies). Similarly, the heterogeneity of organisations, when connected in clusters, can lead to the interaction of heterogeneous behaviours, imitations, and new and different understandings of the innovation. This suggests a more random approach than traditional diffusion theory presupposed.

Finally, Osbourne also argues against the development of overblown and over-ambitious innovation theory. Rather, ongoing reform calls for a series of smaller-scale innovation models within specific contexts. These findings are useful when considering the 'nonprofit organisational lifecycle', as identified at the start of the section.

LEADERSHIP IN CHANGE MANAGEMENT

For disability provider organisations, given the complexity of individualised support arrangements and the evolving recognition of promoting citizenship, the potential need to accommodate for change theoretically matches or even outweighs private corporate companies' need to adapt to change.[84] Given the complexities identified in the previous section, this section examines what the management literature can tell us about handling organisational change. In addition to the management literature, there is also some useful literature on the transformation of support organisations within the disability field.[85]

Despite the importance of being able to undertake change, most efforts, according to the management literature, encounter problems. In particular, change efforts often take longer than expected and desired, they sometimes damage morale, and they often cost a significant amount in terms of managerial time or emotional upheaval.[86] Moreover, change can lead to significant resistance from employees – a feature not uncommon within disability service providers. According to Kotter and Schlesinger this resistance can be a result of (1) a desire not to lose something of value arising from parochial self-interest, (2) a misunderstanding of the change and its implications, (3) a belief that the change does not make sense for the organisation, and (4) a low tolerance for change.[87]

In terms of dealing with resistance and tackling its multiple sources, many managers underestimate both the many ways in which people can react to organisational change as well as the ways they can positively influence specific individuals and

---

[84] Most companies or divisions of major corporations find that they must undertake moderate organisational changes once a year and major changes every four or five years, according to Allen, S. (1978) 'Organizational Choice and General Influence Networks for Diversified Companies', *Academy of Management Journal*, September: 341.

[85] Lord and Hutchison (2007) traced six provider organisations in an examination of how they transformed their support systems: Lord, J. and Hutchison, P. (2007) *Pathways to Inclusion: Building a New Story with People and Communities*. Captus Press, Ontario.

[86] Kotter, J. P. and Schlesinger, L. A. (1979) 'Choosing Strategies for Change', *Harvard Business Review* March/April: 106–114.

[87] *Ibid.*

groups during a change. Again, Kotter and Schlesinger[88] identify the different strategies which managers can use to overcome resistance and bring people on-board with change.

Firstly, *education and communication* are two of the most commonly cited ways to overcome resistance in order to educate people about change beforehand. They are particularly important when resistance is based on inadequate or inaccurate information and analysis of the proposed change agenda. However, they can require time and effort and often a good relationship between initiators and resistors.

Good leaders use the need for a *paradigm change* as the *lever for organisational change*. This ensures that the organisational change is not just associated with a 'tinkering' of working conditions, but rather connected to a wider and more significant philosophical goal (i.e. aligning to the guiding principles of the UN CRPD). Managers must therefore generate a strong vision and set of values to engender a feeling of commitment. Most importantly, it is counterproductive to keep two different paradigms in the same organisation. Resistance to change is minimised with the use of 'paradigm training' in values and attitudes. Also, peer support and putting the right people in place in the training can help to build trust, so that a staff member can hear about the benefits of change from his or her own type of staff worker.

Having *conversations about discontent* is a powerful tool for generating interest in transforming ways of working with people with disabilities. A listening exercise, which accommodates all people's concerns, fears and particular issues across a number of departments, can be a good place to start in instigating change. Setting up a steering group with all the stakeholders can create a boardwalk for all departments to talk through their concerns.

Secondly, *participation and involvement* of all staff, in some aspect of the design and implementation of the change, can often help to forestall resistance. Leaders need to start 'where people are at' in order to create an open process for learning. This can produce leverage for change at the outset and lead to an increased probability that people will take ownership for the change. This can be beneficial at both the start-up stage and for sustaining this change later in the transformation process. This can enable the initiators to listen to the people whom the change involves and use their advice. Considerable research has demonstrated that, in general, participation leads to commitment, not merely compliance. According to Lord and Hutchison, having a good personal touch in this process can help in engendering trust and can encourage a feeling that decisions do not come down from the top without input from employees.[89] This can lead to more creative planning, when managed carefully. It can also secure loyalty further along the organisational path and reinforce relationships between stakeholders. However, the process of participation

---

[88] *Ibid.*
[89] Lord and Hutchison, *supra*, n. 85.

and involvement can have its drawbacks. Not only can it be time consuming, but it can also lead to a poor solution if the process is not carefully managed. It is therefore suited to less immediate changes, as it can take too long to involve all stakeholders.

Thirdly, providing *facilitation and support* is another useful way in which managers can deal with potential resistance to change. This can include providing training in new skills, or giving employees time off after a demanding period, or simply listening and providing emotional support. This practice of nurturing can help to engender a good working culture, particularly in the disability support sector which requires careful and sensitive forms of working. Also, this is an important method for types of work that are prone to regular organisational change – and can help to support people who feel 'burnt out' or are having difficulty adjusting to new work conditions.

Fourthly, engaging in *negotiation and agreement* is another way in which managers can deal with resistance. This can involve offering incentives to active or potential resistors in the form of time off or a bonus payment. Negotiated agreements can be appropriate when it is clear that the staff members involved are going to lose out as a result of a change. However, it may become expensive and open a manager up to the possibility of blackmail. This underscores the points made earlier that the change process should include input from service users, or as the consumer movement asserts: 'nothing about us without us'. Here, *listening and dialogue* are particularly helpful in overcoming resistance to change. Good leadership needs to be proactive and respectful of all stakeholders' views. Given the close proximity of staff to 'service users', managers need to work closely with staff in nurturing and supporting their capacity for change.

Finally, *manipulation and co-optation* are often used by managers to more subtly attempt to influence others. It generally involves the selective use of information and the conscious structuring of events to get selected stakeholders on-board. Similarly, co-optation can involve giving a staff member a desirable role in the design or implementation of the change. This can help to endorse the change and under certain circumstances can be a relatively inexpensive and easy way to gain an individual's or a group's support. There are many potential drawbacks, however, including undermining the trust of staff. Ultimately, different choices require different leadership styles.[90]

While this literature points us to some of the ways organisations have tried to animate change, the international case studies in this book, in particular the more detailed Irish case, identify how different providers have dealt with modernising their support systems within their own jurisdictions. These findings are drawn out and presented in Chapter 11 as options and alternatives for achieving active citizenship and independence.

[90] Despres, C. (1991) 'Information, Technology and Culture', *Technovation* 16 (1): 1–20.

CONCLUSION – DEVELOPING THE FRAMEWORK FOR ANALYSIS

When the aforementioned findings from the reshaping welfare section are translated into the context of disability support provision, they imply that competition is not by itself sufficient to drive innovation. As noted, competition may drive efficiency but it is not sufficient to drive continuous improvement. For improvement to occur, the knowledge system must also be appropriately configured to enable shared and continuous learning.[91] In addition, close collaborations must be made between commissioners and providers and client groups to enable successful personalised outcomes.

As the latter sections examined, at the organisational level, leadership is a key factor underpinning innovation and managing change. Good leadership can shape the internal environment and can cultivate innovative work climates. However, as identified throughout the earlier section on system-wide reform, the external environment also needs to be supportive of change. This includes the legal and policy climate, the funding arrangements and the monitoring and performance management of the delivery system. Otherwise, transformation of support delivery will be met by reorganisation fatigue, staff resistance and a loss of the strategic vision required for change.

This chapter identified what the management and policy evaluation literature can tell us about *how* the change agenda is best managed and identified approaches that can be used in the transformation from older conventional service arrangements. It provides a kind of *blueprint* which is emerging at the domestic level in terms of the changes being developed to enable active citizenship to become a reality for all persons with disabilities. This chapter also sets the parameters by which the comparative chapters are evaluated. It draws on Chapter 2 to identify the important building blocks that *ought* to underpin the reform of support delivery, such as establishing the right values, vision and purpose of change. A number of mechanisms and concepts are explained, which drive approaches to the delivery of services and supports and provide a basis for judging quality. Each of these approaches enables the progression of active citizenship.

Cumulatively, to meet the guiding principles of the CRPD and regional disability policy identified in Chapter 2, and to reach clear blue water from the historical legacies of institutionalisation and service-led group support, the main challenge ahead for all jurisdictions is to successfully harness social supports to achieve genuine dignity for persons with disabilities in a way which can also be affordable and sustainable. At the core of this reform effort should be the recognition that all human beings possess intrinsic worthiness and deserve unconditional respect, regardless of age, sex, health status, social or ethnic origin, political ideas and religion. As stated in

---

[91] Marsh and Spies-Butcher, *supra*, n. 18.

Article 1 of the Universal Declaration of Human Rights, 'All human beings are born free and equal in dignity and rights. They are endowed with reason and conscience and should act towards one another in a spirit of brotherhood'.[92] This is achieved by the provision of good support options, respect for a person's privacy, and a removal of the restrictions on their autonomy on a daily basis. These barriers have been rooted in the sometimes-limiting processes of disability service providers, state organisations and public institutions, and at times in the restrictive practices of professional staff.

The following parts of the book recognise at the outset that to achieve these rights, the policy tools and support delivery mechanisms sometimes need to vary for different levels and types of disability. There are also additional intersectional traits to be considered, such as gender[93] and sometimes complex medical needs.[94] Ultimately, it is understood that any specific or tailored support for distinct groups should be provided in the least restrictive setting. Moreover, the personalisation paradigm is equally relevant for all, including parents and siblings, frail elderly persons, young adults who acquire impairment as well as those with physical, sensory, and intellectual disability, autism or mental health issues. In this regard, the traditional service approach needs to be replaced by a new philosophy of supporting people in the community.

The comparative analysis examines how the purpose of welfare and support is being reframed in each country – in terms of its overarching approach and its localised responses. It also identifies what implications this shift is having in terms of the changing roles and responsibilities of the different stakeholders and how these are accounted for. This chapter thus sets out the 'reckonable variables' – the possibilities and potential mechanisms by which the later comparative case studies will be analysed.

Firstly, in terms of the administration of disability support, the comparative chapters are concerned with whether disability support has an appropriate ministry or

---

92 Article 1 of the Universal Declaration of Human Rights,
93 Council of Europe (2006) *Disability Action Plan to promote the rights and full participation of people with disabilities in society: improving the quality of life of people with disabilities in Europe 2006–2015*, Council of Europe.
94 Hewitt, A., Larson, S. A. and Lakin, K. C. (2000) *An Independent Evaluation of the Quality of Services and System Performance of Minnesota's Medicaid Home and Community Based Services for Persons with Mental Retardation and Related Conditions*. Institute on Community Integration, Research and Training Center on Community Living, University of Minnesota, Minneapolis. An example of an agency which has successfully supported individuals with intellectual disabilities who are considered to have significant needs is Community Association of People for REAL Enterprise (CARPE) in Canada, which assists individuals, provides a unique support network to determine the appropriateness of entrepreneurship as a preferred occupation and assists in the identification and procurement of the necessary resources needed to develop and operate a self-sufficient unit. Over the years they have supported individuals who are considered to have significant needs through person-centred planning, entrepreneurship, innovation, partnerships and community engagement. Please refer to CAPRE Web site at: http://www.capre.org (accessed 5 June 2010).

governance structure in each country. Is it conceptualised as health, community care or general social services? Does government maintain a leadership role in promoting innovation in disability services?

Secondly, what is the overall welfare philosophy in each jurisdiction? How are disability-specific state entitlements configured? Is there a specific strategy to reduce benefits traps or other related barriers to participation? Alongside these benefits, how have services and supports been provided? Are they delivered by the state directly or through local emanations (i.e. the private or nonprofit sector)? Again, are they conceptualised as health, community care or general social services at the local level? Lastly, is there any interaction between services and disability state entitlements?

In terms of the reform of disability support, each chapter attempts to identify the wellsprings for reform. For instance, does it derive from responses to the actions of civil society, major government enquiries, from treaties, legislation, case law, or the need for more cost-effective ways of using public money? From this, each chapter identifies the focus of this reform agenda and assesses whether the focus matches up with the values and vision outlined in Chapter 2.

Next, what is the shape of this reform? Each chapter examines how the government has carved out the reform agenda from the demand side and from the supply side. From the demand side, how has the disability support framework been reconfigured to restore more power to 'consumers'? What various mechanisms have been used in this regard? For instance, is there access to individual funding, support with budgeting, and supported decision making? Also, is there any way of enhancing consumer purchasing power, such as asset-building trusts or savings plans? Also, what kinds of mechanisms have been used to generate a better choice in living arrangements? Finally, what kind of preconditions are needed to make this system work (such as increased capacity in service providers to manage change, for example)?

From the supply side, the study is concerned with identifying what mechanisms have been used to make the support market more responsive. Has there been a system of procurement used to inject market forces into state/service arrangements, such as competitive tendering? Has the state placed service delivery organisations at arm's length from the state and forced them to compete? Has the state insisted on standards for support providers regardless of whether market forces are injected? Moreover, has the state insisted on consequences for failure to meet such standards? Finally, how has the state managed accountability for public money while opening up flexibility room within the sector to innovate? Throughout this area of questions, the study is also concerned with identifying what new roles exist for providers in this new market.

Again, these questions are used to direct the structure of how each jurisdiction has grappled with the reform agenda, and frame the discussion in each chapter.

In addition, the analysis examines to what extent these reform agendas utilise the various mechanisms of reshaping welfare governance and change management outlined in this chapter. Inherent in this approach is a broader analysis of how, overall, each country has tackled the three overarching focus areas of personalisation, choice in living arrangements and a life in the community.

PART II

Learning from Comparative Perspectives

4

Active Citizenship and Disability in the United States

INTRODUCTION

As stated in Chapter 2, the United States has not yet ratified the CRPD. Nonetheless, it still remains in many respects at the forefront of the endeavour to recognise the principles of active citizenship and to ensure the social model of disability is seen through a civil rights prism.[1] The most significant result for disability rights advocates was the 1990 promulgation of the Americans with Disabilities Act (ADA), prohibiting disability-based discrimination. The ADA still remains an exemplar of the principles associated with active citizenship, and has played a leading role in developing disability law around the world.[2] Yet, despite its laudable achievements, the ADA has not – and structurally cannot – bring about equality on its own.[3] For reform of the support sphere in people's lives, legislation and policy need to transform state and society's institutional structures to unlock the many barriers people with disabilities face to engaging and participating in society.

This chapter examines how the United States as a whole as well as a selection of its states have set about tackling the big questions regarding the role of government in the lives of persons with disabilities, in terms of its overall welfare philosophy, the wellsprings of reform in how it administers disability support, and the high-level policy choices in how it has shaped reform in its social policies to enable people with disabilities to re-engage in society. It examines the transformation of both the supply side and demand side of the disability support sector, in terms of how it has given more power to people to guide their own support and how it has tried to make the market more responsive. Before this, the chapter maps out the administrative terrain which governs disability law and policy.

[1] Stein, M. A. and Stein, P. (2007) 'Beyond Disability Civil Rights', *Hastings Law Journal* 58: 1203–1240.
[2] Degener, T. and Quinn, G. (2002) 'A Survey of International, Comparative and Regional Disability Law Reform', in Breslin, M. L. and Yee, S. (eds.) *Disability Rights Law and Policy: International and National Perspectives*, Transnational, Ardsley, New York. pp. 122–124.
[3] *Ibid.* at 1.

AN OVERVIEW OF THE ADMINISTRATION OF DISABILITY SUPPORT

The United States has a unique political and geographical landscape which provides a complex territorial system of administration of disability support policy. It has an intricate federal-state level relationship, with different institutions and actors who can shape disability support policy in many different ways and at various different scales. At the federal level, the United States is a constitutional republic in which the president, Congress and judiciary share powers reserved for the national government, and the federal government shares sovereignty with the state governments. With the separation of powers (between executive, legislative and judicial branches), the role of the executive branch, which is headed by the president and various executive offices, is to enforce the laws. The legislative branch is vested in the two chambers of Congress: the Senate and the House of Representatives. The legislative branch can set national legislation, under certain powers granted to it in the Constitution. These include education, family law, contract law and legislation on most crimes.

Meanwhile, the judicial branch comprising the Supreme Court and lower federal courts exercises judicial power, and its function is to interpret the US Constitution and federal laws and regulations. This includes resolving disputes between the executive and legislative branches. The Supreme Court cannot pass legislation which makes budget decisions for US states, but it has the power to decide what congressional laws mean and how they apply in specific cases (this has become particularly relevant in some instances, such as the *Olmstead* case[4] detailed later in the chapter). The president can introduce executive orders as a response to Supreme Court judgements affirming the United States' commitment to new judicial interpretations.

In terms of the government's role in governing disability policy, the Department of Health and Human Services (DHHS) is the US government's principal agency for protecting the health of all Americans and providing human services, including for people with disabilities and mental health issues. The work of the DHHS is conducted by the Office of the Secretary and eleven separate agencies.[5]

The central agency for health and social care is coordinated by the Centers for Medicare and Medicaid Services (CMS), which administer the two main federal (and state-matched) funding programmes for primary care and long-term care, namely Medicare and Medicaid (examined in the following section). With a budget of approximately $650 billion and serving approximately 90 million beneficiaries, the CMS plays a key role in the overall direction of the health and long-term care system.[6] This body also has a role, through regional offices, in providing primary resources in planning and in implementing agency outreach initiatives relevant to all participants.

---

[4] *Olmstead v. L.C.*, 527 U.S. 581 (1999).
[5] For a full listing, see: http://www.hhs.gov/about/ (accessed 10 December 2010).
[6] Please refer to: *CMS' Strategic Action Plan 2006–2009*. Available at: http://www2.ancor.org/issues/medicaid/cms_strat_plan_06–09_10–06.pdf (accessed 5 December 2010).

At the state level, states governments have the power to make laws on all subjects not granted to the federal government or denied to the states in the US Constitution. In practice, this means that approaches to designing support delivery are as diverse as the fifty states themselves. The main funding programme of disability support, Medicaid, is structured and operated somewhat differently in each state and the District of Columbia. Each state decides how to operate its programme within federal guidelines, establishing or influencing the reimbursement rate, amount, scope and duration of home health and personal care benefits offered.[7]

Several states also fund significant multifaceted disability support programmes from their state general revenues, including Wisconsin's Community Options Program and Michigan's Home Help programme, for example. A state plan must be in effect throughout an entire state (i.e. amount, duration and scope of coverage must be the same statewide). The vast majority of programmes have a legislative mandate, providing a level of recognition and relative stability in the state budget process. Each programme has its own eligibility criteria and service definitions.

The resulting spatial variation in state practices is both an opportunity and a problem. The opportunity is present in the naturally occurring variation and differential innovation. The problem is that access to support and quality assurance can vary substantially within states, across states and for subpopulations. The more states vary beyond federally mandated minimum requirements, the greater the interstate inequities. However, states are often 'blamed' for these differences rather than being credited for going beyond what in many cases may be inadequate federal minimum standards.[8]

This chapter examines the main driving forces in personalisation at the national policy level and identifies some different state responses in developing their own brand of reform throughout. It first provides an overview of the disability support framework before examining the reform effort towards greater personalisation.

AN OVERVIEW OF THE DISABILITY SUPPORT FRAMEWORK

Disability-Specific Federal and State Entitlements

The Supplemental Security Income (SSI) programme was established in 1972 in order to federalise existing state cash assistance programmes for elderly and disabled persons (to which the state could add additional monies). Prior to this, there had only been Social Security for those with a previous work history.[9] This was the first non-contributory welfare programme for elderly and disabled persons, regardless of work history. SSI has since been a means-tested programme which pays benefits

---

[7] Newcomer R. J., Fox P. J. and Harrington C. A. (2001), 'Health and Long-Term Care for People with Alzheimer's Disease and Related Dementias: Policy Research Issues', *Aging & Mental Health* 5(1): 124–137.

[8] *Ibid.*

[9] Introduced as part of the Social Security Act 1935.

based on financial need, requiring that the individual's income and assets fall below a minimum standard.

The other benefit is called Social Security Disability Insurance (SSDI), a contributory payment for those individuals and certain family members who are insured, meaning that they worked long enough and paid Social Security taxes. According to the Social Security Administration (SSA), individuals qualify for SSDI if they have a physical or mental condition that prevents them from engaging in any 'substantial gainful activity' (SGA), the condition is expected to last at least twelve months or result in death, they are under the age of sixty-five, and have worked five out of the last ten years as of the determined date of onset of disability.[10]

In terms of the meshing together of disability-specific government entitlements and services, there has been a substantial effort at overcoming the potential benefit trap with SSI and SSDI through the Social Security's Work Incentives Planning and Assistance programme (WIPA). A person can begin a 'plan to achieve self-support'. If Social Security approve a person's plan for a work goal which will reduce dependence on SSI, any money the person uses for this purpose will not be counted when Social Security figures out how his or her current income and resources affect the payment amount. When a person's other income goes up, his or her SSI payments usually go down. So when a person earns more than the SSI limit, payments will stop for those months – but will restart automatically without further assessment (within a five-year period). If a person with a disability is in receipt of SSI and chooses to work, that person may have to pay for certain items and services that people without disabilities do not pay for. For example, because of a medical condition, a person may need to take a taxi to work, instead of public transportation. They may be able to deduct the cost of the taxi from their monthly earnings before Social Security is determined if they are still eligible for benefits.

SSDI has a Ticket to Work programme which provides opportunities to access support services and extends Medicare coverage for SSDI beneficiaries so employees can return to work without the fear of losing health benefits.[11] The goal of this programme is to increase opportunities and choices for Social Security disability beneficiaries to obtain employment, vocational rehabilitation (VR) and other support services from public and private providers, employers, Employment Networks[12] and other organisations. It is a voluntary programme for beneficiaries, and Employment Networks can also choose which services they want to provide, where and to whom. The person must have a level of earning considered by regulation as

[10]   Please refer to: http://www.ssa.gov/disability (accessed 4 June 2010).
[11]   Ticket to Work and Work Incentives Improvement Act of 1999.
[12]   An employment network is a qualified Social Security–approved organisation or agency that has entered into an agreement with Social Security to provide employment services, VR services and other types of support to beneficiaries under the Ticket to Work programme. All networks are required to provide career counseling, job placement (including job search, job development and job placement assistance) and ongoing employment support.

evidence of one's inability to engage in 'substantial gainful activity', the dollar amount that a disability beneficiary (SSI or Social Security) may earn each month while simultaneously maintaining eligibility for benefits. The SGA amount for 2012 is $1,010.[13]

Disability-Specific Services

Disability-specific services in the United States are administered by state agencies and intermediaries funded either through sole state revenue or through the federal state-matched Medicare and Medicaid, which were both established under President Johnson's leadership in 1965 under the Social Security Amendments. Medicare provides for the medical needs of persons aged sixty-five or older and some people under age sixty-five with disabilities. It primarily covers acute care costs and is not considered a major payer for long-term care.[14] Medicaid, on the other hand, was set up to meet the long-term support needs of people with disabilities and the chronically ill. It is funded through a federal-state partnership, with three coverage programmes in one: (1) insurance coverage for low-income children and pregnant women, (2) additional coverage for low-income elders on Medicare, and (3) acute and long-term care coverage for people with disabilities and frail elders. Under federal law, Medicaid is meant to provide coverage for rehabilitation and other services so that people can attain and retain capability for independence or self-care.[15] Most Medicaid beneficiaries (consumers) receive their long-term care services from agency-based providers which are certified to provide Medicaid services.

When first enacted, federal Medicaid funding had a strong institutional bias. It was available mainly when the person was placed in an institutional setting (e.g. a nursing home or care facility), with few avenues for securing Medicaid dollars to support individuals in their homes. This was because policy makers concentrated primarily on persons with a severe level of disability, on the basis of their presumed extensive service needs.[16] In contrast to private insurance, Medicaid has grown into the dominant funding source for people with disabilities.

Medicaid eligibility rules fall into two basic sets: financial and categorical. The financial eligibility is deeply rooted in the federally financed programmes of cash assistance (i.e. SSI) to help to support low-income individuals and families: states are required to provide Medicaid coverage for most people who get federally assisted

---

[13] http://www.ssa.gov/oact/COLA/sga.html (accessed 19 January 2012).

[14] Family Caregiver Alliance (2003) *Fact Sheet: New Medicare: What Caregivers Need to Know*, http://www.caregiver.org/caregiver/jsp/content_node.jsp?nodeid=890 (accessed 12 March 2012).

[15] Winchester, M. and Frydman, D. (2003) 'Financing Long-Term Care for People with Disabilities', Issue 2 Spring, The Policy Resource Center, Institute for Health, Law, and Ethics, Franklin Pierce Law Center.

[16] Batavia, A. (2003) *Independent Living: A Viable Option for Long-Term Care*. ABI Professional Publications, Clearwater, FL.

TABLE 4.1. *Medicaid beneficiary groups*

Mandatory populations	Optional populations
• Children below federal minimum income levels	• Children above federal minimum income levels
• Adults in families with children (Section 1931 and TMA)	• Adults in families with children (above Section 1931 minimums)
• Pregnant women ≤133% FPL	• Pregnant women >133% FPL
• Disabled SSI beneficiaries	• Disabled (above SSI levels)
• Certain working disabled	• Disabled (under Home & Community Based Services)
• Elderly SSI beneficiaries	• Certain working disabled (>SSI levels)
• Medicare Buy-In groups	• Elderly (>SSI; SSP-only recipients)
	• Elderly nursing home residents (>SSI levels)
	• Medically needy

TMA: Transitional Medical Assistance; FPL: Federal Poverty Level
Source: KFF (2001) Policy Brief: Medicaid 'Mandatory' and 'Optional' Eligibility and Benefits.

income maintenance payments, as well as for related groups not getting cash payments.

In general, Medicaid funding is calculated based on population and need, using capitated rates. It thus varies significantly from state to state. Because of the matching formulas, a state has to pay out a certain percentage to receive matching funds. There are many programmes which are still funded in a block grant, but these programmes are not supposed to offer a ceiling on a person's support.

The categorical set defines particular categories of persons for whom federal law permits coverage (elderly, blind or disabled). Medicaid benefits categories are broken down into 'mandatory' beneficiary groups and benefit categories and 'optional' groups and benefit categories (see Table 4.1). In exchange for receiving federal Medicaid matching payments, states must guarantee coverage to all individuals in certain 'mandatory' groups, including most disabled and elderly people receiving SSI and parents with income and resources below states' welfare eligibility levels.

In terms of the optional service categories, states have the option of covering additional services and receiving federal matching funds for those services, which include prescription drugs, personal care and other community-based services for individuals with disabilities.[17] No state offers only mandatory services in its Medicaid programme. All states cover several, if not most, of the optional service categories. The legislative language of 'State Option' therefore hardly applies to the populations'

[17] For a full listing of mandatory and optional items and services, please refer to KFF (2001) *Policy Brief: Medicaid 'Mandatory' and 'Optional' Eligibility and Benefits*, available at http://www.kff .org/medicaid/loader.cfm?url=/commonspot/security/getfile.cfm&PageID=13767 (accessed 6 March 2010).

need for the services covered; most Medicaid spending *is* optional, making up 65 per cent of the total.[18]

For Medicaid, many exceptions and variations have been enacted over the years to make it work better for low-income persons needing health care but not cash assistance. There is a 'spend down option' available in most states, allowing individuals to use incurred/unpaid medical bills to 'spend down' the difference between their income and the income limit to become eligible. People with higher incomes qualify if they have medical bills equal to or greater than the amount by which their income exceeds the Medically Needy Income Levels.[19]

The federal government, through the Centers for Medicare and Medicaid Services (CMS) provides federal financial participation (FFP) for the covered services. In wealthy states, such as California and New York, the federal matching level is 50 per cent; in other states deemed less wealthy, such as North Dakota, the matching level is 75 per cent. This means that the state has to provide 25 per cent or 50 per cent of the cost of Medicaid services through its own state taxes. In terms of portability, people are allowed to take their Medicaid money to other counties within their state but not to a new state. Importantly, many states are using Medicaid to replace state-only-funded institutions with federally matched community care funding. The federal matching also means that, for states, putting constraints on Medicaid has grave health consequences and effectively little, if any, cost savings. Medicaid cutbacks mean an impact on the state economies through a loss in federal matching funds. Most reports caution that controlling costs through Medicaid – just one component of the health care system – is not sustainable.[20]

Since 2003, after a decision to reform Medicaid by the George W. Bush administration, the open-ended entitlement to Medicaid matching funds was replaced with broader state flexibility over use of funds but with capped federal funding.[21] In practice this meant states would receive a block grant with far more flexibility over how they could use federal funds, albeit with a cap on funding levels.[22]

Prior to Medicaid, institutions were generally operated and funded by the states. The philosophy of segregation and custodial 'care' behind the institutionalisation process was also interwoven with sterilisation, particularly for persons with intellectual disabilities until 1979.[23] As a result of early deinstitutionalisation efforts, a new residential setting, referred to as Intermediate Care Facilities for the Mentally

---

[18] Mann, C. (2002) *The New Era of Medicaid Waivers*, September, Institute for Health Care Research and Policy & Council on Health Care Economics and Policy, Georgetown University.

[19] Kaiser Commission on Medicaid and the Uninsured (2001) *Medicaid's Disabled Population and Managed Care*, March, The Henry J. Kaiser Family Foundation, Washington, D.C. p. 2.

[20] Winchester and Frydman, *supra*, n. 15.

[21] Kaiser Commission on Medicaid and the Uninsured (2003) *Bush Administration: Medicaid/SCHIP Proposal*, May, The Henry J. Kaiser Family Foundation, Washington, D.C.

[22] *Ibid.*

[23] As recently as 1979 it was legal for some state governments to sterilise disabled persons against their will.

Retarded (ICFs/MR[24]), developed in 1971. ICFs/MR are specifically designed to provide twenty-four-hour health care and continuous individualised 'active treatment' for residents. Active treatment is the cornerstone of the ICFs/MR programme and involves a team approach to teaching residents skills and behaviours that help them to function as independently as possible. Despite being set up as 'intermediate' care services in the transition from institutions to communities, they now represent an enduring, outmoded method of support, where residents still remain segregated from the community. State-owned facilities from 2000 account for only 9.3 per cent of total ICFs/MR. Nearly 50 per cent of clients reside in privately operated facilities, funded through federal funding, which represent 83.4 per cent of total ICFs/MR.[25]

In terms of the administration of community services, states began to invest much time and resources into care coordination and case management in the form of Medicaid Managed Care with the Balanced Budget Act (BBA; 1997). This emerged largely in response to previous fiscal crises and to overcome the rising complexity of programmes. Managed care refers to the United States' attempt at providing a comprehensive health and social care system which integrates the delivery and financing of health care services to individuals who are covered by insurance by means of arrangement with selected health care providers. Geographically, managed care in the United States mirrors the 'welfare pluralism' idea of the UK National Health Service.[26] Proponents of Medicaid reform through managed care argued that it would control cost growth; this view has been increasingly challenged, however, given the cost growth in the US health care system.[27] In any case, it has created a 'medical home,' offering Medicaid beneficiaries better and more consistent access to primary care and coordination of services.[28]

With the BBA (1997), most states converted major portions of their Medicaid programmes from individually procured services to managed care models.[29]

---

[24] These are now being referred to as ICFs for the Developmentally Disabled (ICFs/DD).

[25] American Health Care Association (2000) *Intermediate Care Facilities for the Developmentally Disabled: Meeting the Long Term Care Needs and Maximizing the Potential of Individuals with Mental Retardation and/or Developmental Disabilities*, http://www.vor.net/legislative-voice/additional-dd-act-reauthorization-resources/icfmr-program-background-and-history (accessed 2 September 2011)

[26] The landscape of managed care organisations (MCOs) includes several types of network-based managed care programmes such as health maintenance organizations (HMOs) and alternative groups such as preferred provider organizations (PPOs) and Point of Service (POS) plans.

[27] For a review of debates for and against Medicaid managed care, please see discussion by Hurley, R. E. and Somers, S. A. (2003) 'Medicaid and Managed Care: A Lasting Relationship?' *Health Affairs* 22(1): 77–88.

[28] Haslanger, K. (2003), *Medicaid Managed Care in New York: A Work in Progress*, United Hospital Fund, New York.

[29] The government gave states the option of setting up Medicaid managed care programmes, opening up the market for private companies such as the Medical Case Management of America, Inc. (MCMA) to provide case management services. Medicaid managed care grew rapidly in the 1990s; in 1991, 2.7 million beneficiaries were enrolled in some form of managed care. By 2004, that number had grown to 27 million – an increase of 900%. Of the total Medicaid enrolment

Managed care, however, has typically not been part of the Medicaid disability-oriented service array. Managed care organisations' (MCOs)[30] emphasis on primary care and limited access to specialty care has undermined their usefulness at addressing the personal requirements of people with disabilities. Despite this, Medicaid managed care for persons with disabilities is still under active consideration in many states. The care coordination inherent in managed care was conceived as a means of assisting families in navigating through complex Medicaid systems in obtaining information and access to services.[31] Because many beneficiaries with disabilities typically require the services of multidisciplinary teams and other providers, there is some potential for MCOs to mobilise their referral network to fulfil an as yet unfulfilled entitlement. This is achieved through partnerships with the individual, the individual's family, advocacy groups, Centers for Independent Living, other state agencies and the state legislature. Some of these entities can also assist the state Medicaid programme to identify the home and community service infrastructure necessary and help to design support arrangements. Advocacy groups and consumers can be used to educate case managers about the consumer's needs and preferences. Case management also includes arranging for services, following up to ensure that services are in place, developing networks for ongoing support, monitoring the person's situation on an ongoing basis and adjusting the service package as needed.[32] By 2004, Medicaid managed care was available for adults with disabilities in 66 per cent of US counties, up from 43 per cent in 1996.[33]

On the other hand, most disabled Medicaid recipients still secure support outside of managed care networks. These services and supports, in turn, not only are unlikely to be active members of managed care networks, but they also may not have accommodated themselves to capitated payment, and other more commercial aspects of health care delivery. Furthermore, these models often offer too restrictive a menu of service options, and enrolees cannot use their Medicaid dollars to pay for services

in the United States in 2004, approximately 60% are receiving Medicaid benefits through managed care. All states except Alaska, New Hampshire and Wyoming have all, or a portion of, their Medicaid population enrolled in an MCO. States can make managed care enrolment voluntary or seek a waiver of section 1915(b) of the Social Security Act (the Act) from CMS to require certain populations to enrol in an MCO. For more information, please refer to the CMS Web site at: http://www.cms.hhs.gov/MedicaidStWaivProgDemoPGI/MWDL/list.asp?filterType=none&filterByDID=-99&sortByDID=3&sortOrder=ascending&intNumPerPage=10 (accessed 24 August 2011).

30 There are several types of network-based managed care programs, each operating with slightly different business models (e.g. Preferred Provider Organizations, Point of Service plans).

31 Wunderlich, G. S. and Kohler, P. O. (eds.) (2001). *Improving the Quality of Long-Term Care*. National Academy Press, Washington, DC.

32 Smith, G., O'Keeffe, J., Carpenter, L., Doty, P., Kennedy, G. et al. (2000) *Medicaid Coverage of Home and Community Services: Overview*, October, http://www.communitygateway.org/faq/medicaid/chapter_1.htm (accessed 4 July 2011).

33 Burns, M. E. (2009) 'Medicaid Managed Care and Health Care Access for Adult Beneficiaries with Disabilities', *Health Services Research* 44(5): 1521–1541.

outside the remit of their managed care provider. Similarly, MCOs are unlikely to have well-developed relationships with providers of the specialised ancillary services which persons with disabilities may use, such as wheelchair manufacturers or home infusion therapists. Indeed, some disability advocacy groups have spoken out publicly against enrolment in MCOs.[34] As a result, according to Tanenbaum and Hurley (1995), where it has been initiated, the results have been tentative and mixed. Early demonstration programmes in Santa Barbara, California, and in Minneapolis, Minnesota, came into conflict with both advocacy groups and managed care plans, specifically regarding providers' readiness to serve disabled populations. As a result, many people with disabilities prefer to use agencies where they can self-direct their own publicly funded, community-based supports and services. This model, based on individual funding, is examined in more detail in the Shape of Reform section of this chapter.

WELLSPRINGS OF REFORM

The preceding discussion provides an overview of the main framework under which disability support developed leaving aside the introduction of personalisation and consumer-directed support. It identifies the main different mechanisms involved in the administration of conventional non–self-directed services. The following section identifies the main wellsprings of reform, which began to question how the system worked and tested how new approaches could give persons with disabilities more power to direct their own support.

The main wellsprings of reform examined consist of policy responses to a number of factors including the conditions of institutions, the costs of institutional support, the results of self-determination demonstration projects, and the ADA and subsequent *Olmstead* case. Some of these wellsprings of reform predate some of the features of today's system outlined earlier, illustrating the fact that certain legacies of these earlier programmes live on in today's system. Moreover, it serves to demonstrate many of the reforms which were grounded in the principles of active citizenship developed in parallel with service models with contradictory values.

The Conditions of Institutions

The United States began to question the conditions of its institutions starting as far back as the 1970s. At the time, family caregiving in the community operated largely in the shadow of the institutions.[35] In 1967, 190,000 persons with intellectual

[34] See Tanenbaum, S. J. and Hurley, R. E. (1995) 'Disability and the Managed Care Frenzy: A Cautionary Note', *Health Affairs* 14: 213–219.

[35] Metzel, D. S. (2004) 'Historical Social Geography', in Noll, S. and Trent, Jr., W. (eds.) *Mental Retardation in America*, New York University Press, New York. pp. 420–444.

disabilities lived in large, usually state-sponsored institutions.[36] While individuals and families with sufficient resources might have been able to purchase home care and personal care services in the private market, federal, state and, to a lesser extent, local funds largely supported care in nursing homes and other institutional settings.[37]

However, the conditions of many institutions began to increasingly come under public scrutiny. Work by Erving Goffman and others began to describe the destructive effects of institutions on the lives of people who both lived and worked in them.[38] In 1972, Geraldo Rivera made a TV programme which exposed the appalling conditions of those with an intellectual disability in two large institutions in New York. Many considered Rivera's TV exposé the single most important event to give impetus to the shift away from institutional services.[39] However, with community care only in its infancy, the majority of institutionalised persons were displaced back to their family home, put in ICFs/MR or group homes or became homeless.[40] A group home is a typical home in the community where people with disabilities live and receive full-time services. These homes generally range in size from two to ten people and can be publicly or privately owned and operated.[41] Despite their location in the community, multiple problems have been associated with group home arrangements, including inflexible schedules, high levels of staffing, incompatibility/disputes among residents, inability to adapt to residents' changing needs/preferences and low levels of personal choice and autonomy regarding group activities and decisions.[42]

Lawsuits were also filed on behalf of the people living in institutions and their relatives in a dozen states, including New York (Willowbrook), Michigan (Plymouth), Alabama (Partlow) and Pennsylvania (Pennhurst). These early lawsuits were designed to force states to improve the institutions by adequately funding

---

[36] According to the Institute on Disability at the University of New Hampshire.

[37] Knickman, J. R. and Stone, R. (2007) 'The Public/Private Partnership Behind the Cash and Counseling Demonstration and Evaluation: Its Origins, Challenges, and Unresolved Issues', *Health Services Research* 42(1 Pt 2): 362–377.

[38] Goffman, E. (1961) *Asylums: Essays on the Social Situation of Mental Patients and Other Inmates.* Penguin, Harmondsworth.

[39] Mansell, J. and Ericsson, K. (eds.) (1996) *Deinstitutionalization and Community Living: Intellectual Disability Services in Britain, Scandinavia and the USA.* Chapman and Hall, London.

[40] Belcher, J. and Toomey, B. G. (1988) 'Relationship between the Deinstitutionalization Model, Psychiatric Disability, and Homelessness', *Health & Social Work* 13(2): 145–153.

[41] Hewitt, A., and O'Nell, S. (1998) 'Real Lives', in Bestgen, Y. (ed.) *With a Little Help from My Friends... A Series on Contemporary Supports to People with Mental Retardation.* The President's Committee on Mental Retardation, available at: http://www.acf.hhs.gov/programs/pcpid/docs/help3 .doc (accessed 12 October 2010).

[42] See Stancliffe, R. J. and Lakin, K. C. (2005) 'Context and Issues in Research on Expenditures and Outcomes of Community Supports', in Stancliffe, R. J. and Lakin, K. C. (eds.) *Costs and Outcomes of Community Services for People with Intellectual Disabilities.* Paul H. Brookes Publishing, Baltimore. pp. 1–22.

them, hiring and training more staff and providing services that would help people to achieve their potential. The *Pennhurst* case, however, and all subsequent
lawsuits, transformed into judgements which claimed that no amount of money
could remedy the obvious facts of isolation and segregation, which they claimed
led directly to abuse and neglect. Rather than improving the institutions, they ruled
that segregation should be abolished and people should be served in communities
and neighbourhoods just like anyone else.[43] In the *Pennhurst* case, every person
would have to be accorded a new home and a new life in communities around
Pennsylvania. The subsequent surge of litigation also spurred the transformation of
the movement for fair and humane treatment into a true civil rights movement.
The inclusion of Section 504 – 'Nondiscrimination Under Federal Grants and Programmes' – within the Rehabilitation Act of 1973 provided the legislative foundation
for later litigation.[44]

Disability support in the United States has since had two parallel system types: the
congregated care settings typified by ICFs/MR and Home and Community Based
Services (discussed later). In terms of care supports in the community, there are two
major sources of support: state plan services available to all who qualify and Medicaid
Home and Community Based Waiver Services, detailed in the next section. The
most common type of community-based service prior to the personalisation reform
was a package of home care services developed through a care plan and delivered
by a trained aide or personal care worker employed by a formal home care agency.[45]
This continues to remain a popular option, although it is gradually being replaced
by the self-directed model, examined later.

Importantly, the Independent Living movement was an important agent of change
in generating support against the conditions of these institutions and has continued
to draw on the experiences of these early efforts, insisting that states continue to
close their institutions and that there should be no return to the conditions of
the old custodial method of segregating persons with disabilities. In particular,
in 1972, the first Center for Independent Living (CIL) was founded by disability
activists in Berkeley, California. By the turn of the century, there were hundreds
of such centres all across the United States, particularly led by a strong physical
disability community. Additional momentum was given to the movement by the
significant numbers of young war veterans. In addition to the CIL in Berkeley, the
American Coalition of Citizens with Disabilities (ACCD) was a coalition of national,
state and local disability organisations active from 1975 to 1983. ACCD brought a

[43] Conroy, J. and Yuskausakas, A. (1996) *Independent Evaluation of the Monadnock Self-Determination Project*. Center for Outcome Analysis, Ardmore, PA.

[44] Section 504, Rehabilitation Act of 1973, available at: http://www.dol.gov/oasam/programs/crc/sec504 .htm (accessed 30 January 2012).

[45] Kane, R., Kane, R. and Ladd, R. (1998) *The Heart of Long-Term Care*. Oxford University Press, New York.

cross-disability perspective to the movement and took a leading role in the national effort to implement non-discrimination legislation across the United States.[46]

The Costs of Institutional Support

The bias in Medicaid coverage towards institutions also began to change when the federal government in 1981 under President Ronald Reagan authorised a new Medicaid programme called Home and Community Based Services (HCBS), which was designed to permit states to develop programmes specific to the health care and housing needs of low-income individuals eligible for nursing home placement. The decision arose as a result of a case where a three-year-old girl, Katie Beckett, was being treated in a hospital at a cost of $6,000 a month and was refused access to Medicaid support at home. She was singled out by Reagan as a victim of the federal bureaucracy which allowed government payments for her care only in a hospital, even though it could be given at home. The programme was termed the 1915 (c) waiver (referring to the statute being waived) or alternatively the 'Katie Beckett waiver'.[47]

In 1994, the federal government implemented new regulations which empowered states to further expand their Medicaid HCBS Waiver Programmes and eliminated restrictions on the amount of Medicaid funding states could allocate to community-based care, such as assisted living. Medicaid is now better understood as not a single programme, but an array of services and programmes under a single name. Table 4.2 details Medicaid long-term care services currently offered.

The Medicaid waivers represent a significant step to mitigate the Medicaid programme's institutional bias which had led to the extensive development and utilisation of nursing homes and ICFs/MR. Access to funding for community services for those with intellectual and developmental disabilities, for example, has been improving. In 1996, 67.4 per cent was spent on Medicaid institutional services and 32.6 per cent on Medicaid HCBS. In 2006, this rate shifted to 40.5 per cent being spent on Medicaid institutional services and 59 per cent on Medicaid HCBS.[48]

---

[46] For a further discussion of the history of the independent living movement, please refer to UC Berkeley's Web site on the Disability Rights and Independent Living Movement, at: http://bancroft .berkeley.edu/collections/drilm/ (accessed 5 January 2010).

[47] The U.S. Department of Health and Human Services has granted these waivers to allow states to 'waive' certain Medicaid requirements and permit them to reallocate a portion of Medicaid funding from nursing facility care to other forms of care such as case management, personal care services and respite care which are not usually covered by Medicaid, to prevent a person from being institutionalised.

[48] Lakin, K. C., Alba, K. and Prouty, R. W. (2007) 'Utilization of and Expenditures for Medicaid Institutional and Home and Community Based Services', in Prouty, R. W., Smith, G. and Lakin, K. C. (eds.) *Residential Services for Persons with Developmental Disabilities: Status and Trends through 2006*. University of Minnesota, Research and Training Center on Community Living, Institute on Community Integration, Minneapolis.

TABLE 4.2. *Medicaid long-term care services*

Medicaid state plan	Waiver (services vary with each waiver)
Hospital and Physician Services	Adult Day Care
Home Health Nursing Services	Case Management
Nursing Assistant Services	Environmental Modifications
Nursing Facility	Home- and Community-Based Services
Medical Supplies and Equipment	Personal Care
Personal Care	Respite
Physical, Occupational and Speech Therapies	

Source: Winchester, M. and Frydman, D. (2003) *'Financing Long-Term Care for People with Disabilities'*, Issue 2 Spring, The Policy Resource Center, Institute for Health, Law, and Ethics. Franklin Pierce Law Center, p. 4.

However, while the proportion of expenditures for community services continues to increase, a significant institutional bias still remains (although this varies from state to state) when compared to the numbers using HCBS.[49]

As well as the 1915 (c) waivers, the government also introduced Section 1115 waivers, which were granted for experimental, pilot or demonstration projects. Under the statute, the Secretary of Health and Human Services can allow states 'to experiment, pilot or demonstrate projects which are likely to assist in promoting the objectives of the Medicaid statute.'[50] These have been used by states to experiment with new community services and to reduce numbers in costly institutions (see Vermont's 1115 Waiver for an example in Table 4.3).

States often work collaboratively with CMS in designing their waivers from the concept phase, and the process is evaluated throughout its life. While it offers states a chance to experiment with new types of support, restrictions on the 1115 Waivers are liberal, so states have broad authority to waive virtually all aspects of Medicaid law, including statewideness. Some states use the waiver to expand health insurance coverage to populations which would have otherwise been ineligible, or else to target benefits to special populations. While every state has a 1915 (c) waiver, only twenty-eight states have 1115 waivers.[51] Many states now apply for 1115 Waivers in an attempt to provide health care to more of their poorer citizens, while also holding down costs through managed care. The 1115 Waivers are often referred to as Medicaid Managed Care Waivers, because managed care is now common in almost all of these types of waivers.

---

[49] See Anderson, W. L., Wiener, J. M. and O'Keeffe, J. (2006) *Money Follows the Person Initiatives of the Systems Change Grantees Final Report.* CMS, Washington, DC.

[50] CMS, *Research & Demonstration Projects – Section 1115*, https://www.cms.gov/MedicaidStWaivProg-DemoPGI/03_Research&DemonstrationProjects-Section1115.asp (accessed 5 March 2011).

[51] Please refer to the CMS Web site at: http://www.cms.hhs.gov/MedicaidStWaivProgDemoPGI/MWDL/list.asp?filterType=none&filterByDID=-99&sortByDID=3&sortOrder=ascending&intNumPerPage=10 (accessed 24 August 2011).

TABLE 4.3. *Example of 1115 waiver: Vermont long-term care reform waiver*

Official programme name	Vermont long-term care plan
Waiver Authority	1115
Summary	Demonstration to implement system changes which will decrease nursing facility use and increase the number of individuals using community-based services.

Source: CMS, Medicaid Waivers and Demonstration List, available at: http://www.cms.gov/MedicaidStWaivProgDemoPGI/MWDL/list.asp (accessed 5 November 2010).

Early Precedents of Self-Determination

In the United States, 'consumer direction' began in long-term care programmes other than Medicaid. Prominent examples have included programmes in the Department of Veterans Affairs (VA) and some programmes operated by states. These were largely targeted at adults with physical disabilities, who were previously non-disabled and who sought to remain independent in the community. The rationale behind these programmes was driven by the merging of disability rights and independent living concepts, under the guiding philosophy of the CIL, with further support being led by young people challenging the barriers to education and full participation in society.[52] Essentially, individuals with disabilities joined together to protest their exclusion from society's mainstream and to demand more humane, non-medical attention from the nation's service delivery system. The CILs have since been driven by a particular philosophy of persons with disabilities being able to socially and economically engage within society, rather than of providing conventional services per se.

For the past forty years, the VA has operated the Housebound and Aid and Attendance programmes which provide additional cash benefits to qualified veterans or their surviving spouses if they require ongoing personal support services, are housebound or require nursing home services. These cash benefits provide the veteran with additional monthly income to purchase needed services and supports. Importantly, there are no federal restrictions on how these additional cash benefits must be used. The veteran with a disability can determine how to spend the benefit; for example, he or she can hire friends or family members to provide personal support services.[53]

In addition to the federal VA programmes, there are a number of states which established early forms of consumer-directed support options. One of the better

[52] For a full history of the Independent Living movement and its key individuals, including Ed Roberts and Judie Heumann, please refer to Fleischer, D. (2001) *The Disability Rights Movement.* Temple University Press, Philadelphia.
[53] Tritz, K. (2005) *Long-Term Care: Consumer-Directed Services under Medicaid,* Congressional Research Service (The Library of Congress) Report for Congress.

known of these consumer-directed programmes is California's In-Home Supportive Services (IHSS) programme which has been in operation since 1979. IHSS did not include federal funding in its consumer-directed programme until California adopted the Medicaid personal care option in the state plan in 1993. IHSS serves an estimated 200,000 consumers annually and provides up to 283 hours of service each month, including personal care, household and paramedical services, protective supervision and medical transportation. IHSS allows the consumer to choose his or her direct care worker, including a family member. The state then contracts with this direct care worker as an independent Medicaid provider.[54]

The Results of Self-Determination Demonstration Projects

A further move towards self-determination began in the early 1990s as a result of a large-scale demonstration project carried out by the Robert Wood Johnson Foundation (RWJF).[55] In 1993, under its national programme, Building Health Systems for People with Chronic Illnesses, the RWJF provided a demonstration (pilot study) grant to Monadnock Developmental Services based in Keene, New Hampshire, to test a new approach to the delivery of services to persons with developmental disabilities. Monadnock Developmental Services were at the time contracted by the state to administer services to eligible persons living in the south-west of the state. The three-year project, Self-Determination for People with Severe Mental Disabilities, gave individuals, along with their families and advocates, greater control over the services they received.

Under the grant, Monadnock changed the way it provided assistance to a group of forty-five individuals with developmental disabilities. It sought to test whether giving more control to those with developmental disabilities could improve their quality of life while reducing the cost of meeting their needs. The following guiding principles applied:

- Individuals controlled planning for their own support needs, with the assistance of family and friends they designated (often referred to as a circle of support).
- Individuals each controlled a sum of public money that they had the authority to spend on residential, vocational and personal needs.
- Individuals could contract directly for any and all services through individual contracts.
- Individuals could purchase supports from whomever they chose, rather than being limited to providers with whom Monadnock had contracted.

---

[54] *Ibid.*

[55] The RWJF is the United States' largest philanthropy devoted exclusively to health and health care. The foundation's sole purpose is to help US citizens to live healthier lives and get the health care they need. The foundation has significant resources – $10 billion in assets, generating grants approaching $500 million a year – to address the nation's most complex health and health care issues.

The results of this pilot were positive in terms of the personal outcomes and cost-effectiveness of the new funding mechanism. These evaluation findings are detailed towards the end of the chapter in the section on Evaluation and Cost-Effectiveness of Change. Building on the success of this first demonstration, in 1995 RWJF awarded a four-year $744,965 grant to New Hampshire to replicate the principles and structure of the Monadnock self-determination project statewide. In addition, at the end of 1995, the RWJF broadened its scope to help a further eighteen states[56] to implement a demonstration of this new approach.

Meanwhile, in 1998, another major demonstration project took place, this time established by a public/private partnership between the RWJF and the DHHS Office of the Assistant Secretary for Planning and Evaluation (ASPE), the Retirement Research Foundation (RRF) and the Administration on Aging (AoA). It was set up to test the operation of consumer-directed home and community-based care models on a similarly large scale. This was called the Cash and Counseling Demonstration and Evaluation (CCDE) and was set up in Arkansas, New Jersey and Florida (its subsequent programmes have been named the Cash and Counseling model [C&C], which has largely been based on the Consumer-Directed Care model in California, discussed earlier).[57]

The national CCDE project has had a major emphasis on research design and experimentation of programme approaches in order to establish a diverse array of programme and research outcomes whilst at the same time ensuring a scientific evaluation of the process. It used an experimental approach to randomise enrollees into a treatment or control group. Treatment group participants included elderly and younger Medicaid beneficiaries with significant long-term functional disabilities; family caregivers served as representatives, if necessary. The participants were able to self-direct their personal assistance services using a cash allowance to purchase services or items needed to meet their personal care needs.[58] Again, the findings from these evaluations in terms of the level of satisfaction, utilisation and expenditures proved positive and are discussed towards the end of the chapter.

Based on positive evaluation findings from the initial three states in the CCDE study, the partnership is now working on supporting the second phase of the programme, funding twelve additional states[59] to implement a C&C model. Numerous other states are also in the planning stage. Each C&C state has developed its own variation of the model and is using a different programme name; for example,

---

[56] List of states: Hawaii, Kansas, Maryland, Michigan Minnesota, Ohio, Texas, Vermont, Wisconsin, Arizona, Connecticut, Iowa, Oregon, Utah, Florida, Massachusetts, Pennsylvania and Washington.

[57] Cash & Counseling (2007) *Developing and Implementing Self-Direction Programs and Policies: A Handbook*, http://www.cashandcounseling.org/resources/handbook (accessed 14 June 2010).

[58] An equal number of recipients were randomised into a control group where they remained in the conventional service delivery programme.

[59] Expansion states: Alabama, Illinois, Iowa, Kentucky, Michigan, Minnesota, New Mexico, Pennsylvania, Rhode Island, Vermont, Washington and West Virginia.

Arkansas's programme is called Independent Choices, New Jersey's is called Personal Preference, and New Mexico's is called Mi Via (My Way). However, each state which received CCDE grants has to make programme design choices in accordance with the CCDE Vision Statement, principally that participants are allowed maximum flexibility and an individual budget. Self-determination programmes are based on a premise of cost neutrality, which requires federal funding to be no more than the institutional costs which would have been incurred for waiver participants.

The Americans with Disabilities Act and the Olmstead Case

The ADA was indirectly another key wellspring of reform, and represents a landmark federal piece of legislation guaranteeing people with disabilities the same rights to employment and access to public facilities as other citizens enjoy.[60] The ADA presented an opportunity to turn the corner on policies promoting welfare-like dependence and to develop supports for independence in the context of working, living and recreating in the mainstream. In this sense, implementing the ADA was seen as an opportunity to contribute to an improved economy.

Building on earlier protections under Section 504 of the Rehabilitation Act of 1973, the ADA extended antidiscrimination protections well beyond prior law, reaching private employment, publicly funded services and public accommodations, including services operated by private entities. Geographically, then, it was determined that not all states could be counted on to enact serious non-discrimination statutes. Therefore, the legislation moved disability policy towards a national, centralised position. The ADA language went to unusual lengths to specify coverage of state and local governments. It gained unusual widespread cross-political support in Congress and in the White House.[61]

Importantly, Title II of the ADA proscribed discrimination in the provision of public services, specifying, inter alia, that no qualified individual with a disability shall, 'by reason of such disability', be excluded from participation in, or be denied the benefits of, a public entity's services, programs or activities. Congress described the isolation and segregation of individuals with disabilities as a serious and pervasive form of discrimination under this Title of the ADA. It instructed the Attorney General to issue regulations implementing Title II's discrimination proscription. One such regulation, known as the 'integration regulation', requires a 'public entity

[60] Chatterjee, L. and Mitra, M. (1998). 'Evolution of Federal and State Policies for Persons with Disability in the United States: Efficiency and Welfare', *The Annals of Regional Science* 32(3): 347–365.

[61] Percy S. L. (2001) 'Disability Policy in the United States: Policy', in Cameron, D. and Fraser, V. (eds.) *Disability and Federalism: Comparing Different Approaches to Full Participation*. McGill-Queens University Press, London. pp. 231–268, at p. 252.

[to] administer ... programs ... in the most integrated setting appropriate to the needs of qualified individuals with disabilities'.[62]

This part of the ADA had a broader effect for all people with disabilities towards the end of the Clinton Administration, when a case was brought to the US Supreme Court in 1999 by two women who had been institutionalised, despite the fact that professionals had determined that they could be appropriately treated in a community setting. The *Olmstead* case (*Olmstead v. L.C.*, 527 U.S. 581 (1999)), as it became known, was a landmark in disability legislation. The Supreme Court held that the medically unjustifiable institutionalisation of persons with disabilities constituted a form of discrimination and therefore a violation of the ADA (1990). It ruled that when a state's own medical professionals reasonably conclude that an individual is able to reside in the community, the state must make 'reasonable modifications' to furnish community services in the most integrated setting unless the state can prove that to do so would require a 'fundamental alteration' of its programme. In essence, *Olmstead* required that states plan for and undertake two basic reforms: the broad and complex task of restructuring existing programmes and services in order to promote community integration, and the establishment of an individualised assessment process to design community placements.[63]

In *Olmstead*, Justice Ginsburg delivered the opinion of the court concluding that, under Title II of the ADA,

> states are required to place persons with mental disabilities in community settings rather than in institutions when the State's treatment professionals have determined that community placement is appropriate, the transfer from institutional care to a less restrictive setting is not opposed by the affected individual, and the placement can be reasonably accommodated, taking into account the resources available to the State and the needs of others with mental disabilities.[64]

As mentioned at the beginning of the chapter, with the separation of powers, the courts cannot make legislation which makes budget decisions for states. However, given the constitutional responsibilities of the Supreme Court, it is able to determine how Congress *meant* the ADA to apply, as well as how it should be interpreted to assure uniform policies in a top-down fashion. The ruling has stimulated many states to increase community-based alternatives to institutionalisation for people with disabilities of all ages, particularly people with intellectual disabilities. Evidence from state policies suggest that most states are moving ahead with planning and that in

---

[62] See Court Ruling, available at: http://www.laddc.org/main/wp-content/uploads/2008/12/ olmsteadsupremecourtdecision.pdf (accessed 4 March 2011).

[63] Rosenbaum, S. (2001) Olmstead v L.C.: *Implications for Family Caregivers*, Policy Brief No. 6, Family Caregiver Alliance, Washington, DC.

[64] See Court Ruling, available at: http://www.laddc.org/main/wp-content/uploads/2008/12/ olmsteadsupremecourtdecision.pdf (accessed 4 March 2011).

general, states' planning efforts are broad, based on their involvement of community stakeholders, public agencies and programmes.

In response to *Olmstead*, at the federal level, on 1 February 2001, President George W. Bush introduced the New Freedom Initiative, followed by the Executive Order 13217, affirming the United States' commitment to community-based alternatives and programmes that foster independence and participation in the community. This paved the way for a swift implementation of the Supreme Court's *Olmstead* decision to expand community-based services and community living choices for individuals regardless of age. Ten agencies submitted the first report, identifying barriers to full community integration which exist in federal programmes and proposing more than 400 solutions for removing these barriers.

The DHHS has also awarded nearly $158 million for the Real Choice Systems Change Grants for Community Living – a programme aimed to help states and territories to enable people with disabilities to reside in their homes if they wish.[65] Michigan, for example, used its Real Choice Change grant to establish the Person Focussed Quality Management Collaboration for its programme MI Choice. This brought providers and consumers together to design a Quality Outcome review methodology and to update the contract requirement documents and service standards which describe minimum standards for the operation of the waiver programme to assure better outcomes for waiver participants.

SHAPE OF REFORM

Following the wellsprings of reform described earlier, and the demonstrations which showed the benefits of consumer-directed supports for everyone regardless of type of impairment, the focus of the reform agenda has become centred on the guiding principle of self-determination, which, as we saw in Chapter 2, has become a key guiding principle of the UN CRPD. Put simply, the idea of self-determination refers to both the right and capacity of individuals to exert control over and direct their lives. According to the Center for Self-Determination,[66] the philosophy of a self-directed programme is that it allows:

- *Freedom* to decide how one wants to live his or her life;
- *Authority* over a targeted amount of dollars;
- *Support* to organize resources in ways that are life enhancing and meaningful to the individual;

---

[65] Please refer to: http://www.vor.net/Bush.htm (accessed 12 December 2010).

[66] The Center for Self-Determination is a non-profit organisation, established in 2000, operating as the primary information clearinghouse and a source of training and technical assistance on self-determination in the United States and other countries. The Center is devoted to working within the public and private sectors to move power and authority over resources directly to individuals with disabilities, their families and allies. See: http://www.centerforself-determination.com/ (accessed 8 June 2010).

- *Responsibility* for the wise use of public dollars and recognition of the contribution individuals with disabilities can make in their communities;
- *Confirmation* of the important role that self-advocates must play in a newly redesigned system.[67]

In practice, this has meant that the dollars the federal government provides now allow for much more individual autonomy in how the money is spent. The next part of the chapter examines how the United States has developed mechanisms for administering support to persons with disabilities to achieve this vision.

SHAPING THE DEMAND SIDE OF REFORM

This section examines how the United States has sculpted the demand side of reform, in terms of the new ways in which people can access supports, such as individual funding, care management advice and independent facilitation. It uses examples from some states which have pioneered self-directed supports such as Michigan, Wyoming and Wisconsin. Generally, the self-determination programmes use the mechanism of a broker or peer support worker to support individuals to create a personal support plan from a targeted allocation of public dollars. The models used also enable a process of accountability of where the public dollars are being spent. These models and their key design features are discussed in the following section.

New Policy Options for Self-Determination

As a result of the experiences and lessons learned from the states which participated in the demonstrations and pioneered the philosophy of consumer self-direction – as well as *Olmstead*'s preference for home- and community-based care options – on 9 May 2002, Secretary of Health and Human Services Tommy G. Thompson unveiled the Independence Plus initiative. This offered states simplified model waiver and demonstration application templates which would promote person-centred planning and self-directed service options. Importantly, this marked CMS's acceptance that the self-determination programmes outlined earlier afforded people with disabilities or their families the option to direct the design and delivery of services and supports, avoid unnecessary institutionalisation, provide higher levels of satisfaction and maximise the efficient use of community services and supports.

The guiding principles of a comprehensive self-directed programme, or Independence Plus programme, as stated by CMS are 'Person-centered planning, Individual budgeting, and Self-directed services and supports'.[68] The self-direction model that

---

[67] Nerney, T. (n.d.) *Centre for Self-Determination*, http://www.centerforself-determination.com/ (accessed 8 June 2010).

[68] CMS (n.d.) *Self-Directed Services*, https://www.cms.gov/CommunityServices/60_SelfDirected-Services.asp (accessed 3 May 2011).

has since emerged has two basic features, each with a number of variations. The more limited form of self-direction – which the CMS refers to as 'employer authority' – enables individuals to hire, dismiss and supervise individual workers (e.g. personal care attendants and homemakers). This is particularly relevant to persons with physical disabilities who prefer to manage their own support arrangements. The comprehensive model – which CMS refers to as 'budget authority' – provides participants with a flexible budget to purchase a range of goods and services to meet their needs. However, choice is the hallmark of self-direction and this includes the choice *not* to direct or to direct to the extent desired. It was recommended that programme designs should permit individuals to elect the conventional service model if self-direction does not work for them, or to direct some of their services but receive others from agency providers.[69]

At the time of this writing, there are eleven approved Independence Plus waivers in ten states, and several states are working with CMS to submit proposals.[70] Collectively, these states permit 34,456 individuals with long-term support needs to self-direct their services. In addition, there are the other state programmes, as a result of the demonstration projects, two other states with 1115 waiver self-direction demonstrations similar to C&C (Oregon and Colorado), and a multitude of states that offer self-directed programme options in their 1915(c) home- and community-based waivers. The Kaiser Commission on Medicaid and the Uninsured estimated that, in 2008, approximately 1.24 million Medicaid beneficiaries were receiving HCBS at home.[71] While there are no recent data on numbers of HCBS recipients using consumer-directed services, the Office of ASPE in the US DHHS estimated that, in 2004, roughly one third (400,000) of HCBS recipients directed their services (300,000 in California, 100,000 in the rest of the country).[72]

Since the Independence Plus initiative, two further steps have been taken in terms of simplifying the process of expanding consumer-driven approaches. First, the 2005 Deficit Reduction Act (DRA) stated that, as of January 2007, federally approved 'waivers' were no longer required for states to offer flexible budgets to eligible Medicaid consumers and their families so that they may purchase the disability services and supports of their choosing. It authorised states to include HCBS without having to obtain a waiver to provide such services. As a result,

---

[69] Cash & Counseling, *supra*, n. 57.

[70] California (1115 new waiver); Connecticut (1915(c) waiver); Delaware (1915(b)/(c) new waiver); Florida (1115 amendment to Cash and Counseling); Louisiana (1915(c) waiver); Maryland (1915(c) new waiver); New Hampshire (1915(c) waiver); New Jersey (1115 amendment to Cash and Counseling); North Carolina (1915(c) waiver); South Carolina (1915(c) waiver).

[71] The Kaiser Commission on Medicaid and the Uninsured (KCMU) and The University of California at San Francisco's (UCSF) analysis based on The Centers for Medicare & Medicaid Services (CMS) Form 372, December 2011, Table 5. "Medicaid 1915(c) Home and Community-Based Service Programs: Data Update" available at http://www.kff.org/medicaid/upload/7720-05.pdf (accessed 17 July 2012).

[72] Cash & Counseling, *supra*, n. 57.

many states have abandoned their plans to implement Medicaid waivers (although many are still being implemented). The DRA allows states to make changes that previously required a waiver through a simpler mechanism – 'state plan amendments'. So far, CMS has approved DRA-related state plan amendments for seven states: Idaho, Kansas, Kentucky, South Carolina, Virginia, Washington and West Virginia.[73]

Second, in 2010, the Affordable Care Act, passed by Congress and signed by the President on March 23, 2010, authorises a new section 1915(k) of the Social Security Act that allows states, at their option, to provide home and community-based attendant services and supports under their state plan and allows for the provision of services to be self-directed under either an agency-provider model, a self-directed model with service budget, or other service delivery model defined by the State and approved by the Secretary.[74] The Community First Choice (CFC) Option, as it is known, also offers the incentive of a 6 per cent increase in the federal Medicaid matching rate for states that provide community services as an alternative to institutional services for people with disabilities enrolled in Medicaid.

Because of these two pieces of legislation, few states perceive a need to request the Independence Plus designation because it no longer denotes a unique waiver programme. This is a positive sign because it indicates that self-direction is now an integral feature of HCBS programmes in many states. A significant number of states have since developed self-determination options within general HCBS programmes or as additional programmes. The new funding model has also allowed for the extension of the C&C programme across the fifteen states which were involved in the earlier demonstration. These funds come out of the same 'pot' as the general Medicaid funds and allow Medicaid beneficiaries to self-direct a budget and a wide array of services necessary to keep a person from being institutionalised in a hospital, nursing facility or ICF/MR.

To enable the process of partnership and shared learning amongst the C&C states, the National Participant Network (NPN) was established in June 2007. Its remit has been to improve sustainability, develop worker recruitment strategies and lessen differences in existing models (i.e. use of support brokers, fiscal management, etc.). It has also developed leadership and advocacy training, and consults with advocacy and advisory groups to hear participants' experiences.

Although a significant number of states by this time have successfully deinstitutionalised their disabled population, there nonetheless remain considerable numbers still in care facilities with 'institutional practices' such as nursing facilities and ICFs/MR. To speed up the process of movement of persons from institutions to the community,

---

[73] For state plan amendments, see *Families USA, Medicaid Deficit Reduction Act*, http://www.familiesusa.org/resource-centers/medicaid-action-center/dra-implementation.html (accessed 2 February 2011).

[74] Department of Health and Human Services (2012) Medicaid Program; Community First Choice Option; Final Rule, Federal Register, Rules and Regulations, 77(88) 7 May 2012.

a deinstitutionalisation programme called the Money Follows the Person (MFP) Demonstration was established. It is the most ambitious programme to date aimed at helping Medicaid enrollees to transition from institutions to the community. Since its inception, forty-three grantee states plus the District of Columbia provided transition services to 16,638 people who had been institutionalised for six months or more in nursing homes, psychiatric facilities and ICFs/MR.[75] While the MFP programme targets only a small percentage of the approximately one million people who could be eligible each year, the programme nonetheless has the potential to increase the rate of transition for people in long-term institutional care in the grantee states by 15 per cent to 40 per cent annually.[76] The aforementioned Affordable Care Act has now extended and enhanced the MFP programme, in order to continue helping people move out of institutions and into less costly, more independent, community-based settings.

The Individual Funding Allocation System

Many states now have developed self-determination programmes through creative uses of Medicaid funding, as allowed by the new policy options discussed earlier.[77] This has meant states have had to redesign their systems of distributing public funds and put in place mechanisms to ensure equity and accountability.

The C&C states allow participants to receive their support budget as a cash payment if they meet certain requirements. However, most prefer a non-cash individual budget. Many participants in the C&C receive a small portion of their benefit in cash, and a few other current programmes do authorise some portion of participants' budgets to be paid in cash. Sometimes this involves only small cash advances (e.g. for taxi fares) or reimbursements issued by a Financial Management Service (FMS) provider for goods and services – other than attendant care – specifically included in participants' approved spending plans.[78]

---

[75] Kaiser Commission on Medicaid and the Uninsured (2011) *Money Follows the Person: A 2011 Survey of Transitions, Services and Costs*, December 2011. Available at: http://www.kff.org/medicaid/upload/8142-02-2.pdf (accessed 30 September 2012).

[76] Wenzlow, A. T. and Lipson, D. J. (2009) *Transitioning Medicaid Enrollees from Institutions to the Community: Number of People Eligible and Number of Transitions Targeted Under MFP*, The National Evaluation of the Money Follows the Person (MFP) Demonstration Grant Program, Number 1, January, 2009.

[77] While individual budgets and self-determination have been promoted and developed largely for individuals with physical and intellectual disabilities, there are also programmes across the United States which offer self-determination for people with mental health difficulties. The Florida Self-Directed Care Program (FloridaSDC) was created in 2001 and was the first programme of its kind in the nation because it allowed the participant to control how the public mental health resources would be spent.

[78] Each participant agrees to a support and spending plan in advance, which is approved by a fiscal intermediary.

In these programmes, states have oversight over how participants spend the cash – they must say how they are planning to spend it in advance and often have to submit receipts to the FMS provider to document the expenditure. Under a new waiver – a 1915(j) self-directed personal assistance services (PAS) Medicaid State Plan option – states may elect to offer a cash option. It is not yet known how frequently the cash option will be offered, and, if offered, how many participants will take advantage of it. Of the four approved state plan amendments under this option, Alabama, Oregon and Arkansas have elected to offer a cash option.[79] These allow participants to hire friends and relatives as paid caregivers.

Generally, participants have a choice between being the common law employer of their workers and a fiscal/ employer agent to issue pay cheques and file payroll taxes. Alternatively, an organisation – such as a CIL, Area Agency on Aging or even a traditional licensed home care agency – may serve as co-employer. Usually a co-employing organisation serves as the 'employer of record' only for payroll and tax filing or other specific, narrowly defined purposes, while participants exercise the traditional employer prerogatives of hiring, training, scheduling, supervising and dismissing – if necessary – their employees.[80]

At a minimum, self-direction programmes must allow participants or their representative person or agency the employer authority to hire, manage and dismiss their support workers. This includes recruiting job candidates, interviewing applicants and checking their references (if applicants are not already well known to the participant), deciding who to hire, setting or negotiating workers' schedules and training needs, assigning tasks to workers, supervising and evaluating the quality of workers' job performance and deciding to dismiss workers whose performance is unsatisfactory.

If a state maintains a list of qualified 'individual providers' and requires participants to hire providers only from that list, this practice is not compatible, generally speaking, with self-direction (unless virtually any participant-hired worker can be immediately approved). As discussed further later in the chapter, participants do not have to be the legal 'employer of record' in order to direct their workers, but they must have a choice of their attendant worker or provider.

For individualised support options, allocating funding in a manner that equitably meets the needs of individuals is also an essential mechanism for allowing choice in one's own support. Policy makers are being confronted with the need to develop methodologies for equitable allocation of funding. State individual budgeting strategies generally employ one of three approaches to assessing an individual's needs. The first 'statistical' approach uses a standardised needs assessment tool to identify needs and, in some cases, set allocations. The second method can be described as a 'developmental' approach which identifies and evaluates the needs to be supported through the person-centred planning process, relying on the members of the

---

79 Cash & Counseling, *supra*, n. 57.
80 *Ibid.*

individual's programme-planning team or 'circle of support' to select the essential objectives to be achieved. The third method combines elements of the previous two approaches to inform decisions of the circle of support and individual programme-planning team.

Approximately one-third of states have used standardised tools to assess support needs and use data-based procedures for calculating the amount of funding to be allocated to the individual. These states typically use statistical processes based on standardised tools, such as the Inventory for Client and Agency Planning (ICAP) or the Developmental Disabilities Profile (DDP) created by third-party agencies,[81] or other state-specific instruments to determine the individual funding allocation or target budget. In the individual budgeting process, states determine the rates they will reimburse service providers in several ways, including:

- Statistical means that set rates of reimbursement through the application of statistical methodologies that weigh a number of cost- and service-related variables in the development of specific or all-inclusive payment amounts;
- Preset cost or service ranges established by the state and enforced through regulation, waiver programme policy and procedures, negotiation with provider entities or any of a number of other means;
- The establishment of rates and service amounts based on a determination of the actual costs the provider is expected to incur based on past performance or expenditure history.[82]

Self-directed systems of support must be flexible in order to encompass the wide range of different activities offered by both conventional (e.g. day care) and nonconventional (consumer-directed) services.[83]

According to Mosely (2005), almost 70 per cent of the states responding to their survey reported that individual budgets were derived through the second approach – a 'developmental' process based on an individual assessment of the person's needs for support and assistance.[84] The introduction of individualised budgeting, according to a respondent in a demonstration evaluation (1997), was the true turning point in the system's move towards self-determination: 'The individual budget got us away from the insideousness of rate setting that Medicaid had created, and it got us out of the averaging notion. So that when you said how much does it cost to support a person

---

[81] For an example, please refer to: http://www.riversidepublishing.com/products/icap/index.html (accessed 7 December 2011).

[82] Moseley, C., Gettings, R. and Cooper, R. (2003) *Having it Your Way: Understanding State Individual Budgeting Strategies.* National Association of State Directors of Developmental Disabilities Services, Alexandria, VA.

[83] *Ibid.*

[84] Moseley, C., Gettings, R. and Cooper, R. (2005) 'Having It Your Way: Individual Budgeting Practices within the States', in *supra*, n. 42.

who looks like this or fits in that box, as defined by Medicaid, we used averages and rates'.[85]

One example of a 'developmental' approach is Wyoming's DOORS model. Wyoming moved from a five-level payment system to a model based on each person's objectively assessed individual characteristics and his or her service utilisation. This directly provides a unique Individual Budget Amount (IBA) to pay for that individual's supports.[86] According to Fortune et al. (2004), compared to the situation prior to the introduction of DOORS, when the five-level system was used, the proportion of variability in individual funding associated with individual characteristics rose from 37 per cent to 47 per cent and the proportion of variability explained by the total DOORS model increased from 52 per cent to 75 per cent.[87] This substantial increase in the association between individual service users' assessed support needs and the amounts of funding provided to meet those needs indicates that the DOORS model successfully made Wyoming's HCBS funding system more individually tailored.

Role of Independent Planning and Fiscal Intermediary Support

Considering the new responsibilities being given to individuals to govern and manage their own supports, states departments or intermediaries which administer self-direction programmes generally offer independent planning and facilitation services. For people with physical or sensory disabilities, the extent of support planning required is related to their individual preferences and capacity. Generally, people prefer to make their own choices unaided (or with some facilitation managing the budget), but the option should remain open and accessible for all. For many people with intellectual disabilities, support planning is often a key piece of the self-directed community support model.

The facilitation model in the United States is based on having access to an independent consultant (IC) and fiscal intermediary (discussed later in the chapter). The IC enables and assists participants to identify and access a personalised mix of paid and non-paid services and supports which will assist him/her in achieving personally defined outcomes in the most inclusive community settings. Once the individuals are assessed and know what their budget amount is, they must develop a support plan. This identifies self-defined outcomes and the training, supports, therapies, treatments and/or other services, which become part of the person-centred plan. The support plan includes all the services and supports which will be purchased

---

[85] Yuskauskas, A., Conroy, J. and Elks, M. (1997) *Live Free or Die: A Qualitative Analysis of Systems Change in the Monadnock Self Determination Project*, submitted to the Robert Wood Johnson Foundation National Initiative Self Determination for Persons with Developmental Disabilities.

[86] Please refer to Stancliffe, R. J. and Lakin, K. C. (eds.), *supra*, n. 42.

[87] Fortune, J. R., Smith, G. A., Campbell, E. M., Clabby, R., Heinlein, K. B. et al. (2005) 'Individual Budgets According to Individual Needs: The Wyoming DOORS System', in Stancliffe, R. J. and Lakin, K. C. (eds.), *supra*, n. 42.

with the person's budget. The person may develop this plan on their own or with help from a family member, friend or IC (some programmes use terms such as 'support broker', 'consultant', 'advisor' or 'flexible case manager' to describe the facilitation role). This plan must be approved by the case manager or representative before the eligible recipient can begin receiving services or buying goods.[88]

With other forms of self-direction, (e.g. C&C), IC is carried out by professionals who have previously worked in case management and continue to perform eligibility assessments. They act as financial gatekeepers by establishing the amount of the cash benefit payment, based on a client's severity of disability and related needs for assistance; however, their role changes to that of a counsellor or coach. In this instance, person-centred planning is a process, directed by the participant, with assistance as needed from the counsellor. The counsellor's primary function is to help participants to develop the skills necessary to self-direct. According to a policy advisor at the DHHS: 'With Cash and Counseling workers, instead of focusing on diagnosis and prescribing a treatment plan, they are increasingly focusing on finding out what the person wants to do with their life and counseling them toward this'.[89]

In terms of supporting the capacity of the disabled person to make these decisions, the person-driven planning process is intended to identify the strengths, capacities, preferences, needs and desired outcomes of the participant. The process may include other individuals freely chosen by the participant who are able to serve as important contributors to the planning process.

For those with physical disabilities, professionals still have a role in performing eligibility assessments and acting as financial gatekeepers. However, the life-planning piece becomes largely optional, depending on a person's capacity and individual preferences. The focus here becomes more about removing barriers to participation than creating an elaborate life plan. The CILs in the United States have also adopted this role. They often provide facilitation services and advocacy to promote the leadership and independence of individuals. This means that they can deal with all the money and financial requirements such as payroll and assure that all taxes are filed and paid to the appropriate governmental agencies.

When an individual receives an individual budget, a fiscal intermediary (FI) can help to guide the person through unfamiliar territory, making sure that he or she has accounted for all the different taxes and expenses involved in hiring a personal assistant. They will help the person to advertise for new employees. They will also give tips to conduct interviews. When the support services are up and running, the FI collects timesheets and distributes pay cheques on the person's behalf. More generally, they will help an individual to keep track of the amount of public dollars

---

[88] It is currently a requirement of the CMS that customers wishing to hire their support staff directly utilize the services of an FI. For an example of a state model, see Minnesota Department of Community Services (2005) *Consumer Directed Community Supports, Consumer Handbook*, http://edocs.dhs.state.mn.us/lfserver/Legacy/DHS-4317-ENG (accessed 15 January 2011).

[89] Personal communication, interview quote from meeting, June 2009.

the individual is spending in a month, and notify the client when he or she goes over budget.

In most programmes, the funds in a person's budget go directly to the FI. Therefore, choosing an FI is one of the most important decisions a person makes in his or her support plan. Essentially, the FI will be someone available for questions or concerns. There are several qualities which are generally recommended by FI agencies, including accessibility, tax knowledge, ability to communicate, broad experience and flexibility. As well as providing support to the individual, the FI provides an important mechanism to ensure accountability for public money whilst opening up flexibility room within the sector to innovate. FI's are either paid separately by the state government in some states, such as Wisconsin, or through a percentage of the budget, as in Michigan.

One example of how this system operates in practice is Wisconsin's HCBS waiver for individuals with physical and developmental disabilities as well as older individuals who qualify for support called IRIS (Include, Respect, I Self-direct), which began 1 July 2008. Individuals are offered the choice of IRIS or managed care when they enter the state publicly funded long-term care system. Persons using IRIS are able to self-manage their goods and services and may use IRIS to remain in their community and avoid moving into a nursing home or an institution. With IRIS, adults have control over the type of services they receive in home and community settings and can use their individual budget for functional, vocational, medical and social needs.

The process starts with individuals selecting their own IRIS Independent Consultant with help from the IRIS Independent Consultant Agency and FI from the IRIS Financial Services Agency. IRIS participants then create a support and service plan for their long-term supports and services within an individually assigned monthly budget allocation. In IRIS, the individual may hire support workers directly or may purchase goods and services from a provider. The Financial Services Agency pays the bills for services received which the person authorises according to the written IRIS plan. The monthly budget allocation may be adjusted based on an individual's unique circumstances. Help from both of these IRIS sub-agencies is provided at no cost to the person's plan and monthly budget. Individuals may enlist the help of a support broker if desired, and support broker fees are paid out of their individual monthly budget allocation.

Another example of self-direction is found in Michigan's HCBS system, where self-direction has long been an option in their programmes, MI Choice and Home Help, administered through the state Department of Community Health.[90] The MI Choice programme is targeted to persons with disabilities, aged eighteen and older, and to persons aged sixty-five or older who are in need of supportive services and

[90] See Granholm, J. and Olszewski, J. (2009) *Michigan Profile of Publicly-Funded Long-term Care Services*. Michigan Department of Community Health.

choose to receive those services in their home or other community setting. Individuals participating in the self-determination option can choose from an extensive list of support options as well as FI Services and 'goods and services' including equipment and supplies which are authorised in the participant's plan. Home Help is an optional state plan which was created in 1982 and allows individuals to recruit, hire, train and fire their own support workers. They can choose friends, neighbours, relatives or employees of a home care agency; spouses, responsible relatives, or their legal dependents are not reimbursed. Otherwise, they can also use local Department of Human Services registered office or Michigan Quality Community Care Council for registered workers who have had criminal background checks and training.

Service providers, such as the Community Living Network Michigan (CLN), have responded to this new climate of self-determination by offering FI services to adults in Michigan under the MI Choice programme. CLN also works closely with the support coordinators and family members, offering help at every step of the way. At a planning meeting, they are told their options regarding available supports, including the option of becoming an employer of their own PA. The FI helps to determine how many hours the staff can work, what the related costs will be, and what the individual can afford to pay the staff per hour and arrange for the necessary criminal background checks.[91]

Supported Decision Making

To enable all persons with disabilities to exercise the right of self-determination – and be recognised to have decision-making capacity and a personal identity – the importance of having supported decision-making mechanisms available is crucial as articulated by the CRPD. For the intellectual disability population, for example, this may be essential to enable as much autonomous decision making as possible.

Traditionally, guardianship was the sole mechanism used to substitute a person's decision-making capacity. A court appoints an individual (called the guardian or conservator) to protect the person or property of an individual (referred to as the ward). Full guardianship is when a 'Guardian of the Person' or a 'Guardian of the Estate' – or both – is appointed by the court, and the court does not limit the powers of the guardian in the area in which they are appointed. Full guardianship is used only when the court deems that it is not realistic for the ward to retain rights and duties because he/she is unable to care for his/her property or self.

Guardianship is a very restrictive legal mechanism as decisions over a person's capacity are thought to be all or nothing; one either has legal capacity (or is competent) or one does not (or is not competent), and if one is not, he or she needs

---

[91] The FI can also provide the individual with an Employee Packet which outlines required training and where it is offered, as well as forms to conduct criminal background and driver's license checks.

a guardian to substitute as a decision maker.[92] This takes away valuable personal rights and as such should never be taken lightly. It is deemed very restrictive for persons with disabilities or mental health issues, as it removes the full personhood and self-determination of the individual and the right to have a choice in their supports and services. In many cases, with the proper supports and services, guardianship is unnecessary.

In the United States, guardianship has always been an area of state law; there is no one guardianship law nationwide, although many states have adopted in one form or another the Uniform Guardianship and Protective Proceedings Act of 1997.[93] Many state statutes emphasise that guardianship should not be used unless it is the least restrictive means to protect the interests of the allegedly incapacitated person. Indeed, many policy makers and advocates increasingly argue, in the United States and abroad, for supported decision making rather than the surrogate or substitute decision making which characterises guardianship.[94]

It is now understood in the United States that capacity is contextual (decision-dependent as well as individual-dependent) and potentially fluid; a person without capacity in one realm (e.g. health care decision making) may well have capacity in another (e.g. decision making about residence), and a person without capacity today can receive training and be exposed to experiences which will enable him or her to have capacity tomorrow.[95] As such, alternatives to guardianship are generally recommended in the United States before the initiation of guardianship of the person, of the estate, or both. Alternatives include limited guardianship; power of attorney and durable power of attorney; health care power of attorney; Advance Instruction for Mental Health Treatment (AIMHT); social, habilitation, case management and advocacy supports; circle of friends; representative payee for Social Security and other pensions/benefits; and dual signature bank accounts or trust.[96]

With limited guardianship, the ward retains more rights than in a full guardianship, except for the specific rights granted to the guardian. As with full guardianship, however, the individual is adjudicated incompetent. The court is willing, however, to consider tailoring guardianship to the abilities of an individual.[97] In other states, different variations of limited guardianship exist. In Michigan, two types of guardian

---

[92] Fager, S., Hancox, D., Ely, C., Stenhjem, P. and Gaylord, V. (eds.) (2010). *Impact: Feature Issue on Sexuality and People with Intellectual, Developmental and Other Disabilities*, Spring/Summer 23(2). University of Minnesota, Institute on Community Integration, Minneapolis.

[93] Dinerstein, R. D. (2006) 'Guardianship and Its Alternatives', in Pueschel, S. (ed.) *Adults with Down Syndrome*. Paul H. Brookes Publishing, Baltimore. pp. 235–258.

[94] United Nations (2006) *Article 12. Convention on the Rights of Persons with Disabilities*.

[95] Dinerstein, R. D., Herr, S. S. and O'Sullivan, J. L. (eds.) (1999). *A Guide to Consent*. American Association on Mental Retardation (AAIDD), Washington, DC.

[96] Please refer to: http://www.arcnc.org (accessed 7 June 2011).

[97] For example, see The Arc, Dane County, Wisconsin, available at: www.arcdanecounty.org/faq.html (accessed 4 June 2011).

exist: a plenary guardian is appointed when the individual is developmentally disabled and is deemed to be 'totally without the capacity to care for himself'. All the
legal rights that formerly belonged to the individual with developmental disabilities
now belong to the plenary guardian. Meanwhile, a partial guardian is appointed
when the individual is developmentally disabled and is deemed to 'lack the capacity
to do some of the tasks necessary to care for himself'. The protected person keeps
all legal and civil rights except those that have, by court order, been granted to the
partial guardian. If medical care is a responsibility of the partial guardian, this would
have to be stated in a letter of guardianship.[98]

The durable power of attorney (POA) for health care or for finances provides
the opportunity to limit guardianship solely to these elements of a person's life.
Health care decisions include the power to consent, refuse consent or withdraw
consent to any type of medical care, treatment, service or procedure. There is also
the opportunity to make advance directives prior to being deemed incapable, which
might arise from a disabling condition or mental illness. Advance directives put into
writing the type of medical care or decisions one wants made if one is no longer
able to communicate them oneself. Meanwhile, a POA for finance lets individuals
identify another person to make health care decisions for them if they become
unable to communicate what they want.

At the federal level, in terms of decision making with regard to federal benefits,
the Social Security Administration (SSA) can appoint a representative payee for
someone who receives SSI or SSDI benefits if this would be in the person's best
interests because of mental or physical incapacity. Appointing a representative payee
avoids having to define a person's legal incompetence and is limited to only handling
the funds from the government benefits. The payee is to use the money for the
person's benefit and is accountable to the SSA on how the funds are used.

Finally, a dual signature account offers a less restrictive alternative to full conservatorship (a conservator is responsible for making all decisions about the financial
affairs of the ward). On the other hand, dual signature accounts are another method
often used where a trusted friend or family member's name is added to the individual's account. Both persons on the account have ownership of the account, so
great caution should be taken.[99] There is also the opportunity to establish a limited
conservatorship, which is an arrangement like what is described earlier but gives only
those specific powers which are set out in the court order. By doing this, the court
agrees that in all other matters, the ward can still make his or her own decisions.

These options offer a variety of choices for individuals and families which are
less restrictive than full guardianship or ward of court. Limited guardianship, in

---

[98] University of Michigan, Health System (n.d.) *Guardianship*, available at: www.med.umich.edu/
1toolbar/Billing/Guardianship.pdf (accessed 15 February 2011).

[99] The Substitute Decision Makers Task Force for the Iowa Department of Elder Affairs (2001) *Alternatives to Guardianship and Conservatorship for Adults in Iowa*, available at: http://www.state.ia.us/
ddcouncil/Alternatives%20booklet.doc (accessed 15 February 2011).

particular, can ensure that the person loses only those decision-making areas that a court explicitly identifies in the order appointing the limited guardian. Under a limited guardianship, the lawyer for the allegedly incapacitated person (the adult with a disability) can make sure that the individual retains the right to make decisions about, for example, whom he or she wants to live with, sexual relationships, birth control, and other intimate matters.[100] Thus families or allies who can act in the person's best interest can give more opportunity to the individual to retain his or her personhood. This has important implications for persons in choosing the supports which best suit their wishes and goals. These options enable individuals to retain the right to make some decisions; nonetheless, they do not go as far as some other supported decision-making mechanisms used in other jurisdictions such as 'Representation Agreements' in Canada (as detailed in the following chapter). Representation agreements ensure that the 'representative' (a close friend or personal advocate) must endeavour to listen to the person even if he or she does not have sufficient capacity on his or her own to make the decision involved, based on the understanding that the individual will undoubtedly be able to have some opinion about the decision and can process some of the relevant information.

Enabling a Choice in Living Arrangements

Another key area of demand-side reform has been the policy options and other mechanisms used to enable people to have a choice in living arrangements. The CILs have played a key role across the United States in helping people to move out of traditional residential support settings. For example, ARISE in Syracuse, New York, is a CIL which, as part of its ethos, provides support to people looking for independent living options in the community. It provides a residential habilitation coordinator who works with individuals and families to develop an individualised residential services plan to help individuals to achieve their personal goals. Each person receives one-on-one training in the home to enhance independent living skills, such as personal care, preparing a meal and household tasks and health and personal safety. The individuals also have the opportunity to integrate more fully in their community by attending outings that interest them.

ARISE's Housing Search Assistance also helps people to secure affordable, accessible housing. It provides a list of available accessible housing, advice on talking with landlords, help applying for housing support, such as Section 8 rent subsidy (discussed later), as well as information and referrals to other support services. It also provides housing advocacy assistance for people who face disability-related discrimination or are having trouble securing accessible housing. Housing advocates are

---

[100] States such as California, New York and Vermont, for example, go further and specifically recognise in their statutes or regulations that the incapacitated person retains decision-making rights regarding sexual and social relationships unless a court orders otherwise (and sometimes not even then).

also available to deal with landlords who are not willing to accept a person's service or companion animal, as well as offer referrals to community programmes that help with security deposits, paying back utility and phone bill balances and providing moving assistance.

To increase homeownership rates for people with disabilities, the federal government has a programme that permits people with disabilities to use rent subsidy vouchers to make mortgage payments to buy their own homes. The Housing Choice Voucher Program is a type of federal assistance provided by the US Department of Housing and Urban Development (HUD), dedicated to sponsoring subsidised housing for low-income families and individuals. It is more commonly known as 'Section 8', in reference to the portion of the US Housing Act of 1937 under which the original subsidy programme was authorised.

To increase the availability of accessible and affordable housing for individuals with disabilities, the federal government awarded a major national outreach grant as part of the 2001 New Freedom Initiative to help communities to ensure that more apartments are built to be accessible to people with disabilities.[101] The DHHS also awarded a series of grants totaling $119 million to states for the design and implementation of reforms to promote community living. In addition, it launched a programme through the HUD to provide training and technical assistance to the building industry on the Fair Housing Act's (1988 amendment) accessible design and construction requirements.

Currently, the main Section 8 programme involves a voucher programme. Under the voucher programme, individuals or families find and lease a unit (either in a specified complex or in the private sector) and pay a portion of the rent (based on income, but generally no more than 30 per cent of the family's income). The Public Housing Authority pays the landlord the remainder of the rent over the tenant's portion, subject to a cap known as fair market rent (FMR), which is determined by the HUD. The FMR is determined by several factors, including the geographic area (city or county) where the unit is located (generally, a unit in a metropolitan area will have a higher FMR) and the unit size. People with disabilities are then able to pay their percentage of the rent through their SSI benefit or other available funds.

The landlord cannot charge a Section 8 tenant more than FMR and cannot accept payments outside the contract which would cause the total rent to exceed FMR. Landlords, however, are not required to participate in the Section 8 programme. Some choose not to because of such factors as not wanting the government involved in their business, having a full inspection of their premises, a fear that a Section 8 tenant will not properly maintain the premises, or a desire to charge a rent for

---

[101] For the New Freedom Initiative, please refer to Bush White House (2002) *New Freedom Initiative: A Progress Report*, http://www.policyalmanac.org/social_welfare/archive/new_freedom_initiative_2.shtml (accessed 1 February 2012).

the unit above FMR. On the other hand, other landlords willingly accept Section 8 tenants because of the generally prompt regular payments from the Public Housing Authority for its share of the rent, a perceived higher quality of tenants, and a large available pool of potential renters (the waiting list for new Section 8 tenants is usually very long; see discussion later in the chapter).[102]

Section 8 subsidies generally take three forms: project-based, tenant-based, and sponsor-based. These are detailed more comprehensively by the Corporation for Supportive Housing.[103] Project-based subsidies are those that are 'attached' to particular housing units. The project sponsor receives an amount of funds for each subsidised housing unit, equal to the difference between the tenant portion and the FMR. For this reason, project-based subsidies are generally not portable – when a tenant moves, the subsidy remains with the unit. Project-based subsidies generally tend to be used for single-site projects, with the subsidy attaching to some or all of the units in a building.

Tenant-based subsidies attach to an individual or family. With this type of subsidy, the tenant receives the entitlement to a Section 8 voucher that allows him or her to rent a unit in the private market from either for-profit or non-profit owners. Similar to the project-based type of subsidy, the tenant is responsible for the tenant portion and the owner of the property is reimbursed for the difference between the tenant portion and the FMR. Unlike most project-based subsidies, however, tenant-based subsidies remain with the tenant when and if he/she chooses to move.

Finally, a *sponsor-based* subsidy attaches to a specific housing sponsor, typically a non-profit housing developer or supportive-housing provider. The sponsor may use the subsidy to subsidise any unit the sponsor controls, either through ownership or leasing. As with the other forms of subsidy, the sponsor receives an amount of funds for each subsidised unit, equal to the difference between the tenant portion and the FMR. When the tenant in a sponsor-based unit moves, he or she does not retain the subsidy – it remains with the sponsor. Sponsor-based subsidies are moveable in the sense that the sponsor may choose to move the subsidy from one unit to another.

Section 8 also sets aside a programme called the Mainstream Program Vouchers for People with Disabilities. Under this programme, the HUD awards local housing agencies special allocations of Section 8 tenant-based vouchers for people with disabilities through a competitive application process. These programmes are highly competitive, and the housing authority is strongly encouraged to partner with non-profit social service providers to deliver services to the households receiving the vouchers.

---

[102] Please refer to Corporation for Supportive Housing at: http://www.csh.org/index.cfm?fuseaction=Page.viewPage&pageID=3340 (accessed 7 December 2010).
[103] *Ibid.*

However, despite commitments of renewed support in 2003,[104] individuals who wish to receive a tenant-based subsidy must place their name on a waiting list and wait for an extended period of time before receiving a voucher. Because the eligibility criteria for Section 8 are relatively broad (any family with children, senior or disabled person earning at or below 50 per cent of median income is eligible) and funding for new vouchers very limited, waiting lists tend to be very long – it is not uncommon for applicants to wait five years or more for assistance – and are often closed for extended periods of time. One of the greatest challenges for persons with disabilities in the United States, according to the National Council on Disability, is the ability to afford housing: an estimated 14.4 million households with at least one person with a disability cannot afford their housing – this is 41 per cent of all households with disabilities.[105] This remains a core challenge for those wanting to move from segregated care settings.

Enhancing Consumer Purchasing Power

While the previously mentioned reforms represent new ways in which the federal and state governments are restoring power to the consumer, a further mechanism is being developed which poses a radically new approach to enhancing consumer purchasing power, which will help to put people in a better position to purchase the supports they need. An asset-building initiative has been introduced to encourage individuals and families to acquire, accumulate and preserve long-term assets. More generally, it will also allow individuals to overcome issues of funding shortfalls which appear to arise almost cyclically in the United States, which exacerbate many of the problems affecting states, namely the funding to pay for qualified workers available to families.[106]

The United States has initiated legislation to begin offering an incentive to encourage asset building. Research has shown that these savings can enable individuals to bridge short-term cash flow gaps and provide a crucial buffer against life emergencies such as job losses, income reductions, illness or disability.[107] As such, savings and

---

[104] These voucher schemes got renewed support by the Bush administration in a report, entitled *Delivering on the Promise: Preliminary Report of Federal Agencies' Actions to Eliminate Barriers and Promote Community Integration*, in which President Bush requested $40 million in the FY 2003 budget for the Department of Housing and Urban Development to fund approximately 6,000 Section 8 tenant-based rental vouchers for non-elderly disabled families, with an additional $6 million for the Department of Housing and Urban Development to fund 1,000 Section 8 rental subsidy vouchers for people with disabilities who are transitioning from institutions into the community.

[105] National Council on Disability (2010) *The State of Housing in America in the 21st Century: A Disability Perspective*. January.

[106] Gray L. and Feinberg L. F. (2003) *Survey of Californians About In-home Care Services*, March, Family Caregiver Alliance, California.

[107] Lopez-Fernandini, A. (2010) *Unrestricted Savings: Their Role in Household Economic Security and the Case for Policy Action*, New America Foundation, February 15.

other financial assets are often viewed as a source of financial security and economic independence.

The Achieving a Better Life Experience (ABLE) Act of 2011[108] proposes the creation of a savings instrument with significant tax advantages, often called the 'ABLE account', for the support of family members with disabilities and for other purposes. It is designed to encourage savings amongst individuals with disabilities and their families and friends and allow the individual to achieve and maintain a level of financial independence. Incomes earned on amounts contributed to the ABLE account are tax-exempt; withdrawals are also tax-exempt, as long as the funds are used to pay for qualified disability-related expenses.[109] It is believed that these tax-advantaged savings tools will encourage and facilitate savings amongst individuals with disabilities and their families and allow them to build financial resources to achieve and maintain independence and good quality of life. Most importantly, assets in ABLE accounts would supplement, but not replace, benefits provided by other sources, and thus having an ABLE account does not affect an individual's eligibility for other government programmes, such as Medicaid or SSI.[110]

SHAPING THE SUPPLY SIDE OF REFORM

In addition to the aforementioned demand-side approaches to restoring power to the consumer, the United States has also taken a number of steps to try and inject market forces into state/service arrangements, such as competitive tendering, insisting on standards and forcing providers to compete for funding.

The Awarding of Medicaid Funding to Shape the Market

At the federal level, the CMS develops mandates and requirements for the use of Medicaid funds. Within states, the state department responsible for disability support establishes policy guidelines to address the CMS requirements for statewide or county waiver agencies which implement the policy. County waiver agencies in turn are responsible for assuring that all Medicaid waiver service providers meet

---

[108] At the time of this writing (1 February 2012), this bill was at committee stage, the first step in the legislative process.

[109] The list of qualifying disability-related expenses is exhaustive and broad, covering the majority of everyday life expenses. Withdrawals used to pay for the following expenses for the benefit of the designated beneficiary are not subject to federal taxation: education including tuition from pre-school to post-secondary education; housing, including rent or mortgage payments and modifications; transportation including use of mass transit, purchase or modification of vehicles; and employment support including job-related training, assistive technology and personal assistance supports.

[110] Le, H. (2010) *Avoiding the Poverty Trap and Achieving Economic Empowerment for Persons with Disabilities: An Analysis of the United States Legislative Initiative 'Achieving A Better Life Experience' ('Able') Bill of 2009*. Centre For Disability Law & Policy Quarterly Policy Briefing No. 3, National University of Ireland.

the standards established in the state's Medicaid Waivers Manual[111] for the specific service for which they claim payment.

To facilitate choice, states generally offer a managed care option and a self-directed support option. For example, Wisconsin's disability programmes, which are administered by the Wisconsin Department of Health Services' Division of Long Term Care, have a managed care option (Family Care) and a self-directed support option (IRIS) which was discussed earlier.

For the managed care option, generally, the awarding of funding is given by MCOs, in which services can invoice their MCO for a particular volume and type of service offered. In this way, block grants can still exist, although there is now a move towards providers invoicing the MCO for services rendered. MCOs have detailed contracts with the state and are continually given policy guidelines they need to implement or follow. MCOs must establish and maintain provider networks that have the capacity to provide timely and quality services to members.

In terms of competitive tendering, support providers must become Medicaid certified by CMS and must undergo a 'Request for Proposals' (RFP) process with the MCO in the state in order to win a contract to operate. All Medicaid waiver service providers must also execute a State Medicaid Agency (SMA) Provider Agreement and register online with the state department. Contracts are awarded using a process that follows federal and state regulations and CMS programme guidelines. There is a renewal process of the RFP every year for providers.

The RFP is an early stage in the procurement process, issuing an invitation for providers, often through a bidding process, to submit a proposal on a specific service. The RFP process brings structure to the procurement decision and allows the risks and benefits to be identified clearly upfront. Requests for proposals typically reflect the strategy and short/long-term objectives, providing detailed insight upon which suppliers will be able to offer a matching perspective.[112]

For self-directed programmes, there are no MCOs, although some states have an 'allowable spending list' which defines the broad range of goods and services which can be purchased. Providers are funded through the state self-directed programme agency, usually an intermediary of the relevant state department. They are generally only paid through invoices to the FI. For example, in Wisconsin, IRIS has two primary contracts which are made based on an RFP from the state Department of Human Services. One is for the fiscal services and the other is for the IC agency which hires the 'planning consultants'. This means that there is one IC company and one fiscal company for the entire state. This differs from other states, such as Minnesota, which has learned that a choice and selection of regulated fiscal

---

[111] See, for example, Wisconsin Department of Health Services (2010) *Chapter IV: Allowable Services and Provider Requirements*.

[112] Wheaton, G. (2008) *Request for Proposal*, http://www.epiqtech.com (accessed 21 November 2011).

intermediary agencies and 'flexible case management' offering support broker services present a better choice.[113]

Overall, this approach has many built-in requirements and policy guidelines which help to shape the overall market approach and encourage supply-side reform. In particular, providers which offer support to self-determination clients must offer assistance with finding, hiring/firing staff, conducting criminal background checks, billing and paying taxes and support planning, if required. An important aspect of this is the insistence and enforcement of standards, as detailed in the following section.

Insisting on Standards and Regulation of Sector

Regardless of whether market forces are injected, the United States has a strict enforcement of standards for federal programmes, as well as Medicaid procurement agencies and providers. There are four levels of standards and regulations, as illustrated in Table 4.4.

At the federal level, the Office of Inspector General (OIG) has a number of standards to protect the integrity of the DHHS programmes. It is responsible for undertaking internal control assessments of the department's grant award and monitoring processes, and issues recipient capability audits. Through these activities, the OIG independently and objectively provides DHHS with vital information regarding the ability of grantees to manage large grant awards and ensure the integrity of these significant expenditures.[114] This work, however, is largely focussed on financial fraud and is carried out through a nationwide network of audits, investigations and inspections conducted by the different operating components.

The federal government also investigates whether a state's Medicaid authority makes any regulatory violations. For example, in Tennessee, the OIG recommended that the state authority should increase its contracting and monitoring oversight to include tracking documents through the award process, maintaining contracting records, establishing a system to ensure that contracts are monitored in a timely manner, and retaining monitoring reports.[115]

The CMS also provides a monitoring role at the federal level through its Federal Coordinated Health Care Office (Medicare-Medicaid Coordination Office). The Office works with the Medicaid and Medicare programmes across federal agencies, states and stakeholders to align and coordinate benefits between the two programmes

---

[113] This operates under the 'Personal Care Assistance Choice' option. See: https://www.revisor.mn.gov/statutes/?id=256b.0659 (accessed 31 January 2012).

[114] See Office of Inspector General (2010) *Semi-Annual Report 2010*, http://oig.hhs.gov/publications/sar/2010/fall2010_semiannual.pdf (accessed 12 January 2011).

[115] See Office of Inspector General site at: http://oig.hhs.gov/oas/reports/region4/40303025.pdf (accessed 12 January 2011).

TABLE 4.4. *Levels of monitoring standards in US disability support provision*

	Inspecting body	Function
Federal	Federal Office of Inspector General	Undertakes internal control assessments of the DHHS grant awards and monitoring processes
	Center for Medicare and Medicaid Services (CMS) – Federal Coordinated Health Care Office (Medicare-Medicaid Coordination Office)	The Office works with the Medicaid and Medicare programmes, across federal agencies, states and stakeholders to align and coordinate benefits between the two programmes to ensure they operate more effectively and efficiently. It partners with states to develop new support models and improve the way Medicare-Medicaid enrollees receive health care and support.
State	State Departments	Generally oversees Section 1915(c)(b) and 1115 Waivers
	State Medicaid Authority (MCOs, waiver agents, county-wide HCBS commissioning bodies, etc.)	Monitors support providers with annual assessments to check compliance with the standards contained in the State Medicaid Provider Manual
	Private Monitoring intermediaries	The State Medicaid Authority often uses private intermediaries contracted by the relevant state department to undertake provider accreditation and standards certification.

to ensure they operate more effectively and efficiently. They partner with states to develop new support models and improve the way Medicare-Medicaid enrollees receive health care and support.[116]

At state level, the State Medicaid Authority – usually the state department or a quasi-government intermediary – oversees Section 1915(c) (b) and 1115 waivers to provide self-directed HCBS to Medicaid beneficiaries. Each state Medicaid agency is tasked with having in place a system of continuous quality assurance and improvement. The system must include activities of discovery, remediation and quality improvement so that the state learns of critical incidents or events which affect individuals, corrects shortcomings and pursues opportunities for system improvement.[117]

---

[116] See Medicare-Medicaid Coordination Office, https://www.cms.gov/medicare-medicaid-coordination/ (accessed 2 February 2012).

[117] See CMS, https://www.cms.gov/CommunityServices/60_SelfDirectedServices.asp (accessed 12 January 2010).

Evaluation of standards is often carried out by private intermediaries funded by the state department. For example, in Wisconsin, evaluation of MCOs which operate the state managed care option, Family Care, is conducted by an organisation called Metastar contracted by the Department of Human Services. Part of the evaluation is concerned with whether the MCO has developed a method to monitor providers to ensure they are providing timely access to services. In general, quality compliance is focussed primarily on regulations and laws, and billing and financial fraud, while health and safety and personal outcome compliance are managed by case managers working for the MCO.

Another way of checking on providers is the mandate by a number of states to only fund support provider agencies which have received accreditation and provider standards certification. The accreditation body can vary. In some states, an outside accreditation body, such as CARF in Michigan, for example, is used to set standards for and accredit human services organisations. CARF's mission 'is to promote the quality, value and optimal outcomes of services through a consultative accreditation process that centers on enhancing the lives of the persons served'.[118] All waiver agents (commissioners) in Michigan are meanwhile monitored by the Department of Community Health and reviewed on an annual basis.

Waiver agents also monitor providers with annual assessments to assess compliance with the standards contained in the Medicaid Provider Manual. A follow-up site visit is also carried out to review the corrective action plan in correcting the deficiencies noted in the site review survey report. Items reviewed include: adequacy and appropriateness of staff, preparation, timeliness and frequency of service planning meetings and professional monitoring visits; and the degree to which the consumer's choices, preferences and needs are an integral part of the planning using a PCP, family-centred practice process.[119] The contract requirement documents and service standards must describe minimum standards for the operation of the waiver programme to assure the health and welfare of waiver participants. While this system of quality compliance is broadly welcome, arguably even under its most progressive interpretation, the system has chosen *services* as the norm for what constitutes quality rather than outcomes.[120] As discussed in Chapter 3, outcomes-based measurement which tracks consumer satisfaction is still in its infancy, particularly a system which matches funding with positive outcomes. There is a performance measurement and evaluation system used in the intellectual disability field, called the National Core Indicators (NCI).[121] It uses service-level data and research across an agreed set of outcome indicators. Participation in NCI is voluntary. For this purpose, it

---

[118] CARF Mission Statement, http://www.carf.org/About/Mission/ (accessed 2 February 2011).
[119] Michigan Department of Community Health (2009) *Michigan Profile of Publicly-Funded Long-Term Care Services*, Office of Long-Term Care Supports and Services.
[120] Nerney, T. (2010) *Lost Lives: The Paucity of Quality in Human Services*. The Center for Self-Determination, Michigan.
[121] For more information, please refer to: http://www2.hsri.org/nci/ (accessed 20 December 2011).

is useful to compare results across states and inform future planning. In terms of ongoing system-wide outcome measurement – and its link with procurement of best practice – this is an area that remains largely underdeveloped.

In terms of the enforcement of these standards, states vary in their insistence on consequences for providers who fail to meet standards. In theory, providers can lose contracts for such failures. However, for those agencies which are accredited and have been awarded an RFP, quality compliance, as we saw, is focussed primarily on regulations and laws and on billing and financial fraud. In general, there is reluctance by state and county waiver agencies to interfere in the market directly. Once awarded funding, ultimately, clients are encouraged to utilise available appeal and grievance rights to improve the quality of their own services and supports. This puts the emphasis on demand-side quality evaluation by the individual, rather than external regulations on outcomes.

Overall, then, there is a reluctance to regulate the shape of the social care market apart from a clear imperative to limit monopolies. Waiver agents often face capacity limitations because of the downsizing of government workforces in the US privatisation agenda. In addition, there are political disincentives associated with encroaching on private markets.[122] As a result, state and county departments are often limited in their 'smart buyer' role. However, with the majority of self-determination programmes, people with disabilities have the option to purchase support from close friends and allies, registered PAs, or conventional goods and services linked to the goals of a person's support plan. With this power, as more people become enrolled in self-determination options, providers over time will have to become more responsive.

Reconfiguring the Residential Support Market

As well as the demand-side initiatives to enable more choices in living arrangements, the United States has also implemented supply-side reforms in terms of the commissioning of services and allocation of system change grants. As stated earlier, the trend towards institutional closure began in the 1970s and has continued throughout the last number of decades. Between 1970 and 1984, 24 institutions in 12 states were closed. By 1988, 44 institutions in 20 states had been closed. By 2000, there were 125 closures in 37 states.[123] The states of Alaska, Hawaii, Minnesota, New Hampshire, New Mexico, Rhode Island, Vermont and West Virginia and the District of Columbia have closed all of their public institutions. Arizona, Colorado, Maine and Michigan have very few people still living in public institutions. Today, the majority of people with disabilities live at home with their families. In terms of

---

[122] Van Slyke, D. M. (2003) 'The Mythology of Privatization in Contracting for Social Services', *Public Administration Review* 63(3): 296–314, at 301.

[123] Please refer to http://thechp.syr.edu/toolkit/ (accessed 24 November 2010).

choice in living arrangements, service delivery organisations generally do not own community housing, with the exception of state-owned institutions or ICFs/MR.

The support provider market today is still dominated by group homes. These developed similarly to ICFs in response to the earlier deinstitutionalisation movement. Between 1987 and 1999, the use of group homes serving individuals with developmental disabilities and containing six residents or less increased by 240 per cent.[124] Since the passage of the Community Mental Health Centers Act in 1963, state and federal funds such as the Medicaid HCBS Waiver continue to support the majority of group homes. However, some homes operate on donations from private citizens or civic and religious organisations. Most group homes are owned by private rather than governmental organisations and can be either non-profit or for-profit organisations. With a lot of group home providers, the independent living and vocational rehabilitation services operate separately by different providers. Residents receive necessary services from community support providers, including personal assistance, medical care, physical therapy, occupational therapy, vocational training, education and mental health services.[125]

In terms of where transition efforts are today, the ICF model is now outmoded as discussed earlier in the chapter, and group homes are increasingly being seen as a more restrictive option than community living. Group homes have also been criticised for their lack of support in helping the individuals to develop social relationships with their neighbours or the other citizens of the community. The personal networks of residents often involve staff members, with little access to any kind of local association or club.[126]

One significant barrier to the further expansion of the self-determination option for people with disabilities is that the consumer-directed community supports and services are not available to waiver recipients living in residential settings licensed or registered by the state department.[127] These include a hospital or ICF/MR, family or corporate foster care, board and lodge facilities, supported living service facilities and housing with services/assisted living establishments. Therefore, persons have to use the demand-side reforms, such as utilising a CIL or applying for government vouchers to enable a move into the community, in order to become eligible. Alternatively, they can decide to live in their biological or adoptive family's home, or in a relative's home (e.g. sibling, aunt, grandparent, etc.). In particular, the advent of CILs and the increased availability of PAs have spearheaded much of the movement by people

[124] Piat, M. (2000) 'The NIMBY Phenomenon: Community Residents' Concerns About Housing for Deinstitutionalized People', *Health & Social Work* 25(2): 127–138.

[125] Dong Soo, K. (2000) 'Another Look at the NIMBY Phenomenon', *Health & Social Work* 25(2): 146–148.

[126] For critiques of group homes and advocates of self-determination, see the work by Jack Pearpoint and Marsha Forest, John McKnight, John McGee, Herb Lovett, Judith Snow, John O'Brien, Marc Gold, and Jean Vanier.

[127] See http://edocs.dhs.state.mn.us/lfserver/Legacy/DHS-4317-ENG (accessed 31 January 2012).

with physical disabilities to take control over their lives and choices, including their choice of accommodation.

Given the new government policy, there are a number of system change grants mentioned earlier, such as the 'Money Follows the Person' grant and 'Real Choice Systems Change' grant. These are designed to help states to manage the transition from institutions and nursing facilities to the community. Recent efforts have also been made by the Obama administration to further reduce the traditional institutional bias in Medicaid with the inclusion of the previously discussed Community First Choice (CFC) Option in the new health care reform law.[128] As we saw, the CFC Option provides a six per cent increase in Federal Medical Assistance Percentages for HCBS services.[129] However, by definition, it is optional for states so it remains to be seen how many states actually choose the CFC Option.

As a result of the policy direction and these change grants, there is significant evidence of provider-led change towards the goals of active citizenship at the state level across the United States. To illustrate the effects of the supply-side reforms, one example of a successful and innovative residential agency – and one that has transformed its ethos to self-determination – is Michigan's Community Living Services (CLS).[130] CLS is a very large, non-profit organisation (originally state entity) supporting 3,000 people in Michigan. It contracts with eighty-three counties to manage its housing providers through seventeen organisations. It originally had thirteen institutions, but that number has now decreased to one. It also originally contracted with group homes, as well as 128 clinicians, and was very Medicaid-driven. As a result, the individual's lives were deemed by the manager to be expert/clinician-driven, with clinicians' recommendations ending up prescribed as a result of ICFs' requirement that medical practitioners must sign off on Individual Programme Plans (IPPs). People used to 'get better' only when CLS had to move them, not through their own choice.

CLS still has some group homes and ICFs/MR but has worked to separate the owner of the housing from the provider of the services within those homes in order to avoid the conflict of interest and the associated problem of keeping clients in their own services because they need to pay the mortgage. In general, however, CLS has preferred independent tenancies to group homes or the ICF model. Because of this culture change, demand for institutions and group homes has diminished. The Chief Executive Officer (CEO) is aware of the old challenge with group homes being rejected by neighbourhoods, as well as group homes costing $200,000 minimum for an organisation to set up and make available for service users.

---

[128] See http://www.thearc.org/page.aspx?pid=3045 (accessed 31 January 2012).
[129] Ibid.
[130] Adapted from CEO transition story: Dehem, J. (2008) *Community Living Services' Transition Story (a third party summary) and Meetings with CLS*. Available at: http://www.seeingisbelievingnc.com/documents/clsstory.doc (accessed 5 September 2010).

With the RWJF self-determination grant, discussed earlier, CLS established a workgroup and invited providers to submit proposals to transition people into their own homes. The main criteria which they looked at included cost shifting, housing not needing licenses, cutting 'services' that did things to people instead of supporting them to obtain things they had chosen and rewarding effort and excellence among the regional services and staff. CLS incentivised the project by paying an extra dollar an hour when a support worker went into someone's own home because it did not have to worry about the maintenance expense of a group home. As people transitioned, living expenses were covered/absorbed through a variety of measures including live-in companions, sharing a house with a community member (e.g. single mother, student) and decreased maintenance and overhead. In addition, there were clinical services savings of more than $1 million a year from such things as, for instance, not having to pay for services generated by the team for the service provider's benefit (such as speech therapy the person chose not to use). Moreover, better lives led to less challenging behaviour and therefore fewer high-cost interventions.

The achievements of CLS and other organisations have been made through flexing supports and funding through the various mechanisms involved in supporting a life in the community. Its position as a contractor puts CLS in a leveraging position where it can use a combination of carrots and sticks to force the county services to change their practices. Although in the beginning they did not talk or partner well together with providers, from 1995 they began to work with providers and parents better in promoting self-determination.

Provider-Led Change

It may be assumed from the preceding section that individualisation at the provider level can only occur if the whole state system is pursuing this goal simultaneously, on the premise that an *a priori* systems commitment to individualisation is a necessary precondition for agencies to individualise their services. In fact, Kendrick (2009) maintains that many of the progressive agencies in the United States were often either the only agency they knew in their state which had entirely and systematically converted from group to individual service models, or one amongst a very small number of other such agencies.[131]

Examples of other innovative agencies include Onondaga Community Living in Syracuse, New York, Options in Community Living in Madison, Wisconsin, Total Living Concept in Washington, DC and Common Ground in Littleton, New Hampshire. A number of shared key learning outcomes exist, across providers, which offer a useful road map for agencies which wish to alter their service practices from

---

[131] Kendrick, M. (2009) 'Some Lessons Concerning Agency Transformation towards Personalised Services', *The International Journal of Leadership in Public Services* 5(1): 47–54.

an exclusive reliance on group and fixed models of service to models of support which are exclusively individualised for the entirety of the people they serve:[132]

1. The impetus to individualise principally came from values-based leadership within the agency.
2. All agencies believed they had achieved what they had with individualisation by simply moving ahead with individualisation one person at a time, no matter what.
3. The agencies developed individual options for the entirety of the people they served, including those deemed 'difficult to serve'.
4. The agencies paid due respect for and effectively engaged families and other natural supporters.
5. The net costs of individualisation in the aggregate were within the range of normative per capita costs in that system (all of the agencies had been able to maintain a balanced budget throughout the entirety of their period of individualisation).
6. All of the example agencies were fully compliant with system and funder requirements.
7. The agencies were comparatively small and, in some instances, quite self-consciously preferred to be small because of their belief that the quality and viability of their efforts at individualisation were better if the agency did not get too big.
8. All of the agencies had in place some form of functional individual budgets.
9. All agencies were able to coexist and thrive throughout multiple changes in political parties, administrations and policies.
10. All agencies saw their principal task as developmental and ongoing in regards to a person's life at a given moment.[133]

While each of these key lessons points to the characteristics of autonomous, progressive, values-driven providers, importantly many of these outcomes would not have arisen without the demand-side reforms discussed earlier, such as individual budgets, as indicated by item 8 on the list. A sole reliance on either supply-side mandates or on pioneering service providers is therefore insufficient for broader, system-wide change without the necessary demand-side changes. Equally, however, the belief that only systems can create individualisation and that people and agencies must wait until such systems are implemented is also false – change needs to take place from all fronts to transform conventional service systems which fail to encourage independence.

---

[132] *Ibid.* These have been detailed by Kendrick (2009) following an examination of the experience of eight US community-based agencies which were featured at the International Initiative for Mental Health Leadership (IIMHL) conference.
[133] *Ibid.*

EVALUATION AND COST-EFFECTIVENESS OF CHANGE

While each of the aforementioned focus areas has demonstrated the government's commitment to providing more individualised and responsive supports to persons with disabilities, importantly, these changes have been driven by various different evaluations which have tested their cost-effectiveness relative to traditional congregated service arrangements.

From the government's point of view, there has been much evidence of cost-effectiveness which supported the reform agenda. Consistently, the research has shown that ICFs/MR are more expensive to operate than home- and community-based residential services. The 2002 average annual expenditure for ICFs/MR was $85,746 as compared to $37,816 for each HCBS-funded resident.[134] Even when taking into account additional rent paid for a year, this is still a considerably less expensive option. Similarly, Lakin et al. (2005) reported that in Minnesota, costs of services for HCBS recipients were about 78 per cent of that for ICF/MR residents.[135]

Another living option available is the 'semi-independent living' programmes. These involve people living in small homes, apartment buildings, condominiums or agency-owned homes which may be staffed to provide functional skills training and on-site supportive services. Residents generally have basic self-help skills or take responsibility for employing and supervising aides to assist them in meeting their personal needs. Staff may be available on a twenty-four-hour basis or only occasionally, depending on the specific needs of residents. Service costs are substantially lower for the semi-independent settings (mean of $14,602) compared with group homes (mean of $64,105), although the former group did not have night staffing.[136]

Other studies based on historical trend analysis suggest that, by investing in HCBS, certain states (Oregon, Washington, Colorado) have avoided building nursing home beds that otherwise would have been built.[137] In several of these states, the nursing home beds which projections indicate would have been built in the absence of home and community services were replaced by beds in other residential support options including assisted living and adult foster care. Use of these alternative residential care settings has resulted in Medicaid costs savings.

---

[134] Prouty, R. W., Smith, G. and Lakin, K. C. (eds.) (2003) *Residential Services for Persons with Developmental Disabilities: Status and Trends through 2002*. University of Minnesota, Research and Training Center on Community Living, Minneapolis.

[135] Lakin, K. C., Hewitt, A., Larson, S. A. and Stancliffe, R. J. (2005) 'Home and Community Based Services: Costs, Utilization and Outcomes'. In *supra*, n. 42.

[136] Stancliffe, R. J. and Keane, S. (2000) 'Outcomes and Costs of Community Living: A Matched Comparison of Group Homes and Semi-Independent Living', *Journal of Intellectual & Developmental Disability* 25: 281–305.

[137] Doty, P. (2000) *Cost-Effectiveness of Home and Community-Based Long-Term Care Services, June 2000*. USHHS/ASPE Office of Disability, Aging and Long-Term Care Policy, US Department of Health and Human Services.

In terms of the 'economies of scale' debate, which assumes larger residential numbers per setting is cheaper, the recurring finding in the United States is that institutional services have *higher* per-person costs than much smaller-scale community services, which directly contradicts the notion of economies of scale. However, obviously in cases where one staff member is required in a very small setting, further reductions in resident numbers will increase per-resident staff costs.[138] Such diseconomies of very small scale apply only in settings requiring continuous paid staffing. Other opportunities exist to counter this diseconomy, such as semi-independent living or support arrangements which do not involve twenty-four-hour paid support, such as host-family support, companion models or supported living with some unpaid natural support.

In terms of the cost-effectiveness of non-residential day supports, such as the self-determination programmes, the original RWJF demonstration provides a comprehensive cost and personal outcome evaluation. In the original demonstration, independent evaluators at Conroy Outcome Analysts reported an improved quality of life for the participants and a cost savings of 12–15 per cent, even for the participants deemed most 'severely disabled'.[139] Significantly, in Michigan, Head and Conroy (2005) reported that, from 1998 to 2001, average costs (adjusted for inflation) for participants decreased by 16 per cent, although not uniformly across all participants.[140]

The RWJF used the Center for Outcome Analysis to evaluate the effect of the programme on individuals, and the Human Services Research Institute in Cambridge, Massachusetts, to examine institutional changes in the project states. The Center for Outcome Analysis reported a shift in decision making from professionals to individuals with disabilities, and improvement in some, but not all, quality-of-life indicators. The Human Services Research Institute found that flexibility, a system-wide approach and the availability of direct support workers were critical factors in the success of self-determination initiatives. The national programme office at the University of New Hampshire Institute on Disability managed the project selection process and provided technical assistance to the federal and state policy makers. This demonstration operated until July 2001.

From the individual's point of view, specific comparisons between community ICFs/MR (with fifteen or fewer residents) and HCBS-funded residences have shown better self-determination, integration, quality of life, less challenging behaviour and adaptive behaviour outcomes in HCBS settings.[141]

[138] *Supra*, n. 43.
[139] Robert Wood Johnson Foundation (2007) *Self-Determination for People with Developmental Disabilities, Grant Report*, http://www.rwjf.org/reports/npreports/sdpdd.htm (accessed 13 April 2010).
[140] Head, M. J. and Conroy, J. W. (2005) 'Outcomes of Self-Determination in Michigan: Quality and Costs', in *supra*, n. 42.
[141] Conroy, J. W. (1998) 'Quality in Small ICFs/MR versus Waiver Homes', *TASH Newsletter* 24(3): 23–24, 28; Stancliffe, R. J., Hayden, M. F., Larson, S. and Lakin, K. C. (2002) 'Longitudinal Study on

The preliminary evaluation of the RWJF demonstration also provided positive outcome results for individuals. Independent evaluators at Conroy Outcome Analysts reported an improved quality of life for the participants.[142] Mathematica Policy Research, Inc. (MPR) conducted a quantitative evaluation that analyzed differences in consumer satisfaction, quality of life, the amount and types of obtained personal assistance services and cost between participants in the states' C&C programmes and those receiving conventional agency-directed care. Results from Arkansas, the first state to implement the option, found that C&C participants were more satisfied with the quality of their services, had increased access to paid support, had fewer unmet service needs and experienced an improved quality of life.[143]

In addition, ethnographic studies were conducted by researchers at the University of Maryland, Baltimore County, to obtain rich detailed personal accounts of the affects of the CCDE on the lives of individual consumers, their families, workers and counselors in Arkansas, New Jersey and Florida. The results have shown that a C&C programme can successfully serve populations with various impairments and in various age groups. Other evidence shows that consumers in all three allowance programmes were very satisfied with the allowance programme. Further, in Arkansas, satisfaction with support was much increased and unmet need much reduced for those assigned to the allowance programme.[144] The evaluation concluded that this public/private partnership has been effective in working on an important policy issue, and those lessons from the CCDE may ultimately help other states in their efforts to improve HCBS.

However, it was notable that in the first New Hampshire demonstration, control over many service-related issues remained the least available choices to service users and their families. This suggests that professional control continued over personal choice, such as the choice of people to live with, type of work or day programme, amount of time spent at work, etc. Consumer control over services was not achieved to the extent expected.[145] More recently, another evaluation by Head and Conroy (2005) found significant improvements in choice and control, quality of life, satisfaction and community participation, following implementation

the Adaptive and Challenging Behaviors of Deinstitutionalized Adults with Intellectual Disability', *American Journal on Mental Retardation* 107: 302–320.

[142] Robert Wood Johnson Foundation (2007) *Self-Determination for People with Developmental Disabilities, Grant Report,* http://www.rwjf.org/reports/npreports/sdpdd.htm.

[143] Carlson, B. L., Foster, L., Dale, S. B. and Brown, R. (2007) 'Effects of Cash and Counseling on Personal Care and Well-Being', *Health Services Research* 42(1 Pt 2): 467–487.

[144] Phillips, B., Mahoney, K., Simon-Rusinowitz, L., Schore, J., Barrett, S. et al. (2003) *Lessons from the Implementation of Cash and Counseling in Arkansas, Florida, and New Jersey,* The Robert Wood Johnson Foundation, U.S. Department of Health and Human Services, Office of the Assistant Secretary for Planning and Evaluation, New Jersey.

[145] Stancliffe, R. J. and Lakin, K. C. (2004) *Costs and Outcomes of Community Services for Persons with Intellectual and Developmental Disabilities,* Policy Research Brief, Research and Training Center on Community Living, University of Minnesota.

of Consumer Directed Services in Michigan.[146] This involved increased choice in areas such as hiring and firing of direct support staff, choice of agency support person, choice of people to live with, choice of house or apartment and choice of case manager.

In addition, there is research evidence to show that there is better family contact for persons who are transferred from nursing homes to community-based programmes.[147] Baker and Blacher (1993) found that family contact diminishes when a family member is moved to an institution as time passes. This loss of contact, sometimes called 'detachment', involves not only the loss of emotional support, but also the loss of advocacy and protection.[148]

Spreat, Conroy and Rice (1998) compared family contact for persons with intellectual disabilities who either remained in nursing homes or transferred to community-based programmes. Family contact increased by about 31 per cent for persons who transferred to the community, but it was unchanged for persons remaining in the nursing homes.[149] Similar findings were reported by Latib, Conroy and Hess (1984) in a study of persons transferred from a large institution to community-based alternatives. The data reveal that there was an increase in family contact subsequent to placement in supported living arrangements, and that this increased family contact was maintained for as long as four years.[150] This demonstrates that increased levels of family contact were not solely linked to the transition itself but endured over time.

In terms of evidence of better outcomes from the service provider's point of view, there is a lack of large-scale provider-level reactions to self-determination in the United States. However, there are a number of studies which include some mention of the changes which take place in services or studies of large provider agencies which tracked worker satisfaction and other related issues.

In one study of an agency which had implemented self-direction, by Fullerton et al. (2002), it is interesting to note that the five areas which were reported as changing the most since self-determination was implemented were: number of responsibilities, the belief that they are helping people in their jobs, good relationships with the people receiving services, their understanding of their job and their

---

[146] Head and Conroy, *supra*, n. 42.
[147] Spreat, S. and Conroy, J. W. (1999) *The Impact of Deinstitutionalization on Family Contact*, Brief Report Number 10, Submitted to DHS, Developmental Disabilities Services Division, Oklahoma.
[148] Baker, B. and Blacher, J. (1993) 'Out of Home Placement for Children with Mental Retardation: Dimensions of Family Involvement', *American Journal on Mental Retardation* 98(3): 368–377.
[149] Spreat, S., Conroy, J. and Rice, M. (1998) 'Improve Quality in Nursing Homes or Institute Community Placement: Implementation of OBRA for Individuals with Mental Retardation', *Research in Developmental Disabilities* 19(6): 507–518.
[150] Latib, A., Conroy, J. and Hess, C. (1984) 'Family Attitudes toward Deinstitutionalization', in Ellis N. and Bray, N. (eds.) *International Review of Research in Mental Retardation* (Volume 12). Academic Press, Orlando, FL. pp. 67–93.

participation in the individual planning process.[151] The five areas which were reported as changing the least since self-determination started were: participation in the individual budgeting process, their relationships with their employers, their belief that their jobs are secure, their enthusiasm for their jobs and their ability to get things done on time. Significantly, the results from the question, 'do you like your job?' were overwhelmingly positive, with 83.1 per cent of the respondents reporting they either liked their job (37.3 per cent) or liked their job very much (45.8 per cent). Only 11.9 per cent were 'in between' when asked how they liked their jobs. About 5 per cent of the respondents said they either did not like their jobs (3.4 per cent) or did not like their jobs at all (1.7). In another study, the findings showed that self-determination could also improve relationships between families/youths and workers.[152] According to Kendrick (2009), agencies which had implemented individualisation had better-than-average staff retention and took great care to select, keep and nourish the staff who brought a desire to support people in their own lives.[153]

This research – and the lessons learned from the demonstration projects – has led to an expansion of the range of states currently offering consumer-directed services. Overall, these findings suggest that more individualised support arrangements, such as semi-independent living and supported living, are more cost-effective than congregated community living services such as institutions, group homes or ICFs/MR. At the outset, it must be stated that all the research demonstrates that institutions are indisputably undesirable services for persons with disabilities.[154] In addition, financing of congregated facilities has often been based on rate schedules and facility operating costs, cost agreements, local negotiation with service providers and historical reimbursement rates, with little specific attention to the individual needs and characteristics of persons served.[155] Most evaluations have now evolved far beyond the traditional 'cost-effective alternatives to institutional care' paradigm. The available evidence indicates that substantially more individualised supports can be provided without necessarily increasing average per-person costs, but that this is unlikely to

[151] Fullerton, A., Brown, M. and Conroy, J. (2002) *Delaware County Self-Determination, Worker's Survey Results*, Center for Outcome Analysis, www.outcomeanalysis.com/DL/pubs/SD-DelcoY2002.PDF (accessed 2 July 2012).

[152] Center for Outcome Analysis (2006) *Who Are the Young People Involved in the Youth Advocate Program in Pennsylvania, and How Are They Doing? Report on the First Visits*, Brief Report #1 of the Youth Advocate Programs Outcomes Project.

[153] Kendrick, M. (2009) 'Some Lessons Concerning Agency Transformation towards Personalised Services', *The International Journal of Leadership in Public Services* 5(1): 47–54.

[154] European Commission (2009) *Employment, Social Affairs, and Equal Opportunities, Ad Hoc Expert Group on the Transition from Institutional to Community-Based Care*, available at: http://ec.europa.eu/social/BlobServlet?docId=4017&langId=en (accessed 2 February 2012).

[155] Stancliffe, R. J. and Lakin, K. C. (2004) *Costs and Outcomes of Community Services for Persons with Intellectual and Developmental Disabilities*, Policy Research Brief, Research and Training Center on Community Living, University of Minnesota.

be accomplished exclusively through smaller and smaller residences with full-time staffing. It is now better understood that there are undesirable consequences of not reforming ineffective, inappropriate or excessively costly services. These include wholesale across-the-board funding cuts affecting high-quality personalised support arrangements equally with inefficient and ineffective services.

CONCLUSION

Despite financial constraints in many states across the United States, there are examples all over the country showing that self-determination is a legitimate cost-effective and dignifying method of delivering support in people's lives. Self-determination is now a well-established model of support delivery in the majority of states. Transferring further long-term care services to the community remains a priority[156] – and with that, a focus on real membership in, and contribution to, the community with control over the means of support.

There have been a number of mechanisms developed to ensure both demand-side and supply-side reforms. In terms of demand-side reform, these have included new policy options for self-directed supports and the development of an infrastructure of individual funding. This includes fairer resource allocation systems and programmes which combine independent planning and fiscal intermediary services. According to CMS requirements, a broker/consultant/counsellor must be available to each individual who elects the self-direction option.[157] A number of less-restrictive alternatives to guardianship have also been embedded to give individuals and families more options to maintain as much decision-making autonomy as possible. The United States has also begun to address the field of enabling wealth accumulation for persons with disabilities. The recent US ABLE legislation enables trust funds to be built up using targeted and cost-effective tax breaks, which then allow an adult to purchase the services they need – as distinct from those that others think they need. This proposes to reverse the unspoken 'bargain' made with many individuals with disabilities to require all or most of their everyday freedoms to be surrendered in return for support.[158]

In terms of supply-side reform, person-driven support, which is integral to the culture change in disability support, is increasingly viewed as an essential aspect of delivering quality support services. As such, it is included amongst the priority

---

[156] There are a number of initiatives and commitments directed by the Obama administration which seek to promote access to community living and improve educational and employment opportunities, available at: http://www.whitehouse.gov/issues/disabilities (accessed 1 February 2012).

[157] CMS, available at: https://www.cms.gov/CommunityServices/60_SelfDirectedServices.asp (accessed 5 June 2010).

[158] Nerney, *supra*, n. 120.

areas that CMS expects states to focus on under the terms of its scope of work.[159] The awarding of Medicaid funding has a number of mechanisms to ensure strict compliance with standards and requirements. These are enforced by the relevant state departments which commission services and regulate provider organisations. As we saw, each state Medicaid agency is tasked with having in place a system of continuous quality assurance and improvement. It must include activities of discovery, remediation and quality improvement so that the state learns of critical incidents or events which affect individuals, corrects shortcomings and pursues opportunities for system improvement.

Alongside the system-wide changes, many agencies have initiated or responded to the person-driven support agenda by embedding transformation efforts within their own organisations. Examples include Community Living Services (CLS) Michigan and Onondaga Community Living. These agencies demonstrate that service-level change is based on values-based leadership within the agency, paying due respect for and effectively engaging with families and other natural supporters. Importantly, all of the agencies had in place some form of functional individual budgets. They saw their principal task as developmental and ongoing in regards to a person's life at a given moment. These features demonstrate that while financial resources are still important, all agencies believed that vision and values for people's lives were much more important than money as a determinant of good person-centred outcomes.

In terms of choice in living arrangements, the United States has been involved in transformation efforts from institutional 'care' towards supporting people in the community since the 1970s. Given the early origins of this transformation, community-based accommodation in the form of ICF's/MR and large group homes became the norm in the 1970s and 1980s. Evaluations in the late 1990s and early 2000s found poor outcomes and expensive costs with these models, and the United States has since been trying to reconfigure this support landscape. State governments have more recently advocated the development of semi-independent living and 'supported living' settings as its future guiding philosophy. This new approach has the potential to radically progress the idea of active citizenship.

One of the main success factors behind this change has been the independent living movement, which has continually campaigned for the model of self-determination. At the centre of this movement have been the Centers for Independent Living (CIL). They have been driven by a particular philosophy of persons with disabilities being able to socially and economically engage within society, rather than conventional services per se. Accordingly, a key part of the reform agenda has been to assist people into employment. As we saw, this has included non-discrimination legislation such as the ADA, which prohibits discrimination. The

---

[159] CMS, available at: https://www.cms.gov/CommunityServices/60_SelfDirectedServices.asp (accessed 2 July 2012).

reform agenda has also included a number of work-incentive mechanisms, such as the Ticket to Work programme, to encourage people off benefits.

A second success factor has been the degree of continuous testing, evaluation and shared learning of new programmes, which have sought to find better mechanisms to support people. The RWJF and C&C demonstrations ended up establishing sustainable self-directed support programmes across numerous states. Behind the success of the C&C programme has been the National Participant Network (NPN). This was established to enable the process of partnership and shared learning across the states which have implemented C&C models, to improve sustainability, develop worker recruitment strategies and lessen differences in existing models (i.e. use of support brokers, fiscal management, etc.). It has also developed leadership and advocacy training, and consults with advocacy and advisory groups to hear participants' experiences. In addition, there have also been a number of system change demonstration grants such as the Money Follows the Person Grant and Real Choice Systems Change grant to advance the statewide implementation of self-determination. This shows an appreciation for the need for supporting culture (and practice) change and fostering ongoing learning in transformation efforts. These have bolstered state efforts to move people from conventional nursing care organisations to support arrangements in the community.

States continue to expand their self-determination programmes and develop new ones, but the United States still has many challenges ahead. Although states have been making progress in providing community-based alternatives to institutional care, state departments must manage a patchwork of older conventional programmes alongside the newer infrastructure of self-directed support. Moreover, nursing homes and public institutions still capture the largest share of Medicaid long-term care expenditures and therefore large waiting lists exist in all states for HCBS services. As such, many services remain reluctant to embrace self-determination because of fears over loss of resources and power. Many agencies feel that their power is a zero-sum game – that if a person with disabilities becomes more autonomous, then they must lose their power. However, as we saw, research shows that this is not the case; those agencies and staff which embrace personalisation become more empowered and experience greater work satisfaction. In any case, regression in public policy for the benefit of provider agencies at the expense of opportunities for those with disabilities remains the greatest threat to the future of personalisation. Ultimately, however, the United States has turned the corner on its long-held focus on 'services' to a framework which supports persons to actively participate and choose their own path in life, as advocated in the CRPD. The US case provides important lessons of the successes and the challenges inherent in reconfiguring the way in which people with disabilities access support.

5

Active Citizenship and Disability in Canada (British Columbia and Ontario)

INTRODUCTION

This chapter examines how Canada and in particular two of its provinces – British Columbia (BC) and Ontario – have tackled the reform of disability support to enable active citizenship. Canada ratified the CRPD on 11 March 2010, on the eve of the Paralympic Games in Vancouver, imposing a fundamental shift from institutionalisation towards integration of people with disabilities. The ratification has required provincial governments to update a number of laws, and has allowed disabled people to challenge in Canadian courts laws or policies that contravene the international law.

Canada has a strong history of human rights, evident from the Canadian Charter of Human Rights and Freedoms which was incorporated in 1985. Alongside this there has been a steady commitment to deinstitutionalise persons with disabilities and to refocus social policy on removing barriers to employment. Meanwhile, both provinces have introduced the option of individual funding to enable people to have more choice in the supports they require to enable them to live independently. Both provinces in various ways have been at the forefront in developing new initiatives for supporting people with disabilities as well as transforming the landscape of service delivery. At the same time, both provinces have met many challenges and have learned many lessons which are worth drawing on. Despite their successes, both jurisdictions continue to grapple with difficult issues and face common challenges other governments are facing across the world in their efforts to reform support delivery.

AN OVERVIEW OF THE ADMINISTRATION OF DISABILITY SUPPORT

Despite some federal efforts at mainstreaming approaches to disability policy over the last fifty years, the administration of Canadian disability policy is largely provincial.

The governing approach in Canada is based on the British North American Act (Canadian Constitution) (1867). The constitution divided jurisdictional responsibility in the field of health and social care by splitting responsibility between the federal and provincial governments. It specified that the federal government would provide medical care for the military and naval services.[1] It regarded matters of social welfare as local and private, and thus under the jurisdiction of the provinces. It granted to the provinces jurisdiction over the establishment, maintenance and management of local and provincial jails, penitentiaries and asylums, private charities, and municipal/provincial systems of public relief for the poor and destitute.[2]

Since the constitution, funding for provincial programmes was boosted through federal transfers for social services under the Canada Assistance Plan (CAP) (1966). However, it did not contain detailed national standards. This meant that geographically, Canadians had not one welfare system but ten or more. Each relied for its implementation on bilateral federal-provincial agreements negotiated on the specifics of programmes and services.[3]

In the 1970s, Canada saw a growth in the number of grassroots disability organisations. Organised and comprised of persons with disabilities, these groups worked to claim political space in government and influence changes in disability policies.[4] Within the last thirty years, four major organisations have been primarily involved with disability advocacy – The Council of Canadians with Disabilities, the Disabled Women's Network, the Canadian Association of Community Living and the Canadian Disability Rights Council – all of which have worked on strategic litigation to establish benefits and equality for persons with disabilities.[5] There is also the Canadian Mental Health Association which promotes the mental health of all and supports the resilience and recovery of people experiencing mental health issues.

In terms of the federal government's role in disability policy, thinking has evolved on the issue of rights since the early 1980s. Until the 1980s, disability was regarded as a welfare or health care policy issue, not one of human rights or citizenship.[6] A reassessment of the post-war social policy framework was undertaken in 1980 by the Special Parliamentary Committee on the Disabled and Handicapped in response to calls from the civil rights movement, and later from the growing disability

[1] Ruggie, M. (1996) *Realignments in the Welfare State: Health Policy in the United States, Britain, and Canada*. Columbia University Press, New York.

[2] Rice, J. and Prince, M. J. (2000) *Changing Politics of Canadian Social Policy*. University of Toronto Press, Toronto.

[3] Rioux, M. H. and Prince, M. J. (2002) 'The Canadian Political Landscape of Disability: Policy Perspectives, Social Status, Interest Groups and the Rights Movement', in Puttee, A. (ed.) *Federalism, Democracy and Disability Policy in Canada*. McGill-Queen's University Press, Montreal & Kingston. pp. 11–29.

[4] Vanhala, L. (2009) 'Disability Rights Activists in the Supreme Court of Canada: Legal Mobilization Theory and Accommodating Social Movements', *Canadian Journal of Political Science* 11: 981–1002.

[5] *Ibid.* at 4.

[6] *Ibid.* at 7.

rights movement. Released in 1981, the Committee's *Obstacles* Report signalled a substantial shift to understanding disability as a human rights issue more than a biomedical one, and was the first clear statement in the Canadian context of a social model approach to disability in recognising that it was the 'obstacles' to social and economic participation that resulted in the disadvantage of Canadians with disabilities more than their particular disability-related conditions.[7]

The *Obstacles* Report was released at the same time that negotiations were under way between the federal and provincial governments to 'bring Canada's constitution home'[8] from the British Parliament which by now had been enshrined more than a hundred years previous with the British North America Act (1867). A Canadian Charter of Human Rights and Freedoms was incorporated in 1982 in the consolidated Constitution Acts 1867–1982 which signalled Canada's status as a fully sovereign state. The 'Charter' came into effect in 1985 and recognises a right to equal benefit of the law without discrimination on the basis of mental or physical disability and other grounds. The adoption of the Charter made Canada the first country in the world to include such rights in a fundamental constitutional document. Disability groups – both service providers and disability rights groups – were thus ensured equality rights as well as the right to seek clarification of these rights through the courts.[9]

The federal government used symbolic policy reports, such as *Obstacles*, as well as the 1985 Declaration on the Decade of Disabled Persons and the National Access Awareness Week in 1987, to put disability issues on the map.[10] However, on the other hand, in 1984, with the election of the Conservative Party, the federal government embarked on a sweeping review and reform of social programmes, driven primarily by an agenda of deficit reduction (referred to as the 'cap on CAP'). This resulted in the rollback of federal transfers to the provinces for social programmes.

In 1995, the CAP and the Established Programs Finance (EPF) Programme (which provided federal transfers to provinces for health care and post-secondary education financing) were overhauled and combined under the name of the Canada Health and Social Transfer (CHST) in the form of a block grant to provinces ending targeted cost sharing for disability-related and other social services. This decision meant profound changes to both the standards for the programmes and levels of the federal fiscal transfers to the provinces. Immediate cuts totalling CAN$7 billion were made in the first two years. Demands for provincial autonomy meant that no

---

7 Special Committee on the Disabled and the Handicapped (1981) *Obstacles*, February, Ottawa.

8 The Charter of Rights and Freedoms (2011) *History*, http://www.charterofrights.ca/en/26_00_01 (accessed 14 March 2011).

9 The initial version of the charter did not include any antidiscrimination phrase against 'mental or physical disability'. The clause was later added after disability organisations lobbied for inclusion. The charter and the clause are still regarded as outstanding achievements in Canada's government freedoms. For further reading, see: Rioux and Prince, *supra*, n. 3; Prince, M. J. (2004) 'Canadian Disability Policy: Still a Hit-and-Miss Affair', *The Canadian Journal of Sociology* 29(1): 59–82.

10 Sullivan, T. and Baranek, P. (2002) *First Do No Harm: Making Sense of Canadian Health Reform*. Malcolm Lester and Associates, Toronto.

national standards for welfare/social services were negotiated between the two levels of government as the condition for receiving the block grant. Furthermore, there was no designation for use of the funds and no guarantee that provinces would spend the money on welfare or social services. With the decline in cash transfers, it meant the federal government had less leverage to enforce any standards set out in its *Obstacles* report or the Declaration.

In any event, throughout the 1990s and early 2000s, federal policy commitment to disability issues gathered pace. The National Strategy on the Integration of Persons with Disabilities was adopted by the federal government for the period between 1992 and 1996 as a cross-government initiative to advance the independence and inclusion of Canadians with disabilities, following the UN International Year of the Disabled in 1992. A major plank of the initiative was to support provinces and territories in advancing deinstitutionalisation of people with intellectual disabilities.[11] The federal government, through the Federal Task Force on Disability Issues, made a clear expression of its commitment to disability issues in its 1996 report, *Equal Citizenship for Canadians with Disabilities: The Will to Act*.[12] This report made a strong case for a renewed leadership role by the government of Canada on disability issues. Interprovincial and territorial collaboration was also established with the Provincial/Territorial Council (PTC) on Social Policy Renewal, created in 1996 by nine provinces and the territories (with the exception of Quebec).[13]

Shortly after this, there were a number of collaborative statements regarding the disability policy framework by federal, provincial and territorial social service ministers and governments. In 1998, the federal government, the provinces and the territories jointly published *In Unison: a Canadian Approach to Disability Issues*.[14] This expressed a shared vision of full participation of people with disabilities in all aspects of Canadian life. A year later, in 1999, the federal government issued its own disability agenda, called *Future Directions*, and first ministers of the provinces (except Quebec) signed the Framework to Improve the Social Union for Canadians.[15]

This commitment continued into the 2000s with the publishing of a second edition of the joint intergovernmental vision on disabilities, *In Unison*.[16] The thrust of

---

[11] For an evaluation of the deinstitutionalisation initiatives, see The Roeher Institute (1998) *Towards Inclusion: National Evaluation of Deinstitutionalization Initiatives*, The Roeher Institute, Toronto.

[12] Federal Task Force on Disability Issues (1996) *Equal Citizenship for Canadians with Disabilities: The Will to Act*. October 21.

[13] It is worth noting that in 1996, the new Employment Equity Act also came into effect. The act worked with private and public businesses to survey and analyse the workforce to ensure employment equality. See Atkins, C. G. K. (2006) 'A Cripple at a Rich Man's Gate: A Comparison of Disability, Employment and Anti-Discrimination Law in the United States and Canada', *Canadian Journal of Law and Society*, 21(2): 87–111.

[14] Federal/Provincial/Territorial Ministers Responsible for Social Services (1998) *In Unison: A Canadian Approach to Disability Issues*. Human Resources Development Canada, Ottawa.

[15] A Framework to Improve the Social Union for Canadians: An Agreement between the Government of Canada and the Governments of the Provinces and Territories, February 4, 1999.

[16] Federal, Provincial, and Territorial Ministers Responsible for Social Services (2000) *In Unison: Persons with Disabilities in Canada*. Human Resources Development Canada, Ottawa.

this policy statement was to provide a common framework for disability policy across the provinces, with a commitment to advancing the principles that the disability rights community had been advocating – inclusion, self-determination, participation and so forth. It called for coordination between programmes and organisations within and across governments.

Despite the commitment to interprovincial collaboration outlined earlier, the separate political structures operating at provincial and territorial levels, along with the geographical challenges, have made it difficult for Canadian provinces to coordinate their disability strategies. In addition, in April 2004, the CHST was split into (1) the Canada Health Transfer, to cover a portion of provincial-territorial health care costs, and (2) the Canada Social Transfer (CST). The CST is a federal block transfer to provinces and territories in support of social assistance and social services (CA$6.388 billion in 2009–2010), amongst other areas. It is calculated on an equal per capita cash basis to reflect the government's commitment to ensure that general-purpose transfers provide equal support for all Canadians. The CST is also the vehicle through which the government of Canada provides support to provinces and territories in relation to agreements reached on various policy reports.[17] However, in practice, the CST has no mandatory principles or standards attached to it. There is broad acceptance of the level of provincial government autonomy over how they administer these funds in ways they see fit.

More generally, Canada has no national disability strategy. There is also some political resistance to further federal involvement, most notably from the Canadian Conservative government and some provincial governments.[18] To some extent, activists and groups within the disability movement feel that a national strategy is unnecessary and, more seriously, holds certain legal and political risks.[19] There is a fear that such a law risks sidestepping the Charter of Rights and human rights guarantees. Also many disability groups have higher priorities, and this legislation reform process detracts from mobilising efforts to achieve other concrete social programme reforms at the provincial level. For example, rather than discussing wider disability issues, the Accessibility For Ontarians With Disabilities Act Alliance is focussed exclusively on the implementation of accessibility measures in Ontario and the implementation of the accessibility act.[20]

In any case, as a result of federal withdrawal from focussed financing of disability-related services as was the case under CAP, and with provincial governments continuing to finance services largely through contracted-out service provision, the

---

[17] Canada Department of Finance Web site at: http://www.fin.gc.ca/fedprov/cst-eng.asp (accessed 17 July 2010).
[18] Prince, M. J. (2007) *Disability Policy in Canada: Building Blocks or Blocked Building?* CACL Forum, Crowne Plaza Hotel, Ottawa, 23 November.
[19] McCallum, D. (2006) *CACL Analysis of the CDP Private Member's Proposed Bill on Disability.* Report prepared for the Canadian Association for Community Living. Toronto.
[20] Prince, M. J. (2009) *Absent Citizens: Disability Politics and Policy in Canada.* University of Toronto Press, Ontario.

driving force of public policy in the 2000s was a 'devolution of responsibility' for disability-related policy and programming and other social policies to the provincial/territorial level and through them to local communities.[21] As the social policy system devolved, it became harder to maintain standards across the country or across a province. It is worth noting though that the CRPD applies to all levels of government, thus provinces must develop and carry out policies, laws and measures to make sure they put the rights listed in the CRPD in place. Larger and richer jurisdictions have been able to afford better and broader provision of services. Where governments cannot provide the services, voluntary and private-sector organisations are invited to participate.[22] In an effort to provide intra-provincial evaluation of disability policy, the Roeher Institute, located in Ontario, works to generate knowledge across Canada regarding public policies, human rights and equality laws, and how these affect people with disabilities.[23] Given the extent of interprovincial variation, the remainder of this chapter thus examines the disability policy climate in two different provinces in more detail: Ontario and BC.

At the provincial level, in Ontario, the Ministry of Community and Social Services is responsible for administration of support services for people with physical, sensory and intellectual disabilities. Meanwhile, disability services in BC are governed by a few different ministries and agencies: The Ministry of Housing and Social Development is responsible for housing, personal supports and the province's disability strategy, and Community Living British Columbia (CLBC) is responsible for community care supports for adults with developmental disabilities.

AN OVERVIEW OF THE DISABILITY SUPPORT FRAMEWORK

Disability-Specific Federal and Provincial Entitlements

As discussed earlier, in the early 1990s the Canadian government began to eliminate federal cost sharing for disability-related services and supports and has meant millions of dollars for respite services, equipment and supports for people with disabilities are now the full responsibility of the provinces.[24] Despite this, there is an extensive range of Canadian federal disability welfare programmes, as outlined in Table 5.1. Some of these are discussed in more detail later in the chapter.

Both federal and provincial governments provide a wide range of publicly funded and administered income security and social services programmes. The provincial

---

[21] Rice, J. and Prince, M. J. (2000) *Changing Politics of Canadian Social Policy.* University of Toronto Press, Toronto.

[22] *Ibid.*

[23] Atkins, *supra*, n. 13.

[24] Torjmann, S. (1996). *Dollars for Service: aka Individualized Funding.* The Caladon Institute, Ottawa.

TABLE 5.1. *Canadian federal disability programmes*

Programme/initiative	Description	Administering department
Permanent Disability Benefit	For persons with a permanent disability and experiencing exceptional financial hardship repaying their Canada Student Loan(s) because of their disability. Allows for the reduction of loans.	HRSDC*
Opportunities Fund	Provides funding to individuals, employers and organisations to help people with disabilities to prepare for, obtain and maintain employment or self-employment.	HRSDC
Entrepreneurs with Disabilities Program	A grant for persons with a disability who have been unable to get a bank loan for a viable business project. Designed to enable people to start or expand their business and/or to buy or improve facilities. Applies to Western Canada (Alberta, BC, Manitoba and Saskatchewan).	WD$^{\Omega}$
Disability Supports Deduction	If a person has an impairment in physical or mental functions, they may be able to deduct the expenses that they incur in order to work, go to school or do research for which they received a grant.	CRA^
Disability Tax Credit (including supplement for children)	A non-refundable tax credit used to reduce income tax payable for eligible individuals. If a person is 'markedly restricted' or 'significantly restricted in more than one way', then they will likely qualify.	CRA
Caregiver Tax Credit	Provides tax relief to individuals providing in-home care for a parent or grandparent sixty-five years of age or older, or a person deemed 'infirm' by a qualified medical practitioner.[a]	CRA
Labour Market Agreements for Persons with Disabilities (LMAPDs)	Bilateral cost-shared funding for programmes and services which improve the employment situation for Canadians with disabilities. Gives provinces the flexibility to determine their own priorities and approaches to best address the needs of persons with disabilities in their jurisdictions.	HRSDC

(continued)

TABLE 5.1 *(continued)*

Programme/initiative	Description	Administering department
Canada Access Grant for Students with Permanent Disabilities	An up-front grant for students with disabilities who have demonstrated financial need. It is intended to assist in covering the costs of accommodation, tuition, books and other education-related expenses. A *Canada Study Grant for the Accommodation of Students with Permanent Disabilities* is also available.	HRSDC
Enabling Accessibility Fund	A grant to help to cover the cost of improving physical accessibility for people with disabilities within areas in their community.[b]	HRSDC
Working Income Tax Benefit	Includes an additional supplement for low-income working Canadians with disabilities, given that they face even greater barriers to workforce participation.	HRSDC
Residential Rehabilitation Assistance Program for Persons with Disabilities (RRAP-D)	Provides funding to homeowners and landlords of dwellings for low-income persons with disabilities so that they can carry out renovations to improve accessibility.	HRSDC
Social Development Partnership Program – Disability component (SDPP-D)	Provides grants and contributions to help to ensure that people with disabilities can achieve the same quality of life as all Canadians. Supports innovative ways of removing barriers through improved access to programmes and services and encourages a wide range of community-based initiatives to address social issues and barriers.	HRSDC
Tax Exemption of Training	Exemption of training from the goods and services tax / harmonised sales tax (GST/HST) and the expansion of the list of GST/HST-free medical and assistive devices to include service dogs to help people with disabilities.	CRA

* HRSDC – Human Resources and Skills Development, Canada.
Ω WD – Western Economic Diversification Canada.
ˆ CRA – Canada Revenue Agency.
[a] Defined by Canada Revenue Agency as a person who has 'a severe and prolonged impairment in physical or mental functions', http://www.cra-arc.gc.ca/tx/ndvdls/tpcs/ncm-tx/rtrn/cmpltng/ddctns/lns300–350/306/menu-eng.html (accessed 19 April 2011).
[b] See examples of successful proposals at: http://www.hrsdc.gc.ca/eng/disability_issues/eaf/cfp/index.shtml (accessed 19 April 2011).

Source: Adapted from Human Resources and Skills Development Canada (2009) *2009 Federal Disability Report: Advancing the Inclusion of People with Disabilities*, Human Resources and Skills Development, Canada.

governments and, by delegation in some instances, the municipalities have primary responsibility for the administration of social assistance and social services. Social assistance is granted on the basis of a needs test which takes into account both budgetary requirements and the income and resources of the applicant and his or her dependents.

Overall, as evidenced from Table 5.1, there is a strong emphasis on grants and programmes focussed on helping people with disabilities through education, training and employment, guided by an approach which aims to ensure their independence and economic participation in society. The Opportunities Fund, for example, is a programme designed to help people with disabilities to prepare for and obtain employment or self-employment. It also assists people to develop the skills they need to keep a new job. It supports a variety of activities, in partnership with organisations – including the ones in the private sector – to help people with disabilities to overcome the barriers they may face as they enter the job market. These activities include helping individuals to start their own business, increase their job skills and integrate into the workplace through services that meet their required needs, as well as encouraging employers to provide individuals with work opportunities and experience.

There is also a range of programmes which target accessibility for persons with disabilities, including the Enabling Accessibility Fund and the Residential Rehabilitation Assistance Program (RRAP) for Persons with Disabilities.[25] The latter provides funding to homeowners and landlords of dwellings for low-income persons with disabilities so that they can carry out renovations to improve accessibility. These modifications are intended to eliminate physical barriers and imminent safety risks and to improve the tenants' ability to meet the demands of daily living within the home. Therapeutic care, supportive care and portable aid equipment, such as walkers and wheelchairs, are regarded as ineligible modifications for funding.

Both federal and provincial/territorial governments also provide for disability and caregiver-related tax credits and deductions in their personal income tax regimes. These narrowly reduce the base of personal income tax revenues. At the same time, they promote efficiency and mobility by lowering employment barriers and assisting families. In addition, they promote equity between able-bodied earners and those who experience extra expenses because of a disability. However, many Canadians with disabilities do not have a taxable income, and the scheme of credits and deductions does not completely offset the additional disability-related costs for

---

[25] Please refer to: http://www.canadabenefits.gc.ca/f.1.2cl.3nkj.5mp@.jsp?refid=20013&lang=en&url=http%3A%2F%2Fwww.cmhc-schl.gc.ca%2Fcmhc-schl%2Fen%2Fco%2Fprfinas%2Fprfinas_003.cfm (accessed 3 August 2010).

taxpayers and not at all for those without a taxable income – the poorest of Canadians with disabilities.[26]

BC Support Programmes

BC has an additional set of conventional disability benefits for citizens within their province. The Ministry of Housing and Social Development provides the BC Employment and Assistance for Persons with Disabilities programme[27] which allocates 'Disability Assistance', a higher income assistance rate, supplementary assistance and specialised employment supports to qualifying persons with disabilities. Those who leave assistance for employment will keep their designation and maintain their medical assistance. This is an important measure, as it acknowledges that restrictions to daily living activities can be continuous or periodic for extended periods.

The Persons with Persistent Multiple Barriers (PPMB) programme[28] provides financial assistance to those who are unable to achieve financial independence because of specific personal barriers to employment. The person must have received assistance for twelve of the last fifteen months, have severe multiple barriers to employment, and have taken all reasonable steps to overcome barriers. However, all adults (applicant and spouse) in a family unit must experience persistent multiple barriers to be eligible for the full PPMB support rate and for the earnings exemption. It thus has highly restrictive eligibility criteria.

In terms of independent living (housing) benefits, the Independent Living BC (ILBC) programme helps seniors and persons with disabilities to live independently in affordable, self-contained housing. ILBC offers a middle option to bridge the gap between home care and residential care through subsidised assisted living. It provides accommodation, hospitality services such as meals and laundry, as well as personal care services such as assistance with grooming, mobility and medications.[29] Similarly, the Provincial Housing Program[30] provides housing assistance to low- and moderate-income individuals and families. However, as the section on the choice

---

[26] Prince, J. (2002) 'Designing Disability Policy in Canada: The Nature and Impact of Federalism on Policy Development', in Puttee, A. (ed.) *Federalism, Democracy and Disability Policy in Canada.* Institute of Intergovernmental Relations. McGill-Queens University Press, Montreal & Kingston. pp. 29–78.

[27] Please refer to: http://www.canadabenefits.gc.ca/f.1.2cl.3nkj.5mp@.jsp?refid=20484&lang=en&url=http%3A%2F%2Fwww.mhr.gov.bc.ca%2FPUBLICAT%2Fbcea%2Fpwd.htm (accessed 5 August 2010).

[28] Please refer to: http://www.canadabenefits.gc.ca/f.1.2cl.3nkj.5mp@.jsp?refid=20485&lang=en&url=http%3A%2F%2Fwww.mhr.gov.bc.ca%2Ffactsheets%2F2004%2Fppmb.htm (accessed 5 August 2010).

[29] Please refer to: http://www.bchousing.org/Initiatives/Creating/ILBC (accessed 12 February 2012).

[30] Please refer to: http://www.canadabenefits.gc.ca/f.1.2cl.3nkj.5mp@.jsp?refid=20688&lang=en&url=http%3%2F%2Fwww.bchousing.org%2Fprograms%2Fhousing (accessed 5 August 2010).

in living arrangements later in the chapter illustrates, the public housing stock in BC is relatively quite small.

For persons with physical disabilities the Choices in Supports for Independent Living (CSIL) gives people with physical disabilities CAN$3,000 per month to purchase attendant services. The At Home programme for children with significant disabilities funds families for most equipment and medical costs as well as CAN$2,700 annually towards respite costs.[31] Both CSIL and the At Home programmes are not truly individualised, however, because everyone receives the same dollar amount, regardless of need.

Ontario Support Programmes

In Ontario, one of the principal disability programmes from the Ministry for Community and Social Services (MCSS) is the Ontario Disability Support Program (ODSP),[32] which is intended to meet the needs of people with disabilities and help them to become more independent.[33] ODSP is divided into 'Income Supports' and 'Employment Supports'. The former is a programme for people with disabilities who are in financial need; it pays for living expenses like food and housing. The latter is a programme that helps people with disabilities to find work. Individuals are eligible for ODSP Employment Supports if they have a physical or mental disability which is expected to last a year or more and, as a result, makes it hard for them to find or keep a job. It targets assistance to those individuals deemed most able and likely to secure 'competitive' paid employment, defined as no less than minimum-wage levels.[34] However, ODSP from the start has had very strict eligibility requirements. The Social Planning Council of Ottawa has documented several cases in which people determined to be anywhere from 62 per cent to 87 per cent disabled by the ODSP adjudication panel (the Disability Adjudication Unit) have been denied benefits as they are not considered 'disabled enough' to meet the strict eligibility requirements for income support.[35] The Council has pointed out that only people who are substantially disabled can receive benefits, yet people who are deemed not employable in the disability test can no longer qualify for employment

[31] *Ibid.*

[32] Please refer to: http://www.canadabenefits.gc.ca/f.1.2cl.3nkj.5mp@.jsp?refid=20134&lang=en&url=http%3A%2F%2Fwww.adsab.on.ca%2Fssas%2Fodsp%2Fodsp.html (accessed 9 July 2010).

[33] Lord, J. (2006) *Moving Toward Citizenship: A Study of Individualized Funding in Ontario.* Report for Individualized Funding Coalition for Ontario, Canada.

[34] Chouniard, V. and Crooks, V. (2008) 'Negotiating Neo-Liberal Environments in Ontario and Bristsh Columbia, Canada: Restructuring of State-Voluntary Relations and Disability Organisations' Struggles to Survive', *Environment and Planning C* 26: 173–190.

[35] Bernard, G. (2001) *The Experience of People with Disabilities in Ottawa and the Ontario Disability Support Program (ODSP).* Report of the Public Forum, Social Planning Council of Ottawa, Ottawa.

support.[36] In addition, ODSP has been criticised for its complex application and disability adjudication process.

The Special Services at Home (SSAH)[37] programme (also funded by the MCSS) exists for families giving in-home care to a child with a physical and/or developmental disability, or an adult with a developmental disability. These special services provide funding for supports and services for respite, family support, community integration or individualised supports which are not available elsewhere in the community. The main limitation of the SSAH programme is that there is little or no facilitation to assist families with planning and fiscal advice on managing a budget. However, more significantly, in April 2009, the MCSS announced that because of budgetary pressure, no new applications in Ontario for SSAH could be made. Every new approved application is simply directed to a wait list. Understandably, this has angered many disability and family caregiver groups across the province, especially given the province's recent commitment to close institutions and develop community care.[38]

In addition, the Assistive Devices Program[39] provides financial assistance to help Ontario residents with long-term physical disabilities to obtain basic, competitively priced, personalised assistive devices essential for independent living. Meanwhile, the Attendant Outreach Program[40] provides 'visitation attendant services' to people with serious physical disabilities solely in the person's home. These are trained attendants (similar to personal assistants) to help people with physical disabilities to live independently at home. Ontario's Passport Initiative[41] is another important programme. It is targeted at older children with intellectual disabilities facing the transition into adult services. Importantly it starts prior to the end of schooling and requires teachers and/or community-based organisations to build on transition plans that have already been developed by an individual's local school board. The process is designed to encourage individuals' personal development and help them to achieve their potential, smooth the transition from school to life as an adult in

---

[36] Crooks, V. and Chouinard, V. (2005) 'Because They Have All the Power and I Have None': State Restructuring of Income and Employment Supports and Disabled Women's Lives in Ontario, Canada', *Disability & Society* 20(1): 19–32.

[37] Please refer to: http://www.canadabenefits.gc.ca/f.1.2cl.3nkj.5mp@.jsp?refid=20130&lang=en&url= http%3A%2F%2Fwww.cfcs.gov.on.ca%2Fmcss%2Fenglish%2Fpillars%2Fdevelopmental% 2Fprograms%2Ffamily_support.htm (accessed 5 August 2010).

[38] See Petition from ARCH Disability Law Centre, http://www.archdisabilitylaw.ca/?q=petition-improving-and-increasing-passport-and-special-services-home-funding-0 (accessed 14 March 2011).

[39] Please refer to: http://www.canadabenefits.gc.ca/f.1.2cl.3nkj.5mp@.jsp?refid=20591&lang=en&url= http%3A%2F%2Fwww.health.gov.on.ca%2Fenglish%2Fpublic%2Fprogram%2Fadp%2Fadp_mn.html , (accessed 5 August 2010).

[40] Please refer to: http://www.canadabenefits.gc.ca/f.1.2cl.3nkj.5mp@.jsp?refid=20633&lang=en&url= http%3A%2F%2Fwww.health.gov.on.ca%2Fenglish%2Fpublic%2Fprogram%2Fltc%2F21_other .html%232 (accessed 5 August 2010).

[41] Please refer to: http://www.mcss.gov.on.ca/mcss/english/pillars/developmental/programs/young_ leave_school.htm (accessed 5 August 2010).

the community, promote independence, foster social, emotional and community participation skills and promote continuing education and personal development.

Finally, there are also some specifically targeted programmes for tailored groups such as the Northern Health Travel Grant (NHTG) programme to help to defray the transportation costs for eligible residents of Northern Ontario who must travel long distances within Ontario to receive care. The Property Tax Relief for Low-Income Seniors and Low-Income Persons with Disabilities[42] programme offers property tax relief to low-income seniors or persons with disabilities. Eligible persons may have their property taxes deferred, reduced or cancelled.

Overall, then, there is an extensive range of disability-related programmes provided by both federal and provincial governments. These are generally focussed on employment support and offer limited funding to help people to access education and employment-related training.

Disability-Specific Services

Canada has a very different system of funding and administration of disability services from that of the United States, coming out of provincial budgets (with some federal matching funds) and paid through the relevant ministries. Prior to reforming the disability support services, Canada shared a similar history of institutionalisation across its provinces as most other jurisdictions. Today – to provide a snapshot of the conventional (non-self-directed) disability services sector – group homes in Canada typically provide twenty-four-hour support for groups of three to six adults who need supervision or assistance with activities of daily living. These group homes continue to dominate as the standard model of care for people with intellectual disabilities in Canada and funding still largely goes to these care settings.[43] BC has an extensive network of group homes which developed in response to demands for less congregated residential settings. According to the BC Ministry of Housing and Social Development, there are 787 group homes in the province with approximately 2,500 residents and 3,099 home share arrangements.[44] There is now a further transition effort to move more people into semi-independent settings and home-sharing arrangements, as the chapter will explore further. Similarly, in Ontario, since 1975, 6,000 people

---

[42] Please refer to: http://www.canadabenefits.gc.ca/f.1.2cl.3nkj.5mp@.jsp?refid=20152&lang=en&url= http%3A%2F%2Fwww.fin.gov.on.ca%2Fenglish%2Fpublications%2Fbulletins%2Ffrost_9907.html (accessed 5 August 2010).

[43] Braddock, D., Emerson, E., Felce, D. and Stancliffe, R. J. (2001) 'Living Circumstances of Children and Adults with Mental Retardation or Developmental Disabilities in the United States, Canada, England and Wales, and Australia', *Mental Retardation & Developmental Disabilities Research Reviews* 7(2): 115–121; Taylor, S. J. (2001) 'The Continuum and Current Controversies in the USA', *Journal of Intellectual & Developmental Disability* 26(1): 15–33.

[44] BC Ministry for Housing and Social Development (2010) *Community Living BC Service Redesign – Group Homes.*

have been moved out of 13 institutions to live in these group home settings across the province.[45]

Meanwhile, for persons with physical disabilities who require attendant services, there is access to two programme options. The first option is Support Service Living Units (SSLU's), first piloted in 1975, which are accessible and affordable housing units linked to attendant services available twenty-four hours a day, seven days a week. The second programme designed to provide more independent living options is the Outreach Attendant Services (Outreach). This began in 1984 and provides more limited care and housekeeping services to people with disabilities living in their own homes (rented or owned) in the community. Outreach services are only available for scheduled visits and are limited to ninety hours per month. These attendant services are based on people with disabilities self-directing their own care. This second programme emerged from calls by disability activists in the 1980s for personal care options modelled on individualised and direct funding. They also called for a wider set of supports, such as housekeeping, shopping and banking, to be included in public-funded care.[46]

As the following sections show, Canada has moved away from the group home service model to supporting persons in the community. In the last few years, individuals have increasingly chosen more person-driven options, such as home sharing or semi-independent living. Individuals are increasingly living in smaller, individualised arrangements where no more than two people live together.

Community-based developmental services for adults in Ontario are delivered through a network of approximately 370 community-based agencies directed by volunteer boards and managed by sometimes very large staff operations. These agencies are non-profit organisations which contract with the ministry's regional offices and are funded by the ministry through transfer payments for the express purpose of delivering social services. Legislation and policy development are established centrally, while funding and service system management take place locally through nine regional offices.

The Ontario government now spends more than CAN$1 billion annually to provide financial and social supports to approximately 39,000 adults with developmental disabilities, with most of the money flowing through intermediary organisations.[47] Prior to reform, all of these intermediaries were funded through block contracts. Most funding from the MCSS and Ministry of Health continues to be block funding given to agencies, such as associations for community living (for people with developmental disabilities) or support service living units (SSLUs) for people with

45 Lutz, C. (2007) 'Residential Programs Update', *New Leaf Living and Learning Together Inc Newsletter: Life on the Lane* 1(1): 2.
46 Lord, J., Hutchison, P. and Farlow D. (1988) *Independence and Control: Today's Dream, Tomorrow's Reality*. Ministry of Community and Social Services, Toronto.
47 Mackie, R. and Philp, M. (2004) 'Developmental Disability Homes to Be Closed', *The Globe and Mail*, 10 September.

physical disabilities. This has gradually been changing, with new programmes emerging in the 1990s to enable individual funding directly to the person. Ontario and BC have both reconfigured their commissioning and service delivery mechanisms to enable increased personalisation, as detailed later in this chapter.

There also has been an increasing effort at linking disability monetary entitlements mentioned earlier with services. Given the expressed aim of many of the monetary entitlements to enable access to education, training and employment, there has been a joining up of employment-focussed benefits with supported employment services, as illustrated by the ODSP discussed earlier.

WELLSPRINGS OF REFORM

Recognising the Costs of Institutions

To examine the roots of present-day reform, it is important to go back to the original wellsprings of change to examine the earlier processes and dynamics involved in shifting the paradigm of support away from institutions to self-directed support. Governments in both BC and Ontario began to recognise as early as the 1960s that their investment in bricks and mortar was very significant in terms of financial, legal and personal costs.[48]

The first institution for persons with intellectual disabilities in Ontario opened in 1876 in Orillia, and by 1968, it was home to approximately 2,600 individuals.[49] Between 1876 and the mid-1970s, a total of sixteen government-operated institutions which provided residential care existed in the province, including Orillia, Huronia, Smiths Falls and Blenheim. They were originally residences for both children and adults, but in the late 1980s, only adults were housed in these settings.

Similarly, in BC, the institutionalisation of people with mental health issues and intellectual disabilities began in the mid-1880s with the creation of a large institution in New Westminster, first called the Provincial Asylum for the Insane and later known as Woodlands School, or just Woodlands. Other large institutions – Tranquille, Glendale and the Endicott Centre – were later created around the province.[50] People with intellectual disabilities and many with physical disabilities were separated from their families and communities, sometimes for their whole lives.

In terms of financial costs, government panels projected excessive public expenditures if the populations of 'mental hospitals' continued to grow. In the early twentieth

---

[48] Rioux and Prince, *supra*, n. 3.

[49] Ministry of Community and Social Services (MCSS), (2011) *The First Institution*, http://www.mcss.gov.on.ca/en/dshistory/firstInstitution/index.aspx (accessed 17 July 2012).

[50] BCACL (2010) *Institutions and People with Developmental Disabilities*, http://www.bcacl.org/our-priority-areas/disability-supports/institutions (accessed 4 January 2011).

century, one commentator noted in a study that 75 per cent of provincial government expenditures in Ontario were on the asylums.[51] Across the country, more was spent on asylums over the period between 1845 and 1902 than on prisons and other hospitals.[52]

A Canadian Report (1981) later stated that, based on American experiences, there is a remarkable difference in the average annual costs of keeping a disabled person institutionalised compared with assisting him or her to live independently in the community.[53] It estimated that institutionalisation annually costs CAN$30,000 per person, whereas independent living costs CAN$8,000, therefore offering potential yearly savings of CAN$22,000 each time a person can make the transition from institution to community. Similarly, it referred to the Multiple Sclerosis Society of Canada which found that the cost of caring for a person in a nursing home was CAN$11,900 per year. The same service in a private home cost CAN$5,730 per year.

In addition, concern for the legal rights of people committed to mental institutions led to a radical shift of public policy in Canada. Critics argued that hospitals actually harmed individuals rather than helping them, forcing them into a dependent role and allowing them to forget how to cope in the outside world. New psychiatric medicine allowed many individuals to live successfully outside hospitals, especially if they could be given supervised care.[54]

In Ontario, the Ministry of Health and Long-Term Care led the first wave of the deinstitutionalisation movement with mental health institutions in the 1960s. The reduction in Ontario's hospital population for people with mental illness was started with the availability of federal funds, through the CAP on a cost-sharing basis as a stimulus to community care. It was achieved partly through the transfer of patients who neither required nor received active treatment. They were transferred to 'residential units' or to 'approved homes' such as Homes for Special Care, community hospital psychiatric units, private hospitals and other community settings such as nursing homes and residential-care homes. In reality, however, this initial deinstitutionalisation process left many 'ex-patients' to fend for themselves, living in lodging homes or becoming homeless.[55] The lack of bed space in the community prompted the passage of the Homes for Special Care Act (1964), to provide accommodation for discharged persons with psychiatric disabilities. From a virtual standstill in the 1970s,

---

[51] Mulvale, G., Abelson, J. and Goering, P. (2007) 'Mental Health Service Delivery in Ontario, Canada: How Do Policy Legacies Shape Prospects for Reform?' *Health Economics, Policy and Law* 2: 363–389.

[52] Wright, D., Moran, J. and Gouglas, S. (2003) 'The Confinement of the Insane in Victorian Ontario', in Porter, R. and Wright, D. (eds) *The Confinement of the Insane, 1800–1965: International Perspectives.* Cambridge University Press, Cambridge, pp. 100–108.

[53] Smith, D. (1981) *Obstacles*, House of Commons Special Committee on the Disabled and the Handicapped, Canada.

[54] Dewey, R. (2007) *Psychology: An Introduction*, http://www.intropsych.com/index.html (accessed 4 March 2011).

[55] For a full description, see Dear, M. and Wolch, J. (1987) *Landscapes of Despair: From Deinstitutionalization to Homelessness.* Polity Press, Cambridge.

the community mental health and addictions sector has grown to almost 500 agencies with budgets totalling about $670 million.[56] Many of the 500 agencies are, in fact, hospitals that sponsor community mental health and addiction programmes. A second wave of closures and policy initiatives that took place in the 1980s attempted to address the numbers living on the street with no support because of the first wave of deinstitutionalisation. However, this in turn led to many service-dependent ghettos made up of concentrated group home developments throughout the city of Toronto as a result of system-wide retrenchment, system planning and land-use planning. On the other hand, more money was invested back into the community to ensure similar levels of care, albeit in smaller institutions.[57]

A similar story of deinstitutionalisation also occurred in BC, with decreasing populations in their mental health and disability institutions, such as Riverview and the permanent closure of others such as West Lawn in 1983, Tranquille in 1985 and Woodlands in 1996.[58] A limited number of community-based residential settings such as group homes developed alongside sheltered employment-related activities and other segregated day activities specifically for individuals with an intellectual disability.[59]

Meanwhile, beginning in the 1970s, both Ontario and BC began to recognise disability rights and the need for laws and policies to ensure the elimination of barriers for persons with disabilities. There was an increased interest in human rights, and the number of consumer-led organisations pursuing law reform increased.[60] There was also increasing public outcry about the treatment of people with intellectual disabilities within the institutions. For example, on 5 March 1971, Frederick Sanderson, a resident of the Rideau Regional Hospital in Smiths Falls, hanged himself. Walter Williston, the author of the subsequent government review found the conditions in which this man had lived to be 'deplorable'. Indeed, the conditions of the institutions have recently led to a class action lawsuit by former residents against three, now closed, Ontario institutions, with a trial date set for September 2013.[61]

In response to the 1970s scandals, two reports were ordered by the Ontario Premier in the early 1970s to introduce systemic change. The first, known as the Williston

---

[56] Reville, D. and Associates (2006) *On Becoming New Best Friends: Integrating Front and Back Offices in Community Mental Health and Addictions, Final Report*.

[57] Rioux and Prince, *supra*, n. 3.

[58] For a full timeline, see Teachers Law Institute, http://www.teacherslawinstitutes.ca/wp-content/themes/teachers/documents/Mental-Illness-Crime-and-the-Law/History%20of%20the%20Treatment%20of%20Mental%20Illness%20in%20BC.pdf (accessed 3 November 2010).

[59] For a full history, see Ministry of Community and Social Services (2006) *Opportunities and Action: Transforming Supports in Ontario for People Who Have a Developmental Disability*, May, available at: http://www.accesson.ca/en/mcss/publications/developmentalServices/opportunitiesAndAction/perspective.aspx (accessed 14 July 2010)

[60] For example, in 1970, Ontario adopted a law to ensure that blind individuals were permitted access to public and private premises with their guide dogs. See Vanhala, *supra*, n. 4; Atkins, *supra*, n. 13.

[61] Gutnik, D. (2011) *Class Action: Ontario's Developmentally Challenged Go to Court*, CBC News, 25 November.

Report, was presented to the minister of health in 1971.[62] The report recommended phasing down, as quickly as possible, the large hospital institutions. The report was credited for having 'forever altered the custodial mode of caring for individuals with developmental disabilities in large, impersonal, and often inhumane institutions'.[63] Second, in March 1973, the Provincial Secretary for Social Development issued his report, entitled *Community Living for the Mentally Retarded in Ontario: A New Policy Focus*. It outlined, in detail, the new policy direction of the provincial government, which would facilitate the transfer of individuals with intellectual disabilities to the community.[64]

Closing large residences for people with disabilities had the support of all political parties in Ontario. These reports set the stage for the transfer, in 1974, of persons from institutions to the community, marked by the enactment of the Developmental Services Act in 1974. In the period between 1977 and 1986 in Ontario, two five-year plans were implemented to close provincially operated institutions and create community living opportunities for individuals with a developmental disability. Five of the institutions closed and others downsized. Resources from these closures and downsizing were reinvested to develop community-based services.

The process was promoted by the federal government with the publication of *Obstacles* (1981), as mentioned earlier.[65] It stated that independent living for disabled persons, when possible, is more beneficial and less expensive than institutional care. It recommended that the federal government amend the National Housing Act to enable groups to develop more non-profit, cooperative, and group homes for physically and mentally disabled persons, including clusters of units in apartment buildings. It also stated that disabled persons themselves must play a key role in the development and management of these independent living programmes. Put simply, its focus was on unlocking barriers and reducing bureaucratic burden in order to develop a market for the community services.

The closure process gathered pace in 1987, when the ministry published a policy document for the future of developmental services, titled *Challenges and Opportunities: Community Living for People with Developmental Handicaps*. This plan was to create community services throughout Ontario to support people who had a developmental disability, as well as a strategy for closing all the institutions in Ontario within twenty-five years. This government initiative signalled a public policy commitment to phasing out large institutions for people who have a developmental disability. An additional five institutions were closed as a result.

[62] Williston, W. (1971) *A report to the Honourable A. B. R. Lawrence, Minister of Health on present arrangements for the care and supervision of mentally retarded persons in Ontario*, Ontario Department of Health, Toronto.

[63] Spindel, P. (1989) *Protection for Whom? A Brief to the Ontario Cabinet by the Adult Protective Services Association of Ontario*, November, p. 3.

[64] For a more detailed history, please refer to: http://www.kwhab.ca/about-history-of-services.shtml (accessed 5 January 2011).

[65] Special Committee on the Disabled and the Handicapped, *supra*, n. 7.

Pioneering Parents

In BC, one of the major wellsprings of reform behind the transition from institutions to personalised community living was the pioneering work by the Woodland Parents Group (WPG). It was developed in the late 1970s by a group of family members whose sons or daughters had attended the Woodlands School, which was being closed.[66] Families believed that if the money required for community living were allocated by the government directly to people with disabilities (and their personal networks), they could purchase services and supports needed to live in the community with autonomy and dignity. They lobbied the BC government and received a groundbreaking pilot self-managed care programme in 1997. This was the first-ever comprehensive pilot project of individualised funding and brokerage.[67] It proposed that money go directly from government to the individual, based on a personal plan created by the individual and family, and with the aid of a service broker.[68]

Realising that money in itself could not guarantee citizenship opportunities, WPG members identified the need for a place in the community where they could obtain quality information and planning supports. Calling this a service brokerage agency, families understood that such an agency must respect the decisions made by individuals and their personal networks, while operating independently from both government and direct services. In 1977, a proposal to implement individualised funding and establish the Community Living Society (CLS) as an independent brokerage agency to assist individuals to leave Woodlands received initial provincial government approval. However, the CLS was discontinued as a result of service provider and subsequent government resistance.

Another individualised funding/brokerage pilot project called Community Brokerage Services Society took place between 1991 and 1996 for adults with intellectual disabilities.[69] Planners were independent, and money went directly to the individuals and their families. It was regarded as 'the most comprehensive and sophisticated project developed anywhere, and B.C. should be proud of it'.[70] Although it received positive feedback from the individuals with disabilities and families who participated in the pilot project, it was again discontinued by the government. However, it set

---

[66] For a historical overview of the first initiative in the 1970s and an evaluation of outcomes, see The Roeher Institute (1991) *The Power to Choose: An Examination of Service Brokerage and Individualized Funding as Implemented by the Community Living Society.* The Roeher Institute, Toronto.

[67] Salisbury, B. (1997) 'Illusion or Revolution? The International Context', in *Report on the Individualized Funding Conference*, June, B.C. Coalition of People with Disabilities, Vancouver, pp. 14–17.

[68] Salisbury, B. and Collins, D. (1999) *Is Individualized Funding About to Come Full Circle in B.C?*, May, available at: http://members.shaw.ca/bsalisbury/Is%20Individualized%20Funding%20About%20to%20Come%20Full%20Circle%20in%20BC%20-%20revised.doc (accessed 20 July 2010).

[69] *Ibid.*

[70] *Ibid.*, at 7.

in motion the development of subsequent individual funding programmes, detailed later in the chapter.

Subsequently, the BC Coalition of People with Disabilities sponsored a four-year individualised funding project between 1997 and 2000 with the families who wanted 'to keep individualised funding alive [for people with intellectual disabilities] after the closure of the Community Brokerage Services Society'.[71] The goal of the project was to 'enable a ground-up approach to individualised funding so that people with disabilities and family and personal supporters play the lead role'.[72] A Family Summit was set up involving families from across the province and meeting regularly in Vancouver to discuss individualised funding and to bring it back to their communities.[73]

In 2001, a newly elected Liberal government willing to look at system change provided another window of opportunity. Some of the parents and brokers from the WPG who created the original concept of independent support brokerage began redesigning individualised funding for the province.[74] Individuals with disabilities and their families joined with service providers and advocacy organisations to form the Community Living Coalition to assist with proposed system change and budget cuts in a way which could benefit – or (at least) prevent harm to – people with disabilities and their families. The Liberal government accepted their challenge and their proposal for community living. This process led to the creation of Community Living British Columbia (CLBC), a new provincial administration for disabilities in BC in 2005 (detailed after the following section).

Influential Reports on Person-Led Support

In Ontario, a significant wellspring of reform towards personalising support options began in 1988 with the publication of two reports – *Independence and Control: Today's Dream, Tomorrow's Reality*, also known as the Lord Report;[75] and a report by the Ontario Advisory Council for Disabled Persons entitled *Independent Living: The Time Is Now.*[76]

The first report was commissioned as a consultant review by the Ontario Ministry of Community and Social Services. At the time, those living in the Support

---

[71] Gordon, C. (2001). *Individualized Funding – Information Sharing Meeting Notes.* August. B.C. Coalition of People with Disabilities, Vancouver, pp. 3–5.

[72] *Ibid.*

[73] Salter, S. (2002) *Changing the Rules of the Game. Individualized Funding in B.C.: Implications for Families and Social Workers.* Graduating Essay for Degree of Master in Social Work, University of British Columbia.

[74] *Ibid.*

[75] Lord, J. and Hutchison, P. (1988) *Independence and Control; Today's Dream, Tomorrow's Reality: Review of Support Service Needs of Adults with Physical Disabilities in Ontario.* Centre for Research in Education, London, ON.

[76] Ontario Advisory Council for Disabled Persons (1988) *Independent Living: The Time Is Now.* Toronto.

Service Living Units (SSLUs) could not have any control over their attendant services, including who would come into their apartment, how much attendant time might be available to them on short notice and how much portability was available. These services were only available in the SSLU. In the early 1980s, as a result of these limitations, a number of consumers lobbied the government, claiming they had the right to have individualised attendant services (i.e. access to personal assistants) outside of the SSLU programme. Convinced, the government made an Order-In-Council (OIC) (a legal order from the Federal Governor in Council to a statutory authority) which allowed individualised funding contracts with individuals to be administered through a third party. The OIC, according to Yosida et al. (2004), became a catalyst to the growing movement towards direct funding as an option for Ontario citizens.[77] Some of the citizens receiving attendant services through this option organised themselves into the Attendant Care Action Coalition (ACAC).[78]

In response to the growing demand from the ACAC, the Lord Report began a review of attendant services. It found that people with disabilities wanted supports which would encourage personal growth and relationships, and independence and control over their own lives. The report supported ACAC's vision and recommended that direct funding should be provided as an option. It introduced new thinking around direct payments and personalised care in the Ontario context, which were originally developed in the pilot initiatives of WPG in BC in the 1970s, and later in the United Kingdom and Sweden, and promoted a brokerage mechanism for facilitation.

The second report, *Independent Living: The Time Is Now*, was a discussion paper on the future of independent living assistance in Ontario. In the report there was a strong emphasis that whether people are disabled or not, they should have the freedom to choose the most appropriate lifestyle for themselves, and if that requires an attendant care programme, they should also choose who that person is.

These reports injected new ideas into the debate over reform of attendant services. Importantly, shortly after they were published, the Centre for Independent Living in Toronto (CILT) made an official commitment to support persons in using the direct funding initiative. This was important as the Ministry was able to utilise an already established group which had the resources to provide organisational support. Between 1990 and 1993, the CILT and other partners submitted a proposal for a direct funding pilot, which eventually led to the Ontario Direct Funding Program, which is detailed amongst the demand-side reform options later.[79]

77 Yoshida, K. Willi, V. Parker, I. and Locker, D. (2004) 'The Emergence of Self-Managed Attendant Services in Ontario: Direct Funding Pilot Project – An Independent Living Model for Canadians Requiring Attendant Services', in Kronenfeld, J. J. (ed.) *Research in the Sociology of Health Care*, 22, Emerald Group Publishing Limited, Bingley. pp. 177–204.
78 *Ibid.*
79 *Ibid.*

Designing a New Administration for Governing Disability Services

Another key wellspring of reform in Ontario and BC was the reconceptualisation of disability as a general social citizenship issue, rather than being a health or medical issue in the history of Canadian political administration. Significantly in 1974, under the Developmental Services Act, the Ontario Ministry of Community and Social Services took over responsibility for services for people with a developmental disability from the Ministry of Health. This had a profound effect on changing the focus of services from institutional care to living in the community. The change reflected the broader normalisation and deinstitutionalisation movements' agendas, which were being led by parent groups in Ontario and around the world, and the shift away from an illness service model for individuals with intellectual disabilities towards a social model of understanding disability.[80]

In more recent times, as indicated earlier, BC sought a new administration for governing disability services in the 2000s, which has had a significant effect on reconceptualising disability as well as the vision of service delivery. This came about through the creation of CLBC. The process began after a detailed submission process on the future direction for community living services. The majority of submissions felt the previous systems in place to care for adults and children with intellectual/developmental disabilities were rigid, overly bureaucratic and unsustainable in the long term. As a result of this process, then Minister of Child and Family Development (MCFD) Gordon Hogg established the Community Living Coalition, which presented the minister with The Governance Proposal. This proposal outlined changes to community living, establishing 'a single provincial governance body for community living', giving a meaningful and 'permanent voice for individuals and families at the policy government table'; proposed to 'dramatically reform the system with efficiencies that would not impact services to individuals and families'; and finally to provide 'Individualised Funding and Direct Funding to Families as an option for all who wish it'.[81] The Cabinet accepted The Governance Proposal on 12 December 2001. As a result, the BC MCFD entered a period of transition, transferring responsibility for the administration of services to people with intellectual/developmental disabilities to the new agency called CLBC.[82]

The transfer of services from MCFD to CLBC officially began on 1 July 2005. CLBC became a legal entity and a designated Crown agency (statutory body) under the provincial government's Crown agency secretariat.[83] Since that time, the

---

[80] Morris, S. (2003) *Mental Health and Patients' Rights in Ontario: Yesterday, Today and Tomorrow.* Psychiatric Patient Advocate Office (the Ministry of Health and Long-Term Care), Toronto.

[81] Salisbury and Collins, *supra,* n. 68, at 7.

[82] For full details on the transfer of powers, please see the CLBC Web site at: http://www .communitylivingbc.ca/about/history (accessed 14 May 2010).

[83] A Crown agency is an organisation established or acquired by the provincial government outside of a ministry. Crown agencies are accountable to the government through a responsible minister and

authority over children's services has been moved back to the MCFD, with CLBC only focussed on adults.[84,85] In any case, the vision and strategy of CLBC which emerged from the process behind its inception have been an important driver of system change for adults with intellectual disabilities in BC. Since its creation, it has sought to increase utilisation of alternative residential models and further the development of individual funding and independent planning support, as discussed in the following sections.

SHAPE OF REFORM

As a result of the wellsprings of reform, both BC and Ontario, to varying extents, have developed personalisation options in their disability support systems. These include a range of individualised funding mechanisms, sometimes referred to as 'self-managed care' in Canada, and independent planning/support brokerage options for individuals, which will be examined further.

SHAPING THE DEMAND SIDE OF REFORM

New Policy Options for Individual Funding

Following the influential reports in Ontario mentioned previously, the Ontario New Democratic Party government strategy included a commitment to look at individualised funding in the 1990s. A piece of legislation referred to as Bill 101 was passed in 1993, amending the Ministry of Community and Social Services Act to allow individuals with disabilities to receive funding directly from the government or to allow agencies to transfer such a grant on behalf of a person with a disability.[86] On the basis of this, a successful pilot was undertaken, called the Individualised Quality of Life Project in Toronto, in which the Ministry of Community and Social Services Durham Region set up more than sixty individualised funding and support arrangements.[87]

In 1994, the Ontario Ministry of Health created the self-managed Attendant Service Funding Program. The programme was further developed under Ontario's new

---

have assigned/delegated authority and responsibility from government, or otherwise have statutory authority and responsibility to perform specified functions or services.

[84] The MCFD was deemed to be better equipped to administer Early Childhood Development, Youth Services and Child and Youth Mental Health responsibilities.

[85] Letter from Minister for Children and Family Development and Minister of Housing and Social Development to the President of BC Federation of Foster Parent Associations, July 2008. Available at: http://www.bcfosterparents.ca/documents/CLBC20080722/index.shtml (accessed 26 May 2011).

[86] Cranford, C. Fudge, J., Tucker, E. and Vosko, L. F. (2005) *Self-Employed Workers Organize: Law, Policy and Unions*. McGill-Queens University Press, Montreal and Kingston.

[87] Ontario Federation for Cerebral Palsy (2000) *More Choice and Control for People with Disabilities: Individualized Support and Funding*, July, Ontario Federation for Cerebral Palsy, Toronto, p. 12.

Progressive Conservative government party (1995–2002).[88] The new government advocated radical welfare reform in Canada, working to mirror the system already established in the United States. The pilot programme initiated significant funding for disability and was eventually made into a permanent programme under the name of Direct Funding Program in 1998.[89] This allowed up to 700 Ontarians, generally with physical disabilities, to become 'self-managers'.[90] Importantly, the programme has some inbuilt facilitation, in the form of Independent Living Resource Centres across Ontario, which are available to support people who are applying to the programme. Research by the Roeher Institute in 2006 found that Ontario's Direct Funding Program had a lower unit cost to provide services and was more efficient than other community living options.[91]

In the restructuring process of long-term care, the process of extending these options to persons with intellectual disabilities came somewhat later. In 2004, the Ministry of Community and Social Services began a process of consultation with representatives of many of the stakeholders. A Joint Ministry/Developmental Services Partnership Table was established, which was a government consultation forum including representatives from People First Ontario, family and service provider associations, unions, the Ministry of Community and Social Services and the Ministry of Children and Youth Service. An official report from this process was published as *Opportunities and Action – Transforming Supports in Ontario for People who have a Developmental Disability* (May 2006).[92] This set out a vision for 'transformation' of the developmental disability service system. It includes individualised funding as well as independent planning and facilitation. The negotiations behind the report led to Bill 77 – Act to Protect Social Inclusion for People with Intellectual Disabilities, discussed later in the chapter.

Meanwhile, further momentum was gathering towards individualising payments and promoting choice in supports from the Independent Funding Coalition of Ontario (IFCO), a strong lobby for individual funding. IFCO, in partnership with other organisations which were providing creative supports, launched a large-scale project in 2007 funded by Ontario Trillium Foundation, an Ontario government foundation which distributes profits from the province's casinos and lotteries to charitable causes in the province. This pilot was called Modelling Community Change and Innovation (MCCI). MCCI involved collaboration between three community sites in Ontario which were building support for individualised approaches for citizens with a developmental disability. The Trillium grant was used to develop

[88] Spalding, K., Watkins, J. R. and Williams, A. P. (2006) *Self Managed Care Programs in Canada: A Report on Health Canada*, p. 20.

[89] Lightman, E. (2009) 'Not Disabled Enough': Episodic Disabilities and the Ontario Disability Support Program, *Journal of Disability Policy Studies*, 21(2): 70–80.

[90] Spalding, Watkins and Williams, *supra*, n. 88.

[91] *Ibid.*

[92] *Supra*, n. 59.

community readiness, strengthen autonomous groups (self-advocates, families and allies), deepen work in brokerage, develop resource materials and create sustainable community plans.

With this added momentum, Bill 77 was finally enacted in 2008 as the Services and Supports to Promote the Social Inclusion of Persons with Developmental Disabilities Act. Significantly, it permits the use of individualised funding in the province for persons with intellectual disabilities, thus making inroads to providing a dual system to offer individuals and their families a choice between agency support and direct payments. With these changes comes greater potential to create inclusive communities in which people with disabilities participate fully as citizens. However, the minister has yet to authorise regulations for individualised funding for residential supports under the Act. This means that families can choose where to buy their community services, with the exception of choosing a residential service. Given the recent timing of the Act, the transformation is still in its embryonic stage and is being proclaimed in phases (e.g. the new eligibility criteria only came into force on 1 July 2011).[93] Some criticism has centred on the fact that support agencies are accountable to the ministry for the quality of services and supports they provide to people with disabilities. However, there is very little in the regulation to make services and supports accountable directly to the people who receive them.[94] In any case, the Act marks a significant point in the process of transformation of intellectual/developmental services away from a model of 'custodial care' to one that recognises a person's right to make decisions for his or her self.

In BC, a new programme has been initiated, called Choices for Support in Independent Living (CSIL). It was piloted in 1990 and became a permanent programme in 1993. It is funded by BC's Ministry of Health and provides direct funding to individuals (excluding children) with physical disabilities and individuals with both developmental and physical disabilities. Since its inception, the programme has undergone many structural changes. The programme has two phases:

- Phase One is for individuals who are considered mentally capable of self-managing their care. Consumers receive funds directly and assume full responsibility for the hiring and training of personal attendants, as well as all payroll responsibilities of an employer in BC.
- Phase Two is for those who are not considered mentally capable of managing their own care. In order to receive funding, consumers must form a support group including at least five members, and they must register as a non-profit society through the British Columbia Society Act to receive funds on behalf

of the individual. There are no restrictions as to who can be in the consumer support group, although family members are recommended.[95]

In both phases, a case manager determines the amount of funding an individual is eligible for and the funds are administered by the Regional Health Authority. The funding is for a personal assistant only and cannot be used to purchase equipment or supplies.

In BC, the newly created Crown agency CLBC, also introduced a choice for individuals with intellectual disabilities and their families of two payment options through individualised funding: direct funding or host agency funding. Direct funding is an individualised funding payment option where funds allocated by CLBC are paid directly by CLBC to an individual or his/her agent (family member or representative) for the purchase of supports and services.

With the host agency funding option, the funds allocated by CLBC for the purchase of individualised supports and services are paid by CLBC to a host agency which has been approved by CLBC and selected by the individual and family. The host agency administers the funds and works with the individual and family to arrange and manage the supports required. This option provides the benefits of individualised funding, but with less responsibility for paperwork and record keeping.

Role of Independent Planning and Facilitation

Facilitation has emerged as a key element in both provinces' disability policy in response to the growing recognition that citizens with disabilities want to have control over the decisions that affect their lives. The facilitator's role is to help individuals and families to develop their support plan, foster networks and access the resources they need, as well as to provide financial management assistance for direct funding.[96] It is distinct from providing ongoing support and personal assistance. It combines the functions of planning, brokerage, community development and the building of social networks to help people to craft a support plan suitable to their requirements and to navigate through complex programme options. Independent facilitation is seen by many in Canada as an important support to enable the growth of direct, individualised funding, particularly for people with

---

[95] Many who choose this self-managed support option in BC manage the budget through the Vela Microboard Association, a non-profit organisation which assists individuals with disabilities (excluding children) to develop 'microboards' to access government funding for support and to manage it on behalf of a particular individual. Please refer to the CSIL Web site at: http://www.health.gov .bc.ca/hcc/csil.html (accessed 13 November 2010).

[96] Lord, J. (2000) *More Choice and Control for People with Disabilities: Review of Individualized Funding and Support*, July, Ontario Federation for Cerebral Palsy.

intellectual disabilities and others who may need help designing their own support packages.[97]

Both Ontario and BC have created a variety of facilitation options. These vary from province-wide facilitation which is operated by the government, as in BC, to a mixed-model approach in Ontario where there is third-party facilitation from agencies independent from government. These options are detailed later in the section.

Firstly, in BC, there is a province-wide facilitation service offered by CLBC. The Crown agency is committed to providing planning supports independent of funding limitations. Therefore, it has divided the planning and funding roles which were previously undertaken by a single position – the social worker. This means that responsibility for funding decisions, programme management and contract administration has been separated from the provision of planning and support to individuals and families. CLBC developed two roles – facilitator and quality service analyst – to carry out these separate roles.[98]

Facilitators provide information, advice and support to eligible individuals and families, independent from service providers and CLBC funding decisions, to assist individuals in developing and implementing their personal support plans. Facilitators have an important role in working collaboratively with individuals and their families to identify strengths and goals, solve problems and explore opportunities and options within the individual's community, which may assist them to meet their goals. The main focus of the planning is on identifying flexible and innovative ways of providing support. According to CLBC's service plan, facilitators have a 'community first' focus geared to 'empowering and supporting' individuals and families in ways they determine are important to them.[99] The facilitators are trained to work with individuals and the families to make effective use of flexible, individualised funding and plan for greater community involvement in developing appropriate, cost-effective and sustainable person-focussed solutions. This model is

[97] For a full description, see Lord, J. (2008) *Independent Facilitation in Ontario: Governance and Structure Issues.* Presentation to Independent Planning and Facilitation Symposium, Guelph, Ontario, 2 December. Available at: http://www.learningcommunity.us/documents/IndependentFacilitationin-OntarioJohnLord.pdf (accessed on 14 January 2010).

[98] As well as facilitators, CLBC also has two additional roles which are designed to empower citizens. First, a self-advocate advisor meets with self-advocates, finds out what their issues are and learns about the innovative projects they are involved in. This information is gathered to help to guide the work of CLBC. It also tries to create opportunities for self-advocates in the province to develop their leadership skills. Second, a family partnership advisor meets regularly with provincial, regional and local family groups and organisations and gathers information about innovative service and supports, to share with other families and individuals in order to help them to develop their capacity in short-term and long-term planning. Please refer to: http://www.communitylivingbc.ca/individuals-families (accessed 5 January 2011).

[99] *CLBC Service Plan*, available at: http://www.communitylivingbc.ca/policies-publications/publications/service-plans/ (accessed 8 February 2012).

geared towards taking advantage of existing community capacity and taking an interest in creating new capacity. Facilitators work from seventeen Community Living Centres in addition to twenty-three Satellite Offices in BC, which are all funded and managed by the CLBC.

Meanwhile, behind the scenes, quality service analysts determine eligibility, make decisions on requests for funding and/or services, monitor contracts, assess system gaps, develop increased capacity, ensure that a crisis response capacity exists in local communities and work to improve the effectiveness of contracted services. According to CLBC's service plan, their main focus is to ensure that the support and service system infrastructure is in place and working. CLBC has had to ensure that clients understand that the support plan developed by facilitators does not mean an automatic entitlement to all supports identified in the plan – rather, a quality service analyst will review the plan and make a decision about the type and amount of supports and services requested by the individual to be funded to meet his or her disability-related needs.

In general, the onus of responsibility for managing the accountability for the use of funds rests with the individual. They can act personally (as their own agent) or nominate another person or host organisation to become the agent. The agent is responsible for ensuring that the supports and services purchased with government funds comply with CLBC policies and programme standards. The agent employs or contracts directly with all support workers or caregivers. Facilitators must ensure that individuals and families interested in direct funding of more than CAN$6,000 per annum understand that the agent for the individual may be responsible for assuming the financial, managerial, administrative and legal responsibilities associated with being an employer as outlined in their direct funding policy. The agent must be able to demonstrate his/her ability to fulfil their responsibilities, including the ability to arrange and manage the individual's supports and services.

In terms of how well the division between the planning and funding roles works, although some regions have implemented a team approach, generally speaking, according to a review for the ministry, there is a lack of shared reporting, teamwork and communication between the staff groups.[100] Handoffs between facilitators and analysts are areas of concern, introducing a new person into the process and requiring families to tell their stories again (a plan often requires twenty-five hours of consultation with the facilitator). More broadly, there is a general sense of confusion about the role of the facilitator, how they fit in the system, and how families should interact with facilitators. One of their key aims is to encourage a broader 'independent living' focus and reduce the sole focus on funded supports (i.e. to focus on support from mainstream community amenities and natural

---

[100] Queenswood Consulting Group (2008) *Review of the CLBC Service Delivery Model*, Prepared for the Ministry for Housing and Social Development.

support options). However, this function is widely seen as being neglected and under-skilled.[101]

In Ontario, as mentioned earlier, there are a number of different options for accessing facilitation, as detailed by Lord (2008).[102] Firstly, the stand-alone, independent organisation in many ways is the ideal governance structure for independent facilitation. In Ontario, Windsor-Essex Brokerage for Personal Supports best represents this type of governance structure. It is a non-profit agency funded by the Ministry of Community and Social Services and has a board of directors with a majority of family members of young adults with intellectual disabilities. The agency does not provide any direct support provision (e.g. personal assistance) but focusses solely on facilitating individuals with their support plans, providing brokerage and help navigating through the system. The provision of unencumbered facilitation has enabled brokerage to be independent of service provision. It therefore ensures there is no conflict of interest between the provider role and brokerage role.

A second model is embedding independent facilitation within a peer- or family-driven organisation. Families for a Secure Future is an example of such a family arrangement in Ontario, whereas local IL Centers (Canada's variant of CILs) provide peer support. In Ontario, eleven IL Centers already provide support to consumers who are part of the Direct Funding Program for people with physical disabilities. This has merits as well as challenges. The strength of embedding independent facilitation within existing family or peer groups is that individuals and their families have more choice and autonomy in arranging support. The dilemma with this structure is that families may not represent the wishes and goals of their individual son/daughter, which may give rise to a conflict of interest.

Thirdly, the hybrid approach where a number of service providers spin off resources to a new entity exists in several areas of Ontario, where family leaders and service providers are working together to build an independent facilitation entity. One possible outcome of this work is that service providers will spin off staff resources to a new entity. This approach to independent facilitation seems particularly well suited for geographical areas which have widely dispersed and/or remote populations and could benefit from the service providers collaborating around a new structure. With this approach, providers would make a joint commitment to the values and principles of independent facilitation. Each agency would then provide facilitation staff to the new entity and the ministry would provide incentives. For example, the Ministry might provide some core funding to ensure that no one provider was burdened with operational costs. Such an approach requires community development work in order to be sure that family groups and service providers are all committed to the same values and directions. As more and more families receive

---

[101] *Ibid.*, p. iii.
[102] For a full description, see *CLBC Service Plan, supra*, n. 99.

individualised funding, service providers are realising the value of third-party facilitation. This approach to governance requires that trust be built amongst the key service providers and that family members play a driving role in the development.

Finally, in several areas of Ontario, coordinated facilitator networks operate. These are networks of freelance trained facilitators paid by a coordinating body with government funding. These networks create a home for facilitators to hold conversations, solve problems together and reflect on what works best when facilitating. This approach was originally developed in some US states, such as Michigan, where mental health policy requires that independent facilitation be an option for all people who are users of the mental health system. This coordinated network involves a regional committee with a paid chairperson and holds government money to pay facilitators. Individuals and families can choose from a list of trained facilitators. The regional committee provides an oversight role which includes monitoring and training.

This coordinated facilitator network approach may work well in a dispersed-population area. In reality, however, it is an option with real limitations. It is very hard to build freelance facilitation capacity because the pay for facilitators is contingent upon work available. So, for this governance approach to be effective in Ontario or BC, it would require a cadre of part-time facilitators. However, this option would have further potential if based on peer support with other persons with disabilities, as opposed to professional facilitators.

As communities develop their functions and structures for independent facilitation, we may see any one of these four approaches prevailing, or we may witness a combination of approaches. For example, in a rural area, one could imagine a hybrid approach combined with a coordinated roster of facilitators drawn from a network. This would provide some stability, with a core group of full-time professional facilitators and a few part-time peer support facilitators being available as needed.[103]

As well as independent facilitation, it is worth noting that the ministry in Ontario also funds adult protective service workers through agencies which help to protect the rights of people who have a developmental disability living in the community. These are for adults who are capable of living somewhat independently in the community, but who do not have parents or extended family providing them with support and advocacy. In these cases, there needs to be a stronger safety net of support which continues to protect their rights. These individuals often 'fall between the cracks' because they are viewed as both too skilled to benefit from traditional developmental services (e.g. day care activities) and not capable of benefitting from mainstream community supports and services.[104] As a result, they quite often become vulnerable to abuse, exploitation and neglect. Protective service workers play a role similar

---

[103] Please refer to: http://www.facilitationleadership.com/home.html (accessed 5 November 2010).
[104] *Supra*, n. 59.

to that of social workers, but are more focussed on providing service coordination, advocacy and outreach to support independent community living and protecting the rights of adults who have a developmental disability.[105] Protective service workers carry a challenging and complex caseload which can range from assistance with financial management to help with the justice system or abuse prevention.

Overall, the various mechanisms used in BC and Ontario represent a fundamental shift in the power and control over disability supports, with the emphasis shifting to facilitating people to govern and manage their own ongoing supports. The aforementioned examples illustrate how new roles are being developed in the self-directed programmes to provide safeguarding of those deemed vulnerable as well as to ensure accountability.

Supported Decision Making

Another critical demand-side change has been the reform of the legal capacity legislation to enable less restrictive alternatives to guardianship and other forms of substitute decision making. On 6 October 2004, the Montreal Declaration on Intellectual Disabilities[106] was adopted in Canada. It declared that states should

> provide the services and the necessary support to facilitate persons with intellectual disabilities in making meaningful decisions about their own lives. ... Accordingly, where individuals have difficulty making independent choices and decisions, laws and policies should promote and recognize supported decision-making. States should provide the services and the necessary support to facilitate persons with intellectual disabilities in making meaningful decisions about their own lives.[107]

Despite the declaration, there are a number of challenges in implementing a supported decision-making system, as advocated by the Montreal Declaration. These include difficulty in designating the support network – with many not considered 'competent' to designate – as well as developing and maintaining support networks

---

[105] *Ibid.*

[106] The Montreal Conference of the Pan-American Health & World Health Organizations on Intellectual Disability was held on 5–6 October, 2004. This conference was organised by the West Montreal and Lisette-Dupras Readaptation Centers in collaboration with the Montreal WHO/PAHO collaborating centre and with the help of the *Fédération québécoise des centres de réadaptation en déficience intellectuelle*, the Ministry of Health and Social Services of Quebec, and the *Office des personnes handicapées du Québec*. This conference allowed experts in the field from the Americas to come together to discuss the state of fundamental civil rights accorded to intellectually disabled people throughout the world. The accomplishment of this conference was the unanimous adoption and endorsement by the seventy-five participants from seventeen American countries as well as the principal organisations committed to the defence of the rights of persons with an intellectual disability of the Montreal Declaration on Intellectual Disabilities.

[107] *Montreal Declaration* (2004), available at: http://www.opadd.on.ca/News/documents/montreal-declarationMTL.pdf (accessed 5 July 2010).

due to lack of policy, resources, and community capacity.[108] Moreover, people in institutions and in many community services are denied supported decision making and have their rights removed, as are people under the authority of public guardians. However, progress has been made: Bach concedes that CACL and disability rights activists are challenging a few thousand years of law and moral philosophy on who counts as a person before the law.[109]

In terms of mental capacity legislation in Ontario, the Consent and Capacity Board (CCB) holds hearings and makes decisions under the mental health laws of Ontario, the Mental Health Act, the Substitute Decisions Act and the Health Care and Consent Act (1995). The Substitute Decisions Act and Health Care Consent Act refer to capacity as relating to two streams of decision making: decisions in respect to property (banking, day-to-day finance, etc.) and decisions related to personal care (shelter, care, health, etc). However, health care decisions (defined as decisions related to treatment, admission to long-term care homes and personal assistance services in long-term care homes) come under the separate Health Care Consent Act. This was in order to clarify consent and to ensure that all persons had a substitute decision maker for health care, even if that person had not executed a power of attorney for personal care or was not the subject of an order for guardianship. Significantly, the two acts confirm that capacity is issue specific and relates to a particular decision. A person may be capable of personal care but incapable in respect to property in the broadest sense. A person may be capable in respect to some property decisions, such as simple day-to-day financial decisions (shopping for food, paying rent), but incapable of managing extensive assets or a business.[110]

Another important point the legislation confirms is that there is a presumption of capacity.[111] Capacity should not come into question unless there is evidence to question that capacity for any purpose and a decision needs to be made. This presumption has broad implications. It means that it is important to look at the individual and his or her own individual ability to understand and appreciate information relevant to making a decision and not at any labels or diagnoses of disorders or disabilities. This presumption of capacity is consistent with trends in modern legislation around the world.

While these provide safeguards to an individual's personhood, the legislation nonetheless focuses on substitute decision making which involves decisions being made by one person on behalf of another, who is usually determined to be (mentally)

---

[108] Bach, M. (2007) *Supported Decision Making – Lessons from Canada*, Presentation, Canadian Association for Community Living, January.

[109] *Ibid.*

[110] Wahl, J. (n.d.) *Capacity and Capacity Assessment in Ontario, Barrister and Solicitor*, Advocacy Centre for the Elderly.

[111] Substitute Decisions Act, s.2; Health Care Consent Act, s.4.

incapable of making his/her own decisions.[112] In response to concerns about a person's autonomy – and to meet the goals of Article 12 of the UN Convention – there is a growing momentum towards supported decision making. A recent Ontario Human Rights Tribunal decision, for example, strongly endorsed the principle of supported decision making. Ontario's Divisional Court also has recognised the importance of the role of supports.[113] Given these decisions, Community Living Ontario has issued a resolution asking for government policy and legislation to be examined and amended to enshrine the right to legal capacity, as set out in the UN Convention.

In terms of legal capacity law in BC, recent legislation has been passed, as well as provisions for alternatives to guardianship through supported decision making, as provided for under four laws which promote an adult's right to self-determination. These replace the Patients Property Act which reflected a traditional protective and paternalistic approach towards vulnerable adults who lose their capacity to make decisions regarding their personal rights and their property.

These four Acts comprise what is known as the Adult Guardian Legislation:

1. the Representation Agreement Act;
2. the Adult Guardianship Act;
3. the Health Care (Consent) and Care Facility (Admission) Act;
4. the Public Guardian and Trustee Act.

The Acts provide support and protection for those who are deemed vulnerable or incapable of making their own decisions. The legislation attempts to find a balance between protecting and empowering those deemed most vulnerable, including older and disabled persons.

Importantly, as well as the option of an enduring power of attorney as in many other jurisdictions, representation agreements (RAs) allow a trusted person to act as a person's representative. Rather than legal guardianship, which strips a disabled person of their voice and restricts their rights, RAs offer a flexible and effective legal planning tool to allow others to speak on their behalf.[114] A representative must act honestly and in good faith, exercise the care, diligence and skill of a reasonably prudent person and act within the authority given in the representation agreement.[115] When helping the adult to make decisions or when making decisions on behalf of the adult, a representative must consult, to the extent reasonable, with the adult to determine his or her current wishes, and comply with those wishes if it is reasonable to do so. If an adult's current wishes cannot be determined or it is not reasonable to

---

[112] For a comprehensive review, see Bach, M. and Kerzner, L. (2010) *A New Paradigm for Protecting Autonomy and the Right to Legal Capacity*, paper prepared for the Law Commission of Ontario.

[113] *Gray v. Ontario* [2006] O.J. No.266 (Ont. Sup. Ct.) [Gray].

[114] Please refer to: http://www.bclaws.ca/EPLibraries/bclaws_new/document/ID/freeside/00_96405_01 (accessed 14 January 2011).

[115] Part 3, Section 16, Duties of Representatives.

comply with them, the representative must comply with any instructions or wishes the adult expressed while capable. If the adult's current instructions or expressed wishes are not known, the representative must act on the basis of the adult's known beliefs and values, or in the adult's best interests, if his or her beliefs and values are not known.

There are two types of RAs: Section 7 'standard' agreements and Section 9 'enhanced' agreements. It is intended that standard agreements allowing comparatively straightforward decisions, such as authorising a representative to look after the adult's routine financial affairs, may be completed and signed without the involvement of a lawyer. Section 9 agreements are more detailed and deal with more complex decisions, such as authorising a representative to manage the adult's business or refusing to give consent to life support treatments for the adult. Those agreements require consultation with a lawyer.

In addition, new amendments recently enacted make a number of significant changes to the aforementioned four Adult Guardian Acts. These are the Health Statutes Amendment Act (2007) (Bill 26) and the Adult Guardianship and Planning Statutes Amendment Act (2007) (Bill 29).[116] This new legislation came into force in July 2010.[117]

The most significant change from the amending Acts is that there is not going to be a government-funded registry for all RAs, as originally planned in the RA Act. A private registry service has been developed through the Representation Agreement Resource Centre.[118] The second major change is in response to concerns of some people that further protection from potential abuse was necessary if there was not going to be a registry. Therefore, in order to make a standard RA, a person must appoint a monitor. A monitor must make reasonable efforts to determine whether a representative of the adult is complying with the aforementioned duties. If the person does not appoint a monitor, a public trustee may choose someone or become the monitor by default.

The system in BC provides an important and useable legal template for supported decision making, where a person receives support from others who have a trusting and committed relationship based on shared life experiences and personal knowledge, to

---

[116] The Canadian Centre for Elder Law Studies and the British Columbia Law Institute (2006) *Study Paper on a Comparative Analysis of Adult Guardianship Laws in BC, New Zealand and Ontario.*

[117] It is worth noting that the Supreme Court of Canada has struck down some sections of Bill 29, finding that 'the measures adopted by the government constitute a virtual denial of the s. 2(d) right to a process of good faith bargaining and consultation. The absolute prohibition on contracting out in s. 6(2), as discussed, eliminates any possibility of consultation. Section 6(4) puts the nail in the coffin of consultation by making void any provisions in a collective agreement imposing a requirement to consult before contracting out. Section 9, in like fashion, effectively precludes consultation with the union prior to laying off or bumping'. The decision by the Supreme Court is suspended for twelve months, in which period the BC government must ensure provincial legislation is in compliance with the Court's ruling.

[118] See http://www.nidus.ca (accessed 14 January 2011).

express or represent the person to third parties, and/or to process information. It has been hailed by the disability community as highly successful legislative recognition of supported decision making. In particular, the model is notable for its more flexible approach to defining incapability. It recognises shades of grey and establishes four factors to be taken into account, one of which recognises the defining feature of support relationships as being one of trust.[119]

Enabling a Choice in Living Arrangements

In addition to reconfiguring the supply side of the residential service landscape, which is discussed later, there are a number of demand-side initiatives in both Ontario and BC which support persons with disabilities in gaining access to independent living arrangements.

In Ontario, much investment has been made recently in affordable housing. The Canada-Ontario Affordable Housing Program Agreement (2005) comprised an investment of at least CAN$734 million by the federal, provincial and municipal governments. This has led to the development and construction of 15,059 new housing units. The programme was extended an additional two years in 2009 (ending 31 March 2011), leading to another 6,444 units being developed.[120] Despite this, new social housing in Ontario remains limited, given the policy decision by the province to shift the funding and administration of public and social housing to municipalities.[121] This remains a core challenge for persons with disabilities in accessing housing.

The ministry also offers a few programmes to assist with living supports for persons with physical disabilities, which were identified at the start of the chapter. These are the Assistive Devices Program,[122] which provides financial assistance to help residents with long-term physical disabilities to obtain basic assistive devices essential for independent living, and the Attendant Outreach Program,[123] which provides visiting attendant services. There is also the Self-Managed Attendant Services programme which lets people with disabilities choose and hire their own attendants. These offer people with serious physical disabilities the opportunity to remain at home in the community rather than living in a care facility. However, these programmes

---

[119] *Supra*, n. 114.
[120] Ministry for Municipal Affairs and Housing (2011) http://www.mah.gov.on.ca/Page126.aspx#Progress (accessed 14 December 2012)
[121] Swanton, S. (2009), *Social Housing Wait Lists and the One-Person Household in Ontario*, Canadian Policy Research Networks Inc. and Social Housing Services Corporation.
[122] Please refer to: http://www.canadabenefits.gc.ca/f.1.2cl.3nkj.5mp@.jsp?refid=20591&lang=en&url= http%3A%2F%2Fwww.health.gov.on.ca%2Fenglish%2Fpublic%2Fprogram%2Fadp%2Fadp_mn .html (accessed 5 August 2010).
[123] Please refer to: http://www.canadabenefits.gc.ca/f.1.2cl.3nkj.5mp@.jsp?refid=20633&lang=en&url= http%3A%2F%2Fwww.health.gov.on.ca%2Fenglish%2Fpublic%2Fprogram%2Fltc%2F21_other .html%232 (accessed 5 August 2010).

currently have significant waiting lists and remain another challenge for persons choosing their living arrangements.[124]

People in BC face similar challenges to those in Ontario in accessing affordable social housing, despite recent efforts at improving the social housing stock.[125] The provincial government has been focussed in recent years on rental assistance supplements through the Rental Assistance Program, as well as new emergency shelter beds.[126] The former programme goes some way towards offering persons with disabilities the opportunity to rent property. However, only persons whose household income is from employment and who pay 30 per cent of their household income towards rent are eligible. Persons who receive income assistance from the Employment and Assistance for Persons with Disabilities Act or persons living in subsidised housing are not eligible.

There are also some programmes, as identified earlier, which aim to provide support to persons with physical disabilities in their activities of daily living. These include Choices in Supports for Independent Living (CSIL), which gives people with physical disabilities CAN$3,000 per month to purchase attendant services, and the Provincial Housing Program which provides housing assistance to low- and moderate-income individuals and families.

CLBC's goal is to actively support individuals to move from higher-cost residential settings to more person-centred, cost-effective residential options, thus freeing financial resources for the needs of other individuals. In collaboration with individuals, families and service providers, CLBC has completed a comprehensive review of individuals living in group homes to determine if an individual's needs can be better met in an alternative, community-based residential option. It has also begun expanding alternative options including individuals living in family type settings, caregivers living in a person's home, roommate models in which people provide support in exchange for room and board and/or a small payment, living with a roommate who acts in a more formal, paid caregiver role, cluster arrangements which share a live-in caregiver and other options as they are identified. These models have shown demonstrable progress in BC.[127]

At the same time, CLBC has had to maintain existing group home vacancies to allow opportunities to consolidate those homes where residents choose an alternative model. It acknowledges that this increases costs in the short term but creates an opportunity to reallocate resources in the longer term. Where an assessment indicates an opportunity to make a change, individuals and families are offered an

---

[124] Ontario Attendant Services Advisory Committee (2010) *Unleashing Attendant Services for People with Physical Disabilities: Better Quality Service at a Lower Cost to the Health System*, November.

[125] Canadian Center for Policy Alternatives (2010) *Unpacking the Housing Numbers: How Much New Social Housing Is BC Building?* September 2010.

[126] *Ibid.*

[127] *CLBC Service Plan*, *supra*, n. 99.

informed choice to pursue an alternative option. CLBC begins a dialogue with those individuals, families and service providers to explore the opportunity and help to develop a support plan for each individual and start the recruitment and training of an appropriate alternative residential provider. This is supported by developing partnerships with community agencies to identify cost efficiencies and new, more innovative ways to provide needed services.

Ultimately, then, the focus of both provincial governments has been more on redesigning the residential support provider market rather than developing more means to access mainstream housing markets, as explored further in the supply-side reform section. With the restrictive and limiting programmes discussed here, having a choice in living arrangements for those with disabilities remains a challenge.

Enhancing Consumer Purchasing Power

In addition to the provincial benefits and direct funding mechanisms, the Canadian approach to enhancing consumer purchasing power and creating more sustainable resource mechanisms has been the establishment of a Registered Disability Savings Plan (RDSP). This is a savings plan for families to develop long-term financial security for their relatives with significant disabilities. The relevant Canadian legislation is the Canada Disability Savings Act, S.C. 2007, c. 35, s. 136. The purpose of the Act is to encourage long-term savings through registered disability savings plans to provide for the financial security of persons with severe and prolonged impairments in physical or mental functions. According to the BC Minister of Housing and Social Development, 'we are committed to helping families develop solutions which best suit their needs'.[128] The broader aim of the scheme is to provide low-income earners with the tools to achieve financial independence.

Any individual eligible for the Disability Tax Credit may establish an RDSP. In the case of a minor, a parent or guardian can establish and direct the RDSP. There is a CAN$200,000 lifetime contribution limit, but there is no annual limit on contributions. Contributions are permitted by the individual, family member and/or friends. There are no restrictions on when the funds can be used or for what purpose.

Contributions to RDSPs may be supplemented by a Canada Disability Savings Grant and Canada Disability Savings Bond. The government may pay a matching Canada Disability Savings Grant of up to CAN $3,500 a year on contributions. The government may also pay a Canada Disability Savings Bond of up to CAN $1,000 a year into the RDSPs of low-income and modest-income Canadians. The bond is paid into an RDSP even if no contributions were made to the plan.

---

[128] Quoted in Etmanski, A. (2009) *Safe and Secure: Six Steps to Creating a Good Life for People with Disabilities, RDSP Edition*, PLAN Institute.

Upon withdrawal, the investment is taxed in the hands of the beneficiary, but is likely to be taxed at a much lower rate. Most provinces have now exempted the RDSP as an asset and income when determining a person's eligibility for provincial disability benefits. This is especially important because people with disabilities can now accumulate savings without jeopardising disability benefits. Also, in BC, Planned Lifetime Advocacy Network (PLAN) has future planning initiatives which are run for and by a network of families and professionals to ensure that all families and persons with disabilities have an opportunity to set up an RDSP and are provided with ongoing support. The programmes and services are focussed on educating and empowering a person with a disability to articulate his or her preferences. PLAN's programmes were assessed as accessible, cost-effective and administratively simple to implement.[129]

SHAPING THE SUPPLY SIDE OF REFORM

The Awarding of Funding to Foster Service Reform

As stated at the beginning of the chapter, there is broad acceptance of the concepts of provincial sovereignty and flexibility, which has made provincial governments more autonomous from federal interference to administer social programme funds in ways they see fit. This means that provinces are also responsible for commissioning and monitoring the support provider sector. This section focusses on the recent reconfiguration of contracting, standards and monitoring in BC, using the recent policy changes in CLBC as an example, to illustrate the change.

In BC, funding to service providers for persons with intellectual disability is administered by CLBC. In CLBC, the Quality Service Division carries out the commissioning with the network of service providers from across the province and makes decisions on requests for funding for supports and services. Within the Quality Service Division, CLBC analysts undertake a key role in managing the allocation of resources in the face of competing needs. They develop and monitor contracts with service providers to ensure cost-effectiveness and quality and that deliverables are met and outcomes are achieved. In this role, they work with service providers through partnerships with agencies which support progressive, person-centred approaches, to increase their capacity. They also promote innovative support options.[130] Given the policy focus on individualised funding, they also are involved in freeing funds from contracts so people can choose or develop more individualised supports. Finally,

---

[129] Australian Department of Housing, Community Services, and Indigenous Affairs (2009) *International Review of Future Planning Options*, Australian Government.

[130] Annual Report, http://communitylivingbc.ca/wp-content/uploads/CLBCAnnualReport2009–2010 web.pdf.pdf (accessed 23 January 2012).

they must identify service gaps and ensure crisis response capabilities are available in service areas.

In practice, analysts are expected to understand the agencies in their area so they can truly determine whether CLBC is getting good value for the money being provided. There is also now a focus on greater facilitator-analyst collaboration to ensure that the trends emerging in people's support plans are being communicated from facilitators to analysts.

The mechanism through which CLBC administers funding is its new service terms and conditions.[131] In the past, the lack of adequate or industry-standard performance measures, the global nature of contracts and the lack of a monitoring framework hampered the ability of government to ensure that contracts were being performed with the highest degree of effectiveness and efficiency.[132] These new contract documents are being implemented in a phased approach, which began in the autumn of 2010 for new contracts, or later for existing contracts which are being modified or renewed. They include the concept of service levels, representing the amount of service to be purchased, and focus more on oversight and output/outcome monitoring. The contract monitoring framework involves self-reporting by the service provider for service levels as well as reporting designed to assist CLBC to best utilise the purchased services and to gauge the quality of the services. Whilst the new model shows real promise, and is widely seen as an improvement over the system which was inherited from MCFD, the required flexibility that the service delivery model seeks to implement is challenging to realise because such a large proportion of CLBC's contracts are structured under the legacy system, and CLBC has provided its assurances that clients will not be moved to the new system involuntarily.[133]

Ongoing refinements to tools used to standardise resource allocation are also being undertaken to achieve greater equity and consistency.[134] CLBC is working towards agreeing on a common standard for agency programme costs and setting a standard payment for the funding of residential placements. CLBC has developed funding guidelines to provide a standardised approach to fund contracts and to provide fairness and equity across the province. The guidelines define a framework

---

[131] This has been a recent process which CLBC has developed and which will replace their existing Client Service Agreement (CSA) and Component Services Schedule (CSS). The new contract documents are comprised of three key elements that together make up the complete agreement between CLBC and service providers: the contract defining the services being acquired and their payment; the terms and conditions, defining the relationship between CLBC and the service provider and each party's contractual obligations; and the schedules of terms and conditions, a component of the terms and conditions primarily governing quality and reporting requirements. Contract Documents available on CLBC Web site, http://www.communitylivingbc.ca/wp-content/uploads/30-TC063010-and-32-Schedules082510.pdf (accessed 23 January 2012).

[132] *CLBC Service Plan, supra*, n. 99.

[133] *Ibid.*

[134] Annual Report, available at: http://communitylivingbc.ca/wp-content/uploads/CLBCAnnualReport-2009–2010web.pdf.pdf (accessed 23 January 2012).

to determine reasonable costs in discussion with service providers. An optional budget template was developed with a definition of costs to assist service providers with understanding budget submission requirements.[135]

Insisting on Standards

An important aspect outlined in the service terms and conditions is the insistence on accreditation of service providers and on the use of formal safeguards.[136] Formal safeguards include standards, monitoring, licensing, external reviews and a complaints policy.

At the outset, third-party accreditation in BC is required of all contracted service provider organisations with total annual contracts of at least CAN$500,000 with the ministry. Those who fail to gain accreditation are automatically not entitled to participate in the requests for funding process. Service provider organisations with total contracts with the ministry of less than CAN$500,000 annually may also, upon agreement by the contract-spending authority, participate in the accreditation initiative. However, this is not a mandatory component. Nonetheless, all providers must meet the terms of CLBC's formal and informal safeguards to address all concerns and satisfy all assurances that providers are responding to CLBC's vision of fostering good lives in welcoming and inclusive communities.

One of their reviews is an instructional review of a practice, situation or incident in which no serious harm was done to individuals served, staff or others, but a potential for harm was identified. An instructional review serves as a positive learning opportunity to highlight approaches which are more effective for service providers, CLBC and others. An instructional review may be initiated by CLBC or requested by a service provider. Meanwhile, a quality service review is an in-depth audit of specific or overall services a service provider is performing. A quality service review is initiated by CLBC on an as-needed basis or as part of the ongoing evaluation of service provider conformance with CLBC mission, values and contract expectations, including standards.

The director of quality assurance within CLBC has an important role to play with all external reviews by approving funds for the review, tracking results and ensuring that broader organisational learning takes place as a result of the external review. The practice of conducting external reviews also leads to shared learning across all providers. CLBC offers service providers and other stakeholders opportunities to learn from the outcomes and recommendations of external reviews, as appropriate, in general terms, to maximise the benefit of external reviews.[137]

---

[135] CLBC (2010) Funding Guidelines, http://www.clanbc.ca/InfoSessionFeb2010/Fundingguidelines-CLANpresentationFeb2010.pdf (accessed 7 July 2012).

[136] See http://www.mcf.gov.bc.ca/accreditation/contractors.htm (accessed 23 January 2012).

[137] See http://www.communitylivingbc.ca/policies_and_publications/documents/ExternalReviewsPolicy.pdf (accessed 23 January 2012).

For those who are accredited, CLBC can consider and act on recommendations from external reviews, including mortality reviews. Actions resulting from external reviews may include:

- Contract renewal and continuance without change;
- Change or move for an individual to a different service provider;
- Contract modification – for example, changes in expectations of service provider regarding training, supervision and staffing;
- Contract termination;
- Change or modification to CLBC policies or practices;
- Development of specific protocols.

For providers who have been awarded funding, if there has been a failure to fulfil their responsibilities, CLBC notifies them of their failure and gives them thirty days to either correct the failure or develop a plan which will correct it. After this time, if the provider has not corrected the failure or responded to the notification, CLBC can immediately terminate a contract.

CLBC can also terminate a contract if the health or safety of the individual receiving the services is at immediate risk. Other reasons for termination are if the provider becomes insolvent and/or declared bankrupt. In addition, each contractor must have a system for responding to complaints and resolving problems. In addition to the aforementioned reviews, there is also a complaint procedure. Where an individual or family is reluctant to go directly to a service provider with a complaint or has been unsuccessful in attempts to resolve issues, he or she can discuss it with CLBC staff or use the CLBC complaint process.[138]

As a designated agency under the Adult Guardianship Act, CLBC responds to allegations of abuse and neglect towards adults with intellectual disabilities.

Reconfiguring the Residential Support Market

In both provinces, as we saw, the systems change process behind the closure of institutions was significant. This section looks at the main policy efforts which were made to bring about the final institutional closures, and also examines how the relevant ministries have since attempted to reconfigure the community support market to ensure a choice in living arrangements, including community lodgings, group homes, family homes or semi-independent living centres.[139]

It was recognised by the Ontario ministry at the outset that closing institutions is an enormous process which requires the commitment, policy and resources of the

---

[138] Please refer to: http://www.communitylivingbc.ca/policies_and_publications/documents/CLBC-ComplaintsResolutionpolicy.pdf (accessed 23 January 2012).

[139] Ministry of Community and Social Services (2008) *Spotlight on Transformation: A Developmental Services Bulletin.* Issue 7, June.

government as well as the participation of persons with disabilities and communities. In Ontario, this involved government engaging communities, using facilitators to assist individuals and families and developing community resources which reflect the needs and aspiration of individuals and their families. To inform the ministry, the Center for Community Based Research (CCBR) participated with a number of leading researchers, consumers, policy makers and family members in presenting policy alternatives and in documenting the closure of a large institution.[140]

In 1996, a four-year community living initiative was announced to help almost 1,000 people who were still residing in institutions to live in the community and reinvest the savings in community supports. In April 1997, the ministry introduced the Making Services Work for People (MSWFP) policy initiative. Its goal was to set out a new framework for delivering supports and services for children and adults who have an intellectual disability. It also aimed to improve these supports and services by making the most of available resources in each local community and to allocate resources to those most in need. MSWFP has resulted in single points of access to residential programmes in communities across Ontario. To access ministry-funded residential supports, individuals apply to their local single point of access.

By 2000, three more institutions had been closed and the number of people living in the remaining three was reduced. The Ontario government invested CAN$276 million to move nearly 1,000 people into new homes and strengthen community services and supports. In addition, the provincial government had to fight a lawsuit with some families resisting one of the closures. More than 160 families fiercely lobbied and launched a lawsuit to prevent the government from closing down the Rideau Regional Centre (at one time the largest facility of its kind in the Commonwealth).[141]

According to the Ontario Ministry of Community and Social Services (2009),[142] for every resident who moved into the community, the disability support sector had to actively involve family members or advocates. They had to balance their wishes with available resources and the community's ability to support them. The average age of the remaining institutional residents was fifty-one years, and most had lived in institutions for about thirty-nine years. Therefore, the government had to take great care and sensitivity with its plans. That meant working closely with residents, families, agencies and communities to find homes with the supports people needed and the opportunities they wanted. When the Liberal government took office in 2004, three institutions remained. These were closed in 2009. Since then, nearly 1,000 people

---

[140] CCBR (1987) Return to the Community: The Process of Closing an Institution. Please refer to: http://www.communitybasedresearch.ca/Page/View/Deinstitutionalization.html.

[141] For the ruling, please refer to: http://www.rrcassociation.ca/Justice%20Smith%20Decision.pdf (accessed 17 July 2010).

[142] Ontario Ministry of Community and Social Services (2009) The End of an Era: Closing Ontario's Institutions for People with a Developmental Disability, *Spotlight on Transformation*.

with an intellectual disability have moved from these last three institutions into Ontario communities.

One step in the development of Ontario's plan to transform the residential service landscape was the formation of the Joint Ministry/Developmental Services Partnership Table. In October 2004, the Partnership Table prepared a Preliminary Discussion Paper: *Transforming Services in Ontario for People Who Have a Developmental Disability*.[143] The ideas in the document were presented for the purpose of discussion, and Partnership Table members used the paper to obtain feedback from their members in the autumn of 2004. Organisations held discussion sessions with their members, and some posted the paper on their Web site. Additionally, individuals and groups were given the opportunity to provide feedback to the ministry.[144]

Other activities which provided input into the transformation strategy included local meetings throughout the province held by the Minister's Parliamentary Assistant (Disabilities) with individuals and families. The Parliamentary Assistant spoke with more than 180 people, most of whom were not affiliated with one of the Partnership Table member organisations or a local service provider. Also, six Policy Forums were held with approximately 1,000 experts in the field, which provided the ministry with advice and ideas. Detailed research was also conducted by ministry staff of approaches in other jurisdictions.

Several themes emerged from the responses to the consultation, specifically the need to:

- strengthen and support individuals and families;
- create a fair approach to supporting individuals and families;
- provide people with more choice and flexibility;
- create a sustainable service system which provides quality supports;
- improve specialised services for people with specific requirements.[145]

The main message emerging from the consultation was that to enable a choice in living arrangements, the ministry and the disability support providers had to ensure that individuals and families were given the right support to sustain them in independent living settings.

The Ontario Ministry of Community and Social Services also established an Innovative Residential Model and invited individuals, families and agencies to collaborate and propose individually tailored housing arrangements. However, each year, the number of people who need developmental services grows. At the same time, the needs of people already being supported are constantly changing. To serve more people and to meet the changing needs of people already being served, the

---

[143] Joint Developmental Services Sector Partnership Table (2004) *Transforming Services in Ontario for People Who Have a Developmental Disability Preliminary Discussion Paper*.
[144] *Supra*, n. 59.
[145] *Ibid.*

ministry also developed the Increasing Community Capacity (ICC) initiative. ICC has two goals: to serve the extra population and to create flexible supports which fit the needs of the presently served population. In addition, the ministry has invested CAN$21 million extra for the Special Services at Home programme for individuals living at home with their families.[146]

In some cases, institutional organisations have reinvested in residential capacity within the community to move and place people from larger congregate care facilities. One example is Ongwanada, a developmental disabilities service which provides community-based support for approximately 600 individuals in Kingston and eastern Ontario. It operates more than twenty community residences located in neighbourhoods in Kingston, Napanee and Gananoque, as well as an extensive Home Share Programme, in which individuals live with a family other than their own which is contracted to provide ongoing support alongside some targeted support from Ongwanada staff. In April 1977, Ongwanada merged with the L.S. Penrose Centre, a facility housing 120 adults with developmental disabilities. The two buildings were renamed the Hopkins and Penrose divisions of Ongwanada. With the merger came a period of intense public controversy over Ongwanada's future role, particularly in response to the continued use of congregated care facilities. The debate resulted in a positive plan for 'redevelopment', which involved the creation of a range of community services and the eventual closing of both facilities. In the 1980s, all the children living at the Hopkins site were transferred to communities near their families or relocated to seventeen new community residences operated by Ongwanada in the Kingston area. During the late 1990s, redevelopment focussed on the adults living at Penrose, a heritage building constructed in the 1860s as a 'Crown asylum for the mentally ill'. The majority of adults chose, in consultation with their families and staff, to move into eleven new community residences located along the Napanee-Gananoque corridor. While Ongwanada still offers group homes, the organisation has greatly expanded its Home Share programme to enable its service users to live with individuals or families in the community. Penrose closed in April 1997, and the site is now the responsibility of the Ontario Realty Corporation (a private organisation responsible for redeveloping the assets).[147]

More typically, many of the former residents now live in condominium buildings or apartments and are supported by approximately 115 community agencies.[148] One such agency is Montage Support Services, a transfer payment agency (for supporting individual budget holders) in downtown Toronto. Montage operates nine condominiums in the city. Their condo model offers a more independent living setting

---

[146] Ministry of Community and Social Services (2009) *Spotlight on Transformation: A Developmental Services Bulletin*. Issue 11, January.

[147] Please refer to Ongwanada Web site at: http://www.ongwanada.com/index.cfm?CategoryID=11&SubCategoryID=13 (accessed 8 January 2010).

[148] Ministry of Community and Social Services (2007) *Spotlight on Transformation: A Developmental Services Bulletin*. Issue 5, November.

for individuals needing less support from paid staff. The condo units are clustered in groups of three at each building, and staff move from apartment to apartment as needed. Another example is Avenue II based out of Thunder Bay, Ontario. It has an independent living programme called N.E.I.G.H.B.O.U.R.S. that stands for Normalized Entry Into Generic Housing Based on Unique Required Supports.[149] The programme provides individualised support, based on clients' personal preferences and needs, to make it possible for individuals with intellectual disabilities to live independently in their own homes. Some individuals choose to live alone whereas others prefer living with another person with a disability.

In BC, as a result of the earlier deinstitutionalisation process, there is a significant infrastructure of smaller residential facilities and group homes. According to the Adult Services Regional Quarterly Report prepared by CLBC (2006), the greatest percentage of adults with a developmental disability living in BC reside in the family homes and group homes operated by the non-profit sector.[150] Since the mid-1990s, gradual changes have been made in reconfiguring the residential support landscape. Recent trends are now emphasising inclusion and self-determination in BC and have resulted in a shift towards residential alternatives to group homes such as life sharing and semi-independent living. BC has pioneered a number of residential options. According to the BC Community Living Research Project (2006), available options include: (1) supported living, (2) semi-independent living services, (3) family model home/ life sharing/ host family/ foster care, (4) cooperative housing, and (5) homeownership.[151]

Supported living is a residential service model based on the provision of only those supports required by an individual who lives largely independently. Support services are separate from housing options. BC Housing offers subsidised housing to people with disabilities who qualify for the Independent Living BC (ILBC) programme.

Semi-independent living services provide a residential option (apartment, house or condominium) for people with all disabilities (and senior citizens) who live for the most part independently and receive a limited amount of hours of services each week from paid staff. Healthlink BC and North Okanagan Community Life Society are examples of providers that offer semi-independent living apartments. For those who need less assistance, Housing Matters BC has provided more than 3,900 affordable assisted living apartments for persons with disabilities (and elderly persons) across the province to date, with more being allocated. New constructions and conversions are funded in partnership with the federal government through the Canada Mortgage and Housing Corporation (CMHC) and through phase one

---

[149] Community Living Research Project (2006) *Residential Options for Adults with Developmental Disabilities*, School of Social Work and Family Studies, University of British Columbia.

[150] Community Living British Columbia (2006) *Adult Services Regional Quarterly Report*, CLBC.

[151] For a full description and evaluation of each model, see *Residential Options for Adults with Developmental Disabilities, supra*, n. 149.

of the Canada-BC Affordable Housing Agreement, while the rent supplements are funded solely by the provincial government.

Life sharing refers to a planned and deliberate coming together of individuals who choose to share their lives, or a portion of their lives, with one another. It includes a home owned or rented by an individual or family in which they live and provide care and support for one or more unrelated persons. In BC, the Burnaby Association for Community Inclusion (BACI) introduced the Life Sharing Network which has three support options: an individual suite, an apartment, or a respite place.[152] BACI currently receives funding from CLBC to assist with the costs of life sharing for individuals with intellectual disabilities. The individual or host family receives payment from a community-based agency or directly from the provincial government in return for the support they provide to the individual. Matching people in terms of location helps to ensure current support networks will be maintained. Life sharing candidates are also matched in terms of personality characteristics to help to foster the relationship and promote a positive experience for both parties.

Cooperative housing is a type of subsidised housing with fixed rent available to 'frail seniors, people at risk of homelessness, people with disabilities, and low-income families, including women and children fleeing abuse'.[153] Housing cooperatives are jointly owned and managed by residents, who become cooperative members. Members participate in decision making, share the responsibilities of running the cooperative and select new members. In BC, the Co-operative Housing Disability Trust is a programme administered by the Community Housing Land Trust Foundation to help people with disabilities who cannot pay for their shares when they move into housing coops. The Trust provides loans with no fees or interest to qualified beneficiaries.[154]

Finally, for persons who choose the option of home ownership, BC Housing offers subsidised housing to people with disabilities who qualify for the Independent Living BC Program. Also, families can establish discretionary trusts to manage funds necessary for homeownership from the RDSP mentioned earlier, and from other revenue sources for persons with disabilities. Money received or withdrawn from the RDSP and managed through the trust is not counted as 'assets' which would otherwise affect the person's eligibility for social assistance and disability-related benefits.

Clearly, both Ontario and BC are intent on widening the available choices for people with disabilities to decide on where they want to live and who to live with, a key policy goal of the CRPD. The transformation from the exclusive use of group homes has begun, thus, favouring the choice in living arrangements being advocated by the CRPD. However, there are still many obstacles which the provincial

---

[152] Burnaby Association for Community Inclusion (2004) *Life Sharing Resource Manual*, p. 1. Available at: http://www.gobaci.com/programs/lifenetwork (accessed 7 October 2010).

[153] Please refer to BC Housing Web site at: www.bchousing.org (accessed 3 November 2010).

[154] Co-operative Housing Disability Trust (2005) *What Is the Disability Trust?* Available at: http://www.chf.bc.ca/pdf/Disability%20Trust-Dec%2005.pdf (accessed 5 November 2010).

governments and community service providers must overcome. In particular, the group home workforce has resisted threatened closures, with the notable example of the Canadian Union of Public Employees drawing picket lines outside Community Living Association-Lanark County group homes.[155] Government and disability groups are in negotiations with the unions, and some groups have also taken cases to court, to ensure that ultimately people with disabilities are able to live a life in the community not controlled by service providers, the provisions of collective agreements or labour disputes.

New Roles for Providers

Given the new context of service reform centred on enabling citizenship, providers are responding to this new paradigm by carving out new roles to help persons with disabilities to achieve this vision.

Community Living St. Marys[156] provides a good example of an organisation which has shifted its emphasis from 'services' to supporting a person in the community. They were established in 1962 and in the 1980s, the agency helped long-time residents to return from institutions. In response to a severe housing shortage, they created an incorporated company that consisted of providing duplex, fourplex and sixplex residential units. In 1983, St. Mary's began a lengthy process of strategic change, reshaping more flexible supports. They made a commitment to community participation, integration and person-centredness in the provision of all supports. By the end of the decade, they had replaced many of their congregated settings.

Despite these efforts, by 1990, they were still experiencing some shortcomings in their original goals. There was a recognition that planning with individuals *and* providing all their services often created a conflict of interest. In response, they fleshed out the principles which would separate planning from direct supports. The director and board established a new structure consisting of a support services division and a planning and community development division. The main reasons behind this separation of functions were twofold. First, it allowed a more autonomous planning process which freed up options in the community (with St. Mary's only being *one* option); this created the perception that the community was a widely available resource. Second, it supported linkages with other organisations and assisted people in thinking more creatively during the planning process.

Since then, community development has been an essential part of St. Mary's work, with facilitators being committed to 'community as a first resort' and exercising creativity in the way they help people to build a life in the community. By 1996, the last remnants of congregated, traditional services had disappeared. The agency not only supports individuals in finding opportunities in the community; it actively

[155] CUPE (2010) *Group Homes*, available at: http://cupe.ca/group-homes (accessed 6 October 2010).
[156] For a more detailed account of St. Mary's transformation story, see Rioux and Prince, *supra*, n. 3.

engages with others to change community conditions. At the heart of this has been change-oriented leadership, which brought all people along during the change process, with individuals, family members, staff, facilitators and board members all feeling that they had ownership of the change. This task of providing inspirational leadership, as Chapter 3 has shown, remains the core task facing service providers who have become constrained by institutional work practices and who face resistance to change.

Other successful examples of agencies providing independent facilitation for persons with individual funding include Vela Microboards in BC and Windsor-Essex Brokerage for Personal Supports in Ontario. Both are also clearly distinct from direct services. The latter example has separated out residential and vocational services from independent planning and facilitation entirely. Windsor-Essex has set up a separate agency for the planning function. Called brokerage, it now provides information and assists people with a variety of tasks related to planning and individualised funding. These include negotiating, writing contracts, building support networks and hiring attendant care staff.[157]

Another key example of an agency which fosters community connection is Planned Lifetime Advocacy Network (PLAN) Institute. PLAN works to reduce the isolation of people with disabilities at the margins of society, through personal network facilitation and the development of social enterprise. It provides training, consultation and research related to these goals to a wide variety of individuals and organisations. Since its establishment, the provider sector has responded by cultivating a more 'community connection' focus within their support arrangements.[158]

An important lesson to draw from these initiatives is that collective approaches to transformation help to ensure that the initiative builds capacity and becomes sustaining, thus, mirroring the best-practice models discussed in Chapter 3. Regardless of where the source of leadership comes from – a family group, manager or disabled persons organisation – shared leadership creates possibilities for collaborative problem solving and keeps the process going throughout later stages of development.[159]

EVALUATION AND COST-EFFECTIVENESS OF CHANGE

The process of reform in Canada has been driven to some extent by research evidence, from early cost evaluations of institutions in the 1970s and 1980s, as mentioned earlier, to evaluations of living arrangements beyond group homes.[160] Given

---

[157] Windsor-Essex Brokerage for Personal Supports (2009) Available at: http://www.windsoressex-brokerage.com/index.htm (accessed on 18 January 2010).

[158] For more examples of organisations developing such community connector programmes, see Johannes, A. and Stanfield, S. (2010) *A Snapshot of Personal Support Network Related Initiatives*, Spectrum's Personal Support Networks.

[159] Rioux and Prince, *supra*, n. 3.

[160] *Residential Options for Adults with Developmental Disabilities, supra*, n. 149.

that there are no longer large institutions for people with intellectual disabilities in Ontario or British Columbia, the focus of their research has increasingly been on group homes and supported living.[161]

Studies exploring supported living have indicated that individuals in supported living arrangements experience social and community-based activities to a greater extent than individuals receiving traditional services, even though costs were similar.[162] Other favourable outcomes associated with supported living included receiving more staff support, having housemates consistent with preferences and residents being their own decision makers in daily affairs. In a three-way comparison between group homes, supported living and semi-independent living, the Community Living Research Project[163] in BC reported the following outcomes:

Group Homes: Favourable outcomes consisted of twenty-four-hour care/supervision available to individuals and organised access to formal supports in the disability community. However, multiple problems have been associated with group home arrangements, as mentioned in the previous chapter. These include: inflexible schedules, high levels of staffing, incompatibility/disputes amongst residents, inability to adapt to residents' changing needs/preferences and low levels of personal choice and autonomy regarding group activities and decisions.[164] Research also indicates that some individuals residing in group homes do not require such high levels of support and may demonstrate 'better outcomes, at lower cost, by living semi-independently'.[165] In terms of cost outcomes, it was reported that group homes had greater annual accommodation support services costs compared to semi-independent living costs. The mean annual total residential cost was CAN$64,105. Paid staff support was 300 percent greater compared to semi-independent living.[166]

Semi-Independent Living: Favourable outcomes consisted of increased choice in lifestyle, greater empowerment, less social dissatisfaction, increased use of community facilities, often living in own home, increased community participation and smaller households. The main unfavourable outcome reported was that planned activities may be minimal or non-existent, which could result in social isolation.

---

[161] Braddock, D., Emerson, E., Felce, D. and Stancliffe, R. J. (2001) 'Living Circumstances of Children and Adults with Mental Retardation or Developmental Disabilities in the United States, Canada, England and Wales, and Australia', *Mental Retardation & Developmental Disabilities Research Reviews* 7(2): 115–121.

[162] Howe, J., Horner, R. H. and Newton, J. S. (1998). 'Comparison of Supported Living and Traditional Residential Services in the State of Oregon', *Mental Retardation* 36(1): 1.

[163] *Residential Options for Adults with Developmental Disabilities, supra*, n. 149.

[164] See Stancliffe, R. J. and Lakin, K. C. (2005) 'Context and Issues in Research on Expenditures and Outcomes of Community Supports', in Stancliffe, R. J. and Lakin, K. C. (eds.) *Costs and Outcomes of Community Services for People with Intellectual Disabilities.* Paul H. Brookes Publishing, Baltimore. pp. 1–22.

[165] Stainton, T., Hole, R., Charles, G., Yodanis, C., Powell, S. and Crawford, C. (2006) *Residential Options for Adults with Developmental Disabilities: Quality and Cost Outcomes.* The Ministry of Children and Family Development, Province of British Columbia, October.

[166] *Ibid.*

In terms of cost outcomes, semi-independent living options were reported as more cost-effective than group homes or at least similar, and could be provided without increasing average per-person costs. The mean annual total residential cost was CAN$14,602.[167]

Supported Living: Favourable outcomes consisted of increased flexibility and adaptability, greater choice, increased community participation, increased social activities, higher staffing ratios and higher ratios of care staff. Unfavourable outcomes consisted of fewer planned activities, higher rates of home vandalism, greater risk of mistreatment/exploitation and decreased likelihood of having a designated key worker (compared to small group homes). In terms of cost outcomes, it was reported that supported living arrangements were more cost-effective than group homes or at least similar, and could be provided without increasing average per-person costs. A mean annual total residential cost was not available in the study.[168]

One particular model of supported living which has shown demonstrable progress in BC is that of home sharing. This model, as identified earlier, is a residential option in which an adult with a developmental disability shares a home with someone (or a family) who is contracted to provide ongoing support. Homes may be owned or rented by the home-sharing provider or by the individual requiring support. In some situations, people live together as roommates in a reciprocal relationship. This initiative has been well supported in policy and procedures, which were developed with the active participation and support of service providers.[169]

Significantly, evaluations are now showing that rather than group home development alongside deinstitutionalisation, focus should be on other supported living arrangements to minimise the effects of *trans*-institutionalisation.[170] This refers to the process of inadvertently moving people from one type of congregated residential setting (or institutionalised care arrangement) to another in a failed attempt to adequately provide resources for people in the community.

In terms of evaluations of *non*-residential self-determination programmes, there are little publicly available government comparative cost data between traditional service-agency-based care and self-managed support programmes. However, a number of third-party research studies and programme evaluations have identified various cost efficiencies in the latter support model. One finding is that self-managed programmes have the potential to produce cost efficiencies because individuals requiring support are better qualified than third parties to understand their own needs and to find ways of meeting them within available resources. In turn, their choices as consumers drive providers in competitive markets to be responsive and

---

[167] *Ibid.*
[168] *Ibid.*
[169] *CLBC Service Plan, supra*, n. 99.
[170] *Supra*, n. 3.

to achieve innovations in support delivery. Available evidence suggests this may be true at least in some circumstances.[171]

An evaluation of Ontario's Direct Funding Programme by the Roeher Institute (2000) found that the pilot programme's cost-effectiveness was attributable to a lower unit cost to provide services and a more efficient use of services.[172] Additionally, their evaluation of the pilot for another Canadian self-managed programme, 'In the Company of Friends',[173] in 1996 concluded that in twelve out of the fifteen cases studied, costs were on average 8.3 per cent lower than other community living situations.[174]

Another study conducted by Mattson-Prince, Manley and Whiteneck (1995) found that self-managed home care costs less than agency-based home care.[175] The forty-two individuals who received funds to hire their own personal care attendants had a mean daily cost for paid care services that was 10 per cent less than the twenty-nine participants who used agency-based care. These differences remained despite the fact that the self-managed care group received, on average, more hours of care than the agency-based care group. Firstly, the agency-based care group received 10 per cent of their care from skilled providers, versus 8 per cent in the self-managed care group. This difference may explain some of the cost savings for the self-managed care group, as skilled providers would receive a higher wage per hour. Secondly, the self-managed care group received a substantially higher amount of unpaid care, which could reduce the amount of paid care hours used by the self-managed group.[176]

Finally, it was also reported by Spalding et al. (2006) that self-managed support programmes may also benefit consumers' income in terms of the potential for gainful employment. In the 1994 evaluation of the pilot for the Ontario Direct Funding project by the Roeher Institute, consumers reported that the flexibility of managing their support needs led to increased employment opportunities when using the self-managed care programme.[177]

---

[171] Spalding, Watkins, and Williams, *supra*, n. 88.

[172] Roeher Institute (2000) *Individualized Quality of Life Project: Final Evaluation Report.*

[173] This program is funded by the Department of Family Services in Manitoba and is administered through an agency called Living in Friendship Everyday (LIFE). It serves individuals with developmental disabilities. It started as a pilot program in 1993 and has been a permanent program since 1997.

[174] Roeher Institute (1996) *'In the Company of Friends': Final Evaluation of the Pilot Program.*

[175] Mattson Prince, J., Manley, M. S. and Whiteneck, G. G. (1995). 'Self-Managed versus Agency-Provided Personal Assistance Care for Individuals with High Level Tetraplegia', *Archives of Physical Medicine and Rehabilitation* 76: 919–923.

[176] Spalding, Watkins, and Williams, *supra*, n. 88.

[177] Roeher Institute (1994) *Evaluation of the Pilot for the Ontario Direct Funding Project.* Roeher Institute, Ontario.

Despite these positive messages, although individualised funding has been a cornerstone of the service delivery model and its long-term sustainability, there has been very low uptake amongst existing or new clients in BC, partly because of the legacy system but also because of insufficient overall system flexibility for individuals switching from conventional service-driven models. This has been mitigated to some degree by the easier provision and higher uptake of direct respite, but for the residential context it remains challenging.[178]

Some challenges remain in the Canadian transformation towards self-directed supports. Provinces in Canada have experienced substantial cuts to all services, programmes, equipment and supports as a result of federal fiscal cutbacks. A recent study found that BC's per capita funding for voluntary disability organisations in 2006 was lower than in 1998.[179] In BC as in other provinces, there are now lengthy wait lists for scarce services.[180]

BC and Ontario have also had to face obstacles in developing their new systems of allocating funds. At the heart of this, both provinces have grappled with whether direct funding programmes should be attached to service reform efforts. According to Lord and Hutchison (2007), there are both benefits and challenges to attaching direct funding projects to service reform efforts.[181] On the one hand, many feel that direct funding projects should remain a central part of service reform – in other words, unbundling previous block funds into individual support funds. However, there are many challenges to implementing this. First, it takes time to get the major players on board. Throughout the transformation process, issues of power sharing can stifle the initiative and must be addressed. Ultimately, existing service providers must give up some resources or some control. There is also the danger that individualised approaches may remain service driven.

On the other hand, many policy developers feel that direct funding programmes should remain independent of service reform, as has been the case with some programmes in Ontario. In these cases, individualised approaches tend to be central and clearly separate from the service system. In Ontario, examples include Ontario Direct Funding and the Toronto Quality of Life independent planning and individualised funding project (now known as the Options Programme and administered by the Family Services Association of Toronto). Here the key benefit is that the initiative can get under way fairly quickly. However, there are also many challenges to developing and expanding these programmes, as they come out of a different

---

[178] *CLBC Service Plan, supra*, n. 99.

[179] Hanlon, N., Rosenberg, M. and Clasby, R. (2007) *Offloading Social Care Responsibilities: Recent Experiences of Local Voluntary Organisations in a Remote Urban Centre in British Columbia*, Canada.

[180] Salter, S. (2002) *'Changing the Rules of the Game' Individualized Funding in B.C.: Implications for Families and Social Workers*. Graduating Essay for Degree of Master in Social Work, University of British Columbia.

[181] Rioux and Prince, *supra*, n. 3.

source from that which funds services. Resistance from formal service providers can be troublesome and it may take time to gain full community support. In this case, education of individuals, families and service providers is a key to success. Also, it is unlikely that direct funding will be fully endorsed unless the policy framework and priorities support these new programmes. An initial portion carved out of the overall social care budget would help to ameliorate this problem. It could later be grown accordingly, as people moved towards self-directed support.

CONCLUSION

This chapter examined how Canada and in particular two of its provinces – British Columbia (BC) and Ontario – have reconfigured the role of government in the lives of persons with disabilities in terms of its overall welfare philosophy and the shape of support delivery. The Canadian model of disability support, or at least the variants in Ontario and BC, represents an example of an early pioneering model which has transitioned from traditional congregated and paternalistic forms of care to a support model emphasising choice and social and economic participation.

The wellsprings of reform have arisen from responses to the economic and human costs of keeping people in institutional, dependent service arrangements. In the search for alternatives, influential reports and pioneering activists and parent groups called for individual funding and person-led supports. Importantly, in BC, a dynamic of change was embedded by establishing a new administration which sought to regularise personalisation across the province. Meanwhile, in Ontario, the Partnership Table enabled all stakeholders to participate in instigating change.

In terms of how Canada has changed the focus of its disability support and sculpted out reform in its social policies, both the federal government and that in the two provinces have implemented a blend of demand-side and supply-side reforms, to enable people with disabilities to re-engage in society. New policy options have emerged, which enable the use of individualised funding. This model is based on the key mechanism of a facilitator to help persons to utilise these budgets and design personally crafted support plans. Another key ingredient has been the establishment of representation agreements to give voice to persons who may have otherwise lost their capacity to be involved in decision making about their own future. Finally, the new Registered Disability Savings Plans give people the opportunity to build up assets, which can be used to provide for the future support needs of persons with disabilities.

Meanwhile, in terms of supply-side reforms, Canada has established a strictly monitored system of procurement which has been designed to embed a dynamic of change in service providers. In terms of choice in living arrangements, in BC and Ontario, the closing of the provincially run institutions has meant thousands of people have moved into communities over the past twenty-five years. One of the core challenges has been the maintenance of community networks for those who have been traditionally segregated. This has given rise to a new generation of support providers which seek to build community links rather than maintain a person in a closely embedded service structure.

In addition to the political commitment from both federal and provincial governments involved in driving change, similar to that in the United States, an important success factor in this transformation has been a strong disability advocacy movement, working closely with workforce unions and with government to shape the new vision. At the heart of this has been the strong DPO and Parent Movement, as evidenced by groups such as CACL and the Woodlands Parents Group. This created the impetus to pilot new initiatives and demonstration projects.

A second success factor has been the degree of partnership in policy development. The previously mentioned Partnership Table in Ontario serves as an important example of government working successfully with all the different stakeholders. This collaboration, as we saw in Chapter 3, is needed in order to continue driving personalisation reform and to oversee the labour force and infrastructural changes.

Altogether, self-managed support remains a core part of the active citizenship agenda in BC and Ontario. Both provinces provide working examples of the successes and challenges inherent in implementing the guiding principles and obligations of the CRPD. One of the key challenges is that the new model remains in coexistence alongside the conventional service delivery model, and as a result, those administering disability support are caught in a dual paradigm as long as the legacy clients and global contracts remain a distinct and separately structured system. There remain core challenges facing persons with disabilities, including fiscal retrenchment, staff resistance and the erosion of benefits. The transition from this former model has been marked by the growing social movement towards independent living and government commitments towards ensuring meaningful participation, as well as by the work of the 'early adopters' – organisations which are developing new promising initiatives. Cumulatively, according to Lord and Hutchison, we can see the momentum of change in Canada reaching a 'tipping point' where broader change then begins to occur more rapidly.[182]

---

[182] Rioux and Prince, *supra*, n. 3.

6

Active Citizenship and Disability in the United Kingdom (England and Northern Ireland)

INTRODUCTION

This chapter examines the development of personalisation in support delivery in the United Kingdom. It considers the similarities across England and Northern Ireland (NI) in how this process has evolved. In addition, any discerning differences between the two areas will be identified throughout the chapter. The individualising of care budgets became central to the English New Labour government's ambitions for 'modernising' social care, and sits at the heart of the personalisation agenda. This has been attributable in part to campaigning by a vigorous disability movement which has increasingly looked to attain equal rights and participation in society. This agenda has since been highlighted as a part of the more recent coalition government's strategy, albeit with new ways of implementing this policy.[1]

The United Kingdom ratified the CRPD and the Optional Protocol in June 2009 (albeit with some general reservations[2]). It requires government to take action to remove barriers and give disabled people real freedom, dignity and equality. This is being coordinated by the national focal point in government required under the Convention, the Office for Disability Issues (UK-wide). Meanwhile the Equality and Human Rights Commission (EHRC) – together with the Northern Ireland Human Rights Commission (NIHRC) – has a responsibility under the Convention as part of the national implementation mechanism to promote the effective implementation of the Convention (Article 31).

As this chapter shall explore, the United Kingdom represents a model where 'choice' is a central guiding principle in the design of support systems, as set out

---

[1] The coalition government has outlined its vision for personalised social services in its response to the Health Select Committee Report on Social Care. See: http://www.official-documents.gov.uk/document/cm78/7884/7884.pdf (accessed 18 August 2010).

[2] Please refer to: http://www.disabilityaction.org/centre-on-human-rights/human-rights-and-disability/reservations-to-the-convention (accessed 12 February 2012).

by the Independent Living Strategy.[3] It examines the wellsprings of this reform and the different mechanisms which have emerged such as individual funding and new service standards in order to generate change in how persons with disabilities access support.

AN OVERVIEW OF THE ADMINISTRATION OF DISABILITY SUPPORT

Primary legislation concerning the delivery of disability support and community care in the United Kingdom is broadly similar across its devolved parliaments, but it is not generic. England, Wales, Scotland and Northern Ireland have distinct legislation passed by their National Assemblies and Parliaments. Policy direction related to disability and mental health support in the United Kingdom largely comes from the prime minister's Strategy Unit and the Department of Health – and the Department of Health, Social Services and Public Safety in NI. Within the English Department of Health, there are a number of offices related to disability. These include, inter alia, the Director General for Social Care; the National Director for Learning Disabilities, who provides national leadership on the delivery of the cross-government policy such as *Valuing People Now*, the current learning disability strategy; and the National Director for Social Care Transformation. The last post derives from the December 2007 *Putting People First* concordat, signed by government, council and sector leaders, which set out a three-year programme to personalise adult social care in England, backed by a £520 million grant.[4]

The Department of Health also is responsible for the National Health Service (NHS) and controls England's ten Strategic Health Authorities (SHAs), which oversee all NHS activities in England. In turn, each SHA supervises all the NHS Primary Care Trusts (PCTs) in its area.[5] Within England, there are 151 PCTs.[6] These still have responsibility for purchasing services to meet the health needs of persons with disabilities and mental health problems, although since the 1990 NHS and Community Care Act, they do not offer long-term community care. Since its launch in 1948, the NHS has grown to become the world's largest and most comprehensive publicly funded health service. Although funded centrally from national taxation, NHS services in the devolved administrations of Scotland, Wales and Northern Ireland manage their local NHS services separately. Despite this, they remain similar in most respects and continue to be talked about as belonging to a single, unified system. However, in disability, they play more of a residual role, particularly with

---

3 Office for Disability Issues (2008) *Independent Living Strategy*, HM Government, London.
4 For further details, please refer to: http://www.dh.gov.uk/en/Publicationsandstatistics/Publications/ PublicationsPolicyAndGuidance/DH_081118 (accessed 20 August 2010).
5 Please refer to: http://www.nhs.uk/NHSEngland/thenhs/about/Pages/overview.aspx (accessed 20 August 2010).
6 Please refer to: http://www.nhs.uk (accessed 20 August 2010).

the closure of the NHS campuses, and increasingly focus on specialist support for disabled people with medical needs.

The Department of Work and Pensions (DWP) (Department for Social Development in NI) is responsible for most of the allowances and benefits for people with disabilities. These include the Disability Living Allowance and Attendant allowance.[7] As a result, this department can make a large impact on the participation of persons with disabilities in employment and society.

Also at the national level, the Office for Disability Issues (ODI) was set up to help government to deliver on the commitment made in the report, *Improving the Life Chances of Disabled People*.[8] The report says that by 2025, disabled people should have the same opportunities and choices as non-disabled people and be respected and included as equal members of society. The ODI is also the focal point within the UK government for coordinating the implementation of the UN Convention. However, it is the responsibility of individual departments to actively take forward action to implement the Convention in the areas where they have policy responsibility. Each devolved administration including NI coordinates its own work on the Convention and ODI is liaising with each one.

There are also a number of Ministers of State working more specifically on the disability portfolio. The Parliamentary Under Secretary of State for Disabled People (formerly Minister for Disabled People) operates within the DWP. The remit of the position is to promote equality for disabled people. The Minister of State for Care Services (within the Department of Health) is responsible for advancing Long Term Care Reform and social care policy including, inter alia, the following portfolios: Mental Health, Physical Disabilities, Autism, and Learning Disabilities.

At the regional level of governance, the English Local Authorities with Social Services Responsibilities play a key role in commissioning services, thereby giving them a platform for governing the rollout of national policy. The 1970 Local Authority Social Services Act, which introduced social services departments within Local Authorities, is generally considered a watershed in the development of community-based services for disabled people. This gives Local Authority Social Services 'care managers' the responsibility of commissioning services on behalf of their clients but within a predefined overall budget. With the increase of market principles in public sector provision in the late 1980s, the sector saw the establishment of 'quasi-markets', with competition encouraged between providers. The principle is that purchasers, acting on behalf of service users, should be free to buy services from the provider

---

[7] For a detailed description of the UK benefits and services system, please see Disability Alliance (2009) *Disability Rights Handbook* 34th Edition, April 2009–April 2010.

[8] Please refer to: http://www.cabinetoffice.gov.uk/strategy/work_areas/disability.aspx (accessed 20 August 2010).

whose services best meet a particular need.[9] In addition, general practitioner (GP) practices can decide to become fundholders and receive part of the health authority's (purchaser's) budget from which they can pay for specialised care and services from health providers, including some community care.[10] Commissioning has since remained a key mechanism of funding the UK community care structure. Most local authorities no longer provide any direct care services, purely acting as purchasers or commissioners. Others, either for political or geographical reasons, or because their own provision is the best available, have retained some direct provision like home care services, day centres and residential homes. As we shall see, the commissioning from local authorities has been graduating towards enabling individuals themselves to purchase their own services. According to the new Coalition government, 'It is the challenge for local authorities to reflect the growing demand for personalised care in their commissioning strategies. Personalisation will also mean change in the role of the social care workforce, as individuals increasingly become the arbiters of services'.[11]

Within NI, unlike the separate NHS primary care trusts and local authorities, there are five *combined* Health and Social Care Trusts, meaning a closer alliance between primary and community care administration. These are commissioned by one regional Health and Social Care Board (HSCB), replacing the four earlier Health and Social Services Boards.[12] This focusses on commissioning, resource management and performance management and improvement. There are also five Local Commissioning Groups (LCGs) focussing on the planning and resourcing of services. They were set up to actively engage GPs, other primary care professionals and the voluntary and community sector in the planning and redesign of services to secure better services for the communities they serve.[13] The LCGs cover the same geographical area as the health and social care trusts.

---

[9] Douglas, A. and Philpot, T. (1998) *Coping and Caring: A Guide to Social Services*. Routledge, London.

[10] This provides a unique model of commissioning where medical professionals hold real budgets with which they can purchase primarily non-urgent elective and community care for individuals. Some GP practices came together in consortia, creating larger organisations to pool financial risk and share resources. The Labour government abolished GP fundholding in 1997, but it subsequently announced a new form of GP commissioning in 2004: practice-based commissioning (PBC). PBC was not compulsory: practices that chose to participate were given an indicative budget by their PCT. Since then, the coalition government is planning to abolish PCTs and give responsibility for commissioning of most NHS-funded services to new statutory GP consortia. For further information, please see: Smith, J. Curry, N. Mays, N. and Dixon, J. (2010) *Where Next for Commissioning in the English NHS?* Nuffield Trust, 2010 available at: www.nuffieldtrust.org.uk/members/download.aspx?f=/ecomm/files/Where_next_commissioning_KF_NT_230310.pdf (accessed 20 April 2011).

[11] Response to the Health Select Committee Report on Social Care, p. 4. See: http://www.official-documents.gov.uk/document/cm78/7884/7884.pdf (accessed 20 August 2011).

[12] In the wake of a public consultation following the NI Review of Public Administration (RPA) Report 2002.

[13] Please refer to: http://www.engage.hscni.net/about/Background.html (accessed 20 August 2011).

AN OVERVIEW OF THE DISABILITY SUPPORT FRAMEWORK

Disability-Specific State Entitlements

There are three main disability-specific government entitlements available in the United Kingdom – the Disability Living Allowance (DLA), the Attendance Allowance and the Employment and Support Allowance (ESA).

In 1992, the DLA was introduced, replacing and extending the previous Attendance Allowance and Mobility Allowance. Importantly, it is a non-means-tested payment given on top of social security benefits or tax credits for adults who are disabled before the age of sixty-five. It is designed to allow financial assistance for independent living. DLA is not affected by having a job or by the level of earnings. However, if a person saves his or her DLA, the savings may affect other income support eligibility.[14]

The DLA is payable to people who are disabled and who require personal assistance with activities of daily living or mobility or both. The DLA is divided into two parts. Firstly, it includes a section defined as a 'care component' – for help with personal support needs. Secondly, it includes a 'mobility component' – for persons requiring assistance with walking difficulties. It is therefore designed to be a benefit for people who need additional support looking after themselves and those who have difficulty with mobility. It is paid directly to the person with the disability, not a family member. People can qualify for the DLA whether or not they have someone helping them; what matters are the effects of the disability and the help that the people may need, not whether they already get that help. However, it is not designed to act as a payment for one's social supports. Normally, people cannot be paid the 'care component' if they live in a residential home which provides accommodation together with nursing or personal assistance (i.e. group homes). Social supports are funded by the local authority adult social support budget, as detailed later.

At the time of writing, the DLA remains the core disability entitlement in the UK, but from April 2013 a new benefit, Personal Independence Payment, will be piloted and will subsequently replace DLA for disabled people aged 16 to 64. Entitlement is to be based on people's personal circumstances and the impact that their condition or disability has on their ability to live independently. Similar to the DLA, it will have two components; a mobility component and a new daily living component. The exact criteria are not yet known; however, disability rights organisations are concerned about the government's overarching objective to cut 20 per cent of DLA/PIP funding by 2015/16.[15]

---

[14] Income support is a means-tested or income-related benefit intended to provide for basic living expenses for persons out of full-time work.

[15] The rationale for the government plans to introduce a 20% cut expenditure was made clear in Parliament by the Chancellor of the Exchequer in June 2010. The Treasury announced that working age DLA 'caseload and expenditure' would be cut by 20%. This commitment and level of cut were restated by the Minister for Disabled People in December shortly after the consultation was launched for

The Attendance Allowance is a tax-free benefit for people aged sixty-five or older who are physically or mentally disabled and need help with personal assistance or supervision to remain safe. The rules for eligibility are almost the same as the DLA 'care component'.

Meanwhile, ESA is a new benefit paid to people whose ability to work is limited by ill health or disability. Importantly, ESA is not paid simply because a person is found to be incapable of work. The previous assessment system was based on dividing people into two groups: those capable of work and those incapable of work. However, this was seen as a disincentive for people wanting to move from benefits into work and, according to Barbour (2008), did not reflect the reality in people's lives.[16] With the present system, there is a strong focus on the reversal of work disincentives. There has been a purposive link made between ESA and access to local supports. When individuals claim an ESA, they must enter a thirteen-week 'assessment phase' where they must undergo a 'work capability assessment'.[17] During the assessment phase, the person is paid a basic allowance of ESA. ESA claimants after being assessed for having a 'limited capability for work' are divided into two separate groups: the work-related activity group and the support group. The work-related activity group have to meet certain conditions, including attending six work-focussed interviews to identify if there are any barriers to work and what support they could receive to help them to move towards and into work. A work-focussed interview also helps to identify activities, training, education or rehabilitation they could undertake to improve their job prospects. The support group, on the other hand, is for those who have a limited capability for work-related activity and are not expected to undertake these interviews. Those in the support group receive a higher level of ESA than the work-related activity group given their inability to earn a living.

Disability-Specific Services

Disability-specific support services are largely defined by the NHS Act 1948 and National Assistance Act 1948. When enshrined, these Acts established the NHS in the United Kingdom, as well as introduced duties to provide residential accommodation for disabled people. According to Section 21 of the National Assistance Act, the local authority must decide how it will meet identified needs of 'persons aged 18 or over who by reason of age, illness, disability or any other circumstances are in need of care and attention which is not otherwise available to them'.[18] However, at this time, institutionalisation was explicitly prioritised as the government's approach to support

---

the Personal Independent Payment. See Disability Alliance, http://www.disabilityalliance.org/r68.pdf (accessed 23 July 2012).

[16] Barbour, A. (2008) 'Work Incentives in the Benefits System: Increasing Levels of Earnings Disregards', *Community Links Evidence Paper*, No. 12.

[17] For further details, please refer to: Disability Alliance (2009) *Disability Rights Handbook, 34th Edition, April 2009–April 2010.*

[18] s.21 (1)(a) National Assistance Act 1948.

people with disabilities. Home care services were largely ignored when the welfare state was established. A vaguely expressed discretionary power to provide services was contained in section 29 of the National Assistance Act. It gave a general provision to promote the welfare of the aforementioned people including workshops, suitable work in their own homes or elsewhere, recreational facilities and information on services.[19] However, there was nothing like an enforceable duty to provide support services for individuals with disabilities.

In developing the structure of the NHS, institutions for people with intellectual disabilities found themselves under the control of the NHS.[20] The NHS has had a significant role in providing both long-stay 'beds' and residential 'places' (e.g. accounting for 12 per cent of intellectual disability places in 2001).[21] Alongside this provision, the local authority (or more accurately Councils with Social Services Responsibilities) is responsible for arranging social care (but not health care) and has also traditionally been involved in directly managing residential services. However, since the legislative change introduced with the NHS and Community Care Act 1990 to create internal markets in social care (discussed later), between 1993 (when the Act was implemented) and 1998, 85 per cent of each local authority's government grant for new community care services had to be spent in what is referred to collectively as the 'independent sector' (private and non-profit providers). The contracts which had previously been given to 'in-house' council providers were reduced by a percentage amount each year over a specified time.[22] As a result, the extent of direct NHS and local authority service provision fell significantly (e.g. from 12,620 intellectual disability places in 1988/1989 to 6,630 in 2001) and has continued to fall since.[23] With the split in the commissioner-provider roles between government and service providers, local authorities or NI Trusts are no longer expected to deliver services for persons with disabilities. Instead, as stated earlier, they commission independent-sector organisations to deliver direct community services.

The social care budget is administered by the Local Authority Social Service Departments and combines the budgets for Community Mental Health Services, Disability Services, and Services for Older People. It covers the majority of people in state residential care. Nearly 80 per cent of the total social care budget is distributed by local authorities in line with the particular priorities in their areas.[24] Social services since 1993, when the NHS and Community Care Act 1990 was fully implemented, have been funded through the Revenue Support Grant which is paid annually

[19] Disability Alliance (2009) *Disability Rights Handbook: 34th Edition April 2009–April 2010.*

[20] Hamlin, A. and Oakes, P. (2008) 'Reflections on Deinstitutionalization in the United Kingdom', *Journal of Policy and Practice in Intellectual Disabilities* 5: 47–55.

[21] Emerson, E. (2004) 'Deinstitutionalisation in England', *Journal of Intellectual & Developmental Disability* 29(1): 79–84.

[22] Thompson, T. and Mathias, P. (1998) *Standards and Learning Disability*, 2nd Edition. Elsevier Health Sciences, London.

[23] Emerson, *supra*, n. 21.

[24] Please refer to: http://www.nhs.uk/NHSEngland/thenhs/about/Pages/overview.aspx (accessed 15 August 2010).

in a single block to each local authority to pay for all its services. Government uses a Standard Spending Assessment (SSA) as a virtual budget to indicate what it thinks the council should spend on each area under its remit. However, since the personalisation reform effort, there are now numerous mechanisms used by the UK government and local authorities to redirect funds to individuals who can commission their own disability support, which will be discussed in detail later in the chapter.

Since this time, total provision of residential support settings by the independent sector has risen nearly fifteen-fold (e.g. from 3,200 in 1976 to 50,477 in 2001 in intellectual disability residential places[25]). There are a wide variety of legal entities within this sector which carry out the provision of providing services for persons with disabilities. For example, an independent sector residential home could be run by any one (or more) of the following:

- public limited company
- private limited company
- registered charity
- Housing Association
- Friendly Society
- sole trader

- partnership
- consortium
- voluntary association
- trade union
- professional association.[26]

These categories are not mutually exclusive; for example, a union can sometimes run a home using a limited company which is also a registered charity. Furthermore, the 'ownership' of a home does not necessarily imply management of the service. Within this mix of providers, the voluntary sector varies significantly. Some large national organisations can be either highly centralised or highly decentralised, thus having important implications over how decisions are made on individual homes. In addition, each type of provider has their own unique organisational 'culture' in which they operate. This may reflect the different ideals and attitudes towards persons with disabilities, as well as motivational forces to please the different relevant stakeholders.

In terms of the delivery of disability supports, local authority strategies are now aimed at reducing residential care use in favour of supported living. However, there is still an elaborate system of Registered Residential Care Homes (group homes), which dominate the market, particularly in intellectual disability residential services. The mechanisms which have been used to reconfigure this residential support market will be examined in further detail later in the chapter.

In terms of adult day services, ensuring full and fair access to employment opportunities is a key element in the UK government's stated adult support policy in order

---

[25] Emerson, *supra*, n. 21.

[26] Churchill, J. (2003) 'The Independent Sector', in Thompson, T. and Mathias, P. (eds.) *Standards & Learning Disability*, 2nd Edition, Bailliere Tindall in association with the Royal College of Nursing. pp. 46–67.

to enable disabled people to be fully active and independent members of society.[27] There is a strong incentive to align the work of local services with the focus of Jobcentres and the ESA, and for them to understand their roles in encouraging people to work. Responsibility for most elements of employment policy rests with the DWP in England and the Department for Social Development in NI. According to the report of the Secretary of State within the DWP, achieving greater disability equality in employment is a key part of their objectives:

> Our welfare reforms are a major part of the steps we must take and must be allied with equal pressure on employers and service providers to remove discrimination from their decisions of who to employ and how to provide their services.[28]

Reconfiguring the market to make providers more responsive to these objectives, and restoring power to the individual are thus key focus areas of government. Local authorities will also be encouraged to refocus some of their current spending on adult day services onto supported employment. From April 2010, local authorities have also taken on the responsibility for the planning, commissioning and funding of provision of integrated services for sixteen- to nineteen-year-olds, and young people up to age twenty-five where a learning difficulty assessment is in place. Local authorities will be encouraged to use their new responsibility for funding these aforementioned new groups learning to review and align provision of disability services with the broader goals of adult development.

Generally, the disability organisations have been funded via block funding, whereby service providers are given a grant for a specified volume of service.[29] Cost and volume contracts are used to determine the level of funding. These block contracts make up the largest percentage of the adult social care budget. However, this type of funding mechanism, according to the Audit Commission (an independent watchdog for driving economy, efficiency and effectiveness in local public services to deliver better outcomes for everyone), has forced individuals to live in group situations and caused many limitations and restrictions on disabled people's ability to become fully active and independent members of society.[30] To help to dismantle these grants and restore power to people with disabilities, the English and

---

[27] HM Government (2009) *Valuing Employment Now: Real Jobs for People with Learning Disabilities*, Putting People First, HMSO, London. To achieve this goal, 'Getting a Life' is a three-year cross-government (DWP, DH, DCSF, BIS, ODI) programme to identify how to ensure that young people with severe learning disabilities achieve paid employment and full lives.

[28] Department for Work and Pensions (2008) *Secretary of State Report on Disability Equality: Health and Care Services*, December, DWP, HM Stationary Office, December.

[29] Hall, E. (2011) 'Shopping for Support: Personalisation and the New Spaces and Relations of Commodified Care for People with Learning Disabilities', *Social and Cultural Geography* 12(6): 589–603.

[30] Audit Commission (2010) *Financial Management of Personal Budgets*, October, available at: http://www.audit-commission.gov.uk/SiteCollectionDocuments/AuditCommissionReports/NationalStudies/20101028financialimplicationsofpersonalbudgetssummary.pdf (accessed 15 January 2012).

NI governments since the mid-1990s have introduced individual funding mechanisms to reconfigure the way in which disability-specific services are delivered and to transform the adult social care market. Alongside this, both the NHS and councils have also been involved in trying to unpack large PCT block contracts with providers to separate out the health and social care elements. The rest of the chapter examines this transformation in more detail.

Responding to the Crises in Institutions

The roots of the transformation to enable people to achieve a life in the community initially arose from the concerns over the quality of care in the institutions. Deinstitutionalisation policy in England began in the late 1960s and early 1970s and the process gathered pace in the 1980s. It was largely in response to a series of institutional scandals that provided evidence of abuse, such as Ely Hospital in South Wales[31] and the Longcare enquiry into widespread abuse at two large residential homes for adults with learning disabilities in Stoke Poges.[32] Another animator of change was the *Report of the 1954–57 Royal Commission on the law relating to mental illness and mental deficiency* (the *Percy Report*) (1957). The report marked a turning point in official policy from hospital-based to community-based systems of care. The Commission recommended that 'the law should be altered so that whenever possible suitable care may be provided for mentally disordered patients with no more restriction of liberty or legal formality than is applied to people who need care because of other types of illness, disability or social difficulty'.[33]

In retrospect, there was 'a somewhat grim inevitability about the series of scandals that then rocked hospital services in the UK' given their early Victorian origins.[34] Outrage at the conditions uncovered in hospital services led to a significant shift in public policy. Despite these warnings, however, change in the structure of services was slow over the following decades. In England, Tizard's Brooklands experiment is regarded as a defining point of departure for deinstitutionalisation and community living.[35] It was amongst the earliest attempts anywhere to demonstrate that it was possible to support people with intellectual disabilities in smaller, more homely

---

[31] See Mr. Crossman's Statement on Howe Report, BMJ, http://www.bmj.com/content/2/5648/59.full.pdf (accessed 21 August 2010).

[32] See Independent Longcare Inquiry, http://www.adultprotection.freeola.org/Independent%20Longcare%20Inquiry.htm (accessed 22 August 2010).

[33] *Report of the 1954–57 Royal Commission on the law relating to mental illness and mental deficiency* (the Percy Report) (1957).

[34] Hamlin, and Oakes, *supra*, n. 20.

[35] Tizard, J. (1960) 'Residential care of mentally handicapped children', *British Medical Journal* 1(5178) 1041–1046.

circumstances in the community rather than in institutions.[36] Furthermore, similar pilot projects in the United States[37] were beginning to show that alternatives to institutions were possible. By the late 1960s and early 1970s, the policy goal of deinstitutionalisation – the complete replacement of institutions by services in the community – was being articulated by the likes of the Campaign for the Mentally Handicapped in 1972 and pursued.[38]

In 1970, as stated earlier, the local authority social service departments ensured a new shift in the development of community care. The same year, the Chronically Sick and Disabled Persons Act (1970) made the provision of social services for people with disabilities obligatory for councils. The enactment of the Act was a historic event. For the first time, parliament recognised the concept of rights for disabled people. In terms of implementation of this Act, there was much ignorance at the local authority level at the outset as to the expectations and regulations of the Act. In addition, because of local eligibility criteria and the fact that 'criteria of need [were] matters for the authorities to determine in the light of resources', the equitable implementation of the legislation was slow.[39] However, it did begin to slowly change the emphasis from institutional placements to community-based services.

Most significantly, the White Paper titled *Better Services*[40] in 1971 set the agenda for deinstitutionalisation in the United Kingdom. The task of closing hospitals continued in earnest over the following decades. To illustrate the changing paradigm towards supporting people living in the community, the 1971 White Paper was followed by the establishment of the Attendance Allowance, which was introduced that same year. Disabled people needing attendance day and night were eligible for receiving the non-means-tested benefit. Shortly after, in 1974, the first Minister for Disabled People was appointed within the DWP, who was responsible for overseeing the rights and entitlements of people with disabilities.

In the early period of deinstitutionalisation, early initiatives to replace institutions produced relatively large residential homes such as the Wessex experiment in England,[41] similar to the intermediate care facilities in the United States. This saw

---

[36] Mansell, J. (no date) *Deinstitutionalisation and community living: An international perspective*, available at: http://www.institutionwatch.ca/cms-filesystem-action?file=research/international_perspective.pdf (accessed 23 August 2011).

[37] Casey, K., McGee, J., Stark, J. and Menolascino, F. (1985) *A Community-Based System for the Mentally Retarded: The ENCOR Experience*. University of Nebraska Press, Lincoln and London.

[38] See http://www.institutionwatch.ca/cms-filesystem-action/?file/research/international_perspective.pdf (accessed 2 July 2012).

[39] See http://www.communitycare.co.uk/Articles/2010/05/10/114451/pioneering-1970-disability-law-never-fulfilled-its-promise.htm (accessed 17 August 2011).

[40] Department of Health (1971) *Better Services for the Mentally Handicapped*. Department of Health, London.

[41] See Kushlick, A. (1976) 'Wessex, England', in Kugel, R. B. and Shearer, A. (eds.) *Changing Patterns in Residential Services for the Mentally Retarded*, 2nd Edition. President's Committee on Mental Retardation, Washington, DC.

the development of locally based community units designed for twenty to twenty-four residents each to serve a defined geographical area.

Meanwhile, the activist movement of persons with physical disability in England became more vociferous. The Union of the Physically Impaired Against Segregation (UPIAS) in 1976 published its manifesto, *The Fundamental Principles of Disability*. In it, UPIAS stated: 'In our view it is society which disables physically impaired people. Disability is something imposed on top our impairments by the way we are unnecessarily isolated and excluded from full participation in society'.[42] This philosophy began to change the focus on people's disabilities as existing solely from their impairments to a focus on society's impact on disabling people. This embryonic idea was later developed in 1983, by the disabled academic Mike Oliver who coined the phrase the 'social model of disability', in reference to these ideological developments.

The process towards community care continued throughout the 1980s, marked by the 1982 Barclay Report which advocated a shift in social work practice to decentralised community-based work.[43] The larger residential models from the 1970s were superseded by group homes which were piloted in Andover in England in the 1980s in which between three and eight people, including people needing high levels of support, lived together with help from staff.[44] These homes have been provided jointly by the NHS and local authorities with social service responsibilities.[45] The NHS continued to provide both long-stay 'beds' and residential 'places' for people with intellectual disability, although this involvement gradually was phased out.

However, a warning signal was sounded by the 1985 Social Services Select Committee report, *Community care with special reference to adult mentally ill and mentally handicapped people*.[46] It stated that hospital closures had outrun community-care provisions, particularly in relation to people with mental health problems. There were calls for government action and increased spending. In the Committee's own words, 'A decent community-based service for mentally ill or mentally handicapped people cannot be provided at the same overall cost as present services. The proposition that community care should be cost neutral is untenable. . . . Any

---

42 Union of the Physically Impaired Against Segregation (1976) *The Fundamental Principles of Disability*. UPIAS, London.

43 The 1982 Barclay Report emphasised new roles for social workers: to promote community networks and engage in 'social care planning' (that is, work to alleviate existing and future social problems), to act as a 'broker and negotiator' with a knowledge of local community resources, and to promote voluntary activity. Glasby, J. (2005) *The Future of Adult Social Care: Lessons from Previous Reforms*, SSRG Publications, Issue 2, Article 1, available at: http://www.ssrg.org.uk/publications/rpp/2005/issue2/article1.pdf (accessed 8 December 2010).

44 Mansell, J., Felce, D., Jenkins, J., de Kock, U. and Toogood, A. (1987) *Developing Staffed Housing for People with Mental Handicaps*. Costello, Tunbridge Wells.

45 Councils with social service responsibilities (CSSRs) in England provide support to adults in residential accommodation services.

46 Social Services Select Committee (1985) *Community Care with Special Reference to Adult Mentally Ill and Mentally Handicapped People*. MHSO, London.

fool can close a long-stay hospital: it takes more time and trouble to do it properly and compassionately'.[47]

In 1986, the Disabled Persons (Services, Consultation and Representation) Act required social services to provide persons with disabilities with a written assessment if asked to do so by the individual or his or her representative or carer and take into account the abilities of informal carers to continue caring when deciding to provide services. In a sense, it was introduced to strengthen the legislation laid down in the Chronically Sick and Disabled Persons Act 1970.[48] NI passed equivalent legislation with the Disabled Persons (Services, Consultation and Representation) Act 1986 for its own jurisdiction.

Opportunity to Create a New Social Care Market

At the end of the 1980s, another key wellspring of reform was the opportunity accorded to local authorities to sculpt a new social care market within the independent sector. This opportunity came as a result of the Griffiths Report which was published in 1988. Its recommendations included the appointment of a Minister of State for Community Care and the transfer of all community care to local authorities using 'earmarked' grants, partly funded by central government. It also recommended that local authorities be allowed to purchase services from other agencies. By the end of the decade, the 1989 White Paper, *Caring for People*, was published in response to the Griffiths Report. It set out a framework for changes to community care, which included a new funding structure for social care. This would mark the beginning of the purchaser/provider split whereby social services departments were encouraged to purchase services provided by the independent sector.

This process culminated in 1990 with the NHS and Community Care (Assessment) Act (1990) which shifted the traditional local authority provider role to a purchaser/provider split whereby local authority social services departments were encouraged to purchase services provided by the independent sector. Under the Act, people with disabilities have a right to an assessment by local authorities of needs for community care services. The local authorities also became responsible for designing care packages and ensuring their delivery. This was a crucial first step in the reform of the care system in England; it focussed on the idea that the needs of the person should form the basis of an individually tailored, responsive and flexible package of care.

The Act also intended that fewer people would go into care homes because there would be a greater range of support in the community. It was a central part of the Thatcher government policy and came about as a result of a whole range of

---

[47] *Ibid.*
[48] For a more detailed timeline, see Mind Web site: http://www.mind.org.uk/help/research_and_policy/the_history_of_mental_health_and_community_care-key_dates (accessed 23 August 2011).

factors, including a rejection of the nanny-state principles and not least the costs of institutions. In practice, the objective of the Act was to decentralise the use of resources to the local level with a single person controlling the purse and support plan. The ideology was based on the Kent Community Care Experiment and the work by Challis and Davies in the University of Kent[49] where a social worker/care manager coordinates a support plan around the individual and determines the budget and 'places' the person within a service based on a predetermined menu of service options. The care management approach was to develop individual care plans based on detailed assessments of the person's individual needs and circumstances, carried out by budget-holding care managers.[50]

There was a deliberate delay of three years with this Act to allow local authorities to catch up with the policy guidance. Part of the success of this transformation was the 'special transitional grant' of £736 million given to local authorities which came with the Community Care Act 1990. This was to oil the wheels of local government. Each local authority got a number of transitional grants and there was a rule that 75 per cent of the funds had to be spent on the independent sector. That allowed the local authority to get people out of 'mental handicap' hospitals. The local authority was also able to take the 'dowry' money out of the hospitals to help to move people into the community and set up new approaches to support. According to a UK policy representative: 'It gave us an opportunity to do different things and it made us do it with the independent sector. So that made us think about *creating* an independent sector and it gave us an opportunity to be a bit more creative'.[51]

As a result of this legislation, the role of the independent sector increased to fill this gap. The majority of the provision which emerged was in the form of group homes for four or more people.[52] Nonetheless, many local authorities used the funding to animate the provider sector and provide more home support services and to fund new community care posts (e.g. community occupational therapy).

During the three-year implementation time, the government produced some practical guidance, tools for its delivery, transition funds and training. Also, third-party organisations provided training materials. However, according to an interview with a UK policy representative,[53] many local authorities and social workers still struggled with the transition. Professional training did not include care management prior to the Act, so social workers had to rely on in-house training for developing these new skills. There was a large policy expectation from government but implementation was slow. Money did not get devolved in many cases with local authorities unwilling to transfer commissioning powers. Social workers had

---

49　Davies, B. and Challis, D. (1986) *Matching Resources to Needs in Community Care*. Ashgate, Aldershot.
50　Social Care Institute for Excellence (2007) *SCIE Research Briefing 20: The Implementation of Individual Budget Schemes in Adult Social Care*.
51　Personal Communication, representative from relevant disability statutory authority, 21 June 2010.
52　Emerson, *supra*, n. 21.
53　*Supra*, n. 51.

little freedom and person-centred planning was very limited. Moreover, there was a deep-rooted 'Us and Them' pathology to overcome, where 'us' meant trained professionals with the resources and 'them' meant members of the public looking for their services.[54]

Responding to Calls for Individual Funding

The move towards individualised funding began in England in the 1990s. Originally, direct payments (cash payments to individuals in lieu of services) were deemed illegal under the 1948 Social Security Act; however, a number of 'work-around' indirect payment schemes were developed in the early 1990s, whereby funds were channelled from local authorities via third-party organisations such as some Centres for Independent Living to a person to purchase personal assistance. The Conservative government at the time sought the cessation of these programmes, arguing that it was illegal for local authorities to give direct funding under the earlier legislation and there were also concerns about exploitation and fraud.[55] In response, people with physical disabilities guided by the rights focus of UPIAS and the National CIL campaigned for the right to receive a direct payment.

In the meantime, the publication of a significant research report demonstrating the cost effectiveness of Direct Payments by Zarb and Nadash (1994) on behalf of the British Council of Organisations of Disabled People (BCODP)[56] led to the acceptance of direct payments as a future policy option. This culminated in the Community Care (Direct Payments) Act 1996. This was another key milestone in reforming support delivery to enable people to live independent lives in the community. The Act empowered councils to give people with disabilities direct payments. This is considered a turning point in terms of individualised funding of disability services in the United Kingdom. In NI, direct payments were authorised some time later, with the Carer & Direct Payments (NI) Act 2002. This is the Act which permits local trusts to administer direct payments in addition to the provision about the assessment of carers' needs as stated in the English Carers Act 1995. More detail on these Acts and their impacts are examined below.

The Community Care (Direct Payments) Act 1996 enabled local authorities responsible for community care services to make payments to persons to secure the provision of such services and for connected purposes. While the 1996 Act gave local authorities the power to make payments, they did not initially have to. Instead, the New Labour government developed policy through a series of Guidance measures. However, because local authorities did not cooperate, the government

[54] *Ibid.*

[55] Riddell, S., Pearson, C., Jolly, D., Barnes, C., Priestley, M. and Mercer, G. (2005) 'The Development of Direct Payments in the UK: Implications for Social Justice', *Social Policy and Society* 4(1):75–85.

[56] Zarb, G. and Nadash, P. (1994) *Cashing in on Independence: Counting the Costs and Benefits of Cash and Services.* The British Council of Organisation of Disabled People (BCODP), London.

made offering direct payments mandatory in 2001. Eligibility has also been expanded. People who quality for a direct payment can now employ relatives to work as their personal assistant with the exception of close relatives[57] living in the same household. However, exceptions can be made to this rule provided the local authority or trust is satisfied that to do so is in the best interest of the person.

Alongside this development, the initially limited success of direct payments for people with physical disabilities led to the establishment of a parallel initiative amongst intellectual disability stakeholders from 2003. Firstly, In Control, a collaborative venture between the Department of Health, the charity Mencap, six local authorities in England and some disability organisations, developed models of 'self-directed support' and 'Personal Budgets' for, initially, people with intellectual disabilities.[58] Within one of the early local authority 'test sites' in Wigan, Steve Jones, chief executive of Wigan Council, worked together with Simon Duffy and Julie Stansfield from In Control in developing a 'cost-neutral' resource model of self-directed support. Personal budgets were made available as an individualised allocation for social services. Personal budgets are designed to enable people to purchase the services of personal assistants, to contract with people who are self-employed, to buy a service from an agency or to combine a direct payment and a service.[59] In other words, they can be paid as a direct cash payment, care manager-managed 'virtual budget', provider-managed 'individual service fund' or a payment to third-party individuals and trusts. The Individual Service Fund (ISF) option is when a provider holds onto the fund, but it remains ring-fenced to the individual. A direct cash payment is thus one method of providing a personal budget. As a result, the two terms – personal budget and direct payment – are often used synonymously despite meaning quite different things.

Since the early development of direct payments in England, there has been an increasing policy drive to promote 'choice' in support delivery, particularly by the New Labour and subsequent Coalition government, using the tools accorded in the Community Care Act 1996. The Prime Minister's Strategy Unit under Tony Blair was looking for new ideas in the early 2000s in relation to social care. They were particularly committed to developing what they called the choice agenda in social services for children, older adults and people with disabilities. Within the DWP, they were reviewing policies relating to older people.[60] Within the Department of Education and Skills, there was a green paper on children's services (including

---

[57] Spouses, partners, parents, grandparents, aunts, uncles, sons, daughters, brothers, sisters or their spouses are considered to be close relatives.

[58] Poll, C., Duffy, S., Hatton, C. et al. (2006) *A Report on In Control's First Phase, 2003–2005.* In Control Publications, London.

[59] Egan, D. (2008) *Issues Concerning Direct Payments in the Republic of Ireland: A Report for the Person Centre.* November.

[60] Department for Work and Pensions (2005) Opportunity Age – Meeting the Challenge of Ageing in the 21st Century, HMSO, London.

social care and education going together).[61] There was a perceived need, according to a UK policy maker, for 'an organized review and tidy up of adult services'.[62] In the Office of Disability Issues within the DWP, Jenny Morris[63] was recruited to develop their policy on 'Life Chances for Disabled People'. Similarly within the Department of Health, there was a focus on 'individual budgets' within disability services. This culminated in the adult social care green paper, *Independence, Well-being and Choice* (2005), and the 2006 health and social care White Paper, *Our Health, Our Care, Our Say*, which recommended the establishment of a national network to support the development of direct payments and personal budgets.

The reports from the New Labour Prime Minister's Strategy Unit[64] and White Papers[65] set out the personalisation agenda and established pilots for 'Individual Budgets' in thirteen local authorities in England (in the period between 2005 and 2007).[66] There were two objectives: to test whether they could bring all budget streams together and to test the mechanism of individual funding. The first objective failed given the difficulty of the task of alignment across all funding streams as a result of incompatibility in eligibility criteria, lack of control over award decisions, continuing restrictions on how resources could be used and related legal issues and limits of flexibility. However, the second objective was a positive development and brought different departments to work together on developing self-directed support. This also led to national interest in the idea of individual budgets.

Meanwhile, the government also published a paper called *Improving the Life Chances of Disabled People* (2005). In it the government said that 'by 2025 disabled people have full opportunities and choices to improve their quality of life and will be respected and included as equal members of society'.[67] Following this, the governments' policy direction over the following three years moved towards 'empowerment' and 'choice'.

This 'choice agenda' also found its way into learning disability policy in England and Wales with a White Paper in 2001, titled *Valuing People: A new strategy for learning disability for the 21st century*.[68] The report established the principles of inclusion, choice, rights and independence for people with intellectual disabilities.

---

[61] Department of Education and Skills (2003) *Every Child Matters*, Green Paper, September, HMSO, London.

[62] *Supra*, n. 51.

[63] Jenny Morris is a disability activist and disability studies scholar, publishing extensively in the disability studies literature. Please refer to: Morris, J. (1991) *Pride against Prejudice: Transforming Attitudes to Disability*. The Women's Press, London.

[64] Prime Minister's Strategy Unit (2005) *Report to Transform the Life Chances of Disabled People*. HMSO, London.

[65] Department of Health (2006) *Our Health, Our Care, Our Say: Making It Happen*. HMSO, London; Department of Health (2007) White Paper.

[66] Individual Budgets Evaluation Network (IBSEN) (2008) *Evaluation of the Individual Budgets Pilot Programme Summary Report*, October, Social Policy Research Unit, University of York.

[67] Prime Minister's Strategy Unit (2005) *Improving the Life Chances of Disabled People*. HMSO, London.

[68] Department of Health (2001) *Valuing People*. HMSO, London.

Valuing People acknowledged the prejudices and discriminatory practices people with intellectual disabilities often face and proposed changes through which the valuing of people with intellectual disabilities can be realised. Its successor, *Valuing People Now* (VPN) (2008),[69] more explicitly espouses the principles of personalisation, supported living (assured tenancies) and employment. It also recommends that the commissioning for all non-health-related costs be moved from NHS PCTs over to local authority councils.

Alongside the council's budget, the NHS has for a long time received Department of Health money – some £1.7 billion a year to fund care for people with learning disabilities. However, the government's *Valuing People Now* strategy proposed that the funding and associated commissioning responsibilities be transferred from NHS primary care trusts to local authority councils, through local deals in 2009/2010 and 2010/2011, with councils receiving the money directly from the Department of Health from 2011/2012.[70] This signals the government's intention that in the future, the NHS's job is to meet the people's health needs, not offer long-term support. One caveat is those who require long-term care because of a health condition continue to have their costs met by NHS PCTs.

In NI, direct payments and personal budgets are also at the core of the government's aim of personalising adult social care services around the needs of individuals. As identified in the previous section, the legislation concerning direct payments in Northern Ireland is the Carers and Direct Payments Act (Northern Ireland) 2002. As in England, DPs are available to disabled people over the age of sixteen, disabled parents, parents of disabled children and carers over the age of sixteen for services to meet their own needs and of people with mental health difficulties.

In NI, the devolved government did not publish *Valuing People* or its successor, VPN. Instead, the Bamford Review of Mental Health and Learning Disability report, *Equal Lives* (beginning in 2002 and published in September 2005) is considered the most extensive re-examination of policy and legislation in this field ever undertaken in NI. It advocated the following five core values with which all policy and service developments must be underpinned:

- Citizenship: People with a learning disability are individuals first and foremost and each has a right to be treated as an equal citizen.
- Social Inclusion: People with a learning disability are valued citizens and must be enabled to use mainstream services and be fully included in the life of the community.
- Empowerment: People with a learning disability must be enabled to actively participate in decisions affecting their lives.

---

[69] Department of Health (2008) *Valuing People Now*. HMSO, London.
[70] See: http://www.communitycare.co.uk/Articles/2010/01/15/113574/valuing-people-now-one-year-on.htm (accessed 21 August 2010).

- Working Together: Conditions must be created where people with a learning disability, families and organisations work well together in order to meet the needs and aspirations of people with a learning disability.
- Individual Support: People with a learning disability will be supported in ways that take account of their individual needs and help them to be as independent as possible.

Together, these values represent a new policy thrust away from segregated support services towards the personalisation of support delivery in NI. Furthermore, the review proposed that future policy for improving the lives of people with a learning disability is directed towards attaining these values through a set of core objectives over the next fifteen years. In response to the Bamford Review, the Minister for Health, Social Services and Public Safety published their *Response* Report[71] in October 2009. This welcomed the recommendations of the Bamford Review and set out their action plan for implementation of the Bamford Review. The implementation of reform for better support for persons with intellectual disabilities therefore now rests with government.

Since these developments, the policy goal of implementing direct payments and personal budgets across the United Kingdom has been 'mainstreamed' and has culminated with a Department of Health Concordat in 2008 calling on Councils to significantly increase the number of people receiving individual funding. This new policy environment is discussed in further detail in the next section.

SHAPE OF REFORM

As a result of the wellsprings of reform, both England and NI, to varying extents, have developed personalisation options in their disability support systems. These include a range of individualised funding options and a varying mix of sources of support brokerage options for individuals, which will be examined further.

SHAPING THE DEMAND SIDE OF REFORM

New Policy Options for Individual Funding

The commitment to personalisation and the extension of choice and control, as we saw in the earlier sections, were driven by early efforts by DPOs and champions of policy reform. Having resisted direct payments for many years, the government of England and the devolved administrations now strongly promote direct payments

---

[71] Northern Ireland Executive (2009) *The Response of Northern Ireland Executive to the Bamford Review of Mental Health and Learning Disability: Action Plan 2009–2011*, October.

in their policy,[72] as articulating both the social justice and modernising welfare agendas.[73]

In England, the process of expanding individual funding in the United Kingdom has so far culminated with the Department of Health Concordat, *Putting People First*, in 2008, led by Minister for Care Service in the Department of Health Ivan Lewis (2006–2008).[74] It called on Councils to significantly increase the number of people receiving direct payments and for a rollout of a system of personal budgets for all users of adult social care, from 2008 to 2011. In the long term, the government envisages that all users should have a personal budget from which to pay for their social care services, apart from in emergencies. It has been described as 'a massive cultural sledgehammer', by a representative from a relevant disability statutory authority redefining the entire context of social services.[75]

The *Putting People First* (2008) Concordat aimed that significant progress would be made to ensure personal budgets would be available for everyone eligible for publicly funded adult social care support by the end of the Comprehensive Service Review in March 2011. While this goal may have overstated the transformation involved, the discussion within government after this report became 'more about *how* can we do it, rather than *shall* we do it?'[76] In response, the Labour government before their exit from government set a target for 30 per cent of social care recipients to have a personal budget – which may or may not involve a direct cash payment – by April 2011.[77] This would have been a significant increase, given that as of April 2009, only some 86,000 people of the 600,000 receiving social care in England were getting direct payments, with the payments accounting for about 4 per cent of the social care budget.[78] However, by December 2010, the figures showed that 23 per cent of all eligible people under age sixty-five have a personal budget,[79] albeit with some significant disparities across councils.[80]

[72] See Department of Health (2002) *Fair Access to Care Services: Policy Guidance* (LAC(2002)13), Department of Health, London; Department of Health (2003) *Direct Payments Guidance: Community Care, Services for Carers and Children's Services (Direct Payments), Guidance England* 2003, Department of Health, London.

[73] Riddell et al., *supra*, n. 55.

[74] This document is the Department of Health concordat published by the Local Government Association (LGA), the Association of Directors of Adult Social Services (ADASS), the NHS and others.

[75] Personal Communication, interview, July 2010.

[76] Riddell et al., *supra*, n. 55.

[77] Department of Health (2008) *Transforming Social Care*, Local Authority Circular. The 30% target was agreed upon by the Association of Directors of Adult Social Services and the Local Government Association, as well as the Department of Health.

[78] UNISON (2010) *Who Cares: Who Pays? A Report on Personalisation in Social Care Prepared for UNISON*. Report prepared by Land, H. and Himmelweit, S., UNISON, London.

[79] Association of Directors of Adult Social Services (2010) *ADASS Councils on Track to Meet 30 Per Cent Target for Personal Budgets*, http://www.adass.org.uk/index.php?option=com_content&view= article&id=665:adass-councils-on-track-to-meet-30-per-cent-target-for-personal-budgets&catid=127 e:press-releases-2010&Itemid=419 (accessed 25 January 2011).

[80] The Audit Commission has found that while some councils see the 30% target as a stepping-stone, other councils whose performance has generally been less progressive have seen the 30% target as an end

Since these initiatives, with the election of the Conservative-Liberal Democrat coalition government in June 2010, it seems clear that this policy direction will continue. According to the Conservative Government Party Web site, they 'want to see much greater use of direct payments and individual budgets, which give people real control over their care'.[81] Indeed, the government initially sought a dramatic expansion of personal budgets with a target of 100 per cent take up to be reached by April 2013, however, this was subsequently revised in October 2012 to 70 per cent of social care users by the original date.[82]

The resulting funding mechanisms from the policy development discussed earlier include the following options:

Direct payments are cash payments given to service users in lieu of community care services they have been assessed as needing, and are intended to give users greater choice in their care. The payment must be sufficient to enable the service user to purchase services to meet their needs, and must be spent on services that users need. Like commissioned care, they are means-tested, so in many cases, people contribute to the cost of their care.

Direct payments confer responsibilities on recipients to employ people or commission services for themselves. They take on all the responsibilities of an employer, such as payroll, meeting minimum wage and other legislative requirements and establishing contracts of employment. Some of these services can be contracted out and many councils have commissioned support organisations to help service users to handle these responsibilities.

In both jurisdictions (England and NI), qualifying persons are required to account for their direct payment. Individual participants sign an agreement with their local authority or trust which outlines how the direct payment should be used and how they are expected to account for the payment. This means weekly time sheets must be signed by the individual and the PA and returned to the council or Trust on a monthly basis. Individuals who employ a PA are obliged to be familiar with tax and employment legislation. Unlike in the US states, which offer independent facilitation, the direct payment in the United Kingdom is expected to cover the administrative overheads associated with managing the payment. In terms of facilitation, the Centres for Independent Living provide a range of support services including a payroll service for people on direct payments across all disability categories and for older persons who do not have a disability. However, by default, the onus is on the individual to manage the payment.

In NI, no upper limit exists for the number of hours allocated to an individual to meet his or her need. However, direct payments are subject to the same

goal. See Audit Commission (2010) *Financial Management of Personal Budgets*. Audit Commission, London.

[81] Please refer to: http://www.conservatives.com/Policy/Where_we_stand/Pensions_and_Older_People .aspx (accessed 15 August 2010).

[82] Please see Mithran, S. (2012) Lamb scraps 100% personal budgets target, Community-Care, available at: http://www.communitycare.co.uk/Articles/26/10/2012/118640/Lamb-scraps-100-personal-budgets-target.htm (accessed 10 November 2012).

budgetary constraints which affect all social services provided by the NI Health and Social Trusts. Local authority assessors can and do differentiate between critical and noncritical need. Means testing is applicable to qualifying persons for a direct payment, but the scheme does allow some discretion. Although people can be means-tested for what are regarded as core services, such as help in the home, people who require supports which are significantly in excess of core services are unlikely to be means-tested.[83] Service users are allocated a number of hours of personal assistance per week based on their assessed needs. A flat-rate hourly payment, which is decided by the Health and Social Care Trusts, is paid directly to the service user.[84] Payment rates can vary slightly within trusts. Furthermore, in some trusts, direct payments are not given to persons with intellectual disabilities.

Personal budgets are an allocation of funding given to persons after an assessment of needs, which should be sufficient to meet their approved needs. Users can either take their personal budget as a direct payment, or – while still choosing how their care needs are met and by whom – leave councils with the responsibility to commission the services. Or they can have some combination of the two. As a result, personal budgets provide a potentially good option for people who do not want to take on the responsibilities of a direct payment.

In Control developed a resource allocation system (RAS) designed to create an individualised money allocation that operates within existing community care legislation and eligibility rates. They tested it in three local authorities and found cost savings with their model. At present, In Control is developing a major upgrade to its RAS. It is working with subscribing authorities and central government to develop the best possible system to meet government policy commitments to extend the delivery of personal budgets.

Individual budgets differ from personal budgets in that they cover a multitude of funding streams, in addition to adult social care including Supporting People, Disabled Facilities Grant, Independent Living Funds, Access to Work and community equipment services, which are outlined in Table 6.1. The government has only piloted individual budgets – not called for their full implementation. There are currently no plans to extend this pilot scheme, but some councils have chosen to call their direct payments 'individual budgets' instead.

Individual budgets are designed to provide individuals who currently receive services greater choice and control over their support arrangements. In other words,

---

[83] Egan, *supra*, n. 59.

[84] Typically the hourly payment to service users varies between £8 and £10 per hour. There are no incremental payments for night work or Sunday work. The payment is intended to pay the wages of a personal assistant, including holiday pay and unsocial hours. There is no defined payment rate for a personal assistant but it must cover the statutory minimum wage which, in NI, is currently £5.52 for people older than twenty years and £4.60 for those aged between eighteen and twenty. See Egan, *supra*, n. 59.

TABLE 6.1. *Funding streams available in an individual budget*[85]

The Independent Living Fund (ILF)
Established in 1988 as a trust, in response to active campaigning from people with disabilities. It was intended to run for five years but was extended via extension funds. It involved direct cash payments to individuals so they could purchase care from an agency or pay the wages of a privately employed PA.[86] There are currently 21,000 people using the ILF across the United Kingdom. However, earlier in 2010, the ILF announced that it ran out of money for new grants for the rest of 2010–11, as part of government spending cuts.[87] The scheme is now closed to all new entrants.

Access to Work Grant
The Access to Work funding can help if a persons' health or disability affects the way they do their job. It gives support with extra costs which may arise because of an individual's needs.

Supporting People Grant
The Supporting People funding stream was launched in April 2003 and pays for housing-related support to groups in 'vulnerable' positions, including persons with disabilities.

Integrated Community Equipment Services Grant
Integrated Community Equipment Services pays for equipment to help people with disabilities to develop their full potential and maintain their health and independence. This includes toileting and bathing items, handling and lifting equipment, as well as walking frames.

Disabled Facilities Grant
The Disabled Facilities Grant is a local council grant to help with the cost of adapting a person's home to enable him or her to continue to live there. A grant is paid when the council considers that changes are necessary to meet an individual's needs, and that the work is reasonable and practical.

---

they can cover a wider array of supports in a person's life, bundled together in a support package. An individual budget is an individualised allocation based on the individual's care support and impact of his or her disability. It brings together all the money people are entitled to that helps them to get the support they need to live the life they choose.

Supported Decision Making

Given the new choice agenda in the United Kingdom, legal capacity legislation which supports people in their decision making is a crucial element to be considered

---

[85] The latter three grants are discussed in more detail in the 'Enabling a Choice in Living Arrangements' section.
[86] Please refer to: http://www.ilf.org.uk/about_the_ilf/what/index.html (accessed 13 August 2011).
[87] Please refer to: http://www.guardian.co.uk/society/2010/jun/23/disability-fund-has-no-money (accessed 14 August 2011).

in the reform process. In order to restore power to individuals in making decisions about their own lives, the main piece of legal capacity legislation is the Mental Capacity Act 2005 (England and Wales). This aims to protect people with 'mental disorders', who do not have the ability to make certain decisions. It provides clear guidelines for carers and professionals about who can make decisions in which situations. It provides a statutory framework for acting and making decisions on behalf of individuals who lack the mental capacity to do so for themselves. Its five principles are outlined in Section 1 of the Act:

1. A person must be assumed to have capacity unless it is established that he or she lacks capacity.
2. A person is not to be treated as unable to make a decision unless all practicable steps to help him/her to do so have been taken without success.
3. A person is not to be treated as being unable to make a decision merely because he/she makes an unwise decision.
4. An act done, or decision made, under this Act for or on behalf of a person who lacks capacity must be done, or made, in his/her best interests.
5. Before the act is done, or the decision is made, regard must be had to whether the purpose for which it is needed can be as effectively achieved in a way that is less restrictive of the person's rights and freedom of action.[88]

Importantly, the Act also provides for a new Independent Mental Capacity Advocacy (IMCA) Service in England and Wales. The IMCA service will support people who lack capacity and who have no family or friends to support them when serious decisions are taken in their lives.

Under this Act, there is a tipping point between substitute decision making and supported decision making. On the one hand, a hospital or care home must get authorisation in certain circumstances to detain someone deemed to have impaired mental capacity. This is known as the Deprivation of Liberty Safeguards authorisation[89] and is different from being sectioned.[90] It is used in some cases where people who suffer from a disorder or disability of the mind, such as dementia or a profound learning disability, and who lack the mental capacity to consent to their care or treatment need to be deprived of their liberty for treatment or care because this is argued to be necessary in their best interests to protect them from harm.[91]

---

[88] Section 1 Mental Capacity Act 2005.
[89] Based on the European Court of Human Rights (ECtHR) October 2004 judgement in the Bournewood case (*HL v. UK*), which highlighted that additional safeguards are needed for people who lack capacity and who might be deprived of their liberty.
[90] The later Mental Health Act 2007, which received Royal Assent in July 2007, as well as amending the Mental Health Act 1983, was used as the vehicle for introducing deprivation of liberty safeguards into the 2005 Act.
[91] Department of Health (2008) *Briefing Sheet, Mental Capacity Act 2005 Deprivation of Liberty Safeguards in England*, October, Department of Health, MHSO, London.

On the other hand, under the Act, an advance statement or 'advance directive' lets individuals put their preferred care treatment in writing including the treatment they do not want or that does not work for them (e.g. Electroconvulsive Therapy). The advance statement needs to include a named person, guardian or welfare attorney and be signed by a witness. A *named person* is someone the individuals choose to look out for them if they have to have treatment. The named person also helps to make decisions about their care and treatment. A *guardian* is someone appointed by the court to make decisions for the individuals if they are unable to decide for themselves. In most cases, the local authority is named the guardian, although alternatively a friend or relative may be appointed. A *welfare attorney* is someone the individuals choose to take control of decisions about their care and treatment or if they are otherwise unable to make decisions.

In NI, in response to the Bamford Review, a new mental capacity Bill[92] has been proposed and is intended to replace both the mental capacity and mental health legislation. The Bill will introduce the same statutory presumption of mental capacity as the English legislation and considerations of mental capacity will also be decision-specific. The Bill will contain provisions to enable the High Court to appoint Deputies to take decisions on financial, welfare and health matters on behalf of those lacking mental capacity, who have no one else to make decisions for them. The primary safeguards the Bill will provide include acting in the person's best interests and using the least restrictive alternative, with the primary carer and professionals (such as health care professionals) making most decisions.[93]

Enabling a Choice in Living Arrangements

To back up the government's policy commitment to 'supported living', there are a number of programmes to help people to live in their own homes. For adults with disabilities wishing to seek social housing (i.e. council or housing association prop-erties), the first route is through rented housing provided by Housing Associations or Registered Social Landlords using the public capital subsidy. The public capital subsidy is paid through the Homes and Communities Agency (HCA).[94] Individuals apply to their local authority or housing associations directly to go on the housing register, stating their specific housing requirements.

Shared ownership is the second route and has become a realistic option for many people with disabilities.[95] This can be made to work with either the HCA grant

---

[92] Northern Ireland Mental Capacity (Health, Finance and Welfare) Bill.

[93] See Department of Health, Social Services and Public Safety Northern Ireland (2010) *Mental Capacity (Health, Welfare and Finance) Bill Equality Impact Assessment*. DHSSPSNI, Belfast.

[94] The HCA is the national housing and regeneration delivery *agency* for England, enabling local authorities and *communities* to meet the ambition they have for their areas.

[95] Mansell, J. (2010) *Raising Our Sights: Services for Adults with Profound Intellectual and Multiple Disabilities*, Tizard Centre, University of Kent.

subsidy or with investment from the family or another source. The owners are eligible for Income Support on a mortgage and for a housing benefit on the rental element (usually paid to a housing association).

The third route to housing is a rental option administered by charitable housing organisations which are not classified as Registered Social Landlords. These are voluntary organisations which only provide housing and do not provide the support required. Because they are not Registered Social Landlords, they cannot attract the capital subsidy from the HCA. They generally borrow money through private financing and recover the costs through higher rents (they are able to charge higher rents because their rent levels are not controlled by statute in the same way as Registered Social Landlord's). This allows these agencies to be more flexible in their approach to providing and financing more specialist accommodation for people with profound intellectual and multiple disabilities.

Despite this becoming a common option in many local authorities, a judgement by the social security commissioner Charles Turnbull in June 2006 stated that local authority housing payments must be paid at market rent levels. This has meant that many charitable organisations involved in supported living provision[96] have had to lower their rents or evict their tenants. This has created an uncertainty that discourages investment in this provision and cases have been made at the local authority level. Resolving this problem is a goal of the Delivery Plan for VPN and at the time of writing is also being considered by the coalition government.[97]

The English and NI governments also operate a *Supporting People* funding programme to help people to live independently. It began on 1 April 2003, bringing together seven housing-related funding streams from across central government. It is a grant programme administered by 152 top-tier local authorities in partnership with Housing, Health, Social Services and Probation so that local authorities and their partners can plan and deliver support services in a more consistent and accountable way. It is delivered largely by the voluntary and community sector and by housing associations. By and large, the local authorities commission generic floating support services to support people to live in their homes, although it was later recognised that there was a need for a 'portfolio' of services – some generic, some specialist – as well as a need to be careful not to lose specialist services in the rush to rationalise delivery and 'make the money go further.'[98]

The programme helps around 1 million people at any one time including approximately 815,000 older people with support needs, 36,000 people with mental health

---

[96] These organisations had previously been exempt from the general rule limiting housing benefit payment to market rent levels.

[97] Please refer to: http://www.guardian.co.uk/society/2010/oct/27/ministers-negotiate-housing-benefit-cuts (accessed 3 September 2011).

[98] Department of Communities and Local Government (2010) *Government Response to the House of Commons Communities and Local Government Select Committee Report into the Supporting People Programme*. HMSO, London.

issues and 34,000 people with learning disabilities.[99] Those with learning disabilities are getting help from support workers paid for by the Supporting People programme. Most of these people live in hostels or shared housing.[100]

In 2007, the Department of Communities and Local Government published a strategy report, *Independence and Opportunity: Our Strategy for Supporting People,*[101] based on how the *Supporting People* programme had developed since its inception and identified a strategy for its future roll-out. The report set out how government will work with authorities, service providers and service users to ensure that *Supporting People* continues to develop to best meet people's needs.

However, in March 2009, the Communities and Local Government Select Committee announced an inquiry into the Supporting People programme, in particular its ring-fenced funding. The Committee looked at the delivery of the programme and the implications of removing the ring-fence. Following the Select Committee review, from April 2010, *Supporting People* was allocated to local authorities as a non-ring-fenced grant paid as part of the Area Based Grant. The government's decision to remove the ring-fence was made in order to devolve decision making and control over budgets to the local level. The Select Committee's Report agreed that local authorities should be free to manage their own budgets – but they must also be prepared to justify any decisions to redirect *Supporting People* funds to deliver other locally targeted services. A transitional package of support is in place to support local authorities through this change, including a local financial benefits model which enables authorities to understand the impact of investment in housing-related support.

In relation to how it has affected the choice in living arrangements of people with disabilities, the government has declined to issue authoritative guidance on how 'housing-related support' should be defined and this has led to wide variations in operational definitions at the local level. The consequence of this for people with disabilities has been significant differences between authorities in relation to the availability of *Supporting People* funding.[102] Moreover, allowing local authorities to fund the rapid expansion of self-styled supported living schemes has often come at the expense of abandoning the principles of supported living so that, in some cases, it is indistinguishable from residential care. In these cases, the shared tenancies with accommodation-based support were sometimes little different from the registered care homes they had replaced.[103] *Supporting People* guidelines also typically

[99] Please refer to: http://www.communities.gov.uk/housing/housingolderpeople (accessed 7 December 2011).

[100] Department of Health (1997) *Valuing People*. HMSO, London.

[101] Department of Communities and Local Government (2007) *Independence and Opportunity – Our Strategy for Supporting People, Communities and Local Government*, HMSO, London.

[102] Fyson, R., Tarleton, B. and Ward, L. (2007) *The Impact of the Supporting People Programme on Adults with Learning Disabilities*, 15 August, The Joseph Rowntree Foundation, London.

[103] *Ibid.*

preclude money being used to provide support for either social or employment-related activities. As a consequence, tenants with learning disabilities could find themselves well supported in practical aspects of day-to-day life (self-care, cooking, housework), but socially isolated.[104]

Despite these challenges, the impact of *Supporting People* on housing and support for people with disabilities has led to significant positive outcomes for individuals in England and NI. More generally, it signals a new era for the future development of supported living, but this is currently being delayed as a result of budget cuts.

Another means of enabling more people to live in tenancies is investment in access equipment or adoptions to people's homes and assistive technology. As stated at the outset of the chapter, there is a *Disabled Facilities Grant* to pay for equipment or adaptations, which could transform a person's need for personal care, and also reduce social care costs. Local authorities in the United Kingdom, since the removal of a budget ring-fence, have a general discretionary power to help with adaptation or improvement of living conditions by providing grants, loans, materials or other forms of assistance. In England, community equipment, aids and minor adaptations which assist with living at home that cost less than £1,000 are provided free of charge. Larger adaptations, such as facilitating an occupant's access to and from the dwelling, are means-tested.

Enhancing Consumer Purchasing Power

Finally, in order to address the sole dependence of adults with disabilities on state services in the United Kingdom, Britain's financial innovation model is designed as a child savings trust fund. The Child Trust Fund (CTF) in Britain was introduced under the United Kingdom's Child Trust Funds Regulations 2004.[105] It is a long-term savings and investment account which belongs to the child and cannot be touched until he or she turns eighteen. It can either be established as saving accounts or investment accounts (stocks and shares related), which vary in performance, with the latter being associated with higher risk but the possibility of higher gains.

Those who start a CTF receive an initial endowment from the government of £250 with an additional £250 for low-income children. The cost of CTFs is about £240 million for the United Kingdom's 760,000 newborns each year, and there are now more than 3 million CTFs in operation. The United Kingdom will provide an additional contribution at age seven and convert CTFs to adult savings accounts when they mature in 18 years.

For persons with disabilities, from April 2010, children who are entitled to DLA can receive annual payments of either £100 or £200 dependent on the care component of their DLA award. A maximum of £1,200 each year can be saved in the account by

---

[104] *Ibid.*
[105] Please refer to: http://www.investmentuk.org/FactSheets/CTF/default.asp (accessed 15 August 2010).

parents, family or friends. Importantly, it will not affect any disability benefits or tax credits the individual receives. However, some residential care is means-tested and could potentially be counted.

Despite early results showing positive outcomes in terms of increased personal savings rates and additional private contributions which have the potential to finance long-term needs,[106] on 24 May 2010, the government announced that it intended to reduce and then stop government payments to CTF accounts. In its place is a long-term tax-free savings account for children being referred to as a 'Junior ISA' (Individual Savings Account) which was launched in November 2011.[107] These provide families the opportunity to save up to an annual limit of £3,600 tax-free until their child turns eighteen; however they do not offer a voucher to lower income families. At the time of this writing, the United Kingdom is debating whether it will include financial literacy education as an integral component of the savings programme, thus addressing a continuing challenge to educate children about how to spend their money wisely in future.[108]

As a result of the decision, children born after December 2010 are not eligible for a CTF. Nonetheless, those already with one are entitled to continue to benefit from tax-free investment growth and no withdrawals will be possible until the child reaches age eighteen. The child, friends and family will continue to be able to contribute up to an overall total of £1,200 a year, and it will still be possible to change the type of account and/or move it to another provider. The new rules mean that no payments will be made into CTFs for DLA entitlement of any kind in the tax year 2011/12 onwards. Children with a CTF who are entitled to DLA at any point before 6 April 2011 will be eligible for a government payment.

It is not clear yet whether a disability-specific trust fund, rather than a universal account, would have fared better for families with a person with a disability given their often widespread worries for the future. In any case, the CTF, similar to the Canadian RDSP, has set a strong precedent according to the Institute for Public Policy Research (2007), and has informed the development of the model elsewhere.[109] However, according to the Social Market Foundation, the decision to stop government payments to lower-income families means it is poorly targeted and will likely benefit the very families who need it least[110]: a matching contribution at the start has been shown to be an important incentive that increases private saving.[111]

---

[106] Institute for Public Policy Research (IPPR) and the Initiative on Financial Security at the Aspen Institute (2007) *The UK Child Trust Fund: Early Results*. Issue Brief, November.

[107] Please refer to: http://www.direct.gov.uk/en/Nl1/Newsroom/DG_192028 (accessed 12 February 2012).

[108] Institute for Public Policy Research (IPPR) *supra*, n. 106.

[109] *Ibid.*

[110] Social Market Foundation (2011) *Poorly Targeted Junior ISA Shows 'Wrong Lessons' Learned from the Child Trust Fund, Says Think Tank*, http://www.smf.co.uk/media/news/poorly-targeted-junior-isa-shows-wrong-lessons-learned-from-the-/ (accessed 12 February 2012)

[111] Fyson et al., *supra*, n. 102.

Nonetheless, its effect on stimulating private saving and changing savings behaviour over the long term could be powerful.

SHAPING THE SUPPLY SIDE OF REFORM

The Awarding of Funding to Shape the Support Market

In England, local authorities have the discretion to make payments net of any user contribution or else, if they so wish, make payments to the full value of the service, on a gross basis. This means that local authorities may provide the full amount of the cost of the service and consider whether the individual is required to make a contribution later. This places direct-payment users on an equitable basis with people who receive services direct from the local authority.[112] Given the means-testing of government payments, fee-for-service exists for many services, which an individual can pay out of his or her own pocket. In particular, providers in England usually charge for their day care service. This has not been the case to the same extent in NI, where many day care services are still an option covered by the social care budget.

Since February 2010, the process of allocating funding for England has been driven by national policy guidance called Prioritising Need in the Context of Putting People First.[113] This supersedes the previous guidance, Fair Access to Care. Its intention is to address inconsistencies across the country about who gets support, in order to provide a fairer and more transparent system for the allocation of social care services. Additionally, the policy guidance builds on the recommendations made in the Commission for Social Care Inspection's (CSCI) review, titled *Cutting the Cake Fairly*, to support fairer, more transparent and consistent implementation of eligibility criteria.[114]

Despite the introduction of individual funding, domiciliary services are still block contracted to varying extents using cost and volume specifications. Since direct payments and personal budgets were introduced, local authorities have sought ways to continue their commissioning role and maintain some leverage over the quality of providers within their area. Personalisation and the wider requirements of Putting People First have driven recent changes in contracting practice. The Audit Commission is now encouraging councils to reconsider their roles and relationships. Councils will have to work with support providers and other stakeholders

---

[112] Department of Health (2000) Circular No: Ccd4/2000, Community Care (Direct Payments) Act 1996-Community Care (Direct Payments) (Scotland) Amendment Regulations 2000, 30 June.

[113] Department of Health (2010) *Prioritising Need in the Context of Putting People First: A Whole System Approach to Eligibility for Social Care – Guidance on Eligibility Criteria for Adult Social Care, England 2010*. HMSO, London.

[114] The Department of Health recommends that councils should ensure that in applying eligibility criteria to prioritise individual need, they are not neglecting the needs of their wider population. Eligibility criteria should be explicitly placed within a much broader context whereby public services in general are well placed to offer all individuals some level of support.

to influence services and ensure they meet personal budget holder's needs. They will also have a greater role in providing information and support to personal budget holders.[115]

With the rise of market-based approaches to resource allocation and service models being in competition with each other, according to Mansell (no date), there is the threat of less commitment to particular philosophies and models a priori, with increased willingness to judge services on the basis of 'payment by results'.[116] This new approach is based on the idea that people can vote with their feet and choose a provider based on their satisfaction with the results. Consequently, market-based models potentially entail reduced emphasis on broader planning on support models and on locality in favour of 'choice'.

To maintain a focus on broader planning, new approaches have been adopted to ensure that existing services are responsive to the needs of personal budget holders. Local authorities have also established 'Framework Agreements' (zero volume contracts), as mentioned in Chapter 3, as a means of accrediting preferred providers to operate in their jurisdiction. This has involved providers signing up to provide personalised and flexible services without a minimum guarantee of volume or demand. In all cases, the detail of the service delivered to an individual is determined between the personal budget holder and the provider based on information in the support plan, although the framework identifies broad outcomes for the contract overall. The frameworks have also required providers to make ISFs (or their equivalent by another name) available to personal budget holders. Setting up ISFs can involve providers in elements of support planning. The ISF can be commissioned on the basis of a completed support plan, or the provider can work with the person to develop their support plan on the basis of their allocation of money.[117] Generally, with an ISF, the service allocation average break down consists of:

- 13.5 per cent (avg.) – service coordination and development costs (weighted);
- 9.5 per cent (avg.) – company costs (including 3 per cent [avg.] insurance contribution);
- 77 per cent (avg.) – direct support costs (individually determined).[118]

The service coordination and development costs cover the fixed cost of an annual support coordinator and the weighted costs of senior management involvement,

[115] Audit Commission (2010) *Financial Management of Personal Budgets*, October.

[116] Mansell, J. (n.d.) *Deinstitutionalisation and Community Living: An International Perspective*, http://www.institutionwatch.ca/cms-filesystem-action?file=research/international_perspective.pdf (accessed 5 September 2010).

[117] Department of Health (2009) *Contracting for Personalised Outcomes: What We're Learning from Emerging Practice*, DH/Putting People First Programme.

[118] Cooper, O., Sanderson, H., Gorman, R., Livesley, M. and Keely, T. (2008) *What Are We Learning about Developing Individual Service Funds?* IAS Services, September, Support Planning, http://www.supportplanning.org/Support_Planning_Downloads/SP_40_What_are_we_learning_about_Individual_Service_Funds_Sept_08.pdf (accessed 12 March 2012).

allocated average contract hours to a psychologist, social worker, consultants, team leaders and so forth. This is weighted depending on the level of input required in designing, setting up and reviewing a person's supports. The company costs include service management, training, administration, payroll, human resources, recruitment and so on. An insurance contribution is also included to cover the unexpected costs not covered by the commissioner, such as sickness.

Finally, the direct support costs are individually allocated and determined by the individual/circle of support. The money for direct support costs is treated as 'restricted' for the benefit of a named individual. The process involves informing everyone (individual, family and staff) how much money is available and working together to get the best from it. The individual is involved in deciding how to spend the money. Examples of direct support costs may include the hourly rate of personal assistance, night-time support, speech and language therapy, physiotherapy and so on. According to Cooper et al. (2008), families in particular found this much easier to understand as they had an opportunity to work in partnership with their chosen provider where the focus was on working things out together.[119]

To encourage portability, all local authorities have required providers to publish their rates for direct payment holders, self-funders and those who choose the council route for arranging services. In Manchester and Wigan, information is provided on both framework and non-framework contracted providers. In the case of Wigan, a Web site called Shop4Support has an eBay-style marketplace function that enables budget holders to find out what is available from different providers, rate providers' services and to exchange information.[120]

Another method used in the allocation of resources for service delivery has been person-centred 'mini-tenders'. Several local authorities have used processes where anonymised person-centred information, taken from support plans or reviews, is used in 'mini-tendering' to determine which provider from within the framework agreement will offer support to an individual or group of individuals. This information, along with confirmation of the indicative budget, is sent to providers who are encouraged to respond with a plan for how they will support the person or persons. People and families remain involved throughout the process, evaluating bids and determining which provider will deliver the support.[121]

Insisting on Standards

In terms of the regulation of disability support providers, in both England and NI, there is an inspector of social care services. The Care Quality Commission (CQC) is the independent regulator of health and social care in England. It is a

---

[119] *Ibid.*
[120] Please refer to: www.shop4support.com (accessed 15 January 2011).
[121] *Supra*, n. 112.

TABLE 6.2. *Essential CQC outcomes*

Involvement and Information
Regulation 17. Respecting and involving service users
Regulation 18. Consent to care and treatment
Personalised Care, Treatment and Support
Regulation 9. Care and welfare of service users
Regulation 14. Meeting nutritional needs
Regulation 24. Cooperating with other providers
Safeguarding and Safety
Regulation 11. Safeguarding service users from abuse
Regulation 12. Cleanliness and infection control
Regulation 13. Management of medicines
Regulation 15. Safety and suitability of premises
Regulation 16. Safety, availability and suitability of equipment
Suitability of Staffing
Regulation 21. Requirements relating to workers
Regulation 22. Staffing
Regulation 23. Supporting workers
Quality and Management
Regulation 10. Assessing and monitoring the quality of service provision
Regulation 19. Complaints
Regulation 20. Records

Source: http://www.care-plan-management-system.co.uk/cqc-registration (accessed 20 December 2010).

non-departmental public body set up by the Department of Health to assess the performance of individual care providers registered by local authorities.

Since 1 October 2010, the inspection process from CQC has measured five agreed indicators: involvement and information; personalised care, treatment and support; safeguarding and safety; suitability of staffing; and quality and management. Each of these indicators has a number of essential outcomes (identified in Table 6.2) which are used to regulate the sector.

It uses a number of different review mechanisms including seeking the views of people who use services.

The CQC has statutory enforcement powers for providers who fail to meet these standards. This includes the power to issue a warning notice, impose, vary or remove conditions on an organisation, issue a penalty notice in lieu of prosecution, suspend or cancel registration of a provider or prosecute for specified offences. In cases where people's rights or safety is at risk, it can act quickly, including closing a service down if necessary. This includes any service provided by the NHS, local authorities, private companies or voluntary sector, irrespective of their having a framework agreement or not. Rather than a sole focus on compliance, according to their enforcement policy, the CQC will encourage improvement wherever possible, unless a service fails to fulfil its legal obligations, in which case they may take enforcement action.[122]

The CQC Judgement Framework takes assessors and inspectors through a series of questions about evidence against each regulation and whether there are any concerns. The steps in the process are:

Stage 1: determining whether the assessors have enough evidence to make a judgement;

Stage 2: checking whether the evidence demonstrates full compliance or concerns with the quality and safety regulations;

Stage 3: if concerns are found, making a judgement as to the impact on people who use the service and the likelihood that the impact will occur; and

Stage 4: validation.[123]

In the ongoing monitoring of compliance, the CQC uses a model of minor, moderate and major concerns and has procedures for how they trigger enforcement action. In this instance, the recognition by providers that they have an issue with compliance is expanded to include their willingness and capacity to improve. There is a built-in incentive for providers to recognise potential breaches for themselves. This means that if they recognise through their declaration that they have some issues with compliance and may be non-compliant and have developed an appropriate action plan to improve, the CQC will 'lower the bar' for the point at which they apply conditions or take other enforcement action. If the providers are not able to declare that they meet any one or more of the CQC standards, they must state specifically why they do not in each case and offer an action plan to remedy the non-compliance. The CQC will assess the robustness of the providers' action plan using the SMART technique, which requires an action plan to be Specific, Measurable, Achievable, Relevant and Time bound.[124] If an action plan is not SMART, the CQC has the option of asking the providers to redo it, or provide further information.

The local authority also has some leverage for ensuring providers are meeting their standards through their commissioning practices. Many local authorities have set a number of standards which all providers must meet in order to become a contracted provider – for example, having a positive CQC rating. Rather than create an antagonistic relationship between commissioners and providers, local authorities are being encouraged to develop a 'smart buyer' approach and foster good communication with the provider sector.[125] Local authority areas with the most successful outcomes have shown signs of working collaboratively with providers to

---

[122] Care Quality Commission (2010) *Enforcement policy*, CQC.

[123] Care Quality Commission (2010) *Setting the Bar: A Framework for Our Regulatory Response for Existing Providers*, February, CQC.

[124] *Ibid.*

[125] *Supra*, n. 112.

help them to raise their standards if their rating falls. This includes working with the provider to develop and implement an action plan with penalties if the action plan is not met. Also in tendering, West Sussex, in an effort to encourage as many providers as possible to work with the Council, including the very small local services that some customers prefer, invited all tenders from all providers to deliver support services who met the benchmark standards required, had good links with the local community, supported social inclusion, were financially sound and had the capacity to deliver the required services. As a result, there are currently around 100 providers within the framework contract but it is expected that this number will decrease as people stop choosing providers who either do not meet their expectations or who have priced themselves out of the market.[126]

The Department of Health is also keen to promote quality assurance of providers. As part of this agenda, the Department of Health is rolling out the National Indicator 130, Self-Directed Support. The National Indicator 130 is a national performance indicator for councils that counts the number of people who have taken up self-directed support. While there are a number of other social care indicators, 70 per cent of local authorities are signed up for National Indicator 130. As a result, the Department of Health is currently hoping to extend it as a tool for monitoring quality in administering successful individual funding mechanisms.

In NI, the Regulation and Quality Improvement Authority (RQIA) is the independent body responsible for monitoring and inspecting the availability and quality of health and social care services, and encouraging improvements in the quality of those services. There are the RQIA Regulations, Code of Practice and Licensing agreements. Organisations also have to participate in self-assessment. Furthermore, a core objective of the RQIA is to adopt a proactive approach to public participation, including the involvement of persons with disabilities in receipt of supports. All inspection reports are made available to the public. In addition to the RQIA, all social care workers are also registered by the NI Social Care Council.

In NI, the RQIA also has powers to take enforcement action and uses these powers to protect the public interest. Enforcement action is taken when there are serious deficiencies in services which present a risk to the public. However, its intention is to support continuous improvement in services and to build an evidence base in order to encourage shared learning amongst providers.[127] These regulators are thus intent on becoming drivers of quality rather than just focused on compliance.

Reconfiguring the Support Market

Since the *Valuing People* white paper in 2001, continuing efforts have been made to complete the replacement of group homes with supported living options in private

---

[126] *Ibid.*
[127] Regulation and Quality Improvement Authority (2009) *Corporate Strategy 2009–2012*, RQIA.

rented accommodation. Its successor, VPN, recognised the growing dissatisfaction with group homes as an option for people with disabilities and promoted the development of supported living through the use of 'assured tenancies'. This approach is based on the idea that housing and support should be separated, so that people live with individuals they choose, in housing they own or rent, receiving staff support from agencies which do not control the accommodation.[128]

Currently, the English government has replaced all Victorian long-stay institutions for persons with disabilities and is finalising the replacement of the last remaining NHS learning disability campuses which were built when the policy of deinstitutionalisation was first promoted.[129] This signals the end of an era in English social care and demonstrates the continued commitment by the Department of Health towards choice in living arrangements.

The residential services directly managed by the local authority have also been disentangled since the 1990 legislation to move more people into rented accommodation.[130] Since this shift, the current pattern of living arrangements for people with intellectual disabilities in England has been recorded by a report by the Centre for Disability Research, commissioned by Mencap in 2008.[131] According to the report, there has been a notable shift in the types of residential accommodation used from 2000–2001 to 2005–2006, with an emphasis towards supported living arrangements. However, there was still a significant number living in residential homes. There were 3,927 available NHS overnight beds for people with learning disabilities (down 38 per cent from 6,316 available beds in 2000–2001). Of these, there were 1,696 occupied long-stay beds for adults. Of the numbers receiving some form of service from the local authority in 2005–2006, 27,000 people received home care (up 197 per cent from 2000–2001); 58,000 people received day care (unchanged from 2000–2001).[132] There were 35,260 council-supported residents with learning disabilities aged eighteen to sixty-four in 2006 (60 per cent of all council-supported resident adults in this age group), a 13.5 per cent increase from 2001.[133] These included:

- 3,200 people in council-staffed residences (down 45 per cent from 2001);
- 28,080 people in independent-sector registered residential homes (up 23 per cent from 2001);

[128] Allard, M. A. (1996) 'Supported Living Policies and Programmes in the USA', in Mansell, J. and Ericsson, K. (eds.) *Deinstitutionalization and Community Living: Intellectual Disability Services in Britain, Scandinavia and the USA*. Chapman and Hall, London. pp. 97–116.

[129] The Department of Health planned to close all campuses in its learning disability strategy, *Valuing People Now*, and is still currently working towards this goal.

[130] Emerson, *supra*, n. 21.

[131] Emerson, E. and Hatton, C. (2008) *People with Learning Disabilities in England*, Centre for Disability Research, Report: 1 May, Centre for Disability Research (CeDR), Lancaster University, Lancaster.

[132] *Ibid.* p. 21.

[133] *Ibid.* p. v.

TABLE 6.3. *Where people with learning disabilities were living in England*

	Mild or moderate	Severe	Profound multiple	All people
Private Households				
With parent(s)	48%	61%	60%	55%
With other relative	14%	11%	4%	12%
With partner	6%	<1%	<1%	3%
Alone	7%	2%	0%	4%
Sub-total	74%	74%	65%	74%
Supporting People funded	12%	8%	5%	10%
Residential Care Home	13%	15%	19%	14%
NHS Accommodation	<1%	2%	11%	2%
Total	100%	100%	100%	100%

Source: Emerson, E. and Hatton, C. (2008) *People with Learning Disabilities in England, CeDR Research Report 2008: 1, May 2008*, Centre for Disability Research (CeDR), Lancaster University, Lancaster.

- 1,840 people in independent-sector nursing homes (up 87 per cent from 2001);
- 2,140 people in unstaffed or other types of home (up 56 per cent from 2001).[134]

Table 6.3 illustrates the relative locations where people were living. While only 2 per cent of people were in NHS accommodation, those with profound learning disabilities were more likely to be living in residential care homes (19 per cent) and NHS accommodation (11 per cent).[135]

In VPN, a similar picture of those living in private households emerged with 50–55 per cent living in the family home, and 15 per cent renting their own home. When these figures are contrasted with those of the general population, they reveal that 70 per cent of the general population own their own home, and 29 per cent rent their own home.

In NI, according to Mulvany et al. (2007), increasing numbers of people similarly reside in supported living arrangements in which they hold a tenancy to a house or apartment which they may share with one or two others. Some of these housing units are clustered in one neighbourhood to facilitate staffing requirements. The bulk of ordinary housing is managed by statutory agencies (49.8 per cent) followed by non-profit organisations (27.1 per cent), housing associations (17.8 per cent) and private providers (5.3 per cent).[136] Whilst the six large mental health hospitals in NI still remain open, the number of patients in psychiatric beds has fallen from more than 5,400 in 1965 to just 1,500 by the mid-1990s.[137] The development of a range

[134] *Ibid.* p. 20.
[135] *Ibid.* p. 6.
[136] Mulvany, F., Barron, S. and McConkey, R. (2007) 'Residential Provision for Adult Persons with Intellectual Disabilities in Ireland', *Journal of Applied Research in Intellectual Disabilities* 20: 70–76.
[137] Prior, P. (1993) *Mental Health and Politics in Northern Ireland*. Aldershot, Avebury.

of largely state-funded community-based mental health services, particularly in the non-profit sector, was facilitated by the availability of bridging finance and helped to drive the deinstitutionalisation process.[138]

Provider-Led Change

Given the transformation challenges involved in reconfiguring the residential support market identified earlier, the Department of Health made £520 million available as a ring-fenced grant to local councils over a three-year period between 2008 and 2011. This is designed to enable councils to make significant steps towards reshaping their adult social care services to promote independence. Those local authorities demonstrating better outcomes have been found to work closely with disability providers to ensure the development of good practice models of housing support.[139]

Lancashire Council worked with a support provider, Castle Supported Living (Castle), to individualise its services at an early stage. Prior to the closer collaboration, the funding for services provided was unclear, inconsistent and often appeared to be insufficient. Similarly, the expectations of the commissioning body were not clear and often appeared to exceed the levels of funding available. As an organisation, Castle had to calculate and evaluate the real cost of the support they offered. They were able to pass on this clarity around their cost which in turn enabled people with disabilities to make decisions about what support they wanted to buy and how much that would cost them. The director of Castle and the the liaison with the Council worked to create more transparent systems, especially around funding streams, including Supporting People money and ILF and, importantly, costed support plans. They found that if individuals are able to see the actual amounts of money involved and work out what was best value, they seem to gain a sense of real control and autonomy that superseded the existing personalised way of working.[140]

In a lot of cases however, local authorities are not proactively engaging with this process. In reality, it is often local organisations which advance the personalisation agenda and try and work with their local authorities on breaking down block contracts. One example of this has been Choice Support which was established in 1984. It has a budget of £40 million, with 1,700 staff and 800 people with intellectual disability using their service. It currently works in a number of local authority areas

[138] Wilson, G. and Kirwan, G. (2007) 'Mental Health Social Work in Northern Ireland and the Republic of Ireland: Challenges and Opportunities for Developing Practice', *European Journal of Social Work* 10(2): 75–191.

[139] *Supra*, n. 114.

[140] More details about this work are available on Skills For Care North West (n.d.) '*Success Stories*', *Adult Social Care Providers Personalisation Success Stories*, http://www.skillsforcare.org.uk/nmsruntime/saveasdialog.aspx?lID=974&sID=225 (accessed 25 January 2011); and on In Control's Web site, *Lancashire Provider*, available at: http://www.in-control.org.uk/DocumentDownload.axd?documentresourceid=171 (accessed 8 December 2011).

such as Wakefield, Cheshire, Nottinghamshire, Bedfordshire and Southampton. It was established to carry out the first intellectual disability hospital closure in a London Borough. Since 1997, it has expanded to carry out seven closures. It is now working on closing group homes and setting up more assured tenancies for the older population who were previously moved from institutions and with new younger clients with personal budgets. According to a management spokesperson, their largest challenges have been working closely with staff in bringing them along with the transformation; making money work differently, in terms of re-allocating funding from group services; ensuring that risk and safeguarding procedures are balanced and effective and finally moving into unchartered territory, with no road map for change.[141] This process has been ongoing since 2004. In terms of their critical success factors, the same management spokesperson has found that firstly drawing lines in the sand is important, to make it clear that 'this is happening, there will be no other way of delivering support in future'. Secondly, they have brought key prominent people from outside the agency to talk to the staff in order to change the organisational culture. Thirdly, they have worked on getting a new skill mix of worker to make sure they hire creative thinkers, people who can think laterally. Finally, advocacy has been very important in the transformation of disability support, particularly within the cohort of people who are demanding a life in the community.[142]

KeyRing Support Networks is another innovative model of supported living.[143] People with intellectual disabilities live within a Network made up of ten ordinary homes. People who need support live in nine of them. These people are KeyRing members. They help each other out and meet up regularly. A community living volunteer lives in the tenth home. The volunteer is a person who helps members out with such activities like reading bills, forms and letters. The volunteer supports members to explore what is going on in their neighbourhood and to get involved. If members need more support, KeyRing works alongside other support providers who can offer targeted support hours.

Finally, MacIntyre is an organisation which supports more than 1,000 people in supported living and inclusive residential care. It provides an example of a larger organisation involved in broad-scale transformation. It began as a charity in 1966 in South England. At the time, it offered group homes and a school for children and later for adults in two homes. In the 1980s, MacIntyre was asked by the local authority to manage many of the new residential homes. However, the move towards more community-based services and problems maintaining the buildings meant that the future of these sites had to be reconsidered in the 1990s.

It now focuses much more on community-based services with a move towards supported living. Leicester and Warrington were amongst the supported living services

---

[141] Personal Communication with Choice Control, 2010.
[142] *Ibid.*
[143] Please refer to: http://www.keyring.org (accessed 8 December 2011).

developed by MacIntyre in the move away from large institutions and to community living. Their Westoning site – a large residential centre – was sold and people were supported to move into flats and houses.[144] This has meant fundamentally changing the way they offer support. They have had to change the way they develop information to ensure it is accessible and accurate. Staff who may traditionally have had more of a 'back-office' role are required to understand how they need to change their way of working to meet the new customer's needs. This includes training human resources, administration, finance and recruitment teams in human rights so that contracting and administration of support are carefully thought out and adjusted to meet the needs and wishes of individuals rather than a local authority.[145]

In the 2000s, MacIntyre, as discussed earlier, aimed at giving people more of a say in their own support and the way the organisation is run and staffed. They now offer a 'brokerage' role through their 'My Way' service for young adults. With this service, MacIntyre can offer to work with local authorities to establish an individual budget that individuals can use to spend on the support they need, design a plan with them, their family and friends which describes the support they need to live the life they choose and plan how to manage the individual budget and work with them, using their plan, to arrange the support they need.[146]

Given the wellspring of personalisation reform, traditional providers are forced to redirect their focus towards hosting and facilitating a person, including offering brokerage services and personal assistance in their everyday lives. Many agencies are redesigning their support structures to better accommodate people with personal budgets. In terms of personalised planning, organisations in both England and NI have had to improve their responsiveness to individual demands.

EVALUATION AND COST-EFFECTIVENESS OF CHANGE

In the United Kingdom, results of evaluations about the cost-effectiveness of community living differ from those in the United States and Canada in that small community residential services (group homes) were predicted and found to be more costly than institutional services. The reason for this was that it was generally accepted that institutional care had been continually under-resourced, and it was widely viewed as another contributing factor to poor outcomes. For example, Wright and Haycox (1985) estimated that the consequences of transferring residents to community care (group homes) would result in a 22 per cent increase in expenditure.[147] In particular,

---

[144] Please refer to: http://www.macintyrecharity.org/About-Us/?/Our+Heritage/36/1990s/71/ (accessed 9 December 2011).

[145] Skills For Care North West (2010) 'Success Stories', supra, n. 140.

[146] See MacIntyre (2009) My Way, http://www.macintyrecharity.org/Services/?/My+Way/42/ (accessed 14 June 2010).

[147] Wright, K. and Haycox, A. (1985) *Costs of Alternative Forms of NHS Care for Mentally Handicapped Persons*, Centre for Health Economics, University of York, York.

low budget allocations and difficulties in recruiting staff meant that staff-to-resident ratios in former institutions were generally seen as inadequate. Consequently, there was an acceptance that deinstitutionalisation in the United Kingdom should be accompanied by increasing costs per resident as this additional investment was necessary to avoid replicating in the community the often scandalous conditions found in UK institutions.[148]

When deinstitutionalisation began in the United Kingdom in the 1980s and early 1990s, studies showed that the costs of six- to eight-person group homes tended to be more expensive than equivalent large institutions, albeit some only by small margins.[149] Research by Knapp et al. (1992) showed that costs in a number of community care demonstration projects were on average 17 per cent greater than equivalent institution costs.[150]

It is worth noting, however, that in comparison with a more recently provided specialised institution and campus-based service which was resourced at a higher level than was typical of longer-established institutional settings, Hatton et al. (1995) found higher average annual costs per person in the institutions than ordinary group homes.[151]

Despite the findings from the UK cost-evaluation studies, closer inspection reveals that the economies-of-scale argument (which equates larger numbers of residents with cheaper costs) does not adequately explain the cost differential. Given the historical context in the United Kingdom with under-resourced institutions, the research has shown that although the costs in smaller community residences have increased, the size of the service (based on number of residents), is only one factor in explaining the cost variation (accounting for only 23 per cent of the variation), according to Knapp et al. (1992).[152] Additional factors include the other various funding mechanisms and entitlements, the degree to which both models are being properly resourced (to allow for fair comparison), the residents' characteristics, the wage differential between institutional and community staff and the degree of informal support. Therefore, the economies-of-scale argument does not adequately explain the cost differential. In other words, the background context of how both systems

---

[148] Felce, D. and Emerson, E. (2005) 'Community Living: Costs, Outcomes, and Economies of Scale: Findings from U.K. Research', in Stancliffe, R. J. and Lakin, K. C. (eds.) *Costs and Outcomes of Community Services for People with Intellectual Disabilities*, Brooks Publishing, Baltimore. pp. 45–62.

[149] See Davies, L. (1987) *Quality, Costs and 'An Ordinary Life'*. King's Fund Centre, London; Davies, L. (1988) 'Community Care: The Costs and Quality', *Health Services Management Research* 1: 145–155; Felce, D. (1986) 'Accommodating Adults with Severe and Profound Mental Handicaps: Comparative Revenue Costs', *Mental Handicap* 14: 104–107.

[150] Knapp, M., Cambridge, P., Thomason, C., Beecham, J., Allen, C. and Darton, R. (1992) *Care in the Community: Challenge and Demonstration*. Ashgate, Aldershot.

[151] Hatton, C., Emerson, E., Robertson, J., Henderson, D. and Cooper, J. (1996) 'Factors Associated with Staff Support and User Lifestyle in Services for People with Multiple Disabilities: A Path Analytic Approach', *Journal of Intellectual Disability Research* 40: 466–477.

[152] Wright and Haycox, *supra*, n. 147.

are operated and funded plays a significant role in shaping the cost-effectiveness of change.

This has important implications for more conventional service models which continue to use block-type treatment and rigid professionalised support, such as group homes for example. In terms of evaluations of group homes, according to Emerson and Hatton (1994), these community-based services are quite variable in their performance.[153] Case-studies comparing different living arrangements in the UK have found that the ideology of institutions often persists in group homes and can only be overcome by a further move to supported living.[154] This research is evident in the European Commission's classification of institutions, which states they should not primarily be defined by their size but above all by features of 'institutional culture' (depersonalisation, rigidity of routine, block treatment, social distance, paternalism). Size is merely an indicator – the larger the setting, the fewer the chances are to guarantee individualised, needs-tailored services as well as participation and inclusion in the community.[155]

Importantly, Emerson *et al.* (2005) concluded that consistently better outcomes were associated with supported living.[156] Their evaluation revealed that participants in dispersed housing schemes experienced relatively greater choice, more extensive social networks, a more physically active life, fewer accidents in their home, and a greater number and variety of leisure activities. The only negative outcomes were fewer planned activities and more potential exposure to crime and verbal abuse.[157] In the post-institution cost-evaluation literature, in a comparison between small-group homes and supported-living schemes, participants in the latter model experienced greater choice overall, greater choice over with whom and where they lived, and a greater number of community-based activities.[158]

Interestingly, Stancliffe reported that supported living can also be a more cost-effective model given that staff allocations can be individualised (and natural

[153] Emerson, E. and Hatton, C. (1994) *Moving Out: Relocation from Hospital to Community.* HMSO, London.

[154] Ericsson, K. (1996) 'Housing for the Person with Intellectual Handicap', in Mansell and Ericsson, *supra*, n. 125; Stevens, A. (2004) 'Closer to Home: A Critique of British Government Policy towards Accommodating Learning Disabled People in Their Own Homes', *Critical Social Policy* 24(2): 233–254.

[155] European Commission (2009) *Report of the Ad Hoc Expert Group on the Transition from Institutional to Community-based Care*, Directorate-General for Employment, Social Affairs and Equal Opportunities, European Commission.

[156] Emerson, E., Robertson, J., Hatton, C., Knapp, M. and Walsh, P-N. (2005) 'Costs and Outcomes of Community Residential Supports in England', in Stancliffe, R. J. and Lakin, K. C. (eds.) *Costs and Outcomes of Community Services for People with Intellectual Disabilities*, Brooks Publishing, Baltimore. pp. 151–173.

[157] Stainton, T., Hole, R., Charles, G., Yodanis, C., Powell, S. and Crawford, C. (2006) *Residential Options for Adults with Developmental Disabilities: Quality and Cost Outcomes.* October, The Ministry of Children and Family Development, Province of British Columbia.

[158] *Ibid.*

supports interwoven), in contrast to group homes with relatively fixed staffing requirements.[159] In 2001, as discussed there was a renewed commitment by government towards 'supported living'. According to an evaluation by the Department of Communities and Local Government, *Supporting People* is based on an 'invest to save' approach, aimed to prevent individuals from experiencing crises and requiring more costly service intervention; and to enable vulnerable people to live independently through the provision of housing-related support services.[160] Their report acknowledged that the 'invest to save' nature of the programme has been a success and has been demonstrated in robust financial terms. This is based on financial modeling work that was commissioned to Capgemini in March 2009. Capgemini found that the programme was delivering savings to the Exchequer of £3.4 billion for a £1.6 billion investment per annum.[161]

Overall, the experience from the UK shows that countries do differ in how the community support architecture is designed and ultimately funded. Factors include the level of staff costs, the extent of inefficiencies in the system, the relative resource demands in different models, and the poor implementation of one model in contrast to another. One bright spot on the horizon is the new possibilities of better outcomes and lower costs associated with supported living models (in contrast to group homes), as currently being advocated by people with disabilities and government.

In terms of evaluations, there have been many positive outcomes which have emerged from the personalisation agenda. For people with disabilities who use their personal budget to pay for a personal assistant, opportunities for new forms of support relations open up on the basis of individuals having more choice and control over their support arrangements. Personal budgets have seemingly struck a chord with many disabled people (in particular those with physical disabilities), older people and others in receipt of support, as well as with many social workers, other care professionals and family carers.[162] Williams *et al.* (2009) for example, describe the positive change in the power relation between an individual with a learning disability, family member/s and paid care staff.[163] For many, it is simply a pragmatic shift in the funding and management of support, with, in particular, the possibilities for independent living created by employing a personal assistant. For many disability organisations, it has been heralded as much more than this:

[159] Stancliffe, R. J. (2005) 'Semi-Independent Living and Group Homes in Australia', in Stancliffe, R. J. and Lakin, K. C. (eds.) *Costs and Outcomes of Community Services for People with Intellectual Disabilities*, Brooks Publishing, Baltimore. pp. 129–150.

[160] Department of Communities and Local Government (2010) *Government Response to the House of Commons Communities and Local Government Select Committee Report into the Supporting People Programme*. HMSO, London.

[161] *Ibid.*

[162] *Supra*, n. 28.

[163] Williams, V., Ponting, L. and Ford, K. (2009) "I Do Like the Subtle Touch': Interactions between People with Learning Difficulties and Their Personal Assistants', *Disability and Society* 24(7): 815–828.

a key goal of the independent living movement and a 'potentially revolutionary' redistribution of power.[164]

Evaluations of people's experiences of direct payments, individual budgets (in the pilots) and personal budgets have reported greater control over support (72 per cent for personal budgets[165]), improved wellbeing (68 per cent[166]), more choice of forms of support, improved social networks, and more opportunities for engaging in social activities.[167] Significantly however, most benefits were gained by those who were more able, already had care arrangements in place, and had a strong support network of family and friends.

According to the national government evaluation findings from the Individual Budgets Evaluation Network (IBSEN), individual budgets have been found to produce higher overall social care outcomes given the costs incurred.[168] They also have the *potential* to be more cost-effective than standard care and support arrangements. The cost-effectiveness advantage of individual budgets is greater for people with mental health issues and younger physically disabled people than for older people or people with learning disabilities. For this last group, however, implementation delays may have played a part in reducing the cost-effectiveness: once support plans are in place, there is a greater likelihood that individual budgets can be a cost-effective alternative to conventional arrangements.

According to an evaluation of In Control's model of personal budgets,[169] in Phase I (2003–5) of the thirty people in the pilot, ten were in residential care homes at the start of the process, and all moved out: nine into their own tenancies and one back into the family home (however, people in residential homes are not currently eligible for personal budgets). This shift from residential services into supported living was mirrored, although less intensely, in the IBSEN pilot site evaluation.[170] The use of day care centres also fell – the average amount of time spent in day care fell from around 4.5 days per week to 3.5 days per week per person. The biggest increase was in the use of personal assistants: eight people used personal assistants before having a personal budget, 22 people used personal assistants afterwards. Using the money for accessing social and leisure activities was also very popular.[171] The general pattern was that people want more choice and control; they are spending less of their money on day services, and more on social support that can help keep them to be independent and connected to local activities.

[164] Glasby, J. and Littlechild, R. (2002) *Social Work and Direct Payments*. Policy Press, Bristol; for a more detailed discussion, see also *supra*, n. 29.

[165] Tyson, A., Brewis, R., Crosby, N. et al. (2010) *A Report on In Control's Third Phase 2008–09*. In Control, London.

[166] *Ibid.*

[167] *Supra*, n. 65.

[168] *Ibid.*

[169] Bartlett, J. (2009) *At Your Service: Navigating the Future Market in Health and Social Care*. Demos, London.

[170] *Supra*, n. 65.

[171] *Ibid.*

While the above evaluations and examples demonstrate the positive outcomes which have arisen from individualised funding, it is also clear that more needs to be done on ensuring individuals are well supported and have access to information for individualised funding to work. There is considerable variation both by authority and by devolved area in the numbers involved.[172]

In NI, as mentioned there has not been the same level of take-up or national-level political support for direct payments and personal budgets. Notably, *Valuing People* and its successor VPN, with its strong emphasis on personalisation, were not published in NI. Instead, the Bamford *'Equal Lives'* Report in 2005, as discussed earlier, has outlined the NI vision. The NI Executive's Response to Bamford stated that wider promotion of direct payments was supported, but there was a suggestion that the target relating to direct payments needed to be amended to include provision of accurate information and support for parents and families wishing to use them.[173] The total number of Care Packages in Northern Ireland subject to Direct Payments was 1,144 at the end of March 2008, up from 117 in March 2004. Of the total number of Direct Payments, 30 per cent were used by older people, 3 per cent by people with mental health problems, 22 per cent by people with an intellectual disability, 42 per cent by people with a physical disability with the remaining 2 per cent being used by carers over the age of 18.[174]

In addition, an In Control pilot scheme on individual budgets started in the Southern Health and Social Care Trust area in NI in 2009. In that pilot, most of the management of the budget was done on behalf of the individual, but the scheme still gives people control to redirect their support away from standard day care to, for example, innovative use of leisure or recreational facilities. This project is intended to build on the Southern Trust's success in the promotion of direct payments.[175]

Evaluations of personalisation have also reported that whilst, overall, those in receipt of personal budgets reported feeling more in control of their daily lives, the support they accessed, and the activities they were involved in, most individuals and their key carers (usually family members) found the process of securing and managing a budget 'stressful'.[176] Many still 'found it difficult to understand' the package of funding they received and the techniques of financial management.[177] According to Stainton and Boyce, support for care planning and budget management

---

[172] Jolly, D. and Priestley, M. (2004) *Working Paper on Direct Payment Patterns in the UK*, Centre for Disability Studies, Leeds University.

[173] NI Executive (2009) *Delivering the Bamford Vision: The Response of Northern Ireland Executive to the Bamford Review of Mental Health and Learning Disability, Summary of key points arising from consultation*, March.

[174] *Supra*, n. 65.

[175] See http://www.cilbelfast.org/content/personalisation-self-directed-support-and-personal-budgets-0 (accessed 13 February 2012)

[176] *Supra*, n. 65, p. 237.

[177] *Ibid.* p. 155.

was 'inadequate in many cases'.[178] Support schemes are often administered by CILs and are generally given a grant by the authority to undertake this work. Having facilitation in place is being recognised as an important element to be addressed in the future development of adult social support policy.

The variability in access to brokerage and facilitation means that those deemed to have a moderate to severe intellectual disability, those with complex needs, and those who did not have the support or resources to effectively negotiate and manage a budget were less able to take advantage of personalised support.[179] Further, there was concern that those with more complex needs on existing packages of high-cost care could be vulnerable, as the 'cost effectiveness advantages' of individual budgets were less clear than for other groups, such as younger physically disabled people.[180]

In addition, independence of support brokers from both local authority and service provider varies between the local authority and NI Trust areas. In Manchester, independent brokers are just being established. In Lancashire, brokerage is service-provider-led, whilst in West Sussex, it is provided in-house within the local authority. While there is some debate about possible conflicts of interest when providing brokerage as well as services, this is seen as an area of possible expansion and diversification by some providers.[181]

While the IBSEN research has demonstrated that individualised funding can provide better quality-of-life outcomes at the same level or below the cost of traditional services,[182] critics such as many civil sector organisations like Action on Elder Abuse have been skeptical that government sees it as purely a cost-saving exercise. For example, the chief executive of Action on Elder Abuse in the United Kingdom states, 'Unless there is the framework around [self-directed support] which includes active advocacy and a safeguarding agenda, then cash for care is dangerous, and that's almost exclusively what the government is pushing'.[183] There are also concerns from commentators such as Mansell[184] that within a market-based system which relies solely on the decisions on budget-holders, there will be an exclusive focus on price and volume rather than quality, and an under-investment in planning and infrastructure.

In response to these concerns, according to a representative from a community living organisation involved in promoting welfare reform in the UK, 'the arguments over cost and safeguards are as relevant for the conventional model as an individual funding model: the latter system needs to be as rigorously monitored as the traditional

---

[178] Stainton, T. and Boyce, S. (2004) '"I Have Got My Life Back": Users' Experience of Direct Payments', *Disability and Society* 19(5): 443–454.

[179] *Supra*, n. 28.

[180] *Supra*, n. 65, p. 112.

[181] *Supra*, n. 113.

[182] *Supra*, n. 65.

[183] Please refer to: http://www.communitycare.co.uk/Articles/2008/10/22/109761/personalisation-exclusive-poll-of-social-workers-views.htm (accessed 1 September 2010).

[184] Mansell, *supra*, n. 116.

model of service delivery and not more susceptible to rationing'.[185] Indeed, this is the challenge – to see that the new choice agenda is backed up by safeguards to ensure people are not left in vulnerable positions as a result of rationing of state disability entitlements, individual budgets or direct payments.

More generally, the potential for direct payments has only partly been realised as a result of very low and uneven uptake within and between different parts of the United Kingdom. Included in this data is evidence of lower levels of uptake in NI, Scotland and Wales. There are also clear inequalities in relation to access by different user groups, with some local authorities much less likely to sanction payments to people with intellectual disabilities. This is accounted for in part by resistance from some local authorities that have active unions, which regard direct payments as a threat to public-sector jobs.[186] Another reason for geographic variation is the availability of support schemes, which are important in raising awareness and providing assistance to those thinking of or actually using direct payments. In order to further advance personalisation across the United Kingdom, a recent tool called Act Local, Think Personal has been established by a partnership representing the views of providers, local government and service users and carers. It is designed to support providers and commissioners to learn from innovative practice in commissioning and delivering personalised services.[187] It funds a limited number of projects and has a small central delivery team. To encourage better practice, the partnership will also offer clear examples of innovative practice across the country where organisations and individuals are leading the way in delivering personalised and community-based support solutions. Over time, it will establish benchmarks for the sector as a whole to assess their progress in delivering such practices.

CONCLUSION

The personalisation of disability support sits at the heart of the UK support policy. Both England and Northern Ireland to varying extents are focussed on a comprehensive shift away from congregated services towards 'active citizenship', marked recently by the United Kingdom's recent extension of direct payments to a much wider population. The philosophy of personalisation is the keystone of this policy commitment and aims to enable people with disabilities to have a choice in the support they require. Examples of good practice show that, in general, the 'personalisation agenda'[188] – the framework of person-centred planning and highly

[185] Personal Communication, July 2010.

[186] *Supra*, n. 54.

[187] Please refer to: http://www.thinklocalactpersonal.org.uk (accessed 24 February 2012).

[188] Prime Minister's Strategy Unit (2005) *Improving the Life Chances of Disabled People. A Joint Report with the Department of Work and Pensions, Department of Health, Department for Education and Skills, Office of the Deputy Prime Minister.* Cabinet Office, London; Department of Health (2007) *Putting People First: A Shared Vision and Commitment to the Transformation of Adult Social Care.* Department of Health, London.

individualised services, increasingly funded through direct payments and personal budgets (and to a lesser extent individual budgets[189]) – is providing what many people need and want and more broadly fits with the guiding principles articulated in the CRPD.

Ultimately, with this new paradigm, a corresponding shift is being expected away from paternalistic and state-controlled support towards individual responsibility in governing and managing one's own support. With this, individuals must be able to manage direct payments even if they need help to do this on a day-to-day basis. As the discussion showed, the success of direct payments and individual budgets is hinged on the ability and willingness of individuals and families to opt for this model, given the onus of responsibility on personally managing this budget. With support brokerage still in its infancy in many parts of the United Kingdom, there is still some reluctance by some groups of people with disabilities to use this model. Analysis from an ESRC study (2002) has shown that support schemes (which help people to manage their direct payment) undoubtedly have a positive effect on numbers taking up direct payments.[190] Thus the lack of comprehensive support remains a barrier to its uptake, particularly in relation to the slow progress of direct payments in NI.

The option of personalisation also presents a significant shift in control of power and resources and for this reason its implementation will take time, given the range of professionals involved. In particular, according to Stainton (2002), structural conflicts of interest in relation to social workers' roles within the community care system will continue to be a source of resistance.[191] The government is therefore attempting to build confidence and capacity in local authorities and provide a road map for the transformation of adult social support, as outlined in *Putting People First*. The implementation of this policy will be crucial to its future development.

While direct payments offer the potential to reposition people with disabilities as empowered citizens, ultimately the availability of high-quality person-centred supports remains central to supporting individuals. Throughout this chapter, examples of innovative support models have been identified, each of which is committed to providing responsive individualised support. Moreover, the way in which they operate within the legal and funding climate in the United Kingdom offers important lessons about the power of strategic commissioning and political will in shaping local good practice. While evidence is showing that direct payments and individual budgets offer a cost-neutral (and often cheaper) mechanism to avail of these services, concerns about direct payments potentially driving down the cost of support and

---

[189] The further implementation of individual budgets is still being considered given that legal and other obstacles have not all been overcome.

[190] Carmichael, A. and Brown, L. (2002) 'The Future Challenge for Direct Payments', *Disability and Society* 17(7): 797–808.

[191] Stainton, T. (2002) 'Taking Rights Structurally: Disability Rights and Social Worker Responses to Direct Payments', *British Journal of Social Work* 32: 751–763.

deregulating the employment rights for directly employed personal assistants[192] also need to be heeded.

In terms of choice in living arrangements, the United Kingdom has gone a long way in its transformation from institutional 'care' towards supporting people in the community. Given the early origins of this transformation, community-based accommodation in the form of group homes became the norm in the 1970s and 1980s. However, in response to evaluations in the late 1990s and early 2000s which found mixed outcomes with this model, the UK government has more recently begun a secondary transition towards 'supported living' as its future guiding philosophy. This new approach has the potential to radically develop active citizenship.

It is clear from commentators that within the paradigm of 'personalisation' and individual autonomy, safeguards will need to be in place, firstly to ensure people are given the tools and facilitation to effectively manage their own support, and secondly to ensure that a sole focus on individualised support does not lead to a neglect of issues relevant to community connection, such as promoting good mental health, tackling isolation and fostering support networks. At present, the social care system operates in a context that itself creates tensions between individual choice and collective interaction.

Finally, as part of supporting a 'life in the community', accessibility and employment are key goals of the UK government. Given the dual mandate of providing both employment support and state benefits, in particular with the Employment and Support Allowance, Jobcentre Plus and its counterpart in NI, the government is making it clear that economic re-engagement is a core part of the reform. This goal is focussed on supporting people facing the greatest barriers to employment to compete effectively in the labour market, as well as administer employment benefits to persons out of work. It is clear that the new personalisation agenda is being matched with a renewed focus on removing barriers and encouraging people to become socially and economically active in the community.

---

[192] See Spandler, H. (2004) 'Friend or Foe? Towards a Critical Assessment of Direct Payments', *Critical Social Policy* 24(2): 187–209.

7

Active Citizenship and Disability in Sweden

INTRODUCTION

This chapter examines how Sweden is managing personalisation for persons with disabilities, in terms of its overall welfare and rights philosophy and how it has sculpted reform through social policies for the supply and demand side to enable people with disabilities to re-engage in society. It traces the wellsprings of reform and examines the changed focus of its disability support model.

For a long time, the prime goal of Swedish disability policy has been to ensure that people with disabilities have power and influence over their everyday lives. Since the 1950s Sweden has been in a phase of continual change in its transition away from welfare and congregated services to independent living and human rights. In particular, the *Standard Rules on the Equalisation of Opportunities for Persons with Disabilities* has been a cornerstone of Swedish disability policy ever since its publication in 1993. In pursuit of its fundamental goal of promoting independent living, Sweden ratified the CRPD and Optional Protocol on 30 December 2008 and as a result has committed itself to ensuring that its policy goals remain faithful to the Convention's guiding principles.

Reform pushed by a strong movement of disability rights organisations in Sweden has led to, amongst other things, civil rights legislation for support and personal assistance called "Act on support and service for certain individuals with disabilities" (LSS). This is the only civil rights legislation of its kind in Europe. The overall goal now for the Swedish government is to reach higher levels of equality, accessibility and participation for people with disabilities, even though resources in society are considered scarce. The chapter thus offers a particularly pertinent case study for other nations which are grappling with reform.

AN OVERVIEW OF THE ADMINISTRATION OF DISABILITY SUPPORT

Sweden's government structure consists of three levels: the national, the county or regional council and the local authority (municipality). The Swedish health care system, within which lies the responsibility for the administration of disability support, is quite decentralised. The sixteen county councils and the four regions have a general responsibility for health care, public transport and dental health. The 290 municipalities are responsible for local health and social care for seniors and disabled people, including home assistance, housing and housing adaptation and taxi services for persons with disabilities. Because of decentralisation, the distribution of services varies from one area of the country to another. Some county councils have shifted responsibility to the municipalities, which has led to inequality in health care services.[1]

The Ministry of Health and Social Affairs is responsible for social and health care. The National Board of Health and Welfare is a government agency under this ministry with a wide range of activities and duties within the fields of social welfare, medical services, environmental health, communicable disease prevention and epidemiology. The National Board of Health and Welfare is responsible for ensuring good health through social welfare, high-quality health services and social care on equal terms for the whole Swedish population. The largest unit under the Ministry of Health and Social Affairs is the social insurance agency (*Försäkringskassan*). The Swedish social insurance system is designed to provide financial security in case of sickness or disability to older persons or to families with children. Social insurance is based on the case of each individual and provides allowances to cover parts of income loss in cases of sickness or disability, for example.[2] The social insurance covers everyone who lives or works in Sweden and provides financial protection for families and children, the elderly, as well as for persons with disability, illness or work injuries. The social insurance agency is in charge of the financial aspects of family support policy, as well as financial security for people suffering from an illness, people with disabilities and the elderly. It is accountable for payments to the pension system and is also responsible for rehabilitation and getting people back to work.[3]

Disability is regarded as a 'mainstream' issue in Sweden, meaning all ministries are responsible for carrying out government decisions including those concerning disabilities issues. According to the Disability Action Plan[4] (described in detail later

---

[1] See http://www.regeringen.se/sb/d/2462 http://www.regeringen.se/sb/d/2462 (accessed 10 March 2012).

[2] Ministry of Health Social Affairs (2009) *Social Insurance in Sweden*, Fact Sheet, Government, Sweden, http://www.forsakringskassan.se/omfk/om_socialforsakringen (accessed 10 March 2012).

[3] See http://www.forsakringskassan.se/omfk (accessed 10 March 2012).

[4] Skrivelse (2009) Government Communication – *Follow Up of the National Disability Action Plan and Grounds for a Future Strategy*, 10:166, http://www.riksdagen.se/sv/Dokument-Lagar/ Forslag/Propositioner-och-skrivelser/Uppfoljning-av-den-Nationella-_GX03166/?text=true (accessed 12 March 2012).

in the chapter), all sectors have the responsibility for making society accessible. This is an intersectorial responsibility coordinated by the Swedish Agency for Disability Policy Coordination (Handisam). The remit of each ministry includes responsibility for government agencies, including the preparation of budgets, bills and proposals to be presented for government decision.

Since January 2009, Sweden has had one equality ombudsman (*diskriminerings ombudsmannen*) (DO) government agency that deals with discrimination and promotes equal rights and opportunities. The previous four ombudsmen agencies, including the disability ombudsman, were incorporated into this agency with the most recent Discrimination Act (SFS 2008:567),[5] adopted in January 2009. This law prohibits discrimination on grounds of gender, ethnicity, religion, disability, sexual orientation and age. Several laws were replaced by this discrimination act.[6] Before 2009 and the establishment of the DO, people with disabilities had limited protection against discrimination. The previous office of the disability ombudsman (HO) was established in 1994 with the responsibility of monitoring disability policy,[7] in particular questions concerning the rights of people with disabilities and their interests. HO worked to combat the disadvantages faced by people with disabilities. The DO now has a stronger mandate than the HO in investigating cases of discrimination and harassment covered by the Discrimination Act. However, in the process of replacing the earlier laws, the consideration of lack of accessibility as discrimination was not included in this recent legislation in spite of years of lobbying efforts. In any case, the DO can represent in court those people who have been discriminated against[8] and this is free of charge, paid by the government.

Handisam, as mentioned earlier, is the government authority responsible for disability policy coordination. It was created in 2006, having as its mission to take a proactive role in Swedish disability policy and to raise awareness about people with disability, with the goal of enabling their increased participation and equality in society.[9] Handisam has the intersectorial responsibility and the obligation of spreading and anchoring a disability perspective within all parts of society, to enable effective implementation of disability policy and to ensure everyone can participate equally, regardless of their functional ability. Handisam also works for a more accessible society with no physical or mental barriers, including, for instance, the

---

5 http://www.sweden.gov.se/content/1/c6/11/59/03/b463d1e1.pdf (accessed 12 March 2012).

6 These are the Equality Act, the Prohibition against Discrimination on Grounds of Sexual Orientation Act, the Discrimination at Work on Grounds of Ethnicity, Religion and Disability Act, the Equal Treatment of Students at University Act, the Prohibition of Discrimination Act and the Prohibition of Discrimination and Other Offensive Treatment of Children and Students Act.

7 SFS (1994) Law for the Disability Ombudsman, nr. 1994: 749, http://www.riksdagen.se/sv/Dokument-Lagar/Lagar/Svenskforfattningssamling/Forordning-1994949-med-inst_sfs-1994--949/ (accessed 12 March 2012).

8 http://www.do.se/sv/Om-DO/ http://www.do.se/sv/Om-DO/ (accessed 12 March 2012).

9 See http://www.handisam.se/Tpl/NormalPage____1498.aspx (accessed 12 March 2012).

promotion of accessible buses for wheelchair access, smoke-free environments and easy-to-read texts. The work is guided by the goals and strategies of the disability policy. Reporting is done directly to the government.

In terms of the administration of disability supports and services, there are quite complicated arrangements between national, county or regional council and the local authority levels, which are examined in more detail in the section 'An Overview of the Disability Support Framework'.

The Swedish Democratic Process for Disability Support

Some questions concerning the government are more difficult to answer than others and therefore demand a more thorough explanation. The review process in Sweden is well established and is referred to as the national enquiry. This process is used for all issues, which affect society, including disability issues. An enquiry process is used before legislation proposals can be finalised and submitted to the parliament for approval. The process is applied in cases where overarching issues will affect Swedish society at large, and is often used for politically and technically complicated issues. The government appoints the investigator or the committee to lead a national enquiry which reviews the question at hand. Experts are included in the group responsible for the enquiry along with politicians, although one-expert enquiries are often used. When there is a larger enquiry, interest groups are also given the opportunity to be involved in the process.[10] They are included as members of a reference group and/or in the referral procedure. The referral procedure consists of proposals for new legislation being presented to the public for consultation, before the government presents them to the parliament.

The possibility for the ministries, civil society and others to comment on proposed legislation or policy through the referral procedure is an important part of the Swedish democracy and its political decision-making process. The municipalities, county councils and organisations are not obliged to participate in the consultation, but can express their opinions; the ministries, however, are obliged to take part. The aim of the procedure is to identify potential consequences of the proposal. A referral reading is considered important for the promotion of issues and for the inclusion of the public in the community debate which is essential for democracy.[11] In spite of the process, there are often complaints from the disability movement that issues are passed from one enquiry to the next without any action being taken. For example, as indicated earlier, lack of accessibility has been deemed by various enquiries to be an act of discrimination, and has been included in the legislation since the 1970s; however, as mentioned, it has not been incorporated in the latest discrimination legislation of 2009.

---

[10] See http://regeringen.se/sb/d/2461 (accessed 12 March 2012).
[11] Svara på remiss (2009) *Hur och Varför, Stadsrådsberedningens promemoria.*

Apart from disability organisations, one of the most influential organisations included in the referral process for issues concerning disability is the Swedish Association of Local Authorities and Regions (SALAR). The main objective of SALAR is to safeguard the interests of Swedish local and regional authorities. This organisation represents the governing professional and employer-related interests of Sweden's municipalities and county councils. It strives to promote and strengthen local self-government and the development of regional and local democracy. The operation of SALAR is financed through annual membership fees and is politically controlled, meaning that with every election there can be a change in the appointed politicians.[12] With the participation of SALAR in the referral process, there is a guarantee that issues are considered from organisations with various backgrounds, allowing for an all-round perspective on the issues. One of the organisations against the lack of accessibility being classified as discrimination was SALAR.

The Swedish government established a Disability Delegation in 1998 to develop the dialogue between disability organisations and the government. It is an important forum where interests of people with disabilities are discussed. The delegation provides an opportunity for the government to learn more about the situation of people with disabilities and to identify proposals for the development of disability policy. A minister from the social ministry chairs the delegation. Members of disability organisations are elected to the delegation for three years. Disability organisations appoint the members and the government selects them.[13]

The County Administrative Board (Länsstyrelsen) is a government authority existing in each county and, amongst other things, represents its county's citizens to ensure they receive the level of service the government has decided on. The County Administrative Board is an important link between the people and the municipal authorities on one hand and the government, parliament and central authorities on the other. The County Administrative Board is responsible for a wide range of issues and therefore has a wide variety of specialists at its disposal, such as lawyers, biologists, architects, agronomists, forestry specialists, engineers, public relations officers, archaeologists, social workers, veterinarians, social scientists and economists.[14] The County Administrative Board is also responsible for the distribution of national grants for the personal ombudsmen or 'Ombudsmen (PO) for psychiatric patients' to municipalities – an innovative mentoring service for people with mental health issues. The Board initially had the responsibility for monitoring the implementation of disability legislation, but this responsibility has recently been transferred to the National Board of Health and Welfare.

As mentioned earlier, the National Board of Health and Welfare (Socialstyrelsen) is the governmental authority agency under the Social Ministry responsible for

---

[12] See http://skl.se/om_skl (accessed 12 March 2012).

[13] See http://www.regeringen.se/sb/d/1928/a/18947 (accessed 12 March 2012).

[14] See http://www3.lansstyrelsen.se/lst/en/ (accessed 12 March 2012).

elderly and disability issues. This role is set out in legislation, more specifically in the Social Services Act (SoL)[15] and the Act concerning Support and Services for Persons with Certain Functional Impairments (LSS), which are discussed later. The Board is responsible for the monitoring of the services provided by law and now executes judgements and decisions on sanctions, applied to both the municipalities and county councils not fulfiling their obligations.

AN OVERVIEW OF THE DISABILITY SUPPORT FRAMEWORK

Disability-Specific State Entitlements

This section discusses the disability-specific welfare entitlements in Sweden. These are sickness allowance, housing allowance, accessible housing allowance, rehabilitation compensation, car allowance, disability allowance and health care allowance. Disability and health care allowances have a long tradition in Swedish social insurance. The disability allowance was established as an allowance for blind people in 1934, but became the disability allowance in 1975.[16]

Sickness Allowance
Sickness allowance and what is called activity allowance are paid to people with reduced work capacity resulting from sickness or disability and when medical treatment or rehabilitation is not considered able to increase the work capacity. Activity allowance is paid to people between nineteen and twenty-nine years of age and sickness compensation to people between thirty and sixty-four years of age. Activity allowance is limited to a three-year period. Sickness allowance is paid to people having a life-long reduction in work capacity of at least 25 per cent. The allowance can either be full, 75 per cent, 50 per cent or 25 per cent, depending on the degree of work capacity and the ability to make a living.[17]

Housing Allowance
There are two kinds of housing allowance: the first is for people receiving an activity allowance and the second for people with children or low income. The second allowance is based on the income of a person; if a person's income goes up and the allowance is not recalculated, the person may be forced to repay the allowance. The allowance is based on how many people live in the household, income, wealth, living costs and living space. If an individual or family member has a disability, it is possible to obtain the housing allowance for a larger space than what is considered

---

[15] SFS (2001) Social Services Legislation, nr 2001: 453, http://www.riksdagen.se/sv/Dokument-Lagar/Lagar/Svenskforfattningssamling/sfs_sfs-2001--453/ (accessed 12 March 2012).

[16] See www.forsakringskassan.se/irj/go/km/docs/fk_publishing/Dokument/Rapporter/svar_pa_regeringsuppdrag/rupp _45662_07rapport.pdf (accessed 12 March 2012).

[17] See http://www.forsakringskassan.se/privatpers/sjuk (accessed 12 March 2012).

the maximum, as extra space is taken into consideration for technical equipment or the movement of a wheelchair.[18]

Accessible Housing Allowance
The accessible housing allowance aims to give people with disabilities the opportunity to live independently in their own homes. The Environment and Planning Committees decide on the grants and the payment of the premium. Grants are made in an amount equal to a reasonable cost of the measures.

People can apply for the allowance if they:

- have a disability or share a household with a person with a disability;
- are a parent with joint custody of a child with disabilities;
- live at home and have regular responsibility for the support of a disabled person.

Accessibility includes adjustment of property, such as replacing thresholds, widening doors, installing automatic door openers and making adjustments in the bathroom and kitchen. Outside the home, the allowance includes ramps, handrails and adapting patios.[19]

Rehabilitation Compensation
People who take part in rehabilitation programmes according to stipulated rehabilitation plans with the aim of coming back to work are eligible for rehabilitation compensation. The compensation is calculated in the same way as the sickness allowance (see earlier). There is also a compensation for people who leave work to care for sick relatives, for a maximum of 100 days.[20]

Car Allowance
The government finances a car allowance. There are three different applications included in the Swedish car allowance covering purchase of the car, making the car adaptations and fees for obtaining a driving license. To be eligible for a car allowance, the person has to live in Sweden, have a permanent disability with physical difficulties and be employed or studying. The person cannot be working in another country. People with disabilities under the age of sixty-five and families with children under the age of eighteen can apply. The allowance is given for a period of nine years.[21]

---

[18] Social handbok (2009), Grafika förlag AB.
[19] See http://www.notisum.se/rnp/sls/lag/19921574.htm (accessed 12 March 2012).
[20] See http://www.forsakringskassan.se/privatpers/sjuk (accessed 12 March 2012).
[21] For details on the different applications and levels, please refer to Social handbok 2009, Grafika förlag AB.

Health Care Allowance

The health care allowance covers three areas. The allowance provides compensation for loss of income resulting from caring for children with disabilities, compensation for caring for children with disabilities and compensation for additional costs stemming from children's disabilities.

The allowance has four different levels. The maximum allowance is 250 per cent of the price base amount, which in 2011 was 42,800 SEK. That equals 107,000 SEK per year (42,800 x 250 per cent) or 8,900 SEK per month. In the processing of the disability allowance, a distinction is often made between additional costs and need for support. The assessment is based on detailed descriptions of the additional costs. The line between health and support regarding additional costs is less clear when it comes to the health care allowance. In 2006, the cost of the disability allowance for 9,400 individuals was 1.17 billion SEK, while the cost of the health care allowance was 2.6 billion SEK.

Disability Allowance

The disability allowance applies to persons with extra costs resulting from sickness or disability.[22] The allowance is to meet everyday needs for support, as well as work or study needs or additional costs arising from sickness or disability. The allowance is for people nineteen years of age or older. The disability must be acquired before the age of sixty-five for the person to be eligible for the allowance.

The disability allowance is calculated on needs and based on the annual price base amount which was 42,800 SEK in 2009 and can either be 36 per cent, 53 per cent or 69 per cent of the amount. Many things are calculated on the annual price base amount in Sweden (the amount is fixed annually), such as insurances or the amount of salary guarantee which is paid to an individual if, for example, an employer goes bankrupt. The percentage for disability allowance will depend on the need of help for support or additional costs for the person. The disability allowance is not taxed. One cannot receive the disability allowance during a stay at the hospital or when in a nursing home if these are covered by the authorities.[23]

The disability and aforementioned health care allowances have fixed levels and unclear rules on how the amount of compensation is calculated based on a person's needs. This makes it difficult for the individual to calculate, for example, how the approved hours of personal assistance will affect the disability allowance or the health care allowance. For example, if the insured is granted fifty hours of personal assistance per week and wants to keep a certain level of disability allowance, it is unclear how many hours of the assistance the individual then must give up. It is unclear for both the individual and the social worker how the exchange between the personal assistance allowance (discussed in the next section) on one hand and

---

[22] See http://www.forsakringskassan.se/privatpers/sjuk (accessed 12 March 2012).
[23] Social handbok (2009) Grafika förlag AB.

the health care and disability allowance on the other is to be calculated. The disability allowance is a valuable income addition for individuals with small financial resources. If the personal assistance allowance is granted for covering a person's total support costs, the disability allowance may be taken away. This means that some people ask for a smaller amount of personal assistance allowance in order to keep a part of the disability or health care allowance.[24]

Overall, the aforementioned disability entitlements signal a shift towards supporting active citizenship, with a blend of payments and access to adaptations and technologies focussed on enabling people to participate in the community. Alongside these payments, Sweden has established a comprehensive system of personal assistance to further support people to engage in society, as discussed in the following section.

Disability-Specific Services

In addition to the previously mentioned entitlements, disability support in Sweden is based largely on two main pieces of legislation: the Social Services Act (SoL)[25] and the Act on Support and Service for Certain Individuals with Disabilities (LSS).[26] In addition to SoL and LSS, it is worth noting there is also the Health and Medical Services Act (HSL)[27] which was adopted in 1982.[28] Its goal is to provide good health care on equal terms to the whole population.[29] Amongst other acts giving disability support are the Mobility Act,[30] the National Mobility Act[31] and Support for Assistive Technology at Work Act.[32] SoL and LSS are described in detail in this section.

SoL (Social Services)
The Social Services Act (SoL) was adopted in 1982 with the goal to provide:

1. economic and social security;
2. equality in living conditions;
3. active participation in society.

---

[24] SVAR PÅ REGERINGSUPPDRAG 25 (45) Datum Diarienr 2007–04-02 Dnr 45662–2006.

[25] SFS nr: 2001:453: *Social Services Legislation*, http://www.riksdagen.se/sv/Dokument-Lagar/Lagar/Svenskforfattningssamling/sfs_sfs-2001--453/ (accessed 10 March 2012).

[26] SFS nr: 1993:387: Act concerning *Support and Service for Persons with Certain Functional Impairments*, http://www.riksdagen.se/sv/Dokument-Lagar/Lagar/Svenskforfattningssamling/Lag-1993387-om-stod-och-ser_sfs-1993--387/?bet=1993:387 (accessed 10 March 2012).

[27] SFS (1982) Health and Medical Services Act, nr: 1982:763, http://www.riksdagen.se/sv/Dokument-Lagar/Lagar/Svenskforfattningssamling/Halso--och-sjukvardslag-1982_sfs-1982--763/?bet=1982:763 (accessed 10 March 2012).

[28] *Ibid.*

[29] *Ibid.*

[30] SFS (1997) Mobility Act, nr: 1997:736, http://www.riksdagen.se/sv/Dokument-Lagar/Lagar/Svenskforfattningssamling/Lag-1997736-om-fardtjanst_sfs-1997--736/?bet=1997:736 (accessed 12 March 2012).

[31] *Ibid.*

[32] SFS (2000) Support for Assistive Technology at Work Act nr: 2000:630, http://62.95.69.3/SFSdoc/oo/000630.PDF (accessed 12 March 2012).

SoL is the baseline legislation for social services for all people in society, both with and without disabilities. SoL replaced the child-care act as well as earlier social care acts. Its goal is to ensure the provision of supportive and user-oriented services instead of those that are controlling.[33] SoL is a 'framework' legislation, giving municipalities the possibility to design their activities according to their changing needs. It includes both regulations on the right to financial and social support and obligations for municipalities in relation to people living in their area. Free will and self-determination are the basic principles of SoL, defining the way in which the support and services should be provided and guaranteed. The ultimate aim of SoL is that services and support should be designed in a way which will enable personal development within an individual's social situation.[34]

According to SoL,[35] the municipalities should support individuals with physical, psychiatric or other disabilities in order to enable them to participate in society and to live like other people. One possible service is home health care (*hemsjukvård*) or health care for a person in his or her home instead of at a hospital. The municipalities are responsible for the home health care service, whereas the county is responsible for care in the hospital. Another service is 'service homes' (*service hus*), which means that a person lives in a service house, a building fitted for people in need of support. This service is common for seniors. The county councils have the responsibility for medical care and the municipalities for health care (simple medical care like blood tests, controlling blood pressure, tending to sores, etc.) at home, unless the treatment is given by a medical doctor, in which case then the county councils are responsible. The county councils' responsibilities are regulated by HSL, which is a relatively wide act. The entitlements included in the LSS can also be granted through SoL to individuals not belonging to the three groups covered by the legislation.

Municipalities administer disability-specific service coverage included in SoL. These services include home assistance (*hemtjänst*), assistive technology (*hjälpmedel*), a mobility service (*färdtjänst*), a medical travel (*sjuktransport*), an interpreting service for the deaf or hard of hearing (*tolktjänst*), a legal guardian (*god man*) and a personal ombudsman (*personligt ombud*). Some of these services, including home assistance, are subject to a fee.

Home Assistance

Home assistance is a service where a support person comes to one's home and is supposed to support the individual with services in the house such as cleaning, grocery shopping and personal support. The service can include other practical things like laundry. Personal support can involve help with eating, drinking, getting dressed, help with moving around and personal hygiene. Municipalities are responsible for

---

[33] Nordström, C. and Thunved, A. (2005) *De nya sociallagarna*, Norstedts juridik, Stockholm.
[34] SFS (2001) Social Services Legislation, nr: 2001:453, http://www.riksdagen.se/sv/Dokument-Lagar/Lagar/Svenskforfattningssamling/sfs_sfs-2001--453/ (accessed 12 March 2012).
[35] SFS (2001) Social Services Legislation, nr: 2001:453, http://www.riksdagen.se/sv/Dokument-Lagar/Lagar/Svenskforfattningssamling/sfs_sfs-2001--453/ (accessed 12 March 2012).

home assistance. A safety alarm can be installed in the person's home and enables him/her to call for help twenty-four hours a day. Municipalities are responsible for the safety alarm and the setting of the fee for the service. According to SoL, municipalities should provide living quarters when needed, including group homes or service houses (explained in the section 'Reconfiguring the Residential Support Market'). Municipalities are also obliged to establish homes with special services for people with disabilities. When a person applies for living quarters, the municipality establishes the need, and if an individual is dissatisfied with the decision, an appeal is possible according to SoL. The amount charged for home assistance is based on the individual's income and pension and cost of housing.

Assistive Technology

In Sweden, the county councils are often responsible for supplying assistive technology, but in some cases it is the responsibility of the municipality. Assistive technology for people with disabilities can, for example, be a walker, wheelchair, hearing aid, telephone or computer.[36] The social insurance agency is often responsible when it comes to assistive technology for the work situation. In Sweden, a nurse, physiotherapist or an occupational therapist will evaluate the need for assistive technology and then make a prescription. The occupational therapist may do house calls to evaluate the need for assistive technology in the home or for mobility equipment.

Mobility Services and Medical Travel

Mobility services are provided for people with significant difficulties in moving on their own and in travelling with public transport. The national mobility service caters to people with disabilities who do not have the ability to visit family or friends. The conditions are regulated in the Mobility Act[37] from 1997 which is not a rights law, meaning that the transport may not be provided.

Medical travel is another service available for people who are unable to use public transport. Allowance is provided for the use of one's own car, for taking a taxi or for using the special taxi service and a specially adapted vehicle when needed.

Interpreting Service

The interpreting service is available to people with deafness, deaf-blindness or people who are hard of hearing. A person with impaired hearing has the right to interpreting services in different situations such as health care, doctor appointments, parent meetings, outdoor activities or contacts with other authorities. Interpreting centres

---

[36] See http://www.hi.se/sv-se/Arbetsomraden/Hjalpmedel/Om-hjalpmedelsverksamheten-i-kommuner-och-landsting/ (accessed 10 August 2011).

[37] SFS (1997) Mobility Act, nr: 1997:736, http://www.riksdagen.se/sv/Dokument-Lagar/Lagar/Svenskforfattningssamling/Lag-1997736-om-fardtjanst_sfs-1997--736/?bet=1997:736 (accessed 12 March 2012).

offer sign language interpretation and deaf-blind interpreting for someone with visual and hearing impairments.

According to several evaluations,[38] the demand for interpreting for people with impaired hearing is largely not fulfilled. The current system has unclear responsibilities, leading to the authorities not fully applying the responsibility and financial principle. Therefore, an enquiry[39] looked into the situation and showed that within the system, responsibility for interpretation is covered by too many sectors, leading to the need of a new law with a more clear rights regulation. A user-oriented system would need to allow for more self-determination and a choice between those offering the service. In order to be more cost-effective, the resources should be gathered under one authority and go from a care perspective to a language and accessibility perspective.[40]

Legal Guardian

A legal guardian acts on an individual's behalf and is to provide substitute decision making. The legal guardian can support a person with the paying of bills and in taking care of private possessions. Sometimes it is deemed that the service of a legal guardian is not enough; if a person has no control over his or her affairs – for instance, someone deemed incapable of making economic decisions – then the court may appoint a trustee. The person who has a trustee cannot decide on some issues by him/herself. But it is the person's requirements that determine the trustees' assignment, which often is the governing of property.[41] For a discussion of other legal capacity options, see the later section on 'Supported Decision Making'.

Personal Ombudsman

After the closing of institutions, there was a lack of knowledge in meeting the needs of people with psychiatric disabilities. The government therefore invested money during a three-year period between 1995 and 1998 to stimulate the development of social services and living arrangements, employment and rehabilitation for persons who moved out of institutions. Moreover, at ten locations in Sweden, trial operations with personal ombudsmen were implemented. The personal ombudsmen were to provide professional support to people with psychiatric disabilities, enabling them to benefit from the services and support provided by the authorities. According to the evaluation, the trial proved positive with great effects. Results showed that among the people included in the trial, the need for inpatient care was

---

[38] Socialstyrelsen (2008) *Begreppet vardagstolkning*.
[39] Dir. 2010:87 Tolktjänst för döva och hörselskadade.
[40] SOU (2011) En Samlad Tolktjänst, 2011:83, http://www.regeringen.se/sb/d/14017/a/182599 (accessed 12 March 2012).
[41] SFS (1949) The Code Related to Parenthood and Guardianship, nr: 1949:381, http://www.riksdagen.se/sv/Dokument-Lagar/Lagar/Svenskforfattningssamling/Foraldrabalk-1949381_sfs-1949--381/?bet=1949: 381 (accessed 12 March 2012).

reduced, living arrangements were more stable and entitlements were more often approved.[42]

Based on these positive results, the Social Board of Welfare was given the task to develop the personal ombudsmen service together with the county administrative board. A panel was appointed with the SALAR, Labour Market Board, the Social Insurance Agency and representation from the disabled people's organisation, the Swedish National Association for Social and Mental Health (RSMH). The panel wrote the criteria for the profession of personal ombudsman, the duties to be carried out and the principles for the distribution of the government funding. In Sweden, a personal ombudsman is for people older than eighteen years of age with a serious psychiatric disability and with long-term social disability leading to extensive obstacles in everyday life. As their need for care, support and services is complex, individuals in this group can have many contacts with social services, health care, specialised psychiatric care and other authorities. Approximately 300 personal ombudsmen support between 6,000 and 7,000 persons per year with various contacts and other dealings. The values underpinning the work of the personal ombudsman are:

- focus on the individual's perceived needs and wishes, not on the diagnosis or treatment;
- work with the individual's healthy side and possibilities instead of with symptoms, problems and limitations;
- allow individuals to choose the personal ombudsman, not the other way around;
- allow individuals to run the process, not the personal ombudsman.[43]

LSS (Support and Service for Persons with Certain Functional Impairments)
The other key piece of social policy in Sweden derives from LSS (Support and Service for Persons with Certain Functional Impairments), which was adopted in 1994,[44] replacing the Care Act (Omsorgslagen).[45] The LSS forms the centrepiece of the personalisation reform agenda in Sweden and is a key focus of this chapter. LSS is regarded as being the basis of real reform in Sweden, as the act was the first civil rights legislation for certain people with disabilities. With the act, personal assistance became a legalised right. A brief summary of its key tenets is provided here. The background to the passing of this rights legislation and an examination of its key features are provided later in the chapter.

[42] Socialstyrelsen (2009). *Ett nytt yrke tar form, Personliga ombud.*
[43] *Ibid.*
[44] SFS (1993) Act Concerning Support and Service for Persons with Certain Functional Impairments, nr: 1993:387, http://www.riksdagen.se/sv/Dokument-Lagar/Lagar/Svenskforfattningssamling/Lag-1993387-om-stod-och-ser_sfs-1993--387/?bet=1993:387 (accessed 12 March 2012).
[45] Leczinsky, L. (2008) *Handikapplagen LSS.*

LSS sets out rights for the following three groups of people with disabilities:

1. persons with intellectual disabilities and persons with autism or similar conditions;
2. people with major and lasting intellectual disabilities after brain damage in adulthood resulting from violence or disease;
3. people with lasting major physical or psychological disabilities, not attributable to aging, which cause difficulties in everyday life and therefore require support and services.

These groups are defined in the LSS Act. By including groups other than people with intellectual disabilities, the LSS widened the overall coverage of people with disabilities. Besides belonging to one of the groups, the eligible person has to be in need of support, with the need not being fulfilled in other ways. Despite being celebrated as a successful enforcement of rights by persons with disabilities, since its adoption, the administration of the legislation has been the subject of many reviews, as discussed further in the chapter.

According to LSS, services are to allow for equality in living conditions and full participation in community life. The goal is that the individual should have the possibility to live like others. Activities are to be durable and coordinated, and suited to the recipients' needs. Activities are to be designed so that they are easily accessible for people who need them and should strengthen their ability to live an independent life.

Ten entitlements that are disability-specific services can be granted through LSS[46]:

1. *Counselling and other individual support* refer to access to qualified experts who, in addition to their professional knowledge, can supply information on how to solve problems when living with severe disabilities. The professional can be, for example, a counsellor, psychologist, physiotherapist, early childhood consultant, speech therapist, occupational therapist or dietician. Advice and support are complementary to, and not a replacement for, habilitation, rehabilitation and social services.
2. *Personal assistance* is a service through which a person is supported in daily activities. Personal hygiene, dressing, eating, communication and support in participation in society are included in this service.
3. *Guide service* aims to help people with disabilities to get out of their house in order to, for example, run errands, meet relatives and friends, go to a movie or take a walk.
4. *Contact person* is someone who can supplement or replace contact with relatives and friends. The contact will help to break isolation through social

[46] SFS (2010) Amending the Act (1993:387) Concerning Support and Service for Persons with Certain Functional Impairments, nr: 2010:480, http://www.notisum.se/rnp/sls/sfs/20100480.pdf (accessed 20 March 2012).

interaction and leisure activities. The contact can also provide advice or serve as an informal support in different situations.

5. *Relief service* at home is above all an effort for the relief of relatives, allowing them to get rest and have time for other activities. The service can be provided both in regular and emergency situations.

6. *Short stay outside the home* is partly intended to give the individual an opportunity for recreation and change of scenery, and to give relatives a break. A temporary stay may be arranged in short-term homes, in another family or in any other way, for example at a camp or colony.

7. *Short-time supervision of school children* means that children older than twelve years of age can be supervised outside the home in connection to the school day and during holidays.

8. *Housing with special services* is for children and adolescents who cannot live with their parents, and gives a right to live in another family or in special housing. This is complementary to the parental home, both for children who can stay with parents some of the time and for those who cannot live at home at all.

9. *Housing for adults* can take various forms, but the most common forms are group homes with a residential service.

10. *Daily activities* are for people of working age who lack gainful employment and are not in education. The right to daily activities is provided only to persons in groups 1 and 2 covered by LSS, and not the third group.[47]

Along with LSS, the government originally adopted another piece of legislation called the Act for Assistance Allowance (LASS).[48] However, LASS was recently terminated, with its rules being transferred to LSS and the new social insurance legislation coming into force in January 2011.[49] LASS gave the government a responsibility to pay for personal assistance needs of an individual exceeding twenty hours per week (with the first twenty hours being paid by the local government). Under the new system, allocation of personal assistance has continued in the same way as the previous LASS system. The assistance allowance is still partially financed by the government and covers the need for personal assistance. The target group is narrow, including the three groups mentioned under the section on LSS. The needs assessment is carried out through a negotiation between the person in need (or the person's legal guardian) and the social worker from the national social insurance agency (Försäkringskassan). There is a detailed enquiry conducted regarding the

47 *Ibid.*
48 SFS (1993) Legislation on Personal Assistance Compensation, nr: 1993:389, http://www.riksdagen.se/sv/Dokument-Lagar/Lagar/Svenskforfattningssamling/Lag-1993389-om-assistansers_sfs-1993--389/?bet=1993:389 (accessed 12 March 2012).
49 SFS (2010) Social Insurance Code, nr: 2010:110, http://www.notisum.se/rnp/sls/lag/20100110.htm (accessed 12 March 2012).

character and extent of the needed assistance. The number of approved hours of assistance is based on the individual's needs. The hourly amount paid in 2011 for the allowance was 245 SEK for the granted assistance. If an individual has been granted the allowance before the age of sixty-five, the allowance will continue after the age of sixty-five. The need of assistance has to be more than twenty hours per week for what is considered personal needs to be covered through the social insurance. If the need for assistance for personal needs is less than twenty hours per week, it is to be covered through LSS and the local authority. The amount covering the agreed hours of personal assistance[50] is paid to the individual using personal assistance or to the administrator chosen by the individual. The administrator varies and can be a company, a local authority or a user's cooperative. The latter model is an organised cooperation of citizens.[51] The first disability cooperative which was involved in driving the direct payment model of personal assistance was the Stockholm Cooperative for Independent Living (STIL).[52] Since this time, several new cooperatives were formed in Stockholm and other parts of the country, many of which have copied STIL's approach and have received training and financial support from STIL.[53]

In 2005, the assistance enquiry committee presented the report, titled *Good Quality in Personal Assistance – Appropriate Use of the Assistance Allowance*.[54] With this report, there was a change in the political direction towards a more controlling approach to governing assistance. The committee suggested strengthening the monitoring and control of what the assistance allowance is used for, further supervision of anyone organising personal assistance and a requirement of permits for companies and cooperatives providing personal assistance. The committee's suggestions meant that the county took over responsibility for the supervision of providers of personal assistance, which in the meantime has been transferred to the National Board of Health and Welfare. The committee also suggested that the county board authorise

---

[50] The Swedish state sets out a standard hourly amount of the assistance benefit: €28 in 2010. Eighty-seven per cent of this amount has to be used for salaries, bonuses for unsocial working hours (including different supplement rates for evenings, nights, weekends and major public holidays), holiday pay, salary taxes, social fees and retirement insurance contributions. The remaining 13% is to cover the other costs associated with the provision of personal assistance: administration, training of the assistant, costs of the assistant and work environment costs.

[51] Cooperatives have a long and proud tradition in Sweden started by the labour movement, particularly economic cooperatives such as building societies, credit unions, funeral societies or food chains. However, they have a broader goal than economic activity; they have a general interest in human enhancement and the social integration of citizens. In short, they mean an organised cooperation of citizens – with a broad goal of improving the social economy.

[52] From the outset, STIL was organised as a cooperative, and consequently was able to get political support and free technical assistance from the Swedish cooperative movement.

[53] Ratzka, A. (1993). *Kort presentation av STIL* – http://www.independentliving.org/docs3/stil1993.html#14 (accessed 12 March 2012).

[54] SOU (2005) *On Behalf of the User of Personal Assistance – Good Quality and Efficient Personal Assistance*, 2005:100, http://www.regeringen.se/sb/d/10057/a/109952 (accessed 12 March 2012).

all companies and cooperatives providing assistance, meaning more control and limitations for the cooperatives. These proposals were incorporated in the law which took effect in January 2011.

Other results of this national enquiry were, for example, the need for a written agreement between the individual and the assistance provider. This was adopted to protect the user of personal assistance. Banning the use of allowance for anything other than the actual cost of personal assistance was another change. It was also stipulated that 85 per cent of assistance allowance should cover the wages of personal assistants, and if not, the money should be repaid.

As of 2011, there have also been other changes to the personal assistance policy. There is now a requirement of reporting to the Social Board of Welfare for anyone who is entitled to assistance and/or employs assistants. The need of double assistance, meaning assistance from more than one personal assistant at the same time, must now first be established before it can be granted.

Despite the 1994 reform's intention to mandate municipalities to provide LSS supports as a right, services and fees to be paid by the individuals receiving services still vary today from one part of the country to another. The implementation of the SoL[55] and that of the LSS[56] differ from one municipality to the other. [57] This has led to an enquiry on LSS regarding the inclusion of a new assessment instrument to try and ensure equal assessment and distribution of services throughout the country. The Social Board of Welfare, the institute for development of methods and the social insurance agency were appointed to the enquiry. Also, politicians, researchers and representatives from the disability movement were included on the committee. Following the enquiry, the tool was established in August 2011 and is to be used by all authorities when interviewing individuals for decisions on needs of personal assistance.[58]

Another particularity of LSS is that it is the individual's responsibility to apply for the services. The municipality only has the responsibility of providing information concerning the services. The individual applies for LSS through the municipality – and in case the need for personal assistance amounts to more than twenty hours a week, through the National Insurance Agency (FörsäkringsKassan) – and an assessment is made by a social worker of the individual's needs for the services. The services provided are to be adapted to the person's needs and should strengthen

---

55 SFS (2001) Social Services Legislation, nr: 2001:453, http://www.riksdagen.se/sv/Dokument-Lagar/ Lagar/Svenskforfattningssamling/sfs_sfs-2001--453/ (accessed 12 March 2012).

56 SFS (1993) Act Concerning Support and Service for Persons with Certain Functional Impairments, nr: 1993:387, http://www.riksdagen.se/sv/Dokument-Lagar/Lagar/Svenskforfattningssamling/ Lag-1993387-om-stod-och-ser_sfs-1993--387/?bet=1993:387 (accessed 12 March 2012).

57 It is worth noting that the county councils are responsible for the first entitlement, 'counselling and other individual support'; the municipalities are responsible for the other nine entitlements, with the national government sharing the responsibility of financing personal assistance.

58 Socialstyrelsen (2011). *Behov av personlig assistans – Ett instrument som stöd vid bedömning*, http://www. socialstyrelsen.se/Lists/Artikelkatalog/Attachments/18417/2011--8-15.pdf (accessed 12 March 2012).

his/her ability to live an independent life. Every time a person applies for a service, a new assessment is made. When applications are rejected, an appeal is possible.

Since the 1994 reform, national enquiries have continuously been carried out, and bills and acts have been passed changing the original LSS legislation by adding coverage, taking away coverage as well as giving more control to municipalities. Some of the changes are summarized briefly later in the chapter.

The municipalities have had trouble fulfilling their responsibilities and used lack of resources as justification. This has led to the adoption of sanctions by the national government.[59] With these sanctions, if municipalities are found not to be fulfilling their responsibilities under the legislation, they can face a fine. During 1999, another major change in the legislation was the inclusion of people older than the age of sixty-five.[60] Before this change, people who turned sixty-five lost their personal assistance. With the change, those who have personal assistance before the age of sixty-five keep the service, but one cannot apply for personal assistance after the age of sixty-five. This has meant an increase in cost for the government and municipalities.[61] The national enquiries have aimed to ensure that municipalities respect the legislation, but also to investigate the primary causes of increased costs after the reform. The enquiries also aimed to see if there was cheating, irregularities or an overuse of the government assistance allowance.[62]

Ultimately, LSS is a law complementing SoL; however, there are a number of key differences between them. Table 7.1 summarises the distinction between the two laws:

The differences between SoL and LSS can and do cause confusion amongst Swedish people and arguably lead to unequal services. For example, in one locality a person can receive personal assistance through LSS and in another through SoL, even though they have a similar disability. This variation is attributable to the fact that municipalities plan their own services and are to base their decisions on the individual's needs, but may take the local budget into consideration. There is hope that the assessment tool recently adopted will make the distribution of services more equal.

As a result of the legislative and policy climate discussed earlier, people with disabilities are to have the same rights and obligations as other people, implying that access to support and services is to be granted.[63] Services like personal assistance, personal ombudsman, car allowance and interpretation are intended to make it

[59] Prop. 1999/2000:79: From Patient to Citizen – The National Disability Action Plan, http://www.regeringen.se/content/1/c4/14/78/e9da3800.pdf (accessed 12 March 2012).

[60] Prop. 2000/01:5: Personal Assistance for Persons over 65, http://regeringen.se/content/1/c4/14/69/8cb08cb9.pdf (accessed 12 March 2012).

[61] Socialstyrelsen (2008) *Persolig assistans enligt LASS ur ett hälsoekonomiskt perspektiv.*

[62] Dir. 2011:26 Utredning om åtgärder mot fusk, oegentligheter och överutnyttjande av den statliga assistansersättningen.

[63] See http://www.regeringen.se/sb/d/1474 (accessed 12 March 2012).

TABLE 7.1. *Differences between SoL and LSS*

LSS	SoL
The municipalities (up to 20 hours of service) and the government (for more than 20 hours of service) are responsible for personal assistance according to LSS.	The municipalities are responsible for SoL.
If a person is eligible for LSS, the entitlements are free.	The fees charged for SoL services vary and are based on the individual's income.
The level of eligibility for services through LSS or SoL is decided by the social worker from the municipality in discussion with the individual in need of service. The resources accorded through SoL and LSS can vary depending on which municipality a person lives in.	Same
Escort services at no extra cost are available only for the three groups covered in the legislation.	A person needing escort services because of a visual impairment will receive the service through SoL, as visual impairment is not a disability covered in LSS. The extra cost for the service often has to be paid by the individual, depending on the rules in each municipality.

possible for people with disabilities to live an independent and active life. The government funding for these services is an important part of the social welfare politics, as are labour market measures enabling people with reduced work capacity to earn a living.[64]

As one can see, there has been continual development in the different types of disability support through SoL and LSS, and more changes are expected as new national enquiries are launched and completed.

WELLSPRINGS OF REFORM

In Sweden, wellsprings of reform have derived from strong disability politics since the 1960s, a result of the active disability movement with organisations dating back to the 1800s. Another contributing factor to reform is the results of national enquiries. There have been numerous national enquiries and each has contributed to further disability reform. Two enquiries of extra importance were the early committee on social policy from 1958[65] and the disability enquiry from 1966.[66] These two enquires

[64] See http://www.regeringen.se/sb/d/1474 (accessed 12 March 2012).
[65] SOU (1964) *Social Care of the Disabled*, 1964:43, Stockholm, Esselte.
[66] SOU (1976) *Culture for All*, Stockholm, 1976:20, Liber Förlag.

set the foundation for the formation and development of modern Swedish disability support. The strong civil society and the role of the Swedish Inheritance Fund are other important wellsprings of reform. All are described in the following section.

Swedish National Enquiries Lead to Legislation

The first disability enquiry by the committee on social policy was established in 1958. Its report was published in 1964. This government report introduced a revolutionary change in the way to consider disability. It concluded that disability – handicap, as it was referred to at the time – was to be considered as a relationship between the person's physical or psychological impairment and the environment.[67]

The second disability enquiry was appointed 1965 with the aim of investigating how well the state, municipalities and county councils had implemented measures set out in the earlier 1958 enquiry by the committee on social policy. The disability enquiry continued for ten years and had a large impact on disability policy; most notably, it had a key role in leading to the closure of institutions for people with disabilities. Other results were the adoption of financial support for people with disabilities, for example the disability allowance, grants for accessible housing as well as government funding of the mobility services. These were implemented together with the establishment of the institute of disability (Handikappinstitutet) (subsequently renamed the Swedish Institute of Assistive Technology[68]) and the disability councils in the municipalities (*kommunala handikappråd*).[69] The role of the enquiry was to examine questions on housing, health care, technical aids, employment, recreation and home services for people with disabilities. The enquiry led to a programme and the sharing of the responsibility of disability care between the state, the county councils and the municipalities. The municipalities were given the responsibility of implementation of most of the changes. Another important principle was the view that support for people with disabilities was to be formulated as rights.[70] This was an early formulation of the rights principle, which then took thirty years to be implemented for some people with disability through the adoption of the LSS act in 1994.

The responsibility and financial principle mentioned earlier, which entails mainstreaming of disability issues, was already formulated in the social policy enquiry

---

[67] SOU (1964) *Social Care of the Disabled*, 1964:43, Stockholm, Esselte.

[68] A national resource centre on assistive technology and accessibility for persons with disabilities. It works for full participation and equality for persons with disabilities by ensuring access to high-quality assistive technology, an effective provision of assistive devices and an accessible community.

[69] KHR is an agency of local government in which disability movement representatives can monitor and influence policy and ensure that disability aspects are considered in any context in terms of programming of activities and strategies within the municipality. Each municipality has established its own regulations for KHR and decides on the composition (number of representatives from disability movement); SOU 1976:20.

[70] SOU (1964) *Social Care of the Disabled*, 1964:43, Stockholm, Esselte.

from 1964.[71] This principle means that people with disability should be included in mainstream schooling, health care and so on. Disability should not primarily involve special solutions. In carrying out this obligation, a 1968 Care Act shifted the responsibility for social services from the government to county councils.[72] These developments were a result of discontent in how the government had administered services to that point. It was obligatory for the county councils to provide services and habilitation for all persons with disabilities. However, the Act did not include any sanctions against the county councils and the municipalities for not fulfilling decisions on provision of support.

Also during the 1960s, the government wanted to create flexibility in the labour market by adopting labour market training programmes leading to investments in people with disabilities which hinder their employment. Employment possibilities for people with disabilities increased as a result of the integration of the labour market and the financial market. Throughout the 1970s, ideological developments continued to evolve towards greater participation for persons with disabilities.

At the beginning of the 1980s, the Swedish action programme was developed during the 1981 United Nations International Year of Disabled Persons.[73] The basic principle upon which the goals were established was that disability is caused by environmental barriers and a lack of services.

In 1980, the labour market policy was reformed. A salary contribution for employers hiring people with disabilities was introduced. The same reform resulted in the founding of the Institute for Labour Market Policy Evaluation to study the functioning of the labour market. Together with other services, it was then easier for people with disabilities to gain employment training and for companies to hire them.[74]

In the late 1980s, the government decided to appoint a new disability enquiry.[75] The rights to personal assistance were a result of this enquiry, as it led to the acts of LSS and LASS. Both were important elements of the new disability policy implemented in 1994.[76] LSS, as previously mentioned, is a rights act with ten entitlements, through which the position of people with disabilities in society was strengthened. The Act on the Funding of Personal Assistance (LASS), as indicated, is now included in the social insurance. Both these acts enabled access to more independence in everyday life for certain groups.

In the 1990s, there were further developments in promoting accessibility and tackling discrimination. In 1996, the government formulated a disability policy for

---

[71] *Ibid.*

[72] SOU (1992) *Enquiry on the Situation of People with Psychiatric Impairment*, 1992:73.

[73] SOU (1982) *Disability Action Plan*, nr: 1982:46, Swedish Government Offices, Stockholm.

[74] *Supra*, n. 59.

[75] SOU (1988) *Society's Support to People with Disability*, 1988:53.

[76] SFS (1993) Act Concerning Support and Service for Persons with Certain Functional Impairments, nr: 1993:387, http://www.riksdagen.se/sv/Dokument-Lagar/Lagar/Svenskforfattningssamling/Lag-1993387-om-stod-och-ser_sfs-1993--387/?bet=1993:387 (accessed 12 March 2012).

equality and full accessibility.[77] The aim was to ensure that disability goals were fulfilled. The strategy gave a priority to accessibility for the ten years to follow. In 1999, the Discrimination Act was introduced.[78] It was the first time people with disabilities were included in the prohibition against discrimination; this act concerned the workplace. It became illegal to discriminate or treat a person with disability offensively or differently from others on the basis of that disability. An employer was, for example, not allowed to exclude a person from a position because of extra costs caused by accessibility adaptations.

Finally, in January 2000, the national action working plan for disability policy, From Patient to Citizen (*Från Patient till medborgare*),[79] was adopted by parliament. The main objective of this plan is that the disability perspective should permeate all sectors of the community. The plan sees a community of diversity as a basis for a society designed to allow disabled persons of all ages full participation in all aspects of life in the community and equal opportunities in life for girls and boys, women and men with disabilities. The plan was essential in moving the focus from care to rights.[80] Developments in legislation have made it possible for Swedish authorities to create a new social care market, reviewed in the section 'Shaping the Supply Side of Reform'.

People's Movements in Sweden

Another factor with an important role in Swedish disability policy has been the development of the people's movements within Swedish civil society. The people's movements came to Sweden from other parts of Europe and from the United States. The gathering of people for awareness raising was believed to help to solve economic and social problems. Industrialisation and urbanisation broke down rural isolation and gave people the opportunity to come together in the cities for meetings and celebrations. Already in 1830, for example, there was a campaign against alcohol consumption. In the 1840s and 1850s, the Free Church and Sobriety (or 'Temperance') movement started in Sweden. Leaders of these movements were from the middle classes, and they often contributed money and resources that helped their movements to grow.[81] These provided key early examples of strong people's movements in Swedish society that served as important role models for the subsequent disability movement.

---

[77] SKR 1996/97:120: *Government Communication on Disability Politics*, Swedish Government Offices, Stockholm.

[78] SFS (1999) Act on the Prohibition of Discrimination in Working Life for People with Disability, nr: 1999:132.

[79] *Supra*, n. 59.

[80] *Ibid.*

[81] Sköndalsinstitutet, T. L. and Wijkström, F. (1995), 'Defining the Nonprofit Sector: Sweden', in Salamon, L. and Anheier, H. (eds.) *Working Papers of the The Johns Hopkins Comparative Nonprofit Sector Project*. no. 16, The John Hopkins University, Baltimore. pp. 1–28.

Early examples of disability movements include the deaf-mute organisation started in Stockholm in 1868 and the first blind organisation in 1870. It was not until 1924 that people with physical disabilities organised themselves collectively. Special schools were established early for blind and deaf children, but not for children with physical disabilities. The organisation for people with blindness promoted disability allowances for the blind. During the 1930s, the number of cases of tuberculosis (TB) increased and acted as an important mobilising factor for people directly and indirectly affected. The government wanted to adopt a policy to isolate people with TB, leading to the establishment of the lung sickness organisation whose lobbying efforts stopped the policy from being adopted. The next large national disability organisation – the organisation for people with arthritis – was established in 1945. The organisation was founded by people who were experts in the area and nationwide fundraisers, but not by people who themselves had a disability.[82]

Already from the 1930s, government funding was provided for many of these disability organisations, making it possible for them to grow. Through state financing and growth, the disability organisations became important actors in the referral processes, able to influence issues and the adoption of legislation. Their voice was taken into account concerning, amongst others, disability services, inclusive education, access to employment, personal assistance, transport, accessibility and, as in the aforementioned case of people with TB, preventing segregation.

In 1942, the disability organisations came together for the first time. They wanted to make a larger impact on politics. The main question on the agenda was that of employment and how to get people with disabilities into the labour market. In 1963, the perspectives and goals of these organisations were widened with the formation of the 'Handicap Associations Central Committee' (HCK), which gave them a larger platform to articulate their interests. This was a cooperation body for all the disability organisations wanting to be members. This led to the strengthening of the disability organisations during the 1960s and the inclusion of the situation of people with disabilities in the debates shaping society.

One of the significant movements emerging in Sweden was the 'normalisation' agenda. This was first articulated by Bengt Nirje in 1969 and was defined as the principle by which people with a disability have the right to lead a valued ordinary life, based on the belief in their equality as human beings and citizens.[83] The term has since become synonymous with the work of Wolf Wolfensberger in his framework of social role valorisation. Wolfensberger argued that normalisation would be achieved when those with intellectual disabilities were trained in personal and vocational skills. These skills would enable them to live lives as normal as possible through employment, ordinary housing and access to non-segregated services. The use of ordinary housing rather than institutions was therefore increasingly promoted.

---

[82] Ransemar, E. (1981) *Handikapprörelsen växer fram*. Brevskolan i samarbete med ABF.
[83] Ramon, S. (1991) *Beyond Community Care*. Macmillan Education Ltd., London.

The people's movements and civil society, of which the disability movement is now an important actor, are essential for Swedish democracy, influencing the national government, county councils and municipalities. Such movements seek to win political support for their demands and try to get ideas incorporated into the parties' programmes. Once in the programmes, steps can be taken to see that bills or motions written get government support or are successful in redesigning municipal policy. One example would be the movement behind granting access to free insulin for diabetics in the 1960s.[84] The movement helped to shape public opinion and affected relationships with the government and local authorities. This development of disability movements has progressed throughout the last few decades with the participation in the referral process of the national enquiries, without the need for any constitutional amendments to govern the process.

The Swedish Inheritance Fund

Another wellspring of reform has been the Swedish Inheritance Fund – a fund which collects unclaimed assets – which is a distinctive policy tool used to support social policy goals in Sweden. Each year, there are about approximately 600 people who end up in the unclaimed-assets category. The fund was started in 1928 with 10,910 SEK coming from a weaver in Malmö. In 2002, about 232 million SEK came into the fund. The purpose of the fund is to provide financial support to innovative projects for children, young people and people with disabilities. It is used to strengthen civil society and to allow for implementation of ideas on social development. Some examples of successful projects which led to mainstream social programmes are the Swedish special transport system and personal assistance.[85]

The Swedish Inheritance Fund is used to support non-profit organisations and other voluntary associations, with the aim of enabling children, young people and people with disabilities to take part in influencing societal development. The goal is for the projects then to serve as models and spread ideas throughout the country. Programmes must be innovative, stimulate development and lie outside the organisation's ordinary sphere of activities.

Responding to the Crises in Institutions

The building of new mental hospitals continued into the 1960s in Sweden.[86] According to some researchers, Sweden held the world record in the psychiatric hospital beds capacity; by the time the county councils took over the responsibility for mental health services from the government in 1967, there were approximately 36,000

---

[84] See http://www.sbu.se/upload/Publikationer/Content0/1/Mat%20vid%20diabetes/Diabetes_kap1.pdf (accessed 12 March 2012).

[85] Arvsfondsdelegationen (2003) *Allmänna Arvsdonfen 75 år 1928–2003*. Danagårds Grafiska, Ödeshög.

[86] SOU (1992) *Enquiry on the Situation of People with Psychiatric Impairment*, 1992:73.

hospital beds in Sweden and 31 free-standing mental hospitals[87] During the 1950s, new pharmaceuticals and new professionals created new opportunities for development within inpatient care. Their ideas included more active care, with discussions starting in the 1960s about the closure of the institutions. Another related area of reform was the discontinuing of sterilisations on persons deemed mentally 'defective' – an outcome of Sweden's eugenics programme marked by the Sterilization Act of 1934.

What prompted discussions about the closure of the institutions were a number of scandals within the Swedish institutions in the 1950s, mainly because some institutions were poorly equipped and staffed. As the news of the conditions at these institutions became publicly widespread, the government was forced in 1961 to initiate the 'mental health care enquiry'.[88] The new Care Act of 1967 was a result of this enquiry and was to ensure that problems in the institutions were dealt with. One such problem was the unclear directions given to county councils for the transition from institutions. The county councils were uncertain about how to implement this new policy direction.

The economic boom of the 1960s through the early 1970s saw major improvement in the situation of people with disabilities, as high interest was shown for those regarded as the 'weak' in society. The care committee was appointed in 1977, working towards the closing of the institutions.[89] There were lobbying efforts to include children with all types of disabilities in the Care Act, together with the key question of closing the institutions, but the care committee did not succeed in doing that (the disability enquiry of 1989 took over the issue of disabled children). It was not until the 1980s that the closing of institutions started to take place and outpatient care was developed. Directions guiding this process came from the National Board of Social Services.[90]

A referral concerning a bill proposal was sent in 1977 from the care committee to the umbrella disability organisations, including the disability-specific organisations. Their reaction was strongly against the committee's proposals, as the organisations did not want a segregating disability act but rights, which only fifteen years later became enshrined in the LSS act.[91]

In the effort to close down institutions, new group homes were established in the 1980s, which were regarded as a success at the time. Several thousand people with intellectual disabilities and their servicing personnel were involved. The people in the group homes were considered to have:

---

[87] Grunewald, K. (2008) *Från idiot till medborgare*. Gothia, Förlag; Engqvist, U. (2012) 'Mood Disorders in Childhood and Adolescence and Their Outcome in Adulthood', in Juruena, M. F. (ed.) *Clinical, Research and Treatment Approaches to Affective Disorders*, InTech Publishers, Rijeka. pp. 105–142.

[88] SOU (1963) Forfattningsutredningen. Stockholm: Statens Offentliga Utredningar, 1963: 171.

[89] Kylén, G. (1978) *Institutionsboendets psykologiska effekter på utvecklingsstörda*. Ala, Stockholm.

[90] Grunewald, K. (2008) *Från idiot till medborgare*. Gothia, Förlag.

[91] *Ibid.*

- a more person-oriented care;
- a stronger feeling of safety;
- more contact with other people;
- less need for medication, fewer hospital visits and better sleep at night.

The personnel in the group homes:

- had better control over their work;
- had fewer fixed routines;
- were given more freedom to take initiative.[92]

The closure of all the institutions took ten years. In 1997, the Abolition of Institutions Act put the final date for the closure of all traditional institutions at 31 December 1999. One of the reasons for the process taking this long was that most of the relatives of persons with intellectual disabilities had fears and negative attitudes about the closing of the institutions; however, surveys showed that 80 per cent were satisfied afterwards.[93] Since this time, Sweden has recognised that group homes are an outmoded model because they fail to provide independent living.[94]

The Psychiatric Reform

The aim of psychiatric reform in Sweden was to increase the support for relatives, who often play a key role in enabling people to live at home outside of the institutions. The psychiatric reform was adopted in 1995 and was a response to the closing of the institutions. All the political parties were behind the reform. The municipalities were to have the main responsibility for carrying out the reform. The concept of mental illness was replaced with psychiatric disabilities.[95]

The evaluation, carried out five years after the psychiatric reform, showed both positive and negative results. One problem was that the number of people who retired early because of psychiatric problems had increased significantly during the 1990s. The development was in contrast to the ambitions of creating a person-centred, coordinated rehabilitation. It has been deemed that from a humanitarian and socio-economic point of view, it is of great importance that resources are used effectively and early in the process, in order to prevent early retirement, which could lead to isolation, larger social and psychiatric problems and much higher costs later in time. Knowledge regarding this group of people is still found to be lacking.[96]

The evaluation showed that:

- Relatives' involvement in rehabilitation is important and requires support. There is a lack of acceptance from society for this.

[92] *Ibid.*
[93] *Ibid.*
[94] Independent Living Institute (2010) *Personal Assistance in Sweden*, July 2010, ILI.
[95] SOU (1992) *Enquiry on the Situation of People with Psychiatric Impairment*, 1992:73.
[96] *Ibid.*

- "Family support" programmes have had good results, but issues of responsibility need to be clarified.
- Children of parents with psychiatric disabilities are a neglected group, and adequate support is rare.
- The reform predicted that people with psychiatric disabilities would have their needs met through LSS,[97] but many have had difficulties accessing the services.

As a result, more attention is paid to the situation of people with psychiatric disabilities today. Funding has enabled development of a range of services. Interested organisations have been positive about the developments and consider that the reform has led in the right direction.[98]

The Foundation Fokus

A national foundation called Fokus[99] responded to the aforementioned crisis in institutions by providing an important living service (*boende stöd*) option for people with mobility-related disabilities during the 1960s. This was proposed and financed by charity. The project started by establishing 258 apartments in Fokus houses within 13 Swedish cities, working together with municipalities and county councils.

Fokus houses were an alternative to the institutions, with only one similarity being that Fokus houses had common service units, lounge and hygiene areas. The foundation developed guidelines and activities for their services. The common pattern consists of ten to fifteen special apartments dispersed throughout one large apartment complex of perhaps fifty or more units. At the start of the 1970s, the foundation went bankrupt, but as the solution was considered positive and through the political efforts of the Swedish disability organisations and the Fokus Society, local governments in 1973 were charged with the legal responsibility of providing that type of housing and services. Retrospectively, it can be said that the Fokus project influenced the municipalities in supporting this type of living service model, which today is well established. The Fokus project has since been discovered abroad and spread to the Netherlands in the 1980s.

Since then, some of the residents with more extensive disabilities in Stockholm's older cluster housing units have successfully negotiated for their own personal assistants who are not connected to the unit. During the time when they are not serviced by personal assistants, these residents rely on workers from the central staff room as before. Residents who managed to get these personal assistants reported

---

97 SFS (1993) Act Concerning Support and Service for Persons with Certain Functional Impairments, nr: 1993:387, http://www.riksdagen.se/sv/Dokument-Lagar/Lagar/Svenskforfattningssamling/Lag-1993387-om-stod-och-ser_sfs-1993--387/?bet=1993:387 (accessed 12 March 2012).
98 SOU (1992) *Enquiry on the Situation of People with Psychiatric Impairment*, 1992:73.
99 Ritva, G. (2004) *Personlig Assistans, en social bemästringsstrategi*.

significant improvements in their quality of life and increased self-confidence gained from a feeling of being in charge and able to plan their day.[100]

Calls from the Independent Living Movement for Individual Funding

The Swedish Independent Living movement started in 1984 through the efforts of Adolf Ratzka and a group of people whom he brought together.[101] Ratzka had direct payments for personal assistance during his university studies in the United States, and subsequently introduced and defined the term "personal assistance" in Sweden. His vision was that users would be able to purchase their services from competing service providers, and users who were unable or unwilling to contract service providers or to employ their assistants themselves should be able to contract municipal services, paying with their funds from the Social Insurance Agency (Försäkringskassa).[102] This vision was realised a year after he organised a visit of leaders from the Independent Living movement in the United States and the United Kingdom, who shared stories of how personal assistance could work. The Independent Living movement, as mentioned in Chapter 4, started in Berkley, California. The movement in Stockholm, as mentioned earlier, was called Stockholm Cooperative for Independent Living (STIL).

The concept of personal assistance was introduced through the Independent Living movement. The pioneers demanded personal assistance, not health care or conventional care services such as home care, day care or sheltered work. At the beginning, their message was not embraced by the established disability movement, which deemed their demands as elitist because they believed that not every person with disabilities, especially intellectual disabilities, was capable of handling personal assistance.[103] However, STIL felt that conventional care services did not offer the flexibility needed to live independent lives. They stressed the importance of the individuals' active role in the services because they knew what they wanted and needed to become self-sufficient. They also stressed the importance of being able to decide for themselves about the type of service they used. The Independent Living organisation in Sweden differs from those in other countries. As mentioned, in Sweden, it is organised as a user cooperative, with membership composed of those requiring personal assistance. The cooperative is an employer's organisation, and the members are work leaders. Work leaders hire assistants by themselves. The municipality or the national government provides funding for the salary of personal assistants through LSS.

[100] Ratzka, A. (1986) *Independent Living and Attendant Care in Sweden: A Consumer Perspective.* Independent Living Institute, Stockholm.
[101] *Ibid.*
[102] Independent Living Institute (2010) *Personal Assistance in Sweden*, July 2010, ILI.
[103] *Ibid.*

Independent Living in Sweden has mainly promoted:

- the organisation of personal assistance;
- information and counselling through peer support;
- the introduction of public funding for personal assistance through national taxation, to maintain the same conditions for users of personal assistance regardless of where they live.

The Stockholm Cooperative for Independent Living was established in 1987 as an experiment in personal assistance in six municipalities, funded through the Swedish Inheritance Fund. After a difficult start, the pioneers succeeded in acquiring 80,000 hours of assistance in 1988 with a 9 million SEK turnover. The pilot cooperative was deemed a success and after further lobbying, the project was accepted as a permanent programme in 1989. In 1992, four years later, STIL had 10 employees and 90 members in the cooperative, 250,000 hours of assistance, 500 people working as personal assistants and a 48 million SEK turnover. STIL works at the political level to promote giving more power to people with disabilities, through control over services needed to live a normal life. They are also working against repression and discrimination of people with disabilities.

Another group for independent living (GIL) started in Gothenburg in 1989.[104] Its members were employed and wanted an independent life and personal assistance. An important driving force for members of GIL, as for the group in Stockholm, was the discontent with types of service which were available to them. The discontent in the group was formulated as follows:

- The available service is inadequate.
- The service rules restrict the user and require passive adaptation.
- The available service is not personalised.

The Swedish Inheritance Fund also financed the project for personal assistance carried out by GIL. The GIL project ended in 1994, the same year the LSS act was adopted. GIL strongly promoted the inclusion of municipalities in the personal assistance service, but the authorities did not respond to their demands. When the new bill (LSS) for support and service for people with disabilities was presented in 1993, local authorities did not want to comment until the government had made their decision concerning the new bill.[105] Independent Living's efforts (STIL and GIL) were fundamental for the introduction of the LSS bill in 1994.

Despite their successes at reforming the way in which disability support has been funded, the Independent Living organisations in Sweden have been perceived by other disabled people's organisations as not promoting solidarity because they did

---

[104] *Supra*, n. 95.
[105] *Ibid.*

not include all groups of people with disabilities in their work. They have also been criticised for promoting rights which are not important for all people with disabilities. They are not regarded, for example, as organisations fighting for access to education or to rehabilitation services.[106] In essence, the debate over the extent of facilitation in managing individual funding mirrors similar debates in the United States, Canada and the United Kingdom, as we saw in the earlier chapters.

The Enquiry 'A Society for All'

Another key wellspring of reform behind the LSS Act was a 1989 disability enquiry 'A Society for All' (*Ett samhälle för alla*), a report written for the disability enquiry of 1989,[107] which began looking at how municipalities and councils were dealing with people with severe disabilities. The enquiry was to answer the following questions:

- How are services of social support, rehabilitation and habilitation working?
- What are the deficiencies?
- What are the proposed measures and improvements for the areas?

In this report, the enquiry committee pointed out several problems with disability policy and had a number of suggestions on how to change policy. Some of the problems were:

- differences in service fees for people with disabilities;
- poor education on disability issues;
- the need to broaden the Care Act to include additional disability groups;
- the need to reduce waiting times for technical aid;
- lack of socioeconomic input.

Some of the suggestions for change were:

- a law on individual rights;
- inclusion of several smaller disability groups;
- proposed change in technical aid policy;
- care support funding for people with psychiatric disabilities.

The same committee foresaw the following problems in the forthcoming years:

- inflexible labour market for people with disabilities;
- lack of funding within the social care insurance system;
- difficulties achieving a wider acceptance of support for active life.

---

[106] *Ibid.*
[107] SOU (1990) *Handikapp och Välfärd? : en lägesrapport : delbetänkande / av 1989 års handikapputredning*, 1990:19.

The committee described that problems should be tackled with:

- a new social morality;
- greater political commitment;
- technical development.

The conclusion of the committee was that the principles of equality in society are not working for people with disabilities. Many individuals did not have their own living arrangements, and the choice of personal assistants was seen as almost non-existent (as this was before LSS). Accessibility to disabled taxi services was limited. Public places and transportation were not accessible for all. The ability to access leisure activities and work was limited.

Both the enquiries and disability organisations have promoted individual funding or direct payments for services. The Independent Living organisations and the enquiry 'A Society for All' are examples of factors which have promoted the evolution of direct payments in Sweden.

Following this, an enquiry 'Disability, Welfare and Justice' was published in 1991, with proposals that were later included in the LSS reform legislation which came into effect in January 1994.[108] Certain people with severe disabilities were to be given the right to support for functioning, including possibilities to take part in outdoor activities and recreation. The county councils and municipalities were doubtful about the proposal; they considered that the SoL and HSL acts were sufficient, and many were opposed to legislation at the national level, which dictated the services that should be provided at the regional and local levels. This went against the sovereignty of the municipalities, a highly respected tradition in Sweden.

The variation in provided support and the differences in fees charged by the municipalities throughout the country were also investigated, as well as special measures to strengthen the rights of people with disabilities. Suggestions were made on how problems could be solved. This meant analysing how the environment and employment market could become accessible to all citizens. Other suggestions made were on how user organisations and government authorities could cooperate.

Swedish National Disability Action Plan

The first Swedish disability programme was adopted in 1982 and stated that all people are equal.[109] The main goal of the programme was to ensure that all people have the opportunity to enjoy the same living conditions. This disability programme made a great impact stemming from the fact that all the political parties, municipality associations and disability organisations had come to agreement leading to important disability policy change. The programme stated the following: 'People with disabilities

[108] SOU (1991) *Handikapp – Välfärd – Rättvisa*, 1991:46.
[109] SOU (1982) *Handlingsprogram I Handikappfrågor*, 1982:46.

have the same right as everybody else to take part in the welfare system and to live a free and independent life with opportunities of self-realisation. The whole population is responsible for the inclusion of everybody in the community'.

In 2000, Sweden adopted the National Disability Action Plan, called From Patient to Citizen, which governed disability policy from 2000 to 2010.[110] This action plan was considered vital in changing the focus of disability issues from medical to rights issues. Its impact on modern Swedish disability policy was significant. Instead of focussing on the individual's impairment, the focus was on changing the community, so that all citizens could participate and be involved. Barriers to participation were to be removed. The goals of the action plan were the following:

- a municipality based on diversity;
- a society designed to allow people with disabilities of all ages full participation in society;
- equality of living conditions for girls and boys, women and men with disabilities.[111]

The basis for the Swedish equality vision is that all people are equal. The unconditional right to respect for human dignity is no different for someone with a disability than for someone without, nor is it dependent on the degree or nature of the impairment. A person with impairment should not be considered a subject of special measures, but be seen as a citizen with equal rights and equal opportunity to decide how to live his or her life.

According to the action plan, disability policy was to focus on identifying and tearing down barriers to a full, accessible community for people with disabilities. Other focus areas were:

- to prevent discrimination against people with disabilities,
- to provide children, adolescents and adults with disabilities opportunities for independence and self-determination.

Before the halfway mark of the implementation of the plan, a survey was completed on human rights at the national level. The government concluded by reiterating its commitment to follow up on the National Disability Action Plan from 2006–2009.[112] Both the survey and the action plan were to use an open, democratic process, including consultation with many actors of society. This participation was considered important for the government. It was found that an open survey process, as part of the action plan, would provide the opportunity for society to mobilise around human rights and contribute to raising awareness about the plan.

---

[110] *Supra*, n. 59.
[111] *Ibid.*
[112] Skr. 2005/06:110: *Government Communication – Follow-up of the National Disability Action Plan*, http://www.regeringen.se/content/1/c6/06/06/62/ea66b488.pdf (accessed 12 March 2012).

In 2010, the monitoring of the Disability Action Plan took place. The government found that disability policy was well established and that accessibility for people with disabilities had improved within several sectors of society. However, work still remained before people with disabilities could fully participate in the community on equal terms. The focus on human rights had, however, improved the situation, and the government was to continue its ambition to further strengthen the human rights perspective. Diversity within disability was also to be promoted.[113]

Following ratification of the UN CRPD, the government in 2009 designed a strategy on the basis of the Disability Action Plan, which included the following principles:

- Disability policy is intersectional.
- The human rights focus is important for the implementation.
- The responsibility and financial principle shall be applied or the mainstreaming of disability issues, with financial responsibility being covered within each concerned area.
- When implementing disability policy, each government ministry has its particular responsibility.[114]

Through the responsibility and financial principle, activities relating to people with disabilities are to be mainstreamed and financed within the concerned area – for example, within the resources for mainstream schooling or public health care. Disability should not primarily involve special solutions. The overall goals presented in the original national disability plan are still valid. To reach these goals, in June 2011, the government presented a new five-year strategy running until 2016. The strategy has measureable goals,[115] with the central part of the strategy being increased accessibility to employment and education. The goals are to be monitored, with the effect of interventions measured in a more reliable way. The strategy is to lead to increased awareness about the effects of both the actions of the strategy and the living conditions of persons with disabilities. The Handisam is to monitor the strategy's objectives and actions, and is to develop a coherent system for describing and analysing trends. The government is to include development towards the identified orientation objectives and targets in the budget on an annual basis. Authorities have a mandate to submit a special report to the government, setting out actions undertaken, with results and impact. The final follow-up strategy for disability policy will be presented by the spring of 2017.

---

[113] Skr. 2009/10:166: *Government Communication – Follow up of the National Disability Action plan and Grounds for a future Strategy*, http://www.riksdagen.se/sv/Dokument-Lagar/Forslag/Propositioner-och-skrivelser/Uppfoljning-av-den-Nationella-_GX03166/?text=true (accessed 12 March 2012).

[114] *Ibid.*

[115] http://www.regeringen.se/sb/d/14025/a/171269 (accessed 12 March 2012).

SHAPE OF REFORM

The Swedish enquiries, as already illustrated, led to the new legislation governing the LSS and SoL and have shaped reform towards active citizenship. From 1994, LSS gave some people with disabilities a new freedom to become active citizens. This new freedom has constantly been challenged, leading to a continual process of enquiries concerning the legislation and entitlements. The bill for psychiatric reform, with the closure of institutions, has changed the lives of people. The national disability action plan from 2000 emphasised the rights of the disabled as citizens, no longer seen as just patients. Accessibility was also to be a focus of the reform. However, accessibility as a cause of disability was not essentially new, as the principle had been adopted earlier in the social service act from 1979–1980.

Already in the 1950s, disability organisations advocated for change in the concepts of handicap and disability. At this time, the definition of disability was medical instead of being seen as something attributable to a non-accessible environment.[116] During the 1960s, the concept evolved, with the disability organisations playing a central role; in 1972, this culminated in the disability programme called 'A Society for All'.[117] The programme demanded equal living standards and accessibility for all through changes in the urban environment. Handicap was explained as something caused by deficiencies in the society. If the deficiencies were eliminated, no one needed to be handicapped. A person could have a disability, but not a handicap.

In the social service law from 1979, the new definition of disability was publicly acknowledged. This change in concepts had a large impact in designing new measures and the shaping of reform. The new definition was:

> Disability is not a characteristic of a person with an injury or illness. Disability is instead a relationship between the illness or injury and the person's surroundings. This approach moves the handicap from the individual human being to the environment and is very important, because it places the responsibility of accessibility of activities and services on the society.[118]

Adopting a Strategic Approach to Reform

One of the key success factors in the reform of support towards the goals of active citizenship was the adoption of a strategic approach to reframing welfare and services towards supports which enable independent living. This was advocated by the report

---

[116] *Supra*, n. 59.

[117] HCK:s – Handlings- och principprogram från (1972) – Ett samhälle för alla http://www.hso.se/Global/ Material/1972%20_Samhalle_for_alla.pdf (accessed 12 March 2012).

[118] Prop. 1979/80:1: Regerings proposition on Socialtjänsten http://data.riksdagen.se/dokument/G3031/ html (accessed 12 March 2012).

called *Disability and Welfare*[119] in 1990, which was a government-commissioned major review of the situation for people with severe disabilities. The main principle of the report was that all humans are equal. Its guiding principles were of accessibility, influence and self-determination, as well as participation. A holistic approach and continuity in services were also expressed, in order to strengthen the conditions for full accessibility and participation.

In the report, accessibility was to include physical/technical, social, psychological, financial and organisational accessibility, all influencing the possibility to participate in social life. Furthermore, the right to self-determination and the possibility to enjoy social life were considered of major importance for individuals' quality of life and as a measurement of success for a society. The report also prioritised active participation in social life. It advocated the right for people with extensive disabilities to have the same rights and obligations as everyone in society. Finally, the report insisted on a holistic focus and continuity in order to ensure that services and support were person-centred. It recommended that the individuals (and their family) should evaluate their own needs and determine how the services and supports should be planned. It emphasised that it was important for individuals to have the opportunity to decide and to influence, instead of evaluating services and support from an organisational perspective.

The review found that these areas – accessibility, self-determination, participation, person-centeredness and influence – are not equal among people with and without disabilities. At the time, in 1990, some people still lived in institutions, the possibility to choose personal assistance was almost non-existent, and the possibility to access mobility service when one wanted was limited. In order for the principles as described in this section to be a reality for people with disabilities, the review found that much improvement was needed within several areas: social services, habilitation, rehabilitation and the needed financial support to develop the services.

SHAPING THE DEMAND SIDE OF REFORM

Through LSS, the demand side of reform has increased. LSS allows for a variety of service providers, which has led to competition in the delivery of services of personal assistance. Since LSS was enshrined in 1994, another piece of legislation has further copper-fastened the person-driven approach to the way in which services are procured. The Choice Act (*Lagen om valfrihet*) (LOV[120]) (2008) is an alternative to procurement under the Public Procurement Act and can be applied, for example, to care and support activities for persons with disabilities. The law is intended to serve as a tool for local governments adopting the choice agenda and to open up private

---

[119] SOU (1990) *Handikapp och Välfärd? : en lägesrapport : delbetänkande / av 1989 års handikapputred-ning*, 1990:19.

[120] SFS 2008:962 Lag om valfrihetssystem, 'Act on the System of Choice in the Public Sector'.

alternatives. The Choice Act (LOV) has been of great importance to people with disabilities because it opened up the possibility to choose between service providers in other areas. These new policy options, including this recent Act, are examined in more detail in the following section.

New Policy Options for Individual Funding

Persons who receive their assistance allowance from LSS can choose to purchase assistance services from their municipality or from private for-profit companies on the open market or employ their personal assistants themselves individually or collectively by joining a users' cooperative. This freedom of choice has contributed to the establishment of a wider array of cooperatives and many personal assistance agencies. In 2009, of those persons receiving assistance from LSS, 48.6 per cent chose the municipality as provider, whereas 37.7 per cent chose private assistance companies, 10.8 per cent opted for a users' cooperative and another 2.8 per cent employed their assistants by themselves. The figures for private firms have risen since 1994 at the expense of the municipal and cooperative providers.[121]

In response to the growing demand for self-determination, one of the key changes in recent times has been the Choice System enshrined in legislation (the Choice Act [LOV] 2008 mentioned earlier). It rejuvenates the rights enshrined in LSS.[122] The aim of LOV is to increase the choice in services provided by municipalities and county councils. The procurement process for public funding (for example, for home assistance or for the supply of health care through the management of clinics) has increased with more private actors coming into the market.

LOV regulates the terms under which municipalities and county councils can increase the choice of health care providers for users or patients (once the providers get community approval by the council). LOV is for the time being a voluntary tool for the municipalities and county councils in the deregulation of health care and social services. More than 60 per cent of the municipalities have applied for the subsidies and intend to introduce the customer choice model or develop their already existing models.[123] Since 2011, it has been mandatory for county councils to respect LOV regarding outpatient care – in other words, to increase the choice of providers; however, the municipalities are free to choose if they want to abide by the terms set out in LOV.

LOV has moved power from the politicians to the citizens and has promoted a diversity of providers. Providers compete through the quality of service, as the price is settled in advance. There is a Web site where the services within LOV

---

[121] Independent Living Institute (2010) *Personal Assistance in Sweden,* July 2010, ILI.

[122] SOU (2008) *LOV att välja – Lag om Valfrihetssystem,* 2008:15, http://www.regeringen.se/content/1/c6/09/94/54/cf38f67f.pdf (accessed 12 March 2012).

[123] Socialstyrelsen (2008) *Smilulansbidrag LOV delrapport,* Socialstyrelsen, Stockholm.

are advertised, much like the Shop4Support Web site in the United Kingdom.[124] Suppliers of services to municipalities and county councils are also publicised on the Web site along with service requirements.

To some extent this freedom is being curbed by recent initiatives by government to rebalance accountability for funding. These have been partly driven by investigations into misuse of assistance and ongoing issues of control over resources. In 2007, in response to cases of misuse of assistance funding, a report on the costs of personal assistance, *Costs of Personal Assistance. Stricter rules for payment, use and repayment of Assistance allowance* (2007), gave other suggestions for change in the legislation.[125] As personal assistance is financed through the assistance allowance, the social insurance agency proposed that the individual receiving assistance allowance must use the whole amount solely to buy personal assistance or be the employer of personal assistants. Also, the buyer of personal assistance is not allowed to receive contributions from the assistance organiser, unless there are special reasons stemming from the use of personal assistance. The assistance organiser should not pay compensation or benefits to the user of personal assistance, without special reasons coming from the use of personal assistance. In addition, the individual who has assistance allowance should be able to show how the amount of assistance allowance has been used. Excess in the assistance benefit has to be paid back to the assistance organiser. The social insurance agency has the right to control how individuals use the allowance. After discussions with the individual, the agency can decide if the allowance should be paid to another administrator rather than the one chosen by the individual. Ultimately, the report advocated that the government should take a larger responsibility for ensuring that everybody concerned receives relevant information on the rules related to personal assistance.

Following the review, the LSS committee presented a bill with changes to the LSS legislation in 2008. The bill was called 'The Ability to Live Like Others'.[126] The bill reaffirmed LSS as a rights act for people with the most extensive support needs resulting from disability. A child perspective was to be guaranteed through the legislation. The government was to have collective responsibility for personal assistance. The rules on the assessment of personal assistance were to be clearer. As indicated, a committee was appointed to develop a new needs assessment tool which was implemented in August 2011. People with psychiatric disabilities were to be included in the group with the right to daily activities. The committee was also behind the proposal to repeal LASS and include applicable parts in the LSS act and the social insurance act which we saw earlier.

[124] See http://www.valfrihetswebben.se/startsidan.aspx (accessed 12 March 2012).
[125] SOU (2007) *Costs for Personal Assistance*, 2007:73, http://www.regeringen.se/content/1/c6/08/92/91/a71de944.pdf (accessed 12 March 2012).
[126] SOU (2008) *Möjlighet att leva som andra. Ny lag om stöd och service till vissa personer med funktionsnedsättning* (*New LSS legislation on the possibility to live like others*), 2008:77.

In yet another bill proposal, 'Personal assistance and other activities, measures for an increased quality and safety', presented in 2009, the government proposed measures on how to further strengthen the quality, assistance, operation and the control of personal assistance according to LSS.[127] The child perspective required yet further improvement, and a trial project with meaningful activities for people with psychiatric disabilities was to be implemented. Other suggestions affected the municipalities' responsibility for LSS. For example, when the municipality approves a service, the individual is also to be offered an individual plan with approved activities. To enable a better response from authorities, the right to an individual plan was added by the 2009 legislation within LSS. This means that every individual has a right to an individual plan, put together by the administrator in charge of the LSS assessment.

One of the newest developments is the requirement from 2011 for every assistance organiser, including companies and individuals, to apply for a permit to be allowed to run personal assistance programmes. The disability movement is critical of this new control mechanism and finds that the social board of welfare is scaling down the freedom of choice afforded to people with disabilities.[128] In summary, the period of the last five years has involved a continual rebalancing act between the different stakeholders involved in using and providing support. These debates over control are likely to continue in the current era of fiscal retrenchment.

Supported Decision Making

The right to support and advice is also an entitlement of the LSS.[129] Several different initiatives were behind this entitlement. As described earlier, the Independent Living organisations, with their work on personal assistance, played an important role in the development of the LSS legislation and the support service. The cooperatives provide peer counselling and training for their members. There are also programmes for empowerment through peer support.

Already in 1981, before LSS came into existence, a support centre called BOSSE "Counselling, Support and Knowledge Centre" in Stockholm supported people in decision making through the provision of empowerment training and the supply of information about their rights. BOSSE started as another unclaimed inheritance fund project in 1981. The project was for people with disabilities needing to find solutions to problems related to their disability. In response to the national enquiry on

---

[127] Prop. 2009/10:176: *Personlig assistans och andra insatser – åtgärder för ökad kvalitet och trygghet.*

[128] http://www.independentliving.org/assistanskoll/20110516-Socialstyrelsen-odelagger-valfriheten-i-personlig-assistans.html (accessed 12 March 2012).

[129] SFS (1993) Act Concerning Support and Service for Persons with Certain Functional Impairments, nr: 1993:387, http://www.riksdagen.se/sv/Dokument-Lagar/Lagar/Svenskforfattningssamling/Lag-1993387-om-stod-och-ser_sfs-1993--387/?bet=1993:387 (accessed 12 March 2012).

treatment of people with disabilities and the recommendation to establish disability support centers, a three-year programme financed by the Swedish Inheritance fund was carried out.[130] BOSSE subsequently became a permanent activity in the county of Stockholm in 1987. BOSSE helps people with disabilities, particularly those with physical disabilities between the ages of sixteen and sixty-five, living in the Stockholm County. BOSSE's services are free of charge; funding comes from the county council. They offer counselling and support, either individually or in a group. BOSSE helps to answer questions and solve problems regarding living with a disability. This may take the form of advice on studies, on where to find a flat, or where to look for employment.

One other supported decision-making initiative has been the service guarantors based on the JAG model of personal assistance (Jamlikhet Assistans Gemenskap[131]), which allows people to live at home. The JAG cooperative, inspired by and modeled after STIL, targets people with intellectual disabilities or those deemed to have multiple, severe impairments, and has developed what they call the JAG model for personal assistance. JAG has an agreement with a personal representative, which they call a service guarantor, for each of its members, who themselves cannot make decisions concerning support. This person is responsible for the continuity, safety and quality of the assistance for the person with a disability. The personal representative must be a good communicator, have a deep understanding of how the disabled person's impairment affects the individual, and not restrict in any way his or her capacity for self-determination. For the members of JAG it is important that the person appointed as personal representative is someone literally close at hand. The interplay between the member and his or her personal representative is in most cases based on a very close relationship.[132] The task of the service guarantor is to recruit and manage personal assistants, to take responsibility so that the JAG member receives the approved assistance and to see that the quality of assistance complies with LSS and the JAG goals. This model allows people deemed to have complex intellectual and physical disabilities to continue to live in their own homes.[133]

User Support Centers

The disability policy action plan From Patient to Citizen, implemented in 2000, recommended that user support centers should be developed, to improve the contact

---

[130] See http://arvsfonden.se/upload/utvarderingar/Brukarstöd%20sammmanfattning.pdf (accessed 12 March 2012).

[131] The word 'JAG' in Swedish also means 'I'. It is a reminder that people with disabilities are subjects, individuals, and not objects of care. 'JAG' is formed from the first letters of the Swedish words for Equality, Assistance and Inclusion.

[132] See http://enil.eu/wp-content/uploads/2012/02/Pa-manual_ENG.pdf (accessed 4 July 2012).

[133] See http://www.jag.se/pa1.html#toppen (accessed 12 March 2012).

between users and authorities.[134] In response, the government invested 30 million SEK from the Swedish Inheritance fund over a three-year period. The aim was to test how support could be developed, organised and financed. The user centers reached more than 7,000 people. The centers gave the users increased possibilities to exercise their civil rights, increased knowledge and improved quality of life and, as a result, increased power over their own life.[135]

Enabling a Choice in Living Arrangements

Since the closing of institutions, different types of living arrangements have been developed, which are discussed in the supply side of reform. In addition to these, in terms of demand, grants including the housing allowance (described earlier) have helped people with disabilities in finding new living arrangements.

Enhancing Consumer Purchasing Power

While LSS has enhanced the consumer purchasing power, allowing for the choice of the service provided, and LOV is working in the same direction, Sweden does not have a disability asset-building mechanism like the RDSP in Canada. However, another area where purchasing power has increased is technical equipment, thanks to the Free Choice Project described here.

The Free Choice Project

The Swedish Institute of Assistive Technology (SIAT) is a national resource centre for assistive technology and accessibility for persons with disabilities. SIAT was responsible for running an assistive technology programme in Sweden between 2008 and 2010, called 'the free choice project'. This is a project where if the users accepted the offer of free choice for assistive technology, they received a requisition for assistive technology with an indicated amount. With the requisition, the users could buy assistive technology. The users were then the owners of the assistive technology, rather than it being owned by the county council. The aim of the project was to increase the users' influence and participation in the process of choosing assistive technology, based on their requirements. The project was carried out in three Swedish counties, and since then, more county councils showed an interest in adopting the free choice model. The type of assistive technology included in the project varied from county to county, with more products being included throughout the project period. The initial choice was limited because of legal difficulties which had to be solved. At first it was only smaller and easy-to-use assistive technology products which were included. Hearing aids were added later, which increased the

---

[134] *Supra*, n. 59.
[135] Bolling, J. (2007) *Brukarstödcentra – verktyg för empowerment och full delaktiget?*

number of users within the project. The free choice project ended in 2010. The model is now being implemented in those municipalities which are interested in using it.

According to the final project report (2010):[136]

- Eighty per cent felt included in the choice of assistive technology.
- Three out of four felt well treated by sales personnel and suppliers.
- Seventy per cent would use the free choice model again.
- Seven out of ten who have had assistive technology before the project period found that their control had increased as a result of having a choice in buying the assistive technology.

SHAPING THE SUPPLY SIDE OF REFORM

The LSS act, as already mentioned, has been of great importance as far as freedom of choice for users and emergence of an open market in response to choice are concerned. It has also been the catalyst as far as a standard instrument enabling equality among people with disabilities regarding the support and service of personal assistance. Since the closing of institutions, new residential opportunities have been developed, which are described in this chapter.

The Awarding of Funding to Shape the Support Market

The LSS and the newer piece of legislation from 2008, LOV – the Choice Act – have been essential for the awarding of funding and shaping of the support market in Sweden. The aim of LOV[137] as identified is to increase the choice in services provided by municipalities and county councils. The procurement process for public funding (for example, for home assistance or for the supply of health care through the management of clinics) has increased with more private actors coming into the market. As there is at the time of writing a right coalition government in Sweden, there are suggestions to make LOV mandatory for both county councils and municipalities in the near future. Until now, municipalities and county councils have had the freedom of choice as far as respecting LOV, but the government may lay down requirements as to what extent this piece of legislation will need to be respected.[138]

Before LOV, it was only personal assistance that could be contracted through other partners, but now new actors can be contracted within the domains of both

---

[136] http://www.hi.se/Global/Dokument/frittval/Fritt%20val%20av%20hj%c3%a4lpmedel%20slutrapport%20201 0–10320.pdf (accessed 12 March 2012).

[137] SOU (2008) *LOV att välja – Lag om Valfrihetssystem*, 2008:15. http://www.regeringen.se/content/1/c6/09/94/54/cf38f67f.pdf (accessed 12 March 2012).

[138] See http://www.skl.se/vi_arbetar_med/demos/samhallsorganisation_1/valfrihet/valfrihetuppdrag/lag_om_valfrihet ssystem (accessed 12 March 2012).

TABLE 7.2. *Number of persons with granted assistance allowance for December 2010, distributed by social insurance office and type of employer*

Total	Municipality	Cooperative	Other organisation	Employed by oneself	Several employers
16,019	7,191 (44.9%)	1,694 (10.6%)	6,682 (41.7%)	428 (2.7%)	24 (0.1%)

the municipalities and the county councils. For example, private companies are now allowed to supply home care and run service houses using public finance. The coming section gives statistics to show how the LSS market has developed. In 2010, nearly twenty years after the reform, the municipalities were still providing half of the services covered through LSS, with the open market growing and covering the rest.

As mentioned earlier, people with disabilities wanted to be in charge of their own support and independence. An answer to this was the founding of STIL, the JAG cooperative and other assistance corporations. Instead of the governmental institutions, cooperatives and private companies were founded. Individuals gained the possibility of choosing and of changing providers and even of becoming their own employer. Persons are able to decide which assistance is best suited to their needs and lifestyle. This change in systems for the provision of services has also been of importance for home assistance. Today, as mentioned earlier, it is also possible to choose home assistance from different providers through LOV. In addition, if the free choice project, with its focus on assistive technology, becomes permanent, individuals will have more providers from whom to choose their assistive devices.

In the area of support and services, there has also been a change in the provision of the service. There has been an increase in the number of support services for people with disabilities. For example, BOSSE, as mentioned earlier, is one of the providers in the Stockholm area. Another example of a user support organisation is LaSSe.[139] Despite the fact that some of these organisations have existed for some time, they represent the 'new' breed of service providers, according to LSS.

One outcome of reforms and the development of a new social care market is that more providers are coming on the market, making it possible for individuals to participate through choice. Statistics from December 2010 (Table 7.2), based on the distribution of assistance providers divided into type of employer, show that municipalities only provide about 45 per cent of the services. Both cooperatives and other organisations have increased as employers. This means that municipalities have lost half of the market since new service providers have entered the market.

[139] See http://www.lassekoop.se/ (accessed 12 March 2012).

Insisting on Standards

Personal assistance is one area in which standards are being insisted upon. As indicated, the Social Board of Welfare, the institute for development of methods, and the social insurance agency were appointed through one of the enquiries on LSS to construct a scientific tool for evaluating the need for personal assistance, which would enable an equal distribution of the service.[140] The tool is based on the WHO classification tool called the The International Classification of Functioning, Disability and Health (ICF). Using this tool, questions asked during an interview for personal assistance service would be the same for all individuals throughout the country, which would allow for as exact a measurement of need as possible. The new tool has produced mixed reactions, with disability organisations and many users of personal assistance coming out against it.[141] Nonetheless, the tool is to be used as a basis for evaluation of fundamental needs of the individual requiring personal assistance. The tool is supposed to be independent of domestic legislation and is to capture needs which are not included in LSS at the moment.

Insisting on Consequences for Failure to Meet Standards
In the HSL and SoL there are requirements for systematic quality in health services. This entails reporting through registers and notification of problems. Based on the experience with abuse and accidents in health services, Lex Maria, or the responsibility to report injuries or abuse, is included in the HSL legislation, and Lex Sara, or the responsibility to report abuse and failure to deliver good service, is included in SoL and LSS.[142] Lex Maria includes the need to register complaints and take the necessary steps so that the situation will not happen again.[143] One example would be requiring that the service provider improves procedures or makes changes to IT systems. Service providers are obliged to appoint a person responsible for sending notifications under Lex Maria to the national board of welfare. Although not everyone can make such notifications, it is important that all health care workers report a breach in the quality of service, and that the provider has a scheme for dealing with problems. According to Lex Sara, personnel should immediately report accidents or problems in services to the one responsible for the provision of the service. The person responsible should then take immediate action and report the breach without delay. A report should be sent to the Social Board of Welfare if the problem is of a serious nature.

---

[140] http://www.independentliving.org/assistanskoll/20090903-Lennart-Jansson-Bedomningsinstrumentet -avgor-inte-assistans.html (accessed 12 March 2012).

[141] There was a protest and subsequent withdrawal of the disability representatives from the enquiry process; the questions were found to be a gross violation of human integrity.

[142] See http://www.socialstyrelsen.se/lexsarah (accessed 12 March 2012).

[143] See http://www.socialstyrelsen.se/lexmaria (accessed 12 March 2012).

As a piece of civil rights legislation, LSS requires that municipalities provide the needed services. But, in the treatment enquiry of 1999, this was found not to work automatically.[144] Municipalities were found not to be respecting their obligations, such as offering housing to people with disabilities. That is why one of the recommendations of the enquiry was that sanctions should be introduced and that control should be the responsibility of the county administrative boards. This recommendation was then taken up in the national disability action plan From Patient to Citizen, where presently the state can impose sanctions on the authorities and even order them to pay a fine if the rights enshrined in LSS are not applied.

As a result of this policy measure, the county administrative board became responsible for sanctioning a municipality denying an individual his or her approved right according to LSS or SoL. This change in legislation was made in LSS and SoL in 2002, speeding up the process of respecting granted support.[145] One problem for municipalities has been a shortage in the supply of living arrangements, making it difficult to meet the needs within the three given months before sanctions can be decided. Both control and the decisions on sanctions were transferred in 2003 from the county administrative boards to the National Board of Health and Welfare.

Reconfiguring the Residential Support Market

After the closing of institutions, the government has been trying to enable people with disabilities to live at home or in other arrangements depending on their wishes. The housing allowance mentioned has facilitated finding accommodation based on individual choice. Another important service is the allowance covering adaptations to the home in order to make it accessible.[146] The rights from LSS give individuals the possibility to live short term out of their home (the sixth entitlement of the LSS). This also makes it easier for people with disabilities to have leisure activities. The Fokus project mentioned earlier is one project which led to a wider residential market. Group homes and service houses described previously are other examples.

Despite the reforms, a number of congregated residential services evolved which are currently outmoded. In the 1970s, sheltered housing became popular; this was generally a collective of small private bedrooms with large common areas. Demands for housing with better private areas grew from the mid-1980s.[147] During this period,

[144] SOU 1999:21: *Lindqvists Nine – Nine Ways to Develop Treatment of People with Disability.*
[145] Swedish Disability Federation (2006) The Swedish Disability Movement's alternative report on UN International Covenant on Economic, Social and Cultural Rights, available at: http://www2.ohchr.org/english/bodies/cescr/docs/info-ngos/DisabilitiesFederation_Sweden39.pdf (accessed 19 July 2012).
[146] SFS (1992) *Lag om bostadsanpassningsbidrag m.m.*, nr: 1992:1574, http://www.notisum.se/rnp/sls/lag/19921574.htm (accessed 12 March 2012).
[147] Socialstyrelsen (2011) *Bostad med särskild service och daglig verksamhet.*

custom-built housing with four to five apartments surrounding a common area was developed. There were some common rooms and common provision of social services.

Group accommodations also evolved from the original Fokus model where people lived in a number (five to six) of individual apartments situated in the same apartment block, with some common rooms and common provision of social services. The rules were originally that group housing would include up to five apartments, which was amended following a court order. When the group home villas became larger, they were criticised for standing out in the community and for having features of institutional living.

More recently, housing services, including group homes, have come to be located within ordinary flats, where common areas may be in the same staircase, or not available at all. The boundaries between traditional group homes and sheltered housing have thus become increasingly blurred. Stairwell accommodation, as this type of housing is referred to, has led to greater individualisation, but also an increase in the number of homes connected in the same housing unit. The number of residents belonging to the same unit may be up to eight or ten. In addition, there is a tendency to combine various forms of services, including outsourced support to the same area (both for housing for the elderly and housing for people with psychological disabilities). This has become more common despite the initial intent to avoid locating several service units in the same area.

Group homes owned and/or managed by the municipalities became the norm during the first wave of deinstitutionalisation during the 1980s.[148] Group homes over the years have undergone a change from being public housing with a shared kitchen and socialising spaces into being individual apartments with common areas. The studies show that the former smaller units, with three to five residents, have grown into larger units, albeit with individual units. Meanwhile, staff members keep a certain distance from the residents.

One of the ongoing debates regarding living arrangements for people with disabilities is the degree of needed specialisation and the integration involved. The two approaches have conflicting principles.[149] Specialisation is often provided through larger residential homes, and institutions do not enable participation and self-determination, but apartments and small living arrangements might lead to isolation and lack of support (see Table 7.3 for the different living options available). One important step in the development of new living arrangements has been the goal of providing housing so that an individual can stay at home and receive good service and support, without needing to move to a service home.

---

[148] *Ibid.*
[149] Gough, R. (1994) *Personlig assistans, en social bemästringsstrategi för människor med omfattande funktionshinder*, GIL-förlage, Göteborg.

TABLE 7.3. *Housing – from small institutions to smaller and more differentiated housing units*[150]

Small institutions	Units with service homes	Detached housing options
20–40 places	service according to the Fokus model	rehabilitation centres
collective accommodation	10–15 apartments with 24 hour service if needed	food service
treatment home		
Group homes 3–8 places collective accommodation service as needed treatment as needed	Home service 5–10 apartments 24-hour service service if needed	Own home service if needed personal assistance after agreement

Source: Adopted from Gough, R. (1994) Personlig assistans, en social bemästringsstrategi för människor med omfattande funktionshinder, GIL-förlage, Göteborg.

Since the shutting down of institutions, smaller 'service houses' have been dominating the market. These are individual houses and/or apartments situated in the same neighbourhood, with individual support available day and night.

The current policy is focussed on trying to enable all people with disabilities to live at home, and includes different kinds of services. For example, if a person is injured, there is support to enable the person to stay at home or to move to a new home which is accessible. Municipalities can approve grants for reasonable expenditure in making housing accessible through the Home Modification Legislation (1992:1574).[151] Some municipalities own adapted housing for which the housing agency in that municipality is responsible.[152]

Despite the range of options available, several studies show that the choice of housing is relatively limited for persons with disabilities.[153] This is partly a result of needs and family circumstances. In a survey from 2008, *The Ability to Live Like Others (Möjligheten att leva som andra)*,[154] responses showed that 71 per cent have not been able to choose between living arrangements. The municipalities, however, argue that in 77 per cent of the cases, individuals have influence to some extent over where they will live.

[150] *Ibid.*
[151] http://www.notisum.se/rnp/sls/lag/19921574.htm (accessed 12 March 2012).
[152] SFS (2001) *Social Tjänstlagen*, nr: 2001:453, http://www.riksdagen.se/sv/Dokument-Lagar/Lagar/Svenskforfattningssamling/Socialtjanstlag-2001453_sfs-2001--453/ (accessed 12 March 2012).
[153] Gough, *supra*, n. 149.
[154] SOU 2008:77 – New LSS legislation on the possibility to live like others. *Möjlighet att leva som andra. Ny lag om stöd och service till vissa personer med funktionsnedsättning.*

EVALUATION AND COST-EFFECTIVENESS OF CHANGE

There has not been much done in Sweden in the area of research concerning cost-effectiveness of different methods, assistive technologies, help and support and treatment of people with disabilities. A few studies have focussed on costs or effects, but not often on the cost-effectiveness, mainly because of the difficulty in measuring the effects and the costs. Some studies are described in this section, connected to services within SoL and LSS. Resources are found to be scarce within the health care area and, as explained in the section which follows, one measure of cost-effectiveness in Sweden is the use of ethical principles when making priorities in health care.

Ethical Principles

To help to establish priorities in health care, the government has, amongst other initiatives, introduced a cost-effectiveness principle.[155] It means that both costs and effects should be taken into consideration when making decisions in the area of health care.

The ethical platform for control of priorities in health care is based on three fundamental ethical principles:

Human dignity: All human beings have equal dignity and equal rights regardless of personal characteristics and functions in society.

Needs and solidarity: Resources should primarily be allocated to areas of greatest need.

Cost-effectiveness: One should seek a reasonable relationship between cost and effectiveness when choosing between activities or actions in terms of health and quality of life.

The principles are ranked so that the principle of human dignity comes before the needs and solidarity principle, which in turn takes precedence over cost-effectiveness. This means, for instance, that someone deemed to have significant complex needs can be provided with service, although the care of such a person implies a significantly higher cost. It is incompatible with the ethical principles to allow for needs to be overlooked because of the individual's age, weight, lifestyle or economic conditions. However, it is consistent with the ethical principles to take into account in each case the factors limiting the success of such interventions.

---

[155] See http://www.socialstyrelsen.se/ekonomiskaanalyser/resursfordelningochprioriteringar/prioritering-arihalso-ochsjukvarden/etiskplattform (accessed 12 March 2012).

Equality in Living Conditions

A study on the parity in quality of life between people with and without disabilities, conducted by the National Board of Welfare in 2010, aimed to examine the extent to which policy objectives of equal living conditions are met for people with disabilities.[156] The report described the study group according to age, gender, ethnicity and type of disability. Data were gathered on living conditions of both the study group and total population. The study group consisted of 57,500 people.

The results showed significant differences in living conditions between the study group and the population at large. The study group had worse living conditions in all investigated areas except for housing standards. In relation to the population at large, people with disabilities had low educational achievement, faced exclusion in the labour market and had weak personal finances and less active leisure life. Family structure differed in regard to patterns of the general population, with fewer being married or having children. Adults with disabilities receiving support from social services had worse living conditions. Conditions are far from equal for this group. This is particularly the case regarding people with SoL services between the ages of twenty and twenty-nine. Many people with intellectual and psychological disabilities are a part of that group.

The National Board of Welfare intends to continue to analyse the living conditions of people receiving SoL and LSS services. They have identified the following areas which require more research in particular:

- the group's drug consumption and morbidity rate;
- the employment level;
- the degree of influence and autonomy over social services;
- consequences of the lack of accessibility to the environment and services;
- the extent to which the group is affected by the recession that began in 2008.

The National Board of Welfare believes that the government should initiate a review of the economic situation of people with SoL and LSS services. Particularly important are issues relating to the low level of disposable income and the high incidence of long-term financial assistance among young people with SoL services.

Cost-Effectiveness Studies

Cost-effectiveness is on the agenda today, but studies are limited. Several researchers have tried to investigate cost-effectiveness of the prescribed assistive technology. Studies in Sweden have mainly focussed on hearing aids[157] and walkers.[158] The results show that it is cost-effective to prescribe the devices covered by the study, but

---

[156] Socialstyrelsen (2010) *Allt jämt ojämlikt, levnadsförhållanden för personer med funktionshinder.*
[157] CMT Rapport 2008:5 – Kostnader och effekter vid förskrivning av hörapparat.
[158] CMT Rapport 2007:3 – Kostnader och effekter vid förskrivning av rullatorer.

more research is needed. It is difficult to measure the effect, as county councils and municipalities do not have statistics on costs, meaning that these studies are based on assumptions.

According to one study by Socialstyrelsen (2008), taxpayers have saved a minimum of 29 million SEK since 1994, compared to the costs of local governments' home-help services, because the delivery of personal assistance costs less in this competitive market than home-help services' delivery in the protected public sector.[159]

A study on the cost-effectiveness of personal ombudsmen showed that the adoption of the service resulted in huge savings.[160] Costs of psychiatric care are much lower after the introduction of personal ombudsmen in the municipalities. Before the personal ombudsman, the calculated cost to society for one individual was 365,000 SEK, which decreased by 20,000 SEK already in the first year. This was a significant finding showing how support can lead to cost saving.

Another study carried out by JAG has shown that it is more cost-effective to use personal assistance than service homes.[161] The study was based on the cost comparison of a number of group homes for people with extensive functional impairments, and the hours of personal assistance these resources would cover. The result showed that the cost of an individual with extensive functional impairments in a group home often exceeds the cost of personal assistance. The enquiry also showed that, before LSS, many people had their needs for care and service met through relatives' unpaid work. In addition, the individuals were often dependent on a large number of different support measures which have now been replaced by personal assistance. Otherwise, the cost of assistance reform can also be justified by increased equality.[162]

THE CHALLENGES TOWARDS ACTIVE CITIZENSHIP

Despite the extensive reforms of disability services in Sweden, one major challenge today is the rising costs faced by people with disabilities. There is, at the same time, an increased pressure on the government to meet the growing need for services for the population which is growing older and living longer. Efforts are being made for health and social care to be more effective, which is leading to new reforms and ways of delivering services.

Increasing LSS costs have been a great challenge for the municipalities and the national government since 2005.[163] The government is looking for a solution to

---

[159] Socialstyrelsen (2008) *Personlig assistans enligt LASS ur ett samhällsekonomiskt perspektiv Rapport från Socialstyrelsen* (Assistance under LASS from a socio-economic perspective). http://www .socialstyrelsen.se/NR/rdonlyres/E188FA5F-4E0E-4449--8562-9FD8DCE0C7D0/10796 /200813127_Rev1.pdf (accessed 12 July 2011).

[160] Länsstyrelsen, Värmland (2007) *Lönar det sig?* nr. 2.

[161] JAG, Knowledge Project (2006) *The Price of Freedom of Choice, Self-Determination and Integrity.*

[162] *Ibid.*

[163] SOU (2005) *On Behalf of the User of Personal Assistance – Good Quality and efficient Personal Assistance*, 2005:100, http://www.regeringen.se/sb/d/10057/a/109952 (accessed 12 March 2012).

enable the permanent existence of LSS with a cut in the costs. In 2012, a new enquiry got underway to identify ways of addressing the rising cost of personal assistance[164] and to investigate how much cost is attributable to fraud, irregularities and overuse of personal assistance. The enquiry is also to present proposals on how to secure the future of LSS.

With all the enquiries on LSS, the challenge of defending the reform continues. The disability movement is worried about the efforts to cut costs, which would leave people without services and assistance. They consider it more important to improve LSS than to cut costs.[165] The groups covered need to be expanded; at the moment, for example, a person with deaf-blindness will not receive personal assistance according to LSS. To date, there are no innovative savings mechanisms in Sweden to help to sustain the future funding of social care, such as the Registered Disability Savings Plan in Canada, for example.

Another challenge is that of accessibility. Even though all ministries were to be accessible by 2010, they are still not. This leads to an unacceptable exclusion of people with disabilities.[166] Disabled people's organisations in Sweden are trying to make the government follow-up the 1989 enquiry 'Disability and Welfare', which stated the need to view lack of accessibility as discrimination.[167] The aim of the enquiry was to analyse the situation of people with disabilities in society. It has resulted in the LSS legislation and the recommendation that society should be made more accessible by making it illegal to discriminate against people because of disability. To this day, this has still not been implemented, and lack of accessibility remains one of the core challenges of today's disability politics.

Although mainstreaming is a key principle for disability issues, segregated solutions still exist in Sweden.[168] For instance, politicians who do not want to spend money on making public transport accessible defend the well-established system of special transport.

CONCLUSION

Through the creation of LSS and the establishment of ten entitlements, including personal assistance, as civil rights, Sweden still holds a leading role in the world in terms of its consideration of disability issues as mainstream and rights issues. There has been a continual process of improvement of services, with the responsibility for

---

[164] See http://www.independentliving.org/assistanskoll/20110330-Ny-offentlig-utredning-om-assistansens -kostnader-tillsatt.html (accessed 12 March 2012).

[165] See http://www.independentliving.org/assistanskoll/TEMA-utredning-kostandsokning.html (accessed 12 March 2012).

[166] See http://www.funkaportalen.se/Reportage/Politik/Sverige/Handikapprorelsen/Funktionshinder-tar- over-som-begrepp/ (accessed 12 March 2012).

[167] 1994/95:S0236 Uppföljning av handikapputredningen.

[168] See http://www.disability-europe.net/content/aned/media/SE-6-Request-07%20ANED%20Task% 205%20Independent%20Living%20Report%20Sweden_to%20publish_to%20EC.pdf (accessed 12 March 2012).

services shifting from one level of government to the other. Services, allowances and positive discrimination with salary contributions are used to give people equal opportunities and high quality of life, yet studies show that people with disabilities still have worse living conditions than the general population[169] and that segregation persists.[170]

The current disability policy consists of two main areas: the personal support provided to people with disabilities (services, personal assistance, assistive technology and rehabilitation) and measures to make society accessible. These two areas complement and support each other. If personal support is to work effectively, there is a need for the society to be accessible. On the other hand, if there are no community-based services, personal assistance, rehabilitation and assistive technology, people with disabilities will live in isolation. Imbalance between the two areas increases the risk that measures will be ineffective and that full participation of people with disability will not be achieved.

The enquiries investigating the control and use of LSS are continually resulting in changes. Changes to the legislation have led to a more restrictive interpretation of the law and difficulty in acquiring hours for assistance, which have resulted in individuals being referred to the municipalities. This has increased the cost for municipalities, which are being restrictive in granting services.[171,172] The Independent Living organisations and other disability organisations believe that these changes are now reducing the rights covered by LSS to only the right to survival.

Sweden in general has strong disability rights legislation and good practice in terms of personal assistance, yet at times, traditions still act as a barrier to improving life conditions of people with disabilities. In particular, the sovereignty of municipalities still poses many barriers to the full implementation of LSS, and there are ongoing battles with municipalities over their not accepting the duties prescribed by the legislation, as evidenced by the continual enquiries proposing changes to the law. This poses a particular challenge for the full implementation of the UN CRPD at the domestic level. Other traditions in Swedish society are that of believing that change will be made through goodwill, and the failure to accept sanctions for lack of accessibility through discrimination legislation. However, goodwill has not brought about accessibility required by legislation dating back to the 1970s. Goodwill was also not enough for the implementation of LSS, and sanctions had to be adopted to ensure that authorities carried out their obligations.

[169] Socialstyrelsen (2010) *Allt jämt ojämlikt, levnadsförhållanden för personer med funktionshinder.*
[170] See http://www.disability-europe.net/content/aned/media/SE-6-Request-07%20ANED%20Task% 205%20Independent%20Living%20Report%20Sweden_to%20publish_to%20EC.pdf (accessed 12 March 2012).
[171] See http://www.dhr.se/index.php?page=personlig_assistans (accessed 12 March 2012).
[172] See http://www.independentliving.org/assistanskoll/Remissvar/_STIL__Stiftarna_av_Independent_ Living_i_Sverige.pdf (accessed 12 March 2012).

Questions also arise from the recent rebalancing of control over managing personal assistance in disability policy, despite the high level of services for people with disabilities. Will Sweden stay a model of good practice for other countries? How much will the LSS entitlements be affected by the government demand for cost reduction? Will the new assessment tool bring about the goal of equality in services? Will equality in services be achieved through a lower level of services for all or through rising service levels for those who have less?

In conclusion, Sweden has made an important contribution to the global development of active citizenship for people with disabilities by being one of the first countries to implement a right to personal assistance, as part of a broader ongoing project to move away from welfare and congregated services to independent living and human rights. On the whole, there is a strong degree of consensus amongst policy makers and amongst the general population over the key principles embedded in the Swedish personal assistance (LSS) Act of 1993. Furthermore, the national action plan, From Patient to Citizen, fully embodies the vision of a society designed to allow disabled persons of all ages full participation in all aspects of life in the community. The achievements and challenges experienced in Sweden thus serve to illustrate the practicalities of how to embed the guiding principles of the CRPD at the domestic level. Even though the implementation mechanisms in place at the regional level are not always successful in administering the right to personal assistance, Sweden nonetheless provides a full-fledged model of personalisation in practice to be built upon and to facilitate the further development of disability support strategies in other jurisdictions.

8

Active Citizenship and Disability in France

INTRODUCTION

In February 2005, France passed legislation representing a fundamental political and ideological shift in the way that the French government perceived disability: the Act for Equal Rights and Opportunities, Participation and Citizenship of People with Disabilities (Loi Pour L'égalité des droits et des chances, la Participation et la Citoyenneté des Personnes Handicapée) acknowledges a social obligation to enable persons with disabilities to overcome the barriers that disable them, in order to enjoy equal life chances through introduction of a system for *compensating* for disability. The Loi handicap, as it is known in France, allows for persons with disabilities to have a level of choice and control over their own lives unprecedented within the French system, legislating for mandatory accessibility and social and economic inclusion. This legislation has opened new possibilities for disabled French people to exercise their rights as citizens and reframed welfare in line with the goals of active citizenship. However, its initial success must be understood within a context of continuing institutionalisation and an overriding emphasis on access to integration solely through employment. Although the Loi handicap is relatively recent and its implementation is still in process, it is possible to analyse key characteristics of the legislation and the values behind it, as well as to identify challenges to the advancement of personalisation and meaningful inclusion, given socio-historical factors particular to France.

Alongside this legislation, the UN CRPD and its optional Protocol were adopted by the French Senate's Foreign Affairs Commission on 16 December 2009, voted by the Senate on 22 December 2009, and finally ratified on December 31, 2009.[1]

---

[1] European network of legal experts in the non-discrimination field Flash Report: Ratification by France of the UN Convention on the Rights of Persons with Disabilities, France, 21 January 2010.

The new legislation was published on 3 January 2010.[2] However, despite these commitments towards active citizenship and personalisation, as this chapter examines, shortcomings prevail in the implementation of equal rights for people with disabilities in France, particularly in relation to its enduring legacies of institutionalisation.

The intention of this chapter is to examine the French disability support system, looking at the evolution of disability support from the last century to its present system, its relationship to wider welfare approaches and the operation of the current system and to analyse the significance of recent legislative reform as a first step within an integrative process aimed at enabling persons with disabilities in France to take up their rightful positions as equal citizens. The chapter begins with an overview of the development of the disability support system and its administration, including disability-specific entitlements and services. The second half of the chapter provides an analysis of the wellspring of reform in France, assesses market changes linked to reform and finishes with an assessment of the challenges that face the disability support system in its reformed state.

AN OVERVIEW OF THE ADMINISTRATION OF DISABILITY SUPPORT

The administration of the disability support system in France is characterised by a unique relationship between disability organisations (*associations*) at the local level and the government at the national level. This relationship is rooted within the history of the French government's duty to provide for support for persons with disabilities. This section briefly explores the development of the French disability support system within its socio-historical context; it examines the relationship between government and the *associations* and explains the changes introduced to the administration of the system through the 2005 legislation. It then considers the disability-specific welfare entitlements, work-related support and services and laws which comprise the current disability support system in France.

Socio-Historical Context

The French Revolution first recognised a national obligation towards persons with disabilities, but this was subsequently left to charity and private endeavours to provide for. Two major events prompted the attention of French society and government towards the welfare of people with impairments: the first was industrialisation, which saw a rapid rise in incidents of work accidents and occupational disease; the second was the First World War and the return of high numbers of injured veterans. Disability became a topic of daily relevance, with wide concern for social justice

---

[2] Loi 2009–1791 du 31 Décembre 2009 autorisant la ratification de la convention relative aux droits des personnes handicapées, http://www.legifrance.gouv.fr (File: les autres textes législatifs et réglementaires) (accessed 19 January 2010).

and support, to enable the injured to continue being a part of society. Through a law passed in 1898, the Benefits for Accidents at Work Act (Loi sur l'indemnisation des accidents du travail), the idea of industrial accident compensation was introduced and society acknowledged its duty of compensation towards working-class victims of accidents at work.[3]

Disability became dramatically more visible as injured French soldiers returned from the war. A sense of guilt and responsibility emerged in the civilian population, culminating in a desire to take care of and make amends to the injured veterans. A status of 'war disabled' was created, with disability issues and questions being managed by the Minister for Veteran Affairs. In January 1918[4] and March 1919, laws were adopted by the French Parliament to provide free health care for every veteran and the awarding of disability pensions. Through another law passed in 1924, The Mandatory Employment for War Wounded Veterans Act (Loi assurant l'emploi obligatoire des mutilés de guerre), the creation of specific jobs exclusively for people with impairments acquired through injury in war was allowed. Policies for both groups of people were essentially focussed on reparation, rehabilitation and reintegration.[5] These became the hallmarks of the approach to disability support in France throughout the twentieth century.

Organisations formed to defend the rights of those injured by war or industrial work, such as the National Federation of Injured and Disabled Workers (Fédération Nationale des Accidentés du Travail et des Handicapés) (FNATH).[6] These organisations took the legal form of not-for-profit *associations*, by which term they are commonly known. This first wave of *associations* had two objectives: to fight for the right to work and to build and manage rehabilitation centres with government support. Representation of the needs and interests of persons with disabilities spread from those with acquired impairment to encompass those disabled at birth. The concern to protect and defend rights spread to other groups of people with impairment, including those surviving tuberculosis and those with congenital impairments.[7] Organisations were set up by disabled individuals and their families to represent the interests of specific impairment areas, for example the National Federation of Injured and Disabled Workers (Association des Paralysés de France) (APF) and the National Union of Parents, People with Learning Disabilities and Their Friends (Union Nationale des Associations de Parents, de Personnes Handicapées Mentales

---

3 See http://www.lesjeudis.com/Article/CB-315-LINDEMNISATION-DE-L-ACCIDENT-DU-TRAVAIL/?cat=84 (accessed 17 July 2012).

4 *Loi pour Institution de l'Office National des Mutilés et Réformés de guerre, destiné à subventionner des écoles de rééducation.*

5 See http://www.travail-emploi-sante.gouv.fr/IMG/pdf/Loi_du_26_avril_1924.pdf (accessed 15 November 2011).

6 See http://www.triel-sur-seine.fr/federation-nationale-des-accidentes-du-travail-et-des-h-1-973.php (accessed 15 November 2011).

7 Barral, C. (2007) 'Disabled Persons' Associations in France', *Scandinavian Journal of Disability Research* 9(3–4): 214–236.

et de leurs Amis) (UNAPEI), both of which still exist. A number were founded by persons with disabilities themselves; for example, Suzanne Fouché founded L'Adapt in 1929 to provide meaningful occupation for tuberculosis survivors, and André Tamay, a quadriplegic, founded APF.[8] *Associations* grew and consolidated during the period between the wars.

The second wave of *associations* was promoted by the development of the French Social Security (Sécurité Sociale) following the Second World War. The Ordinance of October 1945 outlined the core principles of the French Social Security System. The three main elements of that Ordinance are:

- A system that protects everybody and is financed by taxes, employees and employers. Employees' contributions are deducted directly from their wages.
- An autonomous board, composed of workers and employers, manages the social security system. It is a democratic system that is run by non-governmental agencies. The state only acts as a supervisor and its role is to ensure the financial stability of the system.
- The social security system is based on unity: a single social protection system must protect everyone in the name of solidarity. (The idea of a universal single system was later abandoned. Nowadays everyone benefits from the same compulsory basic protection scheme, but there are other schemes with higher, variable levels of protection.)[9]

The French system largely uses allowances based on the principle of redistribution, while at the same time private, not-for-profit companies called *mutuelles* also play a key role in the system, working in the interests of their members in return for a contribution. The *mutuelles* date back to when they were set up by members of the working class to protect against the risk of industrial accident. In the beginning, *mutuelles* were organised around different industrial activities. Railroad workers and miners each had their own *mutuelle*, financed by the workers themselves. Every active worker paid to the insurance association a social contribution directly taken from his or her salary. This contribution would then be used for the benefit of the members, paying wages during strikes, or giving contributions to former co-workers who could no longer work. *Solidarité*, the notion of unity and a common interest in the welfare of all, was – and still is – the essence of these *mutuelles*. Through the *mutuelles*, there was an established involvement of private not-for-profit companies within the French social security system with a central principle of national solidarity.[10]

---

[8] See http://www.ladapt.net/ewb_pages/h/historique.php (accessed 15 November 2011).

[9] Fontanel, M. (2007). *Le modèle social français*. Odile Jacob, Paris.

[10] See http://www.economie-sociale.coop/index-economie-sociale/mutualite.htm (accessed 15 November 2011).

Social security was intended to protect those who were no longer able to work. This left the question of what about those who could never work, and the need for a welfare system for persons with disabilities became apparent. With the infrastructure of *associations* already in place, the state decided it was a logical step to fund these existing private organisations to be responsible for welfare provision for persons with disabilities. This led to a proliferation of *associations* and the growth of new parent-led organisations. The *associations* had control of 80 per cent of the resources invested in disability support, but did not have complete control, as their activities were under the supervision of the government departments, first health and employment and later health and solidarity. Private institutions run by the *associations* and funded by government expanded to include open schools, physical rehabilitation centres, training centres, sheltered workshops and social services.[11]

Investment in segregated institutions as the foundations of a disability support system has been criticised by many commentators.[12] The avowed intention was to support the rehabilitation of persons with disabilities back into society, yet the system for achieving rehabilitation was based on exclusion and segregation, with little evidence of meeting the target of reinsertion. From the 1950s, and particularly in the 1960s and 1970s, the number of institutions increased considerably, but without national planning; their creation was the result of negotiations between local *associations* and local political authorities, keen to leave a legacy of benevolence but without regard for the question of inclusion into mainstream life. Thus began a partnership which came to dominate the disability support system in France.

Public-Private Partnership

The relationship between the *associations* and government is complex. *Associations* do not have full, independent control of the institutions they run, which remain under government control and are reliant upon state funding. The *associations* are subject to government policy. However, they also exert significant influence over the development of government policy in relation to disability support. Barral describes this relationship as a 'private-public partnership à la Francaise'.[13] Influence is exerted in a number of ways: through official consultative roles on government advisory boards, through organising public protests and through the sharing of personnel between government agencies and senior management positions within the *associations*. This last interaction can be illustrated by the example of Patrick Gohet, who went from executive director of UNAPEI to being the inter-ministerial delegate for persons with disabilities.

---

[11] Barral, *supra*, n. 7.
[12] Stiker, H.-J. (1999). *A History of Disability*. University of Michigan, Ann Arbor, p. 142.
[13] *Ibid*.

Issues around the passage and implementation of disability legislation in 1975 demonstrate the power of the *associations*. This legislation will be examined in more detail later, but it is relevant here to consider firstly, the wider context of the values of social action during this period, and how effectively they were translated to disability support through the 1975 law; and secondly, the impact that this legislation had on the relationship between *associations* and government. The 1960s saw in France the development of social policy based on the concept of integration. This policy direction was applied across different areas of health and social care, covering people with psychiatric support needs (promoting curative and preventative approaches which removed the need for incarceration in asylums), older people and children, with a focus on provision of support in the community, as opposed to institutional segregation. This inclusive approach was directed towards disability support through the Law of Orientation in Favour of Disabled People (Loi d'Orientation en Faveur Des Persones Handicapées), passed in 1975. This law established disability as an issue of national solidarity and promoted inclusive education, employment and universal accessibility.[14] It also introduced many of the welfare benefits for persons with disabilities, like the Disabled Adult Allowance (Allocation aux Adultes Handicapés) (AAH) and the Carer's Compensation Allowance (L'allocation Compensatrice de Tierce Personne) (ACTP).

At the same time as the Loi d'Orientation, a second law was passed, the Health and Social Care Institutions Act (Loi Relative Aux Institutions Sociales Et Médico-Sociales). This was implemented immediately and almost contradicted the Loi d'Orientation in its support for segregated education and institutionalisation. The second law covers the organisation of social and medico-social institutions, defining the missions of these institutions and how they work. It led to the creation and organ-isation of an autonomous medico-social sector, operating separately from the health sector.[15] Meanwhile, the principles of inclusion and accessibility recommended by the Loi d'Orientation remained optional, and as such, integration in response to the legislation was extremely limited.

The *associations* played an important role in the creation of the two statutes. In 1974, they formed an alliance called the Group of 21, through which to exert influence over the development of the legislation. This pressure group continued past 1975 and expanded, becoming the Group of 29 and then the Entente Committee, which today has sixty-three members including disabled persons NGOs and the public authorities (mainly the state secretary for disabled people, the inter-ministries

---

[14] Didier-Courbin, P. and Gilbert, P. (2005) *Éléments d'information sur la legislation en faveur des personnes handicapées en France: de la loi de 1975 à celle de 2005*, RFAS No. 2–2005, available at: http://www.sante.gouv.fr/IMG/pdf/rfas200502-art08.pdf (accessed 23 March 2012).

[15] Winance, M. et al. (2007). 'Disability Policies in France: Changes and Tensions between the Category-based, Universalist and Personalized Approaches', *Scandinavian Journal of Disability Research* 9(3–4): 9.

delegate for disabled people, and ministries of education, social affairs and employment).[16]

The alliance between *associations* ensured an independent channel by which to influence government. In addition to this, the Loi d'Orientation established an official consultative role for the *associations* within national policy. The law set up the National Consultative Council for Disabled People (Conseil National Consultatif des Personnes Handicapées) (CNCPH) through which all government policy relating to disability has to pass. The membership of the CNCPH includes representation from the *associations*, and thus the 1975 legislation made official the public-private relationship between government and the *associations*.

Rather than changing disability support in line with inclusive reforms in other areas of social policy, disability legislation of 1975 served to further strengthen the roles of the *associations* and the multiplicity of institutions and segregated services, dominating support options for persons with disabilities in France.

Building the Current System

Change in favour of more personalised approaches to disability occurred from the beginning of the twenty-first century. Factors leading to this will be examined in more detail in the section on the wellspring of reform, but it is relevant to make a link here with decentralisation and the devolution of power from central to local government. The Decentralisation Act of 1982 and subsequent legislation altered the balance of power between local authorities and the state, and the former acquired greater autonomy. Within local government, there are three levels of administration: the *région*, the *département* and the *commune* or municipality. The most important political body with a remit over social support is the General Council (Conseil generals). These councils operate at *département* level, with members elected by direct universal suffrage every six years.[17] The 2005 Loi Handicap established a disability-related welfare infrastructure at both national and local government levels,[18] which we examine here as the basis for the current administration of disability support in France.

The National Fund for Solidarity and Independence (Caisse National de Solidarité pour l'Autonomie) (CNSA) was created in 2004 as an institution of central government set up to contribute towards independent living costs for people dependent upon state welfare. Funding is divided equally between French territories. The CNSA gives advice and supports research concerning independent living and assessment of need. It works through national and cross-government disability programmes

---

[16] European Disability Forum (n.d.) *Analysis by the European Disability Forum of the Transposition and Implementation of the Council Directive 2000/78/Ec Establishing a General Framework for Equal Treatment in Employment and Occupation.* European Disability Forum.

[17] See http://ambafrance-us.org/IMG/pdf/decentralisation_ang.pdf (accessed 18 July 2012).

[18] CNTERHI, DRESS, DGAS. (2004) *Le handicap en Chiffre.* CNTERHI, Paris.

and collaborates with foreign counterparts. Every four years, an agreement is signed with the French government, setting out the CNSA's strategic aims and priorities for the following period. The last agreement was based on three principles: partnership, quality and equality. Similar agreements are signed by the government with the Sécurité Sociale and the Conseil régional to guarantee standards of performance.[19]

The governing board of the CNSA is composed of members from different government agencies, including the National Assembly, the lower House of the French Parliament (Assemblée nationale) and the Conseil général, representatives from *associations* and unions. A scientific council advises the chair of the board. Funding for the CNSA comes from a state subsidy taken from taxes, such as the Contribution Sociale Généralisée (CSG),[20] as well as from funds provided directly by other government agencies, such as the Sickness Insurance (Assurance Maladie). The CNSA uses its funds in different ways:

- Establishing state-funded services for persons with disabilities. Within services funded by the state, the costs of service delivery are state controlled.
- Providing benefits for persons with disabilities, such as the Personal Independence Allowance (Allocation Personnalisée d'Autonomie) (APA) or the Disability Compensation Allowance (Prestation de Compensation du Handicap) (PCH).
- For research and development work.
- To partially cover the operating costs of the CNSA.[21]

Direct provision of support for persons with disabilities is managed at the local level by the Regional Authority for Disabled People (Les Maisons Departementales des Personnes Handicapées) (MDPH), established through the 2005 legislation. The MDPH acts as the main point of access for persons with disabilities into the disability support system. Its remit extends from initiatives to raise public awareness of disability issues to provision of services to persons with disabilities, such as information resources, counselling and advice, employment support and support with the development and implementation of individual life plans.[22]

The MDPH is a Public Interest Group (Groupement d'Intérêt Public) (GIP), governed by an Executive Commission, whose permanent members are representatives from the Conseil général, the Sécurité Sociale and the Family Allowance Fund (Caisse d'Allocations Familiales) (CAF). GIPs are an administrative structure composed of both public- and private-sector representatives. The aim of a GIP is to facilitate the cooperation between private companies and public services having the

---

[19] Chossy, J.-F. (2006). *Rapport D'information sur la mise en application de la loi n° 2005–102 du 11 février 2005*. Commission Des Affaires Culturelles, Familiales Et Sociales, Paris.
[20] The General Social Contribution is a tax which was created in 1991 to help to finance the French social security system.
[21] See http://www.cnsa.fr/ (accessed 15 November 2011).
[22] See http://www.mdph.fr/ (accessed 20 November 2011).

same activities. Representatives from the *département* make up half of the member-ship of the Commission – one-quarter are from *associations* like the APF and the remaining quarter is made up of representatives from local social welfare agencies. The chair of the Executive Commission is the president of the Conseil général. The chair holds responsibility for the operational and financial management of the GIP, while the *département* and the CNSA provide the funding. The CNSA works in partnership with the MDPH to identify future priorities and annually review MDPH activities.[23]

It can be seen from the preceding description that disability support provision has latterly passed to local government, although central government retains a strategic and supervisory role through the CNSA. The *associations* are represented at every level, and therefore their influence has not diminished through development of new systems brought in by the recent legislation.

AN OVERVIEW OF THE DISABILITY SUPPORT FRAMEWORK

Disability-Specific State Entitlements

Central to the 2005 legislation is a notion of overcoming disabling barriers. To this end, the Loi handicap introduced a new type of benefit, aimed at supporting persons with disabilities to overcome the barriers which prevent them from equal life chances and achieving their goals. The Disability Compensation Benefit (Prestation de Compensation du Handicap) (PCH) is in this way considered different from traditional disability benefits which had a notionally different aim of providing income for persons with disabilities. Each of France's disability-specific entitlements, including the recent PCH, is examined next.

Disabled Adult Allowance (Allocation Adultes Handicapés) (AAH) is one of the oldest post–Second World War disability-specific benefits, introduced in 1975 to give a minimum level of financial support to all adults with impairment. A person with a disability is entitled to AAH if he or she does not have sufficient income through wages, pension or benefits. Although there is an issue with families tending to regard it as a family benefit, it is only payable to and for the disabled person him/herself. AAH is funded by the state and distributed through the Family Allocations Office (Caisse d'Allocation Familliale) (CAF).[24] Eligibility is measured by an 'incapacity rating'; a person must be judged to have an incapacity rating of at least 80 per cent in order to automatically qualify for support. If the rating is between 50 per cent and 80 per cent, a disabled person must also have been unemployed for a year or more and have serious difficulty in finding a job in order to qualify. Another qualification criterion is having income below a certain amount. This amount is recalculated

---

[23] *Ibid.*
[24] https://www.caf.fr (accessed 20 November 2011).

annually. If a disabled person is receiving another benefit or payment allowance, such as an invalidity pension, he or she is still entitled to AAH, but the amount awarded is reduced in proportion to the other income. If a person starts in paid employment, AAH is reduced accordingly.[25]

There are many different initiatives aimed at providing additional resources and support for persons with disabilities based on a concept of national solidarity, and aiming to provide an income for persons with disabilities unable to work. These include Insurance Against Disability (Assurance Invalidité), an insurance funded by contributions from workers, based on a collective provident philosophy, where in the name of solidarity, every worker pays to ensure provision for those unable to work. Persons with disabilities living in the community are also able to choose between the Financial Resource Insurance (Garantie de Ressource) created to ensure that people who cannot work have at least an income representing 80 per cent of the minimum wage, and the Additional Allowance for an Independent Life (Majoration Pour la Vie Autonome) (MVPA), a benefit which corresponds to AAH for disabled adults living in the community receiving Personal Rent Subsidy (Aide Personnalisée au Logement) (APL), who have no income or work-related activity.

The introduction of Prestation de Compensation du Handicap (PCH) represented a very important shift in approach to disability support. It was brought in as one of the core reforms of the 2005 legislation and as one of the elements that compose the Person-centred Compensation Plan (Plan Personalisé de Compensation) (PPC)[26], an overarching personalised life plan outlining the life goals of the individual disabled person and the support he or she will need to get there. PCH provides the financial resources to pay for the support needs identified. It is distributed by the MDPH, with the aim of supporting persons with disabilities to overcome barriers to independence.[27] PCH has replaced another benefit called the Third Party Compensation Allowance (L'allocation Compensatrice de Tierce Personne) (ACTP), although those on ACTP prior to 2005 had the option of staying on it. If a person on ACTP wishes to make the transition to PCH, the MDPH must produce a cost comparison, enabling the person to make the most financially advantageous decision. It can be used by persons with disabilities to purchase five different types of assistance:

- Personal assistance. There is an entitlement to receive funds for this even if relatives provide support for the disabled person. Assistance covers all everyday life activities and can include supervision.
- Equipment not fully covered by contributions from the *Securité Sociale*.

---

[25] See the (2009) *Rapport du Gouvernement au Parlement relatif au bilan et aux orientations de la politique du handicap.* Secrétariat d'Etat chargé de la Solidarité, Paris.

[26] See the CNSA report of 2007: *Handicap et droit à compensation : quelles nouvelles pratiques? Etude sur les Plans Personnalisés de Compensation.*

[27] Please refer to http://vosdroits.service-public.fr/N14201.xhtml (accessed 20 November 2011).

- Adaptations needed to the home or car or alternatively extra transport costs arising from disability.
- Animal assistance, such as a guide dog for people who are blind or visually impaired.
- Financial assistance in exceptional circumstances.[28]

A disabled person's incapacity rate is not taken into account in assessing eligibility, but rather the difficulties encountered in carrying out activities identified in guidelines produced by the CDAPH. The guidelines distinguish between inability and difficulty in performing activities. If a disabled person already receives support from the Carer's Allowance (Majoration pour Tierce Personne) (MTP), the amount is deducted from the PCH. The same applies for people over sixty years of age in receipt of Personal Independence Allowance (Allocation personnalisée d'autonomie) (APA).

There are two stages to the application process for PCH. The first is an assessment of need carried out by the CDAPH. The second is an elaboration of the PPC. PCH is funded by the CNSA and the Conseil général, the latter of which makes the payments directly to the person with the disability. The amount funded depends upon the income and resources of the person, the number of hours of support required and the cost. There is no upper limit, but means testing for the financial contribution is required for every recipient. The level of support is calculated irrespective of the level of contribution.

Work-Related Support

Employment is a central aspect within the 2005 legislation, and the law introduced and strengthened a number of measures to support persons with disabilities into work. Employers are encouraged to hire persons with disabilities, with a bonus of €1,600 for employers who directly or indirectly hire a disabled person for more than twelve consecutive months. Up to 80 per cent of the resources needed to hire a disabled worker, including equipment and specific training, can be reimbursed through public funding.[29] This is also true in the case of measures taken for an employee who has become disabled. Disabled workers are entitled to reasonable adjustments, such as flexible working hours and shifts. They also receive priority access to further training and continuing education, as part of their role. In a redundancy situation, the notice period for a disabled worker is double than for other employees. Disabled workers are also entitled to early retirement from the age of fifty-five, on the basis of thirty working years with a disabled worker status.[30] The

---

[28] Please refer to http://vosdroits.service-public.fr/N14201.xhtml (accessed 20 November 2011).

[29] Please refer to http://www.euroblind.org/convention/article-27–work-and-employment/nr/124 (accessed 20 November 2011).

[30] *Ibid.*

2005 legislation also protects against discrimination of disabled workers, stating that no difference should be made between disabled and non-disabled workers in terms of recruitment or access to company training. Furthermore, an employee cannot be made redundant on the basis of disability. These acts are considered as discriminatory and can be brought before the courts of justice. A specific organisation has also been set up, the High Authority against Discrimination and in Favour of Equality (Haute autorité de lutte contre les discriminations et pour l'égalité) (HALDE), to handle discrimination-based complaints. The range of measures to improve support for persons with disabilities to get into and stay in employment is examined in the following sections.

Centres and Services for Help with Work (Etablissements Et Services d'Aide par le Travail) (ESATs)

ESATs were introduced in 2002 to replace Centres for Help with Work (Centres d'Aide par le Travail). They are state-funded employment specialist settings, combining economic activity with provision of health and social care support, intended to benefit persons with disabilities deemed not able to work in the open competitive workplace. Through delivery of educational and vocational training programmes, they aim to enhance personal development and increase independence and social inclusion.[31]

The ESAT is responsible for guaranteeing an income to people with disabilities attending the programmes. In 2008, the income distributed by the ESATs amounted to around 55–70 per cent of the minimum wage. Of this, the ESAT subsidised 5–20 per cent, with the rest being state funded. The amount of state subsidy depends upon working hours and occasionally covers lack of productivity resulting from a worker's disability.[32] Income received from an ESAT is not considered as a salary within the French labour market, but it does give access to Social Security benefits. The amount of AAH an ESAT worker receives is reduced depending upon earnings from the ESAT. From a legal point of view, the disabled worker is not recognised as a worker: no employment contract is signed and the disabled person does not have the same rights and responsibilities as a regular worker.

ESATs are state funded and must therefore comply with specific requirements, pertaining to such things as the precise type of impairment that the majority of the workforce will need to have. There are, for example, ESATs specifically designed for people with a learning disability. They must also have a limited number of employees whose work capability is measured at more than 33 per cent. An agreement needs

---

[31] Etablissements et Services d'Aide par le Travail, available at: http://annuaire.action-sociale.org. (accessed 20 November 2011).

[32] Direction Generale De La Cohesion (2009) Sociale *Appui Des Services De L'etat A La Modernisation Et Au Developpement Des Etablissements Et Services D'aide Par Le Travail Dans Leurs Missions Medico-Sociale Et Economique*, Rapport Final, November.

to be signed with the state, in which all professional and paraprofessional activities undertaken by the ESAT are outlined. The agreement also needs to designate the exact number of people who will manage the workforce.

Adapted Businesses (Entreprises Adaptées)

Entreprises adaptées are somewhat similar to sheltered workshops. Legally, however, there is no difference between a regular business and an *entreprise adaptée*, except that more than 80 per cent of the employees of an adapted business must have an impairment which affects their productivity. The *entreprise* signs a three-year contract with the state that specifies its production objectives. The state then pays the *entreprise* in advance every year. The contract signed between the state and the *entreprise* guarantees state financial support for the *entreprise* during its first years of activity or compensates for the productivity barriers faced by the workers. The state also meets a portion of the salary costs, to make sure that the pay is not under the legal minimum wage. Other than that, legal rights and duties are the same for adapted as for regular businesses.

Mainstream Employment

A disabled worker has the same rights and responsibilities as other workers. However, the CDAPH permits the employer to reduce the salary of a disabled worker if his or her impairment leads to lower productivity. In such a case, the disabled worker can receive compensation, but this is limited to 20 per cent of the minimum wage and only applicable for an income that is not more than 130 per cent of the minimum wage. In addition, an employer can seek financial assistance for the costs of any adaptations to the workplace required for a disabled worker from the Association for the Management of Resources for the Inclusion of Disabled People (L'Association de gestion du fonds pour l'insertion des personnes handicapées) (Agefiph).

Companies with 20 employees and with less than 6 per cent persons with disabilities within their workforce have to pay a contribution to the Fund for the vocational rehabilitation of disabled persons managed by the Agefiph.[33] The Agefiph uses this money to fund a variety of initiatives focussed on inclusion of persons with disabilities, including financial support for persons with disabilities seeking employment or for firms employing persons with disabilities, research and analysis concerning disability employment issues and supporting employment retention for persons with disabilities. In 2001, Agefiph invested €411.6 million into these activities.[34]

---

[33] Thornton, P. (1998) *Employment Quotas, Levies and National Rehabilitation Funds for Persons with Disabilities: Pointers for Policy and Practice*, GLADNET Collection, Cornell University.

[34] Agefiph (2001) Rapport 2001. The contribution is 400 times the minimum hourly rate per missing unit: approximately €3700. If the company has more than 250 employees, the contribution increases to 500 times, and if the company has more than 500 employees, the contribution is 600. After 3 years of having no disabled employees, the company can be fined 1500 times the minimum wage: €13500.

Self-Employment

If disability hinders the productivity of a self-employed person, he/she can request financial compensation. According to Agefiph, 33,000 persons with disabilities are self-employed in France, and statistics show a marked increase in numbers over the last few years.[35] Persons with disabilities looking to set up self-employment can apply to the Agefiph for funding. They are entitled to support from the National Employment Agency (Agence Nationale pour l'Emploi) (ANPE) to develop a business plan and learn skills such as accounting. A successful Agefiph application entitles a disabled person to receive up to €10,675 in start-up costs, providing he or she invests at least €1,525.[36]

Disability-Specific Services

In France, there is a distinction between an 'institution', which offers residential placements and support, and a 'service', which provides support within the community. Both are funded by the *Sécurité Sociale* and commissioned by the Local Directorate of Health and Social Affairs (Direction Départementale des Affaires Sanitaires et Sociales) (DDASS). Outreach services can be run and managed from institutions. Historically, support services for persons with disabilities were dominated by institutionalised approaches, but once legislation was passed in 2002, giving legitimacy to community-based services, the landscape of support for persons with disabilities began to change. There is now a greater range of community-based support, managed by either statutory agencies or local organisations, depending on the nature of the service.

Until 2004, there was no legislation covering support to live in the community. Government guidelines were concerned only with transport services to assist persons with disabilities with daily living tasks and with buddy schemes to support persons with disabilities to participate in educational and social activities. Four new types of service have come into being through government decrees: two of these relate to older persons and those with disabilities, and the other two are solely for the benefit of persons with disabilities. These services include home and nursing care, support services and rehabilitation (see Table 8.1).

Legislation was also introduced to provide a framework for personal assistance services (*services d'aide à la personne*). Before setting up these services, permission must first be obtained from the local authority. Services must fulfil specifications covering two main areas:

Any company can get a grant if they hire a disabled person since the 1st of January 2012 in order to offset any costs involved in hiring a disabled worker.

[35] Please refer to http://www.euroblind.org/convention/article-27–work-and-employment/nr/124 (accessed 5 December 2011).

[36] Please refer to http://informations.handicap.fr/art-mission-handicap-759–3875.php (accessed 5 December 2011).

TABLE 8.1. *Programmes to support community living*

Services		
UEROS	Unité d'Evaluation de Réentrainement et d'Orientation Sociale et Professionnelle[37]	Support for people who have suffered brain damage and head trauma by providing rehabilitation and training programmes which can be delivered at a location chosen by the service user.
Institutions		
ESAT	Etablissements et Services d'aide par le Travail[38]	Institutions providing employment, training and personal development for persons with disabilities. ESATs are usually focussed on a single impairment.
	Foyer d'Hébergement[39]	Residential placements attached to an ESAT to provide accommodation for the workers.
	Foyer Occupationnel[40]	Residential placements for persons with disabilities who are reasonably able to live on their own, but who are not sufficiently able to have a job even in a specialist employment setting.
MAS	Maisons d'Acceuil Specialisée[41]	Homes for adult persons with disabilities who are not able to live on their own and require constant supervision and medical care.
FAM	Foyers d'Accueil Médicalisé[42]	Residential placements with 24-hour supervision for persons with disabilities judged as completely unable to work or live independently.

- provision of assistance with ordinary daily tasks such as eating, dressing or any other similar activity;
- support with social interaction (e.g. helping to communicate and interact with other people).[43]

These services are organised around a model of a service where the disabled person takes on the role of employer. Disability organisations have developed a quality rating to validate the ethos and standard of these services.

A final category of service within the French disability support system is the Collective Assistance Group (Groupe D'Entraide Mutuelle) (GEM). These are self-help groups, set up to enable persons with disabilities to share their experiences

---

37 Unit for Assessment and Social Professional Rehabilitation.
38 Centres and Services for Help with Work.
39 Accommodation Facility.
40 Occupational Facility.
41 Specialist Residential Unit.
42 Residential Medical Unit.
43 Les Services D'aide À La Personne En France, Par L'una (Union Nationale De L'aide, Des Soins Et Des Services Aux Domiciles).

TABLE 8.1 *(continued)*

SAVS	Services d'Accompagnement à la Vie Sociale[44]	Support to enable disabled persons to lead fulfilling lives, maintaining familial and social relationships. A range of different support workers are involved in the delivery of the service, providing assistance with all essential daily activities, with the goal of increasing independence.
SAMSAH	Services d'Accompagnement Medico-Social pour Adulte Handicapé[45]	Support to assist persons with disabilities in their daily lives, with a striking similarity to SAVSs. The main difference is that SAMSAHs include daily health care provision; whereas the medical perspective is absent from SAVSs, medical professionals including doctors, nurses and assistance nurses are involved in delivery of SAMSAHs.
SSIAD	Services de Soins Infirmier A Domicile[46]	Unlike SAMSAHs, these services are only available to people with a medical prescription. It is exclusively a health care service which does not support any aspect of a disabled person's life. Service delivery is performed by specialist health care professionals and is for the benefit of both older individuals and persons with disabilities.
SAAD	Services d'Aide et d'Accompagnement a Domicile[47]	These services promote social activities and participation through provision of support with domestic tasks. Support is tailored to the needs of the person, according to a plan developed with the individual. Some areas do not have a separate SSIAD and SAAD, but instead have a single service fulfilling both functions, called *Service Polyvalent d'Aide et de Soins à Domicile* (SPASAD).[48]

and provide and receive peer support.[49] They do not run along institutional lines and function more as *associations*.

This overview provides a snapshot of the landscape of support in France. As identified, there have been a number of important shifts in the values underpinning more recent entitlements and services, very much driven by a focus on getting persons with disabilities into the labour market. The wellsprings and implications of these reforms are examined in detail in the following section.

[44] Social Life Support Service.
[45] Health and Social Care Support Services for Disabled Adults.
[46] Home Nursing Care Service.
[47] Home Assistance and Support Service.
[48] Multipurpose Assistance and Care Home Service.
[49] Please refer to http://www.oisis.fr/ (accessed 7 December 2011).

THE WELLSPRINGS OF REFORM

A number of factors can be identified as instrumental in inducing the reform of disability support in France since the turn of the century. These include persons with disabilities' protests and involvement in national policy, the influence of approaches to disability in Europe and attention drawn to disability through the *Perruche* case, a lawsuit dealing with the concept of 'wrongful birth'.

The Role of Persons with Disabilities' Protests

Protest has been one of the key actions that have triggered the lives of persons with disabilities in France to change. Another objective of public protests has been to contribute to a transformation in the way persons with disabilities are viewed within society: through protesting, persons with disabilities were no longer seen as 'helpless', but as empowered people willing to fight for their place in society. In April 1992, L'Association des Paralysés de France (APF) organised one of the first protests of persons with disabilities. Their aim was to initiate a public debate on the aspirations of persons with disabilities and the means required to enable them to freely choose their way of life; it called attention to the ineffectiveness of the 1975 legislation. This protest can be seen as a historical turning point for the French population and the widely held image of disability.

A second protest led by APF and L'Association Française contre les Myopathies (AFM) on 29 May 1999 called for a personalised response to the needs of persons with disabilities. The protest involved twenty-five thousand persons with disabilities and their families who marched on the Bastille.[50] Their aim was to speak out against the barriers persons with disabilities faced to an independent life, but also to raise awareness of a disabled person's right to 'compensation', in other words the resources and support to overcome those barriers. They also called for a review of financial assistance and entitlements and the creation of a single administrative body to manage everything related to persons with disabilities at the local government level. On 25 January 2000, the government announced plans to put in place a coherent and ambitious plan of reforms. The plan included two key elements: to reform and simplify the system of benefits for persons with disabilities and to recognise a disabled person's right to compensation. Two years later, persons with disabilities were critical of a failure to implement the reforms, and the APF and the AFM used the occasion of the second anniversary of the 1999 protest to draw attention to the bureaucratic shortcomings which were holding back the reforms. Through their tenacity, persons with disabilities were eventually able to secure a response to their issues through the 2005 legislation, with its recognition

---

[50] Le Politique de Handicap (2011) *Du Haut Moyen-Age au début du XIXème siècle*, http://www .vie-publique.fr/politiques-publiques/politique-handicap/chronologie/ (accessed 5 December 2011).

of a right to compensation and its introduction of individualised funding through PCH.

The Role of Disability Organisations in the Creation of the 2005 Legislation

The *associations* – and through them persons with disabilities – had a key role in the development of the 2005 legislation, through both official consultation and independent initiative.[51] Work to draft the new legislation began in April 2003. All national policy and legislation pertaining to disability were required, since 1975, to be passed through the National Consultative Council for Disabled People (Conseil National Consultatif des Personnes Handicapées) (CNCPH).[52] Disability associations were represented on this Council. When the first draft of the bill was written, disability *associations* started to propose ways to improve the bill. They formed their own subcommittee to develop a shadow proposal, presented to the government at the end of May 2003. The first official draft of the law contained 48 articles; the shadow proposal had more than 100 articles. The CNCPH used the shadow proposal as a basis for a new proposition to amend the official document. Their final draft was published in December 2003. The Muscular Dystrophy Association (Association Française contre les Myopathies) (AFM) was the first *association* to respond and to publicly demand that a new proposal should be written. In January 2004, the CNCPH presented a slightly amended version that was still contested by disability *associations*. The APF also asked for amendments, on the basis that the proposed legislation did not adequately reflect the needs of people with physical impairment. In February 2004, the CNCPH proposed twenty-six amendments to the proposal. In April 2004, the Federation of Associations for Disabled Adults and Young People (L'association Pour Adultes et Jeunes Handicapés) (APAJH) and the National Association for the Integration of People with Physical Impairment (Association Nationale pour l'Intégration des Handicapés Moteurs) (ANPIHM) called for public protest. Twenty-five other *associations* followed them and formed a new committee called the Committee for the Reform of the 1975 law (Le collectif pour la refonte de la loi de 1975). This level of pressure led to further revision and in February 2005, legislation was finally passed which had had considerable input from persons with disabilities and their representatives.[53]

European Influence

It is possible to discern some inspiration from Europe behind the work undertaken by disability *associations* to influence legal change and disability reform. The

---

[51] Cunin, J.-C. (2008) *Le handicap en France: Chroniques d'un combat politique.* Dunod, Paris.
[52] Conseil National Consultatif des Personnes Handicapées (2011) Rapport 2010.
[53] Cunin, *supra,* n. 51.

Independent Living movement had progressed in countries such as Sweden and the United Kingdom, encouraging approaches to disability based on the social model of disability and independent living philosophy. The year 1993 saw the establishment of the European Forum for Persons with disabilities, with Forum members representing the interests of more than 800 local or national disability organisations throughout the European Union. The French disability *associations* positioned themselves to provide representation from France, and shortly after the Forum was created, Paul Boulinier, chair of the APF, was elected to its vice-presidency. The Forum as a whole was very much in favour of the new disability culture and it prioritised work on inclusion, equal opportunities and tackling discrimination. The work of the French representatives was to pass European recommendations back to French government. Thus the French *associations* came not only to have direct contact with the values and principles of the European independent living movement, but were involved in transferring them to France. Their involvement also allowed them to see that if France did not initiate its own reform of institutional services, European directives would soon force it to.[54]

Wrongful Life and Compensating for Disability: The Perruche Case

Senator Paul Blanc's Report to the Senate, '*sur la politique de compensation du handicap*', laid the foundations for the Loi handicap of 2005. In his opening words to the Senate for his verbal presentation on 24 July, Senator Blanc cited the legal case of Nicholas Perruche as a key factor in precipitating reform. He said:

> In the debate opened up by the Perruche case for the passage of the Loi relatif aux droits des malades,[55] some people believed that there was a conflict between doctors and lawyers. In reality, there was something else at play: although the Parliament had to discuss legislation, this was not the real issue. Behind the debate was in fact another fundamental question: how does society perceive disability?[56]

The *Perruche* case focussed national attention, and even media interest, on disability.[57] Nicholas Perruche was born in 1983 with severe and multiple impairments caused by his mother catching rubella during her pregnancy. Ms Perruche had been tested for rubella during the pregnancy, but had wrongly been told she was clear. Had she tested positively, she wanted an abortion rather than risk having a disabled child. When Nicholas was two, his mother had a breakdown and required

---

54 Barral, *supra*, n. 7.

55 *Loi Relative aux Droits des Malades et à la Qualité du Système de Santé.*

56 Translated from: '*Dans le débat ouvert sur la jurisprudence Perruche, lors de l'examen du projet de loi relatif aux droits des malades, certains ont cru voir un affrontement entre médecins et juristes. En réalité, le Parlement a dû débattre, il est vrai dans l'urgence d'une fin de législation, d'une question autrement fondamentale : celle de notre regard sur le handicap?*'

57 See Ewing, J. (2002) 'The Perruche Case, Journal of Law & Family Studies', *Journal of Law & Family Studies* 4: 317.

psychiatric support. He was placed in an institution. His parents were concerned that, once he reached the age of twenty, he would have to leave the institution and require costly private care.

The parents first took their case to court in 1988, under a claim of 'wrongful birth': had Ms Perruche been given accurate information, she would not have continued with the pregnancy. The parents were awarded damages from the laboratory, as compensation for the harm caused to Ms Perruche by their mistake. The Perruches then went further and introduced to French jurisprudence a concept of 'wrongful life': the idea that Nicholas should never have been born; he had been denied his right to be aborted, and therefore the laboratory staff were responsible for all the costs associated with his care and support for his entire life. The court found in their favour and substantial damages were awarded, only to be overturned on appeal. In July 2001, the Cour de Cassation, the French equivalent of the Supreme Court, upheld the original ruling in favour of the Perruches. There was an outcry from both physicians and persons with disabilities. Physicians were concerned at the implications this ruling could have for medical practice, and in January 2002, the National Syndicate of Gynecologists and Obstetricians began refusing to perform routine ultrasound scans, on the grounds that they could not risk the lawsuits which might arise from disabled babies being born. Persons with disabilities and their organisations criticised the ruling, saying that it questioned their value as human beings with equal rights, and claiming that it encouraged eugenics. In response, the French government called an emergency session of the National Assembly and, in March 2002, passed legislation preventing wrongful-life cases from being taken to court: the Loi Relative aux Droits des Malades et à la Qualité du Système de Santé.

Not long after the *Perruche* affair, Senator Blanc made a report to the Senate, proposing a policy of disability compensation in order to enable persons with disabilities to enjoy a meaningful life. The report contained seventy-five recommendations, which formed the basis for the articles of the Loi handicap which was subsequently set in motion. The recommendations addressed issues that had long been raised through persons with disabilities' protests for better life chances, and can also be interpreted as responding to the concerns of persons with disabilities, that their lives had been diminished by the 2001 Cour de Cassation ruling. The concept of compensating for disability suggests the influence of the *Perruche* case, and the parents' demands that Nicholas be compensated for being born disabled; in a society which supported persons with disabilities to overcome the barriers that prevented them from enjoying an ordinary life, there would be no need for wrongful-life claims.[58] The *Perruche* case, in its involvement with the medical profession, made disability a topic of national interest. It highlighted the conflict between medical and legal

[58] Costiche, J. F. (2006) 'The Perruche Case and the Issue of Compensation for the Consequences of Medical Error', *Health Policy* 78(1): 8–16.

approaches to disability, and impressed upon French government the urgent need for reform.

Building on Earlier Legislation

The 1975 Loi d'Orientation promoted inclusion and access of persons with disabilities to mainstream society. However, without accompanying implementation measures, its precepts remained largely unenforced. A series of statutes over the next twenty-five years sought to strengthen the original Loi. In 1986, a law called the Act on the promotion of employment for disabled persons was passed to enable positive discrimination for persons with disabilities in employment: as we saw, a company employing twenty people or more became obliged to recruit a workforce consisting of at least 6 per cent persons with disabilities and otherwise pay a contribution to the Agefiph. The number of persons with disabilities in mainstream employment remained low, however, with an average of only 4 per cent of workers employed by firms with twenty workers or more being disabled.

The turn of the century saw a consolidated effort to use legislation to enforce the rights of persons with disabilities. In January 2002, the Loi Renovant L'action Sociale et Medico-Sociale was passed, to reform the 1975 Loi Relative aux Institutions Sociales et Medico-Sociale and bring it more in line with the principles of the Loi d'Orientation. It introduced rights and choices for institution service users and required institutions to provide a greater range of services, in order to enable persons with disabilities to have a more varied and higher quality of life.

Building on the earlier wellsprings of reform, in July 2002, the French president Jacques Chirac made the inclusion of persons with disabilities one of the 'three main priorities' (*trois grands chantiers*) for his second presidential mandate. Meanwhile, work was under way to renew and strengthen the Loi d'Orientation. Measures identified as central to enabling the inclusion of persons with disabilities were as follows:

- replacing the current system for assessing incapacity with a person-centred system, based on an understanding of individual needs and potential;
- providing a realistic level of disability compensation to enable a disabled person to overcome the barriers to enjoying a full life;
- supporting integration through development of a global approach to disability access, including:
  - access to buildings and the environment;
  - access to professional development;
  - access to mainstream employment;
  - access to public life;
  - access to sheltered employment;
  - access to citizenship and social life;

- improving residential support through emphasis on user involvement and independence;
- diagnosis, prevention and care.[59]

Finally in February 2005, the Loi Handicapée was passed. The legislation reflects a social model of disability approach and recognises that integration is not to be achieved through focussing on the impairment, but through addressing the *situation de handicap* that a person with a disability is in, and providing individualised support to enable him or her to enjoy the same life chances as other citizens.[60] The main principles of the legislation are: (1) equal treatment through access to mainstream society and solidarity; (2) overcoming the barriers caused by disability through the identification of needs and compensation; and (3) mandatory measures to enforce accessibility.[61] The outcome of this reform relating to the provision of support is examined later in the chapter.

THE SHAPE OF REFORM

This section looks at the mechanisms by which reform of the French disability support system was enacted, how reform was shaped and how the market has been changed to reflect values and principles of the new legislation. This section considers the strategic approach to reform, the creation of a new social care market, and the shaping of the demand side of reform to allow persons with disabilities to exercise consumer power and control.

SHAPING THE DEMAND SIDE OF REFORM

This section focuses mainly on the relationship between the transformation of social care services and national policy objectives to increase the choice and control which persons with disabilities can exercise over the services they use. It looks first at the French policy of individualised funding, then at the reform of supported decision-making processes and finally at enabling a choice in living arrangements. The last

---

[59] See http://lci.tfi.fr/politique/2007–05/trois-grands-chantiers-inacheves-chirac-4883271.html (accessed 5 December 2011).

[60] The legislation gives a definition of disability as 'everything that limits activity or restricts participation in society, for reason of one or more substantial, enduring or serious impairments that are physical, sensory, mental, cognitive, or psychological, or multiple disability or long term health condition'.

[61] The law introduced a concept of universal access, according to which all public areas must be accessible by 2015. Please refer to Larrouy, M. (2007). *L'invention De L'accessibilite. L'invention De L'accessibilite: Des Politiques De Transport Des Personnes Handicapees Aux Politiques D'accessibilite Des Transports Urbains De Voyageurs En France De 1975 A 2005*. Paris; Chossy, J.-F. (2006). *Rapport D'information Sur La Mise En Application De La Loi*, N° 2005–102 Du 11 Février 2005, Commission Des Affaires Culturelles, Familiales Et Sociales, Paris.

part of this section examines different ways to increase the consumer power of persons with disabilities.

New Policy Options for Individualised Funding

With the 2005 legislation and the introduction of PCH, funding for disability support has become more individualised. Legislative and policy reform was predicated upon a need to compensate persons with disabilities for their impairment, in order to enable them to live an ordinary life. The aim of PCH is to provide funds to cover all the extra costs associated with disability. On this basis, the amount of money given differs from one disabled person to another and depends on the type of spending and cost of equipment or services needed. Money is given on a monthly basis directly to the disabled person. Prices for homecare services funded through PCH are fixed and regulated by government decree. If a family member provides a disabled person's personal assistance, the disabled person can choose whether to receive the money or whether this is to be paid directly to the relative.

The legislation which introduced personal assistance services established three different models by which persons with disabilities and their families could employ personal assistants:

- The disabled person directly employs the personal assistant (this method of contracting support is known as *gré à gré*).[62]
- The disabled person uses a professional organisation as a representative, to help to find a worker to employ, but the disabled person is still the employer (*emploi mandataire*).[63]
- The disabled person pays an organisation to be in charge of providing the service, with the disabled person then only having a customer status (*emploi prestataire*).[64,65]

These models are examined in more detail in the section 'Creating a New Social Care Market'. The other factor which has a substantial determining influence on the amount of PCH awarded is the disabled person's individualised plan.

This individualised plan is carried out by the local Maisons Departemental des Personnes Handicapée (MDPH), which was set up in every *département*. The only strategic board within an MDPH is the Commission for the Independence and Rights of Disabled People (Commission des Droits et de l'Autonomie des Personnes

---

[62] By mutual agreement.
[63] Employment by proxy.
[64] Beneficiary of an employment contract held between other parties.
[65] Le Conseil de l'emploi, d. r. (2008). *Les Services A La Personne*. Crec, Paris.

Handicapées) (CDAPH).[66] The CDAPH includes multidisciplinary representation from medical, paramedical, psychological and educational professions.[67] A lead is chosen from among the members, who can change at any time, depending upon the case being reviewed and the particular needs and impairment of the disabled person. The team's aim is to enable the person with the disability to follow a life plan put together with assistance from the MDPH, in consultation with the disabled person and his/her representative. The expertise of specialist resource centres can be utilised in the process of carrying out the assessment process, if needed. The CDAPH works in a democratic way, with decisions being taken by a qualified majority. The CDAPH has the power to:

- Give its opinion on a disabled child's educational prospects.
- Assess the degree of difficulty faced by a disabled person in undertaking daily living tasks. The assessment is to be based on the International Classification of Functioning, Disability and Health (ICF), and the level of benefit awarded is proportional to the identified level of need.
- Designate a disabled person as unable to work (*travailleur handicapé*) and, in so doing, grant access to specific rights.
- Propose a support plan to meet the needs of a disabled person.
- Decide the type and level of support to which a disabled person is entitled. Support can be in the form of financial assistance, equipment or personal assistance. Cases are reviewed every five years.[68]

It is the role of the CDAPH to support persons with disabilities to develop and realise their plans. These plans cover many aspects of life, including education, housing and daily life activities. Every disabled person has at least one plan.[69]

- A Life Plan (Projet de vie) is a general plan covering the desires, dreams, wishes and goals of the disabled person. It is a plan that solely belongs to him/her and nobody can challenge it, although the CDAPH acts as an advisor.
- A Personal Compensation Plan (Plan Personalisé de Compensation) (PPC) is based on the Projet de Vie, but also on a CDAPH analysis. The CDAPH approves the rights and entitlements of the disabled person, taking into consideration the content of his/her Projet de Vie. The Commission then presents the plan to the disabled person to approve.

---

[66] This replaced the Commission Départementale d'Éducation Spéciale (CDES) and Commission Technique d'Orientation et de Reclassement Professionnel (COTOREP),1 which had been set up following the Orientation Act of 1975.

[67] Please refer to http://www.solidarite.gouv.fr/informations-pratiques,89/fiches-pratiques,91/handicap-interlocuteurs-et,1898/la-commission-des-droits-et-de-l,12630.html (accessed 7 December 2011).

[68] *Ibid.*

[69] Baligand, P. (2007) 'Les dispositifs et leurs evolutions consécutifs à la loi de 2005', *mt pédiatrie* 10(4): 211–221.

- A Personal Education Plan (*Plan Personalisé de Scolarisation*) (PPS) is a part of the Plan Personalisé de Compensation, and it is mandatory for every child to have one, regardless of his/her impairment. This plan describes the child's ambitions in terms of education.
- A Care and Assistance Project (Projet d'Accueil et d'Accompagnement) (PAA) is a plan which covers support for all aspects of a person's daily life. For example, if a person does not live in a residential unit, the plan will describe what is needed in terms of equipment and personal assistance in order to live an independent life. If the person lives in a specialist setting, the CDAPH makes sure that the support given corresponds to the Projet de Vie of the disabled person.[70]

The MDPH has a role in ensuring that decisions made by the CDAPH are enforced, but also in referring appeals against decisions made by the CDAPH to an Ombudsman, who will attempt mediation. The Ombudsman will have access to the disabled person's file and will strive for agreement to be reached between all parties. If mediation is not successful within two months, a report has to be written and the case is passed to a court for settlement. Each plan is unique to the disabled person.

Supported Decision Making

The first attempt at reforming the judiciary protection system for persons with disabilities was written in 1968. It stipulated that if a person was deemed not to have mental capacity as a result of old age, sickness or disability, society had a duty to protect his/her personal interests. This law was modified in March 2007. The major change was that protection of a disabled person's interests was no longer limited to material and financial affairs, but extended to cover the personal interests of an individual. Amongst other things, the law reformed the status of guardianship and bodies responsible for supporting the decision-making process of a disabled person.

Judicial Assistance Measure (Mesure D'accompagnement Judiciaire) (MAJ)
A judge has the power to award a MAJ to restore the autonomy of a person over his or her own finances. There are two conditions that have to be fulfilled for the judge to use this measure:

- The security or the health of the person must be compromised.
- Other means of social support must have failed.

70 Patrick, G. (2007). *Bilan de la loi du 11 février 2005 et de la mise en place des Maisons Départementales des Personnes Handicapées*. Ministère du travail, des relations sociales et de la solidarité, Paris.

Mandate for One's Future Protection (Mendat De Protection Future)
Every adult or emancipated minor can choose a representative to assume power of attorney, if in the future he/she loses capacity.

Guardianship (*Curatelle*)
If a person ceases to be able to act independently and requires full-time assistance and supervision in all aspects of his or her affairs, a judge can put in place a *curatelle*. A *curatelle* lasts for five years and can be renewed. The person designated as *curateur* is often the spouse or someone from the person's circle of family and friends; otherwise state guardianship may be decided on and a registered body appointed. The judge can nominate several people: one responsible for the person's health and another in charge of assets. The person who is under a *curatelle* cannot act independently of his/her *curateur's* and the judge's approval, and the *curateur* cannot act without consulting the disabled person. This measure is important for guaranteeing that personhood is still respected. As long as a person is aware of his or her true condition, the guardian is providing only a form of assistance and arbitration rather than actual representation. There are certain exceptions such as:

- Being the disabled person's representative in situations defined by the judge.
- In case of a so-called strengthened *curatelle*, the *curateur* manages all the affairs of the disabled person. In this case, the *curateur* is the only person authorised to sign a contract in the name of the disabled person.

Guardianship (*Tutelle*)
Tutelle is similar to *curatelle*. Usually, the *tuteur* is chosen from amongst the person's family. The main difference between a *tutelle* and a *curatelle* is the fact that the disabled person's family replaces the judge in order to decide what is best for the person. If there are no family members, the *tuteur* is chosen by a judge.[71]

Overall, the French system of legal capacity is largely based on the model of guardianship and substitute decision making. With the exception of a *tutelle*, a person is designated by court appointment and given the responsibility of managing the personal affairs of a person who is legally incompetent to manage his or her own affairs. In cases of medical treatment, if the adult is under a *curatelle* guardianship, the adult can consent to mundane acts; even the guardian cannot decide on treatment against the will of the individual, unless this is treatment which must be imposed in view of the person's state of health. For other medical acts involving serious decisions, like institutionalisation, the relevant medical staff must defer to the guardian or to the judge – for instance, when people are experiencing mental health issues which make it impossible for them to give their consent, but it is imperative that they be

---

[71] Fossier, T. (2009). *Curatelle, tutelle, accompagnements – Protection des mineurs et des majeurs vulnérables*. Litec, Paris.

hospitalised, either to receive treatment or to protect public order and safety (law of 27 June 1990). Apart from these serious instances, the person's consent is always required.[72]

Enabling a Choice in Living Arrangements

The concept of an individualised life plan, as brought in by the 2005 legislation, implies a level of choice for persons with disabilities over their own lives, including their living arrangements. The introduction of new forms of supported living, including the *Logement Transitionel* and the *Maison Familiale D'Accueil Temporaire*, has increased the range of support options open to a disabled person, but the institutional model of support still dominates the market. Where persons with disabilities are agreeing to or even choosing to live in institutional settings, we must ask why. One relevant factor is the attitude of French society towards persons with disabilities, which makes them feel unvalued and excluded to such an extent that they would rather live in segregation. A Market Research Survey carried out by Ifop in 2006, at the request of *l'Association des paralysés de France*, found that attitudes towards persons with disabilities are commonly discriminatory.[73] The survey found that 81 per cent of French people believe that persons with disabilities cannot live alone, 87 per cent think that living with a disabled person 'requires courage', and 61 per cent think that persons with disabilities do not have a sexual life. It was apparent from the survey that the majority of French people do not feel they can interact with persons with disabilities, with 69 per cent saying they could not have a spontaneous face-to-face conversation with a disabled person, and 57 per cent saying they would only be able to speak to 'the carer'. Disabled French people feel unwelcome within mainstream society and, where this prompts them to choose to live in institutions, we must ask how much choice they really have.

Enhancing the Purchasing Power of the Consumer

The French government uses two different tools to increase the purchasing power of persons with disabilities: tax exemption and disability-specific saving schemes, or life insurance, such as the Savings Insurance for Disabled People (Contrat d'Epargne Handicap) or the Subsistence Fund Insurance (Contrat de Rente-Survie). The Contrat d'Epargne Handicap is a form of insurance for persons with disabilities, for whom disability has led to a decrease in income from work. After a minimum of six

---

72 Gromb, S. (1997) 'Ethics and Law in the Field of Medical Care for the Elderly in France', *Journal of Medical Ethics* 23: 233–238.

73 Ifop (2006) *La perception des idées reçues à l'égard des personnes en situation de handicap par les Français*, pour l'Association des paralysés de France.

years, or at the end of the contract, the disabled person can benefit from a lump sum or an annuity. Holding this type of insurance contract also gives access to certain tax exemptions. Every year, the disabled person can deduct from his/her tax return 25 per cent of the value of the insurance, up to a limit of €1,525. As for the Contrat de Rente-Survie, this is life insurance for parents of persons with disabilities. Parents can open this type of insurance if their child's impairment leads to reduction in income. After the death of the parents, the disabled person will receive a life-contingent annuity. If a disabled person is measured to have an incapacity degree of 80 per cent or higher, the fiscal administration views the disability as the equivalent of having 0.5 of an extra person in the household for taxation purposes. People buying personal assistance services can declare 50 per cent of the spending. This means that, for example, if someone has spent €8,000 in one year on homecare services and owes €4,500 in income taxes, he or she can deduct 50 per cent of the homecare spending (or €4,000) from the amount owed in tax, and only pay €500 in income tax. Persons with disabilities are also exempt from some taxes like the Local Residence Tax (Taxe d'habitation).[74] Through such measures, the French government has encouraged the purchase of community-based personal assistance services.

SHAPING THE SUPPLY SIDE OF REFORM

Adopting a Strategic Approach to Reform

In France, there is no single governmental body with exclusive authority over disability issues. In order to identify the measures needed to be taken to enforce the legislation of 2005, a cross-government approach has been taken, involving all government departments. In 2009, a new committee was set up, the Cross-government Committee on Disability (Comité Interministériel du Handicap) (CIH).[75] This new committee replaced the Cross-government Board on Disability (Délégation Interministérielle aux Personnes Handicapées) (DIPH). It was created to allow a cross-cutting approach towards disability policy, and its membership includes every government minister involved with the reform of the French disability system. The head of this new committee is the prime minister. Its aim is to develop, implement and evaluate national policy on disability. The committee is also responsible for the coordination of the National Conference on Disability (Conference national du handicap). The most recent conference took place in June 2011. Introduced shortly after the passage of the 2005 legislation, this event is a governmental initiative which occurs every three years. It serves to bring together every major disability stakeholder,

[74] Apajh La Fiscalite Des Personnes En Situation De Handicap. *Handicap Assistance 2009.*
[75] Please refer to http://www.solidarite.gouv.fr/espaces,770/handicap,775/institutionnel,803/le-comite-interministeriel-du,1711/le-comite-interministeriel-du,11306.html (accessed 5 December 2011).

government officials and enterprises working in the field. The aim of the conference is to review government policy on disability and to initiate discussions on recommendations for further action. This exemplifies the partnership approach adopted by the French government.[76]

Creating a New Social Care Market

Reforms which gave persons with disabilities the power to buy their own services led to a change in the French social care market. The 2005 legislation gave persons with disabilities the choice between living in an institution and living in the community. For the latter aspiration to become reality, a sector of community living support services needed to develop. *Associations* began to diversify into community-based as well as institutionalised support.[77] However, whereas, disability support had previously depended upon commissioning arrangements between the Conseil général and local *associations*, persons with disabilities themselves now had the purchasing power as they made decisions about which services to use. Onto the market came private companies, looking to sell services to individual persons with disabilities. This prompted a sea change among the key stakeholders within the disability sector. In order to compete, economic efficiency and profitability started to become increasingly important in the way institutions were managed. They started to look more like companies, working according to a business model.

Through PCH, local government grants permission for and finances services; it does not recommend them or guarantee business. Persons with disabilities have consumer power and, in order to secure business, service providers need to treat them as customers and attract their interest. As a result, institutions began to offer more community-based services and to tailor their services to be more person-centred, for example providing support on weekends. They also widened their remit, from a focus on single impairment groups to pan-impairment provision. A partial deinstitutionalisation was thereby effected through market forces.

PCH and the PPC opened the way for personal assistance services, and a range of providers entered the market, including both private companies and those run by *associations*. Services proliferated: according to the National Agency for Homecare Services (Agence Nationale Services Personne) (ANSP): 10,288 organisations were granted permission to run care services in 2007.[78] Regarding this figure, it is important to note that many of these organisations are very small and, therefore, economically fragile. There is also a geographical inequality in the market, whereby there are greater numbers of service providers in urban areas than rural ones. It was in order

---

[76] Dossier De Presse De La Conferance Nationale Du Handicap. Ministère des Solidaritées et de la Cohesion Sociales, Paris, 2011.

[77] Barral, *supra*, n. 7.

[78] ANSP (2008) *Rapport d'Activité 2007*, ANSP.

to address gaps in provision that new statutory services like Home Nursing Care Service (SSIAD) were created.

As we saw, there are three different models by which persons with disabilities and their families can employ personal assistants: the *gré à gré* model, the *emploi mandataire* model and the *emploi prestataire* model. The last option is when the disabled person pays an organisation to be in charge of providing the service, with the disabled person then only having a customer status. The *prestataire* model is preferred by the government, as it links to employment targets around creating sector-specific skilled jobs. In the late 1990s, a benefit called Specific Dependence Benefit (Prestation Spécifique Dépendance) (PSD) was introduced for frail older people, allowing the purchase of personal assistance support. Under this scheme, the cost of support through the *prestataire* model was greater, which resulted in the majority of recipients choosing to pay relatives and buy informal support. This did not fit in with the government targets to create secure jobs within a regulated homecare sector and, amongst other criticisms of PSD, it was replaced with APA. Since then, the number of employees in *prestataire* services has increased. In February 2006, a specific plan for the development of personal assistance services announced the creation of between 1 million and 2 million jobs by 2010 and set up a specific agency to organise this sector – the Agency for Personal Assistance Services (Agence des services à la personne).[79]

All disability support services need government authorisation before they can provide services, depending on the type of service they intend to offer. Government thereby retains control over the shape and substance of the market. Organisations offering support other than direct personal care (for example, assistance with domestic tasks) must obtain approval from the Prefet, the head of the local adminisatration, and the Local Directorate for Employment and Professional Training (Direction Départemental du Travail Et de la Formation Professionelle) (DDTEFP) before they can be set up. Approval is granted following an assessment, based not just on the quality of service, but also on price. Pricing is regulated by a government decree.

People who want to open personal care services must obtain authorisation from the Conseil général. The Conseil général only grants authorisation if the scheme is compatible with local health care objectives and meets a need within the existing pattern of service availability. The Conseil général can refuse to grant this authorisation, not only if the service does not meet quality standards, but also for reasons of limiting the number of suppliers and controlling the market. It is also the Conseil général that regulates service pricing.

The social care market has undergone transformation in line with disability reform, to enable persons with disabilities to have greater choice of services and to have more control over the services they choose to buy. The institutions have

---

[79] Da Roit, B. et al. (2007). 'Long-Term Care Policies in Italy, Austria and France: Variations in Cash-for-Care Schemes', *Social Policy and Administration* 41(6): 653–671.

ceased to have a complete monopoly on the social care market, and there is now a multiplicity of services to choose from. However, there is lack of consistency or stability of provision across geographical areas, and the *associations* still dominate the social care sector, as they have diversified into provision of community-based support. Moreover, government retains the ultimate power to shape and limit the market. Reform has also been shaped in line with wider political objectives, favouring models of support which put less power directly in the hands of persons with disabilities, in order to create employment opportunities.

Shaping the Market through Reform

This section looks at how the disability support market in France has been reformed and reconfigured through a range of mechanisms, including enforcement of quality standards, funding to develop services, inspections, audits and penalties to meet standards and the influence of demand.

Funding to Shape the Support Market

Created in 2001, the Fund for the Modernisation of Homecare Services (Fonds de Modernisation de l'Aide à Domicile) (FMAD)' helps to fund programmes for improving home support services.

These programmes can take many forms, for example:

- Measures to improve workforce qualifications.
- Developing agreements in partnership with local government and employers of homecare staff to modernise homecare services. The FMAD has signed an agreement with local authorities to develop, evaluate and monitor local marks of quality.[80] For example, it helped to create the *Label Loire* quality mark, specific to the Loire region.[81]
- Development work to set up new services more economically viable and sustainable.

Until 2008, the FMAD was managed by the DDASS. It is now under the direct supervision of the CNSA. The CNSA now tries to have a more global approach towards its responsibilities, by signing an agreement with every *département* and Conseil général. In 2008, the CNSA signed a protocol for working jointly with the National Union of Assistance, Health Care and Homecare Services (Union Nationale de l'Aide, des soins et des services aux domiciles) (UNA) – an association for professionals working in the homecare sector – to launch a new programme of modernisation,

---

[80] *Enquete sur les conditions de la qualite des services d'aide a domicile pour les personnes agees.* IGAS, Paris.
[81] The Label Loire is a local quality mark developed by the Conseil général of Loire Rhone-Alpe.

including a GPEC[82] agreement. Other agencies have also launched programmes concerned with the modernisation of homecare services. For example, the National Agency for Personal Assistance (Agence National de Service à la Personne) (ANSP) launched the THETIS program in 2008, giving small enterprises and organisations access to accreditation and fifteen days of support. The cost of this program for 2008 was about €7.5 million. The ANSP published a list of the organisations that took part, which numbered nearly sixty in 2007. Benefits like PCH or ACTP – and, therefore, local government – also contribute to the funding for this sector.

Funding for homecare services depends upon the type of service provided. A distinction is made between services that provide homecare and support for daily life activities, and those that provide health care services in the home. Funding for home health care services is distributed for the most part by the social security system and local government. The CAF, National Commission for Health Insurance (*Commission Nationale d'Assurance-Maladie*) (CNAM) and the National Old-age Pension Fund for Employees (Caisse Nationale d'Assurance Vieillesse des Travailleurs Salariés) (CNAVTS) set the eligibility criteria for the funding.

Enforcing Standards

Services require government approval in order to operate. Approval can be retracted for poor performance and thus represents a key mechanism for enforcing quality standards. With the 2002 legislation (the Loi Renovant L'action Sociale et Medico-Sociale), government regulation became compulsory for both institutions and homecare services. This regulation was mainly concerned with the quality of service and enforcing the rights of the persons using the services. In the French market, quality of service is important and is continuously monitored. Even before a service is set up, a document describing the quality of service must be provided, in order to obtain local government approval for the scheme. Gaining this approval also gives access to some tax advantages. This is the case not only for direct service providers, but also for organisations acting as representatives.

Permission to set up community-based support services is granted following a quality assessment of the proposed services by the Conseil général. The assessment asks for a statement of quality, which must contain the following information:

- workforce qualifications of those who will deliver and manage the service;
- operational management of the service;
- a comprehensive outline of the type and standard of different services to be delivered;
- a projection of future costs.

---

[82] Gestion Prévisionnelle des Emplois et des Compétences – Forward Management for Labour Force and Skills.

Local authorities can grant two kinds of permission to open a homecare service: an Agrément qualité and an Autorisation. There are many differences between the two. First and foremost, the Autorisation is only given when the service is exclusively for disabled or older people. The Agrément qualité only lasts for five years, whereas the Autorisation lasts for fifteen years. The Agrément qualité is issued by the Préfet and the Autorisation is issued by the head of the Conseil général.

A quality audit is carried out every year, involving a customer satisfaction survey of the service. The audits check the skill levels of the staff, the needs of the service users and good practice management. Every five years, the findings from these annual audits are compiled and sent to the local authority, to inform the decision whether or not to renew the Agrément qualité. The format of the quality audit has been developed by the National Agency for the Quality Evaluation of Social and Health care services (Agence National de l'évaluation et de la Qualité des Etablissements Et Services Sociaux Et Medico-Socio) (ANSEM), but audits themselves are carried out by independently accredited services.

There is a clear distinction between state approval to open and continue running a service and a quality mark. Professionals from the homecare service field award the quality mark. The eligibility requirements for a quality mark are not as high as the criteria for local authority approval, but a quality mark is reviewed and checked more regularly. There are two different types of processes a company must go through if it wants to achieve a quality mark: one is overseen by the Conseil général and the other by the federation to which the organization belongs. Some Conseil général have set the standards that have to be met. It is not mandatory for organisations to have the quality mark, but it does allow them to profit, for example from tax reduction. When a coalition wants to create a quality mark, it must be recognised by the CNSA. For example, the National Federation of Local Personal Care Services (Federation National des Services à la Personne et de Proximité) (FEDESAP), a coalition of small organisations, has created the QUALISAP label.

Having a quality mark label is a way for companies to set themselves apart from the competition in a market characterised by a vast number of service providers. In a way, a quality mark is a halfway point between a basic commitment to quality and certification. Companies can voluntarily choose to be assessed for certification. Certification represents a guarantee that a service or product meets a certain standard.

The process for achieving certification is set out by the French consumers' code. There are two certifications available in France: the NF X 50–056 certificate and the QUALICERT certificate.

Standards which need to be met in order to achieve certification are as follows:

- There must be a clear description of the level of service a customer can expect, with full information on pricing.
- Staff must be properly qualified, with regular performance management, training and development.

- There must be a complaints policy, and all complaints need to be responded to within two weeks.

Penalties for Failure to Meet Standards

With the multiplicity of quality marks, enforcement of standards has become a key issue. If a service provider ignores its duty to ensure quality and uphold the rights of its customers, the state can start a procedure which will lead to a withdrawal of its permission to operate. However, if an *autorisation* has been granted, the Conseil général does not have the means to stop a service. It is only the Prefet that can withdraw permission to operate. Unfortunately, the only organisations that are properly quality assessed are those providing a service under the *prestataire* model, where the disabled person is a customer and the organisation directly employs the support staff. The only aspect which is quality assessed for services working under the *mandataire* model concerns the service provided and matching of the description. Organisations which have received the *agrément qualité* and operate on the *prestataire* model are assessed by the same authorities that gave them permission to operate. The service provider must prepare an annual report, including both qualitative and quantitative information. The *agrément* can only be renewed for a new five-year period, if the request has been sent a minimum of three months in advance.

It is far easier to withdraw an *agreement* than an *autorisation*, despite the fact that the same level of quality is expected of both. The DDASS is responsible for inspecting the quality of these services, acting under the authority of the Prefet. It is not yet certain, however, how far the authorities will implement their powers of inspection and regulation. Unlike in Sweden or the United Kingdom, services in France are not accustomed to working in the spirit of cost-effectiveness and quality evaluation. The DDASS carries out its quality inspection by interviewing the service user and his/her family. Additional interviews are conducted by a doctor and a psychologist, to check the health and mental well-being of the service user. If abuse is revealed by the inspector, the inspection file is passed over to the local public prosecutor, the Procureur de la Republique. The service provider must then prove that no infraction occurred. From a legal point of view, organisations working under the *prestataire* model are employers with legal rights and responsibilities as any other organisation, as per the labour code. Enforcement of aspects of the employment law is the responsibility of the Local Directorate for Work, Employment and Professional Bodies (Direction Départementale du Travail, de L'emploi et de La Formation Professionnelle) (DDTEFP). The problem is that the DDASS and the DDTEFP do not work together to conduct joint quality inspections. Some *départements* have started to develop guidelines for partnership, improving the effectiveness of the inspection process.

With regard to quality accreditation, if a service provider wishes to retain a particular quality mark, members of the federation owning that quality mark must carry out the assessment. Every five years, findings from the assessments must be given to the local authorities. The assessment focuses on quality of service and does not consider pricing and cost-effectiveness.

Quality enforcement mechanisms are in their infancy in France and an analysis of their effectiveness is not yet possible. It can be seen that there is inconsistency in quality checks across the different models of community-based support service provision. The trend for development of multifarious quality marks can also be seen as potentially confusing.

Reconfiguring the Residential Support Market

Different types of residential placement have been developed in order to strengthen options for community living. However, institutions remain a dominant force on the market, and rather than being phased out, are seen as providing a valid solution to the question of growing support needs.

New options for community living include the Transition Housing (Logement Transitionel), also known as Temporary Homes, and the Temporary Care in a Family Home Service (Maison Familiale D'Accueil Temporaire). This first option is for persons with disabilities living in institutions and wanting to step out into the community, but not feeling ready. The Logement Transitionel is a kind of a halfway house which enables a disabled person to adjust gradually to life outside an institution and to realise the opportunities and potential offered by a life in the community. It allows time to adapt and learn independent living skills to do with socialisation, leisure opportunities and employment. Contact is offered with professionals responsible for equipment and housing adaptations, enabling the disabled person to prepare to live in his or her own home, as well as professionals offering support with daily activities and life tasks, and professionals responsible for psychological support and health care. The transitional housing facility could be physically located within a regular SAVS service.

The Maison Familiale D'Accueil Temporaire is a scheme where persons with disabilities are placed to live with host families in the community. A family wanting to join this scheme must have approval from the head of the Conseil général. There is a limit of three persons with disabilities to each household. Approval is granted for a period of five years. Anyone interested in becoming a community host must undertake specific training and will undergo supervision from the social service authorities. A contract must be signed between the host and the disabled person. The contract sets out the terms and conditions of the placement and the rights and responsibilities of both the host and the disabled person, as well as information about costs and payment. There are two types of placement: a community placement and a therapeutic placement. With the latter type of placement, social support is provided for people who suffer from a mental impairment. The person who is the host is called Acceuilliant familliale. In 2008, there were 9,220 Acceuilliants familliale,

94 per cent of whom were women, and there were 7,327 persons with disabilities in family placements. The contract between a disabled person and the host family is based on a model of direct employment, or *gré à gré*. In France, there are few host families, maybe because the legal status of an *Acceuilliant familiale* is not yet well defined.[83]

The 2005 legislation offered an alternative to institutionalisation, but deinstitutionalisation is far from being under way. By the end of 1998, more than 660,000 people lived in institutional settings, with one-third having lived there for at least five years. Most of these were adults or older people. In 2000, only 40,000 had moved into the community. In 2000, less than 15 per cent of people living in the *foyer d'hebergement* moved back to the community. Between 1998 and 2000, more than 94 per cent of the older people living in institutions continued to do so.[84] Initially, following the reform, there was a tendency to build residential structures that were smaller by French institutional standards and could house only fifty to seventy people. These were not seen as economically viable and so they began to disappear in favour of larger placements.

Increasing the capacity of institutions is the government's approach to tackling the issues of an aging population. The French National Institute for Statistics and Economic Studies (Institut National de la Statistique et des Études Économiques) (INSEE) has predicted that by 2050, one-third of the French population will be older than sixty. This situation will lead to an increase in the number of people dependent on social and health care services. The INSEE has estimated that in 2040, more than 1.2 million senior citizens will need support with their basic daily life activities.[85] Originally, the February 2005 legislation stipulated that by 2010, the age limit for PCH would be removed. In September 2010, the government reneged on this. Instead, institutions are being geared up to increase their capacity by 20 per cent by 2020, to prepare for demographic changes. It is possible that such developments will be funded through financing from both the state and the Conseil général. The French Senate has stated that residential services for persons with disabilities should develop services dedicated to older persons with disabilities. In 2000, the go-ahead was given to build more than 2,000 new residential schemes for older people. There are many different types of residential housing; the Care Home for Older People (Maison d'Acceuil pour Personne Agées) (MAPA) is one of them. MAPAs are residential homes for disabled older people who are no longer able to live independently in their own home. The majority of MAPAs are in the centre of towns, but for disabled older people who do not wish to live in urban areas there are Rural Care Homes for Older People (Maison d'Acceuil Rurale pour Personne

[83] Rosso-Debord, V. (2008). *Vers un nouvel accueil familial des personnes âgées et des personnes handicapées.* Assemblee Nationale, Paris.

[84] Mormiche, P. (2001) *Le handicap en institution: le devenir des pensionnaires entre 1998 et 2000.* INSEE PREMIERE.

[85] Robert-Bobée, I. (2007). *Projections de population 2005–2050.* Économie Et Statistique.

Agées) (MARPA). MARPAs are similar to MAPAs, with a capacity to provide a home for fifteen to twenty older people. The market has also witnessed the development of nursing homes with in-house medical care.[86]

THE CHALLENGES TOWARDS ACTIVE CITIZENSHIP

The French disability support system remains under the shadow of institutionalisation, and as such, the aims of personalisation can only be partly fulfilled. The chapter has considered the socio-historical factors that allow segregationist and medicalised approaches to continue. The 2005 legislation introduced a personalised model of support through the creation of a new disability welfare infrastructure and benefit entitlements. This section considers the challenges faced in implementing the new infrastructure, including issues concerning the structure of the MDPH, insufficient resources and procedural delays and backlogs. The reforms of 2005 have yet to live up to their promise, and the low numbers of disabled French people opting for more personalised support options can be considered as attributable at least in part to the barriers caused by the challenges outlined in the next section. Implementation of the reforms is still a work in progress, but while they aim to enable persons with disabilities to take up their positions as equal citizens, they are held back by the continuing low profile attached to disability issues.

Challenges for the Local Agencies for Persons with Disabilities (MDPH)

Ninety-eight per cent of the Local Agencies for Persons with Disabilities – the MDPHs – have chosen to deliver their own services as a way of responding to the needs of the disabled population. MDPHs across the country do not follow the same structure. There are three different models of governance:

- Some MDPHs are fully integrated within the Conseil général, both in terms of location and administration. It is the head of the Conseil général who appoints the head of the MDPH, who is also a member of the Conseil général. He/she retains his/her duties as a member of the Conseil général, even after he/she has been appointed director of the MDPH. The staff of the Conseil général provide the services of the MDPH.[87]
- Some *départements* choose to have fully autonomous and independent MDPHs. Within this structure, the Conseil général is a stakeholder with the same importance as any other. An independent organisation services the MDPH. Only 4 per cent of MDPHs have this structure.
- The majority of *départements* have chosen a model whereby the MDPH is separated from the Conseil général both geographically and in terms of

---

[86] Inspectioin Generale Des Affaires Sociales (IGAS) (2007) *Rapport D'Activités*, IGAS, Paris.
[87] Blanc, P. (2009). *Le bilan des MDPH*. SENAT, Paris.

administration, but there are nevertheless strong links and a significant part of the workforce comes from other local administrative services. More than 56 per cent of MDPHs have adopted this structure.

One of the major problems facing MDPHs is a difficulty in attracting staff. One reason for this is that staff members do not gain good career prospects through working for the MDPH, as the recognition of the work is low. There is no specific system for recruiting staff to work for a MDPH. Initially, public servants from other local government areas agreed to go on secondment to an MDPH. At the end of their terms, the secondees were released to work in areas outside of the MDPH, according to their preference. In order to make up for the staff shortage, the MDPH started to hire people without a civil servant status on short-term contracts (no longer than two years). This employment policy created a staff turnover that negatively affected MDPH efficiency and the quality of their work. For example, MDPHs are known to provide inaccurate information.[88]

MDPHs do not have much financial resources of their own. The CNSA provides the largest contributions to the funding and there is an imbalance between the amounts received by the CNSA and the other GIP members. From 2005 to 2007, the contribution from the CNSA was approximately €120 million. Over this same period, the state had only given €14 million per year. Central government provides staffing resources from other departments, but the value of this contribution is difficult to evaluate. As for other members of the GIP, their financial or in-kind contribution is not very significant.

The February 2005 legislation also proposed the creation of a Departmental Compensation Fund (Fond Départemental de Compensation) (FDC) within every MDPH. The aim of FDC was to provide an additional source of funding for disability-related costs not fully covered by the PCH. However, in September 2006, only half of all *départements* had an FDC. Furthermore, the amount of money available from the FDC differs greatly from one *département* to another. This is largely because the size of contributions given to the FDC differs so markedly; for example, the *mutuelle* contribution can vary from €5,000 to €160,000 depending on the *département*.

The CDAPH and Its Multidisciplinary Team

Despite the positive measures introduced by PCH and APA which have given individual disabled and older people the opportunity to purchase their own support, the use of these benefits is still tied to traditional support services and is under the supervision of the Commission for the Independence and Rights of Disabled People

---

[88] Branchu C. T. M. (2010) *Bilan du fonctionnement et du rôle des Maisons départementales des personnes handicapées.* IGAS, Paris.

(Commission des Droits et de l'Autonomie des Personnes Handicapées) (CDAPH). According to the 2005 legislation, CDAPH must be comprised of a multidisciplinary team. Most members are professionals from health and social care fields, such as doctors, social workers and nurses. This encourages the view of disability as a medical and impairment issue rather than an environmental one. While large institutions are considered a valid option for disability support, persons with disabilities continue to lack the power to truly significantly shape the market through consumer power. If there was greater representation of other professionals in psychology, occupational therapy, and disability employment, there would be a change in perspective within the commission on how disability is viewed. As things stand right now, however, when *associations* are involved with the commission, they do not have full access to information on an individual's file for reasons of confidentiality, but this means that they cannot fully respond to the situation of the individual.

A final challenge is the amount of time it takes to respond to an application for PCH. On average, it takes between twenty and thirty hours to assess. Although applications for PCH are coming in slower than had been anticipated, MDPH commissions are starting to become overwhelmed. As a result, time taken to process applications is unacceptably long. Disability organisations welcome their involvement in the process, but they all also point to the length of time it takes as a problem for persons with disabilities. The delays are partly attributable to the fact that the MDPH inherited its files from the agencies that preceded it, the COTOREP and the CDES. Since September 2006, it has been noted that the size of the backlog differs from one area to another; some have managed to reduce their processing time, whereas in others this has actually increased.[89]

PCH: A Benefit That Has Yet to Live Up to Expectation

The introduction of PCH was the cornerstone of the 2005 legislation, and was intended to replace the old ATCP benefit. In 2005, the French government estimated that 120,000 people would be eligible for PCH. As of December 2006, only 70,000 persons with disabilities had applied. By this same date, MDPHs have assessed 23,000 applications, but only half were approved. By the end of 2006, only 7,700 benefits were paid. Applications for PCH came in slower than expected. There are a number of reasons which could explain this: first, changing to PCH entailed changing over from what was, for many persons with disabilities, a long-established support system. It was not mandatory for people on ACTP to be assessed for PCH, and initially there were no clear cost comparisons to show the financial implications of the switch.

---

[89] Accueil Association (2007) *Maisons départementales des personnes handicapées: De l'idéal à la réalité*, http://www.arcat-sante.org/JDS/article/758/Maisons_departementales_des_personnes_handicapees_De_l_ideal_a_la_realite (accessed 2 August 2011).

A major issue still facing the PCH system is how to make payments and monitor spending. Benefits paid for the purchase of personal assistance can only be spent on personal assistance; if the money is spent on something other than personal assistance, the disabled person must pay it back to the state. Many MDPHs tried a system whereby they refunded personal assistance costs on production of a receipt by the disabled person. This caused significant difficulty, in that many persons with disabilities did not have the out-of-pocket money to pay before reimbursement; for this reason, this system was abandoned by every MDPH in 2007.

The Enduring Legacy of Institutions

In the French context, it is not appropriate to discuss a 'crisis' in institutions, because there has never been one which has been exposed as a public scandal. The institutional model is still persisting, with plans to increase capacity and demand for places outstripping supply. Under the influence of Europe, legislation was passed in 2002, reforming institutional support to make it more person-centred and to give service users more of a say, but there has never been a situation where the closure of institutions and phasing out of this type of support were publicly declared.

The role of disability institutions was initially defined in the 1975 legislation and was only modernised twenty-seven years later with the law of 2002: the Law Reforming Health and Social Care (Loi rénovant l'action sociale et médico-sociale). That law redefined institutional objectives and widened their remit from just being a place for persons with disabilities to live to having a role in promoting social cohesion, and to enabling persons with disabilities to fulfil their rights and responsibilities as French citizens, free from abuse and mistreatment. This law led to some important changes in the structure of disability institutions, with an emphasis on empowerment. Unlike the 1975 legislation, which was a law created for persons with disabilities, the 2002 legislation was created with them. It was one of the first times that a French law recognised a disabled person's free will. With this new law, the French Parliament changed the rules regulating institutions for persons with disabilities. New measures that guaranteed the rights of the people who lived in these institutions appeared.

First, a charter of rights and freedoms for people living in these institutions was written shortly after the passage of the 2002 legislation. The Order of September 2003,[90] the Charter of the Rights and Freedoms of a Disabled Person in Care (Charte Des Droits Et Libertés De La Personne Accueillie), highlighted the concept of non-discrimination inside an institution, as well as the right to self-determination and protection from harm, the right to access information, respect for family bonds, religious belief, dignity and intimacy. Second, if there is a conflict between a disabled

---

[90] The charter can be consulted at the following Web site: http://www.solidarite.gouv.fr/IMG/pdf/EXE_A4_ACCUEIL.pdf (accessed 25 August 2011).

person and the institution he/she lives in, local authorities are now entitled to appoint someone to help the disabled person to defend his/her interests. Third, the internal policies of any institution must now be developed according to a standard process described in an official decree. The policies for every institution must now contain a charter of rights and responsibilities for every disabled person living and working there. Fourth, every institution must now have a Community Council on which disabled residents or their representatives can sit. This enables everyone to take an active part in the life of the institution. Finally, a personalised contract that describes all the services which will be provided by the institution must be signed by the director of the institution and the individual accessing its services. This is a contract that must be respected by both parties.

The 2002 legislation represented a change in the way people living in such institutions were seen. They were no longer seen as passive recipients of care, and consultation became compulsory. Institutions were no longer reserved exclusively for professional staff and persons with disabilities. Families of persons with disabilities started to have a more active role in the life of these institutions. Greater transparency to persons with disabilities' families has limited mistreatment experienced by persons with disabilities in the institutions.

Nevertheless, the French disability support system has remained largely institutionalised. Information compiled for the 2002 Loi Relative Aux Institutions Sociales Et Médico-Sociales describes a situation where demand for places in institutions outstrips provision. Demand for placements is so high that Belgians describe an 'invasion' Wallonia by disabled and older French people, and in 2009, there were an estimated 6,500 disabled children and adults in Belgian institutions in the region.[91] Over the period between 2001 and 2006, institutional placements for disabled adults in France increased by 20 per cent, with an increase in sheltered workshop placements of 13 per cent and residential placements up by 19 per cent; there was a discharge rate of 6 per cent, but 3 per cent of these were transfers to other institutional placements.[92] We have seen that the French government's answer to an aging population is to increase its institutional capacity, and at the national conference on disability in June 2008, the government announced the creation of 50,000 new places in institutions and community support services. Deinstitutionalisation is not on the French government's agenda. It is also not likely to be the subject of any persons with disabilities' protests, because the main vehicle for voicing protest is represented by the same *associations*, which run the institutions.

In other European countries, revelations of mistreatment and abuse have caused public outcry and led to deinstitutionalisation, with disability organisations leading

91 Please refer to http://www.asph.be/NR/rdonlyres/9026C6C8–6474-401C-8779–1DD3051E3E9D/o/asph17leplacementdespersonneshandicap percentC3 percentA9esfran percentC3 percentA7 aiseenBelgique1.pdf (accessed 21 January 2012).
92 Barral, C. and Velche, D. (2010). *Country Report on Equality of Educational and Training Opportunities for Young Disabled People*, ANED, p. 24.

the campaigns. In France, there has been no equivalent outcry, although abuse must surely occur given the findings of the European Ad Hoc Committee report, which argues that institutions are, by the nature of their set-up, dangerous places which encourage oppression and powerlessness[93]; indeed serious abuse is systemic and endemic within any environment which isolates and segregates a group of people, where the balance of power acts against them. Despite the recent legislative reforms of institutions, it would be unlikely if institutions in France were different in this regard from institutions in any other part of the world.[94]

It is not yet clear the extent to which France's ratification of the CRPD in 2009 will change this legacy of institutionalisation. Similarly, it remains uncertain the level of impact recent European policies will have. As Chapter 2 identified, the EU Charter of Fundamental Rights recognises the right of persons with disabilities 'to benefit from measures designed to ensure their independence, social and occupational integration and participation in the life of the community.' In addition, the recent EC disability strategy 2010-2020, *A Renewed Commitment to a Barrier Free Europe*, also highlights the need to remove barriers to participation in society. Cumulatively, these international and regional policy documents will no doubt serve as an important benchmark for assessing France's continued endorsement of institutions.

COST-EFFECTIVENESS OF THE DISABILITY SUPPORT SYSTEM

There is not a strong tradition of undertaking evaluations of the 'cost-effectiveness' of public programmes in France. Reports and analyses of disability support prepared within France contain instead figures relating to numbers of persons with disabilities and categories of institutions and support services.[95] This is not to say that costs are not a concern relevant to French policy: encouraging private companies to come onto the social care market was motivated by cost-cutting aims. Moreover, disability reform involved decentralisation, devolving power to local government. With greater responsibility for disability support, local government now faces greater responsibility for the fiscal burden. For example, public spending on care needs for older people amounted to approximately 21,602 million francs (approximately

---

93 EC Ad hoc.
94 Moreover, evidence points to the contrary. In 2000, Emile Louis, a special transport driver, confessed to raping and murdering seven young women with learning disabilities during the period between 1975 and 1979. The families of the murdered girls fought for justice for more than twenty years: the day institution the girls attended had not even reported them missing, initially dismissing the incidents as runaway cases. Both Emile Louis and the *directeur* of the institution had been accused of sexually abusing disabled young women in separate incidents, which indicates a prevalence of abuse. Moreover, the fact that such a number of service users could conceivably run away over such a short period, without raising alarm (four of the seven went missing in just one year, 1977), suggests that persons with disabilities were not generally satisfied with their situation.
95 Direction de la Recherche, des Etudes, de l'Evaluation et des Statistiques. Various reports available at: www.sante.gouv.fr/drees/.

€3,293 million) in 1988, with 42 per cent from *département* spending and 58 per cent from health insurance schemes and the pension system; but, with the introduction of APA, the commitment of the health and pension system gradually decreased, whereas *département* spending on older people rose from €2,672 million in 2001 to €5,746 million in 2004.

Local government has an interest in minimising costs for disability-related support, but there is no official correlation between policy trends and costs analyses of relative models of service.

CONCLUSION

Government approaches to disability underwent a significant shift in France with the advent of the new century. Whereas the 1975 Loi d'Orientation had created a notion of *handicap*, according to which all persons with disabilities had a right to support and entitlements regardless of the provenance of their impairment, the 2005 legislation defined disability according to a *situation de handicap*, in which individuals found themselves disabled as a result of society's inability to adequately meet the needs arising from their impairment. Legislation reforming institutions and establishing a concept of disability compensation introduced personalised approaches to disability, in a system previously dominated by medicalised categorisation. The implementation of universalist approaches, introduced through the 1975 legislation, was supported by enforcement measures brought in through the 2005 legislation, to ensure accessibility of public buildings and transport. Personal assistance services providing community-based support were sanctioned as they were seen as more efficient, and alternatives to institutionalisation developed on a cash-for-care basis, which placed consumer power in the hands of persons with disabilities and enabled greater choice and control over the support needed to live an ordinary life. Bureaucratic challenges were faced in the application of the aforementioned measures, but this is to be expected in the development of any new system. The role of persons with disabilities and their representatives in pushing for change, and their subsequent close involvement in the development of the legislation, is notable and accounts for the strong value base of equality and citizenship underpinning the new approaches.

One important point of continuity within approaches to disability in French policy is an emphasis on employment. This is not surprising, given the historical links between work, social protection and welfare. Work is also integral to the concept of *solidarité* that typifies French national identity. Integration to French society is therefore heavily dependent upon access to employment. This attitude was fundamental to the rehabilitative approaches which dominated disability support in the last century. It also persists through recent legislation, whereby a whole raft of measures have been introduced and strengthened to support persons with disabilities into work and to prevent discrimination in the workplace.

The popular belief of French people is that in terms of disability support, France is less advanced than countries like the United States or Sweden. The truth is more complicated. Disabled students' movements of the 1960s and 1970s never grew into an established user-led Independent Living movement. Today, there are only a few French Centres for Independent Living and still no movement to speak about. However, despite the influence of France's unique socio-historical factors on the development of its welfare system, France has matured its very own approach to disability support, based on a recognition of the rights of persons with disabilities made concrete through the 2005 legislation. While this has signalled a radical shift in France's disability policy, overall it has been characterised by Bruno Gaurier, the advisor to the Executive Board of the French Council of Disabled for European Affairs, as 'a glimpse through the keyhole', where instead he wishes for 'an open door for inclusion'.[96]

---

[96] See http://www.kas.de/wf/en/33.30417/ (accessed 15 March 2012).

PART III

The Development of Reform in the Disability Support Sector in Ireland

9

Tracing the Origins of Disability Support in Ireland

INTRODUCTION

In the preceding chapters, we saw how different countries have shaped law and policy reform to enable people with disabilities to achieve greater participation in society. Across all jurisdictions, there is an evolving policy landscape which is increasingly reflecting the goals of the CRPD, particularly its focus on creating a meaningful life in the community. However, at the same time it is possible to evidence the enduring challenges involved in moving from historical institutional service environments. To varying extents, jurisdictions have animated various mechanisms to give people more choice and control over their supports and driven reform within the service sector. These comparative examples thus illustrate the various ways in which countries are trying to ensure that disability supports are implemented consistent with human rights principles and directed towards fostering full citizenship for persons with disabilities.

In this chapter, we turn attention to the case of reform in Ireland. It provides a more in-depth understanding of a site embarking on the transition from conventional welfare and service delivery to a more personalised, individually tailored support system aligned to the broader goals of citizenship. At the same time, it provides a deeper insight into the challenging dimensions of system-wide transformation given its position at the turning point of reform. Despite the challenges facing Ireland, the chapter also identifies the initial strands of reform as well as grass-roots innovation, which demonstrate the potential for change within the Irish context. It identifies how different actors have unlocked deeply entrenched institutional service regimes.

In some respects, Ireland has a history of institutionalisation very similar to the other comparative jurisdictions. Yet the scale and the almost complete reliance on institutions in Ireland at key moments in its history were staggering. As this chapter details, Ireland at one time had the highest rate of institutionalisation in the world.[1] This was, of course, very pronounced when it came to persons with intellectual disabilities – as well as those who were civilly committed to mental institutions. An intrinsic factor in this history of institutional care was the enduring legacy of the Poor Law in Ireland, particularly its philosophy of welfare as a last resort. The rate of institutionalisation peaked in the mid-1980s, and from this time, Ireland has been grappling with the development of providing less congregated support in the community.

A second key theme in this historical account is the considerable imprint of the Protestant and Roman Catholic Churches on the history and evolution of social services for people with disabilities in Ireland. Both churches and religious bodies associated with them, such as the Society of St Vincent de Paul, undertook significant roles in the development and management of support provision. There was nothing inherently wrong with this. However, it tended to perpetuate long-ingrained social assumptions about passivity and policies based on (or in some sense referable to) pity and care as distinct from citizenship. And, as recent official reports of abuse have highlighted, it did create a highly dangerous vacuum of impunity. Religious competition between both churches became apparent, as the religious orders competed to provide denominationally separate services. This particular history marks Ireland as unique in terms of the way in which its support provision developed. Indeed, the role of the Roman Catholic Church throughout this history set the country apart in terms of the mixed model of welfare provision which resulted. The relative withdrawal of the churches from this sector in recent times has exposed a legacy that requires some reform.

While these two themes – Ireland's scale of institutionalisation and the role of the churches – are illustrative of Ireland's distinct cultural and political context, in reality, Ireland shares much of the same history of paternalism, medicalisation and segregation evident in the other comparative countries prior to their processes of reform. Importantly, the tide has been reversed, with Ireland now committed to the same goals of reform as many of the other countries. It has signed but not yet ratified the UN CRPD, but has signalled its intention to do so. Many examples exist where golden threads of reform are already evident. More recently, Ireland has had to re-examine its fledgling community care policy of moving people into community homes with the same organisational restraints, staff work practices, funding models and management as before. Ireland therefore exists at the cusp of transformation towards more person-driven support. As a result, there is an opportunity to learn from the mistakes of other jurisdictions, particularly regarding the *trans*-institutionalisation of people with disabilities from one congregated setting to another. The analysis will therefore resonate not only with an Irish audience but with all people interested in identifying strategic measures to

---

[1] For a more comprehensive history, see Finnane, M. (1981) *Insanity and the Insane in Post-Famine Ireland.* Croom and Noble, London.

ensure disabled citizens can participate effectively in society on an equal basis with others.

To understand the changes which have evolved, this chapter examines the history of policy decisions and legislation which lies behind Ireland's recent shift and the enduring legacies which resist such change. The present chapter examines the history of disability support from the early development of institutional 'care' in Ireland up until 2006. For accuracy, it uses some historical terminology from earlier legislation and policy, which has now become outmoded. The next chapter then provides a contemporary analysis of the initial strands of reform within support delivery as they are emerging today. It examines the current policy commitments and the extent of person-driven quality support in the existing system.

THE EARLY DEVELOPMENT OF ASYLUMS

As stated, Ireland shared a similar history of institutionalisation with many of the previously mentioned comparative jurisdictions. Indeed, Ireland was somewhat of a 'testing ground' for institutionalisation in Britain, which set the country out as a test subject in many respects. As this section examines, by the time Britain had legislated for the development of asylums in England (and similarly in the United States), Ireland had an even greater rate of persons committed to these settings.

Ireland shared much of the legislative history of disability support as England prior to independence in 1922. All Irish legislation had to be sanctioned by the British monarch and the parliament in London during the eighteenth and nineteenth centuries. In 1720, a British Act known as the Sixth of George I gave the English parliament the right to make laws for Ireland. During this time, the Irish parliament in Dublin was prepared to accept a subordinate role in return for England defending the Protestant oligarchy which pervaded Ireland. The only function of the Irish House of Commons, wholly Protestant and largely controlled by wealthy landlords, was its powers of taxation.[2] Irish affairs were managed by a quasi-colonial administration, headed by the Lord-Lieutenant of Ireland, the Chief Secretary and the Under-Secretary at the Chief Secretary's Office.[3]

During this time, there were a small number of almshouses across the country of Ireland. An almshouse was a residential building for the poor, sick or elderly of a parish. They were originally founded by the church and generally became local charities relying on donations for funding. Poorhouses (also known as Workhouses or Houses of Industry) were also established in Ireland. A poorhouse was a place where destitute people who were unable to support themselves could go to live. Those who entered had to give up what they possessed, including their house and any land. Those who were well enough health-wise had to work for their keep. The use of poorhouses was initially on a much smaller scale than was the case in

[2] Foster, R. F. (2001) *The Oxford History of Ireland.* Oxford University Press, Oxford.
[3] Finnane, *supra*, n. 1, at 130.

England and Wales. The first of these was built in Dublin following the Dublin Workhouse Act 1703 at the south-west of James's Street. It provided for four classes of person: disabled men, disabled women, male beggars, and 'strolling women'. The poorhouse also developed a 'lunatic ward' for those with mental health difficulties. Other poorhouses began to appear throughout the century in other cities in Ireland; in Cork (in 1735), Limerick (in 1774) and Waterford (in 1779).[4]

Shortly after the Act of Union 1880, which created the United Kingdom of Great Britain and Ireland, the British government began to enquire into the uses of institutions for the care of persons with disabilities. A Bill was introduced in the session of 1805 to establish four government-funded provincial asylums in Ireland (one in each province: Leinster, Munster, Connaught and Ulster).[5] The Bill was overlooked until later, yet in the meantime, a grant was made by Parliament to build the first public institution solely for the reception of 'lunatics' and 'idiots'[6] between 1810 and 1815 – the Richmond Asylum in Dublin, replacing the lunatic ward in the Dublin poorhouse. It has been more popularly known as Grangegorman because of the street on which it was located.

Shortly after Richmond was built, on 4 March 1817, a Select Committee of the House of Commons was appointed to consider the expediency of making further provision for the 'lunatic' poor of Ireland. The *Report of the Select Committee to Consider the State of the Lunatic Poor in Ireland* (1817) resolved that the poorhouses in Dublin, Cork, Waterford and Limerick should no longer accommodate 'idiots' and 'lunatics'. The Report led to Britain becoming the first nation in the world to pass legislation (in Ireland) to create a system of asylums – the Irish Lunatic Asylums for the Poor Act 1817.

By the middle of the nineteenth century, Ireland was fast becoming entirely dependent on institutional 'care' as it was the only option for people with disabilities outside of local, primarily religious-led, charitable provision.[7] This was copper-fastened by the Irish Poor Law Act 1837 which saw a more extensive development of poorhouses where people with disabilities continued to receive 'indoor relief.' Indoor relief was classified as that provided within the poorhouses.

Significantly, by the mid-nineteenth century, the Irish Famine (1845–1850) caused almost irreparable damage to the fabric of Irish society and had enormous implications on the rudimentary institutional provision of supports for people with disabilities. Both the physical effects of starvation, such as fever and malnutrition, and the social effects of emigration and rural isolation meant that the institutional

---

4 Higgenbothem (n.d.) *History of Irish Workhouses*, http://www.workhouses.org.uk/ (accessed 10 March 2012).

5 Bill for establishing Provincial Asylums for Lunatics and Idiots in Ireland (1805).

6 These were terms used by the medical profession to describe persons with mental health problems and those with intellectual disabilities.

7 The role of the Catholic Church became more dominant in education and social care provision in Ireland after the Catholic Emancipation in 1823.

infrastructure which was developing became quickly overburdened. Indeed, the level of emigration and the disproportionate number of people turned away from the United States and Canada and sent back to Ireland meant the Famine created a context in Ireland where the most destitute were left behind.[8] In addition to the immediate effects at the time, the Famine also led to many intergenerational effects, such as the rupture caused by emigration of informal family care networks for those in need of support, as well as long-term health effects on the cohort of the population who outlived the Famine. Given the resulting deprivation from the Famine throughout the remainder of the century, the Irish Poor Relief Extension Act 1847 permitted the granting of 'outdoor relief' to certain specified groups, such as the sick and disabled, as well as widows with two or more legitimate children.[9] Outdoor relief was where the dependents would be left in their own homes and would be given either a 'dole' of money on which to live or be given relief in kind – clothes and food, for example.[10] However, the local Boards of Guardians varied in their attitude to 'outdoor relief' – some were more liberal in their approach than others.[11] Apart from this residual intervention, most people had to rely on private charities and church-based religious orders.

People with physical disabilities throughout this period shared an equivalent story of paternalism, institutionalisation and abandonment. In general, physical disability was widespread throughout much of the eighteenth and nineteenth centuries and was frequently seen as a medical affliction, with poor nutrition often causing permanent physical disability. According to Cooter (2000), poor health accompanied the lives of the impoverished with such prevalence that disability was widespread and generally accepted as 'normal', and that the degree of severity was the only provision of a vague boundary between ill health and disablement.[12] Children with rickets, for example, were a common sight in the poorer parts of towns and cities, before the introduction of a comprehensive dispensary system.[13] Dispensaries were extensions to infirmaries (early hospitals) where people could attend a medical officer, or ask for them to attend in the person's home. Dispensaries were under the control of the Poor Law Commissioners and were oriented towards the outdoor relief of the sick poor. Until the Famine, dispensaries were only developed in an ad hoc fashion and

---

[8] See O'Gráda, C. (1993) *Ireland: Before and After the Famine*. Manchester University Press, Manchester.

[9] Poor Law Commission Office (1848), Circular to the Clerk of each Union, Dublin, 8 June.

[10] Ironically, the New Poor Law (1838) attempted to curtail outdoor relief in England. However the orders regulating outdoor relief were largely evaded by both rural and urban unions, many of which continued to grant outdoor relief, particularly to unemployed and poor men.

[11] North Clare Historical Society (n.d.) *Outdoor Relief, A Guide to Ennistymon Union 1839–1850*, Clare County Library.

[12] Cooter, R. (2000) 'The Disabled Body', in Cooter, R. and Pickstone, J. (eds.) *Medicine in the Twentieth Century*. London: Harwood Academic Publishers. pp. 368–383. See also: Hutchison, I. (2002) 'Disability in Nineteenth Century Scotland – the Case of Marion Brown', *University of Sussex Journal of Contemporary History* 5:1–18.

[13] *The Oxford Companion to Irish History*. 2007. Oxford University Press, Oxford.

were primarily used for the diagnosis and treatment of tuberculosis.[14] The medical disaster of the Famine persuaded the state to develop the dispensary system further. The Medical Charities Act 1851 divided Ireland into more than 700 districts, each with at least one salaried medical officer.

For blind persons during this time, there was an equal history of hardship and isolation. In addition to the poorhouses and almshouses, a number of charitable institutions were established from largely Protestant benefactors[15] to house blind persons throughout this period (e.g. Simpson's Hospital for Blind and Gouty Men in 1781 and the Richmond National Institution for the Instruction of the Industrious Blind in 1809). The initial purpose of these institutions was largely occupational training for respectable and well-disposed individuals who were rendered incapable of earning a subsistence by the effects of blindness.[16] However, in reality, these institutions did subsequently cater to a broader group of blind persons including those deemed indigent. Some time later, in 1858, a Catholic asylum for the blind was founded on the site of the former Drumcondra Castle in Dublin. Here, the emphasis was on the spiritual and moral guidance of children who were blind. The absence of any meaningful state provision meant that religious charity thus provided for the blind institutions.

The National League of the Blind of Ireland Trust (NLB) marked a shift from these earlier philanthropic institutions. It was established near the end of the century in 1898, and became a blind organisation run *by* the blind for the blind. One of the earliest campaigns of the NLB, latterly and reluctantly supported by the voluntary organisations, was for state aid for the blind, which led to the setting up of the Departmental Committee on the Welfare of the Blind on 7 May 1914. The committee was to sit for three years and reported on 20 July 1917. Its findings and recommendations were to presage the Blind Persons Act 1920 which introduced the Blind Pension in Ireland.

Finally, it is worth noting that many deaf people were also housed in the same poorhouses as individuals with disabilities. They were employed in weaving, hosiery, comb-making and tailoring with the proceeds of their produce funding their maintenance.[17] In terms of educating deaf children, generally, the lack of options available in deaf education in the early nineteenth century meant families, who could afford to, sent their children to England. In response to this, once again the Catholic and Protestant Churches became involved in teaching sign language, with

---

14 Barrington, R. (1987) *Health Medicine & Politics in Ireland, 1900–1970.* Institute for Public Administration, Dublin.

15 One noticeable feature of the institutions is that the same Protestant family names recur. The Crosthwaites, the Wades, trhe Brownes and the Knoxs had been involved with many of these Protestant blind welfare institutions.

16 Callery, F. (2011) *The History of the Blind of Ireland.* National Council for the Blind of Ireland, Dublin.

17 Pollard, R. (2006) *The Avenue: A History of the Claremont Institution.* Denzille Press, Dun Laoighaire.

the Quakers establishing a school in Dublin called Claremont and the Catholic religious orders subsequently establishing two deaf schools in Cabra, Dublin: one school for girls and one for boys.

Ultimately, the support of persons with disabilities became entrenched in institutional care during this early period of 'care' in Ireland. The legacy from this era was an elaborate system of institutions with a broad range of allied professional staff trained to offer support for the individual within the confines of these segregated sites. This established an infrastructure of care which concretised the cultural and societal thinking of the time, which, as we shall later see, has lasted until present times.

IRELAND'S EARLY WELFARE EFFORTS (1922 – MID-1950S)

In the aftermath of the Anglo-Irish Treaty in 1922, Ireland was split into the Republic of Ireland and Northern Ireland. Independence from the United Kingdom had an obvious effect on the future developments of social support in Ireland. At the outset, the Proclamation of Independence in 1916 adopted by Dáil Éireann (Irish Parliament), the revolutionary parliament of the Irish Republic at its first meeting on 21 January 1919, made a bold statement towards protecting the rights of all the children of the nation. It represented a rejection of Victorian Law and set about a new consciousness at the outset, to reach clear blue water from earlier British rule:

> The Republic guarantees religious and civil liberty, equal rights and equal opportunities to all its citizens, and declares its resolve to pursue the happiness and prosperity of the whole nation and all of its parts, cherishing all of the children of the nation equally and oblivious of the differences carefully fostered by an alien government.[18]

Similarly, the Programme for Democratic Action of the First Dáil in 1919 was a broad multifaceted vision of sovereignty which not only signified political independence, but also encompassed social justice and harmony as well as economic prosperity and cultural autonomy as the basic values and aspirations of Irish society. In particular, it stated the need for a shift from earlier degrading forms of care towards a 'sympathetic native scheme':

> The Irish Republic fully realizes the necessity of abolishing the present odious, degrading and foreign Poor Law System, substituting therefore a sympathetic native scheme for the care of the Nation's aged and infirm, who shall not be regarded as a burden, but rather entitled to the Nation's gratitude and consideration. Likewise it shall be the duty of the Republic to take such measures as will safeguard the

---

[18] Ireland's Proclamation of Independence, 1916.

health of the people and ensure the physical as well as the moral well-being of the Nation.[19]

Despite these commitments, the reality over the next couple of decades fell far short. Even though the Irish Free State was founded on the promise of getting rid of the Poor Law, it was the United Kingdom that in fact did so first and more thoroughly. This gap between the 'myth system' of Independence – especially the promise to cherish 'all the children of the nation equally' – and the 'operation system' of law and policy in the 1920s and 1930s was stark. Perhaps it was inevitable given the relative decline of wealth in Ireland until the 1960s.[20] Throughout the 1920s and 1930s, successive Irish governments maintained a conservative ethos after the 'revolution' of separation from the United Kingdom. During the first ten years of independence, there was little development in social welfare for people with disabilities or families. In practice, this meant that the institutional ethos of Victorian times was not challenged and whatever services emerged would do so without direct state provision and without state scrutiny. As a result, the enduring dead hand of the Poor Law lived on.

The new state adopted a very specific philosophy in terms of its support being a 'last resort', which meant that whatever services which emerged in the private or 'voluntary sphere' would be given considerable leeway. This instinctual reflex of the early Irish Free State to remain aloof was copper-fastened into place by the doctrine of subsidiarity which was announced by the Catholic Church in 1931 with the Papal Encyclical, *Quadragesimo Anno* (on reconstruction of the social order).[21] Essentially this doctrine meant that the state's authority to legitimately enter the private sphere of the family (to directly perform functions or provide services or at least regulate the same) was narrowed down to circumstances where actors in the private sphere proved clearly unequal to the task. The Church felt that the state should refrain from intervening in economic and social affairs unless charitable provision and private philanthropy failed to provide the necessary support. The Encyclical stated: 'It is an injustice and at the same time a great evil and disturbance of right order to assign to a greater and higher association what lesser and subordinate organisations can do.'[22]

---

[19] Programme for Democratic Action, 1919.

[20] *Supra*, n. 18.

[21] The principle of subsidiarity was also clearly defined by the earlier Papal Encyclical, *Rerum Novarum* (1891), which stated, 'the contention, then, that the civil government should at its option intrude into and exercise intimate control over the family and household is a great and pernicious error'. However this earlier Encyclical had minimal impact in Ireland, unlike its successor, *Quadragesimo Anno*. (Extract from *Rerum Novarum* Encyclical of Pope Leo XIII on Capital and Labour, 15 May 1891, para 3).

[22] Quadragesimo Anno Encyclical of Pope Pius XI. (1931) *On Reconstruction of the Social Order*, to Our Venerable Brethren, the Patriarchs, Primates, Archbishops, Bishops, and Other Ordinaries.

The Catholic Church had already become heavily involved in welfare and education provision since Catholic Emancipation[23] in 1829. With subsidiarity, people with disabilities and their families came to depend on being supported by the church-based religious orders and charities. In particular, the Catholic and Protestant churches became very proactive in the education and training for employment of persons who were blind or deaf. The involvement of both churches was driven by a broader goal to administer the spiritual and pastoral care to people with disabilities.

This religious involvement culminated in the handing-over of residential intellectual disability services from the state to the control of the Roman Catholic Church at the beginning of the 1950s. Dr Vincent J. Dolphin was appointed Inspector of Mental Hospitals in 1953. He was instructed to 'get in touch with various religious orders in the country with a view to expanding whatever service was already provided'.[24] This would have been suitable if this expansion of service was to form part of a fully comprehensive service designed to work in tandem with the statutory bodies, but this was not what happened. The *entire* service for people with intellectual disabilities was ceded to a few religious orders.[25] While the Church took on the delivery of this care, the government continued to provide funding for these services. It was at this time that all the mental hospitals were renamed with saints' names from the Bible. For example, an overflow of Richmond Asylum was built and called St Ita's; Grangegorman was changed to St Brendan's; Ballinasloe to St Brigid's; and Mullingar to St Loman's.

However, while these measures appear surprising in today's context, it was clear that many actors in both government and the Church thought that this was the best solution to the problems associated with state care of people with disabilities. However, it was also clear that both state and Church motivations were focussed at the time on other bigger issues. The state was focussed on getting Ireland 'back on track' in terms of its economic development. Meanwhile, Church motivations were to underpin religious objectives. It sought the spiritual development of children with disabilities. To a large extent, disability policy was left to one side and remained entrenched in the earlier ideology of care in institutions. It was seen as

---

[23] Catholic Emancipation was a process in Great Britain and Ireland in the late eighteenth and early nineteenth centuries, which involved reducing and removing many of the restrictions on Roman Catholics which had been introduced by the Act of Uniformity (which was designed to establish some sort of religious orthodoxy within the English church) and the penal laws (which sought to discriminate against Roman Catholics and Protestant dissenters in favour of members of the established Church of Ireland).

[24] Ryan, A. (1999) *Walls of Silence: Ireland's Policy Towards People with a Mental Disability*. Red Lion Press, Kilkenny.

[25] This handover was arranged with considerable grants of land and buildings made to religious orders from the government. According to Sweeney (2010), the terms and conditions of this settlement between the Department of Health and the Church were made in private. No explicit White Paper or legislation publicly defined the terms of settlement. For a full discussion on the privacy of this settlement, see Sweeney, J. (2010) 'Attitudes of Catholic Religious Orders towards Children and Adults with an Intellectual Disability in Postcolonial Ireland', *Nursing Inquiry* 17(2): 95–110.

best practice to remove children with disabilities from society and 'care' for them in these segregated sites. The voice of persons with disabilities was ultimately not heard at this time. No matter how well intentioned the state and Church's decision, its result cemented a self-perpetuating cycle of social exclusion, low self-esteem and discrimination.

During this period of change, it was clear that the government needed to respond to the problem of the increasing numbers of persons being involuntarily committed as psychiatric patients in the institutions – which they began referring to as the mental hospitals – which were reaching crisis level. There were some 17,708 individuals resident in asylums in the Republic of Ireland in 1942.[26] In response, the Mental Treatment Act 1945 was enshrined with an explicit intention to stem the ever-rising tide of admission.[27] The legislation mandated the creation of outpatient services, voluntary admissions and research facilities.[28] The Act removed the process of committal from the judicial arena and placed it in the hands of 'authorised medical officers', who were registered medical practitioners.

Significantly, part 15 of the Act introduced the concept of voluntary admissions. Prior to this, persons were only admitted involuntarily, and were often reaching services too late to have a reasonable hope of recovery. Part 2 of the Act allowed the Minister for Local Government and Public Health to appoint an 'inspector of mental hospitals and assistant inspectors of mental hospitals'. The Inspector of Mental Hospitals was required to inspect every mental hospital in the country and report on their conditions once a year, which had positive implications for those with intellectual disabilities living in the institutions. If the hospital was being run privately, the Inspector was required to inspect it twice a year. The Act was regarded as a model of good legislative practice internationally at the time.

Meanwhile, support provision for people with physical and sensory disabilities was largely provided by voluntary initiatives and charitable relief. State intervention was vehemently opposed by the Church in relation to professional social support in the community. Services in the community were particularly led by the female religious and lay Catholic women, with the latter being primarily involved in fundraising.[29] This was seen most clearly in the development of social support and education of people who were deaf or hard of hearing. This was provided in the two separate Catholic deaf schools in Cabra, Dublin. After school age, the religious orders supported deaf people to start apprenticeships, with boys pursuing work in agriculture, horticulture, shoemaking, woodwork, blacksmithing and engraving. The

---

26 Walsh, D. and Daly, A. (2004) *Mental Illness in Ireland 1750–2002: Reflections on the Rise and Fall of Institutional are.* Health Research Board, Dublin.

27 *Ibid.*

28 Kelly, B. D. (2008) 'The Mental Treatment Act 1945 in Ireland: An Historical Enquiry', *History of Psychiatry* 19: 47–68.

29 Kearney, N. and Skehill, C. (eds.) (2005) *Social Work in Ireland: Historical Perspectives.* Institute of Public Administration, Dublin.

females were apprenticed in domestic services, housekeeping, sewing and dress-making.[30]

Similarly for people with physical disabilities, such as cerebral palsy, services were organised locally by pioneers who sought to fill a gap in their local area. Cerebral Palsy Ireland (now Enable Ireland) was founded in 1948. The founder, Dr Robert Collins, was a paediatrician in the National Children's Hospital and Rotunda Hospital in Dublin. He used a £100 donation from the Marrowbone Fund to establish an assessment clinic for children with a disability. The first clinics were held weekly in the Children's Hospital. Initially, assessment and treatment services were provided on a voluntary basis.[31]

The poliomyelitis epidemics which occurred during the 1940s and 1950s serve as another useful example for examining the grass-roots voluntary development of support in response to the effects of having a physical disability. There were several sporadic outbreaks of poliomyelitis throughout Ireland, but more serious epidemics broke out in the Dublin area (in 1951) and Cork (in 1956). This led to many children becoming physically impaired as a result of polio. In Dublin, the Central Remedial Clinic (CRC) was established in 1951 by Lady Valerie Goulding and Ms Kathleen O'Rourke as a small non-residential treatment centre in Dublin.

In response to the development of this emerging local voluntary sector, the Health Act (1953) marked the beginning of a change in the relationship between statutory and smaller voluntary organisations with the introduction of 'Section 65 grants'[32] for such non-profit organisations. Meanwhile, the larger residential institutions, largely ran by the religious orders, continued to be funded through the Department of Health. This led to a two-tier approach between the large non-profit organisations and the smaller community and voluntary associations. This new funding mechanism allowed health authorities to support smaller voluntary organisations providing services 'similar or ancillary' to their own. An exact definition of 'similar' or 'ancillary' was not laid down in the legislation, nor were they defined by the courts. Through this new funding arrangement, it was clear that the state was beginning to recognise the value of the local community and voluntary sector in care support. However, as

---

[30] Pollard, *supra*, n. 17.

[31] Enable Ireland (2009) *About Enable Ireland*, http://www.enableireland.ie/about (accessed 10 November 2011).

[32] Health Act (1953) Section 65. – (1) A health authority may, with the approval of the Minister, give assistance in any one or more of the following ways to any body which provides or proposes to provide a service similar or ancillary to a service which the health authority may provide:

    (a) by contributing to the expenses incurred by the body,
    (b) by supplying to the body fuel, light, food, water or other commodity,
    (c) by permitting the use by the body of premises maintained by the health authority and, where requisite, executing alterations and repairs to and supplying furniture and fittings for such premises,
    (d) by providing premises (with all requisite furniture and fittings) for use by the body.

    (2) A health authority may, with the approval of the Minister, contribute to the funds of any society for the prevention of cruelty to children.

the following sections reveal, the state at this time did not envisage that this fledgling sector would take on core provision of day and community services, as they would when institutional services became increasingly outmoded.

The Section 65 grants were based on a 'grant in aid' model rather than a 'contractual' model, meaning the government could publicly fund a recipient by means of a subsidy, but the recipient would continue to operate through partial fundraising and with reasonable independence from the state. In contrast, a contractual model of funding specifies exact terms of provision and outcomes expected from the recipient.[33] A consequence of the Section 65 grant model has meant that the health authorities were not legally obliged to enter a contractual relationship with voluntary organisations for the provision of certain core services.[34] The discretionary nature of the funding resulted in the absence of guarantees of funding from year to year, which has, since 1953, created planning problems and delays in decision making relating to services. Those through the Section 65 grants also have had to maintain a reliance on charitable fundraising for the remainder of their funding. In addition, there have been considerable differences between health authorities in the interpretation of this section. A focal point of argument in the past was the lack of a definition of a particular set of 'core services'. This funding model is still in use today (albeit under a newer legislative section), and has remained a discretionary payment – a fact which has been much criticised.

GRASS-ROOTS DEVELOPMENT OF COMMUNITY SUPPORT (MID-1950S AND 1960S)

By the beginning of the 1950s, the intention of the state's role was clear – to cement the involvement of the church and charitable resources in supporting persons with disabilities through increased statutory funding. The mid-1950s and 1960s was a time of great change in terms of new ways of thinking about disability. The use of ordinary housing began to be promoted internationally, stimulated by the 'normalisation' movement in Scandinavia, which we saw emerge in Sweden in the late 1960s. Around this time was also the beginning of a movement globally to deinstitutionalise services and move people to community care. This came from increased international concerns for civil rights and over the degrading treatment of people with disabilities in institutions which we saw in the earlier chapters. This new philosophy of community care helped to sustain this commitment to move away from institutions.

The shift in thinking about disability in Ireland began with the establishment of a number of 'Parent and Friends Associations' which were initially focussed on being

---

33 See Donoghue, F. (1998) 'Defining the Nonprofit Sector: Ireland', *Working Papers of the John Hopkins Comparative Nonprofit Sector Project*, no. 28 edited by Lester M. Salamon and Helmut K. Anheier. The Johns Hopkins Institute for Policy Studies, Baltimore.

34 *Ibid.*

support groups, but in time became centrally involved in direct support provision. The first of these was established in 1955 by Patricia ('Patsy') Farrell, a parent from County Westmeath with a young son with intellectual disabilities, who was frustrated by the fact that there were no daytime educational or remedial facilities available for children. She felt that parents did not wish their children to be admitted to one of the existing institutions. A meeting was organised in Dublin and a small advertisement was placed in the national newspapers stating:

> Association for Parents of Mentally Backward Children. Lady wishing to form above would like to contact anyone interested. Box Z 5061 Children.[35]

From these rudimentary beginnings, the Dublin Association of Parents and Friends of Mentally Handicapped Children was established. Following a public meeting of the Association in the Mansion House chaired by Declan Costello, a young Teachta Dáila (TD), St Michael's House was founded (of which Costello would later become president). This was the first day care service for people with intellectual disabilities. Similar localised responses began appearing across the country, such as KARE in Kildare and Western Care in Mayo. Significantly, these were amongst the first generation of day services for children with intellectual disabilities living outside of institutions across the country. Developments such as the Women's and Trade Union Movements and the later National Commission on the Status of Women (1969) proved very influential in the development of the ideology of empowerment, participation, social inclusion and voluntary action, which lay behind much of this fledgling community voluntary sector.[36] Most of these organisations were partially funded through the Section 65 grants, while the earlier large residential services continued to be funded directly by the Department of Health. These voluntary organisations became members of an umbrella association, called the National Association for the Mentally Handicapped of Ireland (NAMHI, later renamed as Inclusion Ireland), which was founded in 1962.

While these were developing, from the mid-1960s, there was an upturn in the Irish economy with a new focus on attracting international investment. In addition, the intrinsic alliance between Catholic Church and state began to loosen. Following Vatican II, the Catholic Church shifted its stance from a suspicion of state intervention towards an advocacy for increased state involvement in social and economic issues. It was in this context that the Irish welfare state was created.[37] This saw the introduction of a number of benefits, such as the Disability Allowance in 1996, which was administered by the health authorities as a disabled person's maintenance allowance.

---

[35] *The Irish Times*, 2 June 1955.
[36] Brennan, 1979, cited in McLaughlin, E. (1993) 'Ireland: Catholic Corporatism', in Cochrane, A. and Clarke, J. (eds.) *Comparing Welfare States: Britain in International Context*. Open University Press, London. pp. 205–237; p. 227.
[37] Coughlan, A. (1984) 'Ireland's Welfare State in Time of Crisis', *Administration* 32(1): 37–54.

Meanwhile, the first signs of potential deinstitutionalisation from the state began to occur. The Department of Health White Paper, *The Problem of the Mentally Handicapped* (1960), favoured an extension of the activities of the voluntary organisations in delivering support in the community. It also gave an impetus for the expansion of nurse training. While the idea of nurse training was well intentioned at the time, this change had the unintended effect of sustaining the medical model of treatment within disability services beyond its initial use within institutional services.

In February 1961, a Commission of Inquiry on Mental Handicap was appointed to examine and report on the arrangements for the care of those referred to as mentally handicapped. Although the report marked a watershed in the development of community-based services in Ireland, it mirrored *The Problem of the Mentally Handicapped* White Paper in terms of specifically favouring the provision of these services through religious orders and voluntary bodies.[38] These political decisions were taken because of the prevailing attitude that the state should not intervene in direct service provision. The philosophy of subsidiarity therefore continued, preventing the state from having any substantial encroachment into territory which the Church and the medical profession regarded as their own.

While the use of institutions was on a much smaller scale for blind persons, the few which existed, according to Callery (2011), were beginning to outlive their time and rationale by then.[39] For example, the Cork Asylum perpetuated an existence which in social terms was becoming untenable. With dwindling numbers, it was reconstituted in the late 1960s as St Monica's Home for the Blind under new trustees. While St Monica's continued in existence until the late 1970s, other institutions closed during this period. For example, the Limerick Asylum for Blind Females Connected with Trinity Church, which had been established in 1834, closed in 1962.

Meanwhile, while the earlier Mental Treatment Act 1945 was seen as an improvement at the time, ultimately it did not prove effective in reducing the numbers living in institutions. The extent of this high rate was uncovered at the start of the decade by a World Health Organisation (WHO) (1961) Report,[40] which undertook an international comparison of the number of psychiatric beds in different countries. According to its findings, Ireland had the largest number of psychiatric beds in the world, at a rate of 10.8 beds per 1,000 total population. This was followed by Northern Ireland (7.4), Denmark (7.2) and Sweden (6.7). England and Wales (5.3) and the United States (5.7) had half as many psychiatric beds per population as Ireland, while countries such as France (3.3) and Australia had only one-third as many. Indeed, a 1966 report from a Commission of Inquiry on Mental Illness deplored the almost exclusively institutional nature of psychiatric care, stating that

---

[38] Robins, J. (1992) *From Rejection to Integration: A Centenary of Service by the Daughters of Charity to Persons with Mental Handicap.* Gill and McMillan, Dublin. p. 55.

[39] Callery, *supra*, n. 16.

[40] World Health Organisation (1961) *Statistics Reports,* 14: 221–245. World Health Organisation, Geneva.

while 'some new buildings have been provided and some old ones have been adequately renovated . . . there are still too many barrack-like structures characterised by
large wards, gloomy corridors and stone stairways'.[41]

While this period saw the emergence of new ways of thinking about supporting
people with disabilities in the community, there were also significant deficits in
the delivery and accountability of support within the system. In particular, it later
appeared that there was a gap emerging in the Inspector of Mental Health Services
Reports of institutions for people with mental health issues and intellectual disabilities. These were last published in 1965 (for the year 1962) and then discontinued for
a period of fourteen years. While the reasons for this gap in accountability remain
uncertain, Ryan (1999) refers to a downgrading of the Inspectorate's Office as a
potential reason.[42] This meant that the vital link to what was going on behind closed
doors at the institutions had been cut, and the voices of those inside the institutions had been effectively silenced. The Assistant Inspector of Mental hospitals and
higher civil servants were reportedly angry with this;[43] however, this was not enough
to reverse this severe lapse of attention until 14 years later.

Meanwhile, in the area of physical disability, support continued to be developed
by secular charitable organisations. In Cork, the Cork Poliomyelitis & General
Aftercare Association was founded in 1957, after it became clear that people who
had contracted polio required special aftercare which was not readily available, and
that a locally based service was urgently needed. Cerebral Palsy Ireland, which was
established the previous decade, began to make an impact on persons with physical
disabilities and became the forerunner of the vocational rehabilitation movement.
Another organisation, the Irish Wheelchair Association (IWA), was formed in 1960 by
a small group of people who used wheelchairs who had returned from the Paralympic
Games.[44] The Cheshire Foundation in Ireland was also established around this time
in 1963. It was based on Leonard Cheshire's philanthropy in the United Kingdom.
He was one of the most decorated Royal Air Force officers during the Second World
War, and later became a charity worker, setting up the first Cheshire Home Le
Court, in Hampshire, in 1948. This was originally for ex-servicemen but later became
a home for other people with physical disabilities. The worldwide movement was
named after him, with Cheshire services in more than fifty countries throughout
the world.[45] Around the country, the further growth of these voluntary organisations
tried to address gaps in state service provision.[46]

---

[41] Commission of Inquiry on Mental Illness (1966) *Report of the Commission of Inquiry on Mental Illness*, Stationary Office, Dublin. p. xiii.

[42] Ryan, *supra*, n. 24.

[43] *Ibid*.

[44] Irish Wheelchair Association (2010) *Spokeout*. Spring 2010.

[45] Cheshire Ireland (2009) *Cheshire Ireland Website*, http://www.cheshire.ie/ (accessed 15 April 2011).

[46] Quin, S. (1996) 'Improving Health Care: Health Policy in Ireland', in Quin, S. (ed.) *Contemporary Irish Social Policy*. University College Dublin Press, Dublin. p. 153.

Meanwhile, the Catholic Church remained central to the support of deaf people. The Catholic Institute for the Deaf became significantly involved in developing deaf clubs around the country. It was also at this time that the National Association for the Deaf (NAD) was founded in 1962 in Cabra by Sister Nicholas Griffey, with a committee composed mainly of prominent figures from the legal and commercial world. After a number of informal meetings, the NAD was formally incorporated on 5 June 1964. The NAD also included parents of deaf children, some prominent members of the legal profession and the then chairman of the National Rehabilitation Board (discussed later), Desmond Doyle. It was modelled on the Royal National Institute for Deaf People (RNID) in Britain. The NAD was a powerful advocate for many deaf individuals facing prejudice and discrimination at the time. One of its earliest campaigns, in 1968, was the lobbying of the Department of Education to award certificates to deaf school-goers who successfully completed the Inter and Leaving Certificate examinations. Before this, they generally did not get a certificate because they did not study Irish, which was a compulsory subject, given the difficulties with learning and speaking another language.[47]

At this time, the barriers to 'active citizenship' were significant; the norm was generally that people lived at home with limited voluntary services, little prospect of employment and near-total inaccessibility of buildings, public services and facilities – or else wound up in institutions.[48] In order to promote training and employment of people with disabilities, the National Rehabilitation Board was established in 1967.[49] Amongst its statutory functions, it was charged with the coordination of voluntary bodies engaged in the provision of rehabilitation and training services for persons with disabilities, and the provision of an employment placement service.[50]

More generally, despite the limited service options available, it is also clear that many of the ideas developing internationally began to be slowly established in Ireland at the grass-roots level, with the emergence of new group homes and day services being run by parents and friends associations. Even though many of these fledgling community services subsequently came under scrutiny, they nonetheless provided an important step towards people with an intellectual disability being viewed as equal members of society. In the words of Declan Costello (one of the founders of St Michael's House), 'We were all inspired to do something because the services were so dreadful. Our aim was to establish a day service to avoid children going into

---

47 DeafHear (2004) *40 Years of NAD – A Look Back*, http://www.deafhear.ie/pages/1_2_1_1.html (accessed 12 April 2011).

48 Irish Wheelchair Association (2009) *IWA website*, http://www.iwa.ie/ (accessed 15 April 2011).

49 Under the Health (Corporate Bodies) Act (1961). It took over the National Organisation for Rehabilitation.

50 Report of a Working Party established by the Minister for Health (1974) *Training and Employment the Handicapped*. Stationery Office, Dublin.

mental hospitals'.[51] The principle that disabled people should be able to live a life as normal as possible became the vision of many of the models of support which emerged in response to these new ideas. This had an impact on a new generation of children with disabilities, but it had little impact for those already in institutions. The institutional infrastructure and policy impediments continued to be a barrier to more wide-ranging reform. Ultimately, Ireland still remained one of the most institutionalised countries in the world, and a widespread response in terms of a transformation strategy failed to emerge.

BEGINNING OF COMMUNITY CARE (1970–1989)

The 1970s saw a shift in the government's role in the lives of persons with disability, as it became more directly involved in administering support. The Health Act 1970 became the principal Act governing health care in Ireland for a period of more than thirty years, until the later change to the Health Service Executive (HSE).[52] The Act set up the Irish Health Board structure to provide primary health services as well as community services for people with disabilities around the country. This dual function marked Ireland's approach as different from many other jurisdictions which separated out the roles of health and disability support, such as Canada[53] and the United Kingdom.[54]

The new Health Boards were also responsible for the development of a new framework of statutory community care, including home help services for people with disabilities and older persons living at home. The Community Care Programme was set out in the Health Board structures which covered a wide range of services and has since had three sub-programmes: community protection (health immunisation), community health services (primary care) and community welfare, the last of which includes a range of cash payments (e.g. domiciliary care allowance), home help service and grants to voluntary welfare organisations.[55] There was considerable investment in the fields of health and community care at this time. The home-help service was established under Section 61 of the Health Act (1970) and has been greatly expanded since its establishment.

The Health Act 1970 also established a new funding grant for disability services through Section 26 of the Act. The Section classified the funding stream as follows:

[51] St. Michael's House (2011) *Tribute to Declan Costello*, http://www.smh.ie/index.php?q=node/658 (accessed 7 March 2012).

[52] Disability Federation of Ireland (2002) *An Overview of Irish Health Legislation*, www.wheel.ie/user/content/download/ 168/730/file/flac.pdf (accessed 15 April 2011).

[53] Ontario Ministry of Community and Social Services (2010) *Community Services*, http://www.accesson.ca/en/mcss/programs/community/index.aspx (accessed 15 April 2011).

[54] Department of Health (2009) *Valuing People Now*. HMSO, London.

[55] Curry, J. (1998) *Irish Social Services*. Institute of Public Administration, Dublin.

A health board may, in accordance with such conditions (which may include provision for superannuation) as may be specified by the Minister, make and carry out an arrangement with a person or body to provide services under the Health Acts, 1947 to 1970, for persons eligible for such services.[56]

In practice, this funding related to agencies or groups providing services which the health boards were now legally and statutorily required to provide. It meant that the health board entered into an arrangement with an outside agency to provide services on its behalf. Significantly, the Health Act 1970 did not repeal the older legislation concerning grants from Section 65 of the earlier Health Act 1953. This meant that two distinct streams of funding would exist side by side: Section 65 and Section 26 grants. In practice, the smaller community and voluntary agencies for disabilities continued to be funded under Section 65 from the earlier Health Act 1953 through the health boards. Many of the Section 65 agencies had come from a parents and friends ethos and had been set up to provide local services, mainly in areas where the large service providers were not operational. Despite the state's shift to develop community care structures, people with disabilities still continued to receive most of their support from the voluntary sector. In intellectual disability support provision, a number of Parent's Associations at this time began to forge links with the institutions around the country.

Alongside these two funding streams, a number of older and larger voluntary organisations continued to receive their funding not by means of Section 65 grants, but directly from the Department of Health. Amongst these organisations were the Daughters of Charity services and the Brothers of Charity services, which had commenced providing services in Ireland in 1855 and 1883, respectively. While this direct funding stream remained, the debates around the new funding structures preceding the Act (relating to the Health Bill 1970) had focussed the minds of the leaders of the service providers. In response, the National Federation of Voluntary Bodies (Providing Services to People with Intellectual Disability) was formally established as a representative organisation of service providers in intellectual disabilities. Today the national 'Federation' is comprised of sixty-two Member Organisations.[57]

Meanwhile, services which had been established for people with physical disabilities had to rely on substantial volunteering in order to meet the need for local assessment and treatment throughout Ireland. For instance, Cerebral Palsy Ireland (the precursor to Enable Ireland) and its constituent members including parents, friends and families of children requiring services established a branch network throughout Ireland to meet the need for local assessment and treatment. These volunteers fulfilled demanding roles as advocates and fundraisers. They provided

---

56 Health Act (1970) Section 26, Part 1.
57 See National Federation of Voluntary Bodies (2010) *NFVB Website*, http://www.fedvol.ie/ (accessed 22 July 2011).

the impetus for the substantial growth of Enable Ireland which is seen today. Partnerships with families grew into strong working relationships and provided a crucial framework to plan, fund and deliver services. They changed their name to Enable Ireland to account for the many people supported by the organisation who did not have cerebral palsy.

During this time, people with physical disabilities began to demand a new paradigm in the way in which they were being supported. Starting from the early 1970s, the way of thinking about disability was increasingly being challenged and rejected by people with a physical disability, in favour of what has been termed the social model of disability (described later in the chapter). Internationally, as we saw in the earlier comparative chapters, in the 1970s, concepts of the independent living philosophy were beginning to be integrated in different countries. This was encouraged by the examples of the African-American civil rights and women's rights movements, which began in the late 1960s. Significantly, as we saw in England, the Union of the Physically Impaired Against Segregation (UPIAS) published *The Fundamental Principles of Disability* in 1976, which spelled out a new model of understanding disability as something which society imposes on top of a person's impairments by way of discrimination and enforcing dependency.[58]

This philosophy began to percolate amongst persons with disabilities in Ireland. At the national level, it is possible to see a gradual shift in thinking towards independent living in the 1980s. There was a plethora of statutory reports concerning disability services in Ireland throughout this decade; the National Economic and Social Council (NESC) Report 50 on *Major Issues in Planning Services for Mentally and Physically Handicapped Persons* (1980), *Report of the Working Party on Services for the Mentally Handicapped* (1980) and the Department of Health Green Paper, *Towards a Full Life: Services for Disabled People* (1984). In particular, the last report, *Towards a Full Life*,[59] which came in the wake of the UN International Year of Disabled Persons (1981),[60] acknowledged the stark gaps in Irish disability thinking:

> When the State was less developed and its social commitments more restricted, the task of supporting the disabled person fell almost exclusively on the family and the charitably minded. Occasionally, through exceptional courage and determination or the availability of extra resources, disabled people were able to establish an independent life for themselves. For the majority, however, survival at minimal

---

[58] UPIAS (1976) *The Fundamental Principles of Disability*. Union of the Physically Impaired Against Segregation, London.

[59] Department of Health (1984) *Towards a Full Life: Green Paper on Services for Disabled People*. Stationary Office, Dublin.

[60] The theme of UN IYDP was 'full participation and equality', defined as the right of persons with disabilities to take part fully in the life and development of their societies, enjoy living conditions equal to those of other citizens and have an equal share in improved conditions resulting from socio-economic development.

levels of subsistence and tolerance was the reality of their lives and they were psychologically conditioned to expect no better.[61]

This was one of the first candid reflections by the Department of Health on its failure to adequately address disability policy. The report acknowledged that progress had been made in terms of a different attitude and noted a greater acceptance that 'the disabled' are entitled, as of right, to the same opportunities and benefits from life as other citizens and that obstacles to their exercising that entitlement should be minimised if not eliminated.

A similar shift in thinking began to emerge in response to calls for deinstitutionalisation. A study group on the development of the psychiatric and intellectual disability services in its report in 1982 stated:

> At present, the psychiatric hospital is the focal point of the patients' psychiatric service in most parts of the country. Large numbers of patients reside permanently in these hospitals – many of them have lived there for years in conditions which in many cases are less than adequate because of overcrowding and capital under-funding. In addition, staff and public attitudes have tended to concentrate effort on hospital care as a result of which community facilities are relatively underdeveloped. The hospitals were designed to isolate the mentally ill from society and this isolation still persists.[62]

In response, the government report, *Planning for the Future*,[63] in 1984 proposed a mental health service that would be comprehensive, community-oriented, sectorised and integrated. As a consequence of this mental health report, significant numbers of long-stay service users, particularly people with intellectual disability, were 'discharged' through a process known as de-designation, which re-categorised the facilities in which persons with intellectual disabilities were living as no longer being part of a mental hospital. Admission numbers thus reached a peak in 1986 at 29,392.[64] However, as later discovered, many people were simply moved to campuses housed on the same land as the institutions or were placed in a separate wing inside the buildings.

Meanwhile, the National Economic and Social Council (NESC) published a Report, *Major Issues in Planning Services for Mentally Handicapped and Physically Handicapped Persons* (1987).[65] It examined a number of community care services

[61] *Ibid.* p. 17.

[62] Study Group on the Development of the Psychiatric Services (1982) *The Psychiatric Services – Planning for the Future: Report of a Study Group on the Development of the Psychiatric Services.* Stationery Office, Dublin. Cited in Garavan, T. N., Costine, P. and Heraty, N. (1995) *Training and Development in Ireland: Context, Policy and Practice.* Dublin: Irish Institute of Training and Development. p. 162.

[63] Department of Health (1984) *The Psychiatric Services – Planning for the Future.* Stationary Office, Dublin.

[64] Walsh, D. and Daly, A. (2004) *Mental Illness in Ireland 1750–2002: Reflections on the Rise and Fall of Institutional Care.* Health Research Board, Dublin.

[65] NESC (1987) *Community Care Services: An Overview*, Report 84, NESC, Dublin, Ch. 6.

and concluded that wide variations in the level of services for the 'handicapped' could be attributed to the lack of national guidelines on the appropriate level of service, the lack of national uniform criteria of eligibility for certain services, and the discretionary nature of some services.[66] It advocated the 'integration' of people with 'mental handicaps' into the community and identified that the voluntary sector would continue its role in supporting people, albeit in a more coordinated manner with the state agencies.

This period saw the development of group homes emerge, which was seen as best practice at the time. In 1981, there were 241 individuals living in such group houses in the community,[67] and four years later this figure more than doubled.[68] Many of the parent and friend's associations, such as KARE, opened their first group homes at this time, as well as adult day care services and sheltered workshops to meet the needs of adults who had grown up through their child services.[69] These mirrored developments in other countries, which favoured residential-style community-based houses, with permanent staff, over larger institutional settings. By 1984, a National Planning Board recommended a 'major shift of emphasis... towards care in the community with... a decline in reliance upon... institutions'.[70] Throughout this period, Rehab Ireland also developed a network of community workshops throughout the country, which helped to transform the lives and work prospects of people with disabilities. Supported Employment arrived in Ireland through Open Road, a three-year project sponsored by St Michael's House in Dublin between 1989 and 1991.

This period was therefore typified by small grass-roots innovative projects which were emerging from the community and voluntary sector. They signalled a new era of disability services committed to the goal of full participation and equality in society by persons with disabilities.

A similar story of local grass-roots provision of essential services was evident in the delivery of support for blind and visually impaired persons. There was a recognition that the issues surrounding disability were much broader than those perceived by the NCBI founders and could no longer be met solely by the founding approach to their work. New service developments in the early 1980s included the employment of people from a social work background who were subsequently trained by NCBI in rehabilitation skills.[71]

---

[66] *Ibid.*

[67] Mulcahy, M. and Reynolds, A. (1984) *Census of the Mentally Handicapped in the Republic of Ireland 1981.* Medico-Social Research Board, Dublin.

[68] Kellegher, A., Kavanagh, D. and McCarthy, M. (1990) *Home Together: A Study of Community Based Residences in Ireland for People with Mental Handicap.* Health Research Board, Dublin.

[69] KARE (2004) *KARE Strategic Plan, 2004–2008,* http://www.kare.ie/KARE%20Strategic%20Plan%202004%20-%202008.pdf (accessed 15 April 2011).

[70] National Planning Board (1984) *Proposals for Plan 1984–1987.* Stationary Office, Dublin.

[71] NCBI (2007) *NCBI Strategic Plan 2007.* NCBI, Dublin.

While these changes signalled new ways of responding to and supporting people with disabilities, regrettably this focus on integration had unintended side effects for others. For the deaf and hard of hearing, there was a reversal in the philosophy of sign language driven by a misguided goal of forcing deaf people to adopt oralism – a method of speaking and lip reading – as a means to integrate in society. The 1970s was ultimately a period when sign language was officially banned from the classroom and oralism was favoured as the sole method of communication. This marked a shift in deaf policy which essentially disconnected younger deaf people from the generations of deaf adults who had previously learned sign language. This also signalled the level of paternalism that was still inherent in disability support policy more generally, which meant that the views of people with disabilities themselves were not considered in policy decisions.

In response to this paternalistic trend within the deaf population, the Irish Deaf Society (IDS) was established on 13 January 1981, during the same year as the UN International Year of the Disabled. It mirrored that of many of the physical disability support and advocacy agencies internationally, in terms of its ethos of 'nothing about us, without us', which had been coined by Disabled Peoples Organisations (DPOs) as part of the global movement to achieve the full participation by and with persons with disabilities. It was established as a voluntary organisation without any state funding and ran *by* and not *for* 'Deaf' people.[72] In other words, Deaf people themselves came together with a philosophy that they should self-advocate for their own rights, not rely on hearing people to advocate for them.

By the end of the 1980s, although the government had for the first time explicitly recognised the stark gaps which had shaped thinking in relation to Irish disability support provision, the reform effort was unfortunately delayed with the 1980s economic recession in Ireland. Ultimately, an implementation gap emerged between the new policy commitments and their delivery. While the 1980s fiscal crisis triggered modern civil service reform in so many other administrations internationally, such as the beginning of the quasi-markets within the NHS in England, this crisis brought about the demise of the first main chapter in Irish reform.[73] In other words, the difficult economic climate potentially offered an opportunity to reform costly institutional structures, but the opportunity was lost in Ireland. In the face of serious economic difficulties of this time, the welfare effort dwindled.

Despite the failed attempt at reforming disability services, it was clear that a new vision was emerging – a vision which the focus of this study is grounded on – that

---

[72] Underlying their philosophy, there was a distinction between the 'big D' Deaf people, who identified themselves as culturally Deaf and have a strong Deaf identity, and 'small d' deaf, who did not associate with other members of the deaf community, strove to identify themselves with hearing people, and regarded their hearing loss solely in medical terms. When used in this cultural sense, the word 'deaf' is often capitalised in writing, as the following sections detailing the 'Deaf community' will do.

[73] Murray, J. A. (2001) *Reflections on the SMI*, The Policy Institute Working Paper, Trinity College, Dublin.

services are only a means to an end, and that ultimately people with disabilities want to be supported to live a life in the community. This new vision was bolstered in 1989, when an Irish film, *My Left Foot: The Story of Christy Brown*, was released in Ireland. It had a significant effect on public attitudes towards disabilities throughout the country as well as giving a new energy to the Irish disability movement. It tells the story of Christy Brown's life as a person with cerebral palsy living in Ireland and his search for a way out of being institutionalised. The escape comes when he takes a piece of chalk from his sister one day with his left foot and begins scrawling a single word on the floor of their Dublin home: 'mother'. With an ethos which advocated residential care at the time, many families found it hard to maintain and care for their young or adult child at home. The film was to give people with disabilities living in Ireland a new confidence, which began to shape their involvement in social politics and create an independent living movement in the country.

ROOTS OF REFORM (1990–1999)

In the 1990s, the new vision of supporting people with disabilities in the community began to take hold. The reform process which was articulated but yet faltered in the 1980s gathered pace in the 1990s with the economic boom mid-decade, dubbed the Celtic Tiger by commentators.[74] This saw a further increase in the role of the state in disability support provision. In addition, the increasing influence of the EU broadened Irish mindsets. A new confidence was emerging amongst people with disabilities in speaking up about the barriers in society. The period saw the emergence of organisations ran *by* people with disabilities themselves, such as the Forum of People with Disabilities. Significantly, this was Ireland's only cross-disability organisation wholly controlled by disabled people themselves at that time. Given the breadth of reforms in the following periods, the following sections are subdivided by theme.

The Commission on the Status of People with Disabilities

The Americans with Disabilities Act 1990, as Chapter 4 examines, set a new precedent internationally based on a 'clear and comprehensive national mandate for the elimination of discrimination' and 'clear, strong, consistent, enforceable standards'

---

[74] The 'Celtic Tiger' is a term that was quickly subsumed into Irish national lexicon to denote two periods (1995–2001 and 2004–2007) characterised by rapid economic growth (e.g. 9 per cent GNP in 1997). This prolonged growth rate was largely a result of globalisation and an inward investment from multinational corporations, which led to Ireland's expanded role as a major high-tech electronic, software and pharmaceutical exporter. See Fahey, T., Russell, H. and Whelan, C. T. (2007) *Best of Times?: The Social Impact of the Celtic Tiger*. Institute for Public Administration, Dublin.

in relation to disability discrimination.[75] This focus on rights framed a new agenda
for people with disabilities across the world, including Ireland. This culminated in
1993 with the Commission on the Status of People with Disabilities being established
in Ireland, which developed a new paradigm of disabled people as citizens requiring
support rather than objects of pity. This came on the back of the Irish government's
establishment of a new Department for Equality and Law Reform. As part of its
brief, the Department was to have a disability equality role. The person appointed
to the new ministerial post was Mervyn Taylor, TD whose role was to ensure that
'responsibility for seeing that equality becomes reality through institutional, administrative and legal reform'.[76] Shortly after this appointment, Taylor established the
aforementioned Commission on the Status of People with Disabilities. The terms
of reference underpinning the appointment of the commission included:

1. To advise the government on practical measures necessary to ensure that
   people with a disability can exercise their rights to participate, to the fullest
   extent of their potential, in economic, social and cultural life.
2. To examine the current situation of people with a disability and the organisation and adequacy of existing services, both public and voluntary, to meet
   their needs.
3. To make recommendations setting out necessary changes, in legislation, policies, organisation, practices and structures, to ensure that the needs of people
   with disabilities are met in a cohesive, comprehensive and cost-effective way.
4. To establish the estimated costs of all recommendations made.[77]

On 18 November 1996, after a period of three years, the Report of The Commission on the Status of People with Disabilities – A Strategy for Equality was finally
published. It is generally regarded as the most definitive policy document regarding
people with disabilities in Ireland, setting out a blueprint for reform and igniting the
transformation agenda in Irish disability policy. Significantly the Commission found
that people with disabilities were the neglected citizens of Ireland. Many submissions
mentioned the lack of coordination between service providers, the fragmentation
of services and the difficulty in getting entitlements. Deficits in education, employment and training, income support, health and personal support and the ongoing
strains, physical, emotional and social, which long-term family caregivers experience
were also brought to the fore. The recommendations included the expansion of the
home help scheme and respite care services and national standards for services for
people with disabilities in the community. The report was highly critical of many of

75 Americans with Disabilities Act (1990), Section 2 (b), Purpose.
76 O'Reilly, A. (2007) The Legacy of the Commission on the Status of People with Disabilities, Contri-
    bution to Conference 'Changing the Landscape' organized by the Forum of People with Disabilities
    and DESSA, Dublin, 12 November.
77 Commission on the Status of People with Disabilities (1996) *A Strategy for Equality: Report of the
    Commission on the Status of People with Disabilities*.

the social barriers, negative attitudes and poor quality of outmoded services, which created social barriers and marginalisation. The absence of services in the health and social care field were highlighted in the report: '[P]eople with disabilities, parents and carers have serious concerns as to the quality of some existing services, and about the lack of some fundamental services'.[78]

The Commission believed it necessary to create an executive body which would monitor the impact of public policy and services on people with disability and argued it should have the power to intervene in particular cases in order to ensure equity. It was against this backdrop that the Commission recommended the establishment of a National Disability Authority which would report to the Department of Equality and Law Reform (now the Department of Justice and Equality). As regards the membership of the National Disability Authority, the Commission took the view that it should include a wide range of interests and represent a balance between key stakeholders (government departments, local authorities, Health Boards and other state and voluntary agencies) and independent users, carers and specialists. It recommended that it should also reflect a balance between the genders, geographical areas and the different types of disability.

Finally, the Commission welcomed and strongly supported the establishment of a representative Council for the Status of People with Disabilities made up of a national board and county networks representing the voice of people with disabilities. The Commission recognised the need to allow the Council to establish itself and to develop its own priorities and ways of working, and believed that it would fulfil a central role in lobbying for the implementation of the Commission's recommendations. The Commission recommended that the Department of Equality and Law Reform should provide ongoing core funding at a level appropriate to the importance of the task facing the Council, which would take into account the additional costs which would arise in respect of disability – for example, sign language interpretation, braille writing, transport and so on. This Council became the precursor to the statutory body, People with Disabilities Ireland (PwDI). PwDI was created by the state as a national organisation to provide an effective, representative structure through which all people with disabilities, their parents, partners, relatives, carers and organisations of people with disabilities can participate in and influence decision making which affects the lives and opportunities of people with disabilities.[79] It ceased operations in 2011.

Equality Legislation

The changing ethos towards social inclusion and the removal of barriers to participation became evident from 1997 onwards in Ireland, which saw an unprecedented

[78] *Ibid.* p. 161.
[79] PWDI (2003), *Strategy 2003–2006*. PWDI, Dublin.

increase in equality legislation (Universities Act 1997, Education Act 1998, Employment Equality Act 1998).[80] Most notably, the Employment Equality Act 1998 was based on the principle that all individuals are entitled to equal treatment in training and employment opportunities on nine grounds, one of which included disability. The Act required providers of goods and services to 'make such reasonable accommodations as are necessary to enable people with disabilities to avail of services which, without such changes, would be difficult or impossible for them to access'. This legislative development won for Ireland the prestigious Franklin Delano Roosevelt award for positive disability developments in 1999.[81]

The Employment Equality Act 1998 also set up the Equality Authority (which started in October 1999) as an independent body to achieve positive change in the situation and experience of disadvantaged groups and individuals experiencing inequality by stimulating and supporting a commitment to equality within the systems and practices of key organisations and institutions and as part of the cultural values espoused by society.[82] A later report for the Equality Authority noted that the quantity of employment equality claims brought by disabled people discriminated against by the public/semi-state sectors was striking.[83]

Employment 'Horizon' Initiative

Another significant development for persons with disabilities in Ireland in the 1990s was the emergence of supported employment as a new service model in Ireland. The supported employment approach developed in the United States in the 1980s as a means of assisting people with disabilities in securing and maintaining employment. Its emergence was influenced by the civil rights and consumer movements and the Independent Living movement. Traditional approaches before then were typically based on a vocational rehabilitation model which involved progressing people with disabilities through a spectrum of social, education and employment training courses with a view to eventual transition into employment in the open labour

---

[80] Other significant legislation enshrined at this time were the Education Act (1998) and the Universities Act (1997). Amongst the objects of the Education Act were the promotion of equality of access to and participation in education, giving practical effect to the constitutional rights of children, including children with disabilities; and the provision of a level and quality of education appropriate to meeting the needs and abilities of all children, 'having regard to the resources available' and 'as far as is practicable'.

[81] The International FDR Award for Disability was announced on the fiftieth anniversary of the United Nations, 24 October 1995, by the Franklin Delano Roosevelt Foundation, in cooperation with the World Committee on Disability. The award is granted annually to the state which best interacts with the key principles embodied in UN programmes targeting persons with special needs and implements, in particular, the principle of equal opportunities.

[82] The Equality Authority (2010) *About Us* and *Mission Statement*, http://www.equality.ie (accessed 1 March 2011).

[83] Equality Authority (2008) *New Research Maps the Social Distribution of Discrimination in Ireland*, Press Release, http://www.equality.ie/index.asp?docID=724 (accessed 2 August 2011).

market.[84] Ultimately, many people with disabilities remained segregated in workshops, many of which were purporting to provide rehabilitation. Supported employment marked a shift in the direction of intervention towards providing the individualised supports required to enable full participation by people with disabilities in open employment. It emphasised the priority of employment placement and the subsequent provision of supports and training in the workplace – summarised by the phrase 'place and train' rather than 'train then place'.[85]

The supported employment model developed in Ireland with support from the EU funded Employment-HORIZON Initiative (during the 1994–1999 period), and it is estimated that approximately 1,000 people with disabilities accessed employment with support from the various pilot initiatives.[86] The success of this initiative led to the National Rehabilitation Board's National Advisory Committee on Training and Employment making recommendations regarding the need to further develop supported employment in Ireland.[87] In response, the government announced in July 2000 a commitment to support the implementation of a national supported employment initiative. The resulting programme which developed, the Supported Employment Programme, is discussed in the 'New Hopes and New Crossroads: 2000–2006' section later in the chapter.

Review of Funding

In addition to the equality legislation, there was also a review of the funding mechanism for the non-profit disability support sector. The report of the review group, *Enhancing the Partnership* (1996), set out a new template for service agreements for Section 26 grants, as detailed earlier.[88] Service agreements became the method used for applying for and allocating these resources (although many providers continued to receive block grants without any such contractual agreements). These were explicit public policy agreements to develop partnership and complementarity between voluntary and statutory agencies, rather than contested procurement. The template included the joint agreement of principles between the two parties (HSEAs and non-profit organisations), the individual obligations of both parties and a system for resolving differences.

---

[84] WRC Social and Economic Consultants (2008) *Research Report on the Operations and Effectiveness of the Supported Employment Programme*, May, Dublin: FÁS.

[85] *Ibid.*

[86] FÁS (2008) *A Profile of Participants on the Supported Employment Programme*, Prepared for FÁS by WRC Social and Economic Consultants, May. p. 5.

[87] NACTW (1997) *Employment Challenges for the Millennium: A Strategy for Employment for People with Disabilities in Sheltered and Supported Work and Employment*. National Rehabilitation Board, Dublin.

[88] Department of Health and Children (1996) *Enhancing the Partnership. Report of the Working Group on the Implementation of the Health Strategy in Relation to Persons with a Mental Handicap*. Stationary Office, Dublin.

The following year, a report titled *Widening the Partnership*[89] extended the application of the principles set out in *Enhancing the Partnership* and recommended that service agreements should be introduced for *all* disability non-profit organisations funded under Section 65 of the Health Act 1953 on condition that they were in a position to meet agreed criteria in relation to good practice, accountability and organisational structures.

Taking its cue from *Enhancing the Partnership*, the broader policy direction in the While Paper *Supporting Voluntary Activity*[90] also suggested the introduction of service agreements and more formalised monitoring arrangements between the state and non-profit organisations. Since the 2001 Health Strategy, these service agreements were extended to all service providers including the larger organisations which had previously received money from the Department of Health and Children. Up to 61 per cent of the total value of funding to non-profit organisations is covered by service agreements – with the remainder obtained largely through fundraising.[91] While this provided a new system of funding allocation, a later audit of the Comptroller and Auditor General would ultimately find many issues with this system, as well as gaps in its implementation, as detailed in the next chapter.

Evolution of Community Care

While many of the grass-roots community services continued to develop throughout this period, there was also a renewed commitment in the 1990s to examine the institutional service arrangements which had been inherited from Victorian times by the Church and larger non-profit service providers.

In 1990, the government published its intellectual disability strategy, *Needs and Abilities*.[92] It outlined the main service developments to enable people with an intellectual disability to live in their local communities with support services to meet their needs. The report examined the issue of whether support in the community was more cost-effective than support in the special residential centres, or indeed in the psychiatric hospitals. The report concluded that 'existing residential facilities which are older [i.e. Victorian] and which are not domestic in scale should be discontinued as soon as possible and appropriate provision made for the present residents'.[93] It

[89] Department of Health and Children (1997) *Widening the Partnership. Report of the Working Party to Examine Financial and Other Issues Relating to Section 65-Funded Mental Handicap Agencies.* Stationary Office, Dublin.

[90] Department of Social, Community and Family Affairs (2000) *Supporting Voluntary Activity – A White Paper on a Framework for Supporting Voluntary Activity and for Developing the Relationship between the State and the Community and Voluntary Sector.* Stationary Office, Dublin.

[91] Comptroller and Auditor General (2005) *Report on Value for Money Examination: Provision of Disability Services by Nonprofit Organisations.* Comptroller and Auditor General, Dublin.

[92] Department of Health (1990) *Needs and Abilities: A Policy for the Intellectually Disabled. Report of the Review Group on Mental Handicap Services.* Stationary Office, Dublin.

[93] *Ibid.* p. 39.

advocated community-based residences such as local authority housing or rented accommodation while using former psychiatric hospitals as day centres. However, it was noted that the Department of Health would need additional capital funding from the Department of Finance in the short term. It recommended first transferring people with an intellectual disability from psychiatric hospitals to community services, and then transferring suitable clients from such services into a community setting. However, the report completely downplayed the scale of large congregated settings in Ireland: 'We have been fortunate in Ireland that our residential centres have generally been small by international standards and many have never had the institutional characteristics which have been a feature of such centres in a number of developed countries'.[94]

In reality, Ireland still had 3,539 people with intellectual disabilities living in residential centres, according to the subsequent National Intellectual Disability Database (1998/1999).[95] However, given the new policy direction, this period did see an increase in numbers of those living in smaller community-based residences, with the National Intellectual Disability Database (1998/1999) recording that 2,835 lived in such community group homes.[96]

Centres for Independent Living (CILs) and their Influence on Physical Disability Services

Meanwhile, in the area of community care for persons with physical disabilities, the Irish CIL was founded in 1992 from the work of the Irish Independent Living movement which led the way in advocating change. Generally speaking, CIL is a grass-roots organisation established by and for people with disabilities. As discussed in Chapter 4, it originated out of Berkeley, California, in the 1970s. From the beginning, the organisation was aware that suitable housing would be pointless for people with significant physical disabilities without the presence of a personal assistance service. The CIL was also aware of the vital role that personal assistants (PAs) play in enabling people with disabilities to take control of their lives.

A personal assistance service commenced in Ireland as an EU pilot programme in Dublin in 1995, called INCARE, which empowered many people to live an independent life.[97] The INCARE programme examined, implemented and secured

---

[94] Ibid.

[95] Mulvaney, F. (2006) Annual Report of the National Intellectual Disability Database Committee. The Health Research Board, Dublin.

[96] At the same time as the Needs and Abilities report was published, the Health Research Board (HRB) also commissioned an evaluation of community-based residences, called Home Together, and its authors reported comparatively better outcomes in these newer settings. Please refer to: Kelleher, A., Kavanagh, D. and McCarthy, M. (1990) Home Together: A Study of Community Based Residences in Ireland for People with Mental Handicap. Health Research Board, Dublin.

[97] Centre for Independent Living in Ireland (2009) Dublin CIL, http://www.dublincil.org (accessed 15 April 2011).

the future provision of a personal assistance service in Ireland.[98] It was operated by the CILs and subsequently taken over by the IWA. The Irish CILs also began to cooperate with Foras Áiseanna Saothair (FÁS) (Training & Employment Authority), the national employment and training agency, in the mid 1990s by recruiting PAs, office staff and other employees through the FÁS Community Employment Scheme (CES).[99] These schemes are still in operation today across the country. Employment of the scheme's participants brings many advantages to both the individual and the organisation, as FÁS not only funds the salary of the participant, but also covers training costs, contributes to the rent and most importantly pays the wages of the FÁS CES supervisor. With this programme, the CIL has since grown to be an active Independent Living movement, with twenty-four CILs across the country. Each centre is run independently, having its own board of directors, funding, services and members. In Dublin, for instance, the PA service offered by the CIL became one of the dominant models by which people with physical disabilities accessed a PA in Ireland.

Most of the earlier secular voluntary organisations by then had reinvented themselves to respond to emerging needs and changes in attitudes and practice driven by the Independent Living movement. The CRC, for example, specialised in the assessment, diagnosis and treatment of children with a wide range of physical conditions including cerebral palsy and spina bifida. Services were provided in an activity centre in Clontarf, Dublin to children throughout the country. Similarly, the Rehab Group (incorporating the former Rehab Institute) developed into a large organisation employing 2,000 people and providing training, employment, social care and commercial services for about 5,000 people each year in Ireland.

Meanwhile, the IWA had by this time a regional network of fifty centres providing a range of services including peer counselling services, transport and assisted living services, and it had implemented many community-based projects such as training and education. These centres also were providing respite and holidays for people with physical disabilities living at home with family members.[100]

Enable Ireland had also grown into a large national organisation supporting a large number of children and adults with disabilities at all stages of their lives and with a wider variety of needs. Their services were aimed to help individuals to have access to advocacy, employment, training, personal assistance, residential services, respite and social and leisure activities. For many adults, this included the development of

98 CIL Network Council (2009) *Irish Centers for Independent Living Report of an Internal Survey*. CIL Carmichael House, Dublin.

99 This is an employment and training programme aimed to help long-term unemployed people to re-enter the active workforce by breaking their experience of unemployment through a return to work routine. The programme assists the participants in enhancing and developing both their technical and personal skills, which can then be used in the workplace.

100 Irish Wheelchair Association (2010) *About IWA*, http://www.iwa.ie/about/history.aspx (accessed 15 April 2011).

independent living skills and getting help to secure independent living options. A core means to meet this aim has been the organisation's PA service.

Despite the PA service being an essential support for people with physical disabilities, much of the funding revenue continued to come from voluntary fundraising (e.g. from the nationwide branch of Enable Ireland retail outlets).[101] This reliance on charitable fundraising was largely a consequence of the state's continued use of Section 65 grants even for disability organisations which had become direct service providers. Many of the Section 65–funded bodies (from the Health Act 1953), including Enable Ireland, were only able to receive a fraction of their costs from the state through grant-in-aid funding, despite moving into direct and essential support provision. This is in contrast with the Section 26–funded bodies (from the Health Act 1970), which generally received between 90 per cent and 98 per cent of funding from the state.[102] This dual system was a further legacy of the traditional charitable ethos from the state towards disability which remains today.

The Cheshire Foundation by this time was also providing a wide range of essential services such as respite and community services to adults with physical disabilities. They were experimenting with individualised housing arrangements for some people, in which individuals lived in their own apartment and received home care services to help with some activities of daily living. However, a core part of their service continued to be a range of eighteen campus-style residential centres around the country. Without bridge-finance to close these centres, and little political will from government to fund individualised housing arrangements, the transformation effort required to move people into less congregated housing was significant.

Ultimately, the 1990s was a time when people with disabilities gained a new confidence in speaking up about the barriers in society, as evidenced by the emergence of organisations ran *by* people with disabilities, such as the Forum of People with Disabilities, and by Deaf persons such as the Irish Deaf Society. In response to this growing momentum, as we saw, the Commission on the Status of People with Disabilities was established, whose report developed a new paradigm of disabled people as citizens requiring support rather than objects of pity. In addition, the Employment Equality Act 1998 and the Employment Horizon initiative marked a shift from earlier traditional philosophies of support, based on being a 'last resort', to supporting the economic participation of people with disabilities in the community. However, it was evident that a number of legacies lived on in the way disability support was funded and administered. As the following section reveals, these would become core elements which would need to be addressed in the future reform effort.

[101] See Enable Ireland's Annual Reports and Strategic Plans (2005–2010), http://www.enableireland.ie/publications-and-research/publications/reports-plans (accessed 15 April 2011).
[102] For an indication of the funding allocations to Section 26-funded organisations, see the financial results from Brothers of Charity Galway Annual Reports (2007–2009) and St Michaels House Annual Reports (2006–2010), for example.

NEW HOPES AND NEW CROSSROADS (2000–2006)

The previous Commission on the Status of People with Disabilities in 1996, as we saw, copper-fastened a new blueprint for change. It was also the initial starting point in the reform of support delivery in Ireland. As this section examines, the early to mid-2000s saw an unparalleled level of change with a number of new acts of legislation, policies and government and third-party reports which set out the new vision ahead. Ireland during this time also experienced a second period of unprecedented growth from 2004 to 2007, which prolonged the 'Celtic Tiger' era. Many of the historical legacies which were still shaping the delivery of support also began to become scrutinised, in the form of financial audits and reports of abuse. However, as the following chapter reveals, the economic climate in Ireland entered an unfavourable downturn with the demise of the 'Celtic Tiger' era, which forced the Irish government to examine the potential for cost-effective reform. The following section examines the new hopes and new crossroads that preceded this downturn – and which crystallised the urgent need for reform.

Recognition and Rights

The beginning of this period was characterised by the passing of the Equal Status Act (2000). The Act prohibited discrimination in relation to the supply of goods, facilities and other opportunities to which the public generally has access on the same nine distinct grounds as the earlier Employment Equality Act (1998), including disability. This set the foundations of the Irish equality agenda which placed Ireland ahead of many other jurisdictions in relation to non-discrimination legislation.

Another key development that year was the establishment of the National Disability Authority (NDA) by the government on 12 June 2000, which was one of the recommendations of the Commission. The NDA is an independent statutory agency originally established by the National Disability Authority Act 1999 (under the aegis of the Department of Justice, Equality & Law Reform [since renamed the Department of Justice and Equality]). Its functions include: to act as a national body to assist in the coordination and development of disability policy; to undertake research and develop statistical information for the planning, delivery and monitoring of programmes and services for people with disabilities; to advise the Minister of Justice and Equality on standards for programmes and services and prepare codes of practice; to monitor the implementation of standards and codes of practice; and to take the lead in both encouraging and recognising the promotion of equality of people with disabilities.[103] When established, the properties, rights and liabilities of the National Rehabilitation Board were transferred to the NDA.[104] The NDA's

---

[103] NDA (2009) *What the NDA Does*, NDA Web site, http://www.nda.ie/cntmgmtnew.nsf/aboutushomepage?OpenPage (accessed 15 July 2012).

[104] Following the National Rehabilitation Board (Transfer of Property, Rights and Liabilities) Order, 2000.

members are drawn from all backgrounds and include people with disabilities, parents and carers of people with disabilities and people working in the disability field. While the research-and-development role has been provided for, some of the NDA's functions differ from those envisaged by the Commission, notably the establishment of a nationwide Disability Support Service which was supposed to offer information, advice, support and advocacy to people with disabilities.[105]

At the same time as the NDA was established, another statutory body, Comhairle, was set up in June following the Comhairle Act 2000 to support the provision of information, advice and advocacy on a broad range of public and social services.[106] The establishment of Comhairle was part of a government commitment to 'provide directly, independent information, advice and advocacy services so as to ensure that individuals have access to accurate, comprehensive and clear information relating to social services and are referred to the relevant services'.[107] It also set up the Resource Database for the Voluntary and Community Sector in Ireland.[108]

Another positive development was the active role of Mary Harney TD, Minister of Enterprise, Trade and Employment (July 1997 – September 2004), in the setting up of the national Supported Employment Programme in 2001 (following the successful HORIZON programme) by the Irish statutory training agency, FÁS. At the outset, FÁS had little experience of working with the client group of people with disabilities, and the agency had to begin developing a strategy to include people with disabilities in its training programmes. Since 2000, the government policy of mainstreaming services for people with disabilities has made a significant impact on the delivery of employment and training services for people with disabilities. More generally, the responsibility for vocational training services and employment for people with disabilities was transferred from the Department of Health and Children to the Department of Enterprise, Trade and Employment in June 2000. This was a particularly welcome development, given the increasing numbers of persons rejecting the option of support in congregated settings and remaining in the community. Indeed, it signalled a new era for persons with disabilities as being considered active and participating citizens in Ireland.

The Disability Bill

Around this time, many national organisations began pushing for a wider statutory basis for the protection of human rights of people with disabilities in Ireland, with an emphasis on the delivery of services as a right. The Disability Bill was drafted in

---

[105] This was originally foreseen as a local service with branches across the country to offer information, advice, support and advocacy. However, these functions became the responsibility of the Citizens Information Board (CIB) and local Citizens Information Centres in an effort to mainstream disability issues.

[106] http://www.citizensinformationboard.ie/about/ (accessed 15 July 2012).

[107] Comhairle Act 2000, Section 7(1) Functions of the Board.

[108] Comhairle (2001) 'The Community and Voluntary Sector', *Relate* 28: 1–9.

2001. However, it offered no social rights to those in need of the services to actually seek redress if the services were not provided. It therefore became a contentious issue amongst disability groups and was debated for a long time in the Oireachtas (Irish House of Parliament). Crucially, it did 'not confer a right of action in any civil proceedings by reason only of a failure by a public body to comply with any duty imposed on it under this Act'.[109] With much outrage from the disability organisations, the original Bill was withdrawn; the government's term of office expired, and the Bill was never passed.

With the subsequent government, a new Bill was debated through a major consultation period with the disability sector in order to be re-drafted. The Department of Justice, Equality and Law Reform at the time established an Expert Consultation Team to consult with all stakeholders and to report to the government. Alongside this, the Minister of State for the same department invited the chairperson of the NDA to 'facilitate meaningful dialogue at the national level with people with disabilities, their families, carers and service providers.'[110] This led to the establishment of the Disability Legislation Consultation Group (DLCG), which included a number of national disability representative organisations, including the Disability Federation of Ireland, the Forum of People with Disabilities, Mental Health Ireland, NAMHI (now Inclusion Ireland), People with Disabilities in Ireland, the National Parents and Siblings Alliance, the National Federation of Voluntary Bodies and the Not-for-profit Business Association which had been formed in 1998 as a representative body for eight leading support provider organisations, principally to people with physical and sensory disabilities.[111]

Reform of the Health Boards

Meanwhile, there was a much broader restructuring of the health board structure, begun in 2003, which had been the main regional body for managing and commissioning disability services for the past thirty years. On 18 June 2003, the government announced a major reform programme for the Irish health services, which, because of the joint health and social services remit, would have significant effects on people with disabilities. This was considered to be the most extensive reform programme since the 1970 Health Act. The primary focus of the reform programme was on the improvement of health care management. This was considered to be necessary to create modern and responsive health care services which would be able to deliver on the government's health strategy and meet the increasingly complex demands placed on the health care system. This was particularly important for disability services

---

109 Disability Bill, 2001.
110 Quoted in Disability Legislation Consultation Group (2003) *Equal Citizens – Disability Legislation Consultation Group*, February.
111 The Not-for-profit Business Association was formed in 1998.

which, as stated by the NDA at the time, were often fragmented and poorly planned because of a range of management, organisational and resource problems.[112]

The change was led by a raft of major reports on the Irish health structures throughout 2003:

- the Brennan Report[113] (January 2003) – carried out by the Commission on Financial Management and Control Systems in the Health Service to undertake a detailed examination and review of the funding of the Irish health service;
- the Prospectus Report[114] (June, 2003) – carried out an Audit of Structures and Functions in the Health System on behalf of the Department of Health and Children;
- the Health Service Reform Programme[115] (June 2003) – offered a government synopsis of the overall reform programme;
- the Office for Health Management (OHM) Report[116] (September, 2003) – requested by the Department of Health and Children to carry out a communication and consultation programme in relation to the Health Service Reform Programme;
- the Hanly Report[117] (October 2003) – carried out by the National Task Force on Medical Staffing to improve primary patient care.

Cumulatively, these reports showed that the health care system was ineffective, cumbersome and fragmented. According to the Brennan Report (2003), for example, 'Management and control of services and resources is too fragmented; there is no one person or agency with managerial accountability for how the overall system performs on a day-to-day basis'.[118] It concluded that there was substantial scope for improving the efficiency and productivity of the health care system so that there could be better value for money and more effective use of resources, and it recommended new financial accountability procedures.

The reports brought in a new era in the health care service, which was outlined in the Health Act 2004. From 1 January 2005, the day-to-day running of services was handed over by the Department of Health and Health Boards to a

---

[112] National Disability Authority (2004) *Towards Best Practice in Provision of Health Services for People with Disabilities in Ireland.* NDA, Dublin.

[113] Commission on Financial Management and Control Systems in the Health Service (2003) *Report of the Commission on Financial Management and Control Systems in the Health Service (the 'Brennan Report'),* June. Stationary Office, Dublin.

[114] Department of Health and Children (2003) *Audit of Structures and Functions in the Health System (the 'Prospectus Report'),* June. Stationary Office, Dublin.

[115] Government of Ireland (2003) *The Health Service Reform Programme,* June. Stationary Office, Dublin.

[116] Office for Health Management (2003) *Dialogue on Implementing Reform,* November, OHM, Health Service Executive.

[117] National Task Force on Medical Staffing (2003) *Report of the National Task Force on Medical Staffing (the 'Hanly Report'),* October.

[118] *Supra,* n. 113. p. 7.

new body called the Health Service Executive (HSE).[119] The HSE has since had four regional offices and a headquarters in Naas, County Kildare, although the old health boards, now called Health Service Executive Areas (HSEAs), continued to have directors of finance and other services in an extensive interim period.[120] The establishment of the HSE represented the beginning of the largest programme of structural change undertaken since the 1970s in the Irish public service. The HSE was now the single body responsible for ensuring that everybody could access cost-effective and high-quality health and personal social services. The objective of the Executive was 'to use the resources available to it in the most beneficial, effective and efficient manner to improve, promote and protect the health and welfare of the public.'[121]

Ultimately, the major reform programme of the health care services did not address the question of whether disability was best placed within the health care services. The reports did not examine the option of repositioning disability as a local authority issue (or a splitting of the HSE into health and social care as in Northern Ireland) rather than a health issue. This was in contrast to the move in the United Kingdom to transfer the funding and commissioning of social care for adults with disabilities from the NHS to local government (with the exception of commissioning responsibilities for specialist health services).[122] Britain's rationale for the shift was that people with disabilities had historically been 'cared for' in old long-stay hospitals managed by the NHS but were now seeking support to live in the community. This shift also enabled NHS Primary Care Trusts to focus on their primary responsibility of meeting the health care needs of individuals. In Ireland, as a result of the government's decision to maintain disability within health services, the role of disability policy and funding remained within the new HSE structure. This emphasis on meeting the needs of people with disabilities within a health 'silo' seemed at odds with the emerging philosophy of supporting active citizenship.

In terms of the funding contracts within the new HSE structure, there were two new funding streams of block grants available through the HSE which disability agencies were able to apply for. These were established through separate sections of the 2004 Health Act:

- Section 38 grants (old Section 26-funded grants) related to agencies / groups providing services on behalf of the HSE. This referred to services which the HSE was legally and statutorily required to provide or to enter into an arrangement with an outside agency to do so on its behalf.

[119] Donnellan, E. (2004) 'Goodbye Health Boards Hello HSE', Health Supplement, *The Irish Times*, 28 December, p. 1.

[120] *Ibid.*

[121] Department of Health (2007) *The Health Service Reform Programme Leaflet*, June. Stationary Office, Dublin.

[122] Department of Health (2008) *Valuing People Now*. HMSO, London.

- Section 39 funding (old Section 65-funded grants) related to agencies / groups undertaking services which were similar or ancillary to those of the HSE and to which the HSE was providing grant aid to do so. However the HSE would not be legally or statutorily obligated to provide such services.[123]

In terms of Section 38 funding, as indicated, there has been an expectation that those in receipt of the grant deliver essential supports on behalf of the HSE. In effect, this arguably makes the non-profit organisations in receipt of the grants somewhat quasi-governmental agencies, given that they are more directly controlled by government in terms of staffing, levels of pay and management. This is limited to agencies currently within the HSE Employment Control Framework.[124] However, there are a range of activities carried out within organisations that could fall under either definition as outlined earlier (Section 38 or 39).[125] For instance, many organisations which have developed out of parents and friends associations, but provide equally essential services, are often under the Section 39 funding stream, whereas many non-statutory, Church-affiliated organisations fall under Section 38.

Progression of Independent Living Amongst User Groups and Providers

In terms of the development of disability supports on the ground during this time period, the non-profit sector continued to pioneer the development of support aimed at enabling people to live and participate in the community. There were at the time twenty-four CIL sites established nationwide, since the first CIL was formed in 1992. The majority of CILs as well as Enable Ireland were providing a PA service through the FÁS Community Employment Scheme (CES). While the PA service was originally used by people with physical disabilities, a small percentage of people with intellectual disabilities also began to use PAs. This was provided for through a mix of HSE funding and the operation of the CES with the balance provided by fundraising (e.g. the Retail and Fundraising department of Enable Ireland). The Irish model of personal assistance service has been dictated largely by the HSE and to a lesser extent by FÁS. The UK model of direct payments, in which individuals with disabilities (Leaders) receive funding to buy their own PA services, has not evolved.[126]

---

[123] For details of each funding stream and templates of the Service Arrangements, see HSE (2010) *National Business Support Unit – Non Statutory Provided Services*, available at: http://www.hse.ie/eng/services/Publications/Non_Statutory_Sector/. For a full list of Section 38 organisations, see http://www.kildarestreet.com/wrans/?id=2010-07-08.1734.0 (accessed 15 April 2011).

[124] *Ibid.*

[125] Disability Federation (2009) *HSE Policy and Procedures for Funding Non-Statutory Organisations.* http://www.disability-federation.ie/index.php?uniqueID=175 (accessed 15 April 2011).

[126] Department of Health (2007) *Putting People First: A Shared Vision and Commitment to the Transformation of Adult Social Care.* HMSO, London.

Meanwhile, the Irish Deaf Society (IDS) became better supported by the Department of Community, Rural & Gaeltacht Affairs to set up a deaf advocacy service. The IDS also began a major management transformation that brought a new vision for campaigning centred around advocacy. Despite varying (and at times contradictory) philosophies, the IDS and the National Association for the Deaf (now called DeafHear) both shared a commitment during the 2000s to the rights of deaf people. This saw a series of achievements such as the Education Act 1998 (ISL for deaf children), the Broadcasting Act 2001 (television access for the deaf), Signlink (interpreting agency) and the Centre for Deaf Studies. However, there were many areas of society that were not accessible to deaf people in their own language. Furthermore, by the mid-2000s, only a tiny pool of less than fifty qualified interpreters were working in Ireland.[127]

During this same period, the National Council for the Blind of Ireland (NCBI) started an expansion of the service delivery role of the organisation. The Independent Living Skills training facility and programme were launched in 2004 by the Minister for Health Mary Harney at the National Headquarters and Training Centre. This focussed on training in living independently with blindness, including life skills such as housework, cooking, as well as education on better lighting of the home for people with vision impairments.

Evolution of the National Disability Strategy

Meanwhile, at the national level, the Department of Health and Children had been negotiating and consulting with the Disability Legislation Consultative Group (DLCG) on a new Disability Bill. After years of deliberation and consultation, the DLCG produced a report, *Equal Citizens: Proposals for Core Elements of Disability Legislation*, in February 2003. It called for the following core elements: (1) Independent Needs Assessment leading to a Statement of Need and coordination of resources, including individual funding where required and services to meet those needs; (2) advocacy; (3) mainstreaming and disability proofing; (4) accessibility of public services: including information, communications and physical accessibility; (5) disability equality awareness training; and (6) public service employment.[128] The thrust of their report signalled a broader paradigm change based on changing values, rights and principles, with equality, participation, quality and inclusion being increasingly regarded as key values and principles underpinning Irish social policy. This was a significant achievement for the disability representative organisations

---

127 The Irish government still had not recognised ISL as the third official language (alongside English and Irish), even though more than forty-five other countries internationally had given legal recognition to their own native sign languages. The Private Members Bill – a version of an ISL Bill – was proposed, which Fianna Fáil Senator Mark Daly planned to put to the Senate, but it received little mainstream attention. If passed, the Bill would allow for the legal recognition of ISL. See RTE (2009) *Hands On*, 8 March, http://www.rte.ie/tv/handson/thisweek08032009.html (accessed 15 April 2011).

128 DLCG (2003) *Equal Citizens: Proposals for Core Elements of Disability Legislation*. DLCG, Dublin.

involved, and for Irish disability politics more generally, as it was the first time these bodies had come together as a unified voice.

In response, the government embarked on a wide-ranging reform of disability legislation with the National Disability Strategy 2004. The core ingredients of the strategy were the new Disability Bill (later to become the Disability Act 2005),[129] Sectoral Plans of the Government departments and the Education for Persons with Special Educational Needs (EPSEN) Act 2004.[130] It also introduced a multi-annual financial package, which was launched the following year, and the subsequent Citizens Information Act 2007, which are discussed in the following chapter.[131]

One of the keystones of the National Disability Strategy was the Disability Act 2005. This was the piece of legislation most strongly deliberated during the consultation period with the DLCG. Its main elements relevant to support delivery were the right to an assessment of need and the requirement of government departments to develop sectoral plans on disability. Under Sections 7 to 23, people with disabilities were given an entitlement to an independent assessment of health and education needs. To date, the government has only implemented this assessment for the zero-to-five age group and has yet to extend it to adults. For the under-five age group, assessments were to be carried out without regard to cost or capacity to provide services. Similar to British Columbia, these assessments were then to be taken into account in the preparation of a service statement. However, unlike the life planning in British Columbia or the 'projet du vie' in France, the service statement in Ireland was relatively limited and was to specify the health or education services, or both, to be provided and time frame within which these services were to be provided having regard to, inter alia, the resources available. Moreover, no entitlement to an assessment was rolled out for adults. To date, there has been no comprehensive review of the assessment of need process; however, the HSE has prepared one report which gives a breakdown of figures for those availing of or requesting assessments of need (and subsequently receiving service statements).[132] In addition, a statutory body called the Health Information and Quality Authority, which was subsequently set up in 2007 to introduce standards in health and social care services (discussed later), also produced standards for the assessment of need.[133]

Secondly, under Sections 31 to 40 of the Disability Act 2005, six Departments were required to draw up Sectoral Plans:

[129] Disability Act 2005.

[130] The EPSEN Act actually predated the launch of the NDS – the Act was passed in July and the Strategy was launched in September. The Act was named as one of the core ingredients of the NDS.

[131] Citizens Information Act 2007.

[132] HSE (2005) *Report to the Minister for Equality, Disability and Mental Health as Provided for under Section 13 of the Disability Act 2005*. Stationary Office, Dublin, available at: http://www.hse.ie/eng/services/Publications/services/Disability/2005actreport.pdf (accessed 15 April 2011).

[133] HIQA (2007) *Standards for the Assessment of Need*, HIQA, Cork, available at: http://www.hiqa.ie/media/pdfs/standards_for_need_assessment.pdf (accessed 15 April 2011).

- Health and Children
- Social and Family Affairs
- Transport
- Environment, Heritage and Local Government
- Communications, Marine and Natural Resources
- Enterprise, Trade and Employment.

The plans were designed to identify *how* the functions of each department, and the key bodies which they oversaw, served the needs of people with disabilities. They also were required to set out a programme for future development. This was a radical change from the traditional 'silo' approach of leaving disability issues with one ministry. However, the Department of Education was not included in the list of departments required to draw up a sectoral plan. Nevertheless, it was a key component of the government's wider policy of mainstreaming, which was affirmed by the Taoiseach in his speech launching the National Disability Strategy, as a 'programme of action . . . to support and reinforce equal participation in society by people with disabilities'. To meet this end, the providers of state services would, 'from today, have the concerns of people with disabilities as part of their core work'.[134]

Overall, the progress of implementation of the National Disability Strategy is monitored by the Senior Officials Group on Disability (SOG-D), which reports to the Cabinet Committee on Social Inclusion. This group consists of officials representing the six government departments responsible for implementing the sectoral plans, as well as the Department of the Taoiseach, the Department of Justice, Equality and Law Reform, the Department of Finance and the Department of Education and Science. A National Disability Strategy Stakeholder Monitoring Group (NDSSMG) was also established to monitor progress on the overall implementation of the strategy. This group is comprised of three different working groups: the Senior Officials group on Disability; the Disability Stakeholder Group[135] and a range of organisations and groups with statutory responsibilities for people with disabilities.[136]

Ultimately, the requirements for public services in the National Disability Strategy did not require a right to services but merely to make mainstream services integrated and accessible for persons with disabilities. Because of the hotly contested issues relating to justiciability and entitlement, particularly for a right to services per se, a number of organizations, specifically the Forum of People with Disabilities (which subsequently disbanded in November 2007), NAMHI (Inclusion Ireland) and the National Parents and Siblings Alliance, left the DLCG. These left because the core

134 Speech by Taoiseach at the launch of the National Disability Strategy, in the Alexander Hotel, Fenian Street, 21 September 2004.
135 Composed of the remaining members of the Disability Legislative Consultation Group, as well as Inclusion Ireland, and the Irish Mental Health Coalition replacing Mental Health Ireland (which left in 2009).
136 This group includes National Disability Authority, Health Service Executive, National Council for Special Education, Irish Congress of Trade Unions, Irish Business Employers Confederation, FÁS, and Commission for Communications Regulation.

commitments which they had identified in their DLCG report were not met in the Disability Bill 2004. This reduced the membership from eight to five organisations. More significantly, two of the three organisations which left were comprised primarily of self-care or family advocates. Although the role of the DLCG in the immediate aftermath of the publication of the Bill and Act was unclear, it has now been reformulated as the Disability Stakeholder Group (with Inclusion Ireland rejoining the group) and given a role in relation to monitoring the National Disability Strategy. Some groups involved also have played an active part in the sectoral plans developed by the six government departments.[137]

Alongside the National Disability Strategy, the Equality Act 2004 was enshrined, which amended the Employment Equality Act 1998 and the Equal Status Act 2000. It introduced some significant new employment rights, including the extension of positive action measures which can assist people, such as greater access to training, 'mentoring' or other forms of ongoing support. It also introduced rights against indirect discrimination, where a particular measure, while appearing neutral on the face of it, has a disproportionate impact on a particular group or individual in the workplace. In addition, people who suffer discrimination because they are associated with a person who has been discriminated against can also make a claim. Given that Ireland had already one of the most advanced equality law frameworks in the EU, with the Employment Equality Act 1998 and the Equal Status Act 2000, the new Irish legislation was regarded as a tidying up exercise, albeit a potentially far-reaching one.[138]

Calls for a 'Developmental Welfare State'

Meanwhile, a firm commitment to innovation in service delivery became evident in a statutory report, the *Developmental Welfare State* (2005), by the National Economic and Social Council (NESC).[139] The concept of the 'developmental welfare state' has attempted to reframe thinking about the direction and role of the Irish welfare apparatus. Rather than a welfare state which enforces dependency, low expectations and low outcomes for a minority – as, it argues, is the way it is currently configured – it advocates for a welfare state which is geared towards encouraging participation, self-reliance and engagement with the labour market. This demonstrated a mainstreaming of ideas which were emerging in disability thinking around the new role for welfare – that all people should be supported to engage and participate in society, rather than being kept in dependent positions away from society. Indeed,

---

[137] Flynn, E. (2011) *From Rhetoric to Action: Implementing the UN Convention on the Rights of Persons with Disabilities*. Cambridge University Press, New York.

[138] Dobbins, T. (2004) *New Equality Law Extends Workers' Rights*, Eurofound, EIROnline, http://www.eurofound.europa.eu/eiro/2004/07/feature/ie0407202f.htm (accessed 15 April 2011).

[139] National Economic and Social Council (2006) *The Developmental Welfare State*, NESC, Dublin. The role of the NESC is to advise the government on strategic issues for Ireland's economic and social development.

it was becoming clear that too many services had become standardised and inflexible to those who needed support.

Specifically, the 'developmental welfare state', as envisaged by the NESC, calls for innovation with respect to services and income supports to ensure real independence. It signals a move away from continuing high levels of benefit dependency towards ways in which welfare payments could be redefined and combined with services to create 'participation packages'. These packages, it recommends, should be adapted to individual needs and capacities and could contain rehabilitation and vocational training, job search support, work elements from a wide range of forms of employment (regular, part-time, subsidised, sheltered) and benefits in cash or in kind. It could also in some circumstances contain activities which are not strictly considered as work, but contribute to the social integration of the disabled person.[140] In short, the approach of the developmental welfare state is towards an 'enabling' welfare state rather than one which creates and sustains dependency.

Similarly, the government's 2006 ten-year Social Partnership Agreement, *Towards 2016*[141] (covering the period 2007–2015), shares a vision of an Ireland where people with disabilities have, to the greatest extent possible, the opportunity to live a full life with their families and as part of their local community, free from discrimination. To achieve this vision, it was stated that the government and the social partners will work together over the next ten years towards long-term goals with a view to continued improvements in the quality of life of people with disabilities. It endorsed a lifecycle approach to social planning for the challenges individuals face at each stage in their lives, from childhood to old age and including disability. It was agreed that each group would require a combination of income supports, services and innovation. In particular, one of their goals was that all individuals with a disability would be supported to enable them, as far as possible, to lead full and independent lives, to participate in work and in society and to maximise their potential.[142]

CONCLUSION

This unprecedented period of disability law and policy in Ireland, marked by the wide-ranging vision and scope of the National Disability Strategy, effectively revolutionised the way in which disabilities issues were dealt with by the state. It was clear from these developments that there was now an opportunity for change within the disability support system in Ireland. As the next chapter details, with this momentum for change, Ireland entered into a period of public scrutiny to identify the legacies and choke points from the earlier landscape of support. The findings from various

---

[140] OECD (2003) *OECD Employment Outlook: Towards More and Better Jobs*. OECD, Paris.
[141] Department of the Taoiseach (2006) *Towards 2016: Ten-Year Framework Social Partnership Agreement 2006–2015*. Stationary Office, Dublin.
[142] *Ibid.* p. 66.

enquiries would provide the impetus for a comprehensive review of disability services in Ireland – and drive the initial strands of reform. Since that time, the Irish government has been at a crossroads. On the one hand, they have been trying to reform the sector in light of modern best practice, and on the other, they have been seeking to identify inefficiencies in the system and reduce costs. These two positions are not necessarily intrinsically opposed. As the other case studies have shown, there is much scope and potential for identifying new cost-effective and innovative practices which can enrich people's lives and encourage independence. However, the state must operate from a strategic position to drive this change rather than simply rationing the existing system without demanding reform.

The history of disability services in Ireland, as this chapter has shown, is littered by the remnants of paternalism, overprotection, medicalisation and segregation. While these elements are by no means unique to Ireland, in many cases the institutional infrastructure within Ireland has been replaced by a community care apparatus characterised by a lack of regulation, monitoring and strategy to promote the new vision of personalisation and active citizenship. Indeed, in many cases, the framework of support has continued to prolong the extensive history of institutional care practices and neglect of persons who continue to live in a state of isolation, dependency and frustration.

Despite these challenges, by the end of 2006, there were many positive developments already on the horizon which began signalling a new era in disability support. The Developmental Welfare State as advocated by the NESC offers a potential road map in shaping a new 'enabling' welfare state. This new vision recognises that contributing by citizens to society is valuable in itself for people with disabilities. This approach was firmly embedded in the national partnership agreement, Towards 2016, which set out a commitment to enable people with disabilities living and participating in society.

Ireland's challenges in many ways are not unique. The other comparative jurisdictions in this book shared similar patterns of institutionalisation and medicalisation of persons with disability; indeed, some still do. All of these other countries also have faced similar crossroads in transforming their systems of support. Moreover, they continue to face ongoing challenges in unravelling the legacies of their history of traditional service delivery. Yet, they are committed to the vision ahead of self-determination and active citizenship. Ireland, as the next chapter reveals, is now at the cusp of this personalisation reform agenda. The potential for shared learning – of both positive lessons and challenges ahead – is significant in setting out upon this journey.

10

Towards Active Citizenship and Disability in Ireland

INTRODUCTION

As the last chapter showed, Ireland's history of disability support on the one hand shared similar patterns of institutionalisation as other jurisdictions, and on the other, had unique political, social and cultural factors, in particular the earlier role of the Catholic and Protestant churches in direct support provision and the reluctance of the state to assume direct responsibility for the development of these services. This provision, as the last chapter identified, was also heavily influenced by the British government's policy during the nineteenth century and relied heavily on intermediaries such as religious orders and charity throughout much of the twentieth century. The state's reluctance to interfere led to a mixture of lay (parent and friends associations) and church-based non-profit agencies which in many cases have provided essential supports for persons with disabilities. As a result, a wide range of service models and providers exist within Ireland partly as a result of the long history of community and voluntary involvement in the disability support sector. However, the support options available to many people are often determined not by their needs but by the history, philosophies and preferences of different providers, as well as available funding arrangements across Ireland.[1] Consequently there is a large variety in terms of the models and quality of supports available.

Whereas this history examined the roots of Ireland's disability policy, this chapter focusses on mapping out the contemporary landscape as it has evolved since 2006, and by taking stock of the current policy commitments and normative values which frame the reform agenda today. In particular, it examines the emergence of a new policy dialogue intent on engaging more directly with the concept of self-determination. This has been marked most clearly by a report by the HSE, *Time*

---

[1] Mulvany, F., Barron, S. and McConkey, R. (2007) 'Residential Provision for Adult Persons with Intellectual Disabilities in Ireland', *Journal of Applied Research in Intellectual Disabilities* 20: 70–76.

to Move On from Congregated Settings (2011) and the Department of Health publication, *A Summary of Key Proposals from the Review of Disability Policy* (as part of a broader review entitled *Value for Money & Policy Review of Disability Services*). Both of these reports acknowledge that a wholly new approach to funding disability services will be required to facilitate the transition to community living.

This recent period of reform has coincided with the emergence of an economic recession since 2008 in Ireland. Despite the clear impact on the public expenditure, given the momentum for change identified in the previous chapter, Ireland has still maintained its commitments to seek reform. Moreover, the policy debates in the aforementioned reports have indicated that the current economic climate presents Ireland with a unique opportunity to restructure funding arrangements to ensure that public expenditure on disability services is reconfigured in a way which allows people with disabilities to purchase the supports they need, thus providing more cost-effective ways of administering services.[2]

Meanwhile, the Irish government has yet to ratify the CRPD, although it has signalled its commitment to do so, thereby creating a renewed interest in disability policy development.[3] Since signing the Convention on 30 March 2007, Ireland has lagged behind the sixteen EU member states which have already ratified the treaty, leaving Ireland amongst the later states to ratify the convention. Its delay stems from the need to reform its legal incapacity laws, in order to comply with the principles of Article 12 in the Convention. As Chapter 2 identified, Article 12 focusses on the right of people with disabilities to make decisions for themselves. This particular chokepoint is examined amongst other challenges later in the chapter, in the section 'The Challenges Towards Active Citizenship'.

AN OVERVIEW OF THE ADMINISTRATION OF DISABILITY SUPPORT

As we saw in the previous chapter, at the national scale, the disability portfolio in Ireland in terms of support delivery comes under the Department of Health.[4] This is largely attributable to the historical development of disability support in Ireland within the medical services. Within this department, the responsibility for disability comes under the Minister of State for Disability, Equality, Mental Health and Older People. Since the Health Act 2004, the Department of Health is now exclusively

---

[2] Health Service Executive (2011) *Time to Move on from Congregated Settings: A Strategy for Community Inclusion*, Report of the Working Group on Congregated Settings, June, Health Service Executive. The report acknowledges that a wholly new approach to funding disability services will be required to facilitate the transition to community living. Despite the current economic climate, the Department of Health has signalled its intention to implement the aforementioned report.

[3] Ireland signed the CRPD on 30 March 2007. See Irish Human Rights Commission (2010) *Joint Committee Meeting in Dublin Calls on British and Irish Governments to Commit to Key International Standards*, available at: http://www.ihrc.ie/newsevents/press/2010/10/15/joint-committee-meeting-in-dublin-calls-on-british/ (accessed 10 March 2012).

[4] Formerly the Department of Health and Children (changed 1 May 2011).

focussed on the policy domain. Alongside this, the Department of Social Protection has a role in administering a range of means-tested disability payments. Finally, the Department of the Environment, Community, and Local Government[5] has responsibility for advancing disability rights more generally.

The government has also undergone a significant mainstreaming process, in which other departments currently have roles in developing sectoral plans. These plans force ministries to identify how they can better serve the needs of people with disabilities as well as develop a programme for future development.[6] With this new emphasis on mainstreaming, the government implemented a new structure for the coordination and integration of support policy for people with disabilities with the establishment of the Office for Disability and Mental Health and Citizen Participation. This is headed by the Minister of State, and a Cross-Sectoral Team, under the aegis of that office, coordinates activities and services across relevant departments and agencies.

Responsibility for the health budget and the planning and commissioning of disability support since the Health Act (2004) lies with the Health Service Executive (HSE). The HSE's overall role is to provide health and personal social services for everyone living in Ireland. The HSE is responsible for ensuring a consistent national approach to the delivery of health services and that best practices within the existing health service delivery structures are replicated across the country. Although the Department is focussed on the policy domain, the HSE, given its role in commissioning and delivery of government policy, also develops its own policy reports, particularly on areas relating to the management and delivery of its services.

At the regional scale, the HSE is divided into four regional HSEAs, called Dublin Mid-Leinster, Dublin North-East, West, and South. The HSEAs have a lot of discretion in commissioning and planning local support in their coverage areas. The HSEAs interfaces with the HSE at the national level and with service providers at the local level. This puts them in an important position of administering national policy and commissioning services. In Ireland, the method of procurement in disability support is through the use of 'service level arrangements' which are informed by the 2000 White Paper, *Framework for Supporting Voluntary Activity and for Developing the Relationship between the State and the Community and the Voluntary Sector.*[7] It outlines the state's funding relationship with the sector, including multi-annual

---

5 Formerly the Department of Community, Equality, and Gaeltacht Affairs (changed 1 May 2011).

6 The Ministries involved include the Minister for Health, the Minister for Social Protection, the Minister for Transport, the Minister for the Environment, Community and Local Government, the Minister for Communications, Marine and Natural Resources and the Minister for Enterprise, Trade and Employment.

7 DOHC (2000) *Framework for Supporting Voluntary Activity and for Developing the Relationship between the State and the Community and the Voluntary Sector*, White Paper. Stationary Office, Dublin.

funding as the norm and best-practice guidelines. In deciding these arrangements, there are Liaison Committees which look at the overall needs for areas of the country and particularly at crisis needs. These committees decide on allocation of resources to meet these needs. These service level arrangements are examined in more detail later in the chapter.

Ireland by international comparison is considered to be a relatively centralised state: Irish local authorities have much less power than their European counterparts. Their main remit is physical planning, rezoning and new housing. The local authorities have a much smaller role in disability support than in the United Kingdom. The commissioning role of disability services is held by the HSEAs rather than local authorities. However, the councils are responsible for administering some housing grants which the 'Enabling a Choice in Living Arrangements' section will examine in more detail. While government and HSE policy has begun advocating a greater role for the local authorities, especially in housing, to date this is still in its infancy, as traditionally people with disabilities had all their services provided by one organisation. This has included accommodation needs and medical and social services.

In terms of informing the policy agenda in Ireland, the independent statutory agency, the National Disability Authority (NDA), provides expert advice to the government on disability issues, universal design, policy and practice. The NDA has published many reports on independent living, employment and training, health and accessibility.

In terms of government monitoring, the Health Information and Quality Authority (HIQA) was established on a statutory basis as the Office of the Chief Inspector of Social Services with specific statutory functions under the Health Act 2007 as part of the government's more recent health care reform programme. The work of the Inspectorate has been focussed primarily on the inspection and registration of residential services in the public, private and voluntary sectors for older people and people with a disability. However, HIQA has only been permitted to publish voluntary standards for residential services for persons with disabilities, as no mandatory standards are enforced. Moreover, given its focus on residential services, there are no enforced standards or quality evaluation of day support provision or support within the wider community.

There are also a number of government policy watchdogs. The Equality Authority acts as an independent monitoring body set up under the Employment Equality Act 1998. The Authority's remit extends beyond promoting best practice and making recommendations on changes to legislation. It also informs, advises, promotes access to legal redress and legally challenges issues of strategic importance, particularly relating to discrimination in employment, vocational training, advertising, collective agreements, the provision of goods and services and other opportunities to which the public generally has access on nine distinct grounds, including disability. However, with recent budgetary constraints, the Equality Authority has had to continue its work with more modest resources.[8] There are two other national policy watchdogs: the Law Reform Commission and the Irish Human Rights Commission (IHRC). The Law Reform Commission published a report examining Ireland's legal capacity legislation,[9] as discussed later. The IHRC published its Enquiry Report into the situation of a group of adults with a severe to profound intellectual disability in the John Paul Centre, Galway.[10] The enquiry found that there were serious gaps in the provision of services to residents or people using the facilities of the Centre.

In terms of national disability representative bodies, there are a number of national organisations representing different stakeholders, which emerged throughout the history of disability supports as examined in the earlier chapter. The Disability Federation of Ireland represents the disability sector on the National Economic and Social Council, which was established to advise the government on the development of the national economy and the achievement of social justice. It is a strong advocacy organisation with a membership that is primarily, although not exclusively, made up of organisations concerned with physical and sensory disability.

In terms of intellectual disability, Inclusion Ireland is a national representative organisation with more than 160 members including parents associations and support groups, professional bodies and service providers. In addition, the Federation of Voluntary Bodies Providing Services to People with Intellectual Disabilities represents the voluntary and community provider sector in intellectual disability. Finally, in terms of advocacy groups, the National Parents and Siblings Alliance is an alliance of interested people advocating a strong rights-based approach on behalf of those with intellectual and developmental disabilities.

In the area of physical disability, there are some large providers at the national level, including Enable Ireland, the Irish Wheelchair Association, Centres for Independent Living (CILs) and the Cheshire Foundation, which contribute to policy debates. In addition, the Not-for-Profit Business Association is a representative organisation of service providers in the physical and sensory area. The Association was formed to formalise cooperation between bodies in this area and to seek to have major funding deficits addressed.

Apart from these representative bodies, there is a relatively weak DPO movement in Ireland, with the absence of a People First organisation. The Forum of Persons with Disabilities was a pan-disability DPO group but was discontinued in 2007. Similarly, People with Disabilities in Ireland (PwDI) was the representative organisation for people with disabilities to advocate on their own behalf. It was established as a pan-disability organisation with a grass-roots approach to give voice to people with

---

8   The Equality Authority was given a 43% cut in funding in 2008, leading its chief executive to resign. Please refer to: http://www.rte.ie/news/2008/1212/equality.html (24 November 2010).

9   Law Reform Commission (2005) *Consultation Paper on Vulnerable Adults and the Law: Capacity.* LRC, Dublin.

10 Irish Human Rights Commission (2010) *Enquiry Report into the Situation of a Group of Adults with a Severe to Profound Intellectual Disability in the John Paul Centre,* 30 March, Galway.

disabilities. However, funding for the organisation ceased in November 2011 on the basis of a value-for-money review (it was decided that the vast majority of the money allocated to PwDI was being spent disproportionately on administration). Therefore, it is vital that the next generation of people with disabilities is tooled up to contribute to policy debates.

AN OVERVIEW OF THE DISABILITY SUPPORT FRAMEWORK

Disability-Specific State Entitlements

In Ireland there are a number of means-tested payments for people with a disability from the Department of Social Protection and HSE. The Disability Allowance is a weekly means-tested allowance paid to people with a disability who are between sixteen and sixty-five years of age. Recipients also get a free travel pass on all state public transport (bus, rail and Dublin's light-rail service),[11] and in some cases a free companion pass may also be available to allow a person to accompany the free-travel pass holder. For eligibility, individuals must have an injury, disease or physical or mental disability which has continued or is expected to continue for at least one year. The individual must be 'substantially restricted' by this disability in undertaking work which would otherwise be suitable for a person of his/her age, experience and qualifications. For the Disability Allowance, at the time of writing, earnings up to €120 per week from 'rehabilitative work' are not taken into account in the assessment of means. For work to be considered 'rehabilitative', a person must get medical evidence from his/her doctor, stating that the work is rehabilitative. If a person's earnings from rehabilitative work are above €120 per week, 50 per cent of the earnings between €120 and €350 will not be taken into account in the means test.[12]

Given the restrictive means testing and definition of 'rehabilitative work' used for the Disability Allowance, there has been some concern over the potential benefit trap for persons interested in taking up regular employment. In particular, the withdrawal of social welfare benefits, medical card (for free primary care services), entitlement to assistive technology and appliances, mobility allowance and secondary benefits (e.g. fuel allowance, free travel pass) constitute a set of powerful disincentives to work.[13]

While the benefit trap is acting as a barrier for people getting back to work and causing more dependency, the government has not yet published plans to amend its eligibility requirements. The Sectoral Plan for the Minister for Social and Family Affairs aims to 'encourage maximum participation in society and do so in

[11] For full details, refer to: http://www.citizensinformation.ie/en/social_welfare/social_welfare_payments/ extra_social_welfare_benefits/free_travel.html (accessed 22 November 2010).

[12] Department of Social and Family Affairs (2010) *Schemes and Services*, available at: http://www.welfare. ie/EN/Schemes/IllnessDisabilityAndCaring/Pages/default.aspx (accessed 5 June 2011).

[13] NDA (2005) *Pre-Budget Submission 2005*. NDA, Dublin.

partnership with other Government Departments and Agencies'.[14] The key features include identifying the potential for rationalisation and integration of social welfare disability schemes including identifying benefit traps and disincentives within the structure.

For those people who acquire a long-term illness or disability and have five years paid contributions since entering social insurance, they may receive an Invalidity Pension. In addition, trainees in foundation training and sheltered workshops can retain their social welfare payments, usually the Disability Allowance, and also receive the Rehabilitation Training Allowance.

Meanwhile, the Blind Pension is a means-tested payment paid to blind and visually impaired people normally living in Ireland. It has the same rates, conditions and means test as the Disability Allowance. There is also a Blind Welfare Allowance, which is a means-tested supplementary payment from local HSE areas and may be paid if an individual already gets Blind Pension or Disability Allowance.

There is also the Mobility Allowance which is a means-tested monthly payment payable by the HSE to people aged between sixteen and sixty-six who have a disability and are unable to walk or use public transport and are deemed to 'benefit from a change in surroundings' (for example, by financing the occasional taxi journey).[15]

Alongside the disability allowances, there are also a number of payments for family carers: the Domiciliary Care Allowance (DCA), Carers Allowance, Carers Benefit and Respite Grant. The DCA is a non-means-tested monthly payment to family carers of a child with a disability. The disability has to be so severe that it requires care and attention and/or supervision substantially in excess of another child of the same age. This care and attention must be provided to allow the child to deal with activities of daily living. The DCA scheme was administered by the HSE before it was transferred to the Department of Social Protection. The Carers Allowance, in contrast, is a strictly means-tested payment for family carers of adults with disabilities. Once a child reaches the age of sixteen, the DCA is discontinued, and the family carer must apply for the Carers Allowance. In many cases, families who previously were receiving the DCA are refused the Carers Allowance on the basis of their means, even though their caring job often remains the same. The Carers Benefit is a temporary allowance for somebody who needs to leave their work to care for a disabled or ill relative for a period of up to 104 weeks. This time restriction precludes the benefit from being a long-term care payment. Finally, those who receive any of the aforementioned care payments are also eligible for the Respite Grant, an annual payment made to carers which they can use in any way they wish.

---

14 Department of Social and Family Affairs (2006) *Disability Sectoral Plan, 2006.*

15 This Allowance was introduced in 1979 by the Department of Health and Children and is payable under Section 61 of the Health Act, 1970.

Disability-Specific Services

In Ireland, alongside the disability welfare payments, most people with disabilities have their services provided by intermediaries within the non-profit community and voluntary sector. In particular, for people with intellectual disabilities, this often includes accommodation and medical and social services in-house, as well as many day services.

Service providers receive a grant from the HSE (either through a Section 38 or Section 39 grant, as discussed in the previous chapter) to cover all the person's various needs, and the individual in many cases has very little, if any, influence over how this allocation is spent. While there are exceptions, generally this has had the effect of tying the person to a particular service provider, often from the transition from childhood into adulthood, leaving the person with few options for changing the aspects of the support. The following section begins with an overview of the residential care sector, proceeds to the day care sector and finally details the staff mix of these services and assesses how they are funded.

Residential Services

In terms of residential care, outside of family care arrangements where the majority of persons live,[16] people with disabilities in general live in residential support services run by a provider in a variety of settings such as independent and semi-independent living, community group homes and residential institutions, on a five-day, seven-day or shared-care basis ranging from high to medium and low support. Many of the disability support agencies began to grapple with the process of moving people from traditional services to individualised supports and making allied links with mainstream services in the 1980s and 1990s, somewhat later than other Western jurisdictions. The origins of this change, as we saw, can be traced back to government policy commitments in the 1980s and early 1990s (e.g. Planning for the Future [1984], Towards a Full Life [1984] and Needs and Abilities [1990]). In response, there has been a slow and steady increase in group home development over the last thirty years.

In many parts of the country, there have been strong legacies of congregated institutional care across all types of disabilities, including St Ita's Hospital, Brothers of Charity Galway and Cheshire Ireland. The government's progress in moving people with disabilities out of institutional care has been slow. There are

---

16 In Ireland, the majority of people with disabilities live at home with parents, siblings, relatives or foster parents. For people with physical and sensory disabilities, the 2008 NPSDD Annual Report revealed that 23,500 (86.1%) of those registered lived with family members. For people with intellectual disabilities, 16,708 (64%) of those registered on the NIDD lived at home with parents, siblings, relatives or foster parents. For people aged eighteen and older, this figure is reduced to 8,812 (49%) living in a home setting.

still more than 4,000 people with intellectual disabilities living in congregated residential settings of 10 or more people.[17] Moreover, according to the National Intellectual Disability Database (2011), 300 people with intellectual disabilities still reside in 'de-designated' wards within psychiatric hospitals.[18] The number remains a policy challenge, although some progress has been made over the last number of years, with numbers gradually decreasing. However, the threat of *trans-institutionalisation* will no doubt continue to remain an issue, given the experience of mental health services in Ireland: In recent years, there has been the development of community residential mental health services. In 2004, the number of people living in community residences reached 3,065.[19] Of the total number, there are 1,805 places in 24-hour nurse-staffed community residences. Worryingly, the Report 'Happy Living Here: A Survey and Evaluation of Community Residential Mental Health Services in Ireland' (2007) found that 'the climate and culture of the residences reflected more those of a 'mini-institution' than of a home-like environment, especially in the high support residences. The medium and low support residences were somewhat more relaxed, but a large number employed constricting rules and regulations, the necessity for which was questionable'.[20] This is particularly important given the statement in the EC report (2009) that institutions are defined primarily by features of 'institutional culture' (depersonalisation, rigidity of routine, block treatment, social distance, paternalism) rather than solely by their size.[21]

In other areas of the country – often in rural counties – there has been a longer history of community development supports, referred to as 'greenfield sites', where campuses or institutions were not built to the same extent. Because of the lack of residential services, support agencies such as parents and friends associations (e.g. Western Care) often were established as a means to 'fill the gap' in state services by developing foster care, day support or carer support arrangements. Over time, many of these organisations began to develop group homes to cater for the children in their services who were progressing into adulthood.

Residents in group homes often have to pay 'contributions' to their residential costs; however, this is not considered rent, and therefore individuals do not

[17] *Supra*, n. 2.
[18] Daly, A. and Walsh, D. (2006) *Irish Psychiatric Units and Hospitals Census 2006*. Health Research Board, Dublin.
[19] Tedstone Doherty, D., Walsh, D. and Moran, R. (2007) *Happy Living Here . . . A Survey and Evaluation of Community Residential Mental Health Services in Ireland*. Mental Health Commission, Dublin. Details available in the Forward section of the document: www.mhcirl.ie/documents/publications/ Happy%20Living%20Here%20A%20Survey%20and%20Evaluation%20of%20Community% 20Residential%20MHS%20in%20Ireland%202007.pdf (accessed 24 November 2011).
[20] *Ibid.* p. 102.
[21] European Commission, Employment, Social Affairs, and Equal Opportunities, Ad Hoc Expert Group on the Transition from Institutional to Community-based Care (2009), available at: //ec.europa.eu/social/BlobServlet?docId=4017&langId=en (accessed 24 November 2011).

have tenancy rights. The legal basis for the 'contribution' paid by people in group homes/residential centres derives from section 4 of the Health (Amendment) Act 2005 and comes under the heading 'in-patient' charges, as well as the HSE (2009) Charges for In- Patient Services National Guidelines.[22]

For people with physical and sensory disabilities, the most commonly used residential services are described as 'nursing home placements' (195, 0.7 per cent) followed by dedicated high-support placements with nursing care and therapy services for people with physical or sensory disabilities (169, 0.6 per cent).[23] Seventy-four people were living independently in the community with high or low support, agency support or with house adapted or re-housing. A total of 730 people (2.7 per cent) were identified as not currently availing of residential services but requiring these services in the future. The reliance on residential centres for those with physical or sensory disabilities, as the figures show, is much smaller than by people with intellectual disabilities, and has diminished in recent years. Nonetheless, because of the historical reliance on congregated settings, there are still 297 people with physical and sensory disabilities living in congregated institutional settings.[24] Many organisations are still trying to dismantle these services to try and develop individualised support arrangements. Often, these are in campus-style settings with a number of bungalows or houses accommodating ten or more persons. In addition, some providers offer places on a five-day basis and/or for forty-eight weeks of the year, with clients returning to their families at other times. These arrangements tend to be a continuation of the boarding school arrangements used in childhood.

Day Support

In terms of day support, day services in Ireland are also generally provided through non-profit providers, many of which offer these 'in-house' within their residential services. PA services for people with disabilities are provided by a number of service provider organisations including the IWA, Cheshire Ireland, Enable Ireland, CILs and RehabCare.

The PA service is still funded mainly through the Irish training agency Foras Áiseanna Saothair (FÁS) (which pays PA workers through the community employment scheme) and the HSE (which funds individual allocations of PA hours).

---

[22] See Chapter 5 of the IHRC (2010) *Enquiry Report on the Human Rights Issues Arising from the Operation of a Residential and Day Care Centre for Persons with a Severe to Profound Intellectual Disability*, IHRC, Dublin; and HSE (2009) *Charges for In- Patient Services, National Guidelines*, HSE, January 2009.

[23] HSE (2008) *NPSDD Annual Report*, HSE.

[24] Lynch, C. (2009) *Presentation to Irish Council for Social Housing 2009 on the Congregated Settings Report*, available at: http://www.icsh.ie/eng/content/download/1773/7346/file/Christy%20Lynch%20-%20Disability%20and%20Housing.pdf (accessed 12 October 2010).

Neither of these agencies contract directly with the individual, opting instead to use service providers. This system, therefore, remains in contrast to many parts of the United Kingdom, Sweden and North America, which allow individuals to use a system of individual funding to pay for a PA. With the regulations of the FÁS Community Employment Programme and the economic downturn Ireland is experiencing, contracts are being awarded to individuals for one year only in most of the cases, and are subject to renewal annually. Once funding has been agreed, a person can continue to use the PA for another year. The PA service is not available to people with mental health problems, and data are not available as to the small percentage of people with intellectual disabilities using the service.[25]

While the PA service model represents the least restrictive model of support in Ireland, there is still widespread use of segregated residential care facilities, in particular for people with spinal injuries and acquired brain injuries. During the consultation for a National Carers Strategy, which the government never proceeded to publish, *Headway* reported that all carers without exception mentioned the absence of services in the community for people with acquired brain injury as a major source of stress. This covered the whole range of services including residential supports, therapeutic interventions, day service places, vocational supports and information.[26] Therefore, people with physical disabilities and their families continue to rely on a fledgling independent living model, which is fraught by resource constraints and a lack of choice of support.

For persons with intellectual disabilities, services include day activation, special high-support and special intensive day services for adults and developmental day care for children. Rehabilitative training is again more typically offered through non-profit providers like Rehab. Rehab provides foundation-level personal, social and work-related skills to individuals to enable them to progress to greater levels of independence and integration. The top three day activities availed of by people with an intellectual disability in 2011, and accounting for more than half of principal day service provision, were activation programmes, rehabilitation services and sheltered work.[27] Sheltered workshops, therefore, still form a significant portion of day services offered, both from private and non-profit agencies around the country.

While the PA service provides a practical model to achieve community engagement, there are many parts of the country where providers have been reluctant to engage in personalisation, preferring to maintain traditional congregated care

---

[25] The income of each CIL varies depending on the size of the organisation (measured usually by number of service users and hours of personal assistance allocated to them) and the nature of the services provided; see http://www.dublincil.org/Documents/Report%20of%20the%20survey.pdf (accessed 24 November 2011).

[26] Headway Ireland (2008) Submission to the Carers Strategy.

[27] Health Research Board (2011) *Annual Report of the National Intellectual Disability Database Committee 2008*: Health Statistics Series 13.

systems, with little or no opportunities to individualise support arrangements.[28] Many organisations remain reluctant or unable to design personalised support. While the practice of locally developing individualised supports is to be celebrated, a more accommodating infrastructure for supporting change is lacking. Therefore, implementation of personalisation can vary substantially across the country and the practice appears to be quite ad hoc and discretionary.

Alongside the disability non-profit provider services, there are a number of programmes offered directly by the state. Home support services are provided to assist persons to continue to live at home. There is a homecare assistant service administered directly through the HSE, which provides personal support including washing, dressing and other activities of daily living, and facilitation in social, leisure and recreational activities. Similarly, there is an HSE home help service which provides domestic type support such as cooking, cleaning and the like. In many cases where home care assistants are not available, the home help may also provide support of a personal nature, such as washing or dressing.[29]

The HSE also funds community-based medical, nursing and therapy services which are provided by a team of professionals who work together to offer an integrated service to persons with a disability. Again, many of these services are provided through intermediaries. Services include social work, occupational therapy, speech and language therapy, physiotherapy, community nursing and psychology. Miscellaneous support services are also available to support people, including counselling and information.[30] Because there is no standardised entitlement to an assessment of need for adults, access to these supports and quality of activities can vary around the country. Most intellectual disability providers offer many of these services within their organisation, but again, the extent to which this is individually tailored varies considerably.

Staffing and Funding of Services

This section examines how the aforementioned disability-specific services are delivered in Ireland. At the outset, one of the most striking aspects of support provision is the level of professionalisation of the direct support workforce. As the last chapter identified, because of the medicalised history of support in Ireland, a significant amount of disability services is still provided by medical nursing staff. The support workforce has thus been relatively well paid, heavily professionalised and well supported by unions in Ireland. There are specific national pay grades for each scale of

---

[28] *Supra*, n. 2.

[29] Read, N. (n.d.) Directory of Services for People with Multiple Sclerosis in the South East Region, MS Ireland

[30] For more information, please refer to the HSE Web site: http://www.hse.ie/eng/services/Find_a_service/Disability_Services/ (24 November 2010).

worker, which have been agreed upon in partnership with national unions. There are three national unions in Ireland: the Psychiatric Nurses Association (PNA), the Irish Nurses and Midwives Organisation (INMO) and IMPACT. It is fair to say that Irish care workers are well represented. This means that at all levels, the disability industry and professionals are crucial players in the implementation phase of disability policy.[31] Indeed, as stated earlier, the 2008 Mental Health Inspectorate report[32] noted, in some areas, strong local industrial relations resistance to the rationalisation of wards in the old buildings and, in others, resistance to the replacement of hospital-based services by community services.

According to Sheerin (2004), the continued use of nurses who are centralised around residential services begins to call into question whether or not it is appropriate for a nurse to be the primary support worker for persons with an intellectual disability within the context of a normalised and holistic model of support.[33] Similarly, in mental health, more than 80 per cent of the mental health services budget is being absorbed by wages and salaries, the greater part of it being to nursing staff. This also needs to be considered in the context of the greatly reduced in-patient base to be supported.[34]

Funding of support-providing organisations is determined by service level arrangements (SLAs) – a successor to the earlier service level agreements. In the SLAs, support providers are expected to detail the numbers of people availing of their services. This is more typical of an Individual Service Fund model, a form of personal budget whereby the money is held by the organisation but restricted to the use of the individual, which has been developing in the United Kingdom. However, a crucial difference is that the funding within Irish organisations is not ring-fenced for the individual's sole use to pay for direct support costs. This type of funding effectively removes the promise of choice and control from disabled people and instead gives 'client capture' to the providers. In respect of the core funding element, non-profit organisations provide aggregated estimates of ongoing services to the HSE. The block funding means that control is entrenched within the disability service provider sector. However, while there is no formal individualised funding system, to some extent there is often enough flexibility in the system to establish individualised support arrangements which service providers have negotiated with

---

[31] Sullivan, M. and Munford, R. (2005) 'Disability and Support: The Interface between Disability Theory and Support – an Individual Challenge', in O'Brien, P. and Sullivan, M. (eds.) *Allies in Emancipation: Shifting from Providing Service to Being of Support*. Thomson Dunmore Press, Victoria. pp. 19–35.

[32] Mental Health Commission (2008) *Annual Report Including the Report of the Inspector of Mental Health Service*.

[33] Sheerin, F. (2004) 'Identifying the Foci of Interest to Nurses in Irish Intellectual Disability Services', *Journal of Learning Disabilities* 8: 159–174.

[34] Walsh, D. and Daly, A. (2004) *Mental Illness in Ireland 1750–2002: Reflections on the Rise and Fall of Institutional Care*. Health Research Board, Dublin.

their HSE areas. This system has been described as a 'relaxed-control' model, where decisions have become decentralised, service providers have a lot of autonomy and there are few or no statutory standards.[35]

If the disability service sector is to move to a more personalised support infrastructure, there will be a need for greater clarity around the cost of services and the services rendered to the individuals supported. There is, however, a need to evolve a costing and funding mechanism which is sensitive to the mix and cost of inputs associated with the various levels of support given to persons from both public and non-profit organisations.

All providers are being currently affected by a 'Value for Money' cut of 2 per cent in the current economic climate.[36] Also, many organisations funded through the Section 38 grants have been affected by a moratorium on new (or replacing of old) staff positions, which is estimated as another 2 per cent cut. The continuing use of the moratorium has meant many agencies have to reduce the breadth of activities in their day services, with a consequent reduction in staff across disability support provision.[37]

IDENTIFYING THE NEED FOR REFORM

As the previous chapter showed, Ireland began its journey towards transformation of disability support in the mid-1990s, somewhat later than most of the other jurisdictions examined earlier in the book. The first key animator of change came from the Report of the Commission on the Status of People with Disabilities – A Strategy for Equality (1996). This was the most definitive policy document regarding people with disabilities in Ireland. It set out a blueprint for reform which kick-started the transformation agenda in the Irish disability policy climate. The consultation behind the report and the comprehensiveness of the review prompted the process of gaining increased recognition and greater rights to enable people with disabilities to live independently and participate in society. In a short span of time, Ireland's national parliament has put in place a strong framework of legislation which promotes equality and prohibits discrimination on nine grounds, including disability. This national legislative framework is also underpinned by European non-discrimination law. The following takes stock of the key policy shifts which have evolved since 2006. Unlike the other chapters, Ireland has still not embarked on a system-wide transformation

[35] Power, A. and Kenny, K. (2011) 'When Care's Left to Roam: Carer Experiences of Grassroots Non-profit Services in Ireland', *Health & Place* 17(2): 422–429.

[36] For further details, please refer to: http://www.irishtimes.com/newspaper/breaking/2010/0707/breaking19.html (accessed 25 October 2011).

[37] The Irish Times (2010) *HSE Embargo on Jobs Created 'Uncontrolled Downsizing'*, available at: http://www.irishtimes.com/newspaper/health/2010/0504/1224269631201.html (accessed 25 October 2011).

of support provision towards individual funding, yet there has been a significant emergence of grass-roots initiatives which provide important lessons for other countries grappling with change. Meanwhile, there have been a number of important national conferences (by the National Disability Authority and Genio) which have sought to draw lines in the sand to ensure older congregated settings become a thing of the past.[38]

Public-Sector Scrutiny

A second wellspring of reform came from a period of public-sector scrutiny in the early 2000s, in which the system of support delivery became an object of detailed enquiry. First, the need for a better mechanism to administer government funding of disability supports was highlighted in a national audit of disability service providers within the non-profit sector by the Comptroller and Auditor General (C&AG). Evidence of the lenient regulation of this sector came to light with this report in 2005. Its investigation found a widespread failure amongst organisations, many of which were secular, to provide audited financial statements or disclose levels of executive pay.[39] The audit of forty-two organisations found that twelve groups did not file accounts for 2003. In particular, one large organisation which received €288 million between 2000 and 2004 had not provided financial statements for these four years.[40] Furthermore, according to the same report, visits to three HSE regional offices found that the information captured from their monitoring processes was not systematically used for evaluating service provision. The C&AG examination also found that, with a few exceptions, the level of supporting detail generally provided was minimal. New service developments and the costs associated with new client placements and enhancements attracted more consideration of costs than the core funding element.[41]

In September 2005, the Competition Authority, in a submission to the Department of Health,[42] also signalled its concerns regarding the manner in which service providers were being selected and funded. In particular, the Authority was concerned that:

---

[38] NDA Annual Conference 2010, www.nda.ie/website/nda/cntmgmtnew.nsf/o/CBC4F81DAB17032380 25773D002CDEDA?OpenDocument (accessed 25 October 2011); and GENIO 'A Day in the Life' Conference, http://www.genio.ie/publications/videos/a-day-in-the-life-presentations (accessed 24 November 2011).

[39] Comptroller and Auditor General (2005) *Report on Value for Money Examination: Provision of Disability Services by Nonprofit Organisations*. Comptroller and Auditor General, Dublin.

[40] *Ibid*. p. 9.

[41] *Ibid*.

[42] The Competition Authority (2005) *Submission to the Department of Health and Children on the Strategic Review of Disability Services*, September.

- Services for people with a disability are currently contracted to service providers with no tendering mechanisms for what often turn out to be contracts of indefinite length. This means that service providers face little incentive to honour their contracts in a satisfactory fashion.
- The provision of new investments and services is bundled, which means there is little scope to allow a new service provider to take over from a provider which does not deliver satisfactory service.
- There is no clear mechanism to allow new service providers to access funding, which means it is extremely difficult for new service providers to offer (potentially more innovative) services.
- Service providers are given 'catchment areas' by the health care services, which hinders service users' ability to switch service providers.[43]

A second area of inquiry focussed on the extent of institutional abuse within statutory organisations. The Ryan Report,[44] the Murphy Report[45] and the Leas Cross Review[46] revealed more sombre findings of institutional abuse within some of the support providers. These reports found evidence of widespread institutional abuse, including abuse of many deaf and hard-of-hearing people who had attended the Cabra schools. While the level of abuse itself was shocking, it also revealed the inadequacies of a system which had been left to develop without any adequate monitoring by the state. And yet, Ireland still has no mandatory inspections for assessing support provided by residential services to people with disabilities. In 2007, a statutory body called the Health Information & Quality Authority (HIQA) was established with a remit to develop standards in public health and social care services. However, the HIQA standards are solely for residential services and do not affect the ways in which day or community-wide services are currently run. Moreover, the HIQA standards are not enforceable. This reluctance is striking given the recent findings of abuse in state institutions.[47]

---

[43] *Ibid.* p. 1.

[44] Commission to Inquire into Child Abuse (2009) *Report of the Commission to Inquire into Child Abuse* 'Ryan Report', http://www.childabusecommission.com/rpt/pdfs/ (accessed 15 November 2011).

[45] Dublin Archdiocese Commission of Investigation (2009) *Report into the Catholic Archdiocese of Dublin*, July–November, http://www.dacoi.ie/ (accessed 25 October 2011).

[46] Health Service Executive (2006) *Leas Cross Review*, 10 November, http://www.hse.ie/eng/services/Publications/services/Older/Leas_Cross_Report.html (accessed 25 October 2011).

[47] The dangers of inappropriate support for disabled people were also laid bare in a recent report by the Mental Health Commission report into St Luke's psychiatric hospital in Clonmel, Co Tipperary. When the commission visited in 2008, it found that 'intellectually disabled patients' were being inappropriately prescribed long-term drugs such as benzodiazepines to control their behaviour, rather than the kind of therapeutic intervention they needed. Despite these findings, there is a lack of standards and inspections, which is a major issue for disability lobby groups. See O'Brien, C. (2008) 'Forgotten People Who Wait in Hope', *The Irish Times*, 19 July.

In response to the findings from this period of scrutiny, there are now new hopes on the horizon for reforming the disability support system in Ireland. The Department of Health and Children set up a Value for Money Review Group, The Review of the Efficiency and Effectiveness of Disability Services in Ireland, in 2008 to identify the inefficiencies and choke-points within the disability service sector.[48] Given the economic crisis which was beginning to emerge, their remit has been to explore new ways of delivering disability support, particularly in less segregated (and less expensive) settings. Following the consultation, the Department of Health and Children published the *Report on Public Consultation: Efficiency and Effectiveness of Disability Services in Ireland* (2010). Alongside this, the department also published a summary of the key proposals emerging from a recently completed Review of Disability Policy (2011). The main proposals are examined in the 'Shape of Reform' section later in the chapter.

There is now a new appreciation from the Department of Health, the HSE and voluntary service providers that the old way of doing things with its spiralling costs is no longer sustainable. A sum of €1.5 billion was spent on disability services in 2010, yet unmet needs continue to grow. The current system is expensive (€80,000 is the HSE average cost for a residential place and €15,000–€20,000 for a day place,[49] although this is subject to change). It is inflexible; the person or his/her family does not have much say in how the money is spent, or have a choice of service provider, and perhaps more importantly, the money is attached to a service not the person.[50] The prospective outcome of this comprehensive review of the existing support system holds the potential for significant reform.

Time to Move On *Report*

In addition to the Value for Money review, the HSE also began a review of congregated settings and day services. The recent publication of its report in July 2011, *Time to Move On from Congregated Settings: A Strategy for Community Inclusion*, indicates that the government is dedicated to reforming the disability support sector and identifying cost-effective new approaches to enabling people to live and participate

---

[48] Members of Review Steering Group include: Laurence Crowley, Chairperson; Gerard Flood; James O'Dwyer; Brendan Broderick, Chief Executive Officer, Sisters of Charity of Jesus and Mary Services; John Dolan, Chief Executive Officer, Disability Federation of Ireland; Bairbre Nic Aongusa, Director, Office for Disability & Mental Health, Department of Health and Children (DoHC); Jim Breslin, Assistant Secretary, Finance, Performance Evaluation, Information & Research, DoHC; Patricia Purtill, Sectoral Policy Unit, Department of Finance (DoF); Cormac Gilhooly, Central Policy Evaluation Unit, DoF; Ger Crowley, Director, Regional Health Office–South, HSE; and Yvonne O'Neill, Assistant National Director, VFM Directorate, HSE. See http://www.dohc.ie/press/releases/2009/20090918.html.

[49] Inclusion Ireland (2009) *Inclusion Ireland Newsletter*, December.

[50] *Ibid.*

in the community.[51] The report identifies best practice internationally and examines the potential for implementation of a more responsive and individualised support system based on living in dispersed housing. More details on this programme for change are examined in the 'Shape of Reform' section later in the chapter.

Genio

Another important development has been the establishment of Genio (formerly the Person Centre), a trust organisation whose aim is to identify and promote innovative practice within disability and mental health support providers and thus animate change more broadly.[52] Given the new era of person-centred planning and individualised of support arrangements, there is also the need for a new period of disability politics which can contribute to informed debates over best-practice models which support people to achieve independence without risking isolation. Moreover, given the range of local pioneering work around the country, there is a need to champion and celebrate the successes within the sector.

TAKING STOCK OF THE INITIAL STRANDS OF REFORM

The main thrust of the reform agenda in Ireland, as the following sections show, has so far been primarily focussed on expanding and reconfiguring the supply side of service delivery. This has included a commitment to reconfigure the administration of disability policy and identify the inefficiencies within the support provider sector to create more responsive and person-centred support organisations.

Alongside this, there have been a few initial strands of demand-side reform, including a commitment to an assessment of need for adults and a review of funding options to advance choice in accessing supports. Given the strong history of provider autonomy in Ireland, there also are a number of grass-roots provider-driven reforms, where organisations have themselves advanced more person-centred support options. Each of these is discussed in detail later in the chapter.

DEMAND SIDE OF REFORM

Assessment of Need

The Irish government made a commitment to providing a right to an Assessment of Need in the Disability Act (2005) under Part 2 (s. 7–23).[53] The legislation provides

---

[51] *Supra*, n. 2.
[52] Genio (2010) *Genio*, http://www.genio.ie/ (accessed 25 October 2011).
[53] The details established under the Disability Act 2005 are available at: http://www.irishstatutebook.ie/ 2005/en/act/pub/0014/index.html (accessed 25 October 2011).

an entitlement to an independent assessment of health and education needs, an assessment report, a statement of the services the individual will receive and the opportunity to make a complaint if the individual is not happy with any part of the process.

This was envisaged as a key first step to reconfiguring the power imbalance inherent in accessing services which have been traditionally provider led. However, to date, this is only available for those aged between zero and five years and has not been extended to adults. According to Citizens Information, it is intended that other age groups will gradually be included so that everyone with a disability will be covered by 2011, although at the time of this writing, this has still not become the case.[54] The likelihood of its further implementation remains unclear.

For now, an independent assessment of need is an assessment of the full range of a child's needs associated with his or her disability. After this the child will receive an assessment report detailing his or her health and educational needs and the services required to meet those needs. The assessments are carried out without regard to cost or capacity to provide services. In other words, the assessment of need takes account of one's needs – it does not address the question of whether or not those needs can be met.

When the assessment is complete, an HSE Liaison Officer prepares a service statement based on the assessment of need and the resources available. The service statement does take into account if those needs can be met and how this can be done. The service statement specifies the health or education services, or both, to be provided and the time frame within which these services are to be provided taking into account, inter alia, the resources available. The service statement then says what services and supports are to be provided to the child and must be prepared within one month of the assessment being completed. The family receives the child's assessment report and service statement at the same time.

The HSE-appointed assessment officers (assessors) are independent in carrying out their functions. They are based in local health offices and may be able to help families to fill in the application form and give them whatever information they need. The assessors can carry out the assessment themselves or authorise other HSE employees or other experienced people to do so. In other words, a broad range of professionals can be involved depending on the HSE area. Meanwhile, for service statements, the HSE has appointed liaison officers to draw up these statements.

HIQA has published standards for the assessment of needs; in them, it has expressed the commitment to make the process take a person-centred approach. It states that the process should ensure that 'the views of the person are listened to, documented and used in relation to the identification and prioritisation of needs'.[55]

---

54 Please refer to: www.citizensinformation.ie/en/health/health_services_for_people_with_disabilities/ assessment_of_need_for_people_with_disabilites.html (accessed 27 October 2011).
55 HIQA (2007) *Standards for the Assessment of Need*, HIQA, p. 9.

While this is a welcome commitment, there are a number of broader concerns relating to the lack of evaluation or available data from the HSE to demonstrate how independent assessments are being conducted.[56] Some evidence exists that meeting the statutory deadlines on providing assessments and service statements has proved challenging to the HSE.[57] This lack of data prevents comparison of the effectiveness of different approaches being taken in various HSE areas and HSE local health office areas at the national level. As a result, neither parents nor assessment teams are fully aware of how the process is developing nationally, which is potentially limiting the assessment team's ability to coordinate strategy and approaches.

Moreover, the process of assessment of need has been solely focussed on assessing the education and health needs of children with disabilities. For a further roll-out of this assessment to adults with disabilities, this focus on health and education offers quite a narrow range of opportunities to access other support options and does not reflect the wider wishes and goals of adults wishing to gain access to community connection or supported employment service options.

For adults requiring access to services, generally the person and his/her family meet a social worker who is linked to a disability service provider for their catchment area. For those already using a service, ongoing support planning ordinarily takes place within organisations. While developing a continuum of support within which an individual feels that the service finding out more about his or her wishes and goals is a welcome development, ultimately there can often be a conflict of interest over the ownership of the plan. Provider-led person-centred planning can potentially restrict the flexibility of the plan, pigeonholing it into a set of services, programmes or treatments which can be offered in-house to meet various needs and goals.

Development of an Advocacy Service

Another step in advancing the demand side of reform has been the implementation of an advocacy service to restore power to persons with disabilities. Advocacy has broad-ranging relevance for people with disabilities who struggle with the transition from congregated setting to the community or deal with issues relating to their service (such as threats to their privacy or dignity). It is likely that embedding an advocacy service is part of the government's growing commitment to move people with disabilities out of congregated settings and into the community.

The National Advocacy Service was a core element of the National Disability Strategy (implemented under the Citizens Information Act 2007). This Act amended the Comhairle Act 2000, which, as we saw in the previous chapter, had established

---

[56] Only one report has been published by the HSE to date on the assessment of needs (in accordance with Section 13), but this report does not address the different methods of conducting assessments used by early intervention teams.

[57] DÁIL QUESTION NO: 120, 18/05/2010, addressed to the Minister of State at the Department of Health and Children (Mr. Moloney) by Deputy David Stanton.

a statutory agency called Comhairle (meaning 'advice' or 'counsel' in Gaelic) to provide assistance and information to citizens, including supporting people with disabilities in identifying and understanding their needs and options and in accessing their entitlements to social services.

Comhairle began some involvement in advocacy in 2004 following the Comhairle (Amendment) Bill 2004, which included a provision for the establishment by Comhairle of advocacy services for people with disabilities. In this context, Comhairle commissioned Goodbody Economic Consultants to undertake a study to identify and examine the components of an advocacy service which would best fit the Irish situation, to set out a framework for such a service and to estimate costs. The Goodbody report, *Developing an Advocacy Service for People with Disabilities*, examined the components of an advocacy service which would meet the needs of people with disabilities in Ireland.[58] It recommended that Comhairle adopt a three-strand approach to advocacy, incorporating a:

- Personal Advocacy Service (PAS) – to be set up on a paid professional basis to deal with critical and complex advocacy issues;
- Support Programme for People with Disabilities in the Community and Voluntary Sector – to focus on the provision of individual advocacy services, employing a range of delivery models;
- Community Visitors Programme – to focus on people with cognitive disability in residential institutions, to be established on a volunteer basis, overseen by a central and regional structure.

Following the report, it was agreed that the two main streams would be concentrated upon: the immediate establishment of the Advocacy Programme for People with Disabilities in the Community and Voluntary Sector (Strand 2) and the preparations required to initiate the PAS (Strand 1) for certain people with disabilities, who would otherwise have difficulty in getting access to those services. The CIB began the process of establishing the advocacy programme by engaging with the community and voluntary sector. In 2005 and 2006, expressions of interest were sought from a range of different organisations representing people with disabilities, including service providers, the voluntary sector and partnership groupings. On a pilot basis, forty-six advocacy projects were chosen for three-year funding (later extended to five) on the basis of their capacity to employ an advocate and reach a service user grouping specified by them.[59]

In 2007, the aforementioned Citizens Information Act 2007 was passed, enabling the delivery of independent, representative advocacy for people with disabilities who seek to enforce their legal entitlements to services. The Act enhanced the functions

---

58 Goodbody Consultants (2004) *Developing an Advocacy Service for People with Disabilities*. Goodbody Consultants, Dublin.

59 Citizens Information Board (2010) *Evaluation of the Programme of Advocacy Services for People with Disabilities in the Community and Voluntary Sector*. Roundtable Solutions and Pathfinder Evaluation, Dublin.

of Comhairle and renamed it the Citizens Information Board (CIB). The CIB began monitoring the pilot programme to ensure the projects were operating in accordance with the board's advocacy guidelines. To give support to the regional advocates, the Irish Association of Advocates (IAA) was also established in 2007 as a national representative organisation. A full evaluation of the community and voluntary sector advocacy programme was published in 2010.[60] It argued strongly for the introduction of a National Advocacy Service which would combine elements of the existing pilot projects with the legislative powers of the Personal Advocacy Service (PAS) envisaged in the Citizens Information Act.

The National Advocacy Service was finally established in January 2011 by the Minister for Social Protection. It consists of five regional advocacy centres across the country with new area offices in Clondalkin (Co. Dublin), Co. Leitrim, Co. Offaly, Co. Waterford and Co. Westmeath, with teams of local advocates working on the ground. It replaces the existing pilot projects which provided assistance to more than 5,000 people with disabilities. The CIB is tasked with the administration of these new services. It remains to be seen whether the advocates will have the necessary statutory powers and resources to gain access to clients in residential centres and to provide full representation and/or support to vulnerable people who are involved in official processes or who wish to pursue a serious complaint against a service provider.[61] Nonetheless, the establishment of the National Advocacy Service is a welcome development as it demonstrates the state's willingness to provide concrete support for people with disabilities in exercising their legal rights.

Involving Individuals in Decisions Regarding Their Support

There has been a new commitment within recent policy guidance to involve individuals in support planning and developing more personalised responses to their needs. The Department of Health report on the public consultation of their Value For Money (VFM) and Policy Review, *Efficiency and Effectiveness of Disability Services in Ireland*, details a number of submissions prioritising the need for 'increased consultation with service users in policy, planning, delivery of services (inclusive of involvement in staff recruitment)'.[62] These are welcome signals for a reappraisal of conventional services. The resulting document from the review, *Summary of Key Proposals from the Review of Disability Policy*, put the key themes emerging from the review in the public domain for consideration and discussion. The final Department of Health report, *Value for Money and Policy Review of Disability Services in Ireland*

---

[60] Mary Hanafin (2009) *Dail Questions*, http://inclusionireland.ie/Dail30April2009.asp#Priority2 (accessed 28 October 2011).

[61] See Flynn, E. (2010) *New Advocacy Service for People with Disabilities Launched, Human Rights in Ireland*, http://www.humanrights.ie/index.php/2010/10/06/new-national-advocacy-service-for-people-with-disabilities-launched/ (accessed 6 August 2011).

[62] Department of Health and Children (2011) *Summary of Key Proposals from The Review of Disability Policy*, p. 50.

was published on 20 July 2012.[63] The Summary document and subsequent report highlight the gap between what people want and current provision: 'The activity of the services is largely focused on providing services in group settings, most of which are segregated from the general community. The current structure and procurement of disability services is focused on continued provision of services in this way'.[64] Significantly, it points to a 'new way' of organising services, recognising that people with disabilities and their families are not necessarily looking for 'more of the same'. They are looking for flexible services which meet their individual needs and systems which vest more control with the service user (and families as appropriate). Therefore, the summary document states, services should focus on aligning themselves with the central policy objective of the national partnership agreement (Towards 2016) – to enable persons with disabilities to 'lead full and independent lives, to participate in work and society and to maximise their potential'.[65] To achieve this, the summary document sets out a new policy vision based on two goals.

Goal 1: Full inclusion and self-determination for people with disabilities. This involves a reframing of the goal of support provision from disability services to individualised supports. These supports will be determined and directed by the person (in collaboration with the family/advocate as required and in consultation with an independent assessor) not the service provider or other 'experts'. The support will be provided on a one-to-one basis to the person and not in group settings (unless that is the specific choice of the person and is part of a 'natural' group activity, such as a team sport). It will be flexible and responsive, adapting to the person's changing needs and wishes and encompassing a wide range of sources and types of support so that very specific needs and wishes can be met, rather than be limited by what a single service provider can provide. Finally, the support will have a high degree of specificity rather than being expressed in terms of residential, day or respite services.

Goal 2: The creation of a cost-effective, responsive and accountable system which will support the full inclusion and self-determination of people with disabilities. This will involve the creation of a strong governance framework in order to underpin the provision of the supports and services for people with disabilities. The elements of such a governance framework will include:

- processes for assessing needs;
- processes for allocating resources;
- processes for procurement and commissioning;
- quality assurance systems, including processes for managing risk;
- processes for performance management, review and accountability;
- appropriate information systems;
- management structure.

---

63 Department of Health (2012) *Value for Money and Policy Review of Disability Services in Ireland*, Stationary Office, Dublin.

64 Department of Health and Children (2011) *Summary of Key Proposals from The Review of Disability Policy*.

65 Department of the Taoiseach (2006) *Towards 2016: Ten-Year Framework Social Partnership Agreement 2006–2015*. Stationary Office, Dublin.

While this is a welcome commitment from government to a new vision of disability supports, and is in line with best-practice thinking, it remains to be seen which of the mechanisms identified earlier will be implemented to ensure these principles are upheld.

Review of Funding Options to Advance Personalisation

As stated earlier, at the time of this writing, Ireland does not have a national system of individual funding. However, there are a number of pilot schemes and funding options being considered by government, which have the potential to restore choice and power to persons with disabilities in accessing supports.

As identified previously, the Department of Health set up a VFM review group. This is largely in response to the C&AG review and a fiscal imperative to identify cost-efficiencies in the provider sector. The VFM review has indicated its intention to move to a system of individual supports; however, it has not gone so far as saying it will implement some form of individual funding option.[66] The former Minister of State for Disability and Mental Health signalled that individual funding could be a future policy option.[67] The *Time to Move On* report recommends that the scope for introducing forms of individualised budgets, giving people as much control as possible over their choice of supports, should be examined by HSE. It also recommends that individuals should get their own personal service level agreement which outlines who is responsible for delivering each aspect of their support provision.[68]

At present, however, people with disabilities in Ireland do not have a right to such an option which would enable them to employ a personal assistant or buy home modifications. The 1999 Progress Report on the Implementation of the Recommendations of the Commission on the Status of People with Disabilities stated that a 'Costs of Disability Payment' would not be introduced, much like the UK Disability Living Allowance. It was argued that such a payment would be very difficult to introduce given the widely varying degrees of disability experienced by individuals. Such a payment would require assessment by a wide range of experts, and the administrative costs, they felt, could be significant.[69] Furthermore, the Costs of Disability Payment was rejected on the grounds that other groups in society, such as travellers, the homeless and seniors, may also claim to have special costs related to their medical or social condition and may seek equality of treatment.[70]

---

[66] CIL Pre-budget Submission 2009–2010.

[67] O'Brien, C. (2010) 'Disabled Should Get Direct Payments, Says Minister', *The Irish Times*, 26 April.

[68] *Supra*, n. 2, p. 148.

[69] Department of Justice, Equality and Law Reform (1999) *Towards Equal Citizenship: Progress Report on the Implementation of the Recommendations of the Commission on the Status of People with Disabilities*. Stationary Office, Dublin.

[70] *Ibid.* p. 60.

According to Breathnach (2006), the main issues for an individualised evaluation system in Ireland therefore are the delivery of value for money considerations, professional issues regarding the undertaking of evaluations, internal non-profit innovative capacities, ensuring and demonstrating non-profit credibility and legitimacy and the developmental role of evaluation as well as that of enabling accountability.[71] However, from looking at other jurisdictions, direct payments have been shown to offer a cost-effective, transparent and fully accountable system of administering support. In addition, they can offer a powerful stimulant to non-profit organisations to adapt to change.

One cause of this resistance to individual funding is a culture where service users must not be exposed to unnecessary risk, as services in many cases are dominated by procedures that aim to minimise risk. In Ireland, according to Egan (2008), there is a particularly strong culture in which risks are often no longer managed but simply avoided.[72] The concept of growth through responsibility has not gained traction in Ireland amongst service users or families who have become accustomed to a service with minimal personal responsibility.

Meanwhile, the HSE is developing a draft protocol of Policy and Procedure for Funding Non-Statutory Organisations. This is a review of the operation of service level arrangements. A national framework is being developed within the HSE which will ensure a consistent approach is taken, which will link funding provided to a quantum of service, and provide for these services to be linked to quality standards, with continuous monitoring to ensure equity, efficiency and effective use of available resources.[73] The HSE is developing comparative cost indicators and is becoming more involved in more detailed contracting practices with support organisations. Previously, the funding was agreed upon by a five-year service agreement; nowadays, however, HSE is operating on the basis of two-year SLAs with providers, with a built-in annual adjustment review.[74]

Alongside these developments, there is a growing family movement in Ireland, particularly within the intellectual disability sector, led by Taking Control, a group of parents, self-advocates and organisations, as well as the CILs and other groups, calling for individual funding and more control in the hands of people with disabilities. Taking Control organised a national conference in 2008 to animate change in the policy debates over the future delivery of support.[75]

---

[71] Breathnach, C. (2006) *The Development of 'Evaluation' as an Exploratory Theme at the Centre for Nonprofit Management.* Dialogue Project on Evaluation: Discussion Paper 1, Centre for Nonprofit Management, School of Business, University of Dublin, Trinity College.

[72] Egan, D. (2008) *Issues Concerning Direct Payments in the Republic of Ireland: A Report for the Person Centre,* November.

[73] Personal Communication, interviews with disability service provider managers, September 2010.

[74] Personal Communication, Disability Representative Organisation, June 2011.

[75] Taking Control Conference, October 2008, available at: http://www.inclusionireland.ie/ TakingControlConferenceOct2008.asp (accessed 13 March 2012).

Individualised funding in the form of direct payments may be part of the solution towards the unmet need for PA services. People with disabilities who are currently residing in 'inappropriate' settings but who cannot live in the community because of service provider waiting lists may be in a position to organise their own services. A direct payment to some extent could circumvent waiting lists. Equally many parents of people with intellectual disabilities feel their children are shoehorned into existing services, with poor outcomes for the individual. Increasingly these parents are asking policy makers within state bodies to give them the means to design and implement their own service plans. Direct payments would allow such state bodies to be proactive in meeting these demands.[76]

There is some degree of local 'piloting' of direct cash grants beginning to take place around the country. The Home Care Support Scheme (also known as the Home Care Support Package) is operated by the HSE. The main priority of the Home Care Support Scheme is older people living in the community or those who are in-patients in acute care hospitals at risk of admission to long-term care. However, there is evidence to suggest that the purpose of Care Packages is liberally interpreted by some HSEAs, including Care Packages being used to support people with disabilities through the provision of personal assistants. In some parts of the country, services under the scheme are provided directly by the HSE; in others they are administered by service provider organisations on behalf of the HSE. According to the HSE, 'Packages may also consist of direct cash grants to enable the patient's family to purchase a range of services or supports privately. In some parts of the country, the package may consist of a combination of direct services and cash payments'.[77]

The Home Care Support Scheme is still largely in its infancy, and there are no national guidelines regarding admission to the scheme. The scheme does allow for means testing, and each HSE administrative area has responsibility for the operation of its own scheme.[78]

In addition to these home care packages, there is also a demonstration of an individual funding programme for persons with physical disabilities in Dublin, called Laying Down New Tracks, which began in 2010. It is being run by an agency called Áiseanna Tacaíochta, which is a person-led organisation based on mentoring amongst people with disabilities and peer-led use of resources to purchase personal assistants. It is being funded by Genio as part of its piloting initiatives.

At the national level, however, there is still no HSE-led pilots of personal budgets for those with intellectual disabilities. However, there is now a new appreciation from the Department of Health and Children, the HSE and voluntary service providers

---

[76] Egan, *supra*, n. 72.

[77] HSE (2010) *Home Care Support Scheme for Carers*, http://www.citizensinformation.ie/en/health/health_services_for_older_people/home_care_packages_for_carers.html (24 November 2010).

[78] Egan, *supra*, n. 72.

that the old way of doing things with its spiralling costs is no longer sustainable. To date, however, it is uncertain what model of individual funding and facilitation may emerge.

Enabling a Choice in Living Arrangements

In terms of specific government housing policy related to enabling more choice in living arrangements, the National Housing Strategy for People with a Disability, published October 2011, aims to reflect the diverse housing needs of people with a disability and to ensure that the appropriate structures and supports, to effectively deliver on these accommodation needs, are in place.[79] Its recommendations were informed in particular by the deliberations and recommendations of the Working Group on Congregated Settings, published by the HSE in 2011.[80] The strategy seeks to mainstream access to independent living for adults living with physical, mental, sensory and intellectual disabilities. This means that it will direct the efforts of housing authorities and the HSE to support people with a disability to live independently in their own homes, with accommodation designed and/or adapted as fit-for-purpose, rather than having to move into residential care settings.

Similarly, the department's overarching statement on housing policy, Delivering Homes, Sustaining Communities, outlines a commitment to the housing needs of persons needing support:

> A clear aim of *Delivering Homes, Sustaining Communities* is to achieve a step change in the provision of housing support to obtain more effective delivery in ways that ensure that individuals in need of support are offered options tailored to their needs. These responses should lead to better life opportunities and break cycles of disadvantage and dependency ... this reflects a central underpinning of the Towards 2016 agreement and the commitments on housing reflected therein.[81]

As indicated in the above quote, Towards 2016 acknowledged that people with a disability often have fewer choices in terms of providing for their housing and accommodation needs, and the vision set out that 'every person with a disability would have access to appropriate housing'.[82] To meet the aims of the new housing strategy for persons with disabilities, the government published a National Implementation Framework in July 2012. The report acknowledges that within the current economic climate, and in light of existing pressures on local authority housing lists, additional and sustainable sources of funding must be identified to support delivery

79 Department of the Environment, Heritage and Local Government (2007) *Press Release: Minister O'Keeffe Launches National Group to Advise on the Development of a National Housing Strategy for People with a Disability*, 25 October.

80 *Supra*, n. 2.

81 Department of the Environment, Heritage and Local Government (2007) *Delivering Homes, Sustaining Communities: Statement on Housing Policy*. Stationary Office, Dublin. p. 10.

82 *Supra*, n. 65.

within the proposed timescales. Nonetheless, the document makes a commitment to respond more quickly and on a larger scale to social housing support needs through a variety of mechanisms, including through increased provision of social housing and more efficient and effective use of the resources, systems and procedures currently allocated to meet the housing and related support needs of people with disabilities.[83]

In terms of current programmes which attempt to meet this aim, the government offers a number of rent relief and housing adaptation grants to individuals who want to live in their house or apartment. In terms of specially adapted housing, the Technical Guidance Document,[84] Part M of the Building regulations requires that new dwellings should be designed and constructed so that people with disabilities can safely and conveniently approach and gain access to the main habitable rooms at entry level. It also requires that a WC should be provided at entry level.

In terms of grants for living independently, the Housing Adaptation Grant for Persons with a Disability scheme replaced the Disabled Persons Grant in November 2007. According to the Department of the Environment, Heritage and Local Government's statement on housing policy, these newer grants were supposed to be more targeted to those most in need.[85] They are targeted to people with disabilities in situations where changes need to be made to a home to make it suitable for a person with a physical or intellectual disability. Grant assistance may be available for changes such as making the home wheelchair-accessible, the installation of a stair lift, the provision of ground-floor bedroom, toilet or shower facilities, and so forth. All grant applications received since 2008 have been processed in line with available funding and prioritised based on terminal illness, age of applicant and urgency of works required. The department's contribution towards the 2010 grant programme was €100 million.[86]

People with disabilities can also apply for the Mobility Aids Grant Scheme through the local authority which provides grants for equipment designed to address mobility problems in the home, such as grab-rails, a level-access shower or chair-lift. It is designed to fast-track essential items required to allow individuals to remain in their own home. The grant is primarily for older people, but people with disabilities can also access the scheme. The amount paid under this scheme is less than the Housing Adaptation Grant for People with a Disability, and the cut-off point for household income is lower; only people with household incomes of less than €30,000 qualify. However, an individual may get essential mobility aids quicker under this scheme

---

[83] Department of Health & Department of Environment, Community and Local Government (2012) *National Housing Strategy for People with a Disability: National Implementation Framework*, Stationary Office, Dublin.

[84] Available at: http://www.environ.ie/en/Publications/DevelopmentandHousing/BuildingStandards/FileDownLoad,1655,en.pdf (accessed 1 December 2011).

[85] Department of the Environment, Heritage and Local Government (2007) *Delivering Homes, Sustaining Communities: Statement on Housing Policy*. Stationary Office, Dublin.

[86] See http://www.greenparty.ie/en/news/latest_news/100m_home_improvement_funding_announced_for_most_vulnerable (accessed 1 December 2011).

and up to 100 per cent of the cost is covered up to a maximum amount of generally under €6,000.

In terms of rent supplement for people with disabilities, if an individual is living in private rented accommodation in Ireland and receives a social welfare or HSE payment, he/she may qualify for a rent supplement. To be eligible for a rent supplement, an individual is means-tested and needs to be on disability allowance, invalidity pension or blind pension. Prior to 1 February 2005, there was a requirement that applicants had to be renting for six months in the preceding twelve months to qualify for rent supplement, but this requirement has been discontinued. The rent supplement is part of the Supplementary Welfare Allowance Scheme for people with little or no income, who have exceptional needs. It is funded by the Department of Social Protection and is administered at the local level by the community welfare officers (CWOs). All the supplementary welfare payments are discretionary, but the CWOs have guidelines within which they work.[87] The amount given is calculated by the CWO and the calculation generally ensures that an individual's income after paying rent does not fall below a minimum level.[88] The minimum contribution which must be made by the individual is €24 per week, or €104 per calendar month.

Given that rent supplement is a discretionary payment, and was originally envisaged as a temporary assistance for people paying rent, the government established the rental accommodation scheme (RAS) as a long-term rent funding option. If individuals are getting rent supplement for more than eighteen months and are in need of long-term housing, they may be eligible for the RAS. The scheme is administered by local authorities and they make the final decision regarding who is eligible under the scheme.

The RAS is an agreement according to which the local authority draws up a contract with a landlord to provide housing for persons with a long-term housing need for an agreed term (e.g. five years). It is designed to give private tenants greater security of tenure. The local authority pays the rent directly to the landlord. The tenants may continue to contribute to their rent but they pay this contribution to their local authority, not to their landlord. The landlord must register their tenancy with the Private Residential Tenancies Board (PRTB),[89] and the property must meet minimum standards for private rental accommodation.[90] Deposits are not required, because the local authority enters into a contract with the landlord.

In some cases, non-profit service providers also operate their own housing associations and manage them separately as 'sister organisations'. The Department of the Environment, Community and Local Government provides funds to the housing associations to buy houses, and the housing associations assist people with moving into the accommodation. The housing association acts as the landlord, and the

---

[87] Under the legislation of the Social Welfare Consolidation Act 2005.

[88] This level is the supplementary welfare allowance minus €13.

[89] http://www.citizensinformation.ie/categories/housing/renting-a-home/private_residential_tenancies_board

[90] The tenancies are governed by the Residential Tenancies Act 2004.

person with the disability pays rent either through the rent supplement from the CWO or privately. In these cases, the disability provider offers targeted support to the individual, such as meals and laundry, by domestic staff and bathing, medication and the like by support staff. The operation of these programmes can vary by HSEA and is largely up to the discretion of the CWO.

Social housing may also be available to persons with disabilities who are in need of housing but who cannot afford to buy their own homes. Local authorities are the main providers of affordable and social housing schemes in Ireland, although voluntary and community organisations also provide social housing to people with disabilities. Local authority housing is allocated according to a scheme of letting priorities, as required by S. 11 of the Housing Act 1988. The 2008 Housing Need Assessment identified a need for 1,155 households where a person with a disability was on local authority housing waiting lists – an increase from 480 in 2005. However, this figure is very small relative to the total number of 56,249 waiting for social housing.[91] Despite the government commitment to increase the number of people with disabilities, it is not known whether those housed in group homes/residential centres are being placed on the waiting list or not.

In relation to local authority social housing, respondents to a survey carried out as part of the Citizens Information Board and Disability Federation of Ireland Report[92] stated that there was an insufficient supply of accessible and adaptable local authority housing, and, as with the general population, people with disabilities can be on the waiting list for several years, particularly those living with parents and relatives. Furthermore, in the opinion of some respondents, local authority waiting lists are incomplete in that some people with disabilities do not apply for local authority housing because they do not believe they have a chance of succeeding.[93]

Similar challenges for people with disabilities accessing social housing were identified by the Irish Council for Social Housing survey of members in 2006–2007.[94] Firstly, the housing needs assessment is the main gateway for individuals to access social housing. Organisations in their survey noted the difficulties with the assessment process and the importance of a clearer system which people with disabilities are aware of and can access. Consequently, it found people with disabilities have been significantly under-represented in previous assessments. Secondly, there was also a reported lack of suitable sites and properties for people with disabilities, particularly given the accessibility requirements of people with physical and sensory disabilities. Moreover, several issues were raised in relation to the capital funding

[91] Housing Agency (2011) *Housing Need Assessment 2011*. Housing Agency, Dublin.
[92] Citizens Information Board/ Disability Federation of Ireland (2007) *The Right Living Space: Housing and Accommodation Needs of People with Disabilities*. Social Policy Report Prepared by Michael Browne, p. 26.
[93] Personal Communication, Disability Representative Organisation, July 2011.
[94] Irish Council for Social Housing (2007) *Enhancing Choices for People with Disabilities in the Community: Survey Findings on Social Housing Provision for People with Disabilities in the Voluntary Housing Sector*. Policy and Research Series, September.

required to provide for assistive technologies and physical adaptations. Thirdly, organisations noted the difficulties with the slowness of the approval process for providing accommodation under the Capital Assistance Scheme. Many organisations felt that the approval process was too drawn out, with some stating that their scheme took more than eighteen months to receive approval.

In terms of the survey recommendations, ensuring collaboration between departments, agencies and providers at all levels was reported as a key aspect of improving the existing system for providing housing for people with disabilities. It also emphasised the need for a coherent approach at national policy level as well as at the delivery/local agency level. It claimed that it is essential that there is a designated person within each HSE area appointed to liaise with the housing officer within each local authority to facilitate the proper planning and coordination of accommodation and support for people with disabilities.

Overall, then, there are many barriers to the implementation of the recent housing strategy for people with disabilities in Ireland – in particular, accessing relief for private rented accommodation, owning private housing or living in council housing. As a result, many people without family connections living in group homes have little avenue for independent living, with the exception of home share options.

Enhancing Consumer Purchasing Power

Finally, in some other jurisdictions, governments have put in place mechanisms for individuals and families to set up trusts or savings plans to enable them to save money for the future. This is a particularly pertinent form of support to sustain a life in the community either after an individual's parents pass away or the individual faces the difficult transition into adulthood. Generally, these savings are held in an account until the child reaches adulthood. The cost savings come from the account's ability to fund a variety of essential expenses for the person with a disability, including educational expenses, assistive technology, personal supports services, transportation, housing and so forth. In addition, funds remaining in the accounts at the individual's death would be used to pay back the state programmes up to the value of services provided to the individual during life. At the same time, such accounts give individuals with disabilities and their families an option to save for their future financial needs in a way which supports their unique situation, and would free them from sole dependence on conventional day care services, making it more feasible to live full lives in their communities.

It is already possible to some extent in Ireland to set up trust funds from the proceeds of public subscriptions to benefit those who are permanently and totally incapacitated under Section 12 of the Finance Act 1999. However, there are various shortcomings with this model. First, there is no state contribution to these trusts, unlike the RDSP in Canada, for example. Second, there is no guarantee that the money saved would be disregarded for the purpose of means-tested eligibility requirements. Finally, Ireland's capacity legislation precludes many individuals from setting up bank accounts in the first place. In situations where individual's capacity is under question, there can be restrictions on the ownership or management of a trust fund, and it becomes a potentially litigious area. As a result, the use of this legislation is problematic. Given the success of disability savings schemes in other jurisdictions, more could be done to develop a programme to support this model. This is particularly relevant given the data from the national intellectual disability database[95] and physical and sensory disability database,[96] which continue to predict increasing numbers of persons needing full-time residential services for those whose parents cannot continue to provide support.

IDENTIFYING THE INITIAL STRANDS OF THE SUPPLY SIDE OF REFORM

Reconfiguring the Administration of Disability Support

The first main development in Ireland's reform agenda from the supply side has been a commitment to reconfigure the public administration of disability support, at both the national level and the regional and local levels, to enable more effective governance of the policy issues affecting persons with disabilities.

A first area of reconfiguration has been a commitment to mainstream disability issues across government departments. Rather than a silo approach, a core ingredient of the National Disability Strategy in 2004, as we saw in the last chapter, was a requirement that six government departments would have to develop sectoral plans. Thus Ireland developed its own mainstreaming process, similar to that envisaged by Sweden with their disability policy *From Patient to Citizen*. These plans have to identify *how* the functions of each department, and the key bodies which they oversee, serve the needs of people with disabilities. They also have to set out a programme for future development. This was a radical change from the traditional silo approach of leaving disability issues solely with the Department of Health.

In terms of the sectoral plan for the Department of Health and Children, the approach to the provision of health and social services for people with disabilities is developed within the context of the overall goal of the HSE. Key features include a new legislative framework to provide for clear statutory provisions on eligibility and entitlement for health and personal social services. S.32 contains particularly relevant clauses in relation to the issue of independent living. S.32 (c) requires the plan to contain information concerning 'arrangements for co-operation by the HSE with housing authorities in relation to the development and co-ordination of the

---

[95] Health Research Board (2011) *Annual Report of the National Intellectual Disability Database 2010*. Health Research Board, Dublin.

[96] Health Research Board (2011) *Annual Report of the National Physical and Sensory Disability Database 2010*. Health Research Board, Dublin.

services provided by housing authorities for persons with disabilities'. Meanwhile, the sectoral plan for the Minister for Enterprise, Trade and Employment[97] aims for enhancing the relevance and effectiveness of vocational training and developing necessary supports to allow greater access to open labour market employment for people with disabilities.

Each sectoral plan also has to include arrangements for complaints, monitoring and review procedures. Reports regarding progress in terms of implementation are to be prepared at least every three years. While these plans are published, the key mechanisms for ensuring progress, however, are (non-judicial) complaints and monitoring reports.

A second area of reconfiguration has been reforming the structures of support delivery within the health system. The national health strategy, *Quality and Fairness: A Health System for You* (2001), set out a number of principles under which these structures should be based. These are equity, people-centeredness, quality and accountability.[98] It contains commitments to increase community-based services for people with intellectual disabilities, support services for people with autism, care services, training and multidisciplinary support services for people with physical and sensory disabilities and increased capacity in community care and acute services in the mental health area. Despite additional investment, however, a decade after this strategy has come into force, there continues to be a substantial area of unmet need with regard to all types of disabilities.[99]

Alongside this, *Primary Care: A New Direction* (2001), the national primary care strategy, stated that 'primary care is the appropriate setting to meet 90–95 percent of all health and personal social service needs' and should 'become the central focus of the health system'.[100] While this signals a new emphasis on mainstreaming of disability supports, it nonetheless places it within the wider health care system. The strategy envisages 'primary care teams' comprising general practitioners, nurses, health care assistants, physiotherapists, occupational therapists, social workers, home helps and administrative personnel. A wider 'primary care network' of other primary care professionals is also planned. This includes community welfare officers, speech and language therapists, community pharmacists, dieticians, dentists, chiropodists and psychologists. It is anticipated that the primary care teams will eventually liaise with specialist teams in the community to provide integration of care. Specialist teams include those with expertise in disability. The strategy stresses a 'single point of entry' to services.

In terms of implementation of this strategy, the report acknowledged that 'such fundamental change will require major investment in human resources, physical

---

97 Department of Enterprise, Trade and Employment (2006) *Sectoral Plan under the Disability Act 2005*.
98 Department of Health and Children (2001) *Quality and Fairness*. Stationary Office, Dublin.
99 *Supra*, nn. 95 and 96.
100 Department of Health and Children (2001) *Primary Care: A New Direction, the National Primary Care Strategy*. Stationary Office, Dublin. See Executive Summary.

infrastructure and information and communications technology'.[101] Ten pilot sites were chosen. However, according to the Joint Oireachtas Committee on Primary Medical Care in the Community, the implementation of this strategy has been slow and cumbersome.[102] It has met with many challenges including the complex transition to the HSE's new governance structure in 2005, and not being sufficiently resourced given the more recent economic downturn. In the disability field, while the strategy advocates choice and easy access, the reality remains troublesome for people with disabilities, with the dominant emphasis on provider-led access to support remaining.

A third area of reconfiguration has been the strategic redevelopment of Ireland's broader welfare policy. As we saw in the previous chapter, a firm commitment to innovation in welfare service delivery became evident in the National Economic and Social Council's report, the *Developmental Welfare State* (2005).[103] The concept of the Developmental Welfare State ensures the basis of future thinking about the direction and role of the Irish welfare apparatus – specifically its calls for innovation with respect to services and income supports to ensure real independence. As detailed in the previous chapter, it conceptualises a new approach to welfare policy which promotes a more active social policy and encourages a life-cycle approach to supporting participation in economic and social life.[104]

Similarly, the government's Ten Year Framework Social Partnership Agreement, Towards 2016, also endorsed a life-cycle approach to social planning for the challenges individuals face at each stage in their lives, from childhood to old age, and including disability. The vision included in the social partnership agreement describes a future in which all persons with a disability would:

- have access to an income which is sufficient to sustain an acceptable standard of living;
- have access to appropriate care, health, education, employment and training and social services in conformity with their needs and abilities;
- have access to public spaces, buildings, transport, information, advocacy and
- other public services and appropriate housing;
- be enabled, as far as possible, to lead full and independent lives, to participate in work and in society and to maximise their potential; and
- carers would be acknowledged and supported in their caring role.[105]

Other priority actions in the partnership agreement relate to the development of a comprehensive employment strategy for people with disabilities, including a range

---

[101] *Ibid.*, Executive Summary, p. 1.
[102] See Joint Oireachtas Committee's Report on Primary Medical Care in the Community, http://www.oireachtas.ie/viewdoc.asp?DocID=14099&CatID=78 (accessed 6 December 2012).
[103] National Economic and Social Council (2005) *Developmental Welfare State*. NESC, Dublin.
[104] Department of Social and Family Affairs (2006) *Disability Sectoral Plan, 2006*.
[105] *Supra*, n. 65, p. 67.

of measures to promote education, vocational training and employment opportunities; the introduction of national standards in respect of health services for people with disabilities; measures to ensure adequate levels of income; the development of information and advocacy services; measures to ensure access to the built environment and public transport; and the development of a National Housing Strategy for People with Disabilities.

These priority actions are high level, but it is possible to read the strategic direction in which services, supports and a variety of measures will be moving during the next decade. It is particularly interesting to note the explicit inclusion in this document of people with significant disabilities – that is, those with ongoing high dependency needs. However, Ireland now faces very significant economic and fiscal challenges which were not foreseen at the outset of Towards 2016. As a result, the government concluded a transitional agreement on pay and workplace issues in order to respond to the immediate challenges facing the economy. The later report, *Towards 2016 Review and Transitional Agreement 2008–2009*, confirms the commitment of the government and the social partners towards the long-term goals set down in Towards 2016 for each stage of the life cycle (children, people of working age and people with disabilities) while recognising that they pose major challenges in terms of availability of resources and building the necessary infrastructure and integrated service delivery.[106]

The aims of both the NESC report and national partnership agreement are best understood against the backdrop of the wider reform agenda which has to do with the reform of welfare services and the consensus amongst the social partners on the need to switch to the concept of life-cycle planning in the delivery of those services.

To concretise these administrative reforms, the government established a new institutional architecture, in the shape of a new Office for Disability and Mental Health under the direction of the Minister of State for Health in 2008. This office oversees the work by the six departments required to carry out sectoral plans under the National Disability Strategy, to ensure coherence between government departments and to maintain the reform momentum. Its coordinating position has been reflective of the state's broader social reform agenda.

Disability Services Reform Policy

As mentioned, service reform policy makes up the core focus of Ireland's approach towards enabling persons with disabilities to achieve independent living to date, rather than on the demand side of empowering persons with disabilities through individual funding.

The core focus of recommendations has been that services should encourage social and economic participation, which was a welcome development. The NDA's 2009 Policy Advice Paper on Sheltered Employment Services states that those

---

[106] Available at: http://www.taoiseach.gov.ie/eng/Publications/Publications_2008/Taoiseach_Report_web
    .pdf (accessed 24 January 2012).

currently engaged in providing sheltered work settings should align with the aim of ensuring people with disabilities are engaged in meaningful employment in integrated, mainstream settings where at all possible.[107] It advocates that a policy framework should identify a clear time frame and target for the transition from sheltered work to open and/or supported employment as appropriate for each individual. Also, since the Needs and Abilities report, mainstream training facilities have become more accessible to persons with disabilities.

The reconfiguration of day services to reflect these aims has been the focus of the HSE day service review, *New Directions* (2012).[108] The review envisages that all the supports available in communities will be mobilised so that people have the widest possible choices and options about how they live their lives and how they spend their time. It recognises that people deemed to have severe and profound disabilities may need specialised support throughout their lives. However, it calls for a blurring of the boundaries between 'special' and 'mainstream' services so that people can access the support most suited to helping them to put their personal plans into action. Importantly, the report acknowledges that many providers have already moved ahead, with new kinds of services and better ways of doing things within the same resource constraints and challenges as others within the sector. Hence there are knowledge, skill and experience amongst service providers and advocacy organisations, which will help to embed cultural and system change. It therefore envisages that to achieve a system-wide transformation, the HSE needs to mobilise a change management process to embed systems to deliver quality and strengthen long-term planning.

For people with physical disabilities, the report of the Review Group on Physical and Sensory Disabilities, *Towards an Independent Future*,[109] identifies the developments in services judged to be required at that time in line with the recommendations of the Commission on the Status of People with Disabilities. It recommends that supports should be better developed to meet more effectively the needs of people with disabilities and their families. It was the first detailed review of services for persons with physical and sensory disabilities since the publication of the Green Paper, *Towards a Full Life*, in 1984. It provided a blueprint for the development of services for people with physical or sensory disability in the coming years.

The main thrust of this report was the development of services to enable people with a physical or sensory disability to live as independently as possible in the community. It recommended that priority be given to the provision of more day care, respite care, nursing and therapy services, personal assistants and residential accommodation. The review group attached great importance to integrating services for people with disabilities with mainstream services wherever possible.

---

[107] NDA (2009) *Policy Advice Paper on Sheltered Employment Services*. NDA, Dublin.
[108] HSE National Review of HSE Funded Adult Day Services 2007/8/9.
[109] Report of the Review Group on Health and Social Services for People with Physical and Sensory Disabilities (1996) *Towards an Independent Future*. Stationary Office, Dublin.

It regarded the independent living arrangement as offering the disabled person 'the opportunity to live in a domestic dwelling, supported with the necessary health and social services'.[110] The review group supported the development of independent living, because it promotes independence and respects the person's right to choose the form of support most appropriate to him or her.

As we have seen, since these reports, the PA service in Ireland has become a more ubiquitous model, with almost 3 million personal assistance home support hours provided since the mid-1990s.[111] People who have personal assistants have their service delivered through a government-approved service provider. Therefore, there is no scope for the disabled persons to become 'leaders' of their own service. After assessment, people are approved for a certain number of hours, and they can then appeal this, but the process is slow and it is difficult to get an increase in the hours. People with disabilities who live in community (group) homes are currently not considered to be 'living in the community' – therefore, they do not receive community living supports, such as personal assistants. Therefore, people trying to move from institutional care to independent living face a significant barrier to meaningful participation in their local area, as they have to be living 'out in the community' before they can apply for assessment for personal assistant services.[112]

Multi-Annual Funding

Another mechanism which the government has used to try and reform the disability support sector has been the agreement on a multi-annual funding package to boost the supply of disability services, which was a cornerstone of the National Disability Strategy. This was an investment programme for the community and voluntary sector for disability support services of €900 million for the period between 2006 and 2009 across all government departments. As part of the Multi-Annual Investment Programme 2006–2009, the government provided the HSE with additional €100 million in both 2006 and 2007. This funding included monies to provide new and enhanced services for people with disabilities, implementing Part 2 of the Disability Act (2005) for a right to an assessment which came into effect on 1 June 2007 for children under the age of five and also for the continuation of the implementation of the transfer of persons with intellectual disability from psychiatric hospitals and other inappropriate placements. While it demonstrated a government's commitment to disability support, the outcomes of this funding have remained unclear given the lack of a transformation strategy to moving people out of hospitals.

---

[110] *Ibid.* p. 79.

[111] HSE (2010) *Annual Report.* HSE, Dublin.

[112] See Expertise Centre Independent Living in cooperation with Nuala Crowe Taft (2009) *Info Sheet 2009,* http://www-en.independentliving.be/upload/EOL/Publicaties/Engels/090622%20info-sheet%20ireland.pdf (accessed 23 March 2012).

While this investment programme was broadly welcomed, when the multi-annual funding package was started, there was no transparent implementation plan to identify where the spending ought to be invested or subsequently where it *had* been invested. Neither the Disability Act nor the National Disability Strategy more broadly had any significant focus on the use of the funding as an 'innovation grant' or to align the investment with a set of core objectives for reform of the support delivery sector. The lack of a national support transformation plan was peculiar given the sum of money agreed upon for the multi-annual investment programme.

The lack of detailed monitoring of this funding has given rise to some criticism. It was discovered by the Disability Federation of Ireland that the 2008 allocation of €50 million as part of the multi-annual funding package was not released. Furthermore, the DFI has argued that the HSE needed to make 'efficiency savings' of 1 per cent per annum, amounting to €25 million from that allocation, by diverting that money to areas of overspending within their budget. On that basis, €75 million of funding voted by the Oireachtas for disability services went instead to solve the HSE budget deficit.[113] The budget therefore had significantly less impact than intended on the waiting list for day or residential services of more than 2,300 people with intellectual disabilities.

Reconfiguring the Residential Support Landscape

The Commission for the Status of Persons with Disabilities in 1996 recommended that housing options for people with disabilities should include a blend of different arrangements, including single houses, houses capable of accommodating four or five people, bungalow units clustered together and groups of town houses with a communal garden. The Commission stated that they should have the appropriate support staff and be situated close to amenities and retail outlets to ensure maximum independence.[114]

In response, as we saw, the government has been moving towards an approach 'to integrate people with disabilities into the community rather than placing them in institutions', as stated in Towards Equal Citizenship[115] and, more recently, with the long-awaited *Time to Move On from Congregated Settings*. Despite the enduring legacies of institutionalisation in Ireland, the latter report is the first policy document specifically focussed on the deinstitutionalisation of persons with intellectual disabilities in Ireland.[116] It builds on previous disability-specific policy documents, such as

---

[113] Disability Federation of Ireland (2008) Paper Submitted by Disability Federation of Ireland to the Joint Oireachtas Committee on Health and Children, 1 July.

[114] Commission, p. 192.

[115] *Supra*, n. 69, pp. 116–118.

[116] The working group behind the report defined congregated settings as living arrangements (whose primary purpose is the provision of services to people with intellectual, physical or sensory disabilities) where ten or more people share a single living unit or where the living arrangements are campus-based.

Needs and Abilities (1990), which recommended that community-based residences such as local authority housing or rented accommodation should be used while using former psychiatric hospitals as day centres. While the period following *Needs and Abilities* did see an increase in numbers of those living in smaller community-based residences (with the National Intellectual Disability Database [1998–1999] recording that 2,835 lived in community group homes), the number of people living in institution settings nonetheless remained significant. Moreover, since this initial shift towards group homes, new styles of support arrangements have likewise proved to be more successful in achieving social inclusion such as supported living.

The key message from Time to Move On is that all those living in congregated settings (recorded as 4,000 people) will move to community settings, with an expressed preference for dispersed housing in the community. Furthermore, it has stated that no new congregated settings will be developed and there will be no new admissions to congregated settings. In addition to the re-accommodating of people, the report has also expressed that arrangements for housing must be part of a new model of support which integrates housing with supported living arrangements based on the principles of person-centredness.

In terms of implementation, the report acknowledges Ireland's current economic climate. Taking this into account, it states that the move to community will be completed within seven years, as well as sets minimum annual targets for each year in order to reach that goal. It delineates responsibilities for the housing authorities and HSE, the former providing dispersed housing and the latter providing for the health and personal social needs of residents moving to the community. To help to achieve these goals, the report recommends establishing five-to-seven 'Accelerated Learning Sites' (demonstration sites) which will demonstrate effective, efficient and sustainable ways of delivering the new model of service. It also recommends the provision of transitioning funding through a Congregated Settings Fund. It has called upon the Department of Health to publish a vision statement in response to its recommendations

The emphasis the Time to Move On report places on supported living has become more common internationally, as we saw. There are also many Irish examples of supported living schemes including for those with significantly challenging behaviour and in both rural and urban settings, which demonstrate that this model can exist within the Irish context.[117] In addition, organisations have piloted various shared-living and host family models (e.g. Contract Families) in various parts of the country.[118] These have been working successfully in many cases, and show

---

117 See Genio for a range of user-led initiatives, available at: http://www.genio.ie (accessed 2 January 2012).

118 Each approved family agrees contractually to provide a specific number of respite sessions (up to sixteen nights) in the course of any one month. Consequently, an allowance is paid for each host person depending on the level of need and length of session. The family is paid a tax-free allowance

that organisations can enable people with disabilities to live in more inclusive environments despite the same constraints by using natural community resources and volunteers alongside targeted paid supports.[119]

Provider-Led Reform

In reality, despite the absence of individualised funding in Ireland, there are many local examples of support providers working with people with disabilities and their families and giving individuals a stronger voice in deciding the type of support services they need and how they want them delivered. Moreover, this type of reform is about establishing the philosophy within organisations that individuals should have a choice in the way they consume supports, and creating a framework that enables that choice to occur. These 'individualised options' can vary between in-house person-driven planning, supporting individuals to rent their own apartments, setting up family share arrangements and so on.

Some service providers have also begun separating out block grants themselves and delivering more personalised support arrangements for their clients (e.g. Western Care, Brothers of Charity Roscommon, Brothers of Charity Clare and St Annes). In some cases, this has led to successful and innovative ways of rearranging funding, as well as linking in with mainstream services, or developing home share arrangements. Some organisations also deliver rights training for staff and people with disabilities and operate their own Human Rights Committees, such as Brothers of Charity Galway.

To aid the process of enabling greater choices for individuals, some providers, such as Sunbeam House, have conducted community service audits to compile a database of all available amenities in the community, which their clients can avail of and build connections with in their local area. Some providers are also making strategic alliances with the Irish National Community and Voluntary Forum and its branch of local county and city fora. This is a national structure established to act, amongst other functions, as an information conduit on models of best practice and to disseminate information on innovative ideas and to facilitate, through the establishment of regional structures, links between forums so that information can be shared and links established to ensure mutual support and shared problem solving. The county and city fora thus offer traditional support providers the opportunity to connect with a wider set of mainstream community and voluntary agencies.

In addition, an alliance of organisations focussed on individualising their support has been established, called the New Options Alliance (NOA), in order to offer

administered pro-rata to the number of sessions delivered in any one month. The organisation works in tandem with the family and provides the back-up and day support.
[119] Brothers of Charity Galway & Ability West (2009) *Room for One More: Contract Families Pilot Scheme* 07–09. September.

support, share best practice and troubleshoot issues with each other on implementing personalisation. In addition, the NOA attempts to animate change in the way disability services have been delivered more broadly, by seeking to change the supply side of support through national conference events and creating a momentum for further transformation amongst providers.

Finally, the trust organisation called Genio[120] identifies a number of 'projects' each year which are local, person-centred initiatives including supports from intellectual disability, mental health, physical disability and cross-disability agencies which promote valued social roles and community inclusion and are able to deploy resources optimally to support self-determination and inclusion. These projects are detailed in their report, titled *Disability and Mental Health in Ireland: Searching Out Good Practice* (2009).[121] Some examples include: Brothers of Charity Clare (Co. Clare) and Western Care (Co. Mayo), both adult intellectual disability services which have sought to provide personalised, flexible supports to individuals in the community; Enable Ireland (national), an organisation for persons with physical disabilities and their families focussed on person-centred supports through the use of personal assistants and targeted training; Headstrong (four sites), a relatively new mental health support organisation which helps to coordinate and integrate services and supports and ensure they work for young people; Microboards Association of Ireland (Co. Offaly), a cross-disability support agency which assists individuals to formulate their own person-centred plan and in all aspects of forming a board; and Slí Eile – Another Way (North County Cork), an organisation which provides housing and support services for people caught up in the psychiatric system.

There are already a number of interesting innovations beginning to operate, which are being supported by the Genio trust (through government and philanthropic funding). There are providers willing to work innovatively in the interests of improving services and supports to people with disabilities. Examples include LEAP – Leading, Education, Advocating and Planning – a training agency for individuals and their families to live self-determined lives, and EVE Ltd., which provides planning for people with mental health difficulties and uses a Recovery Context Inventory tool to enable recovery.[122] There are also older organisations which have developed new promising initiatives, such as Brothers of Charity Services Galway and their Contract Family Scheme designed to enable people to live with families for designated periods of time during the month. To help to scale up these changes further, there is a critical need for shared learning and mutual support for organisations and families to see new possibilities for individuals with disabilities.

---

[120] Genio (n.d.) *The Person Centre Trust*, http://www.genio.ie (accessed 23 November 2010).

[121] Genio (2009) *Disability and Mental Health in Ireland: Searching Out Good Practice*, Genio, http://www.genio.ie/files/publications/Genio_Report_2009_Disability_and_Mental_Health_in_Ireland.pdf (accessed 23 November 2010).

[122] *Supra*, n. 117.

Many of the organisations which are committed to change are applying for accreditation by the Council for Quality and Leadership (CQL), a US organisation which monitors the standards of personal outcomes internationally. During the personal outcomes accreditation review, providers are assessed on whether they deliver basic assurances, shared values and personal outcome measures. The council judges whether a service has helped individuals to attain personally defined outcomes in seven areas: identity, autonomy, affiliation, attainment, safeguards, rights, and health and well-being. It is vital that every key worker ensures that service users have an updated individual plan in place and that all staff support people in achieving their personal goals as much as possible. There are also organisation performance measures to assess whether the organisation meets standard requirements such as health and safety, organisational learning and communication with users, families and communities.[123]

Significantly, Genio has found through their consultation with support providers that, to enable successful person-centred practices, there needs to be strong leadership, a clear understanding of the person-centred approach, committed staff with the necessary competencies, adequate and flexible funding and an ability to work positively with families and others. These features resonate with those found in the management literature as discussed in Chapter 3. They also cite factors which hinder this work – a piecemeal implementation of person-centred approaches, along with a lack of understanding of this approach and inadequate and inflexible funding.

Genio's role will be very important in the future and fills a vacuum which previously existed in the disability policy climate in Ireland. With the input of the different sectors, Genio is strategically well positioned in finding agents of innovation and demonstrating that change can happen within Ireland, given the same resource and system constraints and legislative climate as other providers, and to offer various learning opportunities around the country.

THE CHALLENGES TOWARDS ACTIVE CITIZENSHIP

While many of the developments examined in this chapter are positive and welcome, the transformation agenda still remains significant and will require continued commitment by all stakeholders. While the Disability Act and the National Disability Strategy have no doubt created a new era in mainstreaming disability issues, it must be stated that neither one makes any reference to developing better access to, or quality of, support services which would enable people with disabilities to achieve greater social or economic participation. The legal requirements in the Disability Act 2005 merely call for integrated and accessible mainstream public services. This gap appeared even more glaring because of the hotly contested issues relating to

---

[123] Available at: http://www.thecouncil.org (accessed 14 November 2011).

justiciability and entitlement, particularly in relation to a right to services in the lead-up to the Act.

The direction of the VFM review is recognising the need for change, and the implementation of the policy on the ground will need to be guided by the tools and mechanisms used in other jurisdictions, as well as the various responses to the policy challenges, as discussed in the preceding chapters. To date, there is still no explicit announcement of the tools which will be used to bring about the reform envisaged in the policy, such as access to individualised funding and facilitation, the insistence on standards to drive reform and mechanisms for making the market more responsive. In particular, there are a number of policy issues which continue to block the advancement of supporting persons with disabilities as proper citizens, which are detailed in the following sections.

Legal Capacity

While the policy documentation signals a new era of citizenship and life-cycle supports which promote participation, the Irish mental capacity law poses one of the largest and most significant barriers to reform of the existing support infrastructure for persons with disabilities. At the time of this writing, an outdated mental capacity law, the Lunacy Regulations (Ireland) Act 1871, still prevents many people from independent decision making. Since the 1871 Act, the only system for decision making for adults deemed to be unable to manage their own affairs has been the wardship procedure, where a person is made a ward of court.

There has been growing awareness amongst disability representative groups and government alike of the difficulties in applying the 1871 Act in a contemporary setting. The impact of being made a ward of court on a person's life is significant: a person who is made a ward of court cannot marry or consent to sexual contact; cannot open a bank account or write wills; cannot defend or initiate legal proceedings and cannot buy a house or transfer residence (for example, from a disability service) without the permission of the High Court. Families felt that the ward-of-court system is currently a 'blanket cover' – it covers all decisions a person makes and not just one area of a person's life.[124] This can affect a multitude of people, including those with intellectual disabilities, brain injuries, profound autism, Alzheimer's, learning difficulties, mental illness and Down's syndrome, as well as many older people.

As identified, the wardship system currently operates in Ireland in cases where a formal determination of legal capacity is required, and is a particularly restrictive system, enabling the court to decide where and how an individual is to live.[125] As was

---

[124] Inclusion Ireland (2011) *Submission to the Oireachtas Justice Committee on Proposed New Mental Capacity Scheme*, August, http://www.inclusionireland.ie/documents/Submissiontothe-OireachtasJusticeCommitteeonProposedNewMentalCapacityScheme.pdf (accessed 30 March 2012).

[125] ANED (2007) *ANED Country Report on the Implementation of Policies Supporting Independent Living for Disabled People*, p. 10.

seen in the earlier comparative chapters, many other jurisdictions have introduced supported decision-making legislation. The Law Reform Commission disapproved of the current test for the wardship system which presents capacity as an all-or-nothing status without taking account of contextual variation in decision-making ability. The present system fails to acknowledge a middle ground, for example in cases when an adult can make many decisions independently but is not good at handling money. The Commission proposed replacing wardship with a system of substitute decision making which would embrace a functional understanding of capacity.[126]

A new Mental Capacity and Guardianship Bill 2007 was introduced as a private members Bill in the Seanad in February 2007; however, at the time of writing, it has not been finalised. Lack of progress in this area means Ireland is out of line with the UN Convention on the Rights of Persons with Disabilities, which Ireland is a signatory to. In particular, Article 12, 'Equal Recognition and Capacity on an equal basis with others', relates to the right to make decisions. According to Inclusion Ireland, adults should have the right to make decisions about their lives – for example, to accept or refuse medical treatment, to deal with their property and money and to have consenting sexual relationships.[127] The bill solely focusses on guardianship and falls short of providing supported decision making. Instead it proposes a Public Guardian system to carry out several functions including supervision of personal guardians and enduring powers of attorney, dealing with complaints and nominating personal guardians where there is no one willing or able to do so. There is no reference to supported decision making which is being called for by both disability and mental health groups (Inclusion Ireland[128] and Amnesty International[129]).

Skill Mix of Staff and Working Practices

As stated, given the long history of medicalised care, Ireland has a very profes-sionalised direct support workforce in comparison with other jurisdictions.[130] This has singled out Ireland as having significantly higher unit costs associated with the provision of support than each of the other countries examined. As reported by the NDA in its annual conference (2010), care and support are still provided by professionals, mostly nurses, who in Ireland receive annual salaries of between

---

[126] Law Reform Commission (2005) *Consultation Paper on Vulnerable Adults and the Law: Capacity*, pp. 102–103.
[127] Inclusion Ireland (2003) *Who Decides and How? People with Intellectual Disabilities and Legal Capacity*, http://www.inclusionireland.ie/publications_whodecides.html (accessed 20 April 2011).
[128] Please refer to: http://www.inclusionireland.ie/signup.asp (accessed 20 April 2011).
[129] Amnesty International Ireland (2012) *Mental Health Campaign*, http://www.amnesty.ie/mental-health (accessed 13 March 2012); also see http://www.amnesty.ie/news/new-capacity-law-must-make-supported-decision-making-reality-0 (accessed 13 March 2012).
[130] According to *Time to Move On from Congregated Settings* report, nursing staff (39%) and care staff (35%) accounted for the majority, with 3% being medical or therapy staff. The service is highly professionalised, with a ratio of approximately 1 nurse for every 1.6 residents. *Supra*, n. 2.

€50,000 and €60,000.[131] This factor appears to have a significant impact on the cost of residential group homes in Ireland (approximately €80,000 a year) in comparison to other jurisdictions such as the United States (€38,000) and in England (€62,000).[132]

In addition to the issue of staff costs, the professional control of individuals is another fundamental issue linked to the professionalisation of support staff in Ireland. Many organisational managers and their staff grapple with issues of control over the individuals using their services, and in many cases these relationships become paternalistic and focussed on the elimination of all risk.[133] This can involve multiple complex negotiations over risks, security, health and safety. Moreover, services are often planned, delivered and evaluated without any consumer involvement.

Given the importance of support staff in the lives of persons with disabilities, managers of organisations will have to work very closely with staff in the future to meet the task as outlined in the CRPD, with the emphasis on citizenship, equal opportunities and independent living. The strength of the staffing lobby, as identified in the 'Staffing and Funding of Services' section earlier, remains a significant issue for managers. In the future, all staff will need to be better informed about the outcomes of research and be encouraged to re-evaluate their practice. At the same time, managers must also provide opportunities, training and support for staff to achieve better job satisfaction and the personalisation of support delivery. The unions have a significant role in ensuring staff are supported in this change agenda. However, they also must reconnect with their wider social agenda which ensures that people in their care achieve greater participation and rights, as agreed in the Social Partnership.[134] Ratifying the CRPD will mean that all stakeholders, including staff, must pursue its fundamental goal of promoting independent living and ensure that their work practices remain faithful to the Convention's guiding principles.

Developing Leadership Capacity

Given the challenges identified previously, in terms of developing leadership capacity amongst providers, the Irish government faces an increasing challenge in activating, orchestrating and modulating the activities of a wide variety of stakeholders to ensure that supports of different types are delivered comprehensively and fairly to the Irish disabled population. Statutory agencies have responsibility for developing

---

[131] International Initiative for Disability Leadership (2010) *New Zealand Draft Report from International Initiative for Disability Leadership (IIDL) Exchange and Network Meeting*, 17–21 May, http://www.moh.govt.nz/moh.nsf/Files/disability/$file/iidl-report-may2010.pdf (accessed 22 November 2010).

[132] Lieshout, M. (2010) *International Trends in Contemporary Disability Service Provision: Key Issues*, National Disability Authority Conference, 13 October.

[133] Quinn, G. (2011) *Challenging Times: Ensuring Values Support Ordinary Lives – Exploring Family and Person Centered Approaches*, Keynote, Glenroyal Hotel, Maynooth, Co. Kildare, 23 June.

[134] *Supra*, n. 65.

and overseeing the implementation of legislation and policy aimed at bringing about improvements in services and providing opportunities for people with disabilities.

According to the NESC (2005), one of the core requirements of a modernised public administration is to increase its expertise in 'network management' so as to facilitate diversified regimes for delivering services in each of which the state has responsibility for procuring comprehensive coverage, maintaining standards and ensuring equity.[135] As well as resource constraints, the NESC argues that, as often as not, the design of procurement and delivery systems is at fault. Innovation and radical organisational change frequently need to accompany extra investment if the public is to receive the services it seeks and if staff is to experience a sustained improvement in working conditions.

The provision of developmental funding which encourages good practice is seldom the case in the procurement and delivery of disability support in Ireland, with the exception of Genio pilot funding. With immediate resource constraints, the HSE has been unable to initiate a virtuous circle between reform and higher investment. The Department of Health established the HSE in 2005 with the intention of divesting itself of operational functions so as to concentrate more on policy formulation and entrusting policy implementation to the HSE. However, since the establishment of the statutory agency, it has been placed in the midst of a wider health care restructuring agenda, and the organisation has struggled to adequately provide clear strategic management of the wide and diverse network of voluntary providers.[136] One of the barriers facing reform has been the *ad hoc* monitoring and regulation of the sector by the HSE and HIQA as a result of the Department of Health's failure to enforce mandatory standards and licensing of providers.

As a result, providers in Ireland have been relatively autonomous in delivering their support and in advancing their own agendas. On the one hand, this relative freedom has led to pockets of innovative, person-centred support provision as identified in the 'Provider-Led Reform' section earlier. Managers in many cases are undertaking leadership roles in implementing new types and standards of service provision. Through progressive management, some organisations have been able to lead their workforce through restructuring to improved job satisfaction. Increasingly, more agencies have been developing more individualised support arrangements and have begun grappling with dividing up block grants to enable individuals to take advantage of person-centred support in the community. On the other hand, however, with the lack of a strategic vision from some HSE areas, agencies have struggled with leadership issues in change management, including staff development and sustaining new systems of support. In addition, many support providers have been able to continue to deliver their services in unsuitable congregated settings such as institutions without restriction.

[135] *Supra*, n. 103.
[136] *Supra*, n. 39.

The individualisation of budgets inevitably may cause difficult organisational challenges ahead. If reform efforts are to succeed, providers must reconfigure their service from group arrangements to individualised options. To meet this challenge, some providers have set up separate departments or programmes to move people out of the traditional system into new individual support arrangements. While this can prove successful, it can potentially lead to individuals left in the traditional group settings being ghettoised in more traditional arrangements.

One issue which emerged from the interviews has been that many organisations have struggled with remaining responsive to individuals, and shown themselves prone to use bureaucratic planning to manage every facet of care at a macro policy level. This can lead to scenarios where small issues for individuals can become large problems for the agency, which can in turn lead to the blocking of individualised responses. For example, within one intellectual disability provider, staff are *not* permitted to manually push wheelchairs, even though this is a fundamental support role. This illustrates that in some cases, externally set protocols can become large barriers in the everyday management of individualised supports. In addition, there are complex negotiations with all stakeholders, including family members, staff and volunteers, in reconfiguring support arrangements, particularly those in group homes. According to one manager of a service provider:

> It is delicate. It is. And people don't, I suppose get it right. Sometimes it's about getting it wrong that we learn a bit about how we might do it differently. Especially if there are arrangements where there's paid supports. . . . To do those in areas that are . . . that work well for the family, for the person being supported, that meets our need . . . And we have had difficulties around, for example, I know that there was a meeting last night between parents and a manager and a support staff around the support staff's performance. A very different type of conversation than would normally happen. It's difficult for the staff. It's difficult for us, not to say, well look 'we're the only ones who can do that', it's difficult for the family because this is new for them. And they had to work really hard to say 'yeah ok', so how can we encourage them to say that? how will we say it?, what are the demarcations behind it? – there are some. And trying to work those out . . . so it is difficult.[137]

Organisations also often struggle with reconfiguring their own everyday corporate governance, leading to a scenario where the service operates for the service, not the individual. This issue emerges where there is opposing forces within an organisation between day-to-day management of the traditional model of support and embedding a new model of person-directed support management. Given the new policy context and current economic climate, there is a significant necessity for creatively examining traditional forms of support. However, this requires freeing up key workers to work closely with individuals in identifying and meeting their personal goals.

---

[137] Personal Communication, Service Manager, 21 July 2012.

In particular, larger, more traditional agencies often struggle with this new agenda, given the embedded nature of their systems.

The future role of the Genio trust offers some potential to develop leadership capacity in order for the sector as a whole to transform. Another means of developing better leadership capacity is closer partnerships between stakeholders. One of the most promising partnerships has been a group of service providers coming together as an alliance, called New Options Alliance, which was discussed earlier. Through the mutual support amongst the providers, it has helped to build leadership capacity.

Accountability and Monitoring Mechanisms

To inform continued change within the system and encourage a model of progressive learning, there needs to be much greater attention to evaluation. According to the NESC's (2005) vision for a Developmental Welfare State, this includes: (1) privileging outputs with clear links to desired outcomes in the formulation of targets; and (2) having floor targets in order to keep the variation in performance to a minimum.[138] In addition, according to Noonan, Sabel and Simon (2008), developing useful diagnostic information on the performance of providers helps to inform change.[139] In other words, commissioning of support provision needs to encourage best practice, as measured through outcomes, and ensure an equitable level of provision across different providers; finally there must be a system in place to ensure continual learning to help identify and inform progressive support models as well as providing support to agencies struggling with transformation.

However, as identified earlier, there is a general reluctance by government to formally regulate the disability sector through the use of standards. As we saw, HIQA was established to develop standards in public health and social care services, and yet the standards are solely for residential services and are not enforceable. This reluctance is striking given the breadth of findings of abuse in institutions in Ireland, as noted earlier in the chapter.

Whilst the monitoring of residential services is crucial, the evaluation of individualised support arrangements will increasingly become important in informing best practice and shared learning, particularly as this is relatively uncharted territory for many disability support providers in Ireland. This means having a clear statement as to the outcomes which service providers attempt to achieve so that there is a yardstick against which performance of services can be judged. Internationally, there is greater recognition of personal outcomes as a tool for monitoring individualised support arrangements. In the absence of a national evaluation framework, the

---

[138] *Supra*, n. 103.
[139] Noonan, K. G., Sabel, C. and Simon, W. H. (2008) 'The Rule of Law in the Experimentalist Welfare State: Lessons from Child Welfare Reform', *Columbia Public Law Research Paper* 08–162.

outcomes-based approach promoted by the Council for Quality and Leadership in the United States has attracted much interest in Irish services.[140]

However, more generally, Genio (2009) found that it is difficult for organisations to demonstrate cost-effectiveness in meeting needs, as more sophisticated data are required for such an analysis.[141] Moreover, it found that current funding allocation models are not perceived as facilitating most organisations to use funds in an individualised, flexible manner. There is, therefore, an inherent weakness in current monitoring systems which appear unable to identify different degrees of cost-efficiencies within the support delivery system.

Procurement of Disability Support

Given the reliance on the non-profit sector in the provision of disability support services in Ireland, the area of procurement is an important issue for the future reform of the sector. At the same time, it is an increasingly urgent governance challenge in how best to design procurement structures. The way in which the government and the HSE areas commission organisations to provide services has a strong influence on the culture of practice and the expectations of organisations within the sector. As discussed in Chapter 3, there is a delicate balance between command-and-control types of governance, which can hinder flexibility and innovation, and maintaining some leverage on the sector, which can encourage better practice. On the one hand, excessive intrusions can limit the advantages of the voluntary sector, but on the other, there is a need for strategic commissioning to guarantee a comprehensive and continually improving service across the country.

As identified, the majority of disability provider agencies in Ireland are procured through service level arrangements. These arrangements are now for a period of two years and are subject to annual reviews. The arrangements state that the HSE respects the 'independent identify, operational autonomy, and ethos of the body'. They also state that the service providers will respect the 'body's functions of innovation, advocacy, representation and research'. However, there is little or no emphasis on progressive improvement towards certain goals. Rather, the subject of annual reviews is solely to allow for agreed-upon adjustments to be made to the plan, as well as for the phased development of new services as planned and for upgrading of existing services.

In terms of coverage areas, unlike the quasi-markets in the United Kingdom, which have led to more competition (although the extent of this varies between urban and rural regions), the emphasis in the service level arrangements is towards fixed coverage areas rather than competition. While the arrangement acknowledges that other providers can undertake the support of persons with disabilities, it assigns

---

[140] Council on Quality and Leadership, http://www.thecouncil.org (accessed 23 February 2012).
[141] Genio (the Person Centre) (2009) *Disability and Mental Health in Ireland*. Genio, Ireland.

specific geographic sub-areas of responsibility to reduce the effects of competition. Fixing areas means increased provider autonomy and less choice for persons with disabilities. Competition between agencies in certain areas around the country seems unlikely, given the small numbers of potential clients in some areas. Therefore, people should be free to pay for support from other sources such as relatives, other agencies, and so forth.

Ireland is thus characterised as having a relaxed-control approach to procurement, which gives disability agencies a significant degree of autonomy in the delivery of services in their designated areas.[142] As mentioned earlier, while this autonomy has led to pockets of innovation, some agencies trying to individualise their support argue that they are often left to operate within a climate which is in many cases hostile and resistant to change.[143] While this has some advantages, in terms of giving providers' more financial flexibility, this model lacks enforceability and prohibits 'money following the person' (from congregated service to personal support in the community). The policy of funding following the person rather than the service provider would have the effect of ensuring greater choice and control for the person with the disability. In addition to the broader control issues, the service arrangements also fail to develop and enforce an individualised resource allocation system, based on individual requirements. In reality this money is not specifically earmarked to the individual and is generally lost in the overall budget.

CONCLUSION

It is clear that Ireland's reform agenda has already come a long way since the nineteenth-century custodial care environment characterised in Chapter 9. While policy has continually evolved since then, a key shift was evidenced in the 1970s when a renewed role for the state was identified and recognition for the need for reform in disability services was pronounced. However, it was not until the early 1990s with the Commission on the Status of Persons with Disabilities that an explicit call for change was made and an acknowledgement given that people with disabilities were the neglected citizens of Ireland. As we saw, this was the most definitive policy document regarding people with disabilities in Ireland and set out a blueprint for reform which ignited the transformation agenda in the Irish disability policy climate.

Since this time, there has been a continual policy direction towards supporting the goal of active citizenship. The philosophy of person-driven and individualised support arrangements has taken root, with many national disability conferences advocating a change from expensive and outmoded institutionalised services to more flexible support provision in the community. The government has also indicated its desire to reform support delivery with the VFM and policy review and the HSE

[142] *Supra*, n. 35.
[143] Personal Communication, Service Provider Manager, 21 July 2012.

congregated settings review, both indicating a new direction in supporting people in less restrictive and more cost-effective ways.

In particular, the new policy environment as outlined in *Time to Move On from Congregated Settings* favours a move to dispersed housing (provided by the local authority) for persons with intellectual disabilities who have lived in institutions. In the report, the review group recognised the dangers of continuing to build a costly infrastructure of group homes, and emphasised reducing the chances of trans-institutionalisation which we saw emerge in other jurisdictions (e.g. ICFs/MR in the United States).

Alongside the policy commitment to reform disability services are a number of key actors and organisations which can help to implement the system-wide change needed. The establishment of the Office for Disability and Mental Health within the Department of Health provides a structure for the coordination and integration of support policy for people with disabilities. Meanwhile, the trust organisation Genio provides an important space for organisations to pilot new initiatives and for collectively sharing best practice.

While these changes in the philosophy and delivery of support are welcome, there are a number of significant issues which remain as barriers to further implementation of the active citizenship agenda. Achieving the right skill mix of staff still poses a challenge; the extent of leadership capacity in the commissioning and provider sectors will need to be supported to enable more widespread change; the level of accountability and monitoring of provision is still lacking; and the mechanisms of procurement of disability support and the organisational challenges which providers face in transforming ways of delivering support need to be reviewed.

Moreover, in order to ensure Ireland can ratify the CRPD, it is vital that the government addresses the reform of its legal incapacity laws, in order to comply with the principles of Article 12 in the Convention. Despite signalling its commitment to do so, as noted at the beginning of the chapter, Ireland has lagged behind the sixteen EU member states which have already ratified the treaty, leaving Ireland amongst the later states to ratify the convention. However, according to Flynn (2011), the National Disability Strategy in Ireland makes it a highly instructive case study of how to apply the CRPD to the domestic context, especially since Ireland had developed a ready-made template for disability reform prior to the entry into force of the Convention.[144] For this reason, Ireland has the potential to offer a valuable model for other jurisdictions in addressing most of the key issues in the Convention through legislation and policy documents – albeit with an acknowledgement that much of the strategy has not been fully delivered on to date.

In terms of examining the realisation of Ireland's disability law and policy, there are a number of other factors which have shaped its implementation. These factors also

---

[144] Flynn, E. (2011) *From Rhetoric to Action: Implementing the UN Convention on the Rights of Persons with Disabilities.* Cambridge University Press, New York.

make Ireland a particularly interesting case study for comparative exploration. First, the socio-cultural background to disability support provision is one characterised by the considerable imprint of the Protestant and Roman Catholic churches on the history and evolution of social services for people with disabilities in Ireland. As we saw, both churches and religious bodies associated with them, such as the Society of St Vincent de Paul, undertook significant roles in the development and management of support provision. The relative withdrawal of the churches from this sector in recent times, as we saw, has exposed a legacy which requires some reform.

Second, the political governance of disability policy has for a long time been characterised by the state remaining at arm's length to its citizens with disabilities. Legacies of this reluctance to intervene still exist today, most notably where the state still resists enforcing mandatory standards on disability services providing residential care or support in the community.

Third, unlike other jurisdictions which have had strong disability movements and overt examples of resistance (with some exceptions including the Forum of Persons with Disabilities in the 1990s and early 2000s), the impact of DPOs leading the reform remains minimal in Ireland. Meanwhile, there are clear examples of managers of support organisations trying to drive change, particularly since the introduction of the CILs in Ireland in 1992. These include Brothers of Charity Roscommon and Clare, Western Care and Cheshire Ireland, amongst many others who are grappling with transformation issues to deliver more individually responsive services to persons with disabilities. The lessons from the providers have been telling, notably the challenges involved in facilitating the right to independent living and the complexity of work involved in reconfiguring conventional support arrangements to enable people to live naturally in the community. These provider-led reforms thus need to be supported by system-wide reform to unlock the barriers which providers face.

Perhaps in some ways, the provider-led reform is related to the previously made point regarding the absence of the state; providers have had much more autonomy in shaping different support models (albeit with a strong staff union presence). However, these pockets of innovation must be seen within the broader context of a wider failure by the state to animate change across the entire sector. Geographically, current services can vary from robust, comprehensive and integrative to isolated, patchy and ineffective. Furthermore, as identified, more than 4,000 people still reside in institutional care arrangements and barriers still exist to reforming these services. Rather than advocating more command-and-control governance of the non-profit sector, as discussed in Chapter 3, a middle ground between tight accountability policy design and a hands-off approach by the state could be achieved.[145] An 'experimentalist' social support system, as advocated by Sabel, offers a template for a

---

[145] *Supra*, n. 35.

more progressive, 'learning by doing' approach to managing the provider sector.[146] In particular, with disability services, such a model promises a more flexible and partner-driven approach towards local service delivery.

Finally the economic climate undoubtedly poses a potential challenge to Ireland's reform efforts. However, as stated at the outset of the chapter, it is also a potential catalyst to *reform* policies. In particular, given the timing of the C&AG report and subsequent VFM review, the recession offers the opportunity to help to crystallise thinking around cost-effective alternatives, to review outmoded work practices and to reconfigure dependency-creating services. With a budget of €1.541 billion earmarked for disability services in 2012, there is considerable scope to strategically plan and implement the major change programme for disability services that is under way. However, it is acknowledged that this reform programme must be a collaborative responsibility shared between the HSE, central government and local authorities, the person with disabilities, their families and carers and the multiplicity of agencies within the disability sector.

Given the aforementioned factors, Ireland serves as a pertinent case study for all jurisdictions involved in implementing personalisation. Its position as a country grappling with reform reminds us of the complexities involved in managing such change, in terms of dealing with the financial, legal and policy challenges, as well as the leadership requirements involved. The historical analysis in the Irish case study also helps to reveal many of the false logics which can emerge within current systems; for instance, how outmoded work practices and paternalistic assumptions get fixed in policy and become enshrined in legislation. Confronting these historical legacies is something which every country must continually face, particularly so that meaningful lives in the community can flourish for persons with disabilities in the first instance. According to the Independent Living movement in Sweden, 'memory is short and history repeats itself', particularly with countries building new institutions and pulling back the standards and freedoms which have been obtained.[147]

[146] Noonan, Sabel, and Simon, *supra*, n. 139.
[147] ENIL and JAG (2011) *The "JAG Model" Personal Assistance with Self-Determination*, The JAG Association.

PART IV

The Journey Ahead for Active Citizenship and Independent Living for Persons with Disabilities

11

Options and Alternatives for a New Support Delivery Framework Which Encourages Independence

INTRODUCTION

This chapter draws out the lessons learned from the different jurisdictions in addressing the challenges inherent in providing individualised support arrangements for people with disabilities. Recent years have finally seen a shift away from keeping people in grouped care arrangements with little choice or opportunity to socially and economically participate in the community. The vision of becoming active citizens has become a central goal in national policies and is becoming increasingly reflected in international law and policy, particularly the UN Convention on the Rights of Persons with Disabilities. However, in meeting this vision, as the comparative case studies have shown, there is a significant transformation required in reconfiguring conventional services to become more individually responsive. This chapter begins with drawing out the key mechanisms from each chapter required for achieving a personalised support delivery system. In so doing, it identifies a number of core building blocks to such a model. Then, it identifies the critical success factors for guiding change. It does this at two levels. First, it identifies the different options for policy makers in managing change at the broader domestic system-wide level. Second, it identifies the different options for service providers in managing change at the local frontline level. These two levels must operate interdependently to help to bring about the change required.

OPTIONS FOR ACHIEVING A PERSONALISED SUPPORT DELIVERY SYSTEM

First, as the comparative analysis revealed, there are a number of central elements to create a basic operating system of person-driven support. These include both demand-side and supply-side options. Demand-side options, as we saw, are designed to restore more choice and control to people with disabilities over the types of support they may need or require. They involve embedding important facilitation mechanisms such as independent planning and supported decision making to enable people to take advantage of the opportunities of personalisation. Meanwhile, supply-side options involve reconfiguring the support services market in order to change the ways in which services operate. This includes, for example, reconfiguring the way in which providers are funded and monitored. The following section outlines these core components.

Demand Side of Reform (Restoring Power to Persons with Disabilities)

Independent Planning/Brokerage

At the outset, people require access to independent planning. This does not necessarily involve the design of service statements such as identifying pre-grouped service options such as access to day care, for example, but rather a mechanism which discovers what the wishes and preferences of the individual are and what kind of supports would be useful in enabling that person to achieve these. This involves the design of an individually tailored support plan. This type of planning differs from the ongoing day-to-day coordination and development role in managing a person's support.

One example of this type of work is the plan given by the facilitator, as used in British Columbia,[1] whose role is to help persons with developing an individual support plan prior to accessing any services. A facilitator may also assist with developing an individual support plan when an individual wants to change his/her existing funded services to address new circumstances or goals. Facilitators should also provide assistance with planning for access to generic and informal community supports when funded services are not requested. The plan can include areas such as help with managing the personal assistance programme, housing search, household management, financial management, transportation, health care and recreation.

Another example is the life plan for persons with disabilities in France – a Projet de vie[2] – which is a general plan covering the desires, dreams, wishes and goals of the person.[3] It is a plan which solely belongs to him/her and nobody can challenge it, although the Commission for the Independence and Rights of Disabled People acts as an advisor. The legislation is relatively recent, however, and its implementation is still within the confines of local agencies with medical staff; nonetheless, it serves to illustrate the changing emphasis towards planning for active citizenship.

---

[1] CLBC (2009) *Individual Support Planning Policy*, http://www.communitylivingbc.ca/wp-content/uploads/IndividualSupportPlanningPolicy1.pdf (accessed 4 February 2012).
[2] Please refer to: Life Plan – hal.archives-ouvertes.fr/docs/00/53/ . . . /EUPHA_EHESP_Calvez.pdf (accessed 4 February 2012).
[3] Act for Equal Rights and Opportunities, Participation and Citizenship of People with Disabilities (2005).

Individualised Funding

Individual funding can remove certain barriers towards independent living by giving people more choice in how they want to spend their support budget. Models vary in their scope and flexibility, and generally two different types are offered as potential options. A direct payment is used to purchase hours from a personal assistant to facilitate an individual's ability to live independently. It is generally self-managed or else the onus is on the individual to seek facilitation in managing the payment (including support with ensuring accountability, hiring and firing of personal assistants, etc.). Meanwhile, a personal budget can either be self-managed or include the option of an individual service fund (ISF), which is ring-fenced by a third party for use only by the individual. An ISF can be held by a support provider for those who choose not to manage their daily support. The agency can work with the individual to help with the responsibilities involved.

Fiscal Facilitation

Helping people to manage their individual funding has been emphasised by the disability movement,[4] researchers[5] and policy planners[6] as key for successful policy implementation of individualised support. Indeed, preliminary analysis for the ESRC study showed that support schemes offering facilitation undoubtedly have had a positive effect on direct payment use, encouraging take-up by up to 80 per cent when tested at the UK level.[7] Having access to ongoing facilitation like the fiscal intermediary in the United States, for example – in the form of support with managing budgets, employment regulations and providing assistance in hiring support workers – can help people to govern their own supports and use their individual funding to the best advantage. These can be complicated tasks, given that in most jurisdictions, local authorities which administer individual funding demand detailed spending plans and accounts for public funds. This has the joint benefit of ensuring accountability in the process of tracking a person's budget.

Access to a Support Coordinator/Direct Support Worker

Given that support arrangements are becoming increasingly more diffuse for individuals as a result of personalisation, access to a support coordinator within a support agency is beneficial, particularly for people with intellectual disabilities or those

4   Hasler, F., Campbell, J., and Zarb, G. (1999) *Direct Routes to Independence: A Guide to Local Authority Implementation of Direct Payments*. PSI/NCIL, London.
5   Carmichael, A. and Brown, L. (2002) 'The Future Challenge for Direct Payments', *Disability & Society* 17(7): 797–808; Clark, H., Gough, H. and McFarlene, A. (2004) *'It Pays Dividends': Direct Payments and Older People*. Policy Press in association with Joseph Rowntree Foundation, Bristol.
6   Department of Health (2000) *Community Care (Direct Payments) Act 1996: Policy and Practice Guidance* (2nd edition). Department of Health, London.
7   See Pearson, C., Barnes, C., Jolly, D., Mercer, G., Priestley, M., and Riddell, S. (2005) 'Personal Assistance Policy in the UK: What's the Problem with Direct Payments?' *Disability Studies Quarterly* 25(1): 1–11.

deemed to have complex needs. The coordinator is also referred to as a key worker or lead professional. An important emphasis made by organisations is that the person should have the executive powers to make decisions at the individual level, and be able to liaise directly with other practitioners to ensure the support arrangements remain responsive and flexible enough to meet the individual's needs.

Supported Decision Making

The legal capacity legislation in each jurisdiction has come under increasing scrutiny, particularly regarding the extent to which it accords supported decision making as a right. In this regard, the representative agreements in British Columbia and the JAG model in Sweden are particularly motivated towards maintaining personhood. Operating within a legal climate which enhances people's ability to utilise supported decision-making opportunities is important to ensure that people's voices are heard and not substituted by professionals or other third parties. This is particularly the case if individuals are trying to navigate away from traditional service arrangements and live more independently in the community.

Advocacy

Some of the jurisdictions have developed some form of advocacy service (e.g. personal ombudsman in Sweden). In Ireland, this has been formalised as a national advocacy service which is welcomed by disability groups. Access to an independent advocate is crucial in situations where individuals do not have access to supportive families, or want to choose independently of their family. In particular for Ireland, advocates will have a significant role in helping people who are institutionalised to gain the confidence and to receive the backup required to begin to negotiate living in the community. In addition, self-advocacy support programmes such as the cooperatives in Sweden or CILs in the United States and Canada can help individuals to build capacity and to create opportunities for self-advocates to develop their leadership skills.

Family Leadership

Family leadership programmes such as the Family Leadership and Engagement programme run by the Canadian Association for Community Living, as well as Partners in Policymaking in the United Kingdom, involve training and empowering families to build networks of support. Families are supported to lead inclusion in communities through local workshops, national family conferences, online community building and information resources. The Taking Control group and LEAP (Leading, Education, Advocacy and Planning)[8] in Ireland also have begun to provide family leadership opportunities through training and publicising the opportunities of more

---

[8] See http://www.fedvol.ie/Masterclass_5_presentations_are_now_available_to_download/Default.1627 .html (accessed 4 February 2012).

personalised support arrangements for families.[9] Facilitating family leadership can be an effective way to support family capacity building and resiliency.

Offering Residential Options

Residential institutions worldwide have increasingly been found to create high-risk environments for abuse and neglect.[10] Continual commitment towards their closure should be maintained. The concept of supported living has become the core standard of future living arrangements for people with disabilities, and has been credited with being a cost-effective model[11] and adaptable enough to enable people of *all* levels of disability to live within the least restrictive setting. The model ensures non-duplication of services and an efficient use of existing resources.

With supported living, individuals are able to choose to live at home, with home-share participants, or else access housing through personal finance, rental relief, supported living grants, social housing providers, a relevant trust fund and so forth. Inherent in the model of supported living is the option of *co-housing* – but only in cases where individuals choose to live together. In contrast to co-housing, group homes, where individuals are generally not given a choice to live together, have been found to be often as restrictive as larger institutions, as they are often imbued with features of institutional culture (depersonalisation, rigidity of routine, block treatment, social distance and paternalism).[12]

Enhancing Consumer Purchasing Power

Innovative financial service solutions have been developed by Canada and the United Kingdom, and are being proposed in the United States, to provide an opportunity for individuals and their families to build up and pool assets to pay for future support needs and thus reduce their sole reliance on state support in later life. Examples include the Registered Disability Savings Plan in Canada[13], the ISA in the United Kingdom and the proposed ABLE accounts in the United States.[14] These

---

9   See http://www.inclusionireland.ie/TakingControlConferenceOct2008.asp (accessed 4 February 2012).

10 BCACL (n.d.) BCACL Web site, http://www.bcacl.org/index.cfm?act=main&call=e458c5b1 (accessed 4 February 2012).

11 Massachusetts Rehabilitation Commission (2004) *Supported Living: A Cost Effective Model of Independent Living for People with Disabilities*. Research on the purchasing choices from individual funding shows that the shift from residential services into supported living is common. See also Bartlett, J. (2009) *At Your Service: Navigating the Future Market in Health and Social Care*. Demos, London; and *Ibid*. p. 2.

12 EC Ad Hoc Expert Group Transition from Institutional to Community Based Care (2009) *Report from the EC Ad Hoc Expert Group Transition from Institutional to Community Based Care*, European Commission.

13 Please refer to: http://www.hrsdc.gc.ca/eng/disability_issues/disability_savings/index.shtml (accessed 4 February 2012).

14 See http://www.autismvotes.org/site/c.frKNI3PCImE/b.4119285/k.BFE3/DSA.htm (accessed 4 February 2012).

intend to provide parents with the opportunity to leverage government funds and bolster their assets in order to empower their adult children.

Supply Side of Reform (Making the Market More Responsive)

Enabling Choice in the Support Market
Evaluations of self-directed support models have shown that real change occurs only when people are given greater freedom and control over the supports they need, as well as the assistance to make informed decisions.[15] This, in turn, entails a varied and diverse market made up of large, small, private, not-for-profit and public providers, competing fairly with each other, who can respond in flexible and imaginative ways. Ultimately this means creating a marketplace of different support options available.

To help to inform the development of such a marketplace, and to enable traditional support providers to become more responsive, research by Demos has been able to offer some useful insights into how people, when given control, might want to spend their money.[16] Despite individual funding, there is a strong continuing demand for disability services, which cover domiciliary support (for activities of daily living), residential support and targeted day support. Around half of all those surveyed spent some of their money on such disability services. However, the biggest increases in spending were in the use of personal assistants and access to local mainstream amenities (e.g. swimming pool, exercise classes), which in many cases were previously provided by disability services. In other words, people are spending portions of their budgets on support that can help to keep them independent and connected to local activities. This includes such items as public transport, Internet access, adaptations to the home, help with cleaning and ironing or a mobile phone. The review also showed that there were a number of people choosing to spend their money in innovative and unusual ways: on arts materials, an IT course, hygiene training, driving lessons, a car harness, a shed or skip hire.

These findings have important implications for rural areas, where it may not be feasible for two disability support providers to operate. People should be entitled to use their individual funding to pay for support outside of conventional disability services, such as paying family members or friends for support – or purchasing goods or creative support options from mainstream services, as identified earlier.

---

[15] Stancliffe, R. J. and Lakin, K. C. (eds.) (2005) *Costs and Outcomes of Community Services for People with Intellectual Disabilities.* Paul H. Brookes Publishing, Baltimore.
[16] See Bartlett, J. (2009) *At Your Service: Navigating the Future Market in Health and Social Care.* Demos, London.

Transparent Funding

Transparency of contracting agreements and quality outcomes should be ensured, as with the Care Quality Commission in the United Kingdom and Northern Ireland.[17] In addition, many commissioning bodies provide a publicly available approved list of support providers with accreditation. In many cases, if a provider gets a poor rating, the organisation has to complete an improvement plan. If it fails to show improvement from this time, this could mean deregistration (effectively closure).

Enhancing Community Connection

Efforts by support services that enhance people's community connections have been shown to contribute to increased participation and safety.[18] Examples of such community connecting organisations include PLAN Institute in British Columbia and Keynote in the United Kingdom. Given the increasing decentralisation and mainstreaming of support, community connectors intentionally try to cultivate relationships with volunteers and friends in the community. This is crucial because some studies have found that people with intellectual disabilities may feel more excluded when simply 'placed' back in the community, given the experiences of stigma and feelings of being an outsider.[19] Proponents of self-determination would also argue that if you help participants to cultivate more community connections, they can plan for safeguards, work in partnership with their advocates or family and avoid abuse.

Supporting Employment

It is important to reduce barriers which prevent individuals from moving away from positions of dependency. In practice, there are often disincentives to work such as asset limit tests, referred to as a benefit trap, according to which people lose a funding amount over that which they earn.[20] Building in incentives to work can help to reduce welfare dependency. These can include (1) allowing for a combination of an allowance and income from work; (2) introducing a guarantee that people who no longer have a disability allowance do not lose all secondary benefits (e.g. medical coverage, travel pass); and (3) allowing for a smooth re-entrance into the disability

---

[17] See http://www.cqc.org.uk. Since 1 October 2010, the CQC has been developing a new up-to-date system of assessing an organisation's performance. The profiles for providers will offer a dynamic view of safety and quality and will include their judgements about compliance with registration, which will be updated on an ongoing basis. The profiles will be available to the public and to those people who purchase and provide care.

[18] *Ibid.* p. 47.

[19] See Hall, E. (2005) 'The Entangled Geographies of Social Exclusion/Inclusion for People with Learning Disabilities', *Health & Place* 11(1): 107–115.

[20] Department of Social & Family Affairs (2003) *Review of the Illness and Disability Payments Schemes Report of the Working Group on the Review of the Illness and Disability Payment Schemes.* DSFA, Ireland, September.

allowance system for people who failed in their attempt to go back to work.[21] While the current economic climate facing all countries makes competitive employment a difficult prospect, contributing through volunteering, social enterprises or various forms of work nonetheless should remain a core objective for support organisations.[22]

Long-term Reappraisal of a Commissioning Body
Over the long term, appropriate governance and commissioning of disability support services (e.g. personal assistance) should be established and moved out of health care management, such as the Health Service Executive in Ireland, except for specialist medical support or mainstream primary health care. The creation of the Crown Corporation (semi-state body), Community Living British Columbia, and the move to local authority commissioning in the United Kingdom are examples of this.

Summary

Taken together, the aforementioned core components, when strategically implemented, can make the philosophy of active citizenship a reality. Increasingly, with these policy options, it is possible to see more and more individuals engage in society and realise the benefits of an accessible, inclusive society with individually tailored supports to enable participation.

As evidenced from the case study chapters, most jurisdictions continue to face issues implementing these mechanisms. The following section outlines the critical success factors for managing the transition from conventional service-led, institutionalised services to a self-directed support environment.

THE CRITICAL SUCCESS FACTORS FOR CHANGE

It is important to note that shifting from institutional to community-based models of support is not simply a case of replacing one set of buildings or mechanisms with another. Successful community-based support needs to be carefully planned around the needs and wishes of individuals and then continually monitored and adjusted as people's needs and wishes change.[23] The following section examines the critical

---

21 Samoy, E. (2005) *Beyond the Benefit Trap. Disability Pensions and Incentives for Work*. Research Department of the Flemish Fund for the Social Integration of People with Disabilities, July.
22 See Anderson, A. (n.d.) *Job Development During a Recession*, DTG-EMP (Dover Training Group & Employment Management Professionals), http://www.dtg-emp.com/admin/articles/get_file/14?type=pdf (accessed 4 February 2012).
23 Mansell, J. and Beadle-Brown, J. (2010) 'Deinstitutionalisation and Community Living: Position Statement of the Comparative Policy and Practice Special Interest Research Group of the International Association for the Scientific Study of Intellectual Disabilities, IASSID', *Journal of Intellectual Disability Research* 54(2): 104–112.

success factors which have helped animate change and drive the reform agenda towards active citizenship.

Building an Implementation Strategy for Change

A Strategic Vision

One of the most significant factors behind the shift from traditional service delivery to supporting active citizenship has been a strategic vision which is harnessed by government to animate change. According to a study of deinstitutionalisation in Europe by Mansell et al. (2007), the role of government at the national and regional levels is central to providing a vision for change. A comprehensive vision for community options can incorporate incentives for change and promote positive demonstrations of good practice. This includes making a clear declaration of stopping the building of new institutions and focussing on redirecting resources to develop supports in the community.[24]

In many countries, the government has responded to calls from persons with disabilities for reform and taken a strategic lead to implement change. Governments have worked with disabled persons organisations and the provider sector towards the development of a collective strategic vision. In creating the vision, there is a role for civil society and providers to generate new ideas and to attain clear commitments *within* the different layers of government. In the United Kingdom, for example, according to a representative from the Department of Health, generating support from different sections of government and helping to build political consensus are important in building a strategic vision:

> There is no such thing as 'The Department of Health' or 'The government'. There are groups of people and the directorates and so on, and there are dynamics, and lobbies etc. So, with direct payments, you had going on within the world of disability, the development of a disability movement and academics who developed ideas around the social model and the medical model. So they were powerfully articulating in theoretical terms how things should be and could be.

Ongoing engagement between government and DPOs and civil society in generating change is therefore crucial in this process. Administrators in the United States have commented on the importance of building a strong base of political support for consumer-directed services, particularly within a 'fiscally conservative climate'.[25]

---

[24] Mansell, J., Knapp, M., Beadle-Brown, J. and Beecham, J. (2007) *Deinstitutionalisation and Community Living – Outcomes and Costs: Report of a European Study. Volume 2: Main Report.* Tizard Centre, University of Kent, Cantebury.

[25] Research and Training Center on Community Living (2009) *Implementation of Consumer-Directed Services for Persons with Intellectual or Developmental Disabilities: A National Study, Policy Research Brief*, Institute on Community Integration (UCEDD), College of Education and Human Development, University of Minnesota. 20 (1), January.

As we saw, the US federal government has clearly stated its vision for disability services and has made legal commitments to the 'most integrated setting feasible' as conveyed in the Americans with Disabilities Act and defined in *Olmstead et al v. L.C. et al* (527 U.S. 581). In addition, these commitments have been echoed in the Developmental Disabilities Assistance and Bill of Rights Act (42 USC 15001(101[a])), conveyed as 'the right of individuals with developmental disabilities to live independently, to exert control and choice over their own lives and to fully participate in and contribute to their communities'.[26] Such proclamations can animate change, as we saw in the US example. Meanwhile, the role of the CRPD is crucial in crystallising how nation-states should sculpt this vision.

Building the Infrastructure for Change
Developing a more personalised model is also achieved by taking a strategic approach to *implementation* of the vision – in other words, building the right infrastructure for change. Significantly, when the UK intellectual disability policy, *Valuing People*, was introduced, a national director was appointed who had direct access to the minister and to the director-general for social care, and there was a national team in place to implement the policy which was regionally based. These regional leads had previous experiences in transformation of services and were committed to system change. The successor to *Valuing People*, titled *Valuing People Now*, took a similar approach in embedding a new infrastructure to manage the implementation of the policy. Similarly, in the United States, according to the handbook for the Cash and Counseling (C&C) programme,[27] it was found that it is important that authorities approach system transformation systematically. In most cases this means putting in place the appropriate infrastructure, governance and reporting arrangements (e.g. National Participant Network for states involved in C&C).

Bringing All Stakeholders Along in the Change
For assisting service providers in moving away from significant congregated residential settings, government can play a key role in scaling up the transition process to incorporate external relations with all the stakeholders involved, such as labour relations representatives, service providers, families and, last but not least, people with disabilities. The planning process should therefore involve a wide variety of

---

[26] U.S. Code Title 42, Chapter 144, Subchapter I, Part A, § 15001 Findings, purposes, and policy.
[27] Cash and Counseling (C&C) is a self-directed support model developed in fifteen different states across the United States. It was initially piloted in three states and has been extended since. C&C gives people with disabilities, including older adults, the option to manage a flexible budget and decide what mix of goods and services best meets their personal care needs. Participants may use their budget to hire personal care workers, purchase items and make home modifications that help them to live independently. Those participants who do not feel confident making decisions on their own may appoint a representative to make decisions with or for them. See http://www.bc.edu/schools/gssw/nrcpds/cash_and_counseling.html (accessed 4 February 2012).

individuals who represent different organisations and interests, all centrally oriented around the voice of the person with the disability.

A critical success factor in these negotiations has been the recognition that no stakeholder is seen as a barrier or hindrance. For example, some parents will have great fears about moving their son or daughter from an institution. It is important not to see these parents as a hindrance but to work to answer questions and dispel myths. Clear and constant communication is crucial. Sweden's experience is a good example, where relatives of persons with intellectual disabilities had fears and negative attitudes about the closing of the institutions, yet surveys showed that 80 per cent were satisfied afterwards.[28] Communicating this to families is therefore important in building a shared vision of a 'community for all' amongst different individuals and groups. This process of relationship building between stakeholders has been essential in the C&C programmes in the United States. According to a representative of the national programme office:

> At the beginning, it was just trying to understand each other because we spoke such different languages. Then we had a very good experience in Michigan where we learned to work with each other. [After a bad start], it led us to say we have to talk with each other. And we had this meeting in Detroit where everybody sits – 'this is my problem, this is my problem, these are our issues' and it sort of led to this effort to develop common principles. [...] Every group developed their own principles first; SEI Union, ADAPT, Self-Determination, Cash & Counseling, IL movement. And it was interesting when you put them side-by-side, it was agreement on 70% of all. And it started out with some face-to-face meetings. ... Some of it is literally taking everybody's principles and creating a cross walk. The sheer act of doing that showed the links, and then we went through each of them one by one and say these are going to be easy to write up, these are the two or three that aren't. And now, there's a bunch of them that are the intractable issues. And then how do we go at these.[29]

A key part of this process was developing position statements in order to achieve a memorandum of understanding between the parties involved. Position statements on issues have advanced the US transition process in many ways. They have helped to achieve consensus amongst the members and guide the actions of everyone involved in the organisation. In addition, jointly signed positions allow different stakeholders to come together in a united front. One of the major discussion points in developing these memoranda has been around workforce issues as part of the institutional closure process. These will be outlined in more detail in the 'Motivating the Disability Workforce' section later in the chapter.

[28] *Ibid.*
[29] Personal Communication, July 2009.

Cultivate Leadership and Capacity in Commissioners and Providers

Recognising Leadership

At the heart of managing the transformation is the extent of good leadership in commissioning and provider sector roles. Changing the whole system is clearly a complex process and is susceptible to 'reorganisation fatigue',[30] given all the stakeholders involved. According to the findings in the literature discussed in Chapter 3, as well as interviews with providers, there are a number of styles of leadership which are said to bring deep change; specifically, *transactional* leaders (or managers) focus on processes and procedures, whereas *transformational* leaders focus on cultures and whole systems.[31] Arguably both types of leadership roles are required, given the need for somebody to 'champion' the idea as well as the complexity of procedural change needed.

In jurisdictions where there have been successful system transformations, there is evidence of strong leadership driving the change. In the United Kingdom, for example, Oldham has the most people with personal budgets. The following quote by Paul Davies, service director of Adult Social Care with Oldham Metropolitan Borough Council, illustrates the leadership required to drive through this change:

> It's down to hard work, leadership, belief and determination. There's no reason why all of this cannot be done everywhere. Oldham is a relatively ordinary borough. We manage to move people to do things differently through taking an organised approach to organisational development. We recognised we needed some outside help with that. But, when the direction is clear we're good at taking a consistent line across the entire organisation – from people on the ground to the Chief Executive. Everyone understands that this is how we're going to do business. The message is clear that, if you don't like this direction, then you have to make up your mind if it's the place you want to be.[32]

There have been a number of examples of initiatives supporting leadership from the comparative case studies, such as the innovation grants which give support to service managers willing to try new initiatives (those used by Genio are one such example). This is discussed in more detail in the 'Adopting a Strategic Financial Approach to the Transition' section. In addition, genuine partnership with other managers and stakeholders, as well as initiatives to foster 'policy entrepreneurship' amongst groups, can help to animate change.

---

[30] Ham, C. (1996), 'Editorial: The Future of the NHS', *BMJ* 313: 1277–1278.
[31] In Control (2010) *Third Phase Report Evaluation and Learning 2008–2009*, In Control.
[32] In Control (n.d.) *The Economics of SDS*, http://www.in-control.org.uk/site/INCO/Templates/General .aspx?pageid=632&cc=GB (accessed 4 February 2012).

Genuine Partnership

The other notable feature shared by these leaders is a deeply held sense that transformation will come about only through genuine partnership with others: the old conflict model (conflict with people using services and their families; conflict with other agencies) has to be transcended by an approach which reaches out and recognises shared humanity and joint interests.[33] Leadership involves positive collaboration with peers, the sharing of ideas and information and the recognition and valuing of others' positive contributions.[34] These ideas are closely linked with the ideas for cultivating an innovative climate which seeks to help to percolate innovation, discussed in Chapter 3.

This was seen clearly in the United Kingdom with local authorities which were developing successful personalised supports. According to the Department of Health (2009), in a case study of six local authorities, a collaborative approach between the local authority (commissioner) and the provider was a crucial mechanism in leading change:

> A common feature underpinning the changes in each council has been a shift from traditional and often adversarial relationships towards collaborative and constructive partnerships between commissioners and providers.[35]

Fostering 'Policy Entrepreneur'-type Expertise

To meet the leadership goals in the United States, more supportive and 'policy entrepreneur'-type advocacy groups – with significant expertise – have become leaders at the negotiation tables. The National Resource Center for Participant-Directed Services in the United States is regarded as providing a strong advocacy role by offering an array of services including programme consulting, training and research for policy makers. Its team of subject matter experts are available to help policy makers and managers to design programmes, evaluate existing programmes and recommend improvements in all aspects of operationalising self-direction, including areas of policy development, quality management, financial management services, participant involvement, data management and information systems. Ultimately, they engage with public policy to ensure the growth of self-direction opportunities across the country, informed by existing research, knowledge and practice.

The National Resource Center also offers a National Participant Network (NPN) to enable administrators to receive access to a wide range of critical information resources, as well as to interact with peers, troubleshoot problems and improve operations. The NPN also recognises the important voice of persons with disabilities in the design of their models. This ensures that all of their work is ultimately guided

---

[33] *Ibid.*

[34] *Ibid.* p. 40.

[35] Department of Health (2009) *Contracting for Personalised Outcomes: What We're Learning from Emerging Practice*, DH/Putting People First Programme, p. 4.

by the needs of those for whom self-directed supports are intended. They also offer training modules for support services, as well as research which focuses on good practices and the impact of participant-directed programmes.[36]

EMBEDDING THE VOICE OF PERSONS WITH DISABILITIES

Having a strong voice and a strong representative platform for people with disabilities has proven to be a crucial success factor in the transformation process in the different jurisdictions examined. Importantly, the successful methods of advocacy have had a clear, focussed and strategic approach, as well as being a source of cutting-edge ideas for state or provincial departments and local authorities. The Canadian federal strategy, In Unison, notes that in order to secure the overall goal of 'full citizenship' for people with disabilities, community development in all sectors – a 'healthy infras-tructure of disability organisations' – is needed.[37] Examples of such organisations are provided later in the chapter. Having an infrastructure in place which facilitates consultation between government and people with disabilities is implicit in this, for example the model of disability enquiries in Sweden and the Partnership Table in Ontario.

Strong Advocacy Groups

Strong advocacy bodies such as ADAPT[38] in the United States, L'Association des Paralysés de France (APF) and L'Association Française contre les Myopathies (AFM) in France, STIL in Sweden and the Union of the Physically Impaired Against Seg-regation (UPIAS) in the United Kingdom have had a central role in campaigning against injustices aimed at disabled people. In France, in April 1992, the APF organ-ised one of the first protests of disabled people. Its aim was to initiate a public debate on the aspirations of disabled people and the means required to enable them to freely choose their way of life. This protest can be seen as a historical turning point for the widely held image of disability amongst the French population. A second protest led by APF and AFM on 29 May 1999 called for a personalised response to the needs of disabled people, which ultimately led to the 2005 Act for Equal Rights and Opportunities, Participation and Citizenship of People with Disabilities.

Similarly, ADAPT is a national grass-roots community in the United States which organises disability rights activists to engage in non-violent direct action, including civil disobedience, to assure the civil and human rights of people with disabilities

---

[36] For more details, see http://www.bc.edu/schools/gssw/nrcpds/home.html (accessed 4 February 2012).

[37] See Federal/Provincial/Territorial Ministers Responsible for Social Services (1998) *In Unison: A Canadian Approach to Disability Issues*. Human Resources Development Canada, Ottawa.

[38] ADAPT, http://www.adapt.org/ (accessed 4 February 2012).

to live in freedom. Other forms of strong advocacy have been organised around specific campaigns, such as the Stolen Lives Campaign Stories in May 2003, from the 'Seeking Ways Out Together' (SWOT) team in New Jersey.[39]

New Alliances

In the United Kingdom, the roots of reform largely came from the Independent Living movement of people with physical and sensory disabilities, which fought for and won the landmark direct payments legislation of the 1990s. Some time later, the Inclusion movement of people with learning difficulties and their allies helped to crystallise ideas about self-advocacy and person-centredness. More recently, these strands have been complemented by a new alliance of disabled people, professionals and, particularly, family members (caregivers), under the Community Living movement characterised by a specific strategic focus on advocating for the rights of people with disabilities and their families to live in freedom and dignity, ensuring they have the needed supports to do so, and helping to cultivate inclusive communities (e.g. Canadian Association for Community Living).

Collaboration

In the United States, according to a major self-determination demonstration for persons with intellectual disabilities, funded by the Robert Wood Johnson Foundation (RWJF),[40] collaboration with CILs[41] brought useful experience to the policy table, supported self-determination in the community and offered persons with disabilities a connection in the community. In Arizona, for example, collaboration between the state's developmental disabilities system and local CILs led to shared knowledge between the organisations, involvement in advisory councils and the education of both the organisation and persons with physical disabilities living in the community about issues pertinent to persons with developmental disabilities.[42]

Expanding Leadership Opportunities for Self-Advocates

Keeping people who need support at the heart of designing programmes and expanding leadership opportunities for self-advocates has been a central success factor, according to the RWJF evaluation.[43] This includes ensuring self-advocate

---

[39] See 'Community For All' Toolkit (2004) *Resources for Supporting Community Living*, http://thechp. syr.edu/toolkit/ (accessed 16 April 2011).

[40] Robert Wood Johnson Foundation (2007) *Self-Determination for People with Developmental Disabilities*, RWJF, http://www.rwjf.org/reports/npreports/sdpdd.htm (accessed 4 February 2012).

[41] Federally funded centers across the United States which provide information and other resources to people with disabilities

[42] Project director, Arizona, quoted in Robert Wood Johnson Foundation (2007) *Self-Determination for People with Developmental Disabilities*, RWJF.

[43] Robert Wood Johnson Foundation (2007) *Self-Determination for People with Developmental Disabilities, Grant Report*, http://www.rwjf.org/reports/npreports/sdpdd.htm (accessed 4 April 2011).

representation at all meetings where decisions about self-determination are being made, supporting statewide self-advocacy councils which can make recommendations to service providers on an ongoing basis, holding meetings in accessible places, supporting meaningful self-advocate participation by providing training and technical assistance and providing transportation support so that self-advocates can attend meetings (however, according to the RWJF evaluation, consumer involvement in changing systems of support delivery may need to be mandatory). Proper consultation can identify hidden issues or groups, which is important, particularly given the aim of personalisation, to design support models which are appropriate and responsive to individuals' needs and expectations.[44] Another example of expanding leadership opportunities was the UK consultation for the Supporting People strategy. Through engaging with local communities, the government learned of a great many cases of some of the most vulnerable and 'invisible' groups in society, which were then significantly promoted by the programme.

Specific-Interest Groups on Community Living

In Sweden and Canada, the reform of independent living largely resulted from the lobbying of specific interest groups focussed on deinstitutionalisation and the need for community living. There were a number of scandals within the Swedish institutions, which prompted disability groups to demand change. As we saw, a national foundation called Fokus[45] responded to the crisis in institutions by providing an important living service (*boende stöd*) option for people with mobility-related disabilities during the 1960s. This was proposed and financed by charity.

Similarly, for Canada, at the heart of their transformation process has been a well-positioned and organised group of disability organisations which have a strong strategic vision around community living, rather than engaging with generic disability issues. For example, the Canadian Association for Community Living (CACL) and its provincial counterparts (e.g. BCACL) have a clear mandate around living independently in the community, and are opposed to institutional living. Since 1958, the CACL has been striving for the full inclusion of people with intellectual disabilities. Through its advocacy and hard work, it has ensured a smoother transition from institutions for people with intellectual disabilities.[46]

---

44 UK Government (2001) *Supporting People Strategy*. HMSO, London.
45 Gough, R. (2004) *Personlig Assistans, en social bemästringsstrategi.*
46 CACL promotes awareness of inclusion and provides the tools for making classrooms, workplaces and communities more inclusive. It fosters leadership of families in the community living movement and supports efforts on behalf of all people with intellectual disabilities through local and provincial/territorial associations for community living and grass-roots networks. It leads community change through partnerships like the Community Inclusion Initiative, a program which strengthens the capacity of communities to include and support people with intellectual disabilities and their families in all aspects of community life.

These examples serve to illustrate the strong strategic vision of disability organi-sations in some of the jurisdictions. They also demonstrate through their expertise their commitment towards working in an advisory capacity.

Adopting a Strategic Financial Approach to the Transition from Block Funding and Institutions to Care in the Community

No one would disagree that better outcomes are highly desirable. However, it is clear that decisions about institutional downsizing and closure have economic con-sequences. It is important that research-based information about these consequences is available to policy makers, administrators and advocates, so that deinstitutional-isation can be planned and implemented in a rational, economically sustainable manner. With substantial, growing and often unmet demand for supports, the cost-effectiveness of residential services is highly relevant. As a result, each case study chapter sought to identify any cost-outcome evaluations. This section summarises the key messages emerging from these studies. It is subdivided into four subsec-tions: (1) cost comparisons between institutional and community support; (2) the cost of transitioning from institutions to community support; (3) cost and personal outcome analyses of self-directed support; and (4) transferring from block contracts to individualised funding.

Cost Comparisons between Institutional and Community Support

The cost comparisons between institutional and community support vary from coun-try to country. Economic comparisons between maintaining institutions and engag-ing in deinstitutionalisation (whilst investing in quality community services) are complex. The costs are highly interrelated with numerous other policy decisions. Much depends on other decisions made, such as community infrastructure and enti-tlements, level of capacity-building, wages of community workers, the relationship between funding level and service recipients' support needs, individual budgets, family support and the like. When costs are aggregated, the average per-person cost is the standard, and it is appreciated that the expenses for some will be higher than the expenses for others.[47]

In the United States in 2002, states spent an average of $125,746 per public insti-tution resident, as compared with $37,816 per person served in the community through the Medicaid home- and community-based waiver (HCBS).[48] In studies which looked more closely at the costs of services provided to similar groups of

---

[47] Research and Training Center on Community Living, Institute on Community Integration (UCEDD) (2005) *Status of Institutional Closure Efforts in 2005* 16(1). College of Education and Human Devel-opment, University of Minnesota, Minneapolis.

[48] *Ibid.* p. 47.

people served in both types of settings, costs of community services ranged from 5 per cent to 27 per cent less than state institutional services provided to similar people at comparable intensities of service.[49] However, such comparisons can be misleading, in part because the services differ in many respects, such as the amounts or types of support provided and the characteristics of the people served. The costs of twenty-four-hour formal supports provided in residential homes can make it appear that better-quality support is taking place in these settings. The reasons behind the cost differential, however, have more to do with differences in staff type and staff arrangements (e.g. use of rosters), the extent of built-in natural support (negligible in such settings) and the costs associated with running a large facility.

In terms of the economies-of-scale debate, recent cost comparisons of community and institutional services do not support the position that there are economies of scale associated with institutions.[50] These studies also suggest that costs are associated with a state's traditions as much as with any absolute cost of service which can be identified. That is, one state may spend two or three times as much, per person, as another, based on many factors unrelated to the support needs of the individuals being served.

In Canada, the picture is similar, with cost evaluations demonstrating lower costs in community residential services than in institutions.[51] However, given the successful closures of institutions in British Columbia and Ontario, evaluations of cost-effectiveness are now solely focussed on comparisons between different types of community support options rather than their comparisons with institutions.

In the United Kingdom, cost comparisons have revealed that, as predicted, small community residential services (group homes) are more costly than institutional services. The reason for this was that it was generally accepted that institutional care had been continually under-resourced, which was widely viewed as another contributing factor to its poor outcomes.[52] Therefore, the potential cost savings of community residential services are related to the level of staffing costs, the extent of inefficiencies in the system, the relative resource demands in different models and the poor implementation of one model in contrast to another.

The most positive development emerging from community living evaluations has been the new possibilities of better outcomes and cost-efficiencies associated with the model of supported living (in contrast to group homes), as currently being

49 Stancliffe and Lakin, *supra*, n. 15.
50 *Ibid.*
51 Stainton, T., Hole, R., Charles, G., Yodanis, C., Powell, S. and Crawford, C. (2007) *Residential Options for Adults with Developmental Disabilities: Quality and Cost Outcomes*. The Ministry of Children and Family Development, Province of British Columbia.
52 See Felce, D. and Emerson, E. (2005) 'Community Living: Costs, Outcomes, and Economies of Scale: Findings from U.K. Research', in Stancliffe, R. J. and Lakin, K. C. (eds.) *Costs and Outcomes of Community Services for People with Intellectual Disabilities*. Brooks Publishing, Baltimore. pp. 45–62.

advocated by people with disabilities. In addition, these schemes have had successful cost and personal outcomes across each of the jurisdictions examined; the evidence on the costs of post-deinstitutionalisation residential options indicate that lower costs were observed in supported living and semi-independent living settings when compared with group homes, campus and cluster-style housing.[53] This model signals a new paradigm in living arrangements and posits a new era of post-deinstitutionalisation. Supported living, as stated at the beginning of this chapter, provides people with disabilities the opportunity to live independently in the community with tailored supports. This mirrors the HSE working group findings in *Time to Move On from Congregated Settings* regarding supported living in dispersed housing in Ireland.

The Cost of Transitioning from Institutions to Community Support

In terms of the cost of transitioning from institutions to community support, it is acknowledged that if an institution remains open during the deinstitutionalisation process, many of its 'fixed costs' remain.[54] When states are closing institutions, there is a period during closure when the per-person expenditure increases.[55] Safety must be ensured in the institution for those who have not yet left, and at the same time there must be an expansion of support options in the community. Community service expansion should include the costs of rent contributions, building smaller homes for supporting people with significant disabilities, crisis behavioural response systems, service coordinators and so forth, as well as one-time expenses for start-up, such as housing deposits, furnishings and so on. For these reasons, in the United States, as institution populations decreased from 154,638 to 40,061 between 1977 and 2005, the cost per person of operating institutions increased from $52,077 per year (constant 2005 dollars) to $148,810 per year.[56] As a result, decreasing state institution populations by 74 per cent only yielded real dollar savings of 24 per cent in the same period.

The need for forward planning is crucial, therefore, to achieve a swift closure of institutions and to reduce the length of this transition period. In one of the most comprehensive economic evaluation studies, based on US data, the per diem

[53] Stancliffe, R. J. (2005) 'Semi-Independent Living and Group Homes in Australia', in Stancliffe, R. J. and Lakin, K. C. (eds.) *Costs and Outcomes of Community Services for People with Intellectual Disabilities.* Brooks Publishing, Baltimore. pp. 129–159.

[54] Stancliffe, R. J., Lakin, K. C., Shea, J., Prouty, R. W. and Coucouvanis, K. (2005) 'The Economics of Deinstitutionalization', in Stancliffe, R. J. and Lakin, K. C. (eds.) *Costs and Outcomes of Community Services for People with Intellectual Disabilities.* Paul H. Brookes Publishing, Baltimore. pp. 45–62.

[55] 'All People Can Be Supported in the Community' toolkit, http://thechp.syr.edu/toolkit/ (accessed 4 February 2012).

[56] Prouty, R., Smith, G. and Lakin, C. K. (eds.) (2006) *Residential Services for Persons with Intellectual and Developmental Disabilities: Status and Trends through 2005.* University of Minnesota, Research and Training Center on Community Living, Minneapolis, available at: rtc.umn.edu/residential/pub1 .asp.

institutional costs were compared in states which had dramatically reduced or closed institutions between 1988 and 2000 to per diem costs in states which had very minor declines in institutional populations during the same years.[57] This study found that the high-change states had a greater short-term increase in per-person costs in their institutions than did the low-change states. However, their institutional populations declined rapidly, bringing their overall institutional expenditures down quicker than a dual institution-and-community structure. In such cases, those states that closed institutions had no institutional costs per diem after closure and were able to spend all of their annual allocation in the community. Additionally, many states have been able to sell their institutional facilities and land and to use the proceeds to support more people with disabilities in the community.

It is also important to address local community issues related to institutional closure, such as the economic impact of closure as well as future land use. For instance, during the closure of Brandon Training School in Vermont, some of the citizens of the community of Brandon were concerned about the economic impact which closure would have upon the community (e.g. on small businesses), as well as what would become of the facility and land around it. The Vermont Division of Developmental Services formed a task force to work with the citizens of Brandon to discuss and address these issues.[58] The facility is now used for multiple purposes including a real estate developer office, school supervisory union office, senior housing, day care and a community meeting space. Examples from other states include former institutional facilities which have been converted to use as business/industrial parks and condominiums with golf courses. Ultimately, it is important to be clear that decisions about institutional closure must be based on what is best for people with disabilities.

Cost and Personal Outcome Analyses of Self-Directed Support

Since the mid-1990s, cost analyses of new ways of providing supports, such as consumer-directed services with individual funding, have been carried out. In the United States, the 1996 evaluation of the original Robert Wood Johnson Foundation-funded self-determination project in New Hampshire found that their positive outcomes were achieved at a significantly lower cost (a 12 per cent to 15 per cent lower inflation-adjusted expenditure) than before programme participation.[59] However, it was notable that in New Hampshire, consumer control over many services was not achieved to the extent expected.

---

57 Stancliffe et al., *supra*, n. 54.
58 Shoultz, B., Walker, P., Hulgin, K., Bogdan, B., Taylor, S. and Moseley, C. (1999) *Closing Brandon Training School: A Vermont Story.* Center on Human Policy, Syracuse University, Ithaca, NY.
59 Conroy, J. W. and Yuskausakas, A. (1996) *Independent Evaluation of the Monadnock Self-Determination Project.* Center for Outcome Analysis, Ardmore, PA.

A later study in Michigan[60] found that a substantial transfer of control over services had taken place from staff and other professionals to individual consumers and their families after three years of consumer-directed services. The authors found that from 1998 to 2001, average public costs (adjusted for inflation) for study participants decreased by 16 per cent, although not uniformly for all participants.

More recently, a 2004 Policy Research Brief, Costs and Outcomes of Community Services for Persons with Intellectual and Developmental Disabilities,[61] presented evidence that better outcomes could be achieved at slightly lower cost through provision of individual budgets *and* other elements of consumer-directed support, including expanding the range of choices offered. When individual funding was linked to limited choice options, there was little difference in outcomes. The authors found that small-scale, individualised living arrangements were much more strongly related to the person's degree of choice and control than solely on whether or not they had an individual budget.

Transferring from Block Contracts to Individualised Funding

The transition to self-determination programmes is a complex process involving the design of an individual budget allocation model and embedding short-term and medium-term options for moving people over to the new system.

DESIGNING AN INDIVIDUAL BUDGET ALLOCATION. In the United States, the self-directed support programme in Wisconsin, called IRIS (Include, Respect, I Self-Direct), serves as a useful example. This process of designing a new individual budget allocation (IBA) model began promptly in July 2008, accompanied by a rigorous and long-term plan for refining and improving this new individual budget model during the next five years. The state made a clear mandate of *cost-neutrality* for the new IRIS programme, which meant that IRIS had to ensure not to go over budget.

In terms of designing the IBA, the consulting company Waterhouse and Price developed the predictive models for three target populations: those with physical disabilities, those with intellectual disabilities and older persons. The group studied literature related to the development of similar tools in other states. To ensure cost-neutrality, they used the 2006 Family Care (other long-term care programme in the state) cost history as the basis for comparison. The average Family Care monthly cost was approximately $2,350. The following amounts of funding were taken out of this figure and retained by the IRIS agency (in addition, the state held back funds for licensed residential service costs):

[60] Conroy, J. W. (1998) 'Quality in Small ICFs/MR versus Waiver Homes', *TASH Newsletter* 24(3): 23–24, 28.
[61] Stancliffe, R. and Lakin, C. (2004) *Costs and Outcomes of Community Services for Persons with Intellectual and Developmental Disabilities.* Policy Research Brief, Research and Training Center on Community Living, University of Minnesota, Minneapolis.

administration (6 per cent);
care management (15 per cent);
Medicaid-covered services provided within Family Care;
licensed residential service costs;
one-time-only funds.

The administration and care management costs are taken out and held by IRIS in order to fund its independent consultancy service and fiscal intermediary service to help people to develop their support plan and manage their budget. This meant that the total average available for IRIS Services within the programme was $490 per individual per month. Variance in this amount was also estimated, based on the indicators used and previous service history, with some above the amount (estimated at 61 per cent), some equal to the amount (estimated 6–9 per cent) and some below this amount (estimated at 31 per cent).[62]

For new individuals with no cost history, state staff used the original IRIS individual budget method for people moving into services for the first time. However, continual review of the IBA has been used to inform the amended IRIS IBA method. This has allowed IRIS to gradually build a legacy of increased validity in matching people's costs to their needs.

In England, although it is recognised that self-directed support will not function without a robust, fair, transparent and efficient system, the experience from local authorities has been that too often, a concentration on getting the resource allocation system (RAS) 100 per cent accurate becomes the dominant feature of the work – to the extent that councils become preoccupied with the issue to the exclusion of all others.[63] According to the Department of Health document, *Contracting for Personalised Outcomes*, from the earliest stages, the key designers of successful personalised systems – such as in Hartlepool, for example – understood that the only way of testing a system of personal budgets was through actual trial (and error). The use of pilots and testing various models are useful in building up more accurate budget allocation models.

For Ireland, there is already a long track record of work carried out in designing resource allocation, yet the persistent use of block grants has blurred the lines with regard to accurate individual cost assessments. The findings from the United States and United Kingdom suggest that piloting and ongoing tweaking will need to take place to ensure the appropriate allocations are made.

MOVING FROM EXISTING BLOCK CONTRACTS. One of the main challenges in transforming to an individualised support system is moving from existing block contracts

---

[62] Fortune, J. Agosta, J. and Smith, D. (2008) *Moderating the Impact of the Wisconsin IRIS (Include, Respect, I Self-Direct) Program Individual Budget Methodology*, Wisconsin Department of Health Services, Division of Disability and Elderly Services, Madison.

[63] *Ibid.* p. 40.

to individualised procurement methods.[64] According to the UK Department of Health, it is unrealistic to assume that all block contracts can be dispensed with in the short term without having spent time signalling, developing and testing other approaches with the market. Some councils have used mini-tenders or tapering contracts, enabling block contracts to phase out as demand for personal budgets rises. Other councils are extending existing block contracts on a yearly basis to enable providers to adapt to the new market.[65] In the case of two local authorities (Barking and Dagenham), some of the providers previously contracted with were re-contracted under the new approach to provide services for personal budget holders alongside a traditional service contracted by cost and volume. This is a transitional arrangement which will remain in place only until personal budgets become the norm.[66]

As a result of the different types of commissioning and funding streams, disability provider organisations often receive their funds through several means. The local authority can use mini-tenders to provide a smaller block grant from the social care budget to commission a reduced block of support (e.g. three places within an organisation). To enable the use of personal budgets, the local authority can also design a framework agreement (zero-volume contract) with providers in their jurisdiction. This latter approach allows the local authority to set criteria on best practice for providers to operate in their area. In this case, the contract does not accord any funding directly to the organisation. Instead, individuals with personal budgets are able to access support from providers which have complied with these contracts. This allows the local authority to maintain some leverage over the quality of providers in their area.

This mixed method means that organisations can sometimes get partial funding for a discrete block of support (including the use of mini-tenders) and get the rest of their funding through people's personal budgets. Given the potential increase in separate invoices from individuals with personal budgets, this can increase the need for some back-office support in managing individual accounts, invoicing and non-payment. Some providers also have had to invest significantly in their IT systems to prepare for a larger-scale system of personal budgets.

USE OF INNOVATION GRANTS. A final critical success factor in achieving a strategic financial approach is to arrange the funding mechanisms to encourage ongoing development of good support practice which operates in accordance with the agreed-upon vision. Many governments in the comparative study have developed

---

[64] For a detailed study of commissioning for personalisation, see Needham, C. (2010) *Commissioning for Personalisation: From the Fringes to the Mainstream*, CIPFA, London, http://www.cipfa.org.uk/pmpa/ publications/download/Commissioning_for_personalization_-_from_the_fringes_to_the_mainstream. pdf (accessed 6 July 2012).
[65] Department of Health (2009) *Contracting for Personalised Outcomes: What We're Learning from Emerging Practice*, DH/Putting People First Programme.
[66] *Ibid.*

an infrastructure based on creative learning, innovation and individualised funding options. At the heart of this is an acknowledgement that welfare should not be based on stagnant block funding, but rather on a model which continually searches for creative options, allows for demonstration projects and offers an ongoing effort in tailoring support to different populations. In Ireland, the value of innovation grants such as these is already clear with the work of the trust organisation Genio, which has been funding initiatives to move people towards having a life in the community and facilitating more person-centred support arrangements.

In the United States, the concept of learning by doing is also central to federal and state government's approaches to developing best practice. The Center for Medicare & Medicaid Services (CMS) maintains a repository of promising practices in Home and Community-Based Services (HCBS) to highlight state efforts that enable persons of any age who have a disability or long-term illness to live in the most integrated community setting appropriate to their individual support requirements and preferences, exercise meaningful choices and obtain quality services. These reports are intended to stimulate HCBS programme changes, spark creative ideas, and serve as a launching pad for the next generation of programme innovations.[67]

There also are a number of grant programmes for demonstrations, in order to develop innovation and achieve successful system change. The CMS provides some opportunities for funding to assist in implementing systemic changes to better serve individuals with disabilities in the setting of their choosing. The establishment of Real Choice Systems Change demonstration grants has promoted infrastructure changes which will result in effective and enduring improvements in community long-term support systems. CMS awarded US$5.4 million in Real Choice Systems Change grants to twelve states[68] to develop Independence Plus programs by 2006. Both CMS and the states have learned a lot from work done under the Real Choice Systems Change grants. For example, Colorado used a Systems Change grant to conduct participant focus groups and stakeholder interviews to obtain input on the development of a planned statewide emergency backup system.[69]

With the history and strength of the Real Choice Systems Change grants as a foundation, the Money Follows the Person (MFP) rebalancing demonstration was established with the passage of the Deficit Reduction Act 2005. This initiated grants as part of a comprehensive, coordinated strategy to assist states, in collaboration with stakeholders, to make widespread changes to their long-term support systems. This initiative is meant to assist states in their efforts to reduce their reliance on

[67] Centers for Medicare and Medicaid Services, *Promising Practices*, http://www.cms.hhs.gov/promisingpractices/ (accessed 5 August 2011).

[68] Colorado, Connecticut, Florida, Georgia, Idaho, Louisiana, Massachusetts, Maine, Michigan, Missouri, Montata and Ohio.

[69] Cash & Counseling (2007) *Developing and Implementing Self-Direction Programs and Policies: A Handbook*, http://www.cashandcounseling.org/resources/handbook (accessed 5 February 2012).

institutional care, while developing community-based long-term support opportunities, enabling people with disabilities to fully participate in their communities. In 2007, thirty states and the District of Columbia were awarded grants. The CMS awarded US$1.4 billion in MFP grants, with states proposing to transition 37,731 individuals out of institutional settings over the five-year demonstration period.[70] Another grant has been the Direct Service Worker demonstration grant, to support strategies to help to recruit, train and retain personal assistants for people with disabilities who need help with activities of daily living.

Motivating the Support Workforce

In addition to complex funding issues, motivating the disability support workforce is critical to discussions of a community-based support system.[71] Earlier change in disability support was often achieved by class action lawsuits against state institutions. These still occur to some extent,[72] but increasingly self-determination exponents have found that working closely with community care staff in developing community-based alternatives has worked better. Community living services in Michigan is one such example of system change through participation.[73]

Significantly, studies which have directly examined the outcomes for workers within agencies which have implemented self-direction show that more than 80 per cent (83.1 per cent) of workers reported they either like their job (37.3 per cent) or like their job very much (45.8 per cent).[74] Less than 12 per cent of the respondents (11.9 per cent) were 'in between' when asked how they liked their jobs. About 5 per cent of the respondents said they either do not like their jobs (3.4 per cent) or do not like their jobs at all (1.7 per cent).[75] It is interesting to note that the five areas which were reported as changing the most since before self-determination started were: number of responsibilities, the belief that they are helping people in their jobs, good relationships with the people receiving services, their understanding of their job and their participation in the individual planning process.[76] Significantly, in another study, the findings showed that self-determination could also improve

---

[70] Please refer to CMS Web site: http://www.cms.hhs.gov/DeficitReductionAct/20_MFP.asp (accessed 5 February 2012).
[71] Bleasdale, M. (2000) *Regulating IF – The Case for Union Involvement.* http://members.shaw. ca/individualizedfunding/Articles%20for%20download/Unions%20and%20IF%20-%20Michael% 20Bleasdle.doc. (accessed 4 February 2012).
[72] The Arc of Connecticut, http://www.arcofct.org/617 (accessed 4 February 2012).
[73] Please refer to: http://www.comlivserv.com/ (accessed 4 February 2012).
[74] Fullerton, A., Brown, M. and Conroy, J. (2002) *Delaware County Self-Determination, Worker's Survey Results.* Center for Outcome Analysis, http://www.outcomeanalysis.com/DL/pubs/SD-DelcoY2002. PDF (accessed 4 February 2012).
[75] *Ibid.*
[76] Fullerton et al., *supra*, n. 74.

relationships between families/youths and workers.[77] The five areas which were reported as changing the least since self-determination started were: participation in the individual budgeting process, their relationships with their employers, their belief that their jobs are secure, their enthusiasm for their jobs and their ability to get things done on time.

Despite these positive outcomes, research has indicated that the inability to find, train and keep direct support staff is one of the biggest barriers to continued deinstitutionalisation and the ability to sustain current community supports.[78] For states, continued maintenance and development of a community service system, particularly one which offers quality community supports, are reliant on dealing with issues of recruitment, retention and training of direct support workers. A key component of this is wages and benefits for community support staff. In most states, the wages of community support staff are consistently lower, and institutional staff members have had significantly better wages and benefits.[79] However, this is largely to do with the significant involvement of nursing staff working in institutional settings and trained in medical care. Some states are making efforts to remedy these situations, with initiatives for closer wage parity and better opportunities for working in the community.[80]

Workers are also rightly scared by the loss of jobs or change in working environments. As stated at the beginning of the section, negotiations which address workforce issues as part of the institutional closure process are key to a successful transition process. For example, during the closure of Brandon Training School in Vermont, the Vermont Division of Developmental Services made significant efforts to assist staff in getting jobs in the community care workforce.[81]

Self-directed services have been largely accepted amongst unions in the United States. The Service Employees International Union (SEIU) is the largest healthcare

---

77 Center for Outcome Analysis (2006) *Who Are the Young People Involved in the Youth Advocate Program in Pennsylvania, and How Are They Doing? Report on the First Visits*, Brief Report #1 of the Youth Advocate Programs Outcomes Project.

78 Hewitt, A. and Lakin, K. C. (2001) *Issues in the Direct Support Workforce and Their Connections to the Growth, Sustainability and Quality of Community Supports*. University of Minnesota, Institute on Community Integration, Research and Training Center on Community Living, Minneapolis; Lakin, K. C. and Hewitt, A. (2002) *Medicaid Home and Community Based Services for Persons with Developmental Disabilities in Six States*. University of Minnesota, Institute on Community Integration, Research and Training Center on Community Living, Minneapolis.

79 Polister, B., Lakin, K. C. and Prouty, R. (2002) 'Wages of Direct Support Professionals Serving Persons with Intellectual and Developmental Disabilities', *Policy Research Brief* 14(2). University of Minnesota, Institute on Community Integration, Research and Training Center on Community Living, Minneapolis.

80 Braddock, D. (ed.) (2002). *Disability at the Dawn of the 21st Century and the State of the States*. American Association on Mental Retardation, Washington, DC; Larson, S. A. and Hewitt, A. S. (eds.) (2005). *Staff Recruitment, Retention and Training Strategies for Community Human Services Organizations*. Paul H. Brookes Publishing, Baltimore.

81 Shoultz et al., *supra*, n. 58.

union in the United States, with members including nurses, doctors, nursing home workers and home care workers. Its California branch is generally regarded as a model of good union involvement in working with people with disabilities and the state. The SEIU has accepted the main tenets of self-directed supports that people with disabilities can hire and fire workers (particularly in the direct payment model). It acknowledges that individuals must always have the right to be the "employer" of their personal assistants. Firing a support worker is a serious step, however, and it is recommended by both unions and self-determination proponents that the person with the disability discusses this with a member of the support team before he or she does the actual firing. It is also suggested that someone be with the person when he or she is terminating the employment. However, the SEIU feels that consumer-directed long-term care support systems, including those which utilise individual budgets, must be designed to give workers a practical means to organise.[82] SEIU's main strategy is to develop collective bargaining with the state over a floor to wages, benefits and other types of compensation, access to training and development of career paths. Collective bargaining may include consideration of different compensation floors for companionship-type work or family supports. However, this is a contentious issue given that many 'support workers' are in fact family members, neighbours or part-time workers. In some cases, the public authority remains the employer only for the purpose of collective bargaining.

Similarly, in Canada, it was found that engaging unions in the closure process assisted institutional workers in their adjustment to a significant change in their community. Union agencies have had a very strong presence in Ontario and British Columbia. There is no doubt that the three recent closures of institutions in Ontario had an impact on the institutional workers and the communities where these facilities were major employers. For example, the Local 323 of the Ontario Public Service Employees Union represents care workers and had previously represented staff at the Huronia Regional Centre before its closure. Although institutional workers were reluctant to face change, they ultimately saw that a new era for supporting people had begun, and that the final closures were the end of a twenty-year transformation project. In these closures, many older workers retired, others changed careers and most workers who had wanted to stay in the field have been able to find community employment with people with disabilities (in group homes or community agencies).[83] Government can play a significant role in blunting the economic impact for workers. Efforts to ease the Union's fears have consisted of projects such as the Ontario Direct Funding Project, for example. This developed a fair wage standard for attendants, which must be adhered to across the province.[84]

---

[82] Personal Communication with an SEIU representative, 8 July 2009.
[83] Lord, J. (2004) 'Time to Do It Right: Re-thinking How We Close Institutions', *Community Living Leaders*, 1 November.
[84] *Ibid.*

Rebalancing the Level of Professionalisation

In terms of training a new workforce, the level of professionalisation of support workers – and by extension, the cost of employing the workforce – will need to be examined. In Canada, for example, disability service workers do not receive a nursing qualification and have not done so since as far back as 1968. Since that time, institutions (or facilities, as they came to be called) started offering a two-year Mental Retardation Certification course. Upon completion of the course, students were qualified as both a certified residential counsellor and a medical assistant. Thus, the practice of hiring nurses to care for the residents ended. More recently, as the role of facilities has waned and emphasis has turned to supporting individuals in the community, the earlier Mental Retardation Certification course has evolved into what is now the Developmental Services Worker programme, offered through many community colleges.

Given that the vision of supporting active citizenship is based on the idea of supporting people in their own homes, a broader cross-section of people involved in supporting a person will likely be required. Much of the support in self-directed programmes is through part-time staff, friends and relatives. Mandatory training of such people to give support is a related contentious issue in the United States and is likely to arise in other jurisdictions moving to more individualised options in the community. According to a representative of the Cash & Counseling Demonstration Evaluation (CCDE), multiple issues arise in this debate:

> Like training is a big issue. Here's a place that has a different philosophy. With participant-direction, three-quarters or more [of carers] are family or friends, neighbours. The union picture is one of developing and professionalising. And the two perspectives are very different... the latest one was an issue of the union insisting on 70 hours of uniform mandatory training – even if a family member does [the support]! And there's probably 10 to 15 reasons why we would oppose that. First of all, sometimes the participants are family members who have been caring for persons for years – Some of them are training the agencies! It isn't just issues of expensive mandatory uniform classroom training: from the family point of view, if I'm going to have to do training, it's what's the role of the participants who know less than family care in the training, which is somewhat a sacrosanct issue. But it's also who's going to pay these people who are the family caregivers? So that's the hardest single issue for us to grapple with.[85]

A balanced approach where formal support workers linked to agencies must get training and there is a voluntary approach for family and friends is currently being advocated by a representative of the US Department of Health and Human Services.[86] This appears to be the favoured approach. If support workers want to join a registered agency, they must become a qualified Medicaid worker and accept that training and

[85] Personal Communication, 8 July 2009.
[86] Personal Communication, 12 July 2009.

criminal background checks are part of this process. A participant should then have a choice to use an individual from a listed agency or from a source of "natural" supports. In the first case, these agencies offer considerable opportunity to improve and expand the labour pool available to individuals who want to direct their services. Research evidence indicates that wage and benefit improvements (especially the provision of health insurance in the United States) increase the pool of workers and, in particular, promote worker retention. However, in the latter case, if workers outside these agencies – including participants' family members or part-time informal support workers – are required to join a union, participate in mandatory training and have a criminal background check, these can act as disincentives for many in becoming involved in this work.[87]

Meanwhile in Sweden, the support market has been opened up with the 2008 Choice Act (LOV), to ensure people can have a choice of where they receive their support from. This means that funding for the support market will follow the choice of the users of services. This is having a significant effect on the liberalisation of disability services and the professionalisation of the support workforce.

Each of these issues has arisen in the roll-out of self-directed support frameworks to varying extents in each of the different jurisdictions which involve individual funding and more independent living arrangements. Policy makers and managers of support agencies therefore need to be mindful of workers' concerns and understand the different elements involved in reconfiguring a conventional service landscape towards a self-directed support system. While personalisation has been shown to improve worker satisfaction, as discussed earlier, ultimately for workers to fully embrace personalisation, there needs to be a fair wage standard, as well as access to training and supportive management.

Using Health and Safety to Promote Independence

State officials, health and social services professionals and some families often express concerns about health and safety risks associated with participant-directed support. They worry that self-directed programmes will cover up neglect and allow poor judgement to occur unsupervised. They envision worst-case scenarios in which poor-quality participant-directed support and/or self-neglect and 'bad choices' result in adverse health outcomes, perhaps even death. This fear of self-directed supports is often based on ill-guided assumptions that residential, 'wrap-around' services are safer. However, as discussed later, the research has shown that more flexible individualised and self-directed support arrangements can be a safer option when managed carefully.

Research from the CCDE found that on four out of five measures of adverse health events (contractures, bedsores, respiratory problems, urinary infections and

[87] Personal Communication, US Department of Health and Human Services, 15 July 2009.

falls), the number of reports of such incidents for participants was lower than for non-participants.[88] In practice, the research evidence does not corroborate the afore-mentioned concerns over health and safety. Indeed, several studies indicate that outcomes can be even more positive for individuals in these subgroups, who can designate a representative to handle some or all participant responsibilities.[89] What is clear is that both the traditional service delivery system and self-direction pro-grammes need policies and procedures to manage risk for all participants, not just those with health care needs. However, risk management is a particularly salient issue when participants need skilled nursing services on a daily basis.

The CMS initially urged states to adopt 'systemic' approaches to safeguards based on state and participant feedback. However, the emphasis now is more on individ-ualised approaches, in particular having individuals (and their families, in some cases) identify risks, develop risk management approaches and backup plans to pre-vent them from potential risks as part of a person-centred planning process. CMS now requires that an individualised 'contingency' or backup plan be established as part of a service plan using a person-centred planning process. The focus on individ-ualised planning and risk management means that states are not required to establish a systems response. Individual support plans must address all risks identified during the planning process and provide alternative arrangements for the delivery of critical services, taking the participant's preferences into account.

According to the Cash and Counseling handbook, the essence of the plan for peo-ple self-directing their support typically involves identification of individuals who can be called on to provide backup assistance on an emergency basis or during a period when the participant has lost a regular worker and needs assistance while recruiting a replacement.[90] It is also advised that when backup workers must be paid (often family, friends and neighbours will agree to fill in temporarily without pay), the key task is to complete the employment paperwork for backup workers in advance. In many cases, the best safeguard is to have personal relationships and social networks beyond the service system. Therefore, efforts by support services that enhance people's community connections have been shown to contribute to increased safety.[91] Proponents of self-determination would argue that if you give par-ticipants more choice and control, they can plan for safeguards, work in partnership with their advocate or family and avoid abuse.

---

[88] *Supra*, n. 69.

[89] Social Care Institute for Excellence (2009) SCIE research briefing 20: The implementation of individ-ual budget schemes in adult social care. Published January 2007, updated February 2009, addendum March 2009; Kim K. M., Fox, M. H. and White G. W. (2006) 'Comparing Outcomes of Persons Choos-ing Consumer-Directed or Agency-Directed Personal Assistance Services', *Journal of Rehabilitation* 72(2): 32–43.

[90] *Supra*, n. 69.

[91] *Ibid.* at 47.

Finally, it is also important to bear in mind that conventional and participant-directed services are not in separate, water-tight compartments, requiring beneficiaries to choose to be wholly in one or the other system at any given time. Programmes often permit participants to direct some but not all of their services. For example, in Kentucky in the United States, participants can receive 'blended' services – that is, some agency and some self-directed personal assistant services. Similarly in the United Kingdom, personal budget holders can use some of their budgets as an individual service fund within a support agency, and purchase other goods and services relevant to their support goals outside of the agency.

In each of these cases, the focus of a strategic approach to health and safety is more about problem solving than mere compliance to externally set protocols. Backup plans are designed as part of the support plan with the individual rather than being set by external agencies or departments. It is recognised that overly restrictive health and safety practices in institutions and group homes often have a significant impact on the quality of life (and at times can violate the rights) of residents.[92]

Ensuring Accountability

In terms of accountability, governments are finding new ways of ensuring individuals are accountable in self-directed support models. One of the most significant barriers to introducing individualised supports and budgets in each of the jurisdictions has been the fear of allocating public money to individuals. Therefore, one of the success factors has been the establishment of mechanisms to ensure public accountability of government funding for support services.

In the United States, in most programmes to date, the term 'cash' is a misnomer, because virtually all self-directing participants with individual budgets do not receive cash or even a cheque to deposit in a personal checking account. Rather, they have an individual budget, with the funds in that budget generally held by a financial management service (FMS) provider or fiscal intermediary, to be used to pay for goods and services to meet their needs, as identified in the planning process.

In the programmes that do offer cash payments – for example, Alabama, Oregon and Arkansas[93] – individuals are expected to account for the funds and often use a FMS to help in this regard. Only one programme – in Oregon – authorises the entire benefit to be paid in cash without the involvement of an FMS provider. Participants are allowed to hire friends and relatives as paid caregivers, or else pay support workers. They are responsible for filing taxes, however, so many recipients

[92] EC Ad Hoc Expert Group on the Transition from Institutionalised to Community-Based Care, EC, Brussels.

[93] *Supra*, n. 69.

hire private accountants to help with this task. The state retrospectively reviews a random sample of participants to ensure that funds are being spent appropriately.[94] According to a representative from the Department of Health & Human Services:

> Well in the budget authority programs too, instead of giving people a cash payment, the money is paid to an entity, an organization that serves as their accountant, and pays the payroll taxes for their workers. But if you have to sit down and do a spending plan and you're saying how you're going to spend your money, then this entity is going to pay your bills according to your spending plan. I mean you've really pretty much removed the possibility for fraud and abuse because when you say to begin with, if there is a questionable thing that it has to be pre-approved by the state programme people, and until that approval is given, that organization won't pay a bill that comes in for this questionable item.[95]

The extent of choice accorded to a personal budget holder is a crucial aspect of this form of community care. As identified in the previous section, when individual funding is linked to limited choice options, there is little difference in the quality of outcomes. In some states, there was evidence of the lack of trust in giving an individual choice over how to spend the budget, preferring to offer a predefined list of services.[96] According to a representative of CCDE:

> In some states, we've had big fights. They'll say well, we gave them their allocation based on the fact that they needed x amount of attendant care and if they can get by with only using x amount of their allotted hours, we should take the money back. So there's an irony in the fact that in our public programmes, some of them are fixated on the idea that you should be using attendant services. Whereas if you bought certain pieces of equipment, you might need less attendant hours.[97]

Part of this reluctance to accord choice comes from a fear, particularly from workers unions, that a participant will use all the money elsewhere. In reality, individuals will still need support workers as the evidence from the United Kingdom shows.[98] According to the same representative at the CCDE, this fear is largely unfounded, and the data show that people will primarily use the money for hiring personal assistants:

> In some of the earlier battles, like the [union] honestly didn't want the participant to have control of the budget which just floored us. They said they'd just spend it on

---

94 For more details of the mechanisms of these models, see the Cash and Counselling handbook for managers of agencies and government officials: *Supra*, n. 69.

95 Personal Communication, 23 July 2010.

96 RWJF original demonstration, as noted by Conroy and Yuskausakas, *supra*, n. 59; Conroy, J. et al. (2002) *Outcomes of the Robert Wood Johnson Foundation's National Initiative on Self-Determination for Persons with Developmental Disabilities*. RWJF.

97 Personal Communication, 15 July 2010.

98 *Supra*, n. 16, p. 19.

something other than workers. We said, well, our data shows 90% of all the people used the money to hire the workers.[99]

In an effort to ensure budgeting for meaningful lives is done in tandem with ensuring accountability in spending public money, self-directed support programmes involving personal budgets generally mandate that a person's agreed-upon budget spending plan must be part of the agreed-upon support plan. After the initial assessment of need which identifies a person's IBA, the ongoing support planning is carried out with a fiscal intermediary (this role can be performed by a support organisation, a CIL or an independent agency, for example). The fiscal intermediary helps a person to craft the ongoing support plan, identifying what goods and services would be appropriate for meeting his or her wishes and goals, and agreeing where the IBA will be spent. The fiscal intermediary grants approval for the purchasing of these goods or services based on whether they meet the goals of the person's support plan. Fiscal intermediaries, therefore, can provide much needed assistance in managing a personal budget (with tax, insurance, payroll etc.) whilst guaranteeing accountability.

Informing Progress through Evaluation

Finally, to sustain the political will over time and to be able to demonstrate positive gains, evaluative research has played a central role in a number of countries in re-informing the debate and mapping its progress. As system transformation proceeds, accountability and maintaining a level of quality service across the support sector are important goals. As well as the financial checking measures through the fiscal intermediary, there is also the need for system evaluation of any funded supports and services.

Although there has not been much done in Sweden in the area of research concerning cost-effectiveness of different methods, assistive technologies, help and support and treatment of people with disabilities, a broader method to test whether priorities in health and social care are being met is used, called the ethical platform. The ethical platform is based on three fundamental ethical principles:

Human dignity: All human beings have equal dignity and equal rights regardless of personal characteristics and functions in society.

Needs and solidarity: Resources should primarily be allocated to areas of greatest need.

Cost-effectiveness: One should seek a reasonable relationship between cost and effectiveness when choosing between activities or actions in terms of health and quality of life.

---

[99] Personal Communication, 15 July 2010.

This system is designed so that cost-effectiveness must be compatible with needs and solidarity, which in turn must be compatible with human dignity. This reframing of emphasis towards human dignity is emerging in other jurisdictions which are stressing the need for using personal outcomes as a way of measuring progress in implementing personalisation such as the UK CQC monitoring criteria.

In the United States, there are enormous demands from states and the disability support sector for information on public programmes, especially on determining the impact of new forms of support, better ways of working and improving economic and quality outcomes for people. Carefully conducted evaluations are critically important and can achieve three objectives: determining if programme goals are being met; identifying whether performance improvement is possible; and determining whether similar effects can be achieved more efficiently.[100]

For example, a series of studies were carried out in the 1980s and 1990s, during the transition in the United States from institutions to the community. The first of these was the Pennhurst Longitudinal Study, which was funded by interagency agreements across several federal agencies and lasted from 1979 to 1985. The output of this evaluation was able to reveal that the people who moved from institution to community benefitted in almost every way measured: independence, productivity, integration, choice making, perceived qualities of life, family perception of qualities of life, service intensity, meeting individual goals, freedom from abuse, access to decent health care, freedom from over-medication and so forth.[101]

Similarly, in England, the Individual Budgets Pilot Programme Evaluation (IBSEN) was crucial to the success of implementing personalisation, according to a UK policy representative:

> The Prime Minister's Strategy Unit were active on this and they required the 3 departments – [Department for Communities and Local Government, Department of Work and Pensions, and Department of Health] to establish a pilot programme, which became the Individual Budget Pilot Programme . . . if government hadn't done the IB pilot programme, there wouldn't have been a strong signal sent to the rest of the 150 Local Authorities that this is coming. . . . What we had the opportunity to do was run a government pilot because they weren't going to develop a government policy without doing this, and the Treasury wouldn't have allowed it. And [the IBSEN research] helpfully says individual budgets were cost-effective. They didn't cost any more and they got better outcomes.[102]

In terms of ongoing evaluation of programmes, the Center for Medicaid and Medicare Services (CMS) has used an evaluation strategy called quality assurance and

---

[100] Agency for Healthcare Research and Quality (2007) *Monitoring and Evaluating Medicaid Fee-for-Service Care Management Programs: User's Guide.* US DHHS, Washington, DC.

[101] See Conroy and Yuskauskas, *supra*, n. 59.

[102] Personal Communication, 7 July 2009.

quality improvement (QA/QI). The self-directed QA/QI model builds on the existing foundation formally introduced under the CMS Quality Framework.[103] The framework delineates the functions of quality:

- Design – designing quality assurance and improvement strategies into the home- and community-based programme at the initiation of the programme.
- Discovery – engaging in a process of discovery to collect data and direct participant experiences in order to assess the ongoing implementation of the programme, identifying both concerns as well as other opportunities for improvement.
- Remediation – taking actions to remedy specific problems or concerns that arise.
- Improvement – utilising data and quality monitoring to engage in actions that assure continuous improvement in the self-directed programme.

These ideas are closely linked with the ideas for an experimentalist welfare state approach, as advocated by Noonan, Sabel and Simon (2008),[104] in Chapter 3.

Similarly, in Canada, almost all disability policies and programmes have had extensive evaluations of their initiatives. These evaluation processes have provided opportunities for programmes to learn from practices, including their outcomes and costs. For example, each provider of residential services must complete a checklist of requirements focussed on the personal health and safety of people living in ministry-funded group homes. In addition, service contracts between the ministry and individual service providers are used to establish and monitor accountability and quality. For disability support organisations, quality includes adhering to the principles of community participation, citizenship, safety and security, responsiveness and positive outcomes for people based on an individualised approach.[105]

The paradigm shift to individualised supports and person-centred planning has been accompanied by a shift in how programmes assess improvement and change. The use of personal outcomes determined by the people themselves has become an important way to determine change. Many of the service-transformation projects which have been identified as promising carried out evaluations that assessed outcomes for individuals, and often for other stakeholders as well.[106]

---

[103] As expressed in the state Medicaid director's letter of 29 August 2002 and subsequent correspondence

[104] Noonan, K. G., Sabel, C. and Simon, W. H. (2008) 'The Rule of Law in the Experimentalist Welfare State: Lessons from Child Welfare Reform', *Columbia Public Law Research Paper*, 8–16.

[105] See Council on Quality and Leadership's Personal Outcome Measures, available at: http://www.thecouncil.org (accessed 19 April 2011).

[106] See Lord, J. and Hutchison, P. (2003) 'Individualised Support and Funding: Building Blocks for Capacity Building and Inclusion', *Disability & Society* 18(1): 93–108.

Summary

Overall, as this section has demonstrated, the system-wide change process needs to work on several fronts at once. Moreover, the transition needs to be guided by a clear strategic vision informed by individuals who use supports and services in their everyday lives. Additionally, as the next section examines, a local bottom-up reform effort from support providers is also required in order to bring along the multiple stakeholders involved in working with the individual.

OPTIONS FOR SUPPORT PROVIDERS IN MANAGING CHANGE

To facilitate change at the local frontline level, support-providing agencies across different jurisdictions have played pivotal roles in helping to enable persons to live more independently. This final section draws on fieldwork undertaken as part of this study, as well as published accounts from disability managers and researchers.[107] It identifies the different methods organisations have used to develop better supports within the wider constraints examined throughout the comparative chapters.

Listen to the Individual

At the outset, it is vitally important that support workers and their organisations really tune in to the persons' wishes and goals. While this is crucial for finding out their wishes in the beginning, it also helps in managing appropriate supports and finding appropriate workers and volunteers as the process evolves. With the use of more detailed person-centred planning work, this can help to connect the right staff with individuals. Otherwise, some providers spoke about their support plan failing because of incompatibility issues, with the support worker or other aspects of the support arrangement not working out. At the same time, a thoroughly developed support plan can drive the transformation, instead of change being prescribed from the top by management. Support providers have felt that this has also increased job satisfaction for support staff, because they see for themselves the direct improvements in people's lives. Tuning into the individual can help staff to connect with the preferences and wishes of the individual and thereby provide more opportunity for better work satisfaction.

The concept of a key worker as identified earlier is becoming crucial in the personalisation of support delivery, particularly for people with intellectual disabilities. This concept is not necessarily a new job title – it can be seen as a set of skills

---

[107] For a more detailed examination of organisational change within a disability agency, see Fratangelo P., Olney, M. and Lehr, S. (2001) *One Person at a Time: How one Agency Changed from Group to Individualised Services for People with Disabilities.* Training Resource Network, St. Augustine, Florida.

which all support workers will need to embrace. A key worker is an intensive support worker's role carrying with it the responsibility for developing a relationship with the person and for figuring out support to enable a good life. It is primarily a development and coordination role. A key worker is characterised as being a 'social interpreter' by Ferguson and O'Brien (2005) to denote the importance of helping the person to connect with the local community in a meaningful way.[108] In practice, this means helping an individual and/or family to access help from the range of resources available within most communities and not just from specialist support agencies. According to the Mental Health Commission (2009), a key worker is 'the person who co-ordinates the delivery of the individual [support] plan. The key worker is responsible for keeping close contact with the resident, family/carer and chosen advocate and for advising other members of the multidisciplinary team of changes in the service user's circumstance'.[109] Many organisations interviewed stated that a key worker needs to be empowered to make decisions about the person's support plan without having to defer decisions to regional managers. He or she also has the authority to coordinate the input of different clinicians and professionals such as speech therapists, occupational therapists and others, where relevant.

Individuals with disabilities must have trust in their staff. The crucial issue, then, is how this trust is built and maintained. Some organisations in Ireland are beginning to use more detailed testing in recruitment to ensure they get the right temperament and skill mix of worker, such as being a sensitive communicator or lateral thinker. At the same time, managers are beginning to see the need to work more closely with their human resource departments to ensure that all new frontline workers are able to tailor their work practices to individuals. Similarly, there should be more scope for individuals selecting and employing their own support workers.

With regard to listening to the individual, it has to be acknowledged that sometimes, for one reason or another, people with disabilities may need encouragement and/or practice in self-advocacy because they may not have had the freedom to act on their own behalf in the past. Many may not have the experience or the ability to say what they want. Access to advocates or self-advocacy organisations, therefore, is crucial to help these individuals to realise that they have a voice and that it can be heard.[110]

Finally, the experience from support providers is that listening to the individual can help to simplify the essential role of support provision and help to reduce

[108] Ferguson, P. M. and O'Brien, P. (2005) 'From Giving Service to Being of Service', in O'Brien, P. and Sullivan, M. (eds.) *Allies in Emancipation: Shifting from Providing Service to Being of Support.* Thomson Dunmore Press, South Melbourne, Victoria. pp. 3–19.

[109] Mental Health Commission (2009) Code of Practice on Admission, Transfer, and Discharge to and from an Approved Centre.

[110] Evaluator quoted in Robert Wood Johnson Foundation (2007) *Self-Determination for People with Developmental Disabilities*, RWJF.

incompatibility or disputes. For example, according to the Irish mental health inspectorate, 'the business of any mental health professional is relatively straight forward. Mental health care professionals are in the business of helping the individual service user to lead a more dignified and fulfilling life'.[111] Thus, one of the key recommendations of the Irish mental health strategy, A Vision for Change, is that 'service users should be partners in their own care. Care plans should reflect the service user's particular needs, goals and potential and should address community factors that may impede and support recovery'.[112] This thinking is equally relevant for direct support workers in disability.

Strategic Vision

As with the macro system-wide change, having a strategic vision is also crucial for organisations which are trying to transform their working practices. The quality of management and leadership is pivotal in driving any change.

According to the experience of the RWJF evaluation in the United States, providers commonly fear the risks that system change creates for them, and need education and training to adapt to the changed business environment created by self-directed support. According to one project director, they fear that self-determination will result in 'a situation where [consumers] get their money and exit the system'.[113] In practice, people still need support, as the research has shown.[114] However, providers and local agencies with authority over support delivery need to understand that consumer choice will require their flexibility, inventiveness and regard for customer satisfaction, as is required in most other successful businesses.[115]

Given that every organisation is different and, furthermore, given the wide range of stakeholders, it is important for managers to resist the temptation to force a fixed model on all individuals, staff and families in advance. Rather, successful agencies have given time to bring everyone along through the process of change. This facilitates the ownership of transformation by all stakeholders, including staff and family, rather than individuals being prescribed new terms and conditions of working practices. Management can start with new ideas on the table and communicate what the organisation does *not* want to do anymore. Throughout the process, certain milestones will emerge, where the final decision to agree to a new support arrangement is important.

[111] Mental Health Commission (2009) *Annual Report*.
[112] Department of Health (2006) *A Vision for Change*, Stationary Office, Dublin.
[113] Project Director, Michigan, quoted in Robert Wood Johnson Foundation (2007) *Self-Determination for People with Developmental Disabilities*. RWJF.
[114] Bartlett, J. (2009) *At Your Service: Navigating the Future Market in Health and Social Care*. Demos, London.
[115] *Ibid.* at 126.

(Re)connect with Families/Community

Connecting with families and other community members and building up relationships are particularly important for those who have been in traditional service arrangements for some time. In particular, families can sometimes seem resistant to change and may be disconnected from their child who has been within a service for a long time. This emerges in particular when families think that newer support practices are less secure than traditional placements. Organisations need to work with families to ensure there will be ongoing support in any transformation of service delivery. The experience in Ontario, for example, has been that families which are quite cautious about community alternatives can become quite supportive when they are involved in the planning process for their son, daughter, sibling or cousin.[116] Families understandably are often fearful of this significant change and usually require extensive outreach from those involved in the change. Building social support with families, friends and other community members has been shown to be a strong determinant of health.[117] Understandably, it will not be appropriate in all cases to involve family, but it must be remembered that other community members can be invited to play social support roles. Many agencies have set up 'circles of support' which can include the individual, family or community members, the support worker and an advocate, if required.

In cases where families and other allies in the community are resistant to change, this is often based on their previous experiences of their son or daughter or friend being forced to fit into existing programmes. If there is not a good fit, the person is often faced with the decision to try another support agency or take on the support role him- or herself. As a result, according to Fratangelo et al. (2009), often during these periods of searching and transition, families have no choice except to take care of their child themselves.[118] Organisations therefore need to be sensitive to the multiple fears families may have and ensure that they are not left unsupported under the guise of personalisation. In some instances, according to Tabatabainia (2003), the process of moving people back into the community can break down when the relevant authorities do not adequately prepare families for the deinstitutionalisation process or educate them about normalisation and the expected benefits and services available in the community.[119] Ultimately, organisations need to ensure that a reciprocal shared commitment is agreed upon amongst family members and

---

[116] Lord, J. (2004) 'Time to Do It Right: Re-thinking How We Close Institutions', *Community Living Leaders* 1, November.

[117] Federal, Provincial and Territorial Advisory Committee on Population Health (1999) *Toward a Healthy Future: Second Report on the Health of Canadians*. Ottawa, Canada.

[118] Fratangelo et al., *supra*, n. 107.

[119] Tabatabainia, M. M. (2003) 'Listening to Families' Views Regarding Institutionalization and Deinstitutionalization', *Journal of Intellectual & Developmental Disability* 28(3): 241–259.

community allies to mutually support the individual to become as independent as possible.

Locating the Planning Piece

Locating the planning piece is a crucial issue for organisations which have traditionally provided all the support to an individual in a 'wrap-around' package. With the focus on supported citizenship, managers are increasingly realising that support plans must also incorporate the input of wider stakeholders within the community and outside the boundaries of the organisation itself. As a result, providers which have embraced personalisation have tried to renegotiate the conflict of interest between the service provider role as sole provider of disability-related support and the service provider role as planner, facilitator and administrator. Many organisations have split up these two functions by either setting up a separate agency or else separate departments within one agency.[120] The degree of independence in planning is crucial to ensuring the true freedom of individuals to creatively look at support options available rather than choosing predefined support options within the service offerings of a single service provider.

Support planning should also be an evolving process which facilitates adaptation and change. In other words, support plans should involve a high level of fluidity. To enable this for everyone, including those who, for one reason or another, are unable to achieve what they want in life on their own, service providers should be able to develop an annual plan using a range of people to support the individual, such as:

- friends
- a circle of support
- family
- local community support (e.g. church, etc.)
- volunteers

- independent broker
- key worker
- care managers
- other staff[121]

The circle of support should meet together on a more regular basis and can include some of the people listed above to help individuals with disabilities to accomplish their personal goals in life. Within the circle, there should be a key worker, as identified earlier.

Enable Peer Support and Individual Involvement

People with disabilities can make very important contributions to the transformation of a support agency. Organisations which have achieved transformations have

---

[120] See, for example, *Options* and *St. Mary's* in Canada. Further details are provided in Lord, J. (2007) *Pathways to Inclusion: Building a New Story with People and Communities*. Captus Press, Ontario.

[121] Adopted from the Isle of Wight Council (2008) *Self-Directed Support: Helping You to Get Started, Information Pack*, October.

included the voice of individuals (service users) on their boards. In addition, for many people with disabilities, offering peer support is an important method for gaining more confidence and building bridges back to community life.

The model of active citizenship envisages a society where people with disabilities can act as volunteers themselves. It has typically been assumed that individuals with disabilities solely fit into roles of recipients of services, and have not been given opportunities to reap the substantial benefits associated with being givers of services – as volunteers or peer-support workers. Studies have shown that benefits to the participants with disabilities included pride, skill development and generalisation, empowerment and increases in social interaction and verbal communication.[122]

Examples include the international CIL model (e.g. STIL in Sweden) and Choice Support in the United Kingdom. CILs are based on the idea that people with disabilities are the best experts on their needs, and are run and controlled by people with disabilities. They provide support to people based on the philosophy of self-determination and equal opportunities. Choice Support, a support provider for adults with intellectual disabilities, tries to involve as many service users as possible in all aspects of running the organisation. They encourage and train individuals to establish and run local/regional forums, attend management meetings, develop their own newsletter, review services, plan an annual service user conference and promote greater family involvement.[123]

Get All Personnel Working Together

Organisations reported a much more successful transformation when they brought all different departments or personnel together, including human resources, health and safety and financial management. Each department needs to be close to the change and should be given the opportunity to present its own issues and identify its own challenges. Common issues for the individual service users are then looked at in terms of staffing arrangements, health and safey, funding and so forth. All perspectives are taken into account. For example, Western Care in Ireland set up an Individual Designs Steering Committee which brought all departments together. 'The answer was in getting different departments sitting down together and getting them all to speak to each other. This was all about providing an enabling environment, with the focus on helping circles, problem solving and so on. The key is bringing staff along in the change'.[124]

In order to get all personnel working together on personalised support work, many successful support agencies have involved the use of other organisations which have

---

[122] Miller, K., Schleien, S., Rider, C., Hall, C., Roche, M. and Worsley, J. (2002). 'Inclusive Volunteering: Benefits to Participants and Community', *Therapeutic Recreation Journal* 36(3): 247–259.

[123] Choice Support, http://www.choicesupport.org.uk/index.php?option=com_content&view=article& id=31&Itemid=26 (accessed 9 May 2011).

[124] Personal Communcation, service manager, 3 July 2010.

been involved in personalisation. Staff internships or site visitations are often used where members of staff at an organisation wanting to change go and work in another agency. This greatly helps to develop the level of knowledge transfer, particularly for organisations with staff who find it hard to accept that personalised support arrangements can work for all persons, irrespective of their disability. Annual conferences also provide a great opportunity for networking and sharing ideas amongst staff members. In the United States, staff from the RWJF project states networked during annual conferences and regional meetings and cross-pollinated ideas about how to implement self-determination.[125]

One Person at a Time

The idea of 'one person at a time' was coined by Patricia Fratangelo et al. (2001) after successfully personalising support arrangements within their service.[126] In their book, it was concluded that working with individuals is key to developing good personalised working practices. This philosophy is focussed on evolving from one-size-fits-all approaches to services and supports which more closely fit the unique circumstances of the individual.

In practice, this means detailed individualised planning for each person and a reorganisation of the agency's structures to enable frontline support to operate flexibly and in a responsive manner. One Irish organisation, for example, set each key worker a task of working with one individual. The key worker acted as a lead person to contact the family and help to establish a circle of support. Meanwhile, other key workers simultaneously began working with other individuals. Each of these cases was then reviewed at a meeting with senior management, the health and safety office and the human resources office. This was set up for the purpose of offering advice, as discussed in the previous section.

Another strategy in beginning this complex work, particularly if there is much organisational resistance, is to 'go with the willing'[127] – in other words, start to work where there is already pressure to change within the organisation and let the momentum grow from there. For example, some individual service users emerge in every organisation who continually express disappointment with their traditional support arrangement and want to live more independently. Similarly, often pockets of staff emerge who are keen to try new support arrangements. Organisations should try and leverage this energy and build on these cases, and then learn lessons for others.

---

[125] Evaluator, Project Director/Pennsylvania, quoted in Robert Wood Johnson Foundation (2007) *Self-Determination for People with Developmental Disabilities*, RWJF.

[126] Patricia Fratangelo is the manager of a support organisation in New York. See Fratangelo et al., *supra*, n. 107.

[127] Personal Communication, service manager, August 2010.

Develop a Human Rights Panel

Developing a human rights panel within an organisation can help to support a culture change within an organisation as well as establish a formal mechanism which can reduce the number of rights restrictions which may occur (particularly related to issues of privacy, seclusion, locked doors, etc.). Having such a mechanism can provide guidance to staff on less restrictive alternatives and ensure that service users have a forum to express their views on issues which affect their human rights.

This approach has been used within some Irish disability organisations to confront overly restrictive practices and protocols. It was reported by one such provider that many extremely complex situations were presented to the committee where staff were concerned that removal of a rights restriction would compromise the health, safety and well-being of an individual. The Human Rights Committee helped to talk staff through the various issues and propose alternatives which may not have occurred to staff previously. Restrictions were also lifted as a result of a greater awareness of the importance of respecting the human rights of service users, and the Human Rights Committee has helped to build this awareness through its work.

A key principle of the Human Rights Committee's work is that the persons whose rights are restricted should be given an opportunity to attend the hearings and voice their concerns. Within the service in Ireland, many individuals have chosen to attend meetings, and the committee has also organised visits to services where necessary to understand the individual's situations. Where persons are unable or choose not to attend, the committee tries to compensate for this by asking questions to ascertain the person's views about the restriction on their rights.

Active Community Engagement

Delivering more sustainable individualised support arrangements often involves more significant roles for volunteers and allies in the community. To sustain the ongoing contribution of volunteers, service providers need to work closely with volunteers and develop volunteering pathways for people. Service providers such as Leonard Cheshire Disability, for example, often offer an induction programme to help volunteers to get to know the organisation and settle into their role, a training programme to learn new skills, opportunities to meet other volunteers, staff and people with disabilities, support and supervision to help to carry out their tasks and reimbursement of out-of-pocket expenses, in line with their internal expenses policy.[128] Many disability organisations also now manage befriending schemes for

---

[128] See Leonard Cheshire Disability Volunteering Policy, http://www.lcdisability.org/?lid=3094 (accessed 10 May 2011).

one-on-one relationships between individuals within the service and persons who share similar interests in the community.

'Home share' programmes also enable individuals to live with a single adult or family in their own home. The participants normally receive a small grant or get their rent paid for. Service providers offer a matching and follow-up service for home-sharers and carry out the necessary background checks to ensure the safety of both parties. Each arrangement is custom-made based on the wishes and needs of both the home seeker and the home provider; therefore, services rendered and costs involved vary.[129]

Another aspect of active community engagement is the move away from 'wrap-around' in-house services towards linking in with services in the community. This has significant potential for encouraging a life in the community. To achieve this shift, agencies are undertaking community service audits to examine the extent and potential of mainstream supports, as well as connecting with partnership groups, such as, for example, the Community and Voluntary Forum in Ireland. Their aim is to foster linkages amongst the community and voluntary groups in each county (including disability) and to provide a platform through which members may explore, articulate and organise to advance issues and interests which are of particular concern to them.[130]

Addressing Health and Safety Concerns

In designing individualised supports, a lot of complex issues relating to potential risks in the community have to be worked through. This is an area which has a fine line between protecting the safety of the individual and removing all risk, thereby limiting the life choices of the individual.

As expressed in the earlier section on using health and safety to promote independence, organisations need to individually tailor responsive and flexible backup supports in the person's support plan and be committed to ongoing problem-solving rather than externally setting policies and protocols for all persons. These risk assessments should be as unique and distinctive as the individuals themselves.

Experience from some service providers is that overly formal plans which are set externally have caused support arrangements to fail. For example, the experience of one Swedish organisation is that their health and safety policy of monitoring and background checks disrupted the organic development of relationships between the individual and people in the community. In cases when the

---

129 See National Shared Housing for more information, http://www.nationalsharedhousing.org/ (accessed 10 May 2011).
130 Please refer to Irish National Community & Voluntary Forum Constitution, Adopted 10 September 2005.

organisation worked with a volunteer, the volunteer had to get police clearance. However, if a relationship developed naturally between a person in the community and a service user, the organisation decided not to prescribe background checks which could potentially destroy this relationship. Rather, their key worker was able to check on the relationship using locally informed networks. In another case, an organisation felt that its home share programmes, where a person lives in another families' home, often failed when monitoring visits were too regular and invasive.

Clearly a balance is needed between assessing any potential risk and not limiting individuals' choice or control over what they want to do. Understanding and considering risk are helpful parts of planning how individuals want their needs met. The support plan should therefore consider potential emotional, physical, sexual, financial and institutional abuse as well as potential instances of neglect and discrimination. It should identify ways to reduce risk in advance by giving all people involved in supporting the person good information and ensuring they are aware of their responsibilities.[131] Ultimately, however, taking risks is a part of everyone's life and is a right which everyone has, so it is important that the person can take risks whilst staying safe.

Become a Learning Organisation

In many cases, individualised support work is difficult and can break down. It is crucial to be in a position where important lessons can be learned. Experience from the RWJF demonstration in the United States is that system change is messy; conflict is not necessarily the sign of an initiative falling apart. Despite well-constructed implementation plans and well-orchestrated activities, the process of change is not linear; it happens simultaneously on many fronts and involves many more individuals and diverse interests than can be predicted.[132] At the same time, the demonstration found that opportunity comes when least expected, and programme management needs to retain the conceptual and operational flexibility to seize opportunities where they arise.

It is important, therefore, to build capacity in organisational learning. This means that organisations should develop appropriate mechanisms for quality and outcome management and impact analysis, which embed the personal outcomes of the persons whom they serve. Organisations should be proactive in feedback and evaluation to enable future change.

---

[131] See Isle of Wight Council (2008) *Self-Directed Support: Helping You to Get Started, Information Pack,* October.

[132] National program director quoted in Robert Wood Johnson Foundation (2007) *Self-Determination for People with Developmental Disabilities*, RWJF.

Sustaining Change – Drawing Lines in the Sand

Finally, sustaining individually tailored supports for persons with disabilities is a continual job. This involves having a clear vision of the reform agenda in getting to a place where persons are receiving responsive, individualised support arrangements including the short-term, medium-term and long-term priorities and time frames

In the short term, it is important to establish a steering group and consult with stakeholders committed to change. Organisations can begin to explore all of the options identified previously to set the change process in motion. Support teams and circles of support should be established to build relationships and begin the work of designing support plans for individuals. Meanwhile, appropriate reporting mechanisms will need to be in place to govern and manage the change from the individual level up to management.

In the medium term, the organisation needs to assess and evaluate the lessons being learned from the complex work involved in order to broaden the range of persons being individually supported. Organisational structures will need to be reassessed in order to begin identifying ways of working more flexibly and responsively.

Finally, in the long term, organisational structures will need to be redesigned to become more flexible and responsive in order to continue developing; otherwise dual systems (traditional and individualised) will continue to remain. At each of the milestones reached in each of these time frames, it is crucial to draw lines in the sand. In other words, organisations need to make sure they do not fall back into providing more conventional services for individuals but mark successful milestones along the transformation.

COMBINING NATIONAL SYSTEM-WIDE AND LOCAL ORGANISATIONAL REFORM

In order to accomplish a new support delivery framework that encourages independence, as outlined earlier, it is important to combine national and local frontline reform. According to In Control, the process of reform (which it refers to as Total Transformation) could be classified into four major phases: getting ready for self-directed support (building foundations), developing the tools, making the changes and embedding deeper.[133] In terms of getting ready for self-directed support, this involves adopting a clear vision and strategy for what needs to be done. It also involves nurturing leadership at all levels within support providers. At the local level, it involves unlocking opportunities for persons to govern their own support arrangements and working with individuals in institutional care arrangements to try

---

[133] For a complete discussion of the concept of 'Total Transformation' and each of these four stages, see In Control (2010) *Third Phase Report Evaluation and Learning 2008–2009*, In Control.

and get them to think creatively about a life in the community. It is important in all these processes to build trust and relationships between all stakeholders.

A key part of this phase, as discussed in this chapter, is getting all stakeholders to work together. Crucially at both national and local organisational levels, this involves consulting with the various interested parties and identifying the main concerns and barriers to personalisation. However, this consultation needs to be driven by strong guiding principles and a vision with all stakeholders, recognising that the old way of doing things is no longer sustainable or desirable. As a policy representative from the United Kingdom stated:

> [Our strategy] was saying, 'the way we've been doing this over all these years needs to be fundamentally changed'. And that wasn't something we could have got to, within any reasonable period of time, through the development of careful consensus and stakeholder management etc. It was one of those things where there had to be someone saying, 'we're going to do this' . . . and it wasn't all debugged, and it wasn't all clearly articulated because some of it we hadn't worked out. . . . Because if we tried to debug it, we would have taken 10 years. And we wouldn't have got there because there would have been too much conflict and there would have been so many opportunities for those people who didn't want it to happen to come together in different situations and different places to stop it.[134]

In other words, all stakeholders need to be clear that the new vision of enabling people with disabilities to have a choice in their living arrangements and supports to achieve social and economic participation in society should be fundamentally adhered to and should be the starting point in all consultations. Ultimately, negotiations over different stakeholder interests need to be informed by these principles, particularly given that they are reflected in the guiding principles of the UN CRPD. Here, leadership is crucial to help to develop legitimacy for the vision and engaging with all stakeholders to work through their concerns.

During this time, it is important to begin organising the second phase of developing the tools. These tools characterise the main working elements of a new support system, as identified at the beginning of the chapter. This means designing the administrative and planning mechanisms, funding streams and reporting and evaluation systems. These need to be in place to enable people to transition away from traditional service arrangements. At the same time, it is important to begin to look strategically at ways of unravelling the conventional service system without putting people at risk.

Again, during this time it is important for policy makers not to get stuck in this phase with rigidly defining and proofing every aspect of a new system without recognising the important aspect of 'progressive realisation' and learning by practice

---

[134] Personal Communication, 3 March 2010.

in the latter phases.[135] Therefore, monitoring outcomes and measuring costs are crucial to inform later reviewing and sharing of good practice.

The third phase – making the changes – is centred on scaling up the change and implementing a smart welfare approach in procuring and commissioning innovative models of support which seek to promote independent living. There are a number of mechanisms for moving from block contracts to individualised funding, such as moving to part-funding mechanisms with increasingly smaller commissioned blocks and mini-tenders.[136] Again, ongoing evaluation and research to inform progress are required to enable the last phase.

Finally, the 'embedding deeper' phase is focussed on learning from progress and using the data from outcome monitoring gathered during the earlier phases. This is a period during which all stakeholders look ahead and much of the new learning is to be found.

What is clear from the wellsprings of reform identified in each comparative study is that broader systems change and service provider change do not solely occur from within; change needs an outside force to act as catalyst. While the philosophy of 'one person at a time' helps to change organisational practices, ultimately, experience shows that self-determination will continually need to be pushed along from outside the system or it may stall because of inertia. Without an ongoing advocate or force for the concept, crises or other more urgent organisational issues such as emergency cases, end-of-year accounts, contracting or internal politics will push aside the long-term efforts to implement self-determination.[137] While the regional authorities' systems and processes will need to change, ultimately the processes of change will be led by individuals with their families, allies and communities and advocacy groups as they assert their right to control.

CONCLUSION

The reform agenda outlined in this chapter should be thought of as a pathway to new opportunities in enabling people to gain more control and choice over their own lives. It provides a series of options and alternatives for government and support providers, both of which play a significant role in the lives of individuals with disabilities to remove barriers to participation and to develop the potential of all citizens to engage in society.

---

[135] The concept of progressive realisation was defined in the International Covenant on Economic, Social and Cultural Rights. Article 2 of the Covenant imposes a duty on all parties to: 'take steps . . . to the maximum of its available resources, with a view to achieving progressively the full realization of the rights recognized in the present Covenant by all appropriate means, including particularly the adoption of legislative measures'.

[136] UK Department of Health (2009) *Contracting for Personalised Outcomes, Learning from Emerging Practice*. HMSO, London.

[137] Evaluator quoted in Robert Wood Johnson Foundation (2007) *Self-Determination for People with Developmental Disabilities*, RWJF.

Ultimately the comparative analysis demonstrates a widening trend towards active citizenship rather than a deficit model of welfare, reinforcing dependency and being a continual recipient of welfare. In the words of Williamson:

> What users may value as important in their lives and what they want from services differ markedly from what service providers and professionals believe to be important... an adequate income, a satisfying life, fulfilling relationships, meaningful work, housing, accessible services, choice and information, reducing stigma and equal opportunities.[138]

In particular, for those deemed to have diminished capacity, it has been reported that the more the individual perceives services as controlling or intrusive, the less likely they are to engage and more likely to avoid treatment and support services, which, in turn, can lead to more coercive consequences.[139] This vicious cycle is evident across the whole spectrum of support services and illustrates the balance which must be struck between over-controlling all risks for the individual and allowing them to have a choice in their lives.

While it is acknowledged that the different jurisdictions are at various stages in the process of change, the different options and alternatives identified in this chapter nonetheless provide an important road map for better achieving the principles as set out in the CRPD. They should be regarded as key structural ingredients to form the basis for a more in-depth discussion of the future steps required to further the rights of people with disabilities at the domestic level in line with the CRPD.

[138] Williamson, T. (2003) 'Enough Is Good Enough', *Mental Health Today*, April: 24–27; 24.
[139] Curtis, L. C. and Diamond, R. (1997) 'Power and Coercion in Mental Health Practice', in B. Blackwell (ed.), *Treatment Compliance and the Therapeutic Alliance*. Harwood Academic Publishers, Amsterdam. pp. 97–112.

12

Conclusion

This final chapter outlines the key messages and future directions which emerge from this book. It returns to the original motivation for reform outlined at the beginning of the book and pinpoints how the commitment to transforming welfare and paternalistic forms of care has become crystallised within the guiding principles of the CRPD. It identifies the golden threads to the transformation agenda at the domestic level and traces how it has evolved across different jurisdictions. Lastly, it points towards the future challenges in continuing to implement the principles of personalisation and active citizenship.

MOTIVATION FOR REFORM

This book set out to examine the growing movement away from conventional forms of welfare and care – which, persons with disabilities have argued, enforce dependency, isolation and powerlessness – towards a model which seeks to enable people to have a meaningful life in the community. Traditional approaches to providing support according to a number of comprehensive evaluations have all too often become standardised, inflexible and unaccountable to those they serve.[1] As a result, persons with disabilities have felt that support services have often reinforced ownership and medicalisation of their lives. These forms of support have also been deemed by evaluations to have become costly and have caused multiple problems including inflexible schedules, incompatibility/disputes among persons grouped together, inability to adapt to individuals' changing needs or preferences and low levels of personal choice and autonomy.[2]

---

[1] For different domestic-level evaluations, see Stancliffe, R. J. and Lakin, K. C. (Eds.) (2005) *Costs and Outcomes of Community Services for People with Intellectual Disabilities*. Paul H. Brookes Publishing Co., Baltimore.

[2] See Emerson, E., Robertson, J., Gregory, N., Hatton, C., Kessissoglou, S., Hallam, A. et al. (2001) 'Quality and Costs of Supported Living Residences and Group Homes in the United Kingdom',

These shortfalls prompt us to re-examine the original purposes of welfare. As identified in Chapter 1, the original goal was to combat the ill effects of economic growth such as increased inequality, a break down in social cohesion, emigration and more widespread poor health. The potential alienation contributing to a loss of political support was also identified amongst those affected.[3] The goal of social institutions was to help to achieve full employment, a share in growing prosperity and the satisfaction of certain basic needs to live and participate in society.

As we saw, the NESC's concept of a Developmental Welfare State called into question the assumption that social policy must be at odds with the principles of economic growth. The report argues that economic performance and improved social protection are neither intrinsically opposed nor compelled to occur together in some automatic way, but that they can be made to support each other.[4] If not strategically planned, economic turbulence can damage social cohesion and fracture society unless social policy responses are intelligently designed and well resourced. Similarly, ill-designed social policies can undermine people's cooperation with economic change and contribute to undermining economic performance and, ultimately, the social protection a country can provide its citizens. The NESC envisions an enabling welfare state centred on helping people to achieve meaningful participation in society.

The aim to strategically design cost-effective support systems which encourage participation is crucial, given the broader pressures facing each of the countries studied, particularly the current economic climate around the world. Moreover, providing more services which continue to remain standardised, inflexible and unaccountable to persons with disabilities is not the task facing us in the new millennium, with the emphasis on citizenship, human dignity and independent living. The CRPD affirms that States Parties must 'recognize the equal right of all persons with disabilities to live in the community, with choices equal to others', and that they shall 'take effective and appropriate measures to facilitate full enjoyment by persons with disabilities of this right and their full inclusion and participation in the community'.[5] There is, therefore, a more pressing political imperative to dismantle dependency-creating service structures and ensure that people are given the choice to utilise supports which enable them to become involved in the community. For all European countries, these obligations are reinforced by the goals of the European Commission's disability strategy 2010–2020.

American Journal on Mental Retardation 106(5): 401–415; Howe, J., Horner, R. H. and Newton, J. S. (1998) 'Comparison of Supported Living and Traditional Residential Services in the State of Oregon', *Mental Retardation* 36(1): 1.

[3] Clarke, J. Cochrane, A. and Smart, C. (1987) *Ideologies of Welfare: From Dreams to Disillusion.* Hutchinson, London.

[4] National Economic and Social Council (2005) *Developmental Welfare State.* NESC, Dublin.

[5] CRPD, article 19.

The shortfalls of welfare which solely keep people in dependent, paternalistic forms of care, as we identified, have forced governments around the world to re-examine their own state institutions and welfare apparatuses. Each comparative chapter has provided a snapshot of how jurisdictions have organised both state entitlements and social services, in order to identify how they encourage active citizenship or otherwise. There were instances throughout the comparative study to suggest that when working together, state entitlements and social services can help to ensure that social disadvantage does not become lasting social exclusion. Throughout, examples have shown that these joint social institutions can help people to adapt to pervasive changes and barriers to societal cohesion over time.

As we saw from the comparative case studies, new support structures which are based on the principle of personalisation have led to improvements in people's lives. Evaluations by both state[6] and independent third parties[7] have revealed that self-directed support can enhance choice, control and flexibility, when compared with direct service provision. Sapey (2001) also suggests that direct payments are an important means of challenging the 'culture of welfare' across social service departments.[8]

Despite these positive outcomes, access to cash payments is not in itself enough to secure independent living. A note of caution remains in relation to the sole focus on individual funding as an all-encompassing solution, rather than seeing it as part of a wider transformation effort.[9] Linked to this is a fear from service users of 'a race to the bottom' in terms of quality of service. Experience in Sweden and the United Kingdom has shown that demand amongst persons with disabilities for managing all the responsibilities associated with using direct payments and hiring personal assistants by themselves remains low. Moreover, expectations on people to do so can be unrealistic and potentially harmful. Similarly, a scenario in which individuals pay minimum wage to extract maximum hours in an unregulated market with little support and no recognition of the significant overhead required to administer such a model is something that must be heeded.[10] Instead, a system of self-directed support needs to be as rigorously monitored as conventional services, and in some cases more so, to ensure that neither people receiving support nor staff providing it fall between the cracks or are left susceptible to isolation or abuse.

---

[6] E.g. Individual Budgets Evaluation Network (IBSEN) (2008) *Evaluation of the Individual Budgets Pilot Programme.* Social Policy Research Unit, University of York, York.

[7] Zarb, G. and Nadash, P. (1994) *Cashing in on Independence: Comparing the Costs and Benefits of Cash and Services.* BCODP, London.

[8] Sapey, B. (2001) 'Independent Successes: Implementing Direct Payments (Review)', *British Journal of Social Work* 31(3): 506–508.

[9] Egan, D. (2008) *Issues Concerning Direct Payments in the Republic of Ireland,* Report for the Person Centre.

[10] *Ibid.*

Taking the aforementioned factors into account, an important aspect of successful policy implementation is the role of facilitation to enable people to manage their increased responsibilities in designing their support arrangements. Moreover, individual funding needs to be seen as part of a wider systemic change to animate personalised support, cultivate greater community connection and offer more employment support.

Accomplishing the vision of a personalised and enabling welfare state requires a strategically planned, radical reorganisation of the old social care system. According to the UK Department of Health, 'Personalisation is about *whole system change*, not about change at the margins'.[11] To enable this to happen, this study has been concerned with identifying how different jurisdictions have implemented legal reform and restructured their welfare states and support policy to create cost-effective, individualised support mechanisms which enable people to participate in society.

LEARNING FROM OTHER COUNTRIES

Given the recent nature of the active citizenship reform agenda in which countries are engaged, there is an important incentive to learn from each other in sustaining progress. Moreover, in jurisdictions where much of this reform agenda remains uncharted territory, such as Ireland, the imperative to examine the lessons being learned within other countries is crucial.

According to Article 32 of the CRPD, there is also an obligation to engage in international cooperation through partnerships with other states with relevant international and regional organisations, and with civil society in support of national measures to give effect to the CRPD.[12] There is thus a clear and imperative obligation to learn from other countries and share in best-practice thinking regarding how best states and local agencies have redesigned their support arrangements.

While each jurisdiction examined in this book has been committed to the new paradigm of active citizenship, it becomes clear from the comparative chapters that each country is still grappling with many challenges in implementing this vision. In some cases, the legacies of institutionalisation still live on, particularly in France, Ireland and a few states in the United States. And yet, on the other hand, there are many positive lessons of good practice, successful initiatives and government policies in transforming restrictive structures. Together, it is possible to learn from both the challenges which each country has faced as well as the success stories which have emerged.

In terms of the key building blocks of personalisation, the study has identified a number of demand-side reforms centred on restoring power to persons with disabilities. These include independent planning/brokerage, individualised funding allied

---

[11] Department of Health (2008) *Transforming Social Care*, Local Authority Circular. (emphasis added).
[12] See CRPD, art. 32.

with fiscal facilitation, and access to a support coordinator/direct support worker. Alongside these mechanisms, the national legislation needs to enable supported decision making. For persons who have been institutionalised for some time, access to advocacy services is crucial in negotiating the challenges of moving into the community.

Meanwhile, there is the need to foster family leadership, particularly for cultivating natural community connections for persons at risk of isolation. Governments also need to examine more closely the opportunities which asset-based welfare policy can give to families, according to which the government fosters saving and asset building. These policy mechanisms are designed to restore balance to family members who have previously been left disempowered and solely reliant on the discretion of support providers.

As the comparative case studies showed, there is also the need for supply-side reforms which seek to make the support market more responsive. These options include enabling choice in the support market, more transparent funding models, enhancing community connection and supported employment. In addition, there needs to be a long-term reappraisal of the commissioning body, particularly if it has become entrenched in medical or health fields.

Cumulatively, these options for achieving a personalised support delivery system serve as the basis for further development and restructuring of disability law and policy at the domestic level. Whilst implemented differently in every country, these common threads provide a road map for policy makers seeking to reimagine support delivery. However, it is important to emphasise that reform of disability support policy and implementation structures can only be truly effective where it occurs in conjunction with broader public sector reform – in other words, the mainstreaming of disability issues across all government ministries.

The broader political, social and economic challenges which shape and constrain the development of these various mechanisms are also considered throughout the comparative case studies. The success factors which have led to effective implementation of personalisation at the domestic level were identified. Given the differences in approaches, the book provides a telling example of the complexities involved in implementing international human rights treaties such as the UN CRPD. Shared learning between states parties should help to develop innovative thinking on critical success factors for implementing such disability policy.

In terms of implementation, at the outset, the need to build a broad-ranging strategy for change is crucial with clearly defined responsibilities amongst different stakeholders for each task. This implementation strategy should first include the need to cultivate leadership and capacity in commissioners and managers of providers. It is recognised that the reform of disability services is a significant leadership challenge given the range of stakeholders involved and the different vested interests. Second, embedding the voice of persons with disabilities is vital for a sustained process of reform. Ultimately, people with disabilities need to be at the policy table to ensure the values and guiding principles of the CRPD continually inform the transformation. Third, adopting a strategic financial approach to the transition from block funding and institutions to support in the community is crucial. Otherwise, as evidenced in some cases, dual systems will remain a part of the service landscape.

The other key policy considerations include motivating the support workforce, using health and safety to promote independence and ensuring accountability through the use of fiscal intermediaries. Each of the jurisdictions which have implemented self-directed support models are keenly aware that fears over job security and issues of risk and accountability can pose significant barriers to personalisation. Therefore governments, commissioners and managers need to put in place strategies for supporting workers, as well as safeguards for minimising instances of abuse and fraud.

Finally, it is vital that there are systems in place which can continue to inform progress through evaluation and research. Embedding a system which identifies the personal outcomes of individuals with disabilities as they transition to more personalised support arrangements can help to sustain the process of reform. In addition, independent evidence-based research which seeks to unpack the complexity of implementing community living should be prioritised to ensure it continues to inform effective policy responses.

Through the international comparative study, the book has demonstrated how these mechanisms are being used at the domestic level to unlock paternalistic and dehumanising service models. While these mechanisms began emerging throughout the decades preceding the CRPD, their underpinning philosophy nonetheless closely aligns with the Convention, and can be guided in their future development by the spirit and intention of the treaty. In particular, the overall thrust of the CRPD, as articulated by the first enumerated general principle of Article 3 – 'respect for inherent dignity, individual autonomy including the freedom to make one's own choices, and independence of persons'[13] – should continue to serve as the core guiding principle behind the self-determination mechanisms being developed.

More generally, the personalisation of support delivery is not just for people with disabilities. While this study focussed on these individuals, ultimately, for a true realisation of the vision of active citizenship, the task for us is to design supports which target disadvantaged people across the life course, including those with mental health issues and within different generational boundaries and different social caveats, such as ethnicity and gender. In this context, a personalised social support system should emphasise the individual's dignity, right to self-determination, choice, control and power over the support services they receive. The fulfilment of this approach can help all persons to move away from positions of powerlessness and dependency towards re-engaging and contributing in society.

---

[13] See CRPD, Guiding Principles (a) and (c).

APPENDIX

Questions for Comparative Analysis

These questions were intended to ascertain a common platform in which to examine how different jurisdictions have tackled the active citizenship and personalisation agenda.

What is the overall welfare philosophy of the jurisdiction?

How are disability-specific welfare entitlements configured?

- Is there a specific strategy to reduce benefit traps or other related barriers to participation?

How have services and supports been provided?

- Are they delivered by the state directly or through local emanations (i.e. the private sector)?
- Is there any interaction between services and disability welfare entitlements?

What has been the focus of the reform agenda?

How is it defined and marketed by government (i.e. what kind of language and normative values have been put in place)?

Does it match with the values and vision of the UN CRPD?

What were the wellsprings of reform (i.e. responses to the actions of civil society, government enquiries, treaties, legislation, case law, or need for more cost-effective ways of using public money)?

How has government carved out the reform agenda?

From the demand side – *What various mechanisms have been used in this regard?*

- Is there access to individual funding, independent planning and so forth?
- Are there any ways of enhancing consumer purchase power, such as asset-building trusts or savings plans?
- What mechanisms have been used to generate a better choice in living arrangements?

- What kinds of preconditions are needed to make this system work – such as increased capacity in service providers to manage change, for example?

From the supply side – What various mechanisms have been used in this regard?

- What mechanisms have been used to make the support market more responsive?
- Is there a system of procurement used to inject market forces into state/service arrangements?
- Has the state placed service delivery organisations at arm's length from the state?
- Has the state insisted on standards for support providers regardless of whether market forces are injected?
- Has the state insisted on consequences for failure to meet such standards?
- How has the state managed accountability for public money while opening up flexibility room within the sector to innovate?
- What new roles exist for providers in this new market?

What have been the main success factors?
What challenges or issues have arisen?
How have these been dealt with?

Index

Index

Printed in Great Britain
by Amazon.co.uk, Ltd.,
Marston Gate.